MW01164963

KNOWLEDGE, ECONOMIC ORGANIZATION AND PROPERTY RIGHTS

Knowledge, Economic Organization and Property Rights

Selected Papers

Edited by

Nicolai J. Foss

Center for Strategic Management and Globalization
Copenhagen Business School, Denmark
Norwegian School of Economics and Business Administration,
Norway

Edward Elgar
Cheltenham, UK • Northampton, MA, USA

Published by
Edward Elgar Publishing Limited
The Lypiatts
15 Lansdown Road
Cheltenham
Glos GL50 2JA
UK

Edward Elgar Publishing, Inc.
William Pratt House
9 Dewey Court
Northampton
Massachusetts 01060
USA

A catalogue record for this book is available from the British Library

Library of Congress Control Number: 2008939750

PEFC
PEFC/16-33-111
CATG-PEFC-052
www.pefc.org

ISBN 978 1 84720 821 7

Printed and bound in Great Britain by MPG Books Ltd, Bodmin, Cornwall

Contents

PART III   PROPERTY RIGHTS AND ENTREPRENEURSHIP

Acknowledgements

The author and publishers wish to thank the authors and the following publishers who have kindly given permission for the use of copyright material.

Elsevier for articles: Nicolai J. Foss and Torben Pedersen (2002), 'Transferring knowledge in MNCs: The Role of Sources of Subsidiary Knowledge and Organizational Context', *Journal of International Management*, **8**, 49–67; Nicolai J. Foss and Keld Laursen (2005), 'Performance Pay, Delegation and Multitasking under Uncertainty and Innovativeness: An Empirical Investigation', *Journal of Economic Behavior and Organization*, **58**, 246–76.

Institute for Operations Research and the Management Sciences (INFORMS) for articles: Nicolai J. Foss (1996), 'Knowledge-based Approaches to the Theory of the Firm: Some Critical Comments', *Organization Science*, **7** (5), September–October, 470–76; Nicolai J. Foss (2003), 'Selective Intervention and Internal Hybrids: Interpreting and Learning from the Rise and Decline of the Oticon Spaghetti Organization', *Organization Science*, **14** (3), May–June, 331–49.

John Wiley and Sons Ltd for article: Kirsten Foss and Nicolai J. Foss (2005), 'Resources and Transaction Costs: How Property Rights and Economics Furthers the Resource-based View', *Strategic Management Journal*, **26**, 541–53.

Mohr Siebeck Tübingen for article: Nicolai J. Foss (1999), 'The Use of Knowledge in Firms', *Journal of Institutional and Theoretical Economics*, **155**, 458–86.

Oxford University Press for articles: Nicolai J. Foss (2003), 'Bounded Rationality and Tacit Knowledge in the Organizational Capabilities Approach: an Assessment and a Re-evaluation', *Industrial and Corporate Change*, **12** (2), 185–201; Kirsten Foss, Nicolai J. Foss and Xosé H. Vázquez (2006), '"Tying the Manager's Hands": Constraining Opportunistic Managerial Intervention', *Cambridge Journal of Economics*, **30**, 797–818.

SAGE Publications for articles: Teppo Felin and Nicolai J. Foss (2005), 'Strategic Organization: a Field in Search of Micro-foundations', *Strategic Organization*, **3** (4), 441–55; Nicolai J. Foss (2007), 'The Emerging Knowledge Governance Approach: Challenges and Characteristics', *Organization*, **14** (1), 29–52; Kirsten Foss, Nicolai J. Foss and Peter G. Klein (2007), 'Original and Derived Judgment: An Entrepreneurial Theory of Economic Organization', *Organization Studies*, **28** (12), 1893–912.

Springer Science and Business Media for article: Christian Bjørnskov and Nicolai J. Foss (2008), 'Economic Freedom and Entrepreneurial Activity: Some Cross-country evidence', *Public Choice*, **134**, 307–28.

Taylor and Francis (http://www.informaworld.com) for articles: Kirsten Foss and Nicolai J. Foss (2000), 'Theoretical Isolation in Contract Theory: Suppressing Margins and Entrepreneurship', *Journal of Economic Methodology*, **7** (3), 313–39; Kirsten Foss and Nicolai J. Foss (2001), 'Assets, Attributes and Ownership', *Journal of the Economics of Business*, **8** (1), 19–37; Nicolai J. Foss (2002), '"Coase vs Hayek": Economic Organization and the Knowledge Economy', *International Journal of the Economics of Business*, **9** (1), 9–35.

Taylor and Francis (Routledge) for excerpt: Nicolai J. Foss (2003), 'The Rhetorical Dimensions of Bounded Rationality: Herbert A. Simon and Organizational Economics', in Salvatore Rizzello (ed.), *Cognitive Paradigms in Economics*, London: Routledge, 158–76.

Introduction

Background

Economics

I have been happily employed for two decades at a business school (Copenhagen Business School), I entertain broad and diverse interests (no doubt too many for a serious scholar), I consider myself to be a management scholar, and I have never been to a meeting in the American Economic Association. Still, the dominant disciplinary influence on my research has been, and remains, economics. What is published in the better sociology journals is no doubt serious research of considerable relevance to management research, and the same may be said of much research in social psychology. However, psychologists have little idea of the notion of action relative to constraints, and sociologists usually over-emphasize certain constraints over others. In my opinion, one of the main advantages of economics as a social science is its superior ability to neatly *frame* problems. The framing may often be simplistic (as in the way economists deal with incentives, usually ignoring motivation crowding out effects, Frey and Stutzer, 2007), but it is seldom a bad starting point (those crowding out effects can be modelled as a refinement of the basic model).

I suppose I was an intuitive economist from a relatively early age; at any rate, I remember taking the position, in seventh grade at elementary school, that, on the whole, organized crime should be preferred over un-organized crime, as there would be more crime under the latter situation than under the former. My teacher and classmates reacted with disgust. I remember brief exposures to economics in high school and finding it highly fascinating, not the least because of the moral fervour that my left-wing teachers could mobilize against the latest sinister plots of the sycophants of Anglo-Saxon/US capitalism, that of monetarism (Klein [2008] is really nothing new); predictably, I became a staunch monetarist (buying into the complementary political positions) in University (where I encountered the same attitude, albeit with a bit more sophistication). I had little hesitation that I had made the right choice when I embarked upon the economics program of the University of Copenhagen at the tender age of 18.

Copenhagen University

The study of economics at the University was split between macro-oriented empiricists and mathematical, general equilibrium theorists (luckily, many of the schisms of two decades ago have been overcome today). While the former had much standing in the Danish community, the latter had the standing in the scientific community. Econometric model building was also very strong. Only one or two professors did what may be called 'applied price theory', so the use of economics as a tool to make sense of the choices people make in the real world, and how these choices aggregate to collective outcomes – my main motivation for studying economics – was not stressed. The implications of the missing links between these areas were very clear in the teaching that students were exposed to (although it is nothing like the disciplinary diversity that management students are exposed to): Things didn't really seem to connect, so students made choices rather early in the study program to focus on either 'micro' or 'macro'. Most focused on macro; this was where money and power were, that is, positions with the major banks or ministries.

The majority of the teaching in the bachelor part of the economics program centred on macro-issues, and I rapidly developed a strong dislike for the kind of boring macro-drill that we were exposed to. Things began to change when I realized, in the second year of my economics study, that there were strong alternatives to the Keynesian-macroeconomics-and-macro-econometric-modelling focus of so much of the teaching. The methodological essays of Robert Lucas (1977, 1980) and Milton Friedman's Presidential Address to the American Economic Association (Friedman, 1968) captured my interest, probably because they were bashed by my macro-teachers (I do admit to having a querulous tendency in my nature).

At one of my raids of the Economics Department library, I picked up an old volume with the title, *The Fallacy of the New Economics* (Hazlitt, 1959). It turned out to be an energetic (though over-the-top) smashing of the Keynesian revolution (my Keynesian macro-instructor eagerly picked it up when he saw it on my desk, expecting it to be an attack on new classical macro-economics; after flipping through it he put it down again with a disgusted look). When researching the author, I found out that he had been associated with an 'Austrian School of Economics'. At about the same time I was reading Axel Leijonhufvud's brilliant *On Keynesian Economics and the Economics of Keynes* (1968), a very different attempt (and one with which I felt more sympathetic) to furnish micro-foundations for macro-economics than new classical macro-economics. That book contained references to a 'Friedrich Hayek', and when checking up on that name I again encountered the enigmatic 'Austrian School'.

This led, of course, to the discovery of the writings of Hayek, as well as Mises, Kirzner, Lachmann, and other modern Austrians, as well as the classical liberal tradition in political philosophy. I did not become a die-hard Austrian (I have usually thought of myself as a fellow-traveller), but I found, and continue to find, the basic Austrian vision highly congenial and inspiring. However, I fundamentally like and admire so-called mainstream economics, and although disequilibrium, process, entrepreneurship, and the subjectivism of knowledge and expectations continue to be soft spots in the mainstream corpus, the mainstream seems to me to increasingly make very serious and sustained attempts at coming to grips with the kind of issues that have been central to the Austrians.[1] It was also around this time (i.e., towards the end of the 1980s) that I discovered new institutional economics, that is, transaction cost economics and property rights economics. I remember struggling with Alchian's

---

[1]   Thus, the theme of my 1994 book, *The Austrian School and Modern Economics: Essays in Reassessment*, written as a hobby project while I was working on my PhD thesis, is that although the Austrians, particularly Mises and Hayek, anticipated numerous themes that later became prominent in mainstream economics (e.g., asymmetric information, the agency problem, property rights), they failed to develop these ideas sufficiently and they failed to do concrete theorizing with them. As an example, although the Austrians had many of the necessary ingredients of an economic approach to organization before anyone else, they never thought of piecing them together. Thus, Austrian economics, though sound in its basic vision, seemed to me to constitute an instance of what Lakatos (1970) called a 'degenerating research program' (see also Foss, 2000).

famous 1965 property rights paper, and finally experiencing a sort of epiphany: This kind of reasoning simply made (almost perfect) sense of the world! I have continued to be highly, and in fact increasingly, sympathetic to the new institutional economics, and to pursue applications of this body of economics in management research.

However, in spite of this interest in new institutional economics I decided to write my master thesis, completed in late 1988, on the business cycle theory of Hayek (e.g., Hayek, 1931) (parts of the thesis were later published as Foss, 1996). After submitting the thesis, my thesis supervisor, Professor Hector Estrup – an expert in the now unfortunately largely defunct field of the history of economics – managed to get me a six month stipend at the Economics Department at the University, but it became clear that my interest in pursuing doctrinal history studies in monetary theory did not resonate well with the current research strategies of that Department, so when I was offered a stipend to pursue graduate studies at the Copenhagen Business School, I happily accepted.

Copenhagen Business School
I arrived at CBS in October 1989. In those days CBS was something very far indeed from the present highly entrepreneurial, energetic and research-oriented place: There was little emphasis on research, few senior people seemed interested in assuming a mentoring role (perhaps few could), there was no course work to be done, so as a PhD student one was pretty much left to pursue one's own interests for three years. The only expectation was that one would produce a monograph, typically in Danish, of a minimum of 250 pages long. Quite predictably, most PhD students were not able to finish in time: without the checks on procrastination provided by courses and teaching, time just slipped through the fingers of the students.

However, a cohort of particularly talented PhD students was hired at roughly that time. These included Kirsten Foss, Torben Pedersen, Bent Petersen, and Steen Thomsen who have all since become professors. I was also lucky to become associated with some senior people who were quite research active. In particular, my advisor on the thesis project, Christian Knudsen, took a broad interest in economic theories of the firm, an interest that was clearly contagious for I soon developed a similar interest. Since little or no course work was required, it was to a large extent up to the above cohort to imprint itself. There were obvious negative sides to this (it is difficult to learn statistics in this manner!), but also the benefits that come from the feeling of being part of an exciting emerging perspective (we all shared a fascination with new institutional economics), a certain *esprit de corps*. To illustrate, a number of us were literally lined up at the CBS library eagerly waiting for the arrival of the issue of the *Administrative Science Quarterly* that featured Williamson (1991) (obviously, this was before internet access). The conferment of the Nobel Prize to Ronald Coase in 1992 gave rise to celebrations. The discovery of the emerging resource-based view in the beginning of the 1990s was also a major event. We increasingly found that we shared an emerging perspective (for the rest of the story, including various organizational ramifications, see Foss, 2007).

My PhD thesis, submitted in 1992, was essentially an application of capabilities and transaction cost economics to the issue of the organization of technological innovation, an undertaking that was heavily inspired by the work of David Teece

(1986) and Richard Langlois (1988). I foolishly wrote the thesis in Danish (very few management PhD students and even economics PhD students wrote their theses in English at that time), but I managed to get virtually the whole thesis published as articles translated, of course, from the Danish text.

I was enthused to recognize that many of the ideas on privately held knowledge, dynamics, impediments to exchange and rational agents circumventing those impediments, spontaneous development of institutions, entrepreneurship, and so on that I (perhaps more or less correctly) associated with the Austrian School were part of the core ideas that were taught in business schools. They were also rather closely associated with ideas that were becoming prominent in the business schools in those days, such as insights derived from evolutionary economics (notably the evolutionary theory of the firm and it 'capabilities', 'dynamic capabilities', etc. offspring) (Nelson and Winter, 1982), and transaction cost economics (Williamson, 1985). I decided that a business school would be an ideal research environment, given the basic outlook I held. Not an unusual decision for a failed economist (or failed sociologist, for that matter)!

I have followed the traditional career path of Assistant (1993), Associate (1996) and Full Professor (1998), all at the Copenhagen Business School, and added adjunct professorships at the Norwegian School of Economics and Business Administration and Agder University. During the 20 years I have spent professionally at CBS, I have witnessed the growth of the school from being a sleepy, provincial and almost wholly teaching-oriented university to become one of the world's largest business schools with 400 faculty, about 17,000 students, marked ambitions, and a strong emerging research culture that increasingly results in publications in the best international management and disciplinary journals. This growth has come about as a result of a fruitful interplay between local initiative and a management approach at CBS that has stressed guidance and orchestration of initiatives rather than piecemeal management. Rather than adopting a uniform model of the organization of a research-based organization (e.g., emulating the typical US business school), or dictating research initiatives from the top, the architect of CBS' growth experience, President Finn Junge-Jensen emphasized a bottom-up approach. In his approach to stimulating school-wide research activities, somewhat reminiscent of the Oticon 'spaghetti organization' (treated in 'Selective Intervention and Internal Hybrids: Interpreting and Learning from the Rise and Decline of the Oticon Spaghetti Organization'), local entrepreneurial research initiative would be supported, sometimes very generously, once it had passed an initial and not very rigorous screening procedure. Typically, such efforts would be organized in a research center, encompassing between five and 20 scholars. Currently, CBS has almost 40 such centers. A more serious evaluation would happen later; thus, selection was rather *ex post* than *ex ante*. The whole, largely successful, exercise is a prime example of 'guided evolution' (Ghoshal and Løvas, 2000) in an academic context. I have been a beneficiary of this approach myself, as my research has been generously supported, and I am now the director of The Center for Strategic Management and Globalization, a 12 faculty research center devoted to research in international business and strategic management (more on the Center in Foss, 2007).

Research interests and the papers in this collection[2]

Early work

As is usually the case, the research I did for my PhD thesis has very much shaped my subsequent work. My thesis work drew on the industrial economics tradition of post-Marshallians such as Edith Penrose (1959), George Richardson (1972), and Brian Loasby (1976), evolutionary economics in the Nelson and Winter (1982) tradition, and Williamsonian transaction cost economics (Williamson, 1985, 1996). The thesis was very much taken up with meta-issues, specifically issues of theory comparison and integration and the underpinning of such discussions in the theory of science. This interest has never left me, and although much of my work over the last decade or so has been empirical and relatively conventional management research, I keep returning to it. Although it is easy to risk being branded as somebody who does work that is 'merely conceptual' or writes 'thought pieces' (an academic putdown if there ever was one!), it is my strongly held conviction that in an inherently multi-disciplinary field such as management research, the risk of fundamental confusion is an ever-present danger and the need for a high degree of reflexivity is warranted. Efforts that make an attempt to sort out the fundamental theoretical and methodological issues should therefore be welcomed. Perhaps because this is where my heart (mainly) is, these kinds of papers are over-represented in the present collection, as well as in my paper portfolio in general.

One of the chapters in the thesis was published as Foss (1993a), one of my first and most cited papers (but not included here because I am no longer happy with the style and message of the paper). Much of my PhD thesis dealt with what foundational and conceptual issues, such as the philosophical doctrine of realism and economics (Foss, 1994c), the functionalist mode of explanation of transaction cost economics (Foss, 1994d), and the epistemic assumptions of transaction cost economics (Foss, 1993b, 1994d). Most of this work linked up with the evolutionary research program in economics. The work of Richard Langlois (1992; Langlois and Robertson, 1995) was a huge source of inspiration, as was the work of Brian Loasby (1976, 1991), and the modern semi-formal evolutionary economics associated with Nelson and Winter (1982). Although I have problems with some of the key constructs of this approach (notably, notions of routines and capabilities), in its application to the theory of markets I see it as an interesting and laudable return to and updating of an older and more 'realistic' and processual tradition in economics, one that was taken up with the analysis of changes rather than the comparison of equilibrium states. It is not surprising that it has been such a strong source of inspiration for management scholars.

Around the time I did this research I became one of the co-founders of the Danish Research Unit of Industrial Economics (DRUID), which (established in 1995) has become a highly successful forum for the latest high quality work in industrial dynamics, a sort of European version and blend of the Academy of Management and the Joseph Schumpeter Society. The DRUID was conceived of as a vehicle of disseminating the new evolutionary economics (i.e., post-Nelson and Winter EE), and although this orientation has diminished somewhat it is still strong. Partly inspired by

---

[2]   Check www.nicolaifoss.com for a complete listing of publications plus some downloadable papers.

the ethos of DRUID, I published a number of papers throughout the 1990s on the history of economics and management research. Thus, I published a couple of papers on the work of Edith Penrose, taking issue with the conventional interpretation of this work as the main precursor of strategic management's dominant perspective, the resource-based view (the RBV): Whereas the RBV is an equilibrium approach that focuses on the necessary conditions that must obtain for resources to yield rents in equilibrium, Penrose stressed growth, resource-building, and the dynamics of related diversification, and she was not taken up with competitive advantage *per se* (Foss, 1999b). Brian Loasby (1976) directed my attention to the work of the brilliant but neglected economist George B. Richardson (Foss, 1994f, 1995). With Brian Loasby and John Kay I arranged a conference in honour of Richardson (on the occasion of his 70th birthday) at St. John's College, Oxford University in 1995 (Foss and Loasby, 1998). Richardson had left economics in the mid-1970s to become CEO of Oxford University Press in frustration over the lack of interest in his work.

Capabilities, resources, and economic organization

Richardson was, however, the economist who, building from Penrosian foundations, coined the notion of firm-level 'capabilities'. His thinking on asset specificity and complementarity, particularly in his small monograph, *Information and Investment* (1960), was decades ahead of its time. Richardson was also the first scholar to attempt to explain the boundaries of the firm in terms of capabilities, that is, to provide an (at least seemingly) alternative explanation to the Coasian approach. The capabilities notion and the associated theorizing seemed to dovetail in various ways with what was going on in the exciting field of strategic management that I was discovering at that time, particularly with various extensions of the resource-based view (Barney, 1991). In other words, it provided a very fitting bridge for somebody who was in the process of taking the step from economics to management research.

Capabilities have emerged as one of the key constructs in management research. The central notion goes straight back to Penrose and Richardson, namely that firms should be conceptualized as repositories of routines and capabilities (e.g., Nelson and Winter, 1982; Kogut and Zander, 1992) (see also Foss, 1999a; Langlois and Foss, 1999). It is, furthermore, asserted in this stream of research that routines and capabilities cause firm-level outcomes such as financial performance, innovation, and the boundaries of the firm (e.g., Nelson and Winter, 1982; Kogut and Zander, 1992; Teece, Pisano and Shuen, 1997). Thus, it is argued that explaining firm-level outcomes should take place in terms of other firm-level variables. However, the overall problem with such reasoning is that there are no conceivable causal mechanisms in the social world that operate *solely* on the macro level. There are no macro-level entities on the social domain that somehow possess capacities or dispositions to act (Cartwright, 1989) that make them capable of directly producing macro-level outcomes and there are no direct processes of interaction between macro-entities.

Although this may be obvious to somebody with a methodological individualist background, this recognition has been extremely slow to develop in strategic management and related literatures. Presumably, because of the strong dominance of a mode of research that is all about building firm-level databases and engaging in cross-sectional analysis of firm-level data, the problem of accounting for the causal mechanisms that actually mediate between the analyzed macro- or firm-level has too often been neglected; that is, micro-foundations have been black-boxed, whether consciously or unconsciously. In a very brief paper (a note, really), 'Knowledge-Based Approaches to the Theory of the Firm: Some Critical Comments'; reprinted as the first chapter in this collection, I pointed out that existing accounts of the link between capabilities and economic organization (e.g., the boundaries of the firm) black-boxed or bypassed these micro-foundations so that the link was elusive. The challenge has not, it seems to me, yet been satisfactorily addressed in the capabilities literature.

Micro-foundations and knowledge governance

In retrospect, the 1996 paper is the origin of two closely related research streams: Micro-foundations in strategic management and organization research and what I (borrowing from Grandori, 1997) have termed 'knowledge governance'.

At some point after 1996 I realized that the problem I had diagnosed in the 1996 paper was a general one that beset this literature, that is, a lack of micro-foundations. The recognition emerged partly as a result of being challenged by my then PhD student Volker Mahnke concerning how I, with my Austrian inclinations and therefore presumed sympathy to methodological individualism, could be supportive of notions of capabilities and the like. However, it took me almost a decade, as well as teaming up with a kindred spirit, Teppo Felin (Brigham Young University), before I made the point explicitly. Teppo is a keen thinker with a taste for the radical argument and I have had the pleasure of collaborating with him on quite a number of papers. We realized that we shared a commitment to a basic rationalist and realist outlook and, therefore, a strong aversion to the social constructivist currents that are now rampant in management research (on this, see Felin and Foss, 2008).

In our first collaboration, a brief essay titled 'Strategic Organization: a Field in Search of Micro-foundations', Teppo and I explicitly argue that collective-level constructs in strategic management (and related) fields suffer from a general problem of accounting for their micro-foundations, which makes it hard to understand how they have emerged and how they may be changed.[3] Ultimately, the lack of such micro-foundations means that the managerial relevance of (very prominent) collective level concepts, such as capabilities and absorptive capacity, is unclear: How can managers hope to build capability and absorptive capacity if the way in which these are rooted in individual action and interaction is fundamentally unclear? Somewhat surprisingly, the paper is probably the first explicit statement of the problem of lacking micro-foundations in management research.[4] However, it seems that strategic management is now embarking on a micro-foundations project somewhat similar to, and perhaps inspired by, economics and rational choice sociology (e.g., Teece, 2007).

---

[3] These ideas, explained in greater detail in Felin and Foss (2006) and Abell, Felin and Foss (2009), build a formal model of the micro-foundations of capabilities.

[4] To be sure, micro-foundations were an emerging theme in management research before our paper, though usually implicitly. Scholars realize that understanding such issues as value appropriation (Coff, 1997; Lippman and Rumelt, 2003a), resource value (Lippman and Rumelt, 2003b), strategy implementation (Barney, 2001), and factor market dynamics (Makadok and Barney, 2001), requires that substantial attention be paid to explanatory mechanisms that are located at the micro-level, that is, the level of individual action and interaction.

My concern with the micro-foundations of knowledge-based ideas led – rather naturally, I believe – to an interest in bounded rationality which I (like no doubt many others) had thought of as the natural individual-level underpinning of notions of routines and capabilities. Indeed, modern writers on routines and capabilities refer (routinely) to Simon, Cyert and March as important precursors of their work (e.g., Nelson and Winter, 1982). In 'Bounded Rationality and Tacit Knowledge in the Organizational Capabilities Approach: an Evaluation and a Stocktaking', which was published in 2003 in the Nelson and Winter Festschrift issue of *Industrial and Corporate Change,* I argued that the link between the individual level and the organizational level had not been established in moden work, except metaphorically (by the argument in Nelson and Winter that 'routines are the skills of an organization') and that, at any rate, routines were really more about tacit knowledge than about bounded rationality. Thus, bounded rationality was invoked in a merely ceremonial manner and not fundamentally inquired into. At the same time I argued that this was a broader characteristic of the theory of the firm or organizational economics literature. 'The Rhetorical Dimensions of Bounded Rationality: Herbert A. Simon and Organizational Economics' makes the point that bounded rationality has usually been invoked in a rhetorical manner (in a pre-McCloskeyan sense of the word; McCloskey, 1983). Bounded rationality is not, in general, necessary to drive organizational economics arguments, but is invoked, perhaps partially out of reverence to Simon (or as an appeal to authority?), as a label for a host of things that may make contracts incomplete. I also argued that Simon himself had failed in his attempt to persuade economists that bounded rationality is important: He hammered away at what it was not (namely, maximizing rationality), but failed to truly explain (at least to economics audiences) what it really was.

My interest in the micro-foundations of knowledge-based views in management also led me to what often passes as 'knowledge management'. In particular, I have maintained an interest in issues of managing knowledge in multinational corporations, an interest I have often pursued in collaboration with my CBS colleague, Torben Pedersen, a prominent international business scholar. An example of our collaboration is 'Sources of Subsidiary Knowledge and Organizational Means of Knowledge Transfer' which takes its point of departure in the literature on the 'differentiated MNC', that is, the notion that the such firms can be seen as networks of units that each control heterogeneous and potentially complementary knowledge assets, and that they may derive advantages relative to national firms to the extent that they can build complementarities between such knowledge assets (this literature goes back at least to Hedlund, 1986). In the paper we examine the sources of the knowledge that is held in subsidiaries and argue that these sources matter greatly to the costs and benefits of knowledge transfers inside the MNC. We also argue that MNC headquarters can influence subsidiaries' knowledge sourcing activities. Thus, the paper is an attempt to dig deeper in terms of anteceding and moderating influences on MNC knowledge management activities.

'The Use of Knowledge in Firms', a play on the title of Hayek's (1945) famous essay, reaches back to my Austrian roots and raises some Austrian concerns relating to the treatment of knowledge in the mainstream economics of organization. It examines the drastic simplifications in the knowledge dimension that organizational economists introduce in their attempt to achieve theoretical traction, illustrating a quip by Brian Loasby that most management problems concern the things that are blackboxed in economics models. 'Theoretical Isolation in Contract Theory' is almost like a companion paper, but with a different, theory of science orientation, specifically looking at the kind of 'isolations' theorists perform in trying to make their theorizing determinate, and pinning out the specific 'on-off' modeling approach employed by contract theorists. The 'Use of Knowledge in Firms' paper surely raises many more questions than it gives answers, but I still believe that its basic message is correct, namely that problems of coordination (in the sense of game theory) have been neglected in organizational economics. Notions of capabilities in management and economics have sometimes been presented in the context of examining the coordination of knowledge in the absence of conflicts (see also Foss, 1999b), but as already suggested, they do not seem to me to have been successful here.

One of the many profound insights in Hayek's (1945) essay is that societal institutions should first and foremost be assessed against the extent to which they assist in the creation of new knowledge and exploitation of existing knowledge. To be sure this view is at least implicit in the knowledge-based view of the firm as well as in work on organizational learning (March, 1991) and in work on knowledge management. The idea directs attention to how processes of transferring, sharing, integrating, and creating knowledge can be governed by means of choices of governance structures (i.e., markets, hybrids, hierarchies; cf. Williamson, 1996), as well as the governance mechanisms contained in governance structures, such as authority, reward systems, standard operating procedures, ownership, etc. (see also Grandori, 1997, 2001).

In 'The Emerging Knowledge Governance Approach' I argue that although there has been much interest in how organization and knowledge processes relate in management research since the mid-1960s, there has been a surprising lack of systematic investigation of how formal organization (governance structures and mechanisms) impacts knowledge processes. Organizational governance as a consciously designed effort seems de-emphasized, and the organization-level antecedents that are, in fact, investigated are predominantly variables such as prior related knowledge, organizational practices, or structural conditions such as network positions, centrality, and the like. However, the relative absence of interest in formal organization in large parts of contemporary writing in management research on knowledge, is somewhat worrying for a number of reasons: Managers can often more directly influence formal organization than informal organization; it is usually easier to change job descriptions, reward systems, etc. than to effect changes in, for example, corporate culture. Indeed, the former may drive the latter with a lag. Evidence suggests that managers do change formal organization in an attempt to influence knowledge processes.

Cutting thematically across the fields of knowledge management, human resource management, organization theory, and strategic management, the knowledge governance approach starts from the hypothesis that knowledge processes can be influenced and directed through the deployment of governance mechanisms, in particular the formal aspects of organization that can be manipulated by management, such as organization structure, job design, reward systems, information systems, standard operating procedures, accounting systems, and other coordination mechanisms. It is a systematic attempt to address these issues, paying explicit attention to micro-issues of motivation and cognition (Grandori, 1997; Osterloh and Frey, 2000), which is strongly inspired by the basic explanatory approach of transaction cost economics: Knowledge governance may be conceptualized as a sustained attempt to uncover how knowledge transactions – which differ in their characteristics – and governance mechanisms – which differ with respect to how they handle transactional problems – are matched, using economic efficiency as the explanatory principle (cf. also Nickerson and Zenger, 2004).

Economic organization

'Coase vs. Hayek: Economic Organization and the Knowledge Economy' grapples with knowledge governance issues in a more substantive than methodological way. The context of the paper is arguments that the emerging knowledge economy is going to have strong transformative implications for the boundaries of firms as well as for 'traditional' authority relations, claims that have flourished in the management literature (as well as in popular discourse) over the last decades. The paper develops a framework for examining such claims, making use of organization economics insights to examine claims that, for example, traditional authority relations and firms boundaries (the 'Coasian' dimension) are increasingly breaking down as knowledge workers gain bargaining power and firms increasingly need to source knowledge beyond their boundaries (the 'Hayekian' dimension).

It is a sort of programmatic paper that set the stage for a number of my subsequent research efforts. In particular, it points to the need in organizational economic and management research of devoting more effort to conceptualizing authority and to understanding the distinct incentive liabilities of authority. The standard notion of authority is essentially that of Coase (1937) which assumes that the boss can precisely identify the action that an employee should take and command him to take that action. If this is all authority was about, it is easy to see that it cannot survive 'knowledge economy conditions', that is, an increased reliance on knowledge workers who may have superior information about their own action sets and about which actions should efficiently be taken. However, authority is also about making delegating decision rights to employees (who may be better informed) and deciding on other aspects of organizational design (this is further developed in Foss and Foss, 2008b). The incentive problem arises once it is recognized that authority in this sense also gives managers the right to renege on, for example, delegation with potentially harmful effects on work motivation. Productivity and overall firm performance may suffer.

An example of this line of reasoning is 'Selective Intervention and Internal Hybrids: Interpreting and Learning from the Rise and Decline of the Oticon Spaghetti Organization' which discusses the radical organizational changes that took place in Danish hearing aids producer Oticon in the 1990s. In particular, the paper discusses the implementation of the so-called spaghetti organization, which was a radical move to install market mechanisms inside the corporate hierarchy of Oticon, and why this organizational form ultimately failed. Although the spaghetti organization seemingly represented a coherent organizational design, the paper argues that the very flat spaghetti organization fell victim to managerial meddling with the affairs of sub-ordinates, a meddling that proved strongly demotivating and gave rise to a more structured organizational form with more of a distance between employees and management. From the point of view of strategic management and organizational theory the contribution of the paper is to point to the potential incentive costs of strategies of using organizational means (e.g., emulating market organization) to foster dynamic capabilities. From the point of view of organizational economics, the contribution of this paper is to point to the potential importance of the otherwise neglected (or downplayed) phenomenon of managerial opportunism and to suggest that organizational form is an important antecedent of internal incentive problems.[5] In particular, the paper suggests that for property rights reasons – ultimately, managers do keep residual decision rights and credible commitments to not intervene are difficult to establish inside firms – there are limits to how far firms can go in the direction of emulating markets. This theme is also pursued in 'Tying the Manager's Hands: Constraining Opportunistic Managerial Intervention', co-authored with Kirsten Foss and Xosé Vázquez, which in contrast to the small-N research setting (well, 1) of the Oticon plays out in a large-N setting, namely firms in the Spanish food and electronics industries. The specific contribution of the paper is to look at the factors (reputation effects, informational distance within the hierarchy, unions, etc.) that may constrain the kind of managerial opportunism discussed in the Oticon case.

   The delegation theme is also discussed in 'Performance Pay, Delegation, and Multitasking under Uncertainty and Innovativeness: an Empirical Investigation', which was co-authored with my CBS-colleague, Keld Laursen, a prominent scholar in the economics of innovation (see also Laursen and Foss, 2003). In the paper we employ a database originally designed for innovation research to examine one of the key predictions of agency theory, the risk/incentives tradeoff. Finding that support for this relation is tenuous, we argue, relying on Jensen and Meckling (1992) and Prendergast (2002), that this is likely to be caused by delegation: Firms in uncertainty environments are likely to make more use of delegation, but delegation needs to be backed up with relatively high-powered incentives to check to moral hazard problem. Although agency theory is predicated on delegation (i.e., the principal delegates a task to the agent), our analysis suggests that agency theorists need to pay more attention to delegation and how it is linked to uncertain environments and asymmetric information (i.e., the agent being more knowledgeable about which actions should efficiently be taken than the principal).

Property rights
With Kirsten Foss I have developed a research stream that attempts to apply the economics of property rights (e.g., Coase, 1960; Alchian, 1965; Demsetz, 1967), particularly the work of Barzel (1997) to management issues (see also Foss and Foss, 2008a&b). (Strategic) management scholars have not traditionally been conversant with the economics of property rights so selling these ideas has been a somewhat uphill undertaking. However, economics of property rights seems to have become an increasingly strong voice in the conversation of strategy scholars, particularly in the context of the resource-based view of strategy (e.g., Teece, 1986; Oxley, 1999; Kim and Mahoney, 2002, 2005).

---

[5]   Baker, Gibbons and Murphy (2001) lends formal support to the reasoning in the paper.

The economics of property rights emerged from the recognition that transactions involve the exchange of property rights, rather than the exchange of physical goods *per se* (Coase, 1960). In his pioneering paper, Coase (1960) examines the economic welfare implications of the allocation of legally delineated rights (liability rights) to a subset of the total uses of an asset, namely those that have (non-pecuniary) external effects on the value that agents' can derive from their use rights over assets. Coase argues that these implications can only be grasped if a break is made with the 'faulty concept of a factor of production'; the latter should properly be thought of, not as physical entities but as right to perform certain actions (Coase, 1960: 155). These rights are property rights. Coase's paper gave rise to a spate of work on property rights and ownership (e.g., Alchian, 1965; Demsetz, 1967; Barzel, 1997) that developed more refined categorizations of property rights, for example, introducing distinctions between use rights, income rights, rights to exclude, and rights to alienate resources. Gradually, the economic notion of property rights became dissociated from legal notions. Rights to use, etc. assets may conceivably exist in the absence of the state, legal system, courts, etc. (Umbeck, 1981). Physical force and/or strong social norms may guarantee *de facto* control.

A more recent development is the work of Oliver Hart and his students and colleagues, sometimes called the 'new property rights view' to distinguish it from the work prompted by Coase (1960). As in Williamson's work, a central assumption is that because of transaction costs/bounded rationality, contracts must necessarily be incomplete in the sense that the allocation of control (property) rights cannot specified for all future states of the world. Following legal convention, ownership is defined as the possession of residual rights of control, that is, rights to control the uses of assets under contingencies that are not specified in the contract. By control is meant the ability to exclude other agents from deciding on the use of certain assets. These rights determine the boundaries of the firm: a firm is defined as a collection of jointly owned assets.

In 'Assets, Attributes and Ownership', Kirsten and I argue that this is a view that implicitly starts from the assumption that asset ownership is fully enforceable. However, recognizing with Barzel that assets have multiple attributes, and that these may be subject to capture in world of positive measurement and enforcement costs, implies that the notion of full asset ownership is problematic. Ownership is a function of the costs of enforcement and capture and of agents' abilities to engage in these activities. New property rights theorists sidestep these issues by implicitly assuming that residual rights of control are perfectly enforced. However, if they are allowed into the analysis, a very different rationale for asset ownership (and for who should own an asset) emerges, one that depends on costly measurement and on agents being of different types, rather than on asset ownership creating threat points under *ex post* bargaining. This is not to say that the new property rights economics is wrong; merely that it is different from the ideas of Coase, Alchian, Demsetz and Barzel, and that their approach should not be forgotten under the impact of enthusiasm over the ability to put property rights ideas in formal garb.

This is certainly also the case of strategic management: As Kirsten and I argue in 'Resources and Transaction Costs: How Property Rights and Economics Furthers the Resource-based View' property rights economics brings ideas of transaction costs directly into the picture and thus illuminates the transaction costs dimensions of resource value. If resources have multiple attributes (uses, functionalities, etc.), overall resource value is determined by the benefits of these attributes, net of the costs of protecting property rights to these attributes. Given positive protection costs, some attributes will be left in the public domain. Several implications follow. For example, a 'resource' is an endogenous outcome of processes of economizing with transaction costs and the proper unit of analysis may be the resource attribute rather than the resource itself. Moreover, the ability to reduce transaction costs (e.g., internal agency costs or the costs of transacting with suppliers or customers) can be a distinct source of competitive advantage. Indeed, in a broader perspective, the familiar VRIN conditions of sustained competitive advantage specify the conditions under which property rights to resources are secure.[6] In later work we have applied these ideas to understanding entrepreneurship in the context of the RBV (Foss and Foss, 2008a) and to understanding the transaction cost dimensions of competitive strategy (Foss and Foss, 2008b).

One of my most frequent collaborators has been Peter G. Klein (University of Missouri). Peter's background as a Williamson student and an Austrian has turned to fit out very well with my, roughly similar, theoretical preferences. We have co-authored numerous papers, mainly on issues of economic organization and entrepreneurship. 'Original and Derived Judgment: an Entrepreneurial Theory of Economic Organization' is an example of our collaboration (it also includes Kirsten Foss in the author team). It employs property rights notions and notions of ownership and does so in the context of entrepreneurship inside firms. Traditionally, entrepreneurs have been conceptualized as single persons (or in some recent cases, entrepreneurial teams). This tends to suppress the understanding that an entrepreneur can make employees act in an entrepreneurial manner to further the entrepreneur's vision, what we call 'proxy' or 'derived' entrepreneurship. Building a simple verbal and graphical model we model how much delegation the entrepreneur should optimally choose and we argue (in line with the reasoning in the above-mentioned papers) that an important function of ownership is that it provides the authority to set optimal levels of delegation.

The final paper in this collection 'Economic Freedom and Entrepreneurial Activity: some Cross-Country Evidence' (with Christian Bjørnskov) also brings together ideas on property rights and entrepreneurship, albeit on a much higher level of analysis. Essentially, the paper is an attempt to explain cross-country variation in entrepreneurial activity by means of the prevailing property rights structure, that is, economic policy and institutions. Although entrepreneurship has been much researched in economics lately, and while the same may be said of the link between economic growth and institutions, surprisingly the paper appears to be one the first papers (and perhaps *the* first) dealing empirically with the link between entrepreneurship and institutions in the economics literature, using cross-national data. The institutions/entrepreneurship link is arguably a link in the overall growth/institutions link, so for that reason exploring the former link seems important. We find that the size of the public sector and the instability of monetary policy are particularly harmful to entrepreneurial activity (another link back to my Austrian pedigree).

---

[6] These conditions specify that sustainability of competitive advantage obtains when the resources underlying strategies are valuable, rare and costly to imitate and substitute.

Coda

When approached by Matthew Pitman of Edward Elgar to undertake this project, I was initially somewhat hesitant: 'Collected papers' – like volumes – are usually reliable signals of careers that are approaching their sunset – not necessarily a good signal to send when you are in your early 40s! In my opinion (and no doubt in some readers' opinion!), I have just got started! Another reason I was hesitant has to do with my steadfast attempt to deny Smithian economies of specialization in research: Simply put, I have written about what has interested me, which turns out to have been a lot of different things, and it is not that easy to see how they are connected. After all, my intellectual heroes include thinkers as different as Yoram Barzel, James Coleman, Frank Knight, Axel Leijonhufvud, Ludwig von Mises, George Richardson, David Teece, and Oliver Williamson. I have benefited from interacting with people as different in their outlook as Geoff Hodgson and Yoram Barzel, or J.C. Spender and Anna Grandori, or Ulrich Witt and Oliver Williamson (and I am grateful to them all).

However, I decided to approach this as a sort of mid-career research report, and as a snapshot (or rather, brief documentary) of a series of research programs that I have contributed to get started, programs that surely are still developing. Rather than trying to do a comprehensive tracking of my research by including only well-cited papers, I would include those papers 1) that I liked and 2) which have had a more 'programmatic' function in starting some of my research programmes. Accordingly, the emphasis has been on starting points for research programs rather than very specific manifestations of these. For example, over the last few years I have done extensive empirical work on issues of knowledge governance and micro-foundations, some of it in an organizational behaviour vein. However, these research results are not reported here, either because they are still underway in the relevant journals or because they are (too) specific manifestations of an overall agenda.

I am fortunate to have had excellent co-authors, including Peter Abell, Torben Andersen, Christian Bjørnskov, Teppo Felin, Peter Klein, Thorbjørn Knudsen, Yasemin Kor, Richard Langlois, Lasse Lien, Brian Loasby, Joe Mahoney, Peter Møllgaard, Paul Robertson, Keld Laursen, Torben Pedersen, Xosé Vázquez and, last, but most emphatically not least, Kirsten Foss. A number of the papers in this collection represent joint work with a subset of these. I am happy dedicate this collection to my co-authors.

References

Abell, P.M., T. Felin, and N.J. Foss, 2008. 'Building Microfoundations for the Routines, Capabilities and Performance Link', *Managerial and Decision Economics* (forthcoming).

Alchian, A.A. 1965. 'Some Economics of Property Rights', in idem. 1977. *Economics Analysis of Property Rights*. Indianapolis: Liberty Press.

Baker, G., R. Gibbons, and K.J. Murphy. 2001. 'Bringing the Market Inside the Firm', *American Economic Review* 91 (Papers and Proceedings): 212–18.

Barney, J.B. 1991. 'Firm Resources and Sustained Competitive Advantage', *Journal of Management, 17:* 99–120.

Barney, J.B. 2001. 'Resource-based Theories of Competitive Advantage: A Ten-Year Retrospective on the Resource-based View', *Journal of Management* 27: 643–50.

Barzel, Yoram. 1997. *Economic Analysis of Property Rights*. Cambridge: Cambridge University Press.

Cartwright, N. 1989. *Nature's Capacities and Their Measurement*. Oxford: Oxford University Press.

Coase, R.H. 1937. 'The Nature of the Firm', *Economica* (N.S.) 4: 386–405.

Coase, R.H. 1960. 'The Problem of Social Cost', in idem. 1988. *The Firm, the Market and the State*. Chicago: University of Chicago Press.

Coff, R. 1997. 'Human Assets and Management Dilemmas: Coping With Hazards on the Road to Resource-based Theory', *Academy of Management Review*, 22: 374–402.

Cyert, Richard and James G. March. 1963. *The Behavioral Theory of the Firm*. Oxford: Oxford University Press.

Demsetz, H. 1967. 'Toward a Theory of Property Rights', in H. Demsetz 1988. *Ownership, Control, and the Firm*. Oxford: Basil Blackwell.

Felin, Teppo and N.J. Foss. 2006. 'Individuals and Organizations: Thoughts on a Micro-Foundations Project for Strategic Management', *Research Methodology in Strategy and Management* 3: 253–88.

Felin, T. and N.J. Foss. 2009. 'Social Reality, the Boundary of Self-Fulfilling Prophecy, and Economics', *Organization Science* (forthcoming).

Foss, N.J. 1993a. 'Theories of the Firm: Contractual and Competence Perspectives', *Journal of Evolutionary Economics* 3: 144–60.

Foss, N.J. 1993b. 'More on Knight and the Theory of the Firm', *Managerial and Decision Economics* 14: 269–76.

Foss, N.J. 1994a. *The Austrian School and Modern Economics: Essays in Reassessment*. Copenhagen: Copenhagen Business School Press.

Foss, N.J. 1994b. 'The Theory of the Firm: The Austrians as Precursors and Critics of Contemporary Theory', *Review of Austrian Economics* 7 (1): 31–65.

Foss, N.J. 1994c. 'Realism and Evolutionary Economics', *Journal of Social and Biological Systems* 17: 21–40.

Foss, N.J. 1994d. 'The Two Coasian Traditions', *Review of Political Economy* 6: 35–61.

Foss, N.J. 1994e. 'Why Transaction Cost Economics Needs Evolutionary Economics', *Revue d'Economie Industrielle* 68: 7–26.

Foss, N.J. 1994f. 'Cooperation is Competition: George Richardson on Coordination and Interfirm Arrangements', *British Review of Economic Issues* 16: 25–49.

Foss, N.J. 1995. 'The Economic Thought of an Austrian Marshallian: George Barclay Richardson', *Journal of Economic Studies* 22: 23–44.

Foss, N.J. 1996. 'More on "Hayek's Transformation"', *History of Political Economy* 27 (2): 345–64.

Foss, N.J. 1998. 'The New Growth Theory: Some Intellectual Growth Accounting', *Journal of Economic Methodology* 5: 223–46.

Foss, N.J. 1999a. 'Edith Penrose, Economics, and Strategic Management', *Perspectives in Political Economy* 18: 87–104.

Foss, N.J. 1999b. 'Research in the Strategic Theory of the Firm: "Integrationism" and "Isolationism"', *Journal of Management Studies* 36: 725–55.

Foss, N.J. 2000. 'Austrian Economics and Game Theory: An Evaluation and a Stocktaking', *Review of Austrian Economics* 13: 41–58.

Foss, N.J. 2005. *Strategy and Economic Organization in the Knowledge Economy*. Oxford: Oxford University Press.

Foss, N.J. 2007. 'Knowledge Governance in a Dynamic Global Context: The Center for Strategic Management and Globalization at the Copenhagen Business School', *European Management Review* 4: 183–91.

Foss, N.J. and K. Foss. 2008a. 'Understanding Opportunity Discovery and Sustainable Advantage: the Role of Transaction Costs and Property Rights', *Strategic Entrepreneurship Journal* (forthcoming).

Foss, N.J. and K. Foss. 2008b. 'Hayekian Knowledge Problems in Organizational Theory', *Organization Studies* (forthcoming).

Foss, N.J. and B.J. Loasby, eds. 1998. *Economic Organization, Capabilities, and Coordination: Essays in Honor of GB Richardson*. London: Routledge.

Foss, N.J. and V. Mahnke, eds. 2000. *Competence, Governance and Entrepreneurship*. Oxford: Oxford University Press.

Foss, N.J. and S. Michailova. 2008. *Knowledge Governance: Perspectives From Different Disciplines*. Oxford: Oxford University Press.

Frey, B. and A. Stutzer, eds. 2007. *Economics and Psychology*. Cambridge, MA: MIT Press.

Friedman, M. 1968. 'The Role of Monetary Policy', *American Economic Review* 58: 1–17.

Ghoshal, S. and B. Løvas. 2000. 'Strategy as Guided Evolution', *Strategic Management Journal* 21: 875–96.

Grandori, A. 1997. 'Governance Structures, Coordination Mechanisms and Cognitive Models', *Journal of Management and Governance* 1: 29–42.

Grandori, A. 2001. 'Neither Hierarchy nor Identity: Knowledge Governance Mechanisms and the Theory of the Firm', *Journal of Management and Governance* 5: 381–99.

Grossman, S. and O. Hart. 1986. 'The Costs and Benefits of Ownership: A Theory of Vertical Integration', *Journal of Political Economy* 94: 691–719.

Hayek, F.A.v. 1931. *Prices and Production*. London: Routledge and Kegan Paul.

Hayek, F.A.v. 1945. 'The Use of Knowledge in Society', in idem. 1948. *Individualism and Economic Order*. Chicago: University of Chicago Press.

Hazlitt, H. 1959. *The Failure of the New Economics*. Princeton: van Nostrand.

Hedlund, G. 1986. 'The Hypermodern MNC – A Heterarchy?', *Human Resource Management* 21: 9–35.

Jensen, M.C. and W.H. Meckling. 1992. 'Specific and General Knowledge and Organizational Structure', in L. Werin and H. Wijkander, eds. *Contract Economics*. Oxford: Blackwell.

Kim, J. and J.T. Mahoney. 2002. 'Resource-based and Property Rights Perspectives on Value Creation: the Case of Oil Field Unitization', *Managerial and Decision Economics* 23: 225–45.

Kim, J. and J.T. Mahoney. 2005. 'Property Rights Theory, Transaction Costs Theory, and Agency Theory: An Organizational Economics Approach to Strategic Management', *Managerial and Decision Economics* 26: 223–42.

Klein, N. 2008. *The Shock Doctrine: The Rise of Disaster Capitalism*. London: Picador.

Kogut, B. and U. Zander. 1992. 'Knowledge of the Firm, Combinative Capabilities, and the Replication of Technology', *Organization Science* 3: 383–97.

Lakatos, I. 1970. 'Falsification and the Methodology of Scientific Research Programmes', in I. Lakators and A. Musgrave, eds. 1970. *Falsification and the Methodology of Scientific Research Programmes*. Cambridge: Cambridge University Press.

Langlois, R.N. 1988. 'Economic Change and the Boundaries of the Firm', *Journal of Institutional and Theoretical Economics* 144: 635–57.

Langlois, R.N. 1992. 'Transaction Cost Economics in Real Time', *Industrial and Corporate Change* 1: 99–127.

Langlois, R.N. and N.J. Foss. 1999. 'Capabilities and Governance: the Rebirth of Production in the Theory of Economic Organization', *KYKLOS* 52: 201–18.

Langlois, R.N. and P. Robertson. 1995. *Firms, Markets and Economic Change*. London: Routledge.

Laursen, K. and N.J. Foss. 2003. 'New HRM Practices, Complementarities, and the Impact on Innovation Performance', *Cambridge Journal of Economics* 27: 243–63.

Leijonhufvud, A. 1968. *On Keynesian Economics and the Economics of Keynes*. Oxford: The Clarendon Press.

Lippman, S.A. and Rumelt, R.P. 1982. 'Uncertain Imitability: an Analysis of Inter-Firm Efficiency under Competition', *Bell Journal of Economics,* 13: 418–38.

Lippman, S.A. and Rumelt, R.P. 2003a. 'The Payments Perspective: Micro-Foundations of Resource Analysis', *Strategic Management Journal*, 24: 903–27.

Lippman, S.A. and Rumelt, R.P. 2003b. 'A Bargaining Perspective on Resource Advantage', *Strategic Management Journal*, 24: 1069–86.

Loasby, Brian J. 1976. *Choice, Complexity, and Ignorance*. Cambridge: Cambridge University Press.

Loasby, Brian J. 1991. *Equilibrium and Evolution*. Manchester: Manchester University Press.

Lucas, R. 1977. 'Understanding Business Cycles', in idem. 1981. *Studies in Business Cycle Theory*. Boston: MIT Press.

Lucas, R. 1980. 'Methods and Problems in Business Cycle Theory', in in idem. 1981. *Studies in Business Cycle Theory*. Boston: MIT Press.

McCloskey, D.M. 1983. 'The Rhetorics of Economics', *Journal of Economic Literature* 21: 481–517.

Makadok, R. and J.B. Barney. 2001. 'Strategic Factor Market Intelligence: An Application of Information Economics to Strategy', *Management Science*:1621–38.

March, J.G. 1991. 'Exploration and Exploitation in Organizational Learning', 2: 71–87.

Nelson, R.R. and S.G. Winter. 1982. *An Evolutionary Theory of Economic Change*. Cambridge, MA: The Belknap Press.

Nickerson, J.A. and T. Zenger. 2004. 'A Knowledge-based Theory of Governance Choice: The Problem Solving Approach'. *Organization Science* 15: 617–32.

Osterloh, Margit and Bruno Frey. 2000. 'Motivation, Knowledge Transfer and Organizational Forms', *Organizational Science* 11: 538–50.

Oxley, J. 1999. 'Institutional Environment and the Mechanisms of Governance: The Impact of Intellectual Property Protection on the Structure of Inter-firm Alliances', *Journal of Economic Behavior and Organization* 38: 283–309.

Penrose, E.T. 1959. *The Theory of the Growth of the Firm*. Oxford: Oxford University Press.

Prendergast, C. 2002. 'The Tenuous Tradeoff Between Risk and Incentives', *Journal of Political Economy* 110: 1071–102.

Richardson, G.B. 1960. *Information and Investment*. Oxford: Oxford University Press.

Richardson, G.B. 1972. 'The Organisation of Industry', *Economic Journal* 82: 883–96.

Simon, Herbert A. and James G. March. 1958. *Organizations*. New York: Wiley.

Teece, D.J. 1986. 'Profiting from Technological Corporation', *Research Policy* 15: 285–305.

Teece, D.J. 2007. 'Explicating Dynamic Capabilities: the Nature and Microfoundations of (Sustainable) Enterprise Performance', *Strategic Management Journal* 28:1319–50.

Teece, D.J., G. Pisano, and A. Shuen. 1997. 'Dynamic Capabilities and Strategic Management', *Strategic Management Journal* 18: 509–33.

Umbeck, John. 1981. 'Might Makes Rights: A Theory of the Formation and Initial Distribution of Property Rights', *Economic Inquiry* 19: 38–59.

Williamson, O.E. 1985. *The Economic Institutions of Capitalism*. New York: The Free Press.

Williamson, O.E. 1991. 'Comparative Economic Organization: The Analysis of Discrete Structural Alternatives', *Administrative Science Quarterly* 36: 269–96.

Williamson, O.E. 1996. *The Mechanisms of Governance*. Oxford: Oxford University Press.

PART I

KNOWLEDGE AND MICRO-FOUNDATIONS

[1]

Knowledge-based Approaches to the Theory of the Firm: Some Critical Comments

Nicolai J. Foss

Department of Industrial Economics and Strategy, Copenhagen Business School,
Nansensgade 19.6, DK−1366 Copenhagen K, Denmark

Abstract

It is argued that Kogut and Zander (1992) and Conner (1991) erred in the specific way in which they claimed that a distinct theory of the multi-person firm can be constructed on the basis of a theory of organizational knowledge or from resource-based insights. It is not possible to tell very much of a story about why there should be firms in lieu of notions such as "opportunism" or "moral hazard." However, properly interpreted, knowledge-based theories may help shed light on issues relating to the boundaries and internal organization of the firm.

(*Organizational Knowledge*; *Existence and Boundaries of the Firm*)

Approaches to the Theory of the Firm

A number of recent contributions to the economic theory of the firm have made use of insights that essentially stem from—or are closely related to—organizational theory, and have tried to theorize aspects of economic organization on that basis. Although I treat such contributions under one label, namely as "knowledge-based approaches to the theory of the firm", this should not disguise existing differences.[1] Some of these contributions have emerged from the resource-based literature on the firm (such as Conner 1991), while other contributions are more explicitly evolutionary in focus (Langlois 1992, Dosi et al. 1992, Kogut and Zander 1992, Foss 1993b). Some of them self-consciously make a break with existing theories of economic organization (Conner 1991, Kogut and Zander 1992), while others emphasize complementarities to existing theories (Dosi et al. 1992). However, they are all agreed on the need for a knowledge-perspective on the firm, that is for conceptualizing firms as heterogenous, knowledge-bearing entities.

What is meant by "a theory of the firm" in turn is a theory that addresses the issues of the existence, the boundaries, and the internal organization of the multi-person firm (I neglect the unitary firm.) This conception of the primary requisites of a theory of the firm dates back, of course, to Ronald Coase's 1937 classic,

"The Nature of the Firm." It has since then been given impetus by the likes of Oliver Williamson (1985), Harold Demsetz and Armen A. Alchian (1972), Steven N. S. Cheung et al. (1986), and a host of other theorists. In fact, the modern theory of the firm—or broader, of economic organization—is perhaps the most rapidly expanding field of economics. And as is not unusual with a relatively new and rapidly expanding field, it has already branched into several distinct subfields and diverging approaches (Foss 1993c). What however unites the above mentioned heirs to Coase's approach is the view that the firm should be seen as an efficient contractual entity and that this is—for understanding the issues of the existence, boundaries, and internal organization—the essential and necessary conceptualization of the firm. Property rights, incentives, and contracts occupy center stage.

What is common to all knowledge-based contributions to the theory of the firm that are explicitly influenced by organizational theory is that they reject the *pure* contractual interpretation of the nature of the firm. Some of these contributions argue that the essential thing about the firm is not *only* its "contractualness," but just as much its function as a repository of distinct productive (technological and organizational) knowledge, and as an entity that can learn—and grow—on the basis of this knowledge (Dosi et al. 1992). Such knowledge stocks are associated with differential efficiencies, and are accumulated in a path-dependent way. Thus, they not only help explain why some firms realize competitive advantage while other firms do not, they also help in addressing issues related to diversification and innovation. In this view of the firm, it is Edith Penrose's 1959 classic, "The Theory of the Growth of the Firm," just as much as Coase's, "The Nature of the Firm" that defines the proper lenses through which firm activity should be perceived. Key words are here "capabilities," "competencies," "learning," "social knowledge," and "tacit knowledge," indicating the huge epistemic content in these theories.[2]

But one can quite meaningfully argue that the conceptualization of the firm one chooses should depend

3

on the purpose (cf. Machlup 1967): if that purpose is to investigate successful growth strategies, technological development, imitative strategies, and perhaps the sources of competitive advantage we should apply a Penrosian or some other knowledge-based conceptualization, and perhaps not pay much attention to matters of economic organization. But if the purpose, on the other hand, is to investigate the issues of the existence, boundaries, and internal organization of the firm, we may do with a pure contractual/Coasian conceptualization. As already indicated, there is, however, also a small but growing literature that explicitly emphasize complementarities between the above conceptualizations, placing them on an equal footing. The implicit argument is that some phenomena—such as the organization of innovation activities—can be fully addressed only by such a combined theory. This literature denies, however, that perspectives on the firm that emphasize its knowledge-bearing nature unassisted by Coasian/contractual insights can say anything substantial about the existence, boundaries, and internal organization of the firm.

That something substantial about the existence, boundaries, and internal organization may be said without assistance from the contractual approach is argued by some recent advocates of the view of the firm as *essentially* a knowledge-bearing entity (rather than essentially a contractual one). They argue this on the ground that it is possible to deduct from this conceptualization a theory of economic organization that at least in some respects differs significantly from the contractual approaches. Specifically, it is possible to avoid any reference to concepts such as property rights, incentives, and opportunism for understanding at least the existence of the firm (but probably also the boundaries and internal organization of the firm).

It is this version of knowledge-based approaches— here represented by Kathleen Conner (1991) and Bruce Kogut and Udo Zander (1992)—that I want to take issue with in the following. I start with Kogut and Zander's analysis, and then move on to a brief discussion of Conner's closely related discussion. Briefly, I argue that the implicit assertion of these authors—that they have given *sufficient* reasons for the existence of the firm—is erroneous, since they have indicated only *necessary* reasons. I finally indicate how a knowledge-perspective may *complement*—but not substitute for— the contractual approach.

Kogut and Zander's Analysis

In this section I discuss only a few aspects of Kogut and Zander's (1992) very rich discussion, focusing on

those aspects that have a *direct* bearing on the theory of the firm. Almost in the beginning of their article, Kogut and Zander put forward what appears to be their central conclusion:

> Our view differs radically from that of the firm as a bundle of contracts that serves to allocate efficiently property rights. In contrast to the contract approach to understanding organizations, the assumptions of the selfish motives of individuals resulting in shirking or dishonesty is not a necessary premise in our argument. Rather, we suggest that organizations are social communities in which individual and social expertise is transformed into economically useful products and services by the application of a set of higher-order organizing principles. *Firms exist because they provide a social community of voluntaristic action structured by organizing principles that are not reducible to individuals* (p. 384; my emphasis).

And this is given the following nutshell conceptualization, paraphrasing Michael Polanyi's well-known dictum: "...organizations know more than what their contracts can say" (p. 383). Much of Kogut and Zander's contribution is occupied with clarifying the *meaning* of such statements and with making a number of *implications*, once the meaning has been established.

Concerning the *meaning* of saying that, for example, "organizations know more than their contracts can say," what is meant is that a large part of that stock of knowledge that may be an important co-determinant of firms' competitive advantages and positions is *tacit*[3] and *social*. This, in turn, means that the knowledge is produced and reproduced in a social setting, is inseparable from this setting, and is not fully reducible to individuals. Because of the character of this kind of knowledge and the way it is accumulated through experiences of particularity, particularly in social settings, it is largely *path-dependent*. The firm is very much a distinct social and historical entity. Much of this is familiar from knowledge-based writings on the firm (such as Penrose 1959, Nelson and Winter 1982), although Kogut and Zander's discussion is a great deal more comprehensive and thorough than is usual, supplementing the discussion with subtle insights from group psychology, computer science, and interpretive sociology. The *new* aspect of their discussion seems to me to be primarily the various *implications* they distill from their discussion of the firm as a knowledge-bearing entity.

One such implication (among many) of this conceptualization of the firm as a bearer of tacit, social, and path-dependent organizational knowledge is to throw the issues of the existence, boundaries, and internal organization of the firm into a wholly different light relative to the conceptualizations of the contractual

NICOLAI J. FOSS *Knowledge-based Approaches to the Theory of the Firm*

approaches. The firm, we have seen, is a repository of specialized and tacit knowledge that is fully efficient in use only within that firm, since it is difficult to take a piece—whatever that would mean—of the stock of firm-specific tacit and social knowledge out of the firm and successfully apply it in a different firm.[1]

From this it follows, according to Kogut and Zander, that firms exist, *because* they provide "a social community of voluntaristic action" in which such knowledge can be learned, produced, and commercially applied. The advantage that firms have over market relationships in carrying out (some) complex productive tasks is —according to Kogut and Zander—one that is distinct from the incentive alignment advantages emphasized by contractual theories (for example, in situations characterized by high levels of asset specificity). Specifically, it does not have anything to do with mitigating opportunism/moral hazard. Firms' advantages over markets derive from their being able to supply some, as Kogut and Zander say, "*higher order organizing principles*" that the market supposedly cannot supply, and in which the members of the organizations are embedded. It is not entirely clear what these higher-order organizing principles are, but they would seem to include "shared coding schemes," "values," "a shared language," as well as "...mechanisms by which to codify technologies into a language accessible to a wider circle of individuals" (Kogut and Zander 1992, p. 389).

Conner's Argument

Kathleen Conner's article, "A Historical Comparison of Resource-Based Theory and Five Schools of Thought Within Industrial Organization Economics: Do We Have a New Theory of the Firm" (1991), is a long, scholarly analysis of the two partly separable issues defined by the title of the article. Thus, the emerging resource-based approach is compared to neoclassical price-theory, Bain-type industrial organization economics, Schumpeterian approaches, Chicago-type industrial organization economics, and "Coase/Williamson transaction cost economics." It is this last comparison that interest me here, since Conner's discussion is somewhat different from Kogut and Zander's discussion, although her conclusion—that it is possible to explain the existence of the firm in a resource-based way that is conceptually different from the contractual view—is essentially the same.

On the existence issue, Conner submits that

...existence needs to be explained in terms of a firm's superiority to *two* alternative forms of organization: a collection of market contracts *and* other firms. By the latter, the intention

is to raise the issue of why a particular firm exists, as opposed to its assets being distributed among other firms (1991, p. 139).

Her overall view seems to be that co-specialization of assets holds the theoretical key to *both* the above two existence issues, quite independent of considerations of transaction costs, incentives, and opportunism. On the latter existence issue—why does a particular firm exist in terms of its relation to other firms?—this is because some (co-specialized) assets make "a better fit" (ibid.) with some firms than with other firms. But co-specialization also seems to hold the key to the first existence issue.

To illustrate, consider an example given by Conner (1991) of a research project undertaken to create a product using advances in technology to be developed during the course of the project. The project involves two related activities, S and T. We use the notation ST if S and T are owned in common, and $S + T$ if they are owned separately. Under ST the project is done in-house, whereas under $S + T$ the project involves a contract over the market interface between the owners of S and T. Now, on Conner's view, $S + T$, as compared to ST, should find it more difficult to orient the research so that knowledge and skills can be redeployed, simply because "$S + T$ must try to orient in *two* different directions" (Conner 1991, p. 142). Cooperation in terms of ST is in contrast facilitated by the fact that only cooperation in *one* direction is needed. Essentially, this is because of the presence of what Kogut and Zander call higher order organizing principles, viz. shared codes, language etc. The implication is that the cooperation and coordination gain associated with ST relative to $S + T$ is *sufficient* to explain the *existence* of ST. The general issue can be formulated as follows:

...under certain circumstances, firms have advantage over market relationships in the *joint activity* of creating and redeploying specific capital [*and this explains why they exist, NJF*]. Further, the advantage of firms in the creation-redeployment combination need not stem from an opportunism-control advantage (Conner 1991, p. 140).

Thus, rather than being an "avoider of a negative" (viz. avoider of opportunism), the firm is seen in as a "creator of a positive" (ibid., p. 139). In the following, I argue that these two conceptualizations do not exclude each other, that the advantage Conner identifies is not sufficient to explain the existence of the firm, and that her separation of the existence issue in two parts is a nonissue.

NICOLAI J. FOSS   *Knowledge-based Approaches to the Theory of the Firm*

Discussion

Conner's and Kogut and Zander's views are both non sequiturs and versions—albeit very sophisticated ones—of what Williamson (1985) calls "technological determinism." By this expression he refers to the idea that technology *directly* determines economic organization, so that for example the size of a business organization is directly determined by its minimum efficient scale, that diversified firms exist because of technological economies of scope alone, or that vertical integration takes place because of the need for, say, physical proximity between various pieces of capital equipment. One problem with this idea is that

> [t]echnology is fully determinative of economic organization only if (1) there is a single technology that is decisively superior to all others, and (2) that technology implies a unique organization form. Rarely is there only a single feasible technology, and even more rarely is the choice among alternative organization form determined by technology (Williamson 1985, p. 87).

The kernel of truth in technological determinism is that different technologies yield different constellations of transaction and information costs, and therefore loosely influence economic organization (perhaps define some boundaries for efficient economic organization). But the influence is indirect and the linkage is not tight.

Conner and Kogut and Zander commit the fallacy of technological determinism when they argue that the need for shared codes, languages etc.—easing efficient deployment and utilization of assets—*necessitates* firm organization in a way that can be seen in isolation from considerations of opportunism/moral hazard. It is probably true that the gains identified by Conner and Kogut and Zander are *necessary* to explain firm organization. In fact, this is exactly why value-increasing asset-specificity (Williamson 1985) and/or team-organization (Alchian and Demsetz 1972) are highlighted in the contractual approach, viz. why the conceptualization of the firm as a "creator of a positive" (Conner 1991, p. 139) is *also* important in the contractual approach. But these gains are not sufficient to explain the existence of firm organization.

To fully realize the values of assets/resources, they have—according to Conner and Kogut and Zander—to be embedded within the higher order organizing principles of shared cultures, languages, codes, etc. This may be true for a number of productive tasks. But such embeddedness does not conceptually presuppose common ownership/firm organization; to claim that is to engage in a sophisticated version of technological de-

terminism, viz. to claim that the need for communication channels, shared culture, and other forms of social knowledge *in itself* makes firm organization necessary. In fact, separately owned activities may *conceptually* be much more "embedded" in the above sense than, for example, divisions of the same firm. It is erroneous to think that higher order organizing principles are a *qualitative* differential of the firm relative to the market, although they are probably in reality a *quantitative* one. That is, the qualitative presence of higher order oganizing principles does not necessarily distinguish the market relative to the firm; rather, there may be "more of it" in the firm than in the market, as Arrow (1974) forcefully argued. The argument that firms better cultivate higher order organizing principles demands, however, precisely an argument from opportunism. To see why, consider the following reasoning.

In a moral utopia, characterized by the absence of opportunistic proclivities (the setting that implicitly underlies Conner, and Kogut and Zander's analyses), the gains from resources/assets being embedded in higher order organizing principles could be realized over *the market*. Agents (human resources) could simply meet under the same factory roof, own their own pieces of physical capital equipment or rent it to each other, and develop value-enhancing higher order organizing principles among themselves (as a team). In the absence of opportunism/moral hazard, the degree of co-specialization among the various resources would carry *no* implications for ownership. Or in terms of Conner's example above, $S + T$ could do just exactly as well as could ST. The conclusion on all this is that co-specialization and the presence of higher order organizing principles are not sufficient to explain the existence of the specific constellation of property rights that characterizes the firm.

The argument from the contractual approach would be that because hierarchy can more successfully control opportunism/moral hazard, higher order organizing principles would emerge.[5] This is because the absence of opportunism that the hierarchy may help to create—through internal labor markets, incentive alignment, hierarchical oversight, etc.—stimulates the emergence of trust, cooperation, information exchange, and various sets of commitments, which is precisely what seem to be packed into the concept of higher order organizing principles. In other words, the web of contractual agreements and expectations give employees such incentives that they will invest in accumulating useful social knowledge, and thereby create a "social community of voluntaristic action" (Kogut and Zander 1992, p. 384). This also explains why there normally are more of these higher order organizing principles in firms than in markets. There really is a good reason why we normally speak of corporate culture rather than of industry culture.[6] Conner's and Kogut and Zander's reasoning would not be able to explain this, however, since by dispensing with the notion of opportunism they are fundamentally unable to explain why there should be "more of it" in firms than in markets.

In the contractual approach, the fundamental reason why various resources/assets are brought under common ownership is precisely because of the incentive problems that may arise in situations of (1) high asset-specificity or nonverifiable marginal products under team-production and (2) proclivities to opportunism/moral hazard. This provides a further perspective on Conner's and Kogut and Zander's reasoning, since in this scheme of thought, co-specialized resources/assets are organized more often in the firm than in the market precisely, because co-specialization produces rents that can be appropriated by opportunistic input-owners. This is a general explanation in the sense that it explains both the existence of the firm relative to the market and why a particular firm owns a particular combination of assets/resources. On this reading, Conner's (1991, p. 139) separation of the two is a nonissue. Furthermore, higher order organizing principles may be analyzed as rent-yielding *specific assets*,[7] so the reason why there is "more of it" in the firm than in the market is that firm-organization is the transaction cost-minimizing mode of organizing for this type of asset.

Knowledge-based Approaches and Economic Organization

I have responded to Conner's and Kogut and Zander's analyses by upholding the essential correctness of the contractual approach. We cannot do without concepts such as opportunism if we wish to explain the existence of the firm. That does not preclude, however, that one recognizes the relations of complementarity that exist between a contractual and a knowledge perspective on the firm. These complementarities are particularly fruitful for analyzing the issues of the boundaries and internal organization of the firm. David Teece (1982) in particular has detailed how considerations of appropriability of rent-yielding knowledge resources may influence the firm's boundary choice. But there are other, less developed, points of contact.

For example, one may see knowledge perspectives on the firm as complementing analysis of various

agency-problems of internal organization, so that—for example—the organizational knowledge residing in business culture is also seen as influencing the organization's agency costs. They may also bear some promises for broadening the concept of asset-specificity, as argued by Klein (1988). Furthermore, some aspects of a knowledge perspectives nicely complement the incomplete contract-logic of Grossman and Hart (1986): if long contracts are incomplete, the culture and other higher order organizing principles of the firm may provide clues as to how managers will react to those contingencies that are not stipulated in the contract (Kreps 1990). That is to say, incomplete contracts are made less incomplete because of the presence of higher order organizing principles. Finally, some sort of incorporation of knowledge-perspectives in the contractual approach would allow a more fine-grained analysis of the boundaries of the firm. For example, as the diversifying firm moves increasingly away from its core competencies/core business, it may confront increasing agency costs, as increasingly unfamiliar activities produce more severe moral hazard and adverse selection problems. What is common to all these stories is that the boundaries and internal organization of the firm are all fundamentally understood to involve considerations of opportunism/moral hazard. That is in accordance with the tenor of my argument so far. But I am willing to admit that *some* limited aspects of the boundaries of the firm may be explained in terms that avoid reference to opportunism/moral hazard. I identify these aspects in the following.

One problem in the contractual approach is that it is often implicitly assumed that what one firm can do on the level of production, another firm can do equally well, so that differences in economic organization are not allowed to turn on differences in production costs (Demsetz 1988).[8] Kogut and Zander (1992) rightly take issue with this. The fact that firms simply aren't equally good at producing goods and services—they have "differential capabilities"—may, as Kogut and Zander argue, explain some aspects of the boundaries of the firm. This is the kernel of truth in the claim that not *all* aspects of economic organization demands an explanation in terms of opportunism/moral hazard. But notice that this does not imply a break with an essentially contractual approach. For we can ask why it is that boundary choices are allowed to turn on differential capabilities.

And the answer has not really to do with production costs per se, but rather with *information* (or communication) costs. If a firm internalizes some economic activity because it believes it can carry out the activity

8*Knowledge, Economic Organization and Property Rights*

NICOLAI J. FOSS   *Knowledge-based Approaches to the Theory of the Firm*

in a more efficient way, it has—at least conceptually—already had the possibility of communicating to (say) supplier firms. For the basis for the firm's belief that it can carry out the activity in a more efficient way must the in-house possession of some superior knowledge. But conceptually the firm has the option of communicating that superior knowledge to the supplier firm (viz. of educating it), so that the reason the activity is internalized must be either inability to communicate or very high information costs.

In fact, Morris Silver (1984) suggests an "entrepreneurial" theory of the boundaries of the firm on such reasoning, and Richard Langlois (1992) places Silver's reasoning within the context of a Marshallian perspective on the evolution of industries and technologies. As Silver (1984) notes:

> In my scenario the entrepreneur does not "do it himself" in order to the profitability of good X a secret. Just the opposite is the case! The innovator would prefer to concentrate his managerial resources narrowly on X. His problem is that he cannot, at reasonable cost, convey his implausible "secret" to those with the technical capabilities needed to produce the required operations at the lowest cost (p. 17).

Silver's and Langlois' contributions are interesting, and may usefully complement more standard contractual reasoning, particularly when analyzing economic organization in regimes of rapid technological change. But it is important in the present context to note that these authors do not say that their reasoning can explain *the existence* of the firm, "merely" its boundaries. Furthermore, Silver's story may be argued to be relatively limited. For example, observe how much it has to do with essential disparity in capabilities among firms, and the consequent nonability to communicate about, for example, technical matters. But much productive knowledge is surely shared in communities of firms, so that this forms a basis for communicating about technical matters. Or in Kogut and Zander's terminology, some higher order organizing principles *may* in fact be industry-specific, rather than firm-specific. This is more or less what Marshall (1925, p. 271) meant when he talked about "the industrial district," in which "the mysteries of the trade become no mysteries; but are as it were in the air." The paradigmatic modern example of co-specialized knowledge streams emerging across market interfaces would be firm-networks in Silicon Valley. In such cases, the boundaries of firms are difficult to rationalize except on a standard contractual basis, since the effects of differential capabilities would be negligible.

Conclusion

Summing up, we may conclude that some limited aspects of economic organization may be given to explanation in terms that avoid reference to incentives, property rights, and opportunism/moral hazard. But these aspects probably relate only to the issue of the boundaries of the firm in regimes where firms' capabilities are strongly diverging, and communication is therefore impossible or very costly. At any rate, I conclude that Conner and Kogut and Zander have not given convincing rationales—in the form of sufficient reasons—for the *existence* of the firm that avoid reference to the above terms.

Furthermore, much of what they say—for example, that firms rather than the market supply higher order organizing principles—is perfectly consistent with contractual reasoning. So, although the insight that organizations know more than their contracts can tell is a fundamental one, economists are not well-advised to make a break with an essentially contractual logic, and should not abstain from using concepts such as opportunism or moral hazard. At our current level of knowledge, they are necessary for obtaining significant explanatory power.

That does not mean that we should not try to incorporate some of the insights from knowledge-perspectives in the contractual approach. Understanding some important phenomena, such as the organization of innovation activities, the economic function of corporate culture, or diversification, would seem to necessitate precisely this, as clearly recognized by writers such as Teece (1982), Klein (1988), Kreps (1990), and Dosi, et al. (1992).

Acknowledgements
A number of perceptive comments from three anonymous referees is gratefully acknowledged. All responsibility for remaining errors belongs to the author.

Endnotes
[1] Note the distinction between a "knowledge-based approach to the theory of the firm" and a "knowledge-perspective," I use the last concept in order to distinguish theories of organizational knowledge ("knowledge-perspectives") from theories that *make use* of theories of organizational knowledge in order to address economic organization ("knowledge-based approaches").

[2] Actually, there are many distinct knowledge-based approaches, such as "the evolutionary theory of the firm" (Nelson and Winter 1982), Penrose's (1959) distinctive contribution, the recent "resource-based view of the firm," taking its lead from Penrose (Lippman and Rumelt 1982, Barney 1986, Conner 1991), "the capabilities view of the firm" (Langlois 1991, Chandler 1992), and recent writings in strategic

ORGANIZATION SCIENCE/Vol. 7, No. 5, September–October 1996

management on firms' core competencies (Prahalad and Hamel 1990). Perhaps Harvey Leibenstein's recent work on "effort conventions" (work norms that emerge from the latent prisoners' dilemma games postulated to be played between employees and managers, (Leibenstein 1987) and David Kreps' work on corporate culture (also conceptualized as norms emerging from iterated PD-games, Kreps 1990) should be included here.

[3] That is, not given to direct verbal articulation (non-discursiveness). Such knowledge goes under a number of names, such as "practical knowledge," "know-how," or "knowledge how" [one minor doctrinal quibble: that last concept is really due to British philosopher Gilbert Ryle (1949), not to Bertrand Russell, cf. Kogut and Zander (1992, p. 386)].

[4] This may be a bit of an overstatement, since some competencies may be copied by other firms, and since license markets and franchising exist for the purpose of transferring competencies. So one should distinguish between those competencies that may successfully be transferred and those that may not, on the basis, for example, of Lippman and Rumelt's (1982) concept of "causal ambiguity" (viz. the ability to ascertain the links between competitive advantage and a given resource/competence).

[5] We should not be led to believe that hierarchy does away with all opportunism/moral hazard, however (cf. Grossman and Hart 1986). The hierarchy has its own forms of opportunistic behavior (cf. Miller 1992).

[6] I will certainly not deny that this last concept may be a quite meaningful one. But to the extent that something like industry culture exists, it is probably supported by sets of incentives and commitments in much the same way as corporate culture is.

[7] Klein (1988) explicitly recommends that the concept of asset-specificity be broadened to include what he calls "organizational capital," which is the same as Kogut and Zander's "organizing principles." See Barney (1986) for an analysis of corporate culture as a rent-yielding resource.

[8] See Williamson (1985, p. 88) for some discussion of this. We should not neglect, however, that Williamson has consistently emphasized that efficient economic organization minimizes the sum of transaction *and* production costs.

References

Alchian, A. A. and H. Demsetz (1972), "Production, Information Costs, and Economic Organization," in *Economic Forces at Work: Selected Works by Armen Alchian*, Indianapolis, IN: Liberty Press.

Arrow, K. J. (1974), *The Limits of Organization*, New York: Norton.

Barney, J. B. (1986), "Organizational Culture: Can It Be a Source of Sustained Competitive Advantage?", *Academy of Management Review*, 11, 656–665.

Chandler, A. D. (1992), "Organizational Capabilities and the Economic History of the Industrial Enterprise," *Journal of Economic Perspectives*, 6, 79–100.

Coase, R. H. (1937), "The Nature of the Firm," *Economica*, 4, 386–405.

Conner, K. R. (1991), "A Historical Comparison of Resource-Based Theory and Five Schools of Thought Within Industrial Organization Economics: Do We Have a New Theory of the Firm?" *Journal of Management*, 17, 121–154.

Demsetz, H. (1988), "The Nature of the Firm Revisited," *Journal of Law, Economics and Organization*, 4, 141–162.

Dosi, G., S. G. Winter, and D. J. Teece (1992), "Towards a Theory of Corporate Coherence," in G. Dosi, R. Giannetti, and P. A. Toninelli, (Eds.), Oxford, UK: Clarendon Press.

Foss, N. J. (1993a), "More on Knight and the Theory of the Firm," *Managerial and Decision Economics*, 14, 269–276.

—— (1993b), "Theories of the Firm: Competence and Contractual Perspectives," *Journal of Evolutionary Economics*, 3, 127–144.

—— (1993c), "The Two Coasian Traditions," *Review of Political Economy*, 5, 508–532.

Grossman, S. J. and O. D. Hart (1986), "The Costs and Benefits of Ownership: A Theory of Vertical and Lateral Integration," *Journal of Political Economy*, 94, 691–719.

Klein, B. (1988), "Vertical Integration as Organizational Ownership," *Journal of Law, Economics and Organization*, 4, 201–213.

Kogut, B. and U. Zander (1992), "Knowledge of the Firm, Combinative Capabilities, and the Replication of Technology," *Organization Science*, 3, 383–397.

Kreps, D. M. (1990), "Corporate Culture and Economic Theory," in J. Alt and K. Shepsle (Eds.), *Perspectives on Political Economy*, Cambridge, UK: Cambridge University Press.

Langlois, R. N. (1992), "Transaction Cost Economics in Real Time," *Industrial and Corporate Change*, 1, 99–127.

Leibenstein, H. (1987), *Inside the Firm: The Inefficiencies of Hierarchy*, Cambridge, MA: Harvard University Press.

Lippman, S. A. and R. P. Rumelt (1982), Uncertain Imitability: An Analysis of Interfirm Differences in Efficiency under Competition, *Bell Journal of Economics*, 13, 418–438.

Machlup, F. (1967), "Theories of the Firm: Marginalist, Behavioral, Managerial," in *Methodology of Economics and Other Social Sciences*, New York: Academic Press.

Marshall, A. (1925), *Principles of Economics*, London, UK: MacMillan.

Miller, G. (1992), *Managerial Dilemmas*, Cambridge, UK: Cambridge University Press.

Nelson, R. R. and S. G. Winter (1982), *An Evolutionary Theory of Economic Change*, Cambridge, MA: Belknap Press.

Penrose, E. T. (1959), *The Theory of the Growth of the Firm*, Oxford, UK: Oxford University Press.

Prahalad, C. K. and G. Hamel (1990), "The Core Competence of the Corporation," *Harvard Business Review*, 66, 79–91.

Ryle, G. R. (1949), *The Concept of Mind*, London, UK: Hutchinson.

Silver, M. (1984), *Enterprise and the Scope of the Firm*, Oxford, UK: Martin Robertson.

Teece, D. J. (1982), "Towards an Economic Theory of the Multiproduct Firm," *Journal of Economic Behavior and Organization*, 3, 39–63.

Williamson, O. E. (1985), *The Economic Institutions of Capitalism*, New York: Free Press.

Accepted by Jay B. Barney.

[2]

Industrial and Corporate Change, Volume 12, Number 2, pp. 185–201

Bounded rationality and tacit knowledge in the organizational capabilities approach: an assessment and a re-evaluation

Nicolai J. Foss

The famous three chapters in Nelson and Winter's *An Evolutionary Theory of Economic Change* (1982) that focus on firm routines and capabilities are often taken to be solidly founded on an assumption of bounded rationality. I argue that, in actuality, bounded rationality plays a rather limited role in Nelson and Winter (1982), that the very different assumption of tacit knowledge is much more central, and that the links between bounded rationality and routines/capabilities are not clear. I then argue that the absence in Nelson and Winter of a clear methodological individualist foundation for notions such as routines, capabilities, competencies, etc., has resulted in certain explanatory difficulties in the modern organizational capabilities approach that has taken so much inspiration from their work.

1. Introduction

This paper discusses the respective explanatory roles of bounded rationality and tacit knowledge in the organizational capabilities approach, an increasingly influential approach to the theory of the firm that owes very much to Nelson and Winter's seminal volume, *An Evolutionary Theory of Economic Change* (1982). As befits a contribution to a special issue in honor of Nelson and Winter, particular attention is devoted to their much-cited treatment in chapters 3–5 in that book of bounded rationality and tacit knowledge in the context of firm organization and behavior a treatment that Selten (1990: 649) characterized as having 'brought new impulses to the modeling of bound-edly rational behavior in economics'. However, the examination of their treatment is not just undertaken for its sake, but also because the Nelson and Winter approach to conceptualizing the firm and understanding its organization and behavior has been extremely influential for writers within the organizational capabilities approach (an umbrella term covering capabilities, dynamic capabilities, and competence approaches as well as the evolutionary theory of the firm) (see also Pierce *et al.*, 2003). The organizational capabilities approach is quite often seen as an approach to the theory of the firm that puts much more of an emphasis on bounded rationality than is the case in, notably, transaction cost economics (e.g. Fransman, 1994; Conner and Prahalad, 1996;

10

Marengo *et al.*, 2000). It is also seen as one that goes beyond information processing and stresses the tacit and socially embedded aspects of knowledge (Fransman, 1994). Both of these characteristics hark directly back to Nelson and Winter.

In this paper I engage critically with this influential view. Specifically, the following points are developed. First, the argument is made that the theory of firm developed in Nelson and Winter (1982) is considerably less about bounded rationality than it is about socially held tacit knowledge. Bounded rationality and tacit knowledge do not logically imply each other. It may, in fact, be argued that Simonian bounded rationality and Polanyi's notion of tacit knowledge are ultimately founded on very different, and perhaps incompatible, epistemologies (see Nightingale, 2002). Attempts to combine the two are likely to be unsuccessful, one driving out the other. This is largely the case in Nelson and Winter (1982), in which tacit knowledge looms much larger than bounded rationality. The tip of balance in favor of tacit knowledge has become even more pronounced in subsequent work within the organizational capabilities approach. Second, the emphasis on *socially* held knowledge in the form of 'routines' and the downplaying of bounded rationality in Nelson and Winter (1982) mean that there is very little attention to the level of individual agent. Indeed, the Nelson and Winter theory (as well as many subsequent contributions to the organizational capabilities approach) may be criticized for not being consistent with methodological individualism, at least in the sense that it works with aggregate entities (i.e. routines and capabilities) that are not explicitly reduced to individual behavior. Third, I argue that the absence of a clear behavioral foundation for the organizational capabilities approach is the root cause of the difficulties that the organizational capabilities approach has with respect to illuminating the key organizational economics issues of the internal organization and boundaries of the firm.

2. Nelson and Winter (1982): a high point in the evolution of the organizational capabilities approach

2.1 Briefly on the organizational capabilities approach

What I here call the 'organizational capabilities approach' gets its name after chapter 5 in Nelson and Winter (1982) (see also Dosi *et al.*, 2000). Nelson and Winter (1982) has arguably appealed more to business administration and management (particularly strategy) scholars than to economists.[1] One paper after another, in such fields as strategy, organizational learning, international business and organizational behavior, have generously cited the book, particularly the three chapters (3–5) that deal with issues pertaining to individual and organizational behavior and capabilities. This is not surprising: re-reading the chapters makes one realize that perhaps not so much *essential* has happened in two succeeding decades of work on capabilities, competence, evolutionary, etc., theories of the firm that goes beyond Nelson and Winter's treatment. It is

---

[1] See the citation analysis in Meyer (2001).

arguable that later ideas on competence traps, the central importance of tacit and socially complex 'resources' for explaining competitive advantage, knowledge replication and dynamic capabilities can be found in at least an embryonic, and often quite explicit, form in Nelson and Winter (1982).

Quite appropriately, contributors to the organizational capabilities approach have therefore often treated Nelson and Winter (1982) not only as a source of inspiration, but also as a foundation. At first sight this may appear somewhat surprising, given that building a distinct theory of the firm was never the intention of Nelson and Winter (1982).[2] However, what may appeal to writers within the organizational capabilities approach is the attempt in that book to treat in a unified fashion bounded rationality and tacit knowledge, and at the same time place these in a social context—all of which converges in a single, highly intuitively plausible concept, namely that of 'routine'. These ideas, as well the use of them to help explaining revealed competitive advantages, innovation and limited aspects of economic organization, cannot really be found in any other of the precursors of the capabilities approach. Thus, what unites recent capabilities (Richardson, 1972; Chandler, 1992; Langlois, 1992), dynamic capabilities (Teece and Pisano, 1994), competence approaches (Sanchez, 2001), the knowledge-based view of the firm (Fransman, 1994; Grant, 1996), and, of course, the 'evolutionary theory of the firm' (e.g. Dosi, 2000; Marengo *et al.*, 2000) is indeed an emphasis on the central explanatory importance of experiential, localized, socially constructed and embedded knowledge and learning in understanding firm organization and behavior.

As Langlois and Foss (1999) point out, these approaches are also united in their attempt to increasingly go beyond their traditional explananda of explaining the sources of competitive advantage, localized innovative activity and general rigidity of firm behavior to also include issues, notably the boundaries and internal organization of the firm, that have traditionally been considered the turf of the more mainstream economics of organization. At the heart of these stories are the characteristics, notably tacitness, of the knowledge that is embedded in organizational capabilities (Kogut and Zander, 1992; Langlois, 1992). Some (vaguely specified) mechanism is supposed to link these characteristics to the boundaries of the firm as well as to aspects of internal organization.

It is quite common to interpret this literature as an attempt to provide more room for bounded rationality than is standard fare in the economics of organization (e.g. Fransman, 1994; Conner and Prahalad, 1996). However, it is seldom made clear in exactly what sense the organizational capabilities literature may be characterized as starting from bounded rationality. Because bounded rationality is, unfortunately, a concept that comes with an legacy of diverse and even conflicting interpretations, it does matter where exactly one starts from, and it is rather uninformative to say that the organizational capabilities approach builds on bounded rationality, unless one

---

[2] At the Academy of Management Meetings in Toronto, August 2000, Sidney Winter, in a major address, insisted that there is no theory of the firm in Nelson and Winter (1982). Presumably, what he meant is that there is no theory of the firm in the sense of explaining the existence and boundaries of the firm.

specifies what kind of bounded rationality. Thus, are we talking about Newell and Simon's work on heuristic search, or Selten's aspiration adaptation theory, or Lipman or Rubinstein's axiomatic foundations for bounded rationality, or regularities established in experimental psychological research, or another one of the great number of different—indeed, very different—variations on Simon's Grand Theme?

However, such information is virtually never forthcoming. Indeed, it is easy to become sceptical about the real role played by bounded rationality in the organizational capabilities approach for the basic reason that out of the many sources that the approach builds on, notably the works of Philip Selznick, Alfred Chandler, Edith Penrose, G. B. Richardson, and Nelson and Winter (1982) (see Foss, 1997, for a sampling), only Nelson and Winter explicitly address and try to incorporate bounded rationality.[3] All this raises suspicions that talk of bounded rationality in connection with the capabilities approach may in actuality be more rhetorical (in the pre-McCloskeyan, derogatory sense) than substantive. Understanding the extent to which the organizational capabilities approach builds on a foundation consisting of bounded rationality requires that we take a look at Nelson and Winter, precisely because this contribution has been hugely influential with respect to the conceptualization of business firms as well the understanding of their organization and behavior.

2.2 Nelson and Winter on skills, routines and organizational behavior

Quite early in Nelson and Winter (1982), namely when discussing 'the need for an evolutionary theory', the authors observe that their '. . . basic critique of orthodoxy is connected with the bounded rationality problem' (p. 36), and that, therefore, they '. . . accept and absorb into our analysis many of the ideas of the behavioral theorists' (pp. 35–36), notably Cyert, March and Simon. In particular, they are attracted to the behavioralist notion that short- and medium-run firm behavior is determined by relatively simple decision rules (Cyert and March, 1963).[4] They also make use of behavioralist models of satisficing search (Simon, 1955). In a later contribution they note that 'The view of firm behavior built into evolutionary economic theory fits well with the theory of firms contained in modern organization theory, especially the part that shares our own debt to the "Carnegie School" (March and Simon, 1958; Cyert and March, 1992)' (Nelson and Winter, 2002: 42). However, in the 1982 book Nelson and Winter go significantly beyond behavioralism by examining populations of firms with

---

[3]It may be argued that behavioralist organization theory (notably March and Simon, 1958; Cyert and March, 1992) is also a key input into the development of the approach (Pierce *et al.*, 2003, present such a reading). However, this is quite unusual, and not everybody would agree. For example, Fransman (1994) argues that behavioralism is taken up with information processing, whereas the real concern in the organizational capabilities approach is the use and growth of *knowledge*. The present paper supports Fransman's rather than Pierce *et al.*'s position.

[4]Winter (1964) wrote an early and favorable review of Cyert and March (1963). In a later paper (Winter, 1986), he was quite explicit about the behavioral nature of the theory in Nelson and Winter (1982). However, behavioralism is only one among a large set of inspirations and precursors.

differing decision rules, by addressing the interplay between changing external environments and changing decision rules (see also Pierce *et al.*, 2003), and, the most interesting theoretical innovation in the context of this paper, by trying to bring bounded rationality together with tacit knowledge. It is the last aspect of Nelson and Winter's 'updating exercise' that I shall argue is not entirely successful.

Nelson and Winter's main problem with 'orthodox' theory, and particularly the neoclassical theory of the firm, does not appear to be that this theory rules out diversity in terms of productive or organizational capabilities between firms in an industry *per se* [as some contributors to the organizational capabilities approach have argued (e.g. Connor, 1991)]. Indeed, that theory does allow for variety in these dimensions. For example, to the extent that differences in how well ('competently') a firm is run reflects owners' on-the-job consumption, and these owners are able and willing to bear the consequences of this consumption (Demsetz, 1997), the neoclassical theory of the firm allows for differential competencies to exist in equilibrium. One may also simply postulate differential initial endowments of some costly-to-copy resources, so that firms with differential efficiencies may exist in equilibrium. However, the main point of Nelson and Winter's critique is that in mainstream economics, heterogeneity is at best exogenously determined (as in the cases of differing preferences for on-the-job consumption or different initial endowments). To paraphrase their argument, in the setting of the (basic) neoclassical theory of the firm, it has to be in this way, because the production set is assumed to be not only given (or at best changing through given technological progress functions or similar constructs), but also to be fully transparent. The implication, as Demsetz (1991) notes, is that if information costs are thus assumed to be zero, what one firm can do on the level of production, another firm can do equally well.

Unlike Demsetz, Nelson and Winter do not cast their argument in terms of the information (and other) costs of copying rival firms' resource endowments. Instead, they devote a whole chapter (4) to an analysis of skills. By a skill, they mean '. . . a capability for a smooth sequence of coordinated behavior that is ordinarily effective relative to its objectives, given the context in which it normally occurs' (Nelson and Winter, 1982: 73). The attractions of the notion of skill are apparent. *First*, it provides a way of introducing dynamics on the level of production, since skills need to be nurtured and tend to grow with practice. *Second*, it provides an analogy to the behavioralist notion that behavior is strongly guided by relatively rigid decision rules, and thus serves to underscore Nelson and Winter's critique of maximization in the sense of forward-looking, informed deliberate choice. They put much emphasis on this, noting that '. . . the sort of choice that takes place in the process of exercising a skill is choice without deliberation' (*ibid.*: 82), although they are careful to note that the behavioral 'programs' embodied in skills may be initiated through deliberate, but presumably boundedly rational, choice. However, this and the notion that routines may be changed through meta-routines (i.e. search routines) is the only substantive connection that the notion of bounded rationality make to skills and the organization-level counterpart to individual skills, namely routines. Neither concept is directly derived from from bounded rationality considerations. *Third*, starting from skills and developing the organization-level analogy to skills allow Nelson and Winter to bring considerations of tacit knowledge into the picture and to develop a strong critique of the 'blueprint' view of neoclassical production function theory. *Fourth*, it helps them to establish a link between individual action and organizational behavior. That link is initiated in a rather straightforward way by the observation that '. . . directly relevant to our development here is the value of individual behavior as a *metaphor* for organizational behavior' (*ibid.*: 72; emphasis in original).

In turn, 'organizational behavior' is addressed in terms of 'routines' that serve as organization-level metaphorical equivalents to individual skills. Note in passing that this is not an idea that originates with Nelson and Winter (1982). Thus, Simon (1947) argued that habit may be understood in terms of limits to attention;[5] in turn, habit has an organization-level counterpart, namely organizational routines. Like skills, routines represent stable sequences of actions (i.e. they coordinate actions) that are triggered by certain stimuli in certain contexts and which, in a sense, serve as memories for the organizations that embody them. However, because routines are social phenomena, they go beyond the skill metaphor and raise issues of motivation and coordination. However, Nelson and Winter sidestep the motivation issue, arguing that routines represent 'organizational truces', an idea going back to Cyert and March (1963).

Thus, quite a lot—and perhaps too much—is packed into the notion of routine, including a variety of behaviors (e.g. heuristics and strategies), organizational processes and arrangements, cognitive issues (e.g. 'organizational memories'), and incentives ('truces').[6] Nelson and Winter defend this by noting that, in actuality, '. . . skills, organization, and "technology" are intimately intertwined in a functioning routine, and it is difficult to say where one aspect ends and another begins' (Nelson and Winter, 1982: 104). Although it is true that the boundaries are blurred, it is not clear why one is not excused, for purposes of analytical clarity, to look at one aspect at a time. It is one thing to claim that, ontologically, things are a mess. It is another thing openly to admit the mess into analysis. This is perhaps only a minor problem for Nelson and Winter: because their level of analysis lies higher than the firm, they can afford to keep the firm level messy. However, their all-inclusive notion of routine may have contributed to the considerable terminological soup that characterizes the organizational capabilities approach as well as the difficulties of giving precise content to the notion of routines (cf. Cohen *et al.*, 1996), and derived and related notions, such as capabilities, competencies, etc. In the following, another possible source of conceptual and explanatory problems in the organizational capabilities approach is considered, namely the absence of a clear

---

[5]Nelson and Winter (1982: 85) are hinting at a similar idea when they observe that '. . . there is in a sense a tradeoff between capability and deliberate choice, a choice imposed ultimately by the fact that rationality is bounded'. This attempt to explain skills in terms of attention allocation is, however, not extended to the level of routines.

[6]See also Winter (1986: 165) for a sophisticated further discussion and defence of this.

foundation, rooted in individual, boundedly rational choice behavior, for the notion of routines.

3.   A closer look on bounded rationality and tacit knowledge in the organizational capabilities approach

At first glance, bounded rationality appears to be quite crucial to Nelson and Winter's argument (Fransman, 1994). Thus, firm members can only learn routines through practicing them; routines are simply repeated until they become too dysfunctional; learning is myopic, search is satisficing; etc. All of these very strong assumptions about individual and organizational behavior would seem to make room for a rationality that is very bounded indeed. Apparently, this is Williamson's impression when he argues that Nelson and Winter work with a version of bounded rationality, 'organic rationality', that assumes less intentionality, foresight and calculativeness than his own notion of bounded rationality (Williamson, 1985). However, (re)reading chapters 3–5 in Nelson and Winter (1982) suggests that what ultimately interests them is not really bounded rationality *per se* in the sense of a commitment to building specific models of boundedly rational individual behavior that, in turn, may be fed into models of organization level behavior and outcomes. What interests them is rather tacit knowledge and its embodiment in their firm-level analogy to individual skills, namely routines, and how these notions assists the understanding of sluggish organizational change and adaptation. These claims are substantiated in the following.

3.1   The limited role of bounded rationality in Nelson and Winter

Bounded rationality has a bad reputation for being used as a sort of catch-all category that can 'explain' all observed deviations from maximizing rationality (Conlisk, 1996; Casson and Wadeson, 1997). The Simon dictum that man is 'intendedly rationality, but only limitedly so' is an example. In itself it is vacuous and therefore explains or predicts virtually nothing. Explanation and prediction that begins from a foundation of bounded rationality requires that bounded rationality be focused through specific models of behavior (such as Simon, 1955). This is where the link to the skill metaphor of organizational behavior becomes important, for it is the use of the notion of skill, and particularly its transfer to the organizational level, that steps in and fills the explanatory and predictive vacuum left by invoking bounded rationality in general terms. In other words, it is skills and, particularly, routines that allow Nelson and Winter (1982) to work out an explanatory and predictive theory of firm behavior. However, the additional assumptions that are added to the basic invocation of bounded rationality are not drawn from the existing evidence, notably from psychology, on boundedly rational behavior *per se*, although Nelson and Winter (2002: 31) in a later paper argue that '. . . in contrast to the usual quest for microfoundations in economics, seeking consistency with rationality assumptions, our quest is for consistency with the available evidence on learning and behavior at both the individual and organizational levels'.

In fact, it turns out that what they mean by the 'available evidence' may be somewhat idiosyncratic. They go on to argue, in the 2002 paper, that

> With respect to individual learning, the plausibility of our behavioral foundations for evolutionary economics has received support from an unexpected quarter. Studies linking cognitive abilities and brain physiology have established the existence of anatomically distinct memory processes supporting the skilled behaviors of individuals.
>
> (Nelson and Winter, 2002: 33)[7]

Not only is such memory 'highly durable', it also '. . . functions in some ways that are alien to theories of calculative rationality' (*ibid.*: 34). While this cognitive science support for the notion of skilled behavior seems compelling, the evidence Nelson and Winter present in support for the critical move from individual skilled behavior to the organizational, routine level is less so. The only cited evidence is an experimental study of card-playing teams (Cohen and Bacdayan, 1994) that demonstrated that team level skills (i.e. 'routines') aquired under one specification of the played game made the adaptation to a new specification of the game sluggish. While this has much to do with skilled and inertial behavior and problems of adaptability on the level of teams, it is not clear what exactly all this has to do with bounded rationality. Thus, Nelson and Winter's (2002) recent stocktaking reinforces the tendency in Nelson and Winter (1982) to lump together an almost empty characterization of bounded rationality with a much richer description of skilled behavior. Bounded rationality is, in effect, suppressed as a result of this exercise. This raises the question of *why* bounded rationality is treated as a background assumption while individual and organizational level skilled behavior takes precedence.

3.2   Why tacit knowledge is more important than bounded rationality in Nelson and Winter

Nelson and Winter (1982) explicitly compare skilled behavior to the execution of a computer program.[8] The outcomes of computer programs are predictable, given knowledge of what is fed into them and knowledge of the program itself. When triggered in a certain context, skilled behavior is also predictable, and knowledge of an individual's skill set, the relevant context and the relevant stimulus may also allow for reasonably accurate prediction of his behavior. By implication, organizational routines, the organization-level counterpart to individual skills, may also be understood as programs that make aggregate (i.e. organization-level) behavior predictable and inert.

---

[7]No references are given, but presumably they have in mind the kind of work described in Damasio (1994).

[8]Winter's background at RAND may have played a role here: it was a commonly held view at RAND that the computer is a 'scale free' model of organization. If both organizations and skills can be characterized in terms of computer programs, the metaphorical jump from skills to the organization level of routines seems tempting to make—and may actually be more than merely metaphorical.

And it is inert organizational behavior that Nelson and Winter (1982) are after, because this is a necessary part of their evolutionary mode of explanation. Thus, tacit knowledge, as embodied in skills and routines, can do the job.[9] Can bounded rationality do the job, i.e. can it explain inert organizational behavior?

In Nelson and Winter, bounded rationality is mainly treated to the extent that it provides an underpinning for the behavioralist notion of decision rules, particularly in connection with search. Such decision rules may be understood as manifestations of bounded rationality, on the individual level (cf. Simon, 1955) and, less obviously, on the organizational level (Cyert and March, 1963). One may expect rule-bound behavior also to provide a strong explanation of inert organizational behavior. However, there are two reasons why bounded rationality and the decision rules it gives to may not be a strong foundation for a theory of organizational inertia. First, decision rules that are explicit (i.e. Cyert and March's 1963 'standard operating procedures') may arguably be changed at lower cost than complex routines that embody huge amounts of tacit knowledge. In this sense, routines that are rationalized in terms of skills and tacit knowledge offer a *stronger* explanation of organizational sluggishness than standard operating procedures. Tacitness beats bounded rationality with respect to the explanation of inertia, as it were. Second, it is far from clear that individual bounded rationality produces inert behavior on the aggregate level. To be sure, such stories can be told (e.g. Heath *et al.*, 1993; Egidi, 2000), but they require that bounded rationality and the interaction between boundedly rational agents be specified in certain ways. To take an almost trivial example, if similar agents all suffer from status quo biases, their aggregate behavior may indeed manifest inertia. In contrast, it is not clear that inert aggregate behavior will *in general* follow from individual level rule-following, e.g. in the form of some satisificing model.

Thus, bounded rationality alone cannot do what Nelson and Winter wish their behavioral assumptions for them; hence, the invocation of skills, and the use of the skill metaphor to address aggregate behavior. In the end, bounded rationality is more a sort of background argument that—inspiring other assumptions about tacit knowledge and skilled human behavior—serves to make plausible the notion of organizational routine (including search routines), and therefore the sluggish organizational adaptation that is crucial in Nelson and Winter's evolutionary story.[10] Thus, the whole construct works

---

[9]In fact, tacit knowledge can do the job so well that it is not clear that Nelson and Winter even need bounded rationality for the purpose of understanding such adaptation. For example, if organizational members do not hold the same tacit knowledge, this may be sufficient to explain sluggishness, because of costly communication.

[10]Moreover, those who are not committed to behavioralism may point out that even if one wishes to keep organizational routines central, it is not so obvious how essential bounded rationality really is. This may be argued in a number of ways. One can have perfectly rational standard operating procedures. It is possible to tell a story in which different routines in a population of firms emerge as solutions to appropriately specified games being played in each firms and with agents acting in a maximizing manner. Search behavior is easily reconciled with maximization. It is perfectly possible to tell sophisticated maximization stories about agents following rigid routines and procedures, once a full

from an initial argument about bounded rationality, goes from there to behavioralist decision rules, jumps via analogy to ideas on tacit knowledge as embodied in skilled behavior, and then transfers skills to the level of routines and organizational capabilities. Bounded rationality re-enters the story when changes in routines and capabilities have to be explained, namely in the form of dynamic search routines.

This is a complicated exercise that has some unfortunate consequences. In addition to the various problems identified in the Cohen *et al.* (1996) symposium on the meaning of routines, there are at least two further problematic consequences of this exercise. First, tacit knowledge and bounded rationality tend to become indiscriminately lumped together, because it is not transparent where the one ends and the other begins. Of course, tacit knowledge and bounded rationality are different things and do not necessarily imply each other. Thus, there can be tacit rules for maximization, as Machlup (1946) argued. Or, agents can cope with bounded rationality by means of fully explicit operating procedures. While one can certainly construct an argument that boundedly rational agents make use of experientially produced—and 'skilled'—decision rules that are likely to embody a good deal of tacit knowledge (Langlois, 1999), there is no necessary connection between bounded rationality and tacit knowledge. Second, and perhaps more seriously, bounded rationality on the level of the individual becomes suppressed. This makes it hard to understand the link between bounded rationality on the one hand and routines and other organizational phenomena on the other. In other words, what exactly is the nature of the mechanism that aggregates from individual behavior to routines and organizational behavior? This mechanism is never really identified in Nelson and Winter (1982).[11] It also means that there is a certain interpretative ambiguity surrounding the notion of routines to the extent that it is related to bounded rationality: is organization-level routinization produced by interaction effects among the members of a team or is it ultimately founded in aspects of individual cognition (Egidi, 2000: 2)? These issues are not resolved in Nelson and Winter (1982). In fairness, it should be noted that this is perhaps not surprising, since rather little work existed on this issue when Nelson and Winter wrote their book.

3.3 The organizational capabilities approach and economic organization

As mentioned earlier, Nelson and Winter (1982) is a high point in the development of the organizational capabilities approach, and their work has been foundational for much subsequent work within this approach. It has also been mentioned that the modern organizational capabilities approach aspires to being a theory of economic organization, a point where it goes beyond Nelson and Winter (1982). The argument that will be briefly developed here is that certain characteristics of Nelson and Winter (1982) were carried over into the organizational capabilities approach, characteristics

account is made of all relevant costs (e.g. costs of memorizing, depositing, retrieving, etc., information) (Casson and Wadeson, 1997; Foss and Foss, 2000).

[11]Later work in the evolutionary economics is less vulnerable to this critique, notably the work of Egidi (2000), Marengo *et al.* (2000), Warglien (1995) and Dosi *et al.* (1996).

that may not be so problematic if the analytical purpose is one of explaining rigidity in firm behavior as a part of a broader evolutionary story, but which are much less appropriate for the purpose of building a theory of economic organization.[12] The relevant characteristics are a strong emphasis on aggregate entities, notably routines and organizational capabilities, an emphasis that comes at the expense of attention to individual behaviors, and derives from Nelson and Winter's attempt to establish a metaphorical solution to the aggregation problem of moving from the level of the agent to the level of the organization.[13] Because they fully recognize the metaphorical character of this maneuver, they do not commit the mistake of conflating an ontological claim with a useful research heuristic. Later contributors to the organizational capabilities approach may not have been as careful here as Nelson and Winter.

Problems seem to emerge rather unavoidably as soon as Nelson and Winter's ideas on organizational routines and capabilities are transferred from their original place in the analysis of a changing population of firms to an analysis of the behavior and, particularly, organization of individual firms. While these notions have indeed been of value for the understanding of, for example, the sources of competitive advantage (although much of this literature is also plagued by conceptual ambiguity), their application to economic organization is more problematic. For example, the much-cited Kogut and Zander (1992) paper essentially argues directly from the tacit knowledge embodied in organizational capabilities to the boundaries of the firm. The supporting argument is that 'firms know more than their contracts can tell'. However, there is no attempt to address this is in terms of comparative contracting, and, ultimately, individual behavior. What exactly is it that cannot be written in contracts? Even if writing costs are, in fact, prohibitive, why cannot relational contracting, involving highly incomplete contracts, between independent parties handle the transfer of knowledge? Why is it only vertical integration that economizes with what are presumably writing and communication costs? No compelling answers are given to such questions. This is the case for most of this literature as it is applied to economic organization. A partial exception is the work of Langlois (1992). Langlois attempts to supply the missing mechanism from organizational capabilities to the boundaries of the firm by means of the concept of 'dynamic transaction costs', which are essentially communication costs that arise because of 'dis-similar' (Richardson, 1972) capabilities in a vertical structure of firms. Presumably efficient economic organization minimizes such costs (as well as other more 'traditional' transaction costs, allowance being made for possible tradeoffs between these).

However, this idea may imply another difficulty, one that is also present in Nelson

---

[12]Foss (1996) discusses other problems with organizational capabilities theories as theories of economic organization.

[13]A doctrinal history corollary to this argument is that Nelson and Winter's theory of the firm capabilities and behavior is more in line with the thinking of Thorstein Veblen and prehaps Friedrich Hayek than with the behavioralist tradition that they see as among the most important precursors of their work. On Veblen as a precursor of the organizational capabilities approach, see Foss (1998).

and Winter (1982) and in virtually all of the organizational capabilities literature. This difficulty is that knowledge inside firms is assumed be homogenous (or less strongly: not very costly to communicate), while knowledge between firms ('differential capabilities') is taken to be (very) heterogeneous (and therefore costly to communicate). Thus, Winter (1986: 175) assumes that '. . . the search for information from external sources does not proceed with the same ease as for internal sources'. If this were not the case, it is hard to see how communication costs could carry implications for the boundaries of the firm. However, although there may be some intuitive appeal to the assumption, it is hard to accept as true in general. There are many examples of firms where the bandwidth of the communication channels between some business unit of the firm and external firm (e.g. buyer or seller) is much higher than the bandwidth between the unit and, say, corporate headquarters. Moreover, the implicit assumption that knowledge in hierarchies can be taken, at least as a first approximation, to be communicable at zero cost makes it hard to understand hierarchical organization, since with zero cost communication the managerial task has no economic rationale (Demsetz, 1991; Casson, 1994).

3.4 Methodological individualism

It seems fairly obvious that the essentially *ad hoc* assumptions that knowledge inside firms can be communicated at low cost while knowledge between firms can only be communicated at high cost slip into the analysis when the units of analysis are routines or organizational capabilities. It is then easy to postulate that 'firms know more than their contracts can tell' and that all organizational aspects are 'intertwined in a functioning routine'. If instead the analysis had started in an explicit methodological individualist mode, i.e. from individual choice behavior, the argument that communication costs within, for example, certain business units may be lower than the communication costs between people in the unit and people in a supplier firm might have been derived as an outcome of a properly specified model instead of being postulated.[14] The problem is that there *is* no theory of individual choice behavior in the organizational capabilities approach, so that writers in the organizational capabilities approach have to treat economic organization in a methodological collectivist way, namely in terms of postulating somewhat crude causal relations between capabilities and economic organization, little attention being paid to the microanalytic issues involved. Not surprisingly, these stories are vulnerable to basic critiques from the perspective of comparative contracting (Foss, 1996; Williamson, 2000).

Ironically, it turns out that much of the organizational capabilities approach is vulnerable to the same critique that Winter (1991) forcefully (and justifiably) launched against the neoclassical theory of the firm. Specifically, and borrowing directly from Winter, it is in potential 'conflict with methodological individualism' (Winter, 1991: 181) (because of the emphasis on routines and organizational capabilities), '. . . provides

---

[14]For what I have in mind here, see, for example, Barr and Saraceno (2002).

no basis for explaining economic organization' (*ibid.*: 183) (because transaction costs and comparative contracting are not considered), lacks 'realism' (because of its 'unrealistic' treatment of decision-making as entirely guided by routines), and provides a 'simplistic treatment of its focal concern' (e.g. because it is simply assumed that it is easier to gather, combine, source, etc., knowledge inside firms than between firms). The main underlying problem, it has been argued here, is that too little attention is devoted to individual decision-making. The problem goes at least partly back to Nelson and Winter: It is arguable that their side-stepping of bounded rationality on the level of the individual agent in favor of aggregate notions (i.e. routines and capabilities) is an important source of some of the explanatory difficulties that the modern capabilities approach confront.

4. Concluding comments

In conclusion, it appropriate to cast the argument in this paper in a somewhat broader context. In a fine paper, Paul Nightingale (2002) has made an argument that is parallel to the one that has been developed. Nightingale (2002: 1) argues that Nelson and Winter (1982) seek to '. . . bring together two very different ways of thinking about knowledge', namely the more appreciative '. . . tacit knowledge tradition that derives, in part, from Polanyi's phenomenology' and the more formal '. . . objectivist information processing, problem-solving approach that derives, in part, from Simon'. This is visible in Nelson and Winter's attempt to conceptualize firms both in terms of information processing and in terms of tacit and socially embedded knowledge. Nightingale argues that a number of tensions in the science and technology policy literature are traceable to this problematic attempt in Nelson and Winter to fuse two epistemologies, the tensions between which are what has fueled other recent debates, notably in artificial intelligence research.

Much of the argument in this paper may be cast in similar terms. The attempt in Nelson and Winter to combine ideas on routines and skilled behavior that are derived from Polanyi with ideas on bounded rationality and satisficing search that are derived from Simon has not been entirely satisfactory, and may be an important source of some of the explanatory difficulties that confront the modern organizational capabilities approach. An indication that Nelson and Winter's reconciliation exercise was not entirely successful is that tacit knowledge and bounded rationality simply are not equal partners in the 1982 book; the three central chapters on firm organization behavior and organization are to a much larger extent about tacit knowledge than about bounded rationality. Thus, contrary to a commonly held view, the role of bounded rationality in the organizational capabilities approach is very much a background one.[15] Its precise relation, if any, to the notion of the central concepts of routine and capability is unclear. Its role seems more rhetorical than substantive. At any rate, boundedly rational

---

[15]For the parallel argument that the role of bounded rationality in the modern economics of organization (notably transaction cost economics) is also a background one, see Foss (2001).

behavior on the level of the individual agent is not modeled, neither in Nelson and Winter's seminal 1982 book, nor in the many contributions to the organizational capabilities approach that are so heavily indebted to this contribution.

Finally, lest this paper be taken as a general attack on the organizational capabilities approach, it is important to stress that its real message is a methodogical one: writers in the organizational capabilities tradition should devote more analytical energies to getting the micro-foundations right. It will not do in the long run to continue working with concepts whose micro-foundations are unclear. This is not just a matter of conforming to the conventional methodological individualist approach of most of economics. It is also, and more substantively, a matter of the explanatory and predictive capabilities of the organizational capabilities approach being less impressive than they could be as a result of the lack of micro-foundations for concepts such as routines, capabilities, etc.

Acknowledgements

I am grateful to Kirsten Foss for discussion of many of the issues treated herein, and to Giovanni Dosi, Sarah Kaplan, Richard Nelson, and Scott Stern for comments on an earlier version of this paper. The original version of this paper was written for, and presented at the DRUID Nelson and Winter conference, in Ålborg, Denmark, 12–16 June 2001.

Address for correspondence

LINK-DRUID, Department of Industrial Economics and Strategy, Copenhagen Business School, Solbjergvej 3, 3rd floor, 2000 Frederiksberg, Denmark. Email: njf.ivs@cbs.dk.

References

Barr, J. and F. Saraceno (2002), 'A computational theory of the firm,' *Journal of Economic Behavior and Organization*, **49**, 345–361.

Casson, M. (1994), 'Why are firms hierarchical?,' *International Journal of the Economics of Business*, **1**, 43–81.

Casson, M. and N. Wadeson (1997), 'Bounded rationality, meta-rationality, and the theory of international business,' working paper no. 242 (Discussion Papers in International Investment and Management), Department of Economics, University of Reading.

Chandler, A. D., Jr (1992), 'Organizational capabilities and the theory of the firm,' *Journal of Economic Perspectives*, **6**, 79–100.

Cohen, M. D., R. Burkhart, G. Dosi, M. Egidi, L. Marengo, M. Warglien and S. Winter (1996), 'Routines and other recurrent action patterns of organizations: contemporary research issues,' *Industrial and Corporate Change*, **5**, 653–698.

Conlisk, J. (1996), 'Why bounded rationality?,' *Journal of Economic Literature*, **34**, 669–700.

Conner, K. R. (1991), 'A historical comparison of resource-based theory and five schools of thought within industrial organization economics: do we have a new theory of the firm?,' *Journal of Management*, **17**, 121–154.

Conner, K. R. and C. K. Prahalad (1996), 'A resource-based theory of the firm: knowledge vs. opportunism,' *Organization Science*, **7**, 477–501.

Cyert, R. M. and J. G. March (1963), *A Behavioral Theory of the Firm*. Prentice Hall: Englewood Cliffs, NJ.

Cyert, R. M. and J. G. March (1992), *A Behavioral Theory of the Firm* [1963]. Oxford University Press: Oxford.

Damasio, A. R. (1994), *Descartes' Error: Emotions, Reason, and the Human Brain*. Grosset/ Putnam: New York.

Demsetz, H. (1991), 'The nature of the firm revisited,' in O. E. Williamson and S. G. Winter (eds), *The Nature of the Firm: Origins, Evolution, and Development*. Basil Blackwell: Oxford.

Demsetz, H. (1997), 'Profit maximization and rational behavior,' in *The Economics of the Firm: Seven Critical Commentarities*. Cambridge University Press: Cambridge.

Dosi, G. (2000), *Innovation, Organization, and Economic Dynamics: Selected Essays*. Edward Elgar: Cheltenham.

Dosi, G., L. Marengo and G. Fagiolo (1996), 'Learning in evolutionary environments,' IIASA, working paper.

Dosi, G., R. R. Nelson and S. G. Winter (2000), *The Nature and Dynamics of Organizational Capabilities*. Oxford University Press: Oxford.

Egidi, M. (2000), 'Biases in organizational behavior,' unpublished paper, University of Trento.

Foss, N. J. (1996), 'Knowledge-based approaches to the theory of the firm: some critical comments,' *Organization Science*, **7**, 470–476.

Foss, N. J. (1997), *Resources, Firms, and Strategies*. Oxford University Press: Oxford.

Foss, N. J. (1998), 'The competence-based approach: Veblenian ideas in the modern theory of the firm,' *Cambridge Journal of Economics*, **22**, 479–496.

Foss, N. J. (2001), 'Bounded rationality in the economics of organization: present use and future possibilities,' *Journal of Management and Governance*, **5**, 401–425.

Foss, K. and N. Foss (2000), 'Competence and governance perspectives: how do they differ? And how does it matter?,' in N. J. Foss and V. Mahnke (eds), *Competence, Governance, and Entrepreneurship*. Oxford University Press: Oxford.

Fransman, M. (1994), 'Information, knowledge, vision and theories of the firm,' in G. Dosi, D. J. Teece and J. Chytry (eds), *Technology, Organization, and Competitiveness*. Oxford University Press: Oxford.

Grant, R. (1996), 'Toward a knowledge-based theory of the firm,' *Strategic Management Journal*, **17**, 109–122.

Heath, C., M. Knez and C. Camerer (1993), 'The strategic management of the entitlement process in the employment relationship,' *Strategic Management Journal*, **14**, 75–93.

Kogut, B. and V. Zander (1992), 'Knowledge of the firm, combinative capabilities and the replication of technology,' *Organization Science*, **3**, 383–397.

Langlois, R. N. (1992), 'Transaction cost economics in real time,' *Industrial and Corporate Change*, 1, 99–127.

Langlois, R. N. (1999), 'Rule-following, expertise, and rationality: a new behavioral economics?,' in K. Dennis (ed.), *Rationality in Economics: Alternative Perspectives*. Kluwer: Dordrecht.

Langlois, R. N. and N. Foss (1999), 'Capabilities and governance: the rebirth of production in the theory of economic organization,' *KYLOS*, 52, 201–218.

Machlup, F. (1946), 'Marginal analysis and empirical research,' *American Economic Review*, 36, 519–554.

March, J. G. and H. Simon (1958), *Organizations*. Wiley: New York.

Marengo, L., G. Dosi, P. Legrenzi and C. Pasquali (2000), 'The structure of problem-solving knowledge and the structure of organizations,' *Industrial and Corporate Change*, 9, 757–788.

Meyer, M. (2001). 'Nelson and Winter's *Evolutionary Theory*—a citation analysis,' unpublished paper.

Nelson, R. R. and S. G. Winter (1982), *An Evolutionary Theory of Economic Change*. Belknap Press: Cambridge, MA.

Nelson, R. R. and S. G. Winter (2002), 'Evolutionary theorizing in economics,' *Journal of Economic Perspectives*, 16, 23–46.

Newell, A. and H. A. Simon. (1972), *Human Problem Solving*. Prentice Hall: Englewood Cliffs, NJ.

Nightingale, P. (2002), 'If Nelson and Winter are only half right about tacit knowledge, which half? A Searlean critique of "codification",' *Industrial and Corporate Change*, 12, 149–183.

Pierce, J. L., C. S. Boerner and D. J. Teece (2003), 'The evolutionary theory in dynamic capabilities,' *Industrial and Corporate Change*, forthcoming.

Richardson, G. B. (1972), 'The organisation of industry,' *Economic Journal*, 82, 883–896.

Sanchez, R. (2001), 'Resources, dynamic capabilities, and competences: building blocks of integrative strategy theory,' in T. Elfring and H. Volberda (eds), *Rethinking Strategy*. Sage: Thousand Oaks, CA.

Selten, R. (1990), 'Bounded rationality,' *Journal of Institutional and Theoretical Economics*, 146, 649–658.

Simon, H. A. (1947), *Administrative Behavior*. Macmillan: New York.

Simon, H. A. (1955), 'A behavioral model of rational choice,' *Quarterly Journal of Economics*, 69, 99–118.

Teece, D. J. and G. Pisano (1994), The dynamic capabilities of firms: an introduction, *Industrial and Corporate Change*, 3, 537–556.

Warglien, M. (1995), 'Hierarchical selection and organizational adaptation,' *Industrial and Corporate Change*, 4, 161–186.

Williamson, O. E. (1985), *The Economic Institutions of Capitalism*. The Free Press: New York.

Williamson, O. E. (1996), *The Mechanisms of Governance*. Oxford University Press: Oxford.

Williamson, O. E. (2000), 'Strategy research: competence and governance perspectives,' in N. J. Foss and V. Mahnke (eds), *Competence, Governance, and Entrepreneurship*. Oxford University Press: Oxford.

Winter, S. G. (1964), 'Review of Richard Cyert and James G. March, *A Behavioral Theory of the Firm*,' *American Economic Review*, **54**, 144–148.

Winter, S. G. (1986), 'The research program of the behavioral theory of the firm: orthodox critique and evolutionary perspective,' in B. Gilad and S. Kaish (eds), *Handbook of Behavioral Microeconomics*, Vol. A. JAI Press: Greenwich, CT.

Winter, S. G. (1991), 'On Coase, competence, and the corporation,' in O. E. Williamson and S. G. Winter (eds), *The Nature of the Firm: Origins, Evolution, and Development.* Basil Blackwell: Oxford.

Zandt, T. van (1998), 'Organizations with an endogenous number of information processing agents,' in M. Majumdar (ed.), *Organizations with Incomplete Information.* Cambridge University Press: Cambridge.

[3]

STRATEGIC ORGANIZATION Vol 3(4): 441–455
DOI: 10.1177/1476127005055796
Copyright ©2005 Sage Publications (London, Thousand Oaks, CA and New Delhi)
http://soq.sagepub.com

SO!APBOX
EDITORIAL ESSAY

Strategic organization: a field in search of micro-foundations

Teppo Felin   Brigham Young University, USA

Nicolai J. Foss   Copenhagen Business School, Denmark

Organizations are made up of individuals, and there is no organization without individuals. There is nothing quite as elementary; yet this elementary truth seems to have been lost in the increasing focus on structure, routines, capabilities, culture, institutions and various other collective conceptualizations in much of recent strategic organization research. It is not overstating the matter too much to say that 'organization' has generally entered the field of strategy in the form of various aggregate concepts.

This editorial essay is born out of a frustration on our part for the present lack of focus on individuals in much of strategic organization and the taken-for-granted status of 'organization'. Specifically, the underlying argument of this essay is that individuals matter and that micro-foundations are needed for explanation in strategic organization. In fact, to fully explicate organizational anything – whether identity, learning, knowledge or capabilities – one must fundamentally begin with and understand the individuals that compose the whole, specifically their underlying nature, choices, abilities, propensities, heterogeneity, purposes, expectations and motivations. While using the term 'organizational' may serve as helpful shorthand for discussion purposes and for reduced-form empirical analysis, truly explaining (beyond correlations) the organization (e.g. existence, decline, capability or performance), or any collective for that matter, requires starting with the individual as the central actor.

Our particular focus in this essay is on the organizational capabilities-based literature in strategic management. This focus serves as a specific example of a more general problem of lack of attention to individuals in strategic organization. (Wider implications could be explicated given more space.) As brief support for the fact that our discussion does have wider ramifications, we note that Selznick has also quite poignantly raised the need for micro-foundations on the part of institutional scholars (1996: 274). Whetten (2004) also highlights the fact that scholars are rarely explicit about what they mean by 'organizational'.

441

Our hope is that this essay will serve as a clarion call of sorts for strategic organization (and more broadly organizational) scholars to take individuals and micro-foundations more seriously (beyond calls for multi-level theory or 'meso' research). We advance arguments and call for an even stronger form of methodological individualism. Of necessity we paint with a fairly broad brush and admittedly, in part, our arguments are conjectural and purposefully provocative, all of which, thankfully, this forum allows.

We start with a brief introduction to the organizational capabilities-based literature as it relates to the question of the individual–organization relationship, focusing on deficiencies which result from taking 'organization' for granted. It would certainly be unfair for us to levy heavy criticism on the organizational capabilities literature without pointing out feasible and promising directions for future research; thus, we also offer a rough conceptual framework for thinking about the individual–organization relationship as it relates to the notion of organizational capabilities and underlying micro-foundations.

Capabilities collectivism

Strategy scholars are increasingly converging on organizational capabilities as a key construct (Eisenhardt and Martin, 2000; Winter, 2003). Building on resource-based logic and the notion of organizational routines, the organizational capabilities approach has become one of the predominant ways of thinking about heterogeneity and performance in strategic management. A central argument of capabilities-based work is that routines or capabilities are the fundamental units of analysis, and that the organization should be conceptualized as the central repository of routines and capabilities (Nelson and Winter, 1982). However, despite over two decades of largely theoretical (and some empirical) work, as well as recent efforts to clarify the meanings of organizational routines and capabilities (Winter, 2003), fundamental questions about their origins, micro-foundations, and the theoretical and empirical status still persist. We argue that many of the problems associated with capabilities-based work are a result of the focus on collective level constructs (e.g. routines, capabilities) at the expense of individual-level considerations.

Specifically, a review of the key organizational capabilities contributions suggests that the approach builds on methodological collectivism (see the definition of capabilities by Zollo and Winter, 2002: 340), and perhaps even a strong form thereof. While individuals and managers are mentioned in the theoretical development, nevertheless the assumption is that heterogeneity in collective context, environment and situation drives organizational, as well as individual, outcomes. This is exemplary of the explanatory stance of methodological collectivism.

Thus, the organizational capabilities approach asserts that performance differences between firms are driven by efficiency differences that may somehow be ascribed to collective constructs, such as routines, capabilities, competencies and the like. Furthermore, such performance differences may be sustainable because of certain characteristics of the collective level constructs, for example, social complexity (Barney, 1991). Much of this goes back to Nelson and Winter (1982) (Foss, 2003). They explicitly take the routine as the unit of analysis, and an important aim of their evolutionary theorizing is to understand the changing relative weights of different routines in a population of firms. Although discussion of the level of the individual is not absent in Nelson and Winter (1982), who devote one chapter (chapter 3) to a discussion of knowledge at the individual level (i.e. skills), their arguments nevertheless quickly move to give primary emphasis to organizational routines as largely determining individual behavior (1982: 9, 14, 134–5). While the *metaphor* of individual skills and collective routines seems to have originally been developed by Nelson and Winter as a figurative one (1982: 124) (Foss, 2003), more recent work has moved in a quite literal direction explicitly independent of individuals.

In fact, it can be argued that the approach is founded on an implicit assumption of individual homogeneity (Dansereau et al., 1999; Henderson and Cockburn, 1994). Thus, the extension of explanatory collectivism is that individuals are essentially extraneous (highly malleable by heterogeneous context, situation and surroundings) to the overall theory, and thus in effect can be rounded out (Felin and Hesterly, forthcoming). While the assumption that agents are homogeneous does not imply with logical necessity that they are also malleable, the assumption of malleability is very often made in the organizational capabilities approach. Thus, J. C. Spender specifically notes that 'we must argue that organizations learn and have knowledge only to the extent that their members are *malleable beings* whose sense of self is influenced by the organization's evolving social identity' and thus learning is '*primarily* internalized from the social context' (1996: 53, emphasis added). This line of reasoning has placed all of the explanatory burden on the context and environment (over individual causation).

However, arguing that individuals a priori are homogeneous or largely malleable directly conflicts with established theoretical and empirical arguments from the cognitive sciences emphasizing the role of a priori knowledge, thus challenging the prevalent argument of 'organizations as strong situations' (Davis-Blake and Pfeffer, 1989). But arguing that individuals are heterogeneous does not imply that the collective level is non-existent or unimportant. Rather, it suggests the importance of explicitly linking the individual and the collective levels. However, to our knowledge, specific individual–organization links have yet to be made in at least the strategic management part of the organizational capabilities literature (see Dosi et al., 1999 for an evolutionary economics attempt to model the link). Individuals are rounded out in the analysis, as organizational routines and capabilities are treated as real social facts, which provide the primary causal driver of individual and collective level outcomes. The assumption of the independence as well as the primacy of collectives and routines (rather than individuals) is now a prevalent assumption in the organizational capabilities literature (Dosi, 1995; Nahapiet and Ghoshal, 1998: 247). In other words, and in terms of the philosophy of the social sciences, the field has taken a stand in favor of methodological collectivism and against methodological individualism (Coleman, 1990; Elster, 1989; Hayek, 1952); individual-level explanation is rejected in favor of collective explanation.

Deficiencies of capabilities collectivism

Taking the organization for granted sidesteps numerous critical individual-level questions with regard to strategic organization, questions that arguably should provide the real meat of analysis in this field. Thus, the present collective emphasis in capabilities-based work is problematic on several fronts, which we briefly explicate.

Routines and capabilities ill-defined

No clear definitions of routines and capabilities have been advanced to date (Cohen et al., 1996). Many attempts have been made, to be sure. However, to our knowledge none of these systematically ground the definition in purposeful individual action. Definitions of collective concepts are very often performed in terms of lower-level, constituent elements. For example, an industry is defined in terms of products (and therefore ultimately consumer preferences) and competing firms. No definition of routines in terms of constituent elements appears to exist. (This makes it problematic to define capabilities in terms of routines, as is often done.) In fact, it is noteworthy that when writers attempt to proffer definitions they usually pick concepts on the same analytical level as routines and capabilities, such as strategies, organizational processes and arrangements, organizational memory and the like (Levitt and March, 1988). This is clearly messy, because it conflates the objects that can be routinized (e.g. organizational process) and the definition of what a routine is. However, if there are no individualistic foundations for the analysis of organizational routines and capabilities, we submit that the mess is simply unavoidable. The problem is that because routines and capabilities do not have an anchor in individual antecedents, they can be virtually anything at the organizational level.

The origins of routines and capabilities

A closely related, fundamental problem with existing capabilities-based work in strategic organization is the lack of clear (causal) understanding of the origin of organizational routines and capabilities. In fairness, it should be noted that capabilities-based scholars themselves are painfully aware of this. Winter has recently noted that 'the question of where routines and capabilities come from

... deserves vastly more attention' (Winter in Murmann et al., 2003: 29). Zollo and Winter (2002: 341) further add: 'To our knowledge at least, the literature does not contain any attempt at a straightforward answer to the question of how routines – much less dynamic capabilities – are generated and evolve.' If organizational routines and capabilities indeed are the fundamentally heterogeneous component driving (variations in) firm performance (Eisenhardt and Martin, 2000) – and note that we are not necessarily denying this – the question of their origin is absolutely fundamental.

At present the origin of routines and capabilities is as vague as their existence. Routines originate from previous routines (or meta-routines select among lower-level routines). Thus, origins are largely considered to be collective, and overall, it is argued simply that 'firms tend to do what they have done before' (Kogut and Zander, 1995: 425). What specifically is the source of the observed collective heterogeneity in capabilities? Is it simply the evolutionary history and experience of the firm as it interacts with the environment ('accumulated experience', according to Zollo and Winter, 2002, or 'past routines', according to Nelson and Winter, 1982), or is it possible to argue for more fundamental, individual-level antecedents? As a normative enterprise, strategic management is (and should be), after all, concerned with purposeful heterogeneity, that is, understanding intentional sources of performance differences. Thus, the collectivist orientation underlying the capabilities approach provides a radical departure from the raison d'etre of strategic management, which ought to provide actionable and useful theoretical insights for the practicing manager (Rumelt et al., 1991). While scholars take glee in the irrationality of managerial action (Murmann et al., 2003: 29), we think surface analysis and correlations do not amount to proof. Rather, the origins of collective concepts are likely to be at the individual level and ultimately to be rooted in purposeful and intentional action.

Problems of empirical application

The lack of clean definitions and of understanding the origins of routines and capabilities is almost bound to produce problems of empirical application. Indeed, difficulties of testability and operationalization have plagued the capabilities stream of research since its very origins (Williamson, 1999). Put more bluntly, an agreed upon, or even a simple, rudimentary operationalization has remained elusive despite several decades of work (see Winter's related comments in Murmann et al., 2003: 29; see also Cohen et al., 1996). Empirically, capabilities-based work has recently seen individual-level measurement, though the confounds (including problems of causality and endogeneity) are readily apparent in the clear conflict between collective theorizing and individual-level measurement (Lacetera et al., 2004). Overall, empirical measures for routines and capabilities should be forthcoming as theoretical statements must be subject to empirical verification and falsification (Bacharach, 1989) or else simply give way to more measurable and scientific alternatives.

Routines and capabilities possibly irrelevant for practice

Many fundamental questions of strategic organization are dealt with at the individual level. This is perhaps most conspicuously the case for strategy implementation. Here issues relating to the allocation of decision-making power and the motivation of employees to engage in acts that will support the strategic plan are pressing. However, the fundamental issues of strategic management – the creation and appropriation of value – also ultimately are reduced to issues at the individual level (Lippman and Rumelt, 2003). Thus, as Coff (1999) argues, firms do not appropriate (or perhaps even create value), only individuals do. And individual appropriation influences individual incentives to contribute to creating value. Understanding this involves subtle issues pertaining to the allocation of rights to receive income from and to make decisions over assets (Foss and Foss, 2005). Such micro-specificity is, however, currently outside the purview of current capabilities-based work.

Problems with multi-level theory

There have been numerous calls for multi-level theory in organizational and strategic analysis, which indeed seems like a feasible solution to the argument of individual versus organization we have outlined. Research in strategic organization in fact seems to generally be agnostic to a potentially fundamental level, implying (and often advocating) that all levels are equal, or perhaps more specifically, that analysis depends on sub-disciplinary convention, preference and the question at hand (Dansereau et al., 1999: 349).

There are, however, numerous problems with the call for multi-level theory, which should be explicated. The problems coincide with the above discussion of the weaknesses associated with collectivist capabilities-based work.

First, multi-level theories have often amounted to simply borrowing psychological theories and applying them to higher levels of analysis (Haleblian and Finkelstein, 1999). For example, various behavioral theories (learning by association, stimulus-response) are simply applied from the individual to the collective or organizational level on a one-to-one basis, without consideration for the problem of importing these theories across levels. Nelson and Winter's (1982) metaphorical argument from individual skill to organizational routine does something similar.

Second, and more importantly, there is a tendency to view analysis at all levels as somehow complementary and equally valid, providing various windows into complex phenomena. However, this pluralistic – or, more bluntly, relativistic – approach (which increasingly is the mode in social science, see Boudon,

2004) has in our view been detrimental to the field, because it has led to needless proliferation and often contradictory explanations. Specifically, while one can argue that strategic organization is rich because of its multiple perspectives on phenomena, discerning colleagues from disciplines such as psychology or economics can readily point out the internal inconsistencies and the lack of a coherent and cumulative research program that is caused by the proliferation of perspectives. Thus, as noted by Felin and Hesterly (forthcoming), there are numerous competing papers in strategic management, pointing out the network, industry, firm and individual as the key level of analysis (or locus of knowledge), without apparent resolution and with each having its captive audience (a tension that many have happily accepted in the name of multi-level theory, or richness). This academic insularity is not healthy and does not improve the field's chances for recognition and legitimacy from peers in related disciplines.

Third, the emphasis on ever higher, contradictory collective levels and *loci* has led to a problem of upward infinite regress. Ever higher levels are theorized as the key source of capabilities (Dyer and Singh, 1998; Kogut, 2000); organization–network/alliance–constellation–industry cluster. However, the logic of increasingly higher levels applied *ad infinitum* leads to the field not being able to say anything theoretically useful, particularly from a strategic perspective (Collis, 1994: 147); capabilities and knowledge exist everywhere – and consequently nowhere. That is, each argument for a fundamental level can be 'trumped' by referring to the importance of a higher level of analysis (Collis, 1994). There are several issues with this upward infinite regress that deserve further brief discussion. First, given that 'organization by firm is variety reducing' (Kogut, 2000: 408), it is logically also so at higher levels of organization. As firms become path-dependent as a requirement of specialization, they increasingly become more myopic, which may lead to competency traps and rigidities. Thus, it is argued that path-dependence can be mitigated by (costlessly) focusing on higher collectives, such as alliances and networks (Kogut, 2000). Logically, however, this higher-level organization will also (while perhaps initially beneficial) result in eventual homogeneity. Second, analysis at collective levels leaves findings too open for alternative explanations. Lower, nested levels (Coleman, 1990: 3) may account for outcomes that are attributed to higher-level collectives. Though collective arrangements may provide a component in firm performance (Dyer and Singh, 1998; Kogut, 2000), overall there must be some a priori, hierarchically nested rationale to exchange, and thus collective-level studies may prove rather descriptive and an artifact of unobserved individual qualities. Furthermore, the further the analysis gets from individuals, the less likely it is to discuss or even control for potential individual effects.

A final critical problem that even articles specifically about levels of analysis have not resolved (Dansereau et al., 1999) is the question of transformation, that is, when exactly can we rigorously move from the individual to the collective level? Concepts such as synergy, emergence or embeddedness are frequently used, but fundamentally these conceptualizations have remained fuzzy and have yet to resolve the micro–macro problem. Synergies, relations and so forth must inherently be a function of the individuals that make up the relationship, organization or network. Thus to explain any of these collective structures one must understand the underlying abilities, actions, choices and motivations of the individuals involved.

Overall we have discussed the current collectivist focus of extant capabilities-based work, and have argued for the need for individual-level considerations and micro-foundations. Below we develop some conceptual directions for future research, specifically elucidating what we mean by micro-foundations. It should be noted that while we do not advocate a completely atomistic, individualistic approach, we do believe that a form of methodological individualism provides an adequate amount of consideration for individuals, though we do not want to completely discount the potential causal influence of routines and other collective structures.

Toward individual-level origins for organizational capabilities

A fundamental level?

We argue that taking the individual as the fundamental level is a potentially fruitful and certainly under-researched approach for strategic organization research. Inherently, without individuals there is no collective. As we have argued, scholars often assume random distribution of characteristics when they make arguments at the collective level. For us, this is untenable. Think of the department that you work in and the departments of your colleagues. Are academics randomly distributed into organizational settings with broader collective factors (culture, environment) largely driving outcomes (e.g. publication), or do individuals self-select into and create environments? Given a priori heterogeneity at the individual level, self-selection seems like a more feasible explanation. That is, a talented young academic has multiple offers at various schools and self-selects into the environment where he or she is given the most resources to be productive. (A hypothetical, admittedly extreme, test of the primacy given to the collective environment would be to take a lackluster individual and to put him or her into a productive environment.)

In the interest of moving toward discussing the implications of a fundamental level for the origins of organizational routines and capabilities, we develop a rough conceptual model. First, Figure 1 captures the essential arguments of the capabilities-based work (see arrow specifying focus of extant work), and provides the framework for our arguments for the importance of understanding origins and micro-foundations. Figure 1 builds on the insightful conceptual model of the sociologist James Coleman (1990), who persuasively argues for the critical importance of methodological individualism in social theory

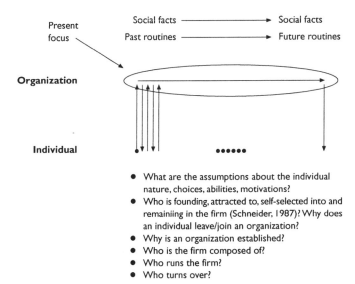

- What are the assumptions about the individual nature, choices, abilities, motivations?
- Who is founding, attracted to, self-selected into and remainiing in the firm (Schneider, 1987)? Why does an individual leave/join an organization?
- Why is an organization established?
- Who is the firm composed of?
- Who runs the firm?
- Who turns over?

Figure 1   Individual–organization relationship

(Coleman, 1990: 2–5). The figure suggests that extant routines and capabilities-based work operate largely at the macro-level. That is, the sources and origins of collective routines and capabilities are explicitly argued to be in previous or past collective routines and capabilities (Kogut and Zander, 1992; Nelson and Winter, 1982: 134–5). Similar to Durkheimian social facts, which originate from previous social facts (Durkheim, 1962: 103–10), routines and capabilities remain at a collective level.

A natural place to study the origins of heterogeneity may be in the past decisions of individuals, notably in the initial conditions, decisions or even the characteristics of the founders and individuals, who make fateful, path-dependent decisions, which affect the company well after these founders have moved. Arrow aptly captures this in his discussion of organizational capabilities, or the 'organizational code', which he suggests is largely 'determined [by the founders] in accordance with the best expectations at the time of the firm's creation' (Arrow, 1974: 56). This implies that individuals play a critical factor in outcomes well into the future of the firm.

The question of who

As we have essentially argued from the outset, the question of who the organization is composed of has important implications for collective outcomes (see

Figure 1). That is, who starts the firm, who is attracted into it, who turns over, who the organization is composed of, etc. is fundamental for overall organizational outcomes and advantage. Similar to much of organization behavior and theory (Davis-Blake and Pfeffer, 1989), however, the underlying assumption in strategy has been that organizations are 'strong situations', and that individuals are malleable, homogeneous, or at least randomly distributed into organizations. This assumption effectively suppresses the 'who' question(s) (and subsequent associated questions regarding motivation, preferences, abilities and so forth.) However, even casual observation of, for example, R&D environments, suggests that the mechanism of self-selection plays a critical role in overall outcomes (Stern, 2004; Zenger, 1994). That is, highly talented individuals self-select and are attracted into (and create) certain environments, thus being largely responsible for overall outcomes (Schneider, 1987).

We should note again that extant arguments in the organizational capabilities literature specifically argue that first, organizational routines are independent of individuals (Levitt and March, 1988: 320; Nelson and Winter, 1982), and given the primacy of routines that second, organizations can withstand significant turnover without material effects on the organization (Kogut and Zander, 1992). We address each point in turn, as it relates to our overall framework.

First, the independence of organizational routines from individuals: from the perspective of methodological individualism, collective structures are dependent on the individuals who make up the organization. How things are done in organizational settings, both in terms of structure and overall efficiency or creativeness, is a function of who is doing. Even in highly routinized environments, the origins of heterogeneous routines are fundamentally at the individual level (Foss and Foss, 2000). While capabilities-based work focuses on exogenous sources of advantage – environment, situation, etc. determining experience – nevertheless the key differential input is the services of the people who make up the organization (Schneider, 1987).

Second, the implications of turnover on organizational capabilities and performance: given the primacy given to collective routines and capabilities, extant work argues that individual turnover does not affect overall organizational routines or outcomes (Kogut and Zander, 1992; Levitt and March, 1988). However, this conceptualization is flawed from an individualistic perspective. That is, who turns over is absolutely fundamental to overall organizational outcomes. Recent work in fact has begun to wrestle with the problem of individual-level measurement and collective-level theory. That is, work, for example by Song et al. (2003; and Lacetera et al., 2004), suggests that capabilities can simply be brought in as a function of certain, key individuals, which implies that capabilities may in the first place reside in individuals rather than in the organization.

Moreover, we should note that much of what happens in organizations can scarcely be labeled as routine (Barnard, 1968: 240; Garicano, 2000: 898; Williamson, 2002: 426). In particular, managers deal with exceptions rather than the routine. Furthermore, in a given organizational setting, perhaps depending on various task- or industry-specific contingencies, certain individuals provide the parameters or constraints within which action is taken (Brennan and Buchanan, 1985; Elster, 1989). This may give way to a two-stage process where (for example) standard operating procedures and rules of interaction are first created and specified by organizational founders or managers, and then individuals interact given these collective structures or constraints, perhaps gradually changing those procedures and rules (Foss and Foss, 2000). However, such a rationalistic, design-oriented approach is admittedly not the only possible approach to understanding the origins and emergence of routines and capabilities.

Invisible hand explanation

We have argued that capabilities work in general rules out a priori the possibility that heterogeneity is located at the individual level. An important question is how exactly collective structure and heterogeneity then emerge.

We do not necessarily wish to rule out the possibility that heterogeneity may conceivably be located at the collective level, but the question we have highlighted throughout this essay is how it arises in the first place. Various bodies of social science research suggest possibilities for understanding the underlying mechanisms (Hedstrom and Swedberg, 1998). For example, game theory shows that many games are characterized by a multiplicity of equilibria, particularly in repeated settings. Thus, different equilibria can emerge, even if agents are relatively homogeneous.

Similarly, we do not wish to argue that routines and capabilities should necessarily be understood as rationally designed. Again, as game theory has clarified, formalizing the traditional intuition of classical liberalism that many of society's most valuable institutions (language, money, norms and conventions, etc.) are the result of 'human action, but not of human design' (Hayek, 1952; Ullman-Margalit, 1977), collective entities may conceivably arise in a wholly unplanned manner (Schotter, 1981; Sugden, 1986). More broadly, we conjecture that 'invisible hand explanations' (Ullman-Margalit, 1977) can be given of routines and capabilities. In an invisible hand explanation, one seeks to explain some 'well-structured pattern' (ibid.) that is the unintended and unforeseen result of the interdependent actions of agents in process, genetic terms, where the explanation involves identifying a plausible mechanism that aggregates individual choices to the relevant 'well-structured pattern'. For example, local imitative behavior among employees may unintentionally lead to organization-level routines or capabilities. Or to return to the question of heterogeneity, it may simply arise out of individual self-selection based on underlying abilities and skills.

Note that when an invisible hand approach is made precise, for example, by means of game theory, it often turns out that processes of emergence of entities such as norms and conventions (and by possible implication also routines and capabilities) are strongly conditioned by historical specificities, such as the characteristics of the initial individuals among which the convention began (Sugden, 1986). And although it addresses the unplanned emergence of collective entities, this approach is squarely in the camp of methodological individualism.

Conclusion

The ultimate consequences of the present collectivist approaches in strategic and their underlying assumptions about individuals have recently been summarized by Howard Aldrich as follows: 'if we truly focused on routines, competencies, practices and so on, we would *not* follow people anymore in our research' (Aldrich in Murmann et al., 2003: 25–7; emphasis in original text). We think that such an approach, which lacks the individual, is fundamentally problematic. Individuals after all provide the nested antecedent to numerous collective phenomena and thus deserve careful theoretical and empirical consideration in our theorizing. As noted by Simon (1985: 303), our underlying assumptions about the humans we are studying are absolutely fundamental to theorizing, and the present assumptions of homogeneity and infinite malleability we think are tenuous at best. Overall we have advocated that more careful consideration is given to individual endowments, characteristics, a priori abilities, motivation and choice of behavior.

Our hope, as we have said, is that this essay will serve as a clarion call for capabilities-based scholars to pay more careful attention to their underlying assumptions and to develop theoretical arguments which give consideration to micro-foundations. We concur with Barnard that 'the individual is always the basic strategic factor of organization' (1968: 139). Thus, with individuals at center stage, the questions for capabilities-based work should shift to explicating how routines are created and emerge (and change) from individual action, and how they evolve with the subsequent interaction between individual and collective. Overall we thus challenge the completely behavioral, organic and structurally-oriented approaches, which have not clearly delineated the origins and micro-foundations of routines and capabilities.

Acknowledgements

Special thanks to Peter Abell, Torben Juul Andersen, Russ Coff, Rachel Hilliard, Lasse Lien, Anoop Madhok, Joe Mahoney, Jackson Nickerson and Steve Tallman for helpful comments. A version of this essay was presented at the 2004 *Academy of Management* conference in the BPS symposium (organized by Teppo Felin and Jamal Shamsie), 'The Role of Individual Stakeholders in Value Creation and Appropriation', and at seminars at Copenhagen Business School and Bristol University Business School. Thanks to participants for helpful comments.

References

Arrow, K. J. (1974) *The Limits of Organization*. New York: W. W. Norton.

Bacharach, S. B. (1989) 'Organizational Theories: Some Criteria for Evaluation', *Academy of Management Review* 14: 496–515.

Barnard, C. (1968) *The Functions of the Executive*, 18th printing. Oxford: Oxford University Press.

Barney, J. B. (1991) 'Firm Resources and Sustained Competitive Advantage', *Journal of Management* 17: 99–120.

Boudon, R. (2004) *The Poverty of Relativism*. Oxford: Bardwell Press.

Brennan, G. and Buchanan, J. M. (1985) *The Reason of Rules: Constitutional Political Economy*. Cambridge: Cambridge University Press.

Coff, R. (1999) 'When Competitive Advantage Dosen't Lead to Performance: Resource-based Theory and Stakeholder Bargaining Power', *Organization Science* 10: 119–33.

Cohen, M. D., Burkhart, R., Dosi, G., Egidi, M., Marengo, L., Warglien, M. and Winter, S. (1996) 'Routines and Other Recurrent Action Patterns of Organizations: Contemporary Research Issues', *Industrial and Corporate Change* 5: 653–98.

Coleman, J. S. (1990) *Foundations of Social Theory*. Cambridge, MA, and London: The Belknap Press of Harvard University Press.

Collis, D. (1994) 'How Valuable Are Organizational Capabilities', *Strategic Management Journal* 15: 143–52.

Dansereau, F., Yammarino, F. J. and Kohles, J. C. (1999) 'Multiple Levels of Analysis from a Longitudinal Perspective: Some Implications for Theory Building', *Academy of Management Review* 24: 346–57.

Davis-Blake, A. and Pfeffer, J. (1989) 'Just a Mirage: The Search for Dispositional Effects in Organizational Research', *Academy of Management Review* 14: 385–400.

Dosi, G. (1995) 'Hierarchies, Markets and Power: Some Foundational Issues on the Nature of Contemporary Economic Organizations', *Industrial and Corporate Change* 4: 1–19.

Dosi, G., Marengo, L., Bassanini, A. and Valente, M. (1999) 'Norms as Emergent Properties of Adaptive Learning: The Case of Economic Routines', *Journal of Evolutionary Economics* 9: 5–26.

Durkheim, E. (1962) *The Rules of the Sociological Method*. Glencoe, IL: Free Press.

Dyer, J. and Singh, H. (1998) 'The Relational View: Cooperative Strategy and Sources of Interorganizational Competitive Advantage', *Academy of Management Review* 23: 660–79.

Eisenhardt, K. and Martin, J. (2000) 'Dynamic Capabilities: What Are They?', *Strategic Management Journal* 21: 1105–21.

Elster, J. (1989) *Nuts and Bolts for the Social Sciences*. Cambridge: Cambridge University Press.

Felin, T. and Hesterly, W. S. (forthcoming) 'The Knowledge-Based View, Heterogeneity, and New Value Creation: Philosophical Considerations on the Locus of Knowledge', *Academy of Management Review*.

Foss, K. and Foss, N. J. (2000) 'Competence and Governance Perspectives: How Much Do They Differ? And How Does It Matter?, in N. J. Foss and V. Mahnke (eds) *Competence, Governance, and Entrepreneurship*. Oxford: Oxford University Press.

Foss, K. and Foss, N. J. (2005) 'Resources and Transaction Costs: How Property Rights Economics Furthers the Resource-Based View', *Strategic Management Journal* 26; 541–53.

Foss, N. J. (2003) 'Bounded Rationality and Tacit Knowledge in the Organizational Capabilities Approach: An Evaluation and a Stocktaking', *Industrial and Corporate Change* 12: 185–201.

Garicano, L. (2000) 'Hierarchies and the Organization of Knowledge in Production', *Journal of Political Economy* 108: 874–904.

Haleblian, J. and Finkelstein, S. (1999) 'The Influence of Organizational Acquisition Experience on Acquisition Performance: A Behavioral Learning Perspective', *Administrative Science Quarterly* 44: 29–56.

Hayek, F. A. (1952) *The Counter Revolution of Science*. Chicago, IL: University of Chicago Press.

Hedstrom, P. and Swedberg, R. (1998) 'Social Mechanisms: An Introductory Essay', in P. Hedstrom and R. Swedberg (eds) *Social Mechanisms: An Analytical Approach to Social Theory*, pp. 1–31. Cambridge: Cambridge University Press.

Henderson, R. and Cockburn, I. M. (1994) 'Measuring Competence? Exploring Firm Effects in Pharmaceutical Research', *Strategic Management Journal* 15: 63–84.

Kogut, B. (2000) 'the Network as Knowledge: Generative Rules and the Emergence of Structure', *Strategic Management Journal* 21: 405–25.

Kogut, B. and Zander, U. (1992) 'Knowledge of the Firm, Combinative Capabilities, and the Replication of Technology', *Organization Science* 3: 383–97.

Kogut, B. and Zander, U. (1995) 'Knowledge, Market Failure, and the Multinational Enterprise: A Reply', *Journal of International Business Studies* 26: 417–26.

Lacetera, N., Cockburn, I. and Henderson, R. (2004) 'Do Firms Change Capabilities by Hiring New People? A Study of the Adoption of Science-Based Drug Discovery', in J. A. Baum and A. M. McGahan (eds) *Business Strategy over the Industry Life Cycle – Advances in Strategic Management* 21: forthcoming. Oxford: Elsevier/JAI Press.

Levitt, B. and March, J. (1988) 'Organizational Learning', *Annual Review of Sociology* 14: 319–40.

Lippman, S. A. and Rumelt, R. P. (2003) 'The Payments Perspective: Micro-foundations of Resource Analysis', *Strategic Management Journal* 24: 903–27.

Murmann, J. P., Aldrich, H., Levinthal, D. and Winter, S. (2003) 'Evolutionary Thought in Management and Organization Theory at the Beginning of the New Millennium', *Journal of Management Inquiry* 12: 1–19.

Nahapiet, J. and Ghoshal, S. (1998) 'Social Capital, Intellectual Capital, and the Organizational Advantage', *Academy of Management Review* 23: 242–66.

Nelson, R. R. and Winter, S. (1982) *An Evolutionary Theory of Economic Change*. Cambridge, MA: Harvard University Press.

Rumelt, R. P., Schendel, D. and Teece, D. J. (1991) 'Strategic Management and Economics', *Strategic Management Journal* 12: 5–29.

Schneider, B. (1987) 'The People Make the Place', *Personnel Psychology* 40: 437–54.

Schotter, A. (1981) *The Economic Theory of Social Institutions*. Cambridge: Cambridge University Press.

Selznick, P. (1996) 'Institutionalism "old" and "new"', *Administrative Science Quarterly* 41: 270–7.

Simon, H. A. (1985) 'Human Nature in Politics', *American Political Science Review* 79: 293–304.

Song, J., Almeida, P. and Wu, G. (2003) 'Learning-by-Hiring: When is Mobility More Likely to Facilitate Interfirm Knowledge Transfer?', *Management Science* 49: 351–65.

Spender, J. C. (1996) 'Making Knowledge the Basis of a Dynamic Theory of the Firm', *Strategic Management Journal* 17 (Winter special issue): 45–62.

Stern, S. (2004) 'Do Scientists Pay to be Scientists?', *Management Science* 50: 835–53.

Sugden, R. (1986) *The Economics of Rights, Cooperation and Welfare*. Oxford: Blackwell.

Ullmann-Margalit, E. (1977) 'Invisible-hand Explanations', *Synthese* 39: 263–91.

Whetten, D. A. (2004) 'In Search of the "O" in OMT', Organization and Management Theory (OMT) Division Distinguished Speaker Address presented at the Academy of Management Conference (August), New Orleans, LA.

Williamson, O. E. (1999) 'Strategy Research: Governance and Competence Perspectives', *Strategic Management Journal* 20: 1087–108.

Williamson, O. E. (2002) 'Empirical Microeconomics: Another Perspective', in M. Augier and J. March (eds) *The Economics of Choice, Change and Organization: Essays in Memory of Richard M. Cyert*, pp. 419–41. Northampton, MA: Edward Elgar.

Winter, S. G. (2003) 'Understanding Dynamic Capabilities', *Strategic Management Journal* 24: 991–5.

Zenger, T. R. (1994) 'Explaining Organizational Diseconomies of Scale in R&D: The Allocation of Engineering Talent, Ideas and Effort by Firm Size', *Management Science* 40: 708–29.

Zollo, M. and Winter, S. G. (2002) 'Deliberate Learning and the Evolution of Dynamic Capabilities', *Organization Science* 13: 339–52.

Teppo Felin is an Assistant Professor at the Marriott School of Management, Brigham Young University, and was formerly a Visiting Assistant Professor at Goizueta Business School, Emory University. His research interests include the knowledge-based view, individual and organizational learning, micro-macro link, social theory and the philosophy of social science. He has a manuscript (closely related to this essay) forthcoming in the *Academy of Management Review*, and he has also published in the *Human Resource Management Journal* and other outlets. *Address:* 587 Tanner Building, Marriott School, Brigham Young University, Provo, UT 84602, USA. [email: teppo.felin@byu.edu]

Nicolai Foss is Professor of Economic Organization and the Director of the Centre for Strategic Management and Globalization. His research interests include the resource-based view, organizational economics and the philosophy of social science. His work has appeared in journals such as *Strategic Management Journal, Organization Science* and *Journal of Management Studies*. *Address*: Porcelainshaven 246, 2000 Frederiksberg, Denmark. [email: njf.smg@cbs.dk]

[4]

The rhetorical dimensions of bounded rationality

Herbert A. Simon and organizational economics

Nicolai J. Foss

Introduction[1]

In this chapter I make a couple of connected arguments about the status of bounded rationality (henceforth, "BR") in modern economics and the role of Herbert Simon with respect to understanding this status. Following McCloskey (1983), emphasis is placed on the rhetorical aspects, the attempts to persuade, of scientific development in economics. Following Sent's (1997) fine study of Thomas Sargent's (rhetorical) appeal to BR, economists' actual use of BR is examined. The economists whose use of BR I consider are economists of organization. This choice is far from arbitrary. In his key papers directed at an economics audience (Simon 1978, 1979), Simon made several explicit references to the emerging economics of organization and he himself contributed fundamentally to the neighboring field of organization theory. His examples of BR and its implications usually involved the business firm. Indeed, he sometimes took the notion of "administrative man" to be *synonymous* with a boundedly rational agent. Perhaps not surprisingly, then, the economics of organization was probably the first sub-field of economics where BR was systematically invoked, and it is perhaps still today the sub-field being invoked with the highest frequency.[2]

More specifically, it will, first, be argued that the use of BR arguments in the economics of organization is primarily rhetorical in the somewhat pre-McCloskeyan (McCloskey 1983) sense of dressing up a theory with arguments that are essentially empty in an explanatory sense, but are nevertheless made because they help to persuade. Specifically, BR is invoked in the rhetorical practice of organizational economists, because it represents a way of conveying the intuition of another, much more central point; however, it is not invoked because it itself is in any way central. Specifically, BR is used in order to explain in a loose, background way the notion of contractual incompleteness. Thus, if people do not have the wits to imagine and make contractual provision for a number of contingencies, they will leave the contract incomplete, giving rise to the kind of externality problems that drive the modern economics of organization. However,

H.A. Simon and organizational economics 159

asymmetric information (a well-defined concept) can do, in these models, what BR (a concept with a multitude of different connotations, but arguably no clear definition) supposedly does, and can do so more "cleanly". This raises the question why BR continues to be invoked, leading to the second argument.

Second, I argue, admittedly in a more speculative vein, that there are strong reasons to suspect that the status, as well as the rhetorical practice, of Herbert Simon plays a decisive role for understanding the way in which BR is presently used. The fact that a Nobel Prize was bestowed upon Simon for his work on BR, and that it was the brainchild of one of history's more impressive polymaths, should make it hard for almost anyone to simply dismiss it.[3] Arguably, however, the rhetorical practice of Simon made it hard for most economists to *not* in the end dismiss it, if perhaps only discreetly; namely, by tacitly refusing to incorporate it in their theoretical work. Here, rhetorics is understood in a more authentic manner as the "art of discovering good reasons, finding what really warrants assent, because any reasonable person ought to be persuaded" (Booth 1974: xiv; quoted by McCloskey 1983: 482). Thus, although Simon certainly wrote as if "any reasonable person ought to be persuaded" by his arguments, he did not, I argue, give the "good reasons," those that would "really warrant assent," for BR. He failed to persuade. Most importantly, in his most "rhetorical" papers, directly aimed at persuading economists, Simon never provided any precise definition of what BR really *is*. Moreover, he never really gave good heuristic advice on how to incorporate BR into economic models, and simply noted that how exactly notions of BR developed in the theory of computational complexity – his favorite example of successful modeling of BR – would be incorporated into economic models "remain[s] to be seen" (1978: 12). These failures form part of the explanation of why most economists, including economists of organization, so far have not fundamentally taken BR seriously.

Some implications and wider implications, notably with respect to the future of BR in the economics of organization, are finally briefly discussed. A conclusion is that there is reason to be more optimistic on behalf of the use of BR in economic reasoning, since there are now better critical and constructive foundations for BR than when Simon tried to make economists take BR seriously, as partly signaled by the publication of the present book.

Economists' use of bounded rationality: the case of organizational economics

Bounded rationality in organizational economics

In his autobiography, Simon (1991a: 270–271) recounts increasingly violent disagreements with mainstream economists, leading him to abandon, for a period, economics in favor of psychology and computation science. "By the time I returned to a concern with economics in the 1970s," he observed, "the war was open and declared." Indeed, many of Simon's writings from that period (Simon 1976, 1978, 1979) are so sharply formulated that it seems quite likely that at least Simon himself felt that he was part of a war.[4] (It is actually harder to find specific and concerted critique, at least in print, of Simon and BR, such as one would expect of a genuine war.)

However, at exactly the time when the supposed war was going on, an important part of economics, namely the theory of the firm, seemed to be increasingly influenced by considerations of BR. New, serious approaches to various aspects of the theory of the firm that all appeared to be solidly based on bounded rationality were mushrooming. Thus, team theory (Marschak and Radner 1972), transaction cost economics (Williamson 1971), and the evolutionary theory of the firm (Nelson and Winter 1973) all appeared in the beginning of the 1970s (although their roots go further back). These, still flourishing, approaches all seemed to start from bounded rationality,[5] exactly as Simon would like them to. And the explicit motivation for such a starting point was that neoclassical theory of the firm and its behavioral starting point in substantive rationality excluded concern with such vital phenomena as incomplete contracts, the role of organizational structure and organizational routines.

Today, many – if not all – economists of organization would likely agree that BR is important to the study of economic organization (Milgrom and Roberts 1988, 1992). Indeed, some argue that it is *indispensable*; that is, a necessary assumption in the theory of economic organization (Williamson 1996; McLeod 2000). References to the need to draw more on psychological research for understanding the workings of organization are quite common now, even among the economics profession's foremost symbol manipulators (e.g., Holmström and Tirole 1989; Lazear 1991).

Thus, a newcomer to the field may, by glancing at contemporary organizational economics, easily get the impression that Simon's lessons have been absorbed, and that organizational economists have acknowledged the need to place BR centerstage in their theorizing. This is not the case. If anything, the use (or invocation) of BR may have declined.[6] To some extent this is because the mainstream economics of organization has developed into a highly formal and axiomatic enterprise, and BR has a bad reputation of only being given to formalization if that formalization is

H.A. Simon and organizational economics 161

fundamentally *ad hoc* and the axiomatic basis is unclear or non-existent. That reputation may not be entirely justified (Rubinstein 1998), but many economists of organization (particularly contract theorists) certainly act as if it is. Oliver Hart arguably sums up the attitudes of many formal economists when he argues that

> I do not think that bounded rationality is necessary for a theory of organizations. This is fortunate because developing a theory of bounded rationality in a bilateral or multilateral setting seems even more complicated than developing such a theory at the individual level; and the latter task has already proved more than enough for economists to handle.
>
> (Hart 1990: 700–701)

In fact, some parts of the economics of organization, particularly contract theory, bear little substantial imprint of BR.[7] This is not surprising: contract theory is based entirely on information economics and game theory, which at least in their standard, "toolbox versions" have no room for BR at all. Still, even contract theorists occasionally invoke BR, usually to explain in a loose way why some contingencies may be left out of a contract.

Bounded rationality and transaction cost economics

It is sometimes argued that transaction cost economics provides considerably more room for BR than contract theory (e.g., Brousseau and Fares 2000). There is something to this claim; for example, Williamson (1975) does invoke BR in connection with, for example, explaining the M-form, and other aspects of organizational structure. He puts much emphasis on the need for adaptation that arises in a world of uncertainty and bounded rationality. Governance mechanisms in Williamson's work are more than efficient (i.e., second-best) *ex ante* allocations of property rights (as in Grossman and Hart 1986; Hart and Moore 1990); they are mechanisms for *ex post* adaptation and conflict resolution. Williamson's works are replete with references to Simon.

Still, however, Williamson refrains from being explicit about how to model BR on the level of the individual agent. He is quite explicit here, noting that "[e]conomizing on bounded rationality takes two forms. One concerns decision processes and the other involves governance structures. The use of heuristic problem-solving ... is a decision process response" (Williamson 1985: 46). However, in transaction cost economics, "heuristic problem solving" is not central. Instead, transaction cost economics "is principally concerned ... with the economizing consequences of assigning transactions to governance structures in a discriminating way."[8] In other words, Williamson is interested in making use of bounded rationality for the purpose of developing a theory of discriminating alignment rather than for the purposes of explaining administrative *behavior*, as in Simon (1947). He is not interested in BR as a "decision process response." For the purpose of explaining why contracts are incomplete, Williamson apparently thinks that it is not necessary to model BR itself; it may be asserted as a "background assumption" that while vital – indeed, necessary – does not need to be explicated itself. Milgrom and Roberts (1992: 128), as well as most other mainstream economists of organization who invoke BR, adopt the same procedure.

Thus, BR enters organizational economics reasoning in a loose background sort of way, in which it lends credence to exogenously imposing constraints on the feasible contracting space, but is not modeled itself. It supplies the rhetorical function of lending intuitive support to the notion of incomplete contracts. A Simonian information-processing argument is sometimes invoked in order to be more concrete about how BR produces incomplete contracting (Hart 1990: 698; Schwartz 1992: 80): if agents do not have the mental capacity to think through the whole decision tree (for example, in complicated bilateral trading relations), it seems reasonable to assume that some of the branches of the tree (such as those relating to some future uses of assets) cannot be represented in a contract; the contract is left incomplete. This is indeed a BR argument. However, agents are supposed to deal with this manifestation of BR in a substantively rational manner, as numerous critics have pointed out since Dow (1987). As he observed, this approach provokes a lurking suspicion of a basic inconsistency, for whereas BR is loosely invoked as a background assumption (yet still a necessary one), there is no hesitation to appeal to substantive rationality when the choice between governance structures must be explained. I discuss this next.

The irrelevance of bounded rationality: the incomplete contract controversy

A recent theoretical debate on the coherence and foundations of incomplete contract theory – called the "incomplete contract controversy" (Tirole 1999) – is pertinent to the issues under consideration here. The debate concerns whether satisfactory foundations for incomplete contracts are offered in the works of Hart and associates (e.g., Grossman and Hart 1986; Hart and Moore 1990). The main critics are Eric Maskin and Jean Tirole (Maskin and Tirole 1999; Tirole 1999). At the core of this debate is the explanatory tension between invoking transaction costs – which may be understood as a consequence of BR – on the one hand and postulating farsighted and substantively rational contracting on the other (i.e., the parties to a contract can foresee the utilities from the relation). Whereas Dow (1987) interpreted this as an inconsistency in transaction cost economics, Maskin and Tirole show that there is no formal inconsistency

H.A. Simon and organizational economics 163

here, and that on this point the incomplete contracts literature has got it right. However, the main thrust of their argument is that the use of transaction costs (i.e., BR) in models of incomplete contracting does not provide additional explanatory insight relative to models that make no use of these (i.e., complete contracting models). The obvious implication is that there is no reason for making use of BR, not even in the "homeopathic" (Dosi 2002) way in which it has hitherto been used.

Organizational issues have largely motivated the upsurge in incomplete contract modeling during the last decade. In fact, the founding incomplete contract paper, namely Grossman and Hart (1986), was explicitly motivated by an attempt to model the emphasis in transaction cost economics on asset specificity as a key determinant of the scope of the firm, using modeling conventions and insights already developed in (complete contracting) agency theory and its basis in mechanism design theory. However, whereas Williamson (1996) puts much emphasis on inefficient *ex post* bargaining, the incomplete contracting approach assumes that *ex post* bargaining is efficient. Thus, what drives these models are misaligned *ex ante* incentives, particularly with respect to investment in vertical buyer–supplier relationships. The problem is to motivate what may cause such misalignment. The point of contention in the incomplete contracts controversy is whether transaction costs arising from the inability to perfectly anticipate or describe all relevant contingencies or enforce contract terms – all of which may derive from BR[9] – constrain the set of feasible contracting outcomes relative to the complete contracting benchmark. If this is *not* the case, transaction costs (BR) do not suffice to establish the possibility of inefficient investment patterns. Therefore, they do not suffice to establish a role for ownership, and in turn for a theory of the boundaries of the firm.[10]

The Maskin and Tirole argument builds on the key assumption in the incomplete contract approach that although valuations may not be verifiable, they may still be observable by the parties (Hart and Moore 1990). This implies that trade can be conditioned on message games between the parties. These games are designed *ex ante* in such a way that they can effectively describe *ex post* (where bargaining is efficient) all the trades that were not described *ex ante*. A further crucial step in the argument is the typical contract theory assumption that parties allocate property rights and choose investments so that their expected utilities are maximized, knowing (at least probabilistically) how payoffs relate to allocations of property rights and levels of investment (i.e., they can perform "dynamic programming"). Given this, Maskin and Tirole (1999) provide sufficient conditions under which the undescribability of contingencies does *not* restrict the payoffs that can be achieved. In other words, there are no differences in the allocations that can be achieved under incomplete contracting and complete contracting; no real economic content is achieved by adding considerations of BR/undescribability of contingencies/transaction costs. This is their "irrelevance of transaction costs" theorem. We might as well call it the "irrelevance of bounded rationality theorem."

Bounded rationality and mainstream modeling

BR, it has been argued, is very much a background assumption that is introduced in order to help explaining in an "intuitive" way incomplete contracting, a key ingredient in understanding the efficient boundaries of the firm, and efficient alignment more generally. BR is never explicitly modeled on the level of the individual agent. It is never fundamentally taken seriously in the way economists take arguments seriously, namely by modeling them. After Maskin and Tirole (1999), there would indeed seem to be little reason to take BR seriously at all; its use can at best be "rhetorical."[11]

However, one may argue that it is exactly the very "thin" way in which BR is treated in organizational economics that allows for the Maskin and Tirole argument, which purportedly demonstrates the complete irrelevance of BR (Kreps 1996; Foss 2001). After all, a main notion in incomplete contract theory and transaction cost economics is that a very thin Simon may join hands with a rather corpulent Savage, as it were, and it is not really surprising if the very thin Simon turns out to matter very little indeed for the explanatory weight of the whole construct.

Still, the puzzle remains why organizational economists have chosen to work with models in which BR occupies at best a small corner – of a mainly rhetorical nature – of the model, the rest of the space being taken up by common priors, dynamic programming, etc. Not only was Simon critical of, for example, dynamic programming (Simon 1978), his work was taken up with rather concrete manifestations of BR often explored in detailed computational models (e.g., Newell and Simon 1972). Simon himself published prolifically on firms and other organizations (e.g., Simon 1947, 1951, 1991a, 1997; March and Simon 1958). Given all this, how can it be that organizational economists have been reluctant to be serious about BR, in the sense of actually modeling BR?

The presumably most obvious reason is because of the well-known difficulties of aligning BR with the basic machinery of neoclassical microeconomics and game theory (Conlisk 1996; Rabin 1998; Camerer 1998). Thus, fundamental notions and modeling principles, such as subjective expected utility, common priors, rational expectations/dynamic programming, backward induction, etc., are not too easily aligned with fundamental findings of cognitive psychology (such as gain–loss asymmetries, role-biased expectations, etc.). Moreover, from the mainstream economist point of view, there is a huge price to be paid in terms of analytical tractability and clarity to the extent that one wishes to factor findings from cognitive psychology into economic models. This would seem to be consistent with BR becoming increasingly squeezed out of the economics of organization, as the latter has become increasingly formalist, the Maskin and Tirole argument being the culmination of the squeeze-out operation. However, this may not be the entire story. In the following, I argue that Simon himself is partly responsible for the way in which economists have used (rather, not used) BR.

Simon lecturing economists on rationality

In a series of papers, Simon (1976, 1978, 1979) made a sustained attempt to convince economists to take BR seriously. Two of these are particularly noteworthy in the present context, namely his Richard T. Ely lecture, "Rationality as Process and as a Product of Thought" (Simon 1978) and the Nobel lecture, "Rational Decision Making in Business Organizations" (Simon 1979). Needless to say, an Ely lecture, held at the annual meeting of the American Economic Association, and a Nobel even more, represent excellent platforms for persuasion exercises. It is therefore worth looking a bit into these papers.

The Ely and the Nobel lectures

The lectures differ primarily in the dimensions of depth and broadness, the Nobel being more survey-oriented and less analytically engaging. The similarities are, however, much more striking than the differences. First, they cover much the same themes. Second, both lectures are very strongly rhetorical in a number of senses. Thus, they employ a host of familiar rhetorical devices, such as metaphorical reasoning (particularly the Nobel), analogies, reference to authority, and, yes, quotations from *Alice in Wonderland*. Moreover, the lectures are rhetorical in the sense that they are very much taken up with "probing what men believe they ought to believe, rather than prove what is true according to abstract methods" (Booth 1974: xiii; cited in McCloskey 1983: 482). An aspect of this "probing" is that the lectures are highly polemical, with much strong critique of economists such as Fritz Machlup, Milton Friedman, Edward Mason and other defenders of the neoclassical theory of the firm. Also, there is indeed no attempt to "prove what is true according to abstract methods"; quite the contrary, "abstract methods" (axiomatic, non-empirical, etc.) are criticized and a rather sturdy elementary empiricism is promoted, one that involves "straightforward 'anthropological' field study" (1978: 12). General equilibrium theory is condemned as mere intellectual puzzle-solving, it being noted that "[p]erhaps some of these intellectual mountains have been climbed simply because they were there" (1979: 493–494).

All these aspects are signaled at the beginning of both lectures. Thus, they begin with the traditional opening gambit for talks of this kind – namely, invoking authorities. The relevant authorities are Richard Ely and Alfred Marshall. Citing and quoting them is motivated by their taking a different, and more "realistic," view of economics from the abstract one associated with Lionel Robbins of how to best allocate scarce means among competing ends, an understanding that is, of course, closely related to the notion of maximizing. The richer and more realistic view of behavior in Marshall and Ely leads directly into the rationality theme.

Particularly in the Ely lecture, Simon handles this in a strikingly rhetorical manner. He begins by arguing that indeed most of human behavior has a rational element; however, maximizing rationality may not adequately describe this rational element. He then shows that economists in fact do use weaker forms of rationality, particularly in connection with institutional issues, where economists are as methodologically functionalist as sociologists and anthropologists (transaction cost economics is mentioned here). In general, Simon continues, it will not do to separate the various human and social sciences on whether they ascribe to rationality to human beings or not; they *all* do (Freudian psychology and sociological social exchange theory are provocatively mentioned as examples), and economics differs only by having adopted a particular, narrow conception of rationality. In particular, economics is not concerned with the process of choice, such as what are effective procedures for searching for solutions, only with the results. However, if attention is not in unlimited supply, it is necessary to account for the allocation of attention in search processes. A theory of this is a theory of procedural rationality. However, Simon admits, he is not aware "that there has been any systematic development of a theory of information and communication that treats attention rather than information as the scarce resource" (1978: 13).

The Nobel lecture is slightly more specific about concrete manifestations of BR than the Ely lecture. Here, as in many other places in the two lectures, Simon employs the mode of argumentation of beginning by criticizing a mainstream position and then arguing that the behavioral alternative is superior. Thus, he begins by strongly criticizing the methodological notion (endorsed in economics by Machlup and Friedman) that theories can only be tested with respect to their predictions of aggregate phenomena. This is a methodologically unsound idea; instead, attention should indeed be directed toward the soundness of basic assumptions, not the least with respect to behavior. Moreover, it is insufficient to help discriminating between mainstream and behavioral perspectives, as some of the. central mainstream predictions, notably negatively sloping demand curves and first-degree homogeneity of production functions, might be as well explained by a behavioral theory. This leads into a lengthy discussion of "normative decision theory," much of which, quite appropriately for a Nobel lecture, surveys Simon's own work. Later in the lecture there are other references to "advances in the behavioral theory," notably the works of Tversky and Kahneman, Simon's own work on the psychology of problem-solving, theories of organizational decision-making, and various theories of firm organization, such as the work of Nelson and Winter,

H.A. Simon and organizational economics 167

Cyert and March, Degroot, Radner, Leibenstein, Kornai, Williamson, and, rather surprising, Baumol's managerialist theory of the firm (which is entirely based on maximization).

Perspectives on the lectures

In both lectures Simon makes critical and constructive arguments and observations. His main critical targets are the von Neumann/Morgenstern/Savage model, game theory, information economics, oligopoly theory, rational expectations theory on the level of theory and instrumentalism on the level of methodology. These are treated rather harshly. Thus, of subjective expected utility theory we are told "it is hard to take SEU seriously as a theory of actual human behavior in the face of uncertainty" (Simon 1978: 9), and of game theory, we are told that it "is embarrassing in the wealth of alternative solutions it offers" (1978: 10). Not only do these involve excesses of rationality, they also may not lead to determinate solutions (oligopoly theory is mentioned a number of times as an illustration; see also Simon 1976). Simon also offers a number of observations on how bounded rationality has a bearing on economic organization, as well as brief surveys of specific work on boundedly rational behavior.

With the substantial benefit of hindsight we can discern a number of reasons why the rhetorics of Simon's two lectures failed to convince contemporary (and succeeding) economists. Most obviously, Simon's *oeuvre* suffered from unusually bad timing (hardly his fault, of course). Thus, the end of the 1970s, the time when Simon gave his two key lectures, is the beginning of the information economics and game theory revolution. Path-breaking work by Arrow, Mirrlees, Stiglitz, Ross, Myersbon, Wilson and others was between five and ten years old. The first statements of contract theory were about five years old; the revelation principle was almost contemporaneous. The first really convincing applications of non-cooperative game theory – incidentally to the part of economics, oligopoly theory, that Simon characterized as "the permanent and ineracidable scandal of economic theory" (1976: 140) – by Spence, Dixit and others were being worked out at about the same time. Rational expectations were moving from being strictly associated with Lucas and Sargent (and with specific policy positions), to becoming a generally acceptable modeling tool, etc. Thus, Simon was fighting a battle that even he, in that particular historical context, was bound to lose.

However, even if the historical context had been more favorable to Simon's arguments, there are still a number of fundamental problems with how Simon tried to convince his economist audiences of the soundness of his ideas. These have to do with the lack of definitions of BR, and the lack of modeling heuristics in Simon (1978, 1979). Consider these in turn.

A fundamental problem which many discussions of BR have pointed to is that the concept is defined negatively rather than positively: BR tends to be seen as all those aspects of decision-making that substantive rationality is *not*. The problems with this are, first, that BR only assumes a real existence when viewed against its substantively rational counterpart, and, second, that the set of candidates for boundedly rational behaviors is without bounds. Of course, the problem is inherent in the name of the concept itself, and Simon may have committed a fundamental labeling blunder here. This may explain why he, from about the mid-1970s, used the notion of "procedural rationality" rather than BR, and why he, in fact, uses the concept very little in Simon (1978, 1979). In a discussion of his earlier work, he mentions that

> In *Administrative Behavior*, bounded rationality is largely characterized as a residual category – rationality is bounded when it falls short of omniscience ... There was needed a more positive and formal characterization of the mechanisms of choice under conditions of bounded rationality.
>
> (Simon 1979: 502)

The theory of satisficing search is, of course, one such characterization, and it, as well as other instances of behavioral decision theory, is discussed in Simon (1978, 1979). It has often been argued that a basic problem with satisficing search is that there is virtually nothing in the theory itself about the merits of alternative search procedures, and certainly not in economics. Simon explicitly argues that in order to understand the relative advantages of different procedures, it is necessary to step outside of economics and consider, for example, work on integer programming. However, his comments on the subject are extremely vague, and he chooses to "leave the topics of computational complexity and heuristic search with these sketchy remarks. What implications these developments in the theory of procedural rationality will have for economics ... remain to be seen" (1978: 12).

Thus, Simon essentially admits that the theoretically developed basis for theorizing on satisficing is virtually non-existent, and, at any rate, will likely emerge outside of economics. The conclusion for a listener to these 1978 or 1979 lectures can only be that work based on satisficing search must make use of rules for search and postulate aspiration levels that are essentially arbitrary, and at best justified by loose empirical considerations of a dubious sociological nature. In other words, Simon's alternative program would not seem to present any non-arbitrary modeling heuristics.

It is not surprising, then, that Simon's economist audience, being first severely criticized for their methodical practice and listening to a wholesale condemnation of what they likely saw as hot new ideas, then being instructed to take seriously a fundamentally undefined notion, and finally being exposed to examples and applications of procedural rationality that came close to what they would consider sociological reasoning, was not persuaded, and that the use of BR in economics remains, at best, rhetorical in a pre-McCloskeyan sense of the word.

Could Simon have done it differently, and perhaps more successfully? A fundamental problem is that his message was in many ways so radically counter to most economists' ingrained habits of thought, and they no doubt must have seen him as someone who refused to play by the rules of the game. Arguably, there was little Simon could have done, and would have wanted to do, about this. However, he could have done *something*, such as cutting down on the polemical elements, which arguably take up a disproportionate amount of space in the lectures. More importantly, he could have done more to present economists with precise behavioral models and the computational models associated with these (Newell and Simon 1972) in order to more convincingly present the case of a genuine behavioral alternative to mainstream modeling of behavior. It is indeed striking that when Simon talks to economists about BR, he is much less specific than when he addresses audiences in artificial intelligence and psychology about the same subject. Perhaps he felt that what was necessary was conveying the big idea and not go into formal detail (which might not have been appropriate in an Ely or Nobel lecture anyway). That may have been a mistake, for most modern economists like to be told about big ideas in a formal manner (the rational expectations revolution and the new growth theory comes to mind; Lucas 1972 and Romer 1986 are quite formal pieces, indeed).

Discussion

Simon's influence on organizational economists

There can be little doubt that Simon has had a strong influence on many of those economists who have directed their analytical efforts toward firms and organizations. Williamson, Winter and Radner immediately come to mind.[12] When various economics approaches to firms and organizations began to emerge in the beginning of the 1970s, Simon's fundamental work on the subject was already two to three decades old (Simon 1947, 1951; March and Simon 1958). For some of the pioneers it was natural to look to Simon's work for inspiration, perhaps particularly those who stressed the routinized nature of firm behavior (i.e., Nelson and Winter 1973). Bounded rationality seemed to link up directly with the notion of routines, since these may be interpreted as firm-level equivalents to individual behavioral rules that are adopted to reduce complexity under bounded rationality. To others the contribution of Simon's thought lies elsewhere and is, in a sense, less direct. Thus, what Williamson appears to have gained from Simon is, first of all, a rationale for incomplete contracting, and, second, the notion that institutional choice is discrete (see Simon

170   *Nicolai J. Foss*

1978). Although he is, of course, familiar with Simon's work in economics from the 1950s which is taken up with actually modeling boundedly rational behavior (e.g., Simon 1955), it is the Simon of the 1978 lecture – the interdisciplinary Simon who goes into institutional choice as a discrete one at considerable length[13] – that seems to loom largest in Williamson's thinking. As mentioned earlier he explicitly dissociates himself from understanding economizing with BR in terms of, for example, heuristic problem-solving.

It is notable that those economists that have been able to utilize aspects of Simon's thought in their work on economic organization were graduate students in the 1950s and early 1960s when Simon's influence was perhaps more readily felt, and when he was around for interaction. In contrast, the works of those theorists of economic organization who began to publish from the mid-1970s are arguably much less, and usually not at all, influenced by Simon. One reason why this is so is simply that they were busy assimilating, applying and extending the new information economics and game theory tools when Simon presented his fundamental ideas to economists, and that Simon's vision was simply too far from what they were up to. A part of that explanation, however, is that the Simon papers they were likely to know would be his two end-of-the-1970s papers. And, as has been argued, there is very little in these papers that may instruct economists wanting to build a BR research program in the economics of organization about the exact nature of BR and how to go about doing it. His later papers are equally barren in this respect. Thus, one of his last papers on organizational issues (Simon 1991b) surprisingly does not go into BR *at all*, but mostly takes issue with various themes in organizational economics, notably the assumption of opportunism. This has arguably contributed to the absence of a distinct BR research program in the economics of organization.

The future of bounded rationality in the theory of economic organization

So, what will happen to Simon's Grand Theme of BR in the theory of economic organization? Will it gradually disappear, as contract theory takes over the whole field, everybody realizing that what some theorists try to say using BR may be said more elegantly with notions of asymmetric information, drawing on standard methodology? Although this may have been a reasonable prediction, say, ten years ago, there are reasons to think that the situation is different now.

First of all, the evidence from psychology and experimental economics about the relative failures of expected utility theory is now so large that it cannot be ignored. Although various findings that are contradictory to EU theory were certainly well known at the time Simon gave this lectures, the amount of findings today is many times larger (Camerer 1998), and the

H.A. Simon and organizational economics 171

scientific quality of the relevant experimental methods is superior. There is, in other words, a much better *critical* foundation for BR.

Second, there is now a much-improved *positive* foundation for theories of BR. Economists do not have to look at (at least to them) esoteric branches of computational theory or AI.[14] In the fields of psychology and decision theory, perhaps closer neighbors to economics than AI, theorists and experimentalists have been at work since the end of the 1970s trying to align some aspects of BR with EU theory or develop distinct alternatives to EU theory (see Camerer 1998 for a fine survey and discussion). While economists may still be uncertain or ignorant about alternatives to EU theory – one wonders how many economists are familiar with cumulative prospect theory with rank-dependent weights which Camerer (1998: 166) singles out as the best alternative to EU theory in the light of the evidence – at least they may be increasingly *alert* to the new alternatives.

Third, within mainstream contract theory, the Maskin and Tirole paper (Maskin and Tirole 1999) is not taken to be the last word about BR (and Maskin and Tirole do not appear to think of it in this way, either). Rather, it may be taken as a contribution that demonstrates the inherent limitations of a certain class of models (Kreps 1996), and points to the need to overcome these limitations, possibly by means of sophisticated treatments of BR (see Segal 1999). However, it is far from clear how to incorporate BR in contract theory. A main problem is that BR threatens to complicate drastically the link between current actions (e.g., investments) and anticipations of future payoffs, because BR is hard to square with the rational expectations of these payoffs. There is no BR theory of expectations (as far as I know), and although notions of satisficing may perhaps be invoked we are up against the usual problem that virtually anything can be postulated to be a reasonable aspiration level. Still, there are other uses for BR within contract theory, such as understanding the limitations of hold-up (Carmichael and McLeod 1999) and providing more refined understanding of why contracts are incomplete than merely postulating this by fiat (Mokerjee 1998; Segal 1999; McLeod 2000).

Fourth, writers associated with transaction cost economics have increasingly begun to look into the BR component of the approach. Thus, Williamson (1998) himself has put forward a possible modeling strategy for how to incorporate richer notions of BR in transaction cost economics. He argues that the many ramifications of bounded rationality should be explored with a view to first identify those regularities in decision-making that differ from the classical model of von Neumann–Morgenstern–Savage, then work out the implications of these regularities for efficient organization, and finally fold these into the organizational design. The implication is that the efficiency questions of the economics of organization may usefully be reformulated, relying on more elaborate models of BR, so that "organization can and should be regarded as an instrument for utilizing varying cognitive and behavioral propensities to best advantage"

(1998: 12). A limitation of Williamson's (1998) paper (if not of the program he sketches) is that he seems mostly intent on demonstrating that findings of cognitive psychology are entirely consistent with "[t]he transaction cost economics triple for describing human actors – bounded rationality, farsighted contracting, and opportunism." Therefore, he is not very specific about what exactly to do with these findings. However, Foss (2001) sketches various ways in which findings from the bias and heuristics literature may be utilized in transaction cost economics. The main idea is to interpret these findings as potential sources of transaction cost problems (e.g., contribution biases may increase bargaining costs) and argue that such problems influence the choice of governance structure.

These ideas have been criticized by Loasby (2002), who argues that they continue an unfortunate tendency in most of organizational economics to only look at organization as something that exists in order to avoid the negative aspects and consequences of human behavior and not to stimulate the positive ones. There is certainly something to this critique. Transaction cost economics needs to address how governance choice influences alternative methods of search and learning. A recent, very interesting attempt at building a theory of this is Nickerson and Zenger (2002). Relying on complexity theory, they argue that Simonian heuristic search, which is usually necessary for problems that involve many, highly interdependent knowledge sets, is likely to require substantial knowledge sharing and ongoing interaction of knowledge sets. However, this exposes those who control the relevant knowledge sets to various knowledge exchange hazards (e.g., the Arrowian paradox of information). Because firm organization makes such hazards less severe and also better enables the building of a specialized language in terms of which the relevant communication may take place, complex problem-solving requiring heuristic search will be organized inside firms. Simpler problems, which may be decomposed into sub-problems, and correspondingly simpler search, may be well organized by market governance. Thus, Nickerson and Zenger elegantly combine key ideas from Simon (notably Simon 1962) with key transaction cost economics ideas in a theory of how governance structures both avoid the negative and promote the positive.

Conclusions

This chapter has treated BR as a mainly rhetorical part of the practice of organizational economists. Thus, BR is invoked in a loose, intuitive manner to explain more central concepts, notably incomplete contracting, but it is not itself treated in much detail; it is not defined and modeled in any precise manner. I also argued that this practice may be related to the fact that Simon never really explained, at least to his economist audiences, what BR is, how it may be modeled so that it may be of use to economists, and how exactly BR impacts on those issues that interest economists of organization (i.e., existence, boundaries and internal organization of firms; contract design). Thus, although the study of economists' rhetorical practice may be helpful for illuminating aspects of scientific development, it has also been suggested that there are limits to the role of rhetoric in scientific development. At least, rhetoric in the sense of mere eloquence is not sufficient, because the successes of persuasion attempts are highly context-dependent. Thus, although Simon in his two major attempts to win economists over to the behavioral side (Simon 1978, 1979) exhibited rather considerable eloquence he failed to persuade, arguably because the context was so unfavorable to his arguments. However, that context has changed. Had Simon given his Ely and Nobel lectures in, say, 2001 and 2002 he would have found considerably more receptive audiences than he did in 1978 and 1979.

Notes

1 The comments of Mie Augier are gratefully acknowledged.
2 Game theorists may refer to BR more frequently, but game theory is hardly a distinct sub-field in economics; rather, it is a workshop that supplies machine tools to the various fields.
3 Giovanni Dosi (2002) reports that a few years ago, he (and a couple of co-authors) had a paper on industrial dynamics rejected from *Econometrica*, based on a review report, the main conclusion of which was that the paper would bring "back the discussion of industrial change to the Dark Ages of Herbert Simon." Such bluntness is, however, rare.
4 Simon also published in economics in the 1970s on issues that are not directly related to BR – for example, Ijiri and Simon (1974) and Seskin and Simon (1973).
5 Albeit rather different conceptions of BR. Thus, BR in team theory is in actuality maximizing with costly communication, BR in transaction cost theory is the factor that explains why contracts are incomplete, and BR in evolutionary theory is a matter of search.
6 An impressionistic example: in Williamson's work, bounded rationality looms larger in *Markets and Hierarchies* (1975) than in *The Mechanisms of Governance* (1996).
7 For example, rational expectations are central in most contract theory models. Applying the notion (any notion, really) of BR to expectations formation would imply that much contracting would produce unintended consequences, producing a need for *ex post* governance; however, this is not explored in contract theory.
8 Thus, Simon may be justified in his critique that "the new institutional economics has not drawn heavily from the empirical work in organizations and decision-making for its auxiliary assumptions" (Simon 1991b: 27). See also Simon (1997).
9 In the last case (non-verifiability), it is the enforcing party, such as a judge, that is boundedly rational.
10 That is, within the particular set-ups adopted in contract theory.
11 In contract theory courses at American universities, BR is often introduced (and finished) in the following manner: "We may use BR as a shorthand for anything that makes a contract incomplete."

174   *Nicolai J. Foss*

12 For a brief essay on the Simon–Williamson relation, see Augier and March (2001).
13 Incidentally, Simon (1978) presents this theme as somehow intimately connected with BR, and mentions that discrete institutional choice is at variance with marginalism. While discreteness in choice indeed may require other tools (notions of complementarity and the underlying mathematical lattice theory) than conventional marginalist ones, it is entirely consistent with mainstream economics.
14 However, it should be mentioned that various computational approaches have been very usefully applied in the context of the theory of the firm by a number of evolutionary economists. See, for example, Marengo *et al.* (2000). Also, game theorists have made much use of AI notions of BR (see discussion and references in Lipman 1995).

References

Augier, M. and March, J.G. (2001) "Conflict of Interest in Theories of Organization: Herbert A. Simon and Oliver Williamson," *Journal of Management and Governance*, 5: 223–230.

Brousseau, E. and Fares, M.H. (2000) "Incomplete Contract Theory and New Institutional Economics Approaches to Contracts: Substitutes or Complements?," in C. Ménard, *Institutions, Contracts, and Organizations: Perspectives From New Institutional Economics*, Aldershot: Edward Elgar.

Camerer, C. (1998) "Bounded Rationality in Individual Decision Making," *Experimental Economics*, 1: 163–183.

Carmichael, L. and MacLeod, W.B. (1999) "Caring About Sunk Costs: A Behavioral Solution to Hold-Up Problems with Small Stakes," Olin working paper 99–19, University of Southern California Law School.

Conlisk, J. (1996) "Why Bounded Rationality?," *Journal of Economic Literature*, 34: 669–700.

Dosi, G. (2002) "A Very Reasonable Objective Still Beyond Our Reach: Economics as an Empirically Disciplined Social Science," Working paper.

Dow, G. (1987) "The Notion of Authority in Transaction Cost Economics," *Journal of Economic Behavior and Organization*, 8: 13–31.

Foss, N.J. (2001) "Bounded Rationality in the Economics of Organization: Present Use and (Some) Future Possibilities," *Journal of Management and Governance*, 5: 401–425.

Grossman, S. and Hart, O. (1986) "The Costs and Benefits of Ownership: A Theory of Vertical Integration," *Journal of Political Economy*, 94: 691–719.

Hart, O. (1990) "Is 'Bounded Rationality' an Important Element of a Theory of Institutions?," *Journal of Institutional and Theoretical Economics*, 146: 696–702.

Hart, O. and Moore, J. (1990) "Property Rights and the Nature of the Firm," *Journal of Political Economy*, 98: 1119–1158.

Holmström, B. and Tirole, J. (1989) "The Theory of the Firm," in R. Schmalensee and R.D. Willig (eds), *The Handbook of Industrial Organization*, Amsterdam: North-Holland.

Ijiri, Y. and Simon, H.A. (1974) "Interpretations of Departures from the Pareto Curve Firm-size Distributions," *Journal of Political Economy*, 82: 315–332.

Kreps, D.M. (1996) "Markets and Hierarchies and (Mathematical) Economic Theory," *Industrial and Corporate Change*, 5: 561–595.

Lazear, E.P. (1991) "Labor Economics and the Psychology of Organizations," *Journal of Economic Perspectives*, 5: 89–110.

Lipman, B.L. (1995) "Information Processing and Bounded Rationality: A Survey," *Canadian Journal of Economics*, 28: 42–67.

Loasby, B.J. (2002) "Economics After Simon," Working paper, Department of Economics, Stirling University.

Lucas, R.E. (1972) "Expectations and the Neutrality of Money," *Journal of Economic Theory*, 4: 103–124.

McCloskey, D. (1983) "The Rhetoric of Economics," *Journal of Economic Literature*, 21: 481–517.

McLeod, W.B. (2000) "Complexity and Contract," *Revue d'Économie Industrielle*, 92: 149–178.

March, J.G. and Simon, H.A. (1958) *Organizations*, New York: Wiley.

Marengo, L., Dosi, G., Legrenzi, P. and Pasquali, C. (2000) "The Structure of Problem-Solving Knowledge and the Structure of Organizations," *Industrial and Corporate Change*, 9: 757–788.

Marschak, J. and Radner, R. (1972) *The Theory of Teams*, New Haven, Conn.: Yale University Press.

Maskin, E. and Tirole, J. (1999) "Unforeseen Contingencies and Incomplete Contracts," *Review of Economic Studies*, 66: 83–114.

Milgrom, P. and Roberts, J. (1988) "Economic Theories of the Firm: Past, Present and Future," in N.J. Foss (2000) *The Theory of the Firm*, Vol. 1, London: Routledge.

—— (1992) *Economics, Organization, and Management*, Upper Saddle River: Prentice-Hall.

Mokerjee, S. (1998) "Ambiguity Aversion and Incompleteness of Contractual Form," *American Economic Review*, 88: 1207–1231.

Nelson, R.R. and Winter S.G. (1973) "Towards an Evolutionary Theory of Economic Capabilities," *American Economic Review*, 63: 440–449.

Newell, A. and Simon, H.A. (1972) *Human Problem Solving*, Englewood Cliffs, N.J.: Prentice-Hall.

Nickerson, J. and Zenger, T. (2002) "A Knowledge-based Theory of Governance Choice – A Problem-solving Approach," Unpublished paper.

Rabin, M. (1998) "Psychology and Economics," *Journal of Economic Literature*, 36: 11–46.

Romer, P. (1986) "Increasing Returns and Long-Run Growth," *Journal of Political Economy*, 94: 1002–1037.

Rubinstein, A. (1998) *Modeling Bounded Rationality*, Cambridge, Mass.: The MIT Press.

Schwartz, A. (1992) "Legal Contract Theories and Incomplete Contracts," in L. Werin and H. Wijkander, *Contract Economics*, Oxford: Blackwell.

Segal, I. (1999) "Complexity and Renegotiation: A Foundation for Incomplete Contracts," *Review of Economic Studies*, 66: 57–82.

Sent, E.M. (1997) "Sargent versus Simon: Bounded Rationality Unbound," *Cambridge Journal of Economics*, 21: 323–338.

Seskin, E.P. and Simon, H.A. (1973) "Appendix to the article 'Residential Choice and Air Pollution: A General Equilibrium Model,'" *American Economic Review*, 63: 966–967.

Simon, H.A. (1947) *Administrative Behavior*, New York: Macmillan.

176   *Nicolai J. Foss*

Simon, H.A. (1951) "A Formal Theory of the Employment Contract," *Economet-rica*, 19: 293–305.

—— (1955) "A Behavioral Model of Rational Choice," *Quarterly Journal of Economics*, 69: 99–118.

—— (1962) "The Architecture of Complexity," in S. Masten and O.E. Williamson (eds), *Transaction Cost Economics*, Aldershot: Edward Elgar.

—— (1976) "From 'Bounded' to 'Procedural' Rationality," in S. Latsis (ed.), *Method and Appraisal in Economics*, Cambridge: Cambridge University Press.

—— (1978) "Rationality as Process and as a Product of Thought," *American Economic Review*, 68: 1–14.

—— (1979) "Rational Decision Making in Business Organizations," *American Economic Review*, 69: 493–513.

—— (1991a) *Models of My Life*, New York: Basic Books.

—— (1991b) "Organizations and Markets," *Journal of Economic Perspectives*, 5: 25–44.

—— (1997) *An Empirically Based Microeconomics*, Cambridge: Cambridge University Press.

Tirole, J. (1999) "Incomplete Contracts: Where Do We Stand?," *Econometrica*, 67: 741–781.

Williamson, O.E. (1971) "The Vertical Integration of Production: Market Failure Considerations," *American Economic Review*, 61: 112–123.

—— (1975) *Markets and Hierarchies*, New York: Free Press.

—— (1985) *The Economic Institutions of Capitalism*, New York: Free Press.

—— (1996) *The Mechanisms of Governance*, Oxford: Oxford University Press.

—— (1998) "Human Actors and Economic Organization," Paper for the 1998 Paris ISNIE Conference.

NORTH-HOLLAND

Journal of International Management
8 (2002) 49–67

THE FOX SCHOOL
of Business and Management
TEMPLE UNIVERSITY

Transferring knowledge in MNCs:
The role of sources of subsidiary knowledge and organizational context

Nicolai J. Foss[a], Torben Pedersen[b,*]

[a]*Department of Industrial Economics and Strategy, Copenhagen Business School, Howitzvej 60, 6,
DK-2000 Copenhagen F, Denmark*
[b]*Department of International Economics and Management, Copenhagen Business School, Howitzvej 60, 2,
DK-2000 Copenhagen F, Denmark*

Abstract

We link up with the recent literature on the differentiated MNC and in particular with its stress on intra-MNC knowledge flows. However, rather than focusing on the characteristics of knowledge as determinants of knowledge transfer within MNCs, we focus instead on levels of knowledge in subsidiaries, the sources of transferable subsidiary knowledge and on the organizational means and conditions that realize knowledge transfer as the relevant determinants. We find largely positive support for the relevant hypotheses. These are tested on a unique dataset on knowledge development in subsidiary firms [the Centre of Excellence (CoE) project]. © 2002 Elsevier Science Inc. All rights reserved.

Keywords: Sources of knowledge; Subsidiary knowledge; Transfer of knowledge

1. Introduction

It is generally accepted that knowledge ranks first in the hierarchy of strategically relevant resources (e.g., Grant, 1996). More precisely, the issue of the degree to which valuable knowledge can be imitated by rival firms is seen as crucial to the understanding of competitive advantage and its sustainability (Lippman and Rumelt, 1982; Simonin, 1999). Accordingly, a

* Corresponding author. Tel.: +45-3-815-2522; fax: +45-3-815-2500.
E-mail addresses: tp.int@cbs.dk (T. Pedersen), njf.ivs@cbs.dk (N.J. Foss).

1075-4253/02/S – see front matter © 2002 Elsevier Science Inc. All rights reserved.
PII: S1075-4253(01)00054-0

cottage industry has emerged on the various characteristics of knowledge that may hinder the imitability of rent-yielding knowledge assets, such as causal ambiguity (Lippman and Rumelt, 1982), complexity and tacitness (Barney, 1991). Much of this has taken place in the context of work on the resource-based (Wernerfelt, 1984; Barney, 1991), knowledge-based (Grant, 1996) and evolutionary theories of the firm (Nelson and Winter, 1982).

However, the issues of the knowledge-based determinants of competitive advantage and the creation and renewal of knowledge have not yet been satisfactorily integrated in the above literatures. Moreover, the literatures on the connection between knowledge and competitive advantage have paid rather little attention to the organizational aspects of the connection. For example, little attention has been paid to which organizational mechanisms may decrease "internal stickiness" (Szulanski, 1996) and help diffusing valuable knowledge inside the firms while still keeping knowledge hard to imitate to would-be imitating rivals.

A parallel interest in knowledge as a strategic resource has characterized much research in international business, perhaps particularly during the last decade and a half (Bartlett and Ghoshal, 1986; Gupta and Govindarajan, 1991; Kogut and Zander, 1993).[1] Some of this research has drawn upon the above type of research into those dimensions of knowledge assets that hinder imitability (e.g., Kogut and Zander, 1993; Simonin, 1999).[2] A concern with knowledge as a source of competitive advantage and on the renewal of competitive advantage through building new knowledge has also characterized the literature on the differentiated multinational corporation (Bartlett and Ghoshal, 1986, 1989; Birkinshaw, 1996). A well-known argument posits that the differentiated MNC is in fact more favorably positioned than the nondifferentiated MNC or the purely domestic firm with respect to mobilizing knowledge in the creation and renewal of competitive advantage, ceteris paribus, simply because of its access to more knowledge networks, internal as well as external (Hedlund, 1986; Bartlett and Ghoshal, 1989). In different terms, the differentiated MNC can strike an exploitation/exploration tradeoff (March, 1991) that may not be available to, for example, purely domestic firms.

In such a perspective, the organizational design problem is to choose organizational instruments of control, motivation and context in such a way that (1) subsidiaries actually access and produce knowledge, for example, through tapping into local knowledge bases, (2) communication is established between those who need and those who possess knowledge and (3) the relevant subsidiary knowledge is actually made available to those MNC units that need it.

---

[1] One may rightly point out that knowledge has been central in the theory of the MNC since Hymer's (1960/1976) early work. However, the focus on knowledge has traditionally been a (static) matter of explaining the existence of the MNC by focusing on failures in markets for knowledge rather than on (dynamically) stressing the MNCs distinct capabilities of realizing competitive advantages through managing knowledge flows.

[2] However, even as late as 1994, Crossan and Inkpen (1994, p. 271) could point out that "…while much of the MNC research has dealt with static theories of the firm and investigations of structural questions, very little research has delved into the process of knowledge transfer and the barriers to successful intraorganizational learning."

N.J. Foss, T. Pedersen / Journal of International Management 8 (2002) 49–67   51

Among other things, this has led to a renewed conceptualization, understanding and appreciation of subsidiaries, which are now seen as potential sources of MNC-wide strengths (Bartlett and Ghoshal, 1986, 1989; Birkinshaw, 1996; Forsgren et al., 1999) and perhaps even as "centres of excellence (CoE)" (Moore and Birkinshaw, 1998; Holm and Pedersen, 2000a). In fact, recent research has emphasized the need for direct *lateral* mechanisms between individual subsidiaries (Moore and Birkinshaw, 1998).

However, much of the empirical (if perhaps not the theoretical) research on the differentiated MNC still tends to focus on characteristics of knowledge and characteristics of senders and receivers rather than on organizational means of transferring knowledge. Moreover, much of this literature is silent on the sources of transferable subsidiary knowledge (but see Porter and Sölvell, 1999; Forsgren et al., 1999), for example, whether transferable subsidiary knowledge is largely internally produced or acquired through interacting with firms in networks or acquired through interaction with local knowledge institutions, etc. However, not only may the sources of subsidiary knowledge strongly condition the characteristics of knowledge but it may also be of more direct managerial relevance. Thus, while it may not be directly helpful for a manager to be told that competitive advantage is best sustained if the rent-yielding knowledge asset conforms to certain criteria (like tacitness, ambiguity, etc.), it may be quite helpful to be told that certain sources of knowledge are more likely to be associated with these criteria than other sources. This is because it may be difficult to change the characteristics of knowledge by managerial action, but managerial action may change the mode of knowledge acquisition.

In the present paper, we link up with the recent literature on the differentiated MNC. However, rather than focusing on the characteristics of knowledge that hinder or stimulate knowledge transfer within the MNC, we focus instead on the sources of potentially transferable subsidiary knowledge. We distinguish between knowledge sourced from internal development of knowledge in the subsidiary, knowledge sourced from network relations and knowledge sourced from local clusters. We argue that these sources condition the characteristics of knowledge in specific ways. Therefore, they require different organizational means and conditions of transfer. For example, the extent of interdependence among the MNC units, the amount of intra-MNC trade and the autonomy of the subsidiary are all conditions that we argue influence in different ways the expected success of transferring knowledge from different sources.

In sum, our contributions in this paper are (1) to examine how well knowledge acquired by subsidiaries and stemming from diverse sources is transferred within an MNC and (2) to examine the organizational means and conditions specific to individual MNCs that condition the success of transferring knowledge, arguing in effect that knowledge stemming from different sources requires different organizational means and conditions for successful transfer. Both of these two contributions are, to our knowledge, novel to the literature. Moreover, the hypotheses related to how the sources of knowledge and organizational context influence knowledge transfer are tested on the basis of a unique and dataset on subsidiary knowledge development that has been constructed in connection with the cross-national research project "Centres of Excellence" (Holm and Pedersen, 2000a). The dataset covers more than 2000 subsidiaries located in seven different European countries.

52   *N.J. Foss, T. Pedersen / Journal of International Management 8 (2002) 49–67*

2. Theoretical model (Fig. 1)

Although it is widely accepted in the literature that the MNC owes its existence to its superior ability (relative to markets) to transfer knowledge and that this superior ability may at the same time be a source of competitive advantage (relative to purely domestic firms), it is also widely recognized that the resource costs of knowledge transfer are likely to be substantial. Thus, Teece (1981) estimated that transfer costs for the intra-MNC technology transfer cases he examined ranged from 2.24% to 59% with a mean of 19.16%. In the view of Kogut and Zander (1993, p. 630) "...these costs are derived from the efforts to codify and teaching complex knowledge to recipient."

Along similar lines, Szulanski (1996) showed that his findings imply that the barriers to knowledge transfer were only to a very small extent motivational (at least in the sense of, for example, agency theory). Rather, the barriers to knowledge transfer had to do with causal ambiguity, the receiver's absorptive capacity and the general atmosphere in the relation between sender and receiver. However, his findings did not relate to the context of cross-border knowledge transfer. In fact, rather little is known about the determinants of intra-MNC knowledge flows in spite of their obvious importance to theoretical arguments about the MNC. Thus, Gupta and Govindarajan (2000, p. 474) observe that with some notable exceptions (e.g., Zander and Kogut 1995) "...very little systematic empirical investigation in the determinants of intra-MNC knowledge transfers has so far been attempted."

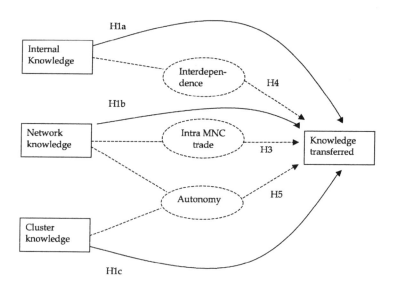

Fig. 1. The hypothesized model.

N.J. Foss, T. Pedersen / Journal of International Management 8 (2002) 49–67 53

In this section, we develop the theoretical arguments that intra-MNC knowledge transfer is influenced by the intensity of knowledge production and knowledge absorption of subsidiaries, the sources of knowledge and the organizational instruments and conditions that surround the transfer of knowledge within an MNC. These determinants are discussed seriatim in the following.

2.1. Intensity of subsidiary knowledge production and absorption

As a trivial matter, for knowledge transfers from a subsidiary to the MNC headquarters or to other subsidiaries to take place, transferable knowledge has to exist. As we later discuss, we focus on three main sources of such transferable knowledge, namely internal development, networks and local clusters. Less trivially, a basic organizational problem is to motivate the subsidiary to actually transfer knowledge that may be useful to other subsidiaries. One set of problems is who should bear the resource costs of transferring knowledge and how the parties to the knowledge exchange are to be compensated. We shall abstract from this problem and assume that it can be handled by the subsidiaries and the headquarters through structuring compensations in the right way (O'Donnell, 2000). A rather different motivational problem is that to the extent that a subsidiary possesses a knowledge monopoly, it controls a lever of bargaining power in the MNC, since it controls a crucial complementary asset (Hart, 1995). Transferring knowledge is tantamount to giving up this power (Holm and Pedersen, 2000b), which may be quite unattractive. Gupta and Govindarajan (2000, p. 475) briefly point to such a problem.

However, whether this is a serious problem depends not only on whether MNC headquarters can somehow force or motivate subsidiaries to transfer knowledge to other subsidiaries or to headquarters but also depends on the time frame. Thus, the knowledge monopoly problem is likely to be much more serious in a static context than in a dynamic one. In a dynamic setting, generalized knowledge exchange may catch on in a network of subsidiaries, so that subsidiaries are motivated to transfer knowledge to each other through the discipline of repeated dealings (Klein and Leffler, 1981). In fact, in a dynamic context, one may *gain* power by transferring knowledge. This is because influence is likely to flow to a subsidiary that is able to continuously transfer knowledge to other subsidiaries.[3] In contrast, the argument that knowledge transfer diminishes power implicitly assumes that once knowledge is transferred, the subsidiary is on par with everybody else in the MNC in terms of knowledge held and therefore cannot exercise any power based on the control of knowledge assets.

Here, we deal with subsidiaries that are involved in lengthy relations with headquarters and other subsidiaries and hence engage in repeated interaction with these. Thus, we believe it is justified to assume that in fact subsidiaries will be motivated to transfer knowledge. The ability of headquarters to influence the transfer of knowledge through control and incentive

---

[3] Thus, the power-wielding asset is the dynamic capability to produce and transfer new knowledge. For further discussion, see, for example, Forsgren et al. (1999, p. 184).

mechanisms only reinforces this. In other words, to the extent that subsidiaries control knowledge that may be useful to other units in the MNC, they will in fact make an attempt to transfer this knowledge. Therefore, we state the following set of hypotheses:

Hypothesis 1: The more knowledge that the subsidiary creates and absorbs, the more knowledge will be transferred to other units in the MNC. (a) The more knowledge that the subsidiary creates through investing in internal production of knowledge, the more knowledge will be transferred to other units in the MNC. (b) The more knowledge that the subsidiary creates and absorbs through network relations to external partners (customers, suppliers, etc.), the more knowledge will be transferred to other units in the MNC. (c) The more knowledge that the subsidiary creates and absorbs by tapping into the knowledge base of a local cluster (e.g., a well-educated workforce, high-quality research institutions, etc.), the more knowledge will be transferred to other units in the MNC.

Two things should be noted in connection with these hypotheses. First, transfer of knowledge does not imply a "full" replication of knowledge in a new location. Indeed, transfer of knowledge is often associated with modification of the existing knowledge to the specific context. Therefore, what is transferred is not the underlying knowledge but rather applications of this knowledge in the form of solutions to specific problems. Second, note that the hypotheses are cautiously stated so that a qualitative change leads to another sign-preserving qualitative change. This is because of the many nonmotivational barriers to the process of transferring knowledge. We treat this next.

2.2. Sources of subsidiary knowledge and barriers to knowledge transfer

The basic premise for work on the differentiated MNC is that subsidiaries control heterogeneous stocks of knowledge and that competitive advantages can be achieved from orchestrating knowledge flows between MNC units in such a way that knowledge is transferred to those MNC units where it will increase value-added. In this connection, much has been made out of the directionality of knowledge flows (e.g., Gupta and Govindarajan, 1991), the centrality of certain subsidiaries (Birkinshaw, 1996) and patterns of corporate control (Egelhoff, 1988). Arguably, less attention has been devoted to the determinants of intra-MNC knowledge transfer, although work has been done on motivational and cognitive barriers to knowledge transfer (Zander and Kogut, 1995; Gupta and Govindarajan, 2000). In Section 2.1, we briefly discussed motivational barriers to transfer. Nonmotivational barriers to transfer are usually conceptualized in terms of such factors as causal ambiguity, complexity, tacitness, absorptive capacity and the like. Although they make perfect theoretical sense, these variables are hard to operationalize.[4] A more operational approach may be to examine how the *sources* of subsidiary knowledge influence intra-MNC knowledge transfer.

---

[4] However, a few successful attempts do exist (Kogut and Zander, 1993; Simonin, 1999; Gupta and Govindarajan, 2000).

N.J. Foss, T. Pedersen / Journal of International Management 8 (2002) 49–67 55

Although an internal element necessarily enters into the production of all subsidiary knowledge, it makes sense to distinguish between

1. knowledge that is produced mainly through investing in the internal production of knowledge (e.g., much R&D) or from learning by doing, using, etc.,
2. knowledge that is to a large extent created on the basis of knowledge inputs from network relations to external partners (customers, suppliers, etc.) and
3. knowledge that is to a large extent created on the basis of knowledge inputs from a local cluster (e.g., a well-educated work force, high-quality research institutions, etc.).

The first category of knowledge is the kind of internal knowledge that has been highlighted in resource- and knowledge-based theories of the firm. In this literature, the focus has been on production and organization knowledge that is embodied in bundles of routines of a highly tacit and social nature. Because of their characteristics, such knowledge is strongly intertwined with the organization itself and are therefore hard (very costly) to trade in the market. This leads us directly to the conventional argument for the existence of the MNC, which asserts that MNCs exist because of their comparative advantages of transferring knowledge. However, that argument fails to distinguish between the transfer of knowledge that differs in terms of its sources. We argue that the ease of transfer of knowledge will be influenced by the sources of the knowledge.

Of course, no knowledge is entirely internally accumulated (Nohria and Eccles, 1992). For example, parts of the knowledge base of a subsidiary firm are likely to be the result of previous knowledge transfer from other MNC units.[5] Nevertheless, it makes sense to say that some knowledge is largely internally produced, while some other knowledge is strongly based on external knowledge inputs. We distinguish among two external sources of knowledge that may be available to subsidiary firms. The first category may be called "network-based knowledge." We here have in mind the gaining of knowledge from long-lasting interaction with *specific* external parties, notably customers or suppliers, and the use of that knowledge in the firm's activities (Ford, 1990). In contrast, "cluster-based knowledge" is not to the same extent the result of long-lasting interaction with specific parties. Rather, it refers to knowledge controlled by the subsidiary that to a substantial extent is based upon knowledge inputs from, for example, a well-educated work force or local knowledge institutions, such as technical universities, etc. (Porter, 1990).

Our distinction between three types of sources of knowledge that enter into the subsidiary knowledge base is different from the conventional distinction between, for example, production, marketing or R&D knowledge. The latter types of knowledge may all in principle have internal, network and cluster components. The advantage of our distinction

---

[5] We shall, however, treat such knowledge inputs as internal (to the MNC network) in nature.

is that it may be *more* plausibly discussed in terms of general characteristics of knowledge than the activity-based definitions of knowledge. For example, it is hard to argue on a priori grounds that, for example, production knowledge is inherently more complex, ambiguous or tacit and therefore harder to transfer than marketing knowledge. In contrast, we consider it more justified to make this kind of arguments with respect to our distinction, although with considerable cautiousness.

Cautiousness is necessary because the three sources of knowledge might be highly correlated and intertwined in a way, so it is rather the combination of the different types of knowledge than each of the knowledge sources that matters. However, as we have no a priori expectations on how the knowledge sources should interact, we will leave it as an empirical problem to what extent the knowledge sources are, in fact, correlated.

Sidestepping motivational issues (which have been dealt with earlier), the success of knowledge transfer is primarily a matter of the existence and richness of transmission channels (Bartlett and Ghoshal, 1989; Ghoshal et al., 1994), the characteristics of the transferred knowledge in terms of such dimensions as tacitness, ambiguity, etc. (Zander and Kogut, 1995; Szulanski, 1996), and the absorptive capacity of the target unit(s) (Gupta and Govindarajan, 2000).

Thus, of the three knowledge sources that enter into the subsidiary knowledge base, we submit that internally accumulated knowledge is likely to be the type of knowledge that is most easily transferable and of which most will be transferred. This is because such knowledge to a large extent is based on knowledge that has already been transferred to the subsidiary from other MNC units. Moreover, one reason why some subsidiaries control a knowledge base that is characterized by many internally accumulated elements may have to do with a strategic decision at the MNC level concerning the localization of processes of knowledge creation. Thus, there is likely to be considerable understanding of the knowledge developed internally in the subsidiary at least at a headquarters level. In sum, internally accumulated knowledge may be relatively easily transmitted through existing transmission channels, and although it may contain, for example, tacit elements, the absorptive capacity of target units is likely to be relatively high.

Network-based knowledge is likely to be less easily transferable than internally accumulated knowledge. This is because it is largely derived from the specific problems and needs of external local counterparts. It is therefore likely to contain many tacit elements. Still, because network-based knowledge relates to the subsidiary's products or processes, much of it will still be transferable, at least to those other MNC units that have similar products or processes. Finally, cluster-based knowledge will be the kind of knowledge that will be least transferred. This seems counterintuitive: Arguably, some cluster-based knowledge, for example, knowledge inputs from local universities, may be less characterized by tacit elements than, say, internally accumulated knowledge. However, knowledge inputs from local universities may constitute a rather small part of cluster knowledge, given that the tendency in most MNCs is to source this kind of inputs in centrally placed R&D departments and not in local subsidiaries (Gassman and von Zedtwidtz, 1999). Therefore, much of the content of cluster-based knowledge is likely consist of knowledge of local skill levels, tastes, regulatory authorities, etc., much of which

N.J. Foss, T. Pedersen / Journal of International Management 8 (2002) 49–67 57

may be hard to transfer or of no or little use for other MNC units. Thus, to sum up, we put forward the following hypothesis:

Hypothesis 2: More internally accumulated knowledge will be transferred from subsidiaries to other MNC units than network-based knowledge, which in turn will be more transferred than cluster-based knowledge.

2.3. Organizational means and conditions of knowledge transfer

Because knowledge built from different sources (internal, cluster and network) is associated with different degrees of ease of transfer, the process of knowledge transfer is likely to be supported by different organizational means and conditions. By "organizational means and conditions," we refer to such issues as the degree and type of interdependence between MNC units and the management of that interdependence through formal systems and informal processes (Bartlett and Ghoshal, 1989; Gupta and Govindarajan, 1991, 1995; Buckley and Carter, 1999; O'Donnell, 2000). A key theme in many recent contributions to the theory of the MNC is that—under norms of administrative rationality—the degree and type of interdependence strongly condition the choice of types of management systems and processes for managing subsidiary relations (ibid.).

We agree with the basic thrust of this literature. However, the type and degree of interdependence is not the only determinant of the choice of administrative and managerial systems and processes. We argue that the concern with this link be supplemented with attention to how the sources of subsidiary knowledge conditions the choice of such systems and processes. For example, subsidiary knowledge with a large component of network-based knowledge may require different administrative mechanism for its successful transfer than subsidiary knowledge with a large component of internally accumulated knowledge. Transfer of network-based knowledge may require nonroutine communication, such as the temporary transfer of people from the transferring to the receiving MNC unit (e.g., cross-unit teams and job rotation), for its successful transfer.

In general, network-based subsidiary knowledge is likely to require close and rich communication between the transferring and the receiving MNC unit/subsidiary. Further, such communication is likely to be stimulated by the transfer of goods and/or services between MNC units. First, the transfer of goods and/or services, that is, intra-MNC trade, is in itself a force pulling in the direction of a widening of the bandwidth of communication channels. Second, network-based knowledge is per definition derived from needs and problems of counterparts. To the extent that such knowledge is embodied in products and services, which are then transferred to other MNC units, it is likely to give rise to communication about possible modifications in goods and/or services, so that these may better be adapted to the needs of the receiving MNC unit. We may therefore put forward the following hypothesis:

Hypothesis 3: Network-based knowledge will be more successfully transferred to other MNC units if there is substantial transfer of goods and/or services between the transferring and the receiving units.

We argued earlier that when the knowledge bases of some subsidiaries show a high proportion of knowledge that is mainly accumulated internally, this may reflect MNC level strategic choices, in the sense that headquarters establish a pattern of specialization in the accumulation in certain types of knowledge within the MNC. Such MNC-wide specialization evidently implies a high degree of interdependence. Thus, we hypothesize that

> *Hypothesis 4:* Knowledge that is mainly accumulated internally will be more successfully transferred to other MNC units if there is a high degree of interdependence between the transferring unit and the receiving units.

Finally, we argue that a very important aspect of the management of subsidiaries in the MNC network is the autonomy granted to the subsidiary. If subsidiary knowledge is mainly based on external knowledge (i.e., network and cluster-based), it is hard for MNC headquarters and top management to direct the subsidiary's acquisition of such knowledge in any detailed manner because of the knowledge asymmetry (Jensen and Meckling, 1992). In that case, it may be better to delegate decision rights to the subsidiary (Aghion and Tirole, 1997), that is, increase its autonomy. We have earlier argued that to the extent that a subsidiary is engaged in knowledge trading with other subsidiaries, this counteracts the control loss that accompanies giving a subsidiary increased autonomy. Thus, giving a subsidiary more autonomy allows it to better tap into networks and local clusters and also means that more knowledge will be more successfully transferred to other MNC units. Hence, we have the following hypothesis:

> *Hypothesis 5:* Knowledge that is strongly based on participation in networks and local clusters will be more successfully transferred to other MNC units if the transferring unit has been given a high degree of autonomy.

The hypotheses are summarized in the following model.

3. Data and method

3.1. Data collection

The data that we use here have been collected as part of the CoE project that engaged researchers in the Nordic countries, the UK, Germany, Austria, Italy, Portugal and Canada. The CoE project was launched in May 1996 with the purpose of investigating headquarter–subsidiary relationships and the internal flow of knowledge in MNCs. In order to collect quantitative data on acquisition of subsidiary knowledge, it was decided to construct a questionnaire that could be applied in all the involved countries. After several project meetings and extensive reliability tests of the questionnaire on both academics and business managers, the construction of such a questionnaire was accomplished.[6]

---

[6] For more information on the CoE project, see Holm and Pedersen (2000a).

N.J. Foss, T. Pedersen / Journal of International Management 8 (2002) 49–67 59

For practical reasons, it was decided that each project member would be responsible for gathering data on foreign-owned subsidiaries within their own country. Thus, all subsidiaries in the database belong to MNCs. In the process of data gathering, subsidiary managers, rather than headquarters, were respondents. One advantage of choosing subsidiary respondents is that they are directly engaged in the market and therefore are more acquainted with its characteristics. Although we can expect that the subsidiary has a reliable awareness of its own competencies, it would clearly be an advantage to gather information on intra-MNC knowledge flows from other corporate units as well. However, it would be an unmanageable task first to identify the subsidiaries in each country and then to identify the relevant management units in the foreign MNCs.

The paper is based on empirical data from seven countries: Austria, Denmark, Finland, Germany, Norway, Sweden and the UK. All countries are located in the northern part of Europe, and the four Nordic countries are considered to be relatively small, while Germany and the UK are among the largest in Europe. Approximately 80% of the questionnaires were answered by subsidiary executive officers, while financial managers, marketing managers or controllers in the subsidiary answered the remaining 20%. The response rate varies between 20% (UK) and 55% (Sweden), depending on the country of investigation. The quality of the data is quite high, with a general level of missing values of not more than 5%.

As shown in Table 1, the total sample covers information on 2107 subsidiaries. It comprises all kinds of subsidiaries in all fields of business. Between countries, the sample ranges from 202 (UK) to 530 (Sweden). With the exception of Sweden, the size of the sample is rather similar in the other six countries. The average number of employees in the subsidiaries is 742 and the median is 102. Within the five smaller countries, the average size of the subsidiaries are very similar, while Germany and UK — due to their larger market sizes — comprise substantially larger subsidiaries. As we expect larger subsidiaries to comprise more knowledge and therefore more potential for knowledge transfer, we need to control for this bias in the data material when conducting our tests of the hypotheses.

For all these, subsidiaries are covered information on the level of subsidiary competencies, the sources of this competence and to what extent the knowledge has been transferred to other MNC units. The subsidiaries were asked to indicate the level of competence for six different activities performed by the subsidiary on a seven-point Likert scale from 1 = very weak competence to 7 = very strong competence. The six activities are research (basic and applied),

Table 1
Sample size and subsidiary employees in the different countries

Country	Sample size	Subsidiary employees (mean)
Austria	313	318
Denmark	308	284
Finland	238	200
Germany	254	1.574
Norway	262	130
Sweden	530	244
UK	202	3.787
Total	2.107	742

development (of products and processes), production (of goods and services), marketing and sales, logistics and distribution and purchasing. The average score on the seven-point scale of the level of competence is shown in Table 2.

In general, the subsidiaries are indicating that they comprise a relatively high level of competence for all activities with average values ranging from 4 to 6 in the upper level of the seven-point scale. The pattern is very similar for all the six countries with the highest competence levels for production and marketing/sales and somewhat lower levels for the four other activities. As expected, the larger German and UK subsidiaries have higher competence levels than the other subsidiaries in the sample. They have slightly higher values than the total sample for all six activities.

3.2. Measures

All data were collected through the questionnaire and most items were measured using seven-point Likert scales. However, items such as the number of employees were measured using actual values. The following sections provide the exact wording used for question-naire items.

3.2.1. Knowledge transfer

Recall that our definition of knowledge transfer was capturing the application rather than the physical transfer of the subsidiary knowledge in other MNC units. Accordingly, in the questionnaire, the subsidiaries have been asked to what extent the subsidiary knowledge has been of use to other MNC units. Respondents have indicated this on a seven-point Likert scale, where 1 was defined as "to no use at all for other units" and 7 was defined as "very useful for other units" for all the six abovementioned activities. *Knowledge transfer* is a multi-item construct calculated as the average score reported by respondents across these six items ($\alpha = .69$).

3.2.2. Internal knowledge

The construct of internal knowledge captures the subsidiaries' own effort of knowledge production. This construct was measured by asking respondents to assess the level of

Table 2
The average score on a seven-point scale of the level of competence

Country	Research	Development	Production	Marketing/sales	Logistics/distribution	Purchasing
Austria	3.1	4.4	5.8	6.1	5.7	5.2
Denmark	4.8	5.2	6.0	5.9	5.7	5.3
Finland	4.3	4.9	5.9	5.9	5.5	5.3
Germany	4.6	5.3	6.3	6.2	5.9	5.7
Norway	4.2	4.9	5.6	5.7	5.3	5.2
Sweden	4.7	5.3	5.9	5.9	5.5	5.2
UK	4.9	5.3	6.1	6.1	5.9	5.5
Total	4.4	5.1	6.0	6.0	5.6	5.3

N.J. Foss, T. Pedersen / Journal of International Management 8 (2002) 49–67 61

investments in the subsidiary in the past 3 years, where 1 = very limited, 7 = substantial. The level of investments was assessed for all the six abovementioned activities. In the models used to test our hypotheses, we use a composite measure, *Internal knowledge*, based on the average across all six items ($\alpha=.70$).

3.2.3. Network knowledge

The variable of network knowledge captures the importance of external counterparts like customers and suppliers as sources of knowledge creation in the subsidiary. It was measured by asking respondents to assess the impact of various external organizations on the development of the subsidiary's competencies, where 1 = no impact at all, 7 = very decisive impact. Four organizations were identified: external market customers, external market suppliers, specific distributor and specific external R&D unit. Our measure, *Network knowledge*, is the average of the individual scores ($\alpha=.62$).

3.2.4. Cluster knowledge

Building on the elements of Porter's (1990) diamond model, respondents were asked to assess the business environment in which they compete along the following dimensions: availability of business professionals, availability of supply material, quality of suppliers, level of competition, government support, favorable legal environment and existence of research institutions (1 = very low, 7 = very high). In the diamond model, the items are presented as different dimensions. However, Porter's (1990) own emphasis on the holistic nature of the model and the high intercorrelation between many of the items motivated us to construct a composite index. *Cluster knowledge* is calculated as the average score reported by respondents across these seven items ($\alpha=.66$).

3.2.5. Interdependence

This variable measures the extent to which the MNC units are dependent on the subsidiaries and vice versa. The MNC dependence on the subsidiary knowledge were assessed by asking the respondents the following question: "What would be the consequences for other units in the Foreign Company if they no longer had access to the competencies of the subsidiary?" (1 = no consequences, 7 = very significant consequences). In a similar vein, the subsidiary dependence on knowledge from other MNC units was captured by the following question: "What would be the consequences for the subsidiary if it no longer had access to the competencies of other MNC units?" (1 = no consequences, 7 = very significant consequences). Taken together, these two items reflects the interdependence between the focal subsidiary and other MNC units.

3.2.6. Intra-MNC trade

The level of intra-MNC trade is an indicator of the breadth of the internal trade links. It is measured as a single item, as the share of subsidiary sale going to other MNC units in 1996. The subsidiary sale to other MNC units includes both semiproducts and final goods and services.

3.2.7. Autonomy

Based on the scale developed by Roth and Morrison (1992), respondents were asked to identify the level at which certain decisions were made, where 1 = foreign corporate (HQ), 2 = subcorporate (e.g., division), 3 = subsidiary level. Decisions were as follows: hiring top subsidiary management, entering new markets within the country, entering foreign markets, changes to subsidiary organization, introduction of new products/services and approval of quarterly plan/schedules. Our measure, *Autonomy*, is based on the average of these six items ($\alpha=.61$).

3.2.8. Controls

To control for structural characteristics of the subsidiary that might also influence the extent of knowledge transfer, we controlled for the following factors: number of subsidiary employees in 1996 (a proxy for size), the age of the subsidiary (a proxy for accumulated experience) and its mode of formation (greenfield or acquisition). We expect that larger, more established (i.e., older) subsidiaries will be more likely to transfer knowledge to other MNC units, consistent with our theoretical arguments of a cumulative process of knowledge development in foreign subsidiaries. We have no predictions with respect to the role of entry mode for the extent of knowledge transfer.

4. Results

4.1. Tests of hypotheses

A correlation matrix of all the independent variables in the model is presented in Appendix A. As can be seen, no more than 21 out of 36 pairwise correlations are highly significant (1% level). However, this is hardly surprising given the large number of observations (2.107). The highest correlation coefficient is between age and formation with the value of .37, which is well below the usual threshold of .5 (Hair et al., 1995). However, in order to detect potential multicollinearity problems, we have included the tolerance values where the tolerance is the amount of variability of the selected independent variable not explained by the other independent variables. The tolerance value for each variable is shown in Table 3. The lowest values are for the two control variables, mode of formation (.78) and age of subsidiary (.81). However, both are well above the usually applied thresholds (Hair et al., 1995). Therefore, we do not expect any multicollinearity problems.

The correlation matrix suggests that there is a high correlation among the three sources of subsidiary knowledge with all three pairwise correlations being significant at 1% level. This indicates that there might be leeway for exploring complementarities among the knowledge sources in future research. However, as already mentioned, the high correlations do not create a multicollinearity problem since the tolerance values of internal knowledge (.83), network knowledge (.87) and cluster knowledge (.90) are far above the threshold (Hair et al., 1995). The tolerance values indicate that only 10–17% of the variation in each of the knowledge source variables are explained by other independent variables included in the model.

Table 3
Factors affecting the extent of knowledge transfer to other MNC units

	Parameter estimates	Tolerance
Constant	0.039** (0.020)	
Internal knowledge	0.375*** (0.021)	0.83
Network knowledge	0.178*** (0.020)	0.87
Cluster knowledge	0.083*** (0.020)	0.90
Interdependence	0.166*** (0.021)	0.80
Intra-MNC trade	0.146*** (0.020)	0.87
Autonomy	0.056*** (0.020)	0.92
Internal knowledge × Interdependence	0.065*** (0.019)	0.96
Network knowledge × Intra-MNC trade	0.029 (0.019)	0.97
Network knowledge × Autonomy	− 0.014 (0.019)	0.97
Cluster knowledge × Autonomy	0.044** (0.020)	0.95
Number of employees	0.795*** (0.159)	0.92
Age of the subsidiary	0.039* (0.021)	0.81
Formation (1 = Greenfield, 2 = Acquisition)	0.086*** (0.022)	0.78
F-value	89.76***	
R^2	41.9	
N	1.629	

* Significant at the 10% level.
** Significant at the 5% level.
*** Significant at the 1% level.

Since all variables in the model are measured as continuous variables or dummies (as in the case of mode of formation), we can apply standard regression techniques. However, since Hypothesis 2 is about the relative strengths of the three different sources of subsidiary knowledge and the variables is not measured on the same scale, we have standardized all variables in the model with mean = 0 and standard deviation = 1. This makes it possible to use the parameters in the model to compare the relative strengths of the variables.

It is straightforward to test Hypothesis 1a–c, while 3–5 are tested by including the interaction term between the knowledge source and the organizational mechanism. The result of the total model is reported in Table 3. Numbers in parentheses represent standard errors.

Overall, the model works very well with a highly significant F-value of 89.8 and an R^2 of 41.9. This indicates that almost half of the observed variation in the extent of knowledge transfer is explained by the variables in the model. We turn now to the tests of our explanatory hypotheses.

Hypothesis 1a–c posited a relationship between sources of subsidiary knowledge and the transfer of that knowledge to other MNC units. These hypotheses are strongly supported. All three knowledge sources (internal, network and cluster knowledge) have a significantly positive relationship with the extent of knowledge transfer (all at the 1% level). However, the parameter for internal knowledge (.375) is substantially higher than for the two external knowledge sources (.178 and .083), indicating that internal knowledge is transferred to a much larger extent transfer than network and cluster knowledge. The parameter for network knowledge is somewhat higher than for cluster knowledge. All in all, Hypothesis 2 is supported which points to the conclusion that not all knowledge is transferred to the same extent, and the sources of knowledge seems to be a good indicator for the extent to which knowledge is actually transferred. We argue that this is because the sources of knowledge are determining the characteristics of knowledge, and in this case of internal MNC knowledge transfer, the context specificity of the knowledge turn out to be of major importance.

Hypotheses 3–5 were concerned with the organizational mechanism as facilitators of the knowledge transfer for the different sources of knowledge. In Hypothesis 3, we posited that intra-MNC trade would interact positively with network knowledge in the process of knowledge transfer. However, the interaction term between network knowledge and intra-MNC trade does not meet the requirements for significance, although with a value of .12, it is close to reaching the acceptable level. Therefore, Hypothesis 3 is not supported.

In the same vein, we posited that interdependence would interact positively with internal knowledge (Hypothesis 4). This hypothesis is strongly supported by the highly significant (at 1% level) and positive interaction term. Hypothesis 5 on the positive interaction between cluster and network knowledge, respectively, and autonomy is supported with regard to cluster knowledge (at 5% level), but not for network knowledge.

The three organizational mechanisms—interdependence, intra-MNC trade and autonomy—are also significantly and positively affecting the knowledge transfer in itself.

Moreover, all three control variables—the size, age and the formation of the subsidiary—turn out to be highly significant, indicating that larger experienced subsidiaries and acquisitions rather than greenfields do transfer more knowledge to other MNC units.

5. Concluding comments

In this paper, we have addressed the issue of intra-MNC knowledge transfer in a novel way. Whereas most of the literature has focused directly on either the characteristics of knowledge in terms of causal ambiguity, tacitness, etc., or the links between interdependencies and administrative systems and processes, we have taken a perhaps more direct approach and focused on the levels of subsidiary knowledge, the sources of this knowledge and organizational means and conditions as important determinants of knowledge transfer.

We found support for the main argument of the paper that the sources of knowledge are determinative of the characteristics of knowledge-to-be-transferred and that knowledge with different characteristics needs different organizational mechanism to facilitate the transfer of that knowledge. The source of knowledge—whether internal, network or cluster-based—has a profound impact on the characteristics of knowledge. In turn, this affects the extent of knowledge transfer. In particular, the context specificity of the knowledge has an effect on the extent of knowledge transfer, both because the more context specific the knowledge is, the smaller the absorptive capacity of the received and the less it can be used in other MNC units.

Moreover, given the different characteristics of the knowledge, it cannot be transferred in the same way. Thus, even in the case of MNCs, internal knowledge transfer is not an easy task. MNCs need to apply different organizational mechanisms in order to facilitate knowledge transfer and depending on the specific characteristics of the knowledge. For a differentiated MNC engaged in global knowledge sourcing, a main organizational task is to develop a large spectrum of different organizational mechanism. In some instances, as with subsidiaries tapping into local cluster knowledge, the autonomy of the subsidiary seems to be important for the knowledge transfer, while interdependence between the subsidiary and the other MNC units are very important for the knowledge transfer in the case of internal production of subsidiary knowledge.

However, there are various problems with our approach that need to be briefly commented upon. First of all, the measures that proxy organizational means and context (interdependence, intra-MNC trade and autonomy) admittedly do so only rather imperfectly, and we would have preferred to have much more direct measures. For example, it is somewhat unclear what kind of organizational means or context the measure intra-MNC trade exactly represents. However, these are unavoidable limitations of the dataset. Another limitation that is also dictated by the nature of dataset concerns the role of motivation factors. However, we may invoke the Szulanski (1996) findings that motivational factors were of relatively minor importance for understanding the efficiency of knowledge transfer as a partial justification for neglecting motivational issues.

Acknowledgments

We gratefully acknowledge the helpful comments of Udo Zander, Anna Grandori, Stephane Saussier and participants at the LINK workshop in Copenhagen, 25–26 October 2000, and the EIBA Meeting in Maastricht, 10–12 December 2000.

Appendix A. Correlation matrix of the independent variables

	1	2	3	4	5	6	7	8
(1) Internal knowledge	1.00							
(2) Network knowledge	.31***	1.00						
(3) Cluster knowledge	.19***	.21***	1.00					
(4) Interdependence	.12***	.20***	.13***	1.00				
(5) Intra-MNC trade	.18***	.09***	.14***	.30***	1.00			

(6) Autonomy	.12***	.01	− .03	− .20***	− .06 **	1.00			
(7) Employees	.03	.001	.003	.02	.08***	− .02	1.00		
(8) Age	.003	.01	.07***	.14***	.05 **	− .06 **	.001	1.00	
(9) Formation	.17***	.08***	.03	− .15***	.08***	.11***	.03	− .37***	

All the variables have mean = 0 and standard deviation = 1.
* Significant at the 10% level.
** Significant at the 5% level.
*** Significant at the 1% level.

References

Aghion, P., Tirole, J., 1997. Formal and real authority in organizations. J. Polit. Econ. 105, 1–29.

Barney, J.B., 1991. Firm resources and sustained competitive advantage. J. Manage. 17, 99–120.

Bartlett, C.A., Ghoshal, S., 1986. Tap your subsidiaries for global reach. Harv. Bus. Rev. 64 (4), 87–94.

Bartlett, C.A., Ghoshal, S., 1989. Managing Across Borders: The Transnational Solution. Harvard Business School Press, Boston.

Birkinshaw, J., 1996. How multinational subsidiary mandates are gained and lost. J. Int. Bus. Stud. 27, 467–495.

Buckley, P.J., Carter, M., 1999. Managing cross-border complementary knowledge. Int. Stud. Manage. Organ. 29, 80–104.

Crossan, M.M., Inkpen, A.C., 1994. Promise and reality of learning through alliances. International Executive 36, 263–273.

Egelhoff, W.G., 1988. Organizing the Multinational Enterprise: An Information Processing View. Ballinger, Cambridge, MA.

Ford, D., 1990. Understanding Business Markets: Interaction, Relationships, Networks. Academic Press, London.

Forsgren, M., Pedersen, T., Foss, N.J., 1999. Accounting for the strengths of MNC subsidiaries: the case of foreign-owned firms in Denmark. Int. Bus. Rev. 8, 181–196.

Gassman, O., von Zedtwitz, M., 1999. New concepts and trends in international R&D organization. Res. Policy 28, 231–250.

Ghoshal, S., Korine, H., Szulanski, G., 1994. Interunit communication in multinational corporations. Manage. Sci. 40 (1), 96–110.

Grant, R.M., 1996. Toward a knowledge-based theory of the firm. Strategic Manage. J. 17, 109–122.

Gupta, A.K., Govindarajan, V., 1991. Knowledge flows and the structure of control within multinational corporations. Acad. Manage. Rev. 16, 768–792.

Gupta, A.K., Govindarajan, V., 1995. Organizing for knowledge flows within MNCs. Int. Bus. Rev. 3, 443–457.

Gupta, A.K., Govindarajan, V., 2000. Knowledge flows within multinational corporations. Strategic Manage. J. 21, 473–496.

Hair, J.F., Anderson, R.E., Tatham, R.L., Black, W.C., 1995. Multivariate data analysis, fourth ed. Prentice-Hall, Englewood Cliffs, NJ.

Hart, O., 1995. Firms, Contracts, and Financial Structure. Oxford Univ. Press, Oxford.

Hedlund, G., 1986. The hypermodern MNC — a heterarchy? Hum. Resour. Manage. 21 (1), 9–35.

Holm, U., Pedersen, T., 2000a. The Emergence and Impact of MNC Centres of Excellence. Macmillan, Basingstoke.

Holm, U., Pedersen, T., 2000. The Dilemma of Centres of Excellence: Contextual Creation of Knowledge versus Global Transfer of Knowledge, LINK Working Paper no 8.

Hymer, S.H., 1960. The International Operations of National Firms: A Study of Direct Foreign Investment. MIT Press, Cambridge, MA.

Jensen, M.C., Meckling, W.H., 1992. Specific and general knowledge and organizational structure. In: Werin, L., Wijkander, H. (Eds.), Contract Economics. Blackwell, Oxford.

N.J. Foss, T. Pedersen / Journal of International Management 8 (2002) 49–67 67

Klein, B., Leffler, K., 1981. The role of market forces in assuring contractual performance. J. Polit. Econ. 89, 615–641.

Kogut, B., Zander, U., 1993. Knowledge of the firm and the evolutionary theory of the multinational corporation. J. Int. Bus. Stud. 24, 625–646.

Lippman, S., Rumelt, R.P., 1982. Uncertain imitability: an analysis of interfirm differences in efficiency under competition. Bell J. Econ. 13, 418–438.

March, J.G., 1991. Exploration and exploitation in organizational learning. In: Cohen, M.D., Sproull L. (Eds.), 1996. Organizational Learning. Sage, London.

Moore, K., Birkinshaw, J., 1998. Managing knowledge in global service firms: centers of excellence. Acad. Manage. Exec. 12, 81–92.

Nelson, R.R., Winter, S.G., 1982. An Evolutionary Theory of Economic Change. The Belknap Press, Cambridge, MA.

Nohria, N., Eccles, R.G., 1992. Networks and Organizations: Structure, Form and Action. Harvard Business School Press, Boston.

O'Donnell, S.W., 2000. Managing foreign subsidiaries: agents of headquarters, or an independent network? Strategic Manage. J. 21, 525–548.

Porter, M.E., 1990. The Competitive Advantage of Nations. Free Press, New York.

Porter, M.E., Sölvell, Ö., 1999. The role of geography in the process of innovation and the sustainable competitive advantage of firms. In: Chandler, A.D., Hagström, P., Sölvell, Ö. (Eds.), The Dynamic Firm — The Role of Technology, Strategy Organization, and Regions. Oxford University Press, Oxford.

Roth, K., Morrison, A.J., 1992. Implementing global strategy: characteristics of global subsidiary mandates. J. Int. Bus. Stud. 23, 715–736.

Simonin, B., 1999. Ambiguity and the process of knowledge transfer in strategic alliances. Strategic Manage. J. 20, 595–623.

Szulanski, G., 1996, Winter. Exploring internal stickiness: impediments to the transfer of best practice within the firm. Strategic Manage. J. 17, 27–43 (Special Issue).

Teece, D.J., 1981. The market for know-how and the efficient international transfer of technology. Ann., AAPSS 458, 81–96.

Wernerfelt, B., 1984. A resource based view of the firm. Strategic Manage. J. 9, 443–454.

Zander, U., Kogut, B., 1995. Knowledge and the speed of the transfer and imitation of organizational capabilities. Organ. Sci. 6, 76–92.

[6]

The Use of Knowledge in Firms

by

NICOLAI J. FOSS*

Austrian economics allows us to identify a number of weak spots in the modern economics of organization that all relate to the treatment of knowledge. Specifically, this body of theory is open to the same kind of objections that HAYEK [1937, 1945] raised against economics, namely that it does not incorporate truly dispersed knowledge, and therefore significantly understates the nature and severity of the coordination problems that confront social systems. However, rather than rejecting the modern economics of organization and opting for an alternative research program, this paper suggests that a combined research effort may be worthwhile. (JEL: B 15, B 25, L 22, D 81)

> "... from time to time it is probably necessary to detach one's self from the technicalities of the argument and ask quite naïvely what it is all about. "(F. A. v. Hayek)

1. Introduction

In line with the epigraph for this paper, which is drawn from Hayek's 1936 presidential address to the London Economic Club (HAYEK [1937, 56]), I want to "quite naïvely" make some basic points about the theory of the firm, or, more broadly, the modern economics of organization (henceforth MEO). These points are related to Hayek's, because they are non-technical, relating to the treatment of knowledge in economics, and Austrian in flavor. Recall that HAYEK [1937], [1945], [1946] made the fundamental point that economists routinely neglected or sidestepped the division of knowledge and the coordination problem this division raises. This was not only illegitimate, Hayek argued, but also made many phenomena incomprehensible to the economic theorist. The present paper applies this basic Hayekian critique to the MEO, and argues that an Austrian perspective raises issues that are not considered in the MEO. Hence, the title of the paper, which, of course, is a paraphrase of the title of Hayek's famous 1945 paper.

* The comments of two anonymous referees, Thráínn Eggertson, George Richardson, Viktor Vanberg, Richard Wagner and Ulrich Witt, and discussions with Kirsten Foss and Frederic Sautet are gratefully acknowledged. All errors are entirely the author's responsibility.

Journal of Institutional and Theoretical Economics (*JITE*), Vol. 155 (1999)
© 1999 Mohr Siebeck – ISSN 0932-4569

Briefly summarized, the points are as follows. Although proponents of the MEO (principal-agent theory, incomplete contract theory, transaction cost economics) can point to many scientific advances, it will be argued that this body of theory has a number of weak spots that relate to the treatment of knowledge. Others, too, have argued this[1]; however, the critique here is different, centering on the neglect in the MEO of the kind of dispersed knowledge that HAYEK [1937], [1945], [1946] highlighted. The dispersal of knowledge creates coordination problems that go beyond the incentive coordination problems that are treated in the MEO, and are consequently sidestepped in this body of theory (section 2). A consequence of this neglect is that the MEO tends to neglect the role of management, leadership, routines, capabilities, and shared cognitive categories (e.g. corporate culture) in coordination, except when these can be interpreted as either manifestations of *ex ante* incentive alignment (e.g., HERMALIN [1998]) or *ex post* governance (WILLIAMSON [1996]). While section 3 discusses the nature of coordination problems that are non-standard in the context of the MEO, section 4 discusses what Austrian economics has to offer with respect to insights into economic organization.

It should be emphasized that the ambition of the present paper is not to take steps towards an alternative Austrian theory of the firm. Rather, it is the more humble one of suggesting that Austrian economics is a challenge to the MEO, that economists of organization may derive inspiration from Austrian economics, and perhaps even that some sort of combined research program may be a worthwhile endeavour. Although Austrian economics raises good questions, arriving at satisfactory answers is likely to involve the efforts of more mainstream economists of organization.

2. Contracting and Coordination in the Modern Economics of Organization

This section provides an overview of the basic explanatory structure of the main streams in the MEO, namely the complete and the incomplete contracting approaches.[2] The purpose of this overview is to identify a number of assumptions about agents' knowledge that are often made as a matter of routine, and which may be defended by pointing to analytical convenience.

---

[1] For example, KREPS [1996] criticizes the routine assumption in much of the MEO that agents can perform dynamic programming, that is, agents can anticipate expected pay-offs from a relation, even when they have no or little knowledge about the character of the good that they intend to trade (e.g. in an R&D joint venture). And DEMSETZ [1988], HALLWOOD [1997], LANGLOIS AND FOSS [1999], and HOLMSTRÖM AND ROBERTS [1998] have argued that there may be knowledge-based determinants of the boundaries of the firm that are not identified in the MEO.

[2] I shall primarily discuss more formal work. This is not to say that such work is necessarily superior to less formal work, such as Williamson's, but rather that the formal work is less guarded and more explicit. For an Austrian discussion of Williamson's work, see SAUTET [1999].

However, the effect of making these assumptions is that a number of issues related to the coordination of knowledge in firms are hard or impossible to conceptualize and address. Among the relevant assumptions are that the best present uses of assets and rights to those assets are known to agents, that the principal knows the full range of actions available and that transactors can perform dynamic programming.

2.1. Problems of Coordination

The overarching theme that runs through all the many and diverse contributions to the MEO is the theme of coordination, reflecting that the essence of organization is indeed coordinated response to volatility of whatever type and source. However, the word "coordination" comes with a number of meanings. One meaning that has become prevalent – in fact, almost completely dominant – in the MEO is that of mitigating the effects of incentive-conflicts.[3] Thus, incentive-conflicts are ubiquitous and all-important; in contrast, coordination problems that do not turn on incentive conflicts are implicitly taken to be either empirically rare, theoretically trivial or both.

To illustrate, we can in an abstract manner think of economic agents as choosing game forms and equilibria thereof for regulating their trade. Efficiency requires that if agents can find a game form, and an equilibrium thereof, that allows them to do better, they will do so. For example, we may think of two agents that confront the following two possible games, each one being a simple coordination game (WERNERFELT [1994]).

Figure 1

	Game 1			Game 2	
	B			B	
	x	y		x	y
A x	1/1	0/0	A x	1/1	0/0
y	0/0	2/2	y	0/0	3/3

In this situation, Pareto efficiency requires that agents choose game 2 and play the (3/3) equilibrium. In such simple situations, problems of economic organization are taken to be absent, because there are no incentive conflicts.[4]

---

[3] Here understood in a broad sense as also encompassing the paradigmatic "hold-up" problem.

[4] It may be argued that, in the absence of incentive conflicts, the first-best solution is always obtainable, but this can only be claimed if all other coordination problems are already assumed away.

Indeed, many would deny the absence of any real coordination *problems* in games 1 and 2, simply because rational players will have no problems choosing the Pareto-dominant equilibrium (LUCE AND RAIFFA [1957, 59]).[5] However, it is easy to see that a slight modification of pay-offs, as in game 3, may spell trouble.

Figure 2

		Game 3				Game 4	
		B				B	
		x	y			x	y
A	x	2/2	0/0	A	x	2/2	0/0
	y	0/0	4/1		y	0/0	$4-u/1+u$

The problem here is, of course, that the Pareto criterion is too weak to select a unique equilibrium, since both the (2/2) and (4/1) outcome may be equilibria on this criterion. Now, obviously the (4/1) equilibrium has a higher joint surplus than the (2/2) equilibrium, and therefore it will be in A's interest to bribe B to play the *y*-strategy. If *u*, the bribe, lies between 1 and 2, the equilibrium corresponding to both A and B playing *y* will be efficient, and, hence, be chosen. Thus, efficiency now implies that the agents agree on maximizing and somehow splitting the joint surplus. In this situation, a market failure occurs when bribes cannot be sustained in equilibrium, something that may be crucially dependent on the timing of the game.[6] Such market failures may often be remedied through contractual means,[7] but contracts may fail too in the sense that they cannot completely safeguard against the reduction of surplus/loss of welfare stemming from incentive conflicts. This sort of "contract failure" may take various forms.

2.2. Contracting in the Modern Economics of Organization

It is customary in the literature to make an overall distinction between complete and incomplete contract theories, the former category including principal-agent theories and the latter including transaction cost economics

---

[5] An assumption that is not warranted; see, for example, COLMAN AND BACHARACH [1999].

[6] For example, if A gives B the bribe before the game begins, B will not choose the *y*-strategy, which means that A will decide not to give B any bribe. Or, A may promise B to pay the bribe after the game, but B will realize that this will not be in A's interest, and will still choose the *x*-strategy. Although the (2/2) equilibrium is still efficient, it is not joint-surplus-maximizing.

[7] For example, A may agree to pay B a compensation if they do not pay *u*, or B may agree to pay A a compensation if they do not choose the *y*-strategy after receiving *u*.

(COASE [1937], WILLIAMSON [1996]) and property rights theories (HART [1995]).

Under complete contracting, the parties can (costlessly) write a contract that describes their actions given all the future contingencies that may influence their contractual relation. In this context, there may be failure to reach the first-best outcome because of asymmetric information and differing risk-preferences, but given these constraints (and a specification of the parties' bargaining power), there is a determinate preferred outcome, on which the parties can coordinate without any problems.

Under incomplete contracting, some contingencies are left out for whatever reasons, such as information costs, the limitations of natural language, etc. For example, in the context of the example above, A may be confronted with a contingency that is not covered by the contract, refuse to pay B the bribe, and B can do nothing about it. Or, while it may be possible for partners to agree on contract terms, these may not be enforceable by a third party, such as a court (i.e. are non-verifiable). In these cases, it may not be possible to sustain the first-best outcome, that is, the one that unambiguously maximizes joint-surplus. Since complete contingent contracts cannot be written, parties to a contract may find it necessary to renegotiate their contracts after the contract has been signed, either because they encounter states of nature about which the contract is silent or where the contract specifies inefficient terms (WILLIAMSON [1996]). In the Grossman-Hart-Moore version of this idea,[8] it is assumed that the outcome of the renegotiation process can be foreseen at the time of drafting contracts and that the process does not involve costly bargaining – hence, is efficient (GROSSMAN AND HART [1986], HART AND MOORE [1990], HART [1995]). Nevertheless, the very fact of the possibility of renegotiation may be sufficient to cause inefficient levels of investment in relation-specific assets.

This directs analytical attention to property rights, or more precisely residual control rights, that is, the rights to control the use of assets in states of nature that are not described in the contract. The interest then centers on which pattern of ownership rights leads to the most efficient outcome, where this depends on the characteristics of the assets involved (e.g., whether they are complementary), on whose assets are most important to the joint surplus, and on who is most responsive to incentives, since ownership by one of the parties will attenuate the incentives of the other party. The bottomline is that the efficient ownership arrangements primarily turn on the trade-off between incentives for the buyer and the seller.

2.3. Coordination in the Context of Incomplete and Complete Contracting

The Grossman-Hart-Moore property rights approach has recently given rise to substantial debate within the MEO. For example, it has been argued that

---

[8] If not in WILLIAMSON's [1985], [1996] story.

property rights are not always necessary for reaching efficient outcomes, but that various cleverly designed mechanisms can handle the problems of unverifiable contract terms, so that one returns to the complete contracting (principal-agent) tradition (TIROLE [1999]). Relatedly, there has been some uneasiness about the supposedly less rigorous and more *ad hoc* type of modeling that characterizes the incomplete contracts literature relative to the principal-agent literature (MASKIN AND TIROLE [1997]).

However, these are, as it were, *internal* debates, and many things are therefore taken for granted and not contested. In the following, I shall launch a critique that is more of an external nature, namely one based on an Austrian point of view. To anticipate matters somewhat, it can be argued that the MEO makes a number of strong assumptions about the coordination of economic agents' actions and plans, and the way in which this should be analytically approached. Thus, on the overall level, agents are assumed to be able to coordinate on any desired game form and equilibrium thereof, subject to constraints such as attitudes to risk, incentive trade-offs, bargaining power, and asymmetric information. Thus, coordination takes place by means of pure reasoning, and there is no mention of discovery, trial-and-error learning and the like. With respect to the conceptualization of coordination problems, only alignment of incentives is considered. In the context of the examples above, game 4 is the ruling paradigm. But surely, we can imagine interesting coordination problems that do not turn on incentive problems and we can surely imagine agents having difficulties coordinating on an equilibrium (CRAWFORD AND HALLER [1990]).

From an Austrian point of view, the strong powers of coordinative ability that are ascribed to agents in the MEO are perhaps particularly striking in the context of the literature on contractual incompleteness. Thus, incompleteness is often explained by arguing that although the parties to the contract are symmetrically informed, certain things are not verifiable (in essence shifting the bounded rationality of the parties to the courts). Not only are the agents in a contractual relation symmetrically informed; they are also assumed to be able to foresee the pay-offs from their relation, even if they have no knowledge at all the physical characteristics of the good they are trading (TIROLE [1999]) and even if unforeseen contingencies occur.[9] Thus, the parties

---

[9] Of course, the motivation for this assumption is that otherwise the whole theory threathens to fall apart. As MOORE [1992, 180] comments: "If parties cannot foresee certain events, let alone anticipate how surplus would be divided in the event of renegotiation, then how is this likely to affect the size and nature of their specific investments?". However, MASKIN AND TIROLE [1997] point out that there is a tension between the assumption of dynamic programming and the presence of transaction costs. If agents can in fact perform dynamic programming, then transaction costs (of describing actions or the nature of goods in advance) will not restrict the set of outcomes that contracts can implement.

to a contract can correctly anticipate the distribution of utility, but cannot describe the sources of that utility. Of course, this reflects the basic modelling approach of assuming that everything except a few variables is common or shared knowledge.

Such an approach often makes perfect sense. However, at other times it is vulnerable to the critique that HAYEK [1937], [1945] launched against the economics of his day, namely that it assumes from the outset the coordination of activities that it should be the prime task of economists to inquire into.[10] From such a perspective, the MEO may be criticized for assuming that virtually all that is worth discovering has already been discovered. There are a few spanners in the works – all of which are only related to misaligned incentives – but there is no genuine knowledge problem of the sort that Hayek talked about.[11]

The bottomline is that, in the MEO, knowledge is not truly dispersed and coordination problems are trivialized. One may press the claim that the MEO has not fully absorbed one of the main messages of the socialist calculation debate (see LAVOIE [1985]): That knowledge is dispersed, subjectively held and tacit, and that there is more to efficient ressource allocation (in socialist economies or firms) than providing managers with the right incentives. There is also the problem of the coordination of knowledge, which is not necessarily an incentive issue. The following section develops these Austrian critiques further.

3. An Austrian Starting Point

In this section, I clarify the ways in which an Austrian approach differs from a more mainstream approach, and how it challenges the MEO. I also argue that Austrian economics focuses on "non-standard" coordination problems that go beyond those considered in the MEO.

---

[10] Relatedly, FURUBOTN AND RICHTER [1997, 442] criticize the modern mainstream modelling approach on the grounds that it portrays decision-makers as having "...split economic personalities. They are perfectly informed about some matters yet completely ignorant about others."

[11] For example, in the following quotation: "The peculiar character of the problem of a rational economic order is determined precisely by the fact that the knowledge of the circumstances of which we must make use never exists in concentrated or integrated form but solely as the dispersed bits of incomplete and frequently contradictory knowledge which all the separate individuals possess. The economic problem of society is thus not merely a problem of how to allocate 'given' resources – if 'given' is taken to mean given to a single mind which deliberately solves the problem set by these 'data'. It is rather a problem of how to secure the best use of resources known to any of the members of society, for ends whose relative importance only these individuals know. Or, to put it briefly, it is a problem of the utilization of knowledge which is not given to anyone in its totality." (HAYEK [1945, 77 f.]).

3.1. Austrian Subjectivism

Because of some diversity in the school, it is difficult to precisely and briefly summarize what is the essence of Austrian economics (but see O'DRISCOLL AND RIZZO [1985], BOETTKE [1994], VAUGHN [1994]). Some hold that the crucial concept is that of market process (KIRZNER [1992], [1997]). However, a conceptualization of the market process is likely to be derived from underlying notions of individual behavior (LITTLECHILD [1986]). Accordingly I shall take Austrian economics to be primarily distinguished from mainstream economics by its much more thoroughgoing *subjectivism*. Austrian subjectivism is not only a matter of accepting the subjectivism of preferences; it is a more radical matter of stressing the subjectivity of beliefs, expectations, plans, etc.

This may sound as a banality, but it is not. To see this, contrast Austrian subjectivism with mainstream (game theory) modelling of agents' knowledge (GEANAKOPLOS [1989], RASMUSSEN [1994], DEKEL AND GUL [1997]). In the latter type of modeling exercise, it is assumed (1) that there is an isomorphism between the real world and an agent's image of it, (2) that agents differ only with respect to decision-making capabilities in terms of how fine or coarse their information partitions are, (3) that information partitions are given, and (4) that genuine knowledge gaps, such as mistakes and surprises, can be ruled out. For example, in the standard principal-agent model, the only true knowledge difference between the principal and the agent is that the principal's information partition is coarser than the agent's partition.[12]

In essence, the Austrian perspective is a call for breaking with all four assumptions. For example, in a subjectivist perspective, learning must involve more than Bayesian updating of priors; it must also involve setting up new interpretive frameworks for handling new types of problems. Action – including entrepreneurial action – is mediated by such mental constructs (see DENZAU AND NORTH [1994]). A subjectivist perspective on action thus implies that the essence of economic behavior is not merely maximizing. It also consists in understanding the environment, making sense of incoming information, and generating procedures which can help to solve problems (LACHMANN [1978], CHOI [1993], DOSI AND MARENGO [1994]). It certainly includes alertness to hitherto neglected opportunities (KIRZNER [1973], [1992], [1997]), that is, the overcoming of sheer ignorance. Crucially, in the Austrian view the subjectivity of mental constructs, problem-solving procedures, etc., translates into a postulate that such constructs, procedures, etc., differ across agents (BUTOS AND KOPPL [1997]). A direct implication is that communication costs are non-negligible in a world of Austrian agents. Another is that the overcoming of ignorance is an important economic

---

[12] LEWIS AND SAPPINGTON [1993] introduce "ignorance" into the principal-agent model, but only in the rather restricted sense of making the agent know as little about a critical parameter as does the principal.

activity. Both implications have further implications for economic organization.

3.2. The Subjectivist Challenge

A response may well be that taking Austrian subjectivism seriously merely amounts to introducing unnecessary complications. However, in the perspective of this paper it is exactly by taking a subjectivist starting point that we are able to see and conceptualize problems that are crucial to the understanding of economic organization, but which have disappeared from the focus of the MEO. Among these is truly dispersed knowledge. This goes beyond the conventional asymmetric information paradigm to also include the possibility of different ways of mentally representing economic reality and sheer ignorance.[13] In the Austrian perspective, agents often hold different mental constructs for making sense out of reality, they may be ignorant about what knowledge they are ignorant about (sheer ignorance), and they will, therefore, experience unforeseen contingencies. I shall characterize these epistemic conditions as *truly dispersed knowledge*.

Not only can we better see these aspects of knowledge from an Austrian perspective, there is a further constructive dimension to it. Truly dispersed knowledge leads directly to a concern with the coordination of subjectively held and formed plans, and to an appreciation of the institutions – such as firms (MALMGREN [1961]) – that promote the coordination of plans. Moreover, the set of coordination problems is considerably broader than that considered in the MEO. Thus, at issue is not only the alignment of incentives which is the predominant form that plan-consistency takes in the MEO; it is also a matter of discovery of things hitherto unknown – including discovering the best uses of assets – and of aligning mental frameworks.

Thus, Austrian subjectivism poses a challenge. It does so by radicalizing the Hayekian knowledge problem of how to make best use of dispersed knowledge to go beyond the standard asymmetric information paradigm and also consider sheer ignorance, unforeseen contingencies and differential cognitive frameworks. Applied to the organization of firms, and paraphrasing HAYEK [1945], the subjectivist challenge may be formulated thus: How is rational firm organization possible when we *cannot assume from the outset* that (a) all contracting action can be compressed into one initial grand contract, as in the principal/agent paradigm – because of the occurrence of unforeseen contingencies; (b) principals know all the possible actions that are open to agents – because of truly dispersed knowledge; (c) agents, for

---

[13] As KIRZNER [1997] carefully explains, sheer ignorance goes beyond asymmetric information in that the latter essentially assumes that agents know what they are ignorant about (and can search to reduce their ignorance), whereas the former implies that agents are not aware of what it is that they are ignorant about. Discovering such hitherto unthought-of knowledge is bound to produce surprise.

example, division managers in a firm, hold the same cognitive constructs – because of different subjective perceptions of reality; (d) decision rights are efficiently assigned – because entrepreneurial activity may discover better assignments; (e) agents can perform dynamic programming and perfectly foresee their pay-offs (or at least the distribution thereof) – because of the occurrence of novelties; (f) that all present uses of all assets, including the optimal ones, are known to economic agents – because entrepreneurial activity may discover better uses; (g) we can pay lip service to issues of communication – because Austrian subjectivism implies the presence of non-negligible communication costs, but must think of these as either non-permissible abstractions (e.g., the complete contracting assumption) or as *explananda* rather than data (e.g., the efficient assignment of decision rights, the optimal use of assets).

In short, the subjectivist challenge consists in portraying coordination problems as a good deal more complicated and messy than they are normally portrayed in the MEO. In the latter, attention is focused on situations in which everything is coordinated, but for a few variables or relations. For example, in the canonic principal-agent set-up, the principal knows the range of courses of action that is open to the agent, their preferences and the probabilities distribution of the stochastic variable that impinges on the agent's output. The principal's basic problem is that they cannot observe the agent's effort and Nature's move. However, they are able to design a second-best incentive scheme (at no contracting cost). More generally, all the best present uses of all assets are known to the parties; what may be uncertain is the future use of these assets when unexpected contingencies emerge (Foss [1999]), but even this can be cast in an equilibrium mould, as in the Grossman-Hart-Moore approach. Thus, in virtually all of the MEO, knowledge is not truly dispersed.

3.3. Coordination Problems and Knowledge Problems

A proponent of the MEO may argue that not only are the above complications far-reaching and hard to model, they may also be unnecessary. In many realistic settings (small firms and partnerships?), coordination problems indeed reduce to giving people who already are on "the same wavelength", as it were, the right incentives – that is, the problem studied in virtually all of the MEO. This may be granted, and it bears repeating that the purpose here is not to attack the MEO *per se*. There is much to admire in this body of theory, but what should be kept in mind is its limited nature. Thus, we may certainly make the routine assumptions that are made in the MEO, provided we keep in mind that making them is only a first step.

In the perspective taken here, the MEO is, however, likely to lead attention away from coordination problems that do not necessarily involve problems of incentive alignment. To repeat, there are (many) coordination problems that go beyond the simple paradigmatic one portrayed in game 4 above, and the Hayekian knowledge problem (HAYEK [1945]) is one such problem. For example, we can have a completely simple symmetric coordination game (game 5):

Figure 3

Game 5

B

		x	y
	x	2/2	0/0
A			
	y	0/0	2/2

It is well-known that there is nothing in classical game theory to help us predict the outcome in this situation,[14] and that one must rely on *ad hoc* constructions – such as focal points or appeal to mediators (SCHELLING [1960, 144]) – for rationalizing any particular outcome. One may of course argue that such arbitrariness can be an advantage rather than a problem – for example, it may help us make sense of, for example, firm heterogeneity[15] – but that is not the point here.

The normal form games 1-5 have been made extremely simple on purpose, because nothing more is required to illustrate some basic points about game theoretic modeling in the MEO (see also KREPS [1996]). Most notably, game theory representations tend to obscure some rather fundamental questions in order to analyze well-defined situations. Among these questions are, How do players come to know the pay-offs? Or each other? Or the available strategies? Will they hold the same views of the pay-offs? Of each other? Of the available strategies? How do they know which game, and type of game, they are playing? Such questions are suppressed by assuming from the outset that players have commonly known, identical beliefs about all other players' strategies, and that those beliefs are consistent with some equilibrium in the game.[16] Given this the analyst then proceeds to examine the design of incentive schemes, the sharing of the surplus from a relation, the support of certain outcomes by implicit contracts, etc. However, this is not unproblematic for the basic reason that a number of real difficulties of coordination have been shunted aside.

The claim may be pressed that much of game theory is characterized by the conflation of what objectively exists and what is subjectively perceived, a

---

[14] For example, the usual refinement techniques are not helpful here.

[15] Firms all play game 5 but choose different equilibria.

[16] There are expections, such as CRAWFORD AND HALLER [1990] and HUYCK, BATTALIO AND BEIL [1990].

conflation that Hayek criticized so strongly more than six decades ago in his discussions of the coordination problem in economics (HAYEK [1937]). Ironically, one possible reason for the strong upsurge in the popularity of game theoretical models in the last 10–15 years may have to do with these models being perceived as solving the coordination problem: Agents reason (instantaneously) their way to equilibrium (GUESNERIE [1992]). But as we have seen (see game 5), this is not always possible. And more generally, the coordination problem of course is not thereby solved at all, merely side-stepped.

While an "eductive" (BINMORE [1991]) approach may have some plausibility for simple non-symmetric coordination games with few players,[17] it becomes increasingly implausible as we increase the number of available strategies, players, and equilibria. And while we also know that when simple pure coordination games are repeated, the players will, through trial and error, eventually coordinate on an equilibrium (CRAWFORD AND HALLER [1990]), in a more realistic setting the game itself may change during play. For example, the players may discover some "particular circumstances of time and place" (HAYEK [1945]) that affect the pay-offs and require that they restart play. Both when the number of players expand and when the presumed "data" of the game change, we increasingly confront the Hayekian knowledge problem of how to coordinate truly dispersed knowledge. To some extent, however, the Hayekian knowledge problem is alleviated by the presence of numerous, largely spontaneously grown, institutions – a theme intimately connected with Hayek's own work (HAYEK [1973], but see also SCHLICHT [1998, 260 ff.]). It is such insights, I submit, that may be applied to understanding firm organization.

To anticipate this somewhat, consider the case of the multi-divisional form, or "the M-form". While CHANDLER [1962] in his early analysis had argued that information overloads on the part of top-management under the U-form explained the adoption of the M-form, the economic analysis of the M-form is cast almost entirely in terms of aligning incentives. For example, MASKIN, QIAN AND XU [1998] argue that different organizational forms give rise to different information about managers' performance and therefore have different implications with respect to the effectiveness of incentives. The M-form will be adopted because under certain conditions it promotes relative performance evaluation better than do the alternatives.

However, another – Austrian-style – interpretation is possible (SAUTET AND FOSS [1998], SAUTET [1999]). In this story, the advantages of the M-form have more to do with the knowledge-related advantages of changing the internal division of labour. Rather than focusing on the information overload that top-management confronts, an Austrian perspective focuses on the knowledge

---

[17] However, even in very simple interaction situations, coordination failure may arise (see HUYCK, BATTALIO AND BEIL [1990] for experimental evidence).

that is dispersed in the corporation and which management cannot possibly centralize. The M-form is one way of coping with this knowledge-dispersal problem (SAUTET [1999]). This is because it allows decentralized decisions to be made in an efficient manner, and frees top-management from daily operational control, so that they become more able to specialize in overall strategic judgment. The reason for the existence of the M-form is thus not information overload but rather that it is an organizational structure that allows top-management to cope with the problem of dispersed knowledge.

4. Austrian Insights and the Economics of Organization

Austrian economics is normally taken to be first and foremost a theory of the *market* process (KIRZNER [1997]). In contrast, it is not seen as containing a theory of the firm, and one seeks in vain for any details about firm organization in the Austrian literature.[18] A basic reason for this neglect is easy to discern: In the view of the Austrians, economics – and social science in general – is about tracing the unintended consequences of intentional human action (HAYEK [1952], LACHMANN [1978]). And in the view of the Austrians, unintended consequences are only manifest in large-scale, complex systems characterized by a substantial division of knowledge, notably whole economies. Smaller scale systems, such as firms, have no room for unintended consequences and are therefore not a proper domain of inquiry for the economist.

Bearing in mind that this is a rational reconstruction, one may argue that a problem with this Austrian view is that we are never being told *when* a social system is so large that it is sufficiently complex to produce non-trivial unintended consequences. Moreover, perhaps because this is not made clear, it is not fully recognized that firms may manifest a substantial division of dispersed knowledge, and that organizational forms may reflect attempts to grapple with the coordination problems introduced by dispersed knowledge. As this suggests, there is in fact a potential for applying key Austrian ideas on the organization of the process of knowledge utilization and creation. The following sections discuss some of these ideas.

4.1. Firms and the Dispersal of Knowledge

In contrast to markets, firms are planned by identifiable historical individuals with the purpose of earning a profit and they normally operate under a designed framework, such as a mission statement, a formal organization

---

[18] Most work on the theory of the firm with an Austrian flavor has been done by "fellow-travellers", for example, LANGLOIS [1995] and LOASBY [1991]. However, younger Austrians have recently begun to apply Austrian ideas to the theory of the firm, for example, KLEIN [1996], COWEN AND PARKER [1997] and SAUTET [1999].

structure, etc.[19] Firms are set in motion, as it were, by conscious intention and are therefore "pragmatic" institutions in the sense of MENGER [1883/1985]. However, the distinction between "pragmatic" and "organic" systems really only refers to the *origins* of these systems. Thus, systems with an organic origin may become heavily regulated, and systems with a pragmatic origin may develop spontaneous elements (LANGLOIS [1995]).

To the extent that such spontaneous phenomena are treated in the MEO, they are cast in a somewhat negative light; for example, they tend to be placed under the rubrics of rent-seeking, sub-goal pursuit, on-the-job consumption, etc. In the MEO, equilibria of decentralized firms are thus taken to be inefficient because of various conflicts of interest among the decision-makers within the firm. Given this, attention turns to the design of various devices, such as Groves-Vickrey-Clarke mechanisms (GROVES AND LOEB [1979]), which may remedy incentive conflicts.

From an Austrian point of view, it is striking that the MEO has focused almost exclusively on the negative aspects of decentralization, that is, to the extent that it has treated decentralization in organizations at all.[20] Large firms may confront knowledge dispersal problems of a magnitude comparable to those that confront the social planner in a socialist economy (GHOSHAL, MORAN AND ALMEIDA-COSTA [1995]). Clearly, such a dispersal of knowledge may be unavoidable, for example, because attempts to put all tacit dispersed knowledge in the hands of top management may be exceedingly costly (JENSEN AND MECKLING [1992]), accompanied by information loss (WILLIAMSON [1970]), and perhaps even impossible (LAVOIE [1985]). Moreover, even assuming that all dispersed knowledge could in fact be centralized, there is of course no guarantee that top-management would be competent to efficiently utilize the knowledge (PELIKAN [1989]).

Not only is dispersal of knowledge in firms unavoidable; there may also be a beneficial aspect to it. HAYEK [1945] stressed that economic problems only arise as a consequence of change, particularly unforeseen contingencies. One may argue that the MEO to some extent incorporates this Hayekian point *via* its emphasis on incomplete contracts, renegotiation, *ex post* governance and so on. However, the Hayekian point that decentralization is an effective response to the local emergence of unforeseen contingencies[21] is either neglected or given a static mechanism design interpretation.

---

[19] VANBERG [1992] talks in this connection of the firm's "constitution".

[20] However, the works of M. AOKI (e.g., AOKI [1990a], [1990b]) and, to a smaller extent, RADNER [1993], are outstanding exceptions to this.

[21] To quote Hayek directly: "If we can agree that the economic problem of society is mainly one of rapid adaptation to changes in the particular circumstances of time and place, it would seem to follow that the ultimate decisions must be left to the people who are familiar with these circumstances, who know directly of the relevant changes and of the resources immediately available to meet them. We cannot expect that this problem will be solved by first communicating all this knowledge to a central board which, after integrating all knowledge, issues its orders." (HAYEK [1945, 83 f.]).

Hayek's point appears to have been that an economy with alienable property rights promotes a tendency towards allocating property rights to those who can make best use of them and in this way ensures that the best use possible is made of dispersed knowledge.[22] However, as JENSEN AND MECKLING [1992] point out, this reasoning makes it hard to account for the existence of firms; why not have complete decentralization?[23] Suppose firms existed. We then know that management will generally not be able to centralize all dispersed knowledge inside the firm. An implication is that employees will not only have less coarse information partitionings than their bosses – they will quite simply know and discover things about which their bosses have no idea.[24] Therefore, they may arrive at different conclusions as to how certain events that influence firm profitability should be handled. This in turn implies a powerful argument for extensive decentralization of control rights, and an argument against direction, since the latter normally presumes that the principal possesses knowledge that is superior to that of the agent (DEMSETZ [1988], CASSON [1994]). But why then have firm organization? Driven to its extreme, an emphasis on dispersed knowledge may easily lead to a denial of the need for firms.

Of course, we know from the MEO that for all sorts of reasons the benefits from efficient utilization of dispersed knowledge may be swamped by the incentive conflicts attendant upon a decentralization of decision rights. Indeed, the MEO has emphasized these conflicts to such an extent that, while it may provide strong reasons why control rights in firms should be centralized, it has a hard time explaining why (some) control rights should ever be decentralized. However, even if we suppress such incentive conflicts, we are not necessarily led to the conclusion that firms will not exist. I shall argue that this conclusion is too hasty, and is likely to only hold true (if at all) in a static context. In a dynamic context – which is the setting that interests Austrians – firms may have distinct advantages relative to markets in terms of their planning ability. Given that a main message of Austrian economics is that there are strong inherent limitations to planning, this may indeed seem to

---

[22] This point has been reflected in much recent management thinking (SEMLER [1989], MEYER [1994], NONAKA AND TAKEUCHI [1995]). The recent strong emphasis on cross-functional teams that are given extensive decision rights and where payment is based on team-output reflects the recognition that it is to some extent possible to combine "high-powered" incentives with efficient utilization of local knowledge in firms.

[23] Indeed, in some recent, and explicitly Austrian, work on these issues, the very distinction between firms and markets is argued to be insubstantial (COWEN AND PARKER [1997]). According to these authors, the coordination problems solved by firms and markets are essentially similar, and firms cannot realize production possibilities that cannot be realized by markets.

[24] As SAUTET [1999] points out, management therefore confronts a "double Hayekian knowledge problem": It is not just that it doesn't know what it doesn't know in the *market*; it is also the case that it doesn't know what it doesn't know about the firm's *employees*.

be a strange conclusion to reach in a paper with an Austrian orientation. However, there are different meanings of planning, and some of these are fully compatible with an Austrian point of view.

4.2. Types of Coordination and Planning

As we have seen, HAYEK's [1945] discussion of spontaneous coordination by means of the price mechanism and alienable property rights may lead to a denial of the need for planning. But here it is pertinent to remember HAYEK's [1944] famous quip that the issue is not planning versus no planning but rather who should do the planning. Furthermore, as KLEIN [1997] reminds us, there is a sense of the word "coordination" that is different from the sense in which HAYEK [1945] used it. This may be best associated with the work of SCHEL-LING [1978] (or with much of recent game theory work on coordination games). Here, coordination is typically smaller scale than in the market settings discussed by Hayek; moreover, it is intended and desired by the interacting parties. At one extreme, coordination takes place in a completely unintended manner; at another extreme, it is intended, and possibly a product of pure reasoning.

We may illustrate these two extremes by referring to two different overall modeling strategies in the theory of the firm. One of these is to model the firm as an adaptive network (e.g., DOW [1990]). In this modeling approach, agents in a network initially do not know what they and others are doing, but fall back on naive adaptive learning procedures. Over time they may home in on some sort of equilibrium (absorbing state or the like) consisting of stable decision rules. This equilibrium is then interpreted as an organization (e.g., as in MARCH [1988]). The other modeling approach is that favored by the MEO. In its mechanism design guise, this rational design approach implies that the codes and rules that coordinate local decisions and plans are designed by top-management. In other words, management is presumed to know the basic game(s) that is (are) being played and can rationally influence its (their) outcome(s) (e.g., HURWICZ [1986]).

From an Austrian point of view, none of these modeling strategies seem very attractive. The basic problem with the rational design approach is that the designer needs to undertake much pre-play communication in order to establish the optimal codes and decision rules[25] – which runs counter to an Austrian emphasis on dispersed knowledge. The basic problem with the adaptive network approach is that it completely eliminates the intentional and hierarchical elements that we know characterize real-world firms. Thus, while the former strategy suffers from a "pretense of knowledge" (HAYEK [1975]), the

---

[25] Technically, they must know the complete range of possible realizations of the agent's private information.

latter plays down rationality too much. Both by assumption suppress the entrepreneurial process of discovery.[26]

The Austrian perspective suggested in this paper implies that coordination in firms is intermediate between these two extremes. The fact that fully informed and detailed top-down planning that incorporates all dispersed knowledge in a firm is not possible does not mean, of course, that firms cannot be characterized by some measure of planning. Note that many firms actually regularly carry out strategic planning exercises, and continue to do so, which to the economist suggests that such exercises on average influence firms' returns positively.[27] What may be the source of that value? Although not all dispersed knowledge can be fully revealed, a regular strategic planning exercise may still update management's knowledge. Thus, it may become more informed about what sort of knowledge is present in the organization, which learning processes are going on locally (say, in a foreign subsidiary), and which knowledge and practices may profitably be transferred to other parts of the organization.[28] These activities may all influence returns positively.

4.3. Planning and Uncertainty

From an Austrian point of view, the dispersal of knowledge is not the only obstacle to successful, comprehensive planning. Another is radical uncertainty (WISEMAN [1953]), which I will here interpret to refer to the emergence of unforeseen contingencies. That unforeseen contingencies matter for the understanding of contracts, governance structures and even constitutions has been a recurrent theme in the MEO for quite some time (WILLIAMSON [1985], GROSSMAN AND HART [1986], KREPS [1990], DEKEL, LIPMAN AND RUSTICHINI [1998]). However, unforeseen contingencies *per se* are seldom modeled. This is not surprising, since they raise some very basic problems: Does it make sense to claim that economic agents can "anticipate the unanticipated"? If the efficiency of a governance structure depends on how well it copes with unforeseen contingencies, how can agents choose an efficient governance structure on an *ex ante* basis? These problems are central to the understanding of, for example, the efficiency hypothesis in transaction cost economics

---

[26] Furthermore, none of these modeling strategies tell us much that helps us to discriminate between different types of coordination and planning; in principle, the adaptive networks and the mechanisms identified in the two approaches may refer equally to the intra-firm or the inter-firm level.

[27] Admittedly, strategic planning may have fallen somewhat out of favor relative to its heydays in the 1960s and 1970s. However, the type of planning that has fallen out of favor is precisely the detailed, top-down planning, so strongly criticized by MINTZBERG [1994].

[28] Indeed, there is a strong argument that it is precisely the ability to transfer at low cost successful practices that gives multinational firms a competitive edge not only over domestic firms but also over the market (BARTLETT AND GHOSHAL [1989]).

(WILLIAMSON [1996]) or the assumption in the incomplete contract approach that agents can perform dynamic programming (MOORE [1992], KREPS [1996]).

It has been a recurring theme in the Austrian tradition that rationality and unexpected contingencies are not mutually exclusive. Thus, MENGER [1871/ 1976] stressed the holding of reserves in various forms as rational behavior in the presence of unforeseen contingencies. And HAYEK [1945, 82] argued that, in the absence of unforeseen contigencies, the task of "drawing up a comprehensive plan governing all economic activity would be much less formidable... and that" economic problems arise always and only in consequence of change. In Hayek's view, decentralization was one, society-level, response to unforeseen contingencies. This is related to LACHMANN's [1971, 81] discussion of the limits of social engineering:

> "In a society in which it is generally known that frequent change of undesigned institutions is inevitable, the designers of designed institutions may deliberately confine their activity to designing a framework which leaves room for a good deal of change ... In such a society it might be said that the undesigned institutions which evolve gradually ... accumulate in the *interstices* of the institutional order. The interstices have been planned, though the sediments accumulating in them have not and could not have been."

Thus, unforeseen contingencies are a challenge to constitutional design. However, the problem remains of how one can meaningfully speak of anticipating the unforeseen, a problem that must be addressed to the extent that we wish to claim that economic agents can rationally choose contracts, governance structures or constitutions that help them adapt to unforeseen contingencies.

LANGLOIS [1986] discussed a similar problem in a splendid but neglected paper. He argued that the crux of the matter is that most events have both foreseeable and unforeseeable aspects, or that they have "typical" and "unique" features (LANGLOIS [1986, 182]).[29] Typification is an important aspect of the way in which agents perceive their environment (O'DRISCOLL AND RIZZO [1985]). Typical features are those elements of the environment that are stable and unique features are those that are non-repeatable and idiosyncratic. While we can often clearly foresee typical features, we often also have to let time pass before we can fill in the unique features (see also DEKEL, LIPMAN AND RUSTICHINI [1998, 524]). As COASE [1937, 21; my emphasis] explained, this is indeed the essence of the employment contract:

> "It may be desired to make a long-term contract for the supply of some article or service ... Now, owing to the difficulty of forecasting, the longer the period of the

---

[29] The latter terminology derives from the philosopher-sociologist, Alfred Schütz. See also BUTOS AND KOPPL [1997] for an interesting Austrian discussion of expectations.

contract is for the supply of the commodity or service, the less possible, and indeed, the less desirable it is for the person purchasing to specify what the other contracting party is expected to do ... Therefore, *the service which is being provided is expressed in general terms, the exact details being left until a later date* ... When the direction of resources ... becomes dependent on the buyer in this way, that relationship which I term a firm may be obtained".

This suggests that the distinction between typical and unique features of events may be relevant to understanding economic organization. The following section pursues this theme further.

4.4. Coherence and Flexibility: The Firm in a World of Radical Uncertainty[30]

Dividing events up into typical and unique features may be a general way of approaching unforeseen contingencies and one that allows us to understand why agents may, after all, be able to rationally choose contracts and governance structures on an *ex ante* basis. For example, agents may entertain the expectation that in this particular type of relation, such and such types of contractual problems typically take place unless the right safeguards are built into the contract, but they do not have to be able to anticipate precisely which contractual problems might arise. Something similar is the foundation of KREPS' [1990] theory of corporate culture. Kreps argues that firms may develop implicit contracts that align incentives by signaling to employees that management will not opportunistically take advantage of them in the case of unforeseen events, although nothing specific is being said (or can be said) about the event. However, we can certainly think of such typification taking place inside firms quite independently of considerations of incentive conflicts. Thus, coordination problems are greatly reduced if employees categorize emergent contingencies in the same way so that the "convergence of expectations" that MALMGREN [1961] saw as a primary benefit of firm organization may be realized (CREMER [1990]). The firm may indeed be characterized by plan consistency (HAYEK [1937], MALMGREN [1961]), but only of a sort that relates to the typical features of events (see O'DRISCOLL AND RIZZO [1985]).

We may now suggest that an important aspect of what a firm's leaders can do is to influence and steer the development of schemes of typification that are flexible enough to accommodate unforeseen events, and that help agents coordinate their interdependent activities. If that is an essential part of what a firm's leaders do, it is potentially misleading to portray these activities in terms of simple situations of interaction such as those portrayed in games 1 to 5. It is more true to say that leaders often define what is the relevant game and the feasible strategies, communicate the pay-off structure of the relevant games, and determine which strategies should be played in the face of an

---

[30] Apologies to LANGLOIS [1986].

emergent event. It is often as much a matter of defining what are the relevant problems and of providing solutions to these as it is of inducing agents to choose the right actions. There are both cognitive qualities and incentive aspects to coordination problems. For example, the problem of adapting to an unexpected event has the cognitive dimension of categorizing and interpreting the event, and it may also have the incentive dimension of avoiding that one of the parties to a contractual relation utilizes the unexpected contingency to effect a hold-up.

Many real-life coordination problems are likely to contain such a mix, and the various problems may to some extent be thought of as hierarchical.[31] As CALVERT [1992, 12] points out, the ongoing interactions of real life – for example, inside large firms – are not simple repeated games. There is unlikely to be an exact correspondence between players, strategies and outcomes in various repetitions of the game, and players are likely to have incomplete (or none at all) information about other players, previous plays, etc. In this situation, there is likely to be multiple equilibria, but, unfortunately, behavior that is appropriate for play in one equilibrium may be inappropriate for another equilibrium; equilibrium strategies are not interchangeable. The problem of selecting the right equilibrium is, in a sense, a higher-order coordination problem.

We may in an abstract way think of the activities of the firm's leaders as a matter of solving such higher-order coordination problems. They may do so by direct intervention or by influencing the formation of typifications that assist the coordination of actions and expectations. However, both incentive problems (see WILLIAMSON [1985, ch. 6]) and the dispersal of knowledge inside firms mean that the top manager's task is inherently rather circumscribed. It is mostly a matter of choosing the right interstices. To quote LACHMANN [1971, 13] again:

> "[T]he central problem of the institutional order hinges on the contrast between coherence and flexibility, between the necessarily durable nature of the institutional order as a whole and the requisite flexibility of the individual institution ... the relative immutability of some institutions is always a necessary prerequisite for the relative flexibility of the rest."

To combine relative immutability with "flexibility" optimally is indeed a central problem not only of the design of an institutional order, but certainly also of organization design (see also MARCH [1988]). For example, problem-solving capability (flexibility) may be supported by a shared understanding (relative immutability) of the nature of the businesses the firm is in, such as may happen when corporate mission and vision statement become not only "corporate" but also "personal".

---

[31] See also HAYEK [1973] for the idea that coordination problems and the institutions that solve them have a hierarchical character.

4.5. Economic Organization

Arguably, the main issues in the MEO are the issues of the existence, boundaries and internal organization of firms. We have seen that an Austrian perspective may have something to say, albeit on a very abstract level, about internal organization. But what about the remaining issues?

With respect to the issue of the existence of the firm, an Austrian perspective suggests casting this in terms of coordination in dynamic environments, for example, environments characterized by unforeseen contingencies.[32] Although much of the argument in favor of market turns precisely on the ability to adapt to unforeseen contingencies, there are certain types of activities that may be hard to coordinate via the market in the presence of unforeseen contingencies. As RICHARDSON [1960] suggested, markets often have difficulties handling emergent events in the context of complementary activities. Of course, on the abstract level, this has been a recurrent theme in the MEO (e.g. HART [1995]). However, here the problems are seen to stem from incentive conflicts; it is the mutual hold-up threat that is the problem. In contrast, Richardson held a coordination perspective: Under market relations and in the absence of communication (i.e., infinite communication costs) and forward markets, agents would not have a clue about how to coordinate their actions. Planning, for example, in the form of collusion, might handle the coordination problem.

Richardson's argument may be generalized to cover planning inside firms and positive (but finite) communication costs, so that firm organization may be a communication cost minimizing governance structure for certain types of transactions.[33] More generally, it may be suggested that firms can exercise a degree of "directedness" that is not in general available to markets (Foss [1997]). Although there are strong knowledge-related constraints on the type and amount of planning and intervention that top management can engage in, it still possesses the right to control adaptation to unforeseen contingencies, to delegate decision-making rights, to evaluate units, and to implement new strategies. All of this may be less costly to accomplish inside a firm because, as we have seen, firms can develop certain typifications or cognitive constructs that are shared among the firms' employees.

---

[32] LOASBY [1976, 134] long ago argued that we should in fact look to emergent events in order to find a rationale for the firm. "The firm exists", he explained, "because it is impossible to specify all actions, even contingent actions in advance; it embodies a very different policy to emergent events. Incomplete specification is its essential basis: For complete specification can be handled by the market". Unfortunately, Loasby did not make clear why markets cannot handle incomplete specification.

[33] See WERNERFELT [1997] for an attempt to explain the employment contract along such lines, and LANGLOIS AND ROBERTSON [1995] for an ambitious attempt to address economic organization issues in terms of how well firms handle change relative to markets.

With respect to the issue of the boundaries of the firm, intuitively, there is much in Austrian economics that is helpful for understanding this issue.[34] Thus, the very idea that knowledge is dispersed inside firms suggests that there are limits to the size of firms that turn on the costs of centralizing dispersed knowledge (see also COASE [1937], WILLIAMSON [1970]). Moreover, the idea that firms may be differentiated in terms of the dispersed knowledge they contain and the typifications and rules they develop to handle the attendant coordination problems has implications for the issue of the boundaries of the firm. For example, firm-specific knowledge implies the presence of communication costs between firms that may influence the make-or-buy decision (LANGLOIS AND ROBERTSON [1995], HALLWOOD [1997], FOSS [1999]).

Thus, Austrian ideas do have implications for economic organization, although these have only been sketched here in an extremely intuitive fashion. Moreover, Austrian ideas link up with established insights of both a mainstream and a not so mainstream character. The following section briefly surveys a few recent developments in the MEO that have a bearing on the issues that interest Austrians. Linking up with these recent developments may help Austrians address the issues of economic organization that their perspective naturally raises, such as: How do we model the knowledge-based determinants of economic organization? How can we make room for entrepreneurship in firms? How do incentives and the use of knowledge interact in firms? How should we model truly dispersed knowledge? What is the role of rules in firms and how should their emergence be modelled?

4.6. Austrian Economics, the Firm, and Recent Advances in the MEO

According to the line of reasoning pursued in this paper, it is possible to carve out a niche for a distinct Austrian perspective on economic organization. Table 1 maps alternative approaches within the MEO and suggests that the

Table 1
Mapping Alternative Approaches to the Theory of Economic Organization

| | | KNOWLEDGE | | |
		Symmetric	Asymmetric	Dispersed
COORDINATION	Incentive conflict	*The property rights approach*	*Principal/ agent theory*	*The Austrian theory of the firm*
	No incentive conflicts	*Arrow-Debreu contracting*	*Team theory*	

---

[34] Thus, ROTHBARD [1962] and KLEIN [1996] draw on MISES' [1949] analysis of economic calculation to argue that the firm's boundaries are partly determined by the increasing calculational problems it encounters as it internalizes more and more markets.

niche carved out for Austrian economics relates to the inclusion of (truly) dispersed knowledge.

Thus, what distinguishes an Austrian perspective is that it asks questions related to truly dispersed knowledge that have not so far been comprehensively addressed in the MEO, even if they may not have been entirely neglected (e.g., DEMSETZ [1988], KREPS [1990], JENSEN AND MECKLING [1992], MINKLER [1993], AGHION AND TIROLE [1997], DEKEL, LIPMAN AND RUSTICHINI [1997], WERNERFELT [1997]). Now, Austrian economists may be better at asking questions than at providing answers – at least of the sort that will satisfy the mainstream economic theorist. Austrians may not care much about this, invoking their own standards of scientific excellence. However, there seems to be an opportunity for Austrians in linking up with some recent developments in the MEO, because these have begun treating issues that are close, if not identical, to key Austrian ideas.[35]

For example, AGHION AND TIROLE [1997] argue that real authority (effective control over decisions) in a firm depends on the structure of information existing in that firm, which in turn is determined by the exercise of formal authority (the formal right to decide). If agents obtain more real authority, their initiative is promoted (consistent with HAYEK [1945] and KIRZNER [1973]), but there is also an agency problem stemming from the principal's loss of control. There is a similar thrust to JENSEN AND MECKLING's [1992] analysis of the optimal co-location of knowledge and decision rights, which, they argue, is determined by the trade-off between effective use of dispersed knowledge and the agency problem. Thus, these contributions go a long way towards examining the interplay between knowledge and incentive problems in firms.[36]

The team-theory tradition initiated by MARSCHAK AND RADNER [1972] goes some way to represent the problem of communication when it is necessary to make use of dispersed knowledge and yet some coordination of decision-makers is required (RADNER [1993]). Thus, BOLTON AND DEWATRIPONT [1994] model the firm using the idea of an information network in which each agent handles a particular type of information, and the different types of information are aggregated through the network. When the benefits to specializing outweigh the costs of communication, teams (firms) arise. Much of Aoki's (e.g., AOKI [1990a], [1990b]) and Casson's (e.g., CASSON [1994]) work also belong to the small sub-group of contributions to the MEO in which

---

[35] Die-hard Austrians may argue that this work is still mainstream in its nature, because it of its predominant emphasis on coordinated states and optimizing behavior. And they are right, but the point here is that, in spite of the shared emphasis on optimization, etc., some mainstream work is surely closer to Austrian ideas than other mainstream work.

[36] However, the only contribution within the agency framework known to this author that grapples with truly dispersed knowledge (sheer ignorance) is MINKLER [1993].

incentive conflicts are suppressed, and knowledge considerations take center stage.[37] This kind of work clearly helps addressing the Austrian issue of how to optimally handle dispersed knowledge in an organization.

However, there are many questions that the Austrian perspective raises which are not dealt with by the MEO. Notably, how should truly dispersed knowledge be modelled? The complete contracting paradigm seems to be inadequate for handling this, particularly if neither the principal nor the agent fully know the latter's action set *ex ante*. In that case, both may be surprised *ex post*, and some flexibility in the form of contractual incompleteness may be rational. In the market, entrepreneurial processes of discovery, stimulated by the lure of pure arbitrage opportunities, tend to eliminate pockets of ignorance (KIRZNER [1997]). How do firms stimulate similar discovery processes? May incentives in firms also stimulate entrepreneurial processes of discovery (SAUTET [1999])? If so, how are such incentive best designed? Indeed, what is the meaning of efficiency in the presence of truly dispersed knowledge?

Firm-specific conventions and communication codes and the like also reduce the coordination problems stemming from dispersed knowledge, just as the rules of just conduct that characterize "the great society" do (HAYEK [1973]). How should we model the emergence of these conventions and codes?

Of course, we have partial answers to such questions. For example, the emergence of firm-specific conventions and norms may be modelled as iterated coordination games. And although monitoring is likely to be inefficient in general as a solution to principal-agent problems involving ignorance, profit-sharing may be one way of making a less ignorant agent work in the interests of a more ignorant principal (MINKLER [1993]). But there is a long way to go before the MEO will fully come to grips with the issues raised by Austrian insights into the dispersal of knowledge.

5. Conclusion

"If I have ... shown not only that the answer to this question [of how knowledge is coordinated] is not obvious but that occasionally we do not quite know what it is, I have succeeded in my purpose." (HAYEK [1937, 56]).

The aim of this paper has been to apply a well-known Austrian theme – that of dispersed knowledge – to a somewhat unusual context, namely firm organization and theories thereof. I have argued that much of the MEO can be criticized by means of much the same arguments that were employed by HAYEK [1937], [1945], [1946] in his classic critique of economics. Thus, truly dispersed knowledge is suppressed in the MEO.

---

[37] AOKI AND DORE [1994] is a fascinating account of how in practice Japanese firms handle knowledge dispersal problems.

From a model-building point of view, it may be claimed that there are good reasons for suppressing dispersed knowledge and other Austrian themes because we are dealing here with phenomena which are difficult to model. All who have invested resources in familiarizing themselves with contract theory will know how even seemingly simple interaction situations can lead to rather mind-boggling complications. Better then to forget about all the seeming additional mess introduced by the Austrians. In response, one may argue that Austrian issues, such as dispersed knowledge, entrepreneurship and emergent rules, in fact may be formally modelled (e.g., LITTLECHILD AND OWEN [1980]). Hence the problem is not that they cannot be modeled; rather it is that most modern economists of organization follow a methodological convention that dictates a very specific and arguably narrow modeling heuristic – that literally all issues of economic organization must be cast in the incentive-conflict mold – to the exclusion of alternative modeling heuristics. However, I have suggested that economists of organization may be gradually transcending this narrow modeling heuristic. There are signs of an increasing interest in issues of communication, organizational codes, unforeseen contingencies, etc. Perhaps in this way Austrian insights may make their way back into the MEO.

References

AGHION, P. AND J. TIROLE [1997], "Formal and Real Authority in Organization", *Journal of Political Economy*, 105, 1–29.
AOKI, M. [1990a], "Toward an Economic Model of the Japanese Firm", *Journal of Economic Literature*, 28, 1–27.
– – [1990b], "The Participatory Generation of Information Rents and the Theory of the Firm", pp. 26–52 in: M. Aoki, B. Gustaffson and O. E. Williamson, (eds.), *The Firm as a Nexus of Treaties*, Sage: London.
– – AND R. DORE [1994], *The Japanese Firm: The Sources of its Competitive Strength*, Oxford University Press:. Oxford.
BARTLETT, C. AND S. GHOSHAL [1989], *Managing Across Borders: The Transnational Solution*, Hutchinson: London.
BINMORE, K. [1991], *Essays on the Foundation of Game Theory*, Blackwell: Oxford.
BOETTKE, P. [1994], *The Elgar Companion to Austrian Economics*, Edward Elgar: Aldershot.
BOLTON, P. AND M. DEWATRIPONT [1994], "The Firm as a Communication Network", *Quarterly Journal of Economics*, 115, 809–839.
BUTOS, W. N. AND R. G. KOPPL [1997]. "The Varieties of Subjectivism: Keynes and Hayek on Expectations", *History of Political Economy*, 29, 327–59.
CALVERT, R. L. [1992], "Leadership and its Basis in Problems of Social Coordination", *International Political Science Review*, 13, 7–24.
CASSON, M. [1994], "Why Are Firms Hierarchical?", *Journal of the Economics of Business*, 1, 47–76.
CHANDLER, A. D. [1962], *Strategy and Structure*, MIT Press: Cambridge, MA.
CHOI, Y. B. [1993], *Paradigms and Conventions*, Michigan University Press: Ann Arbor.
COASE, R. H. [1937], "The Nature of the Firm", *Economica* (N.S.), 4, 386–405.
COLMAN, A. M. AND M. BACHARACH [1999], "Pay-Off Dominance and the Stackelberg Heuristic", *Theory and Decision*, forthcoming.

COWEN, T. AND D. PARKER [1997], *Markets in the Firm: A Market Process Approach to Management*, The Institute of Economic Affairs: London.

CRAWFORD, V. P. AND H. HALLER [1990], "Learning How to Cooperate: Optimal Play in Repeated Coordination Games", *Econometrica*, 58, 571–595.

CREMER, J. [1990], "Common Knowledge and the Coordination of Economic Activities", pp. 53–76 in: M. Aoki, B. Gustafsson and O. E. Williamson (eds.), *The Firm as a Nexus of Treaties*, Sage: London.

DEKEL, E. AND F. GUL [1997], "Rationality and Knowledge in Game Theory", in: D. M. Kreps and K. Wallice (eds.), *Advances in Economics and Econometrics*, Cambridge University Press: Cambridge, MA.

– –, LIPMAN, B. L. AND A. RUSTICHINI [1998], "Recent Developments in Modeling Unforeseen Contingencies", *European Economic Review*, 42, 523–542.

DEMSETZ, H. [1988], "The Theory of the Firm Revisited", *Journal of Law, Economics, and Organization*, 4, 141–161.

DENZAU, A. T. AND D. C. NORTH [1994], "Shared Mental Models: Ideologies and Institutions", *Kyklos*, 47, 3–31.

DOSI, G. AND L. MARENGO [1994], "Some Elements of an Evolutionary Theory of Organizational Competences", pp. 157–178 in: R. W. Englander (ed.), *Evolutionary Concepts in Contemporary Economics*, University of Michigan Press: Ann Arbor.

DOW, G. K. [1990], "The Organization as an Adaptive Network", *Journal of Economic Behavior and Organization*, 14, 159–185.

FOSS, K. [1999], "Economic Organization and the Accumulation of Rent-Yielding Assets", in: N. J. Foss and P. Robertson (eds.), *Resources, Technology, and Strategy*, Routledge: London, forthcoming.

FOSS, N. J. [1997]. "On the Rationales of Corporate Headquarters", *Industrial and Corporate Change*, 6, 313–339.

FURUBOTN, E. AND R. RICHTER [1997], *Institutions and Economic Theory: The Contribution of the New Institutional Economics*, The University of Michigan Press: Ann Arbor.

GEANAKOPLOS, J. [1989], "Game Theory Without Partitions", Yale Cowles Foundation Discussion Paper #914, Yale University.

GHOSHAL, S., MORAN P. AND L. ALMEIDA-COSTA [1995], "The Essence of the Megacorporation: Shared Context, not Structural Hierarchy", *Journal of Institutional and Theoretical Economics*, 151, 748–759.

GROSSMAN, S. AND O. HART [1986], "The Costs and Benefits of Ownership: A Theory of Lateral and Vertical Integration", *Journal of Political Economy*, 94, 691–719.

GROVES, T. AND M. LOEB [1979], "Incentives in Divisionalized Firms", *Management Science*, 25, 221–230.

GUESNERIE, R. [1992], "An Exploration of the Eductive Justifications of the Rational-Expectations Hypothesis", *American Economic Review*, 82, 1254–1278.

HALAL, W. E., GERANMAYEH A. AND J. POURDEHNAD (eds.) [1993], *Internal Markets: Bringing the Power of Free Enterprise INSIDE Your Organization*, John Wiley: New York.

HALLWOOD, P. [1997], "Competencies as Private Information: An Efficient Capital Asst Pricing Theory of the Firm", *Journal of Institutional and Theoretical Economics*, 153, 532–544.

HART, O. D. [1995], *Firms, Contracts, and Financial Structure*, Oxford University Press: Oxford.

– – AND J. MOORE [1990], "Property Rights and the Theory of the Firm", *Journal of Political Economy*, 98, 1119–1158.

HAYEK, F. A. v. [1937/1948], "Economics and Knowledge", pp. 933–956 in: F. A. v. Hayek (ed.), *Individualism and Economic Order*, University of Chicago Press: Chicago.

–– [1944], *The Road to Serfdom*, Routledge and Kegan Paul: London.
–– [1945/1948], "The Use of Knowledge in Society", pp. 77–91 in: F. A. v. Hayek
   (ed.), *Individualism and Economic Order*, University of Chicago Press: Chicago.
–– [1946/1948], "The Meaning of Competition", pp. 92–106 in: F. A. v. Hayek (ed.),
   Individualism and Economic Order, University of Chicago Press: Chicago.
–– [1948], *Individualism and Economic Order*, University of Chicago Press: Chicago.
–– [1952/1979], *The Counter-Revolution of Science*, ed. Liberty Press: Indianapolis.
–– [1973], *Law, Legislation, and Liberty, Vol. 1: Rules and Order*, University of
   Chicago Press: Chicago.
–– [1975/1996], "The Pretence of Knowledge", pp. 442–451 in: M. D. Lamberton
   (ed.), *The Economics of Communication and Information*, Elgar: Cheltenham.
HERMALIN, B. E. [1998], "Toward an Economic Theory of Leadership: Leading by
   Example", *American Economic Review*, 88, 1188–1206.
HOLMSTRÖM, B. AND J. ROBERTS [1998], "The Boundaries of the Firm Revisited",
   Journal of Economic Perspectives, 12, 73–94.
HURWICZ, L. [1986], "On Informationally Decentralized Systems", pp. 297–336 in:
   C. B. McGuire and R. Radner (eds.), *Decision and Organization*, 2nd ed.,
   University of Minnesota Press: Minnesota.
HUYCK, J. v., R. BATTALIO, AND R. BEIL [1990], "Tacit Coordination Games, Strategic
   Uncertainty, and Coordination Failure", *American Economic Review*, 80, 234–
   248.
JENSEN, M. C. AND W. H. MECKLING [1992], "Specific and General Knowledge and
   Organizational Structure", pp. 251–274 in: L. Werin and H. Wijkander (eds.)
   Contract Economics, Blackwell: Oxford.
KIRZNER, I. M. [1973], *Entrepreneurship and Competition*, University of Chicago Press:
   Chicago.
–– [1992], *The Meaning of the Market Process*, Routledge: London.
–– [1997], "Entrepreneurial Discovery and the Competitive Market Process: An
   Austrian Approach", *Journal of Economic Literature*, 35, 60–85.
KLEIN, D. B. [1997], "Convention, Social Order, and the Two Coordinations",
   Constitutional Political Economy, 8, 319–335.
KLEIN, P. [1996], "Economic Calculation and the Limits of Organization", *Review of
   Austrian Economics*, 9, 3–28.
KREPS, D. M. [1990], "Corporate Culture and Economic Theory", pp. 90–143 in: J. Alt
   and K. Shepsle (eds.), *Perspectives on Positive Political Economy*, Cambridge
   University Press: Cambridge, MA.
–– [1996], "Markets and Hierarchies and (Mathematical) Economic Theory",
   Industrial and Corporate Change, 5, 561–595.
LACHMANN, L. M. [1971], *The Legacy of Max Weber*, Heineman: London.
–– [1978], *Capital, Expectations, and the Market Process*, Sheed Andrews and
   McNeel: Kansas City.
LANGLOIS, R. N. [1986], "Coherence and Flexibility: Social Institutions in a World of
   Radical Uncertainty", pp. 171–181 in: I. M. Kirzner (ed.), *Subjectivism, Intelligi-
   bility, and Economic Understanding: Essays in Honor of Ludwig M. Lachmann*,
   Macmillan: London.
–– [1995], "Do Firms Plan?", *Constitutional Political Economy*, 6, 247–261.
–– AND FOSS, N. J. [1999], "Capabilities and Governance: The Rebirth of Production
   in the Theory of Economic Organization", *Kyklos*, forthcoming.
–– AND P. L. ROBERTSON [1995], *Firms, Markets, and Economic Change: A Dynamic
   Theory of Business Institutions*, Routledge: London.
LAVOIE, D. [1985], *Rivalry and Central Planning*, Cambridge University Press:
   Cambridge, MA.
LEWIN, P. [1999], *Capital in Disequilibrium*, Routledge: London.

LEWIS, T. R. AND D. E. M. SAPPINGTON [1993], "Ignorance in Agency Problems", *Journal of Economic Theory*, 61, 169–183.

LITTLECHILD, S. [1986], "Three Types of Market Process", pp. 27–39 in: Richard N. Langlois (ed.) *Economics as a Process: Essays in the New Institutional Economics*, Cambridge University Press: Cambridge, MA.

– – AND G. OWEN [1980], "An Austrian Model of the Entrepreneurial Market Process", *Journal of Economic Theory*, 23, 361–379.

LOASBY, B. J. [1976], *Choice, Complexity, and Ignorance*, Cambridge University Press: Cambridge.

– – [1991], *Equilibrium and Evolution*, Manchester Univesity Press: Manchester.

LUCE, R. D. AND H. RAIFFA [1957], *Games and Decisions*, John Wiley & Sons: New York.

MALMGREN, H. B. [1961], "Information, Expectations, and the Theory of the Firm", *Quarterly Journal of Economics*, 75, 399–421.

MARCH, J. G. [1988], *Decisions and Organizations*, Basil Blackwell: Oxford.

MARSCHAK, J. AND R. RADNER [1972], *The Economic Theory of Teams*, New Haven: Yale University Press.

MASKIN, E. AND J. TIROLE [1997], "Unforeseen Contingencies, Property Rights, and Incomplete Contracts", *Review of Economic Studies*, 66, 83–114.

– –, Y. QIAN AND CH. XU [1998], "Incentives, Information, and Organizational Form", working paper, Harvard University.

MENGER, C. [1871/1976], *Principles of Economics*, New York University Press: New York.

– – [1883/1985], *Investigations Into the Method of the Social Sciences with Special Reference to Economics*, New York University Press: New York.

MEYER, C. [1994], "How the Right Measures Help Teams Excel", *Harvard Business Review*, 95–103.

MINKLER, A. P. [1993], "Knowledge and Internal Organization", *Journal of Economic Behavior and Organization*, 21, 17–30.

MINTZBERG, H. [1994], *The Rise and Fall of Strategic Planning*, Prentice-Hall: New York.

MISES, L. v. [1949], *Human Action*, William Hodge: London.

MOORE, J. [1992], "Comment", in: H. Wijkander and L. Werin (eds.), *Contract Economics*, Blackwell: Oxford.

NONAKA, I, AND TAKEUCHI [1995], *The Knowledge-Creating Company*, Oxford University Press: Oxford.

O'DRISCOLL, G. P. AND M. RIZZO [1985], *The Economics of Time and Ignorance*, Blackwell: Oxford.

PELIKAN, P. [1989], "Evolution, Economic Competence and Corporate Control", *Journal of Economic Behavior and Organization*, 12, 279–303.

RADNER, R. [1993], "The Organization of Decentralized Information Processing", *Econometrica*, 61, 1109–1146.

RASMUSSEN, E. [1994], *Games and Information*, 2nd ed., Blackwell: Oxford.

RICHARDSON, G. B. [1960], *Information and Investment*, Oxford University Press: Oxford.

ROTHBARD, M. N. [1962], *Man, Economy, and State*, 2 Vols., Nash: Los Angeles.

SAUTET, F. [1999], *An Entrepreneurial Theory of the Firm*, Routledge: London, forthcoming.

– – and N. FOSS [1998], "The Organization of Large, Complex Firms: An Austrian Perspective", mimeo.

SCHELLING, T. [1960], *The Strategy of Conflict*, Harvard University Press: Cambridge, MA.

– – [1978], *Micromotives and Macrobehavior*, Norton: New York.

SCHLICHT, E. [1998], *On Custom in the Economy*, Clarendon Press: Oxford.

SCHOTTER, A. [1981], *The Economic Theory of Social Institutions*, Cambridge University Press: Cambridge, MA.
SEMLER, R. [1989], "Managing Without Managers", *Harvard Business Review*, 3, 76–84.
TIROLE, J. [1999], "Incomplete Contracts: Where Do We Stand?", *Econometrica*, forthcoming.
VANBERG, V. [1992], "Organizations as Constitutional System", *Constitutional Political Economy*, 3, 223–253.
VAUGHN, K. I. [1994], *Austrian Economics in America*, Cambridge University Press: Cambridge, MA.
WERNERFELT, B. [1994], "An Efficiency Criterion for Marketing Design", *Journal of Marketing Research*, 31, 462–470.
– – [1997], "On the Nature and Scope of the Firm: A Adjustment Cost Theory", *Journal of Business*, 70, 489–514.
WILLIAMSON, O. E. [1970], *Corporate Control and Business Behavior*, Englewood Cliffs: Prentice Hall.
– – [1985], *The Economic Institutions of Capitalism*, Free Press: New York.
– – [1996], *The Mechanisms of Governance*, Oxford University Press: Oxford.
WISEMAN, J. [1953], "Uncertainty, Costs and Collective Economic Planning", in: J. M. Buchanan and G. F. Thirlby (eds.) *LSE Essays on Cost*, Weidenfeld & Nicholson: London.

Nicolai J. Foss
Department of Industrial Economics and Strategy
Copenhagen Business School
Nansensgade 19, 6
1366 Copenhagen K
Denmark

[7]

Journal of Economic Methodology 7:3, 313–339 2000

Theoretical isolation in contract theory: suppressing margins and entrepreneurship

Kirsten Foss and Nicolai J. Foss

Abstract We discuss contract theory from a combined Austrian/new institutional view. In the latter view, the world is seen as shot through with ignorance and transaction costs, but, as a tendency, entrepreneurial activity responds to the problems caused by these. All modelling must critically reflect this. This ontological commitment is contrasted to various isolations characteristic of contract theory, specifically the modelling strategy of introducing often ad hoc and unexplained constraints that suppress margins and possibilities of entrepreneurial actions that would be open to real-world decision-makers. We illustrate this by means of, for example, the treatment of asymmetric information under complete contracting and the notion of control rights under incomplete contracting.

Keywords: contract theory, new institutional economics, Austrian economics, entrepreneurship

1 INTRODUCTION

In this paper, we shall develop a critique of the increasingly important body of modern economics that is commonly referred to as 'contract theory',[1] and which encompasses 'complete contract theory' (alias principal–agent theory) and 'incomplete contract theory' (alias 'the new property rights theory'). In the eyes of the profession at large, this field is arguably where the pioneer research in economic organization takes place. In some dimensions, contract theory is related to transaction cost economics (Williamson 1996), the nexus of contract approach (Alchian and Demsetz 1972), and other branches of new institutional economics. For example, there is a shared focus on various types of contracting problems, stemming from misaligned incentives, as the causes of different types of economic organization. Indeed, the initial motivation of one of the classic contributions of contract theory, Grossman and Hart (1986), appears to have been to cast the essential insights of Williamson (1985) in more mainstream terms, and the incomplete contracts approach that they founded is often seen as a formalization of '. . . the intuitions of transaction cost economics, as created by Coase and Williamson' (Salanié 1997). However, as we shall point out, contract economics is in a number dimensions at variance with new institutional economics.[2]

Journal of Economic Methodology ISSN 1350-178X print/ISSN 1469-9427 online © 2000 Taylor & Francis Ltd
http://www.tandf.co.uk/journals

In order to identify points of disagreement, we shall make use of the meta-theoretical framework on the role of 'theoretical isolation' that has been developed by Uskali Mäki in a string of publications (e.g. 1992, 1994) and applied to specific debates by Mäki (1999) himself and by Kyläheiko (1998). 'Isolation' broadly refers to items which are included or excluded in the attempt to comprehend economic reality, something that is accomplished by means of 'idealizing assumptions'. Mäki argues that isolation plays an important role in the dynamics of dispute and the progress of economics. Specifically, much of these dynamics revolve around charges that a given theory isolates too little, too much, or wrongly. Certainly, the critique of contract economics that we develop in this paper is based on an argument that contract theory isolates too much and sometimes wrongly. We shall therefore apply ideas on isolation *normatively*. Thus, like most economists, we do think there are proper and improper – or, to put in weaker terms, less problematic and more problematic – isolations in economic theorizing. However, we also recognize that justifiably criticizing the isolations of a given theory is a very thorny epistemological issue.

In order to find some criteria for criticizing contract theory for the isolations it adopts, and to help identifying these isolations as well, we rely in particular on insights from two perspectives that have both been argued[3] to be parts of new institutional economics. These are the (Austrian) entrepreneurial discovery perspective advanced by, in particular, Kirzner (1973, 1997), and the property rights perspective associated with, for example, Ronald Coase (1988), Alchian (1965), Demsetz (1964, 1967), Cheung (1969a, b, 1983), and Barzel (1997). To repeat, we rely on these perspectives because they are particularly helpful for identifying those isolations used in contract theory that we consider particularly problematic.[4]

We shall argue that the basic problem with contract theory is that in some respects it goes too far with respect to what agents can do, while in other respects it does not go sufficiently far. To put it less mysteriously, contract theorists consistently adopt an 'on–off' approach to theoretical isolation in which, for example, agents are either fully informed about some variable or not informed at all, property rights are either perfectly enforced or not enforced at all, actions are either fully verifiable or not verifiable at all, etc. Thus, as a matter of modelling convention extreme values are chosen for many choice variables, because some (usually unspecified) information and/or transaction costs are supposed to prohibit agents from choosing certain actions. These particular isolations mean that a number of *margins* that would be relevant to real-world decision-makers are *suppressed*, and agents are not allowed to exercise *entrepreneurship* to somehow circumvent the interaction problems caused by the suppression of margins. Although it will sometimes be legitimate to suppress margins, making these particular isolations without consulting the real world in order to understand whether the suppressed margins may be important to understanding the phenomenon under consideration will result in arbitrary models (Coase 1988).

Setting aside for the moment any possible defences of the modelling strategy of contract theorists, there are two sets of critical reactions to these isolations, both turning on the issues of suppressing margins and entrepreneurship. One reaction is to criticize contract theory on the ground that it illegitimately abstracts from supposed *essential* features of the social world, such as the inherent propensity of agents to discover new opportunities for gain (e.g. Kirzner 1973) or the generality of bounded rationality (Furubotn and Richter 1997; Brousseau and Fares 1998). This may be called an 'ontological critique', since it takes the exclusion by means of idealizing assumptions of essential features of reality to be inexcusable.

Although we shall present such an argument, we realize that it may be too 'metaphysical' and too much of a conversation-stopper to have much 'bite'. We therefore also argue that taking seriously the inherent propensity of agents to discover new opportunities for gain is likely to substantially change some important conclusions derived from contract theory models. In other words, this is a critical reaction that relates more to what comes out of these models than to how well they capture the structure of the world. Thus, we discuss and invoke both ontological and more model specific criteria for criticizing the isolations that suppress margins and entrepreneurship.

The paper is organized as follows. We begin by briefly discussing what we take to be a shared view of the essence of the economy, and an ontological commitment shared by Austrians and new institutionalist economists. The shared view is that although the economy is shot through with ignorance and transaction costs, agents will nevertheless as a tendency evolve institutional means to cope with these problems. Thus, ignorance, transaction costs, bounded rationality, and learning constitute the essence of the economic problem. The ontological commitment is that these essential features should be prominently featured in modelling (section 2). We contrast this view with the modelling strategy – characteristic of not only contract theory but of much of modern formal economics – of arbitrarily introducing constraints that suppress the margins over which agents may optimize (section 3), a procedure that is typical of so-called 'no-fat MIT style theory' (section 4). Modern contract theory is an important instance of this modelling strategy (section 5). As a general matter, the coordination problem is here narrowed to only concern the alignment of incentives in extremely stylized non-cooperative game theory settings. In these settings, many of the margins that would be relevant to real-world decision-makers are suppressed, and agents are not allowed to evolve alternative institutional solutions that can cope with the problems caused by these suppressed margins. We illustrate this by means of the treatment of asymmetric information under complete contracting and the notion of control rights under incompete contracting (section 6). Section 7 concludes.

2 ONTOLOGICAL COMMITMENTS IN ECONOMIC MODELLING

In the view of Knight (1921) – the founder of the theory of the firm – firm organization, profit, and the entrepreneur are closely related phenomena. As he saw it, they arise as, respectively, an embodiment, a result and a cause of commercial experimentation – a view that he explicitly founded on an ontological view of the world as essentially open-ended and non-deterministic (1921: chapter 7). Few economists have followed Knight in linking together the firm, profit, and entrepreneurship (not to mention his philosophical starting points).[5] Thus, entrepreneurship is not stressed in the modern economics of organization in general, and certainly not in contract theory. As we see it, this difference reflects different ontological commitments.

Consider the basic view of the economy adopted by both Austrian (von Hayek 1937, von Mises 1949, Kirzner 1973) and new institutionalist (Coase 1988; Furubotn and Richter 1998; Williamson 1998) writers. They stress that the economy is at any moment characterized by substantial ignorance and shot through with transaction costs, but that entrepreneurial activity, prompted by the lure of profit, is continuosly closing pockets of ignorance in the market, devising ways of overcoming transaction difficulties and reducing the bounds on rationality.[6] A formal contract theorist may certainly also accept such an ontology. The difference rather lies in the sort of commitments with respect to how economic modelling should be carried out that is believed to flow from such an ontology, that is, which constraints ontology places on isolation. On this issue, many positions are possible, and the history of economics witnesses many different ontological commitments (see also Foss 1994). Different extremes are defined by Shackle (1972), who came close to denying the possibility of virtually any modelling for the reason that such modelling would inherently misrepresent the nature of human choice, and Debreu (1959: x), who from a mathematical formalist point of view stressed that his theory be '. . . logically entirely disconnected from its interpretations'. Much of the long debate on the reality of assumptions also reflects different ontological commitments.

Most economists steer a course between these extremes: they stress both the need for (formal) modelling, and the need for their theories and models to possess some sort of correspondence to economic reality. However, many possibilities of disagreement still exist, and many debates that go beyond checking the logical consistency of a given model often relate to how much of the contact to reality is sacrificed by the choice of a given set of isolations. However, criteria for putting forward justified critique of the isolations of a given theory or model do not often appear to be explicitly stated by debating contemporary economists. What are permissible and not permissible isolations are arguably partly dictated by schools of thought (Mäki 1992), presumably often in a tacit manner. They are part of the 'positive heuristic' of a research tradition. Of course, this does not immunize them from critique. Moreover, one may still argue that it is in fact possible to find (non-trivial) criteria of what are good and what are bad isolations that are independent of one's adherence to a certain research tradition.

One such criterion was suggested by Morgenstern. He (1964; quoted in Furubotn and Richter 1997: 444) acknowledged that isolations are necessary in all theorizing, but added that '. . . [r]adical simplifications are allowable in science so long as they do not go against the essence of the given problem'. Thus, a given isolation should be considered '. . . faulty if it bypasses a fundamental feature of economic reality'. Even accepting Morgenstern's criteria that isolations should not discard the 'essence of the given problem' and 'a fundamental feature of economic reality' leaves a wide margin of choice, for disagreements may certainly exist with respect to what are the true 'essences' or 'fundamental features'. For example, Coase's (1988) famous criticism of 'blackboard economics' is founded on the position that '[r]ealism in assumptions forces us to analyze the world that exists, not some imaginary world that does not' (Coase 1981: 18) – a statement that surely is open to a great deal of interpretation (see Mäki 1998). Moreover, we may be back to the problem that what is deemed essential, etc. depends on a given research tradition.

The least one should do in this situation is to make explicit one's conception of what are essential and fundamental features that economic modelling should not bypass. We here adopt what we earlier in this section characterized as a shared Austrian and new institutionalist ontology. Moreover, like Austrian and new institutionalist writers we believe that this ontology places certain constraints on economic modelling that are typically more restrictive than the constraints imposed by modelling by, for example, a practitioner of modern contract theory. Thus, there are certain things that economic modellers should not do.

A possible starting point lies in Coase's and various Austrians' (von Hayek 1948, von Mises 1949) insistence that the analysis of 'imaginary worlds' can have only a very limited role, an insistence that appears to be followed by practicising new institutionalists and Austrians (e.g. Demsetz 1969, Kirzner 1973, Williamson 1996, Furubotn and Richter 1997). Extreme models and arguments (e.g. competitive equilibrium, the Coase theorem) do have a role, but this role is restricted to that of an *argumentum a contrario*, that is, they show the conditions that must obtain, for example, for money not to exist, for the law to have no allocative consequences, etc. (Mises 1949, Coase 1988). In itself, this may imply that new institutionalist economists tend to impose a stronger ontological commitment on themselves than many formal economists do. A clear instance of this is Furubotn and Richter's (1997: 446) claim that once the ideas of bounded rationality and transaction costs are accepted, one must recognize that:

> . . . [T]ransaction costs must appear *everywhere* in the system because of the nature of the individuals making decisions . . . Thus, once we reject

the notion of the omniscient decision maker who is 'completely rational', the economic model undergoes a basic transformation.

Thus, according to Furubotn and Richter, one cannot have agents that are only boundedly rational some of the time or with respect to only a few variables or parameters, because the '*nature* of the individuals making decisions' is such that agents are always – albeit to a varying extent – boundedly rational, and economic theorizing should reflect this.[7]

This argument is, in a sense, a call for *symmetry* with respect to what is assumed about the rationality of agents and the consequences (i.e. transaction costs) of this. We may call this 'weak symmetry' in the sense that it is not required that agents are completely homogeneous with respect to, for example, their decision rules, risk preferences, beliefs, expectations, etc. (which would be 'strong symmetry').[8] Rather, agents are only assumed to be homogeneous in the very general sense of all being boundedly rational, and this bounded rationality will have different behavioural implications across agents. In a wider sense, it is a warning against the widespread procedure in modern economics of arbitrarily assuming that certain margins are completely closed to agents while others are completely open (i.e. invoking what we may call 'strong asymmetry'). Just as agents are not omniscient, they are not completely stupid either. Thus, one should be careful with assumptions that, for example, an agent is completely ignorant with respect to a certain variable, because margins are seldom completely closed and this may have a bearing on the phenomenon that one scrutinizes.

This boils down to our first new institutionalist/Austrian criterion for proper isolation in economics: in economic modelling, one should as a minimum give strong reasons for closing certain margins that may be open to real world decision makers in comparable situations, where these margins may be critical to the understanding of the phenomenon. Margins may be closed to the extent that they do not add to the understanding of the phenomenon.[9]

It is pertinent here to also consider an instance of Austrian economics, namely the entrepreneurial discovery perspective developed by Kirzner (1973, 1997). In Kirzner's view, the entrepreneur is an agent who by exercising alertness '. . . grasps the opportunities for pure entrepreneurial profit created by temporary absence of full adjustment' (1997: 69). According to Kirzner (1973), the alert entrepreneur should be contrasted with the Robbinsian maximizer of conventional neoclassical economics who acts in a mechanical fashion within a given means-ends structure. In contrast, the entrepreneur sets up new means-ends structures. However, according to Kirzner, this ability to discover and grasp hitherto unnoticed opportunities for profit is not limited to people with special cognitive qualities; it is a quite general aspect of human action. Thus, people in fact have a tendency to discover those margins on which they can optimize.[10] Now, what does this imply for economic modelling?

It is tempting to interpret Kirzner's theory of entrepreneurship as a denial of the very possibility of economic modelling, except, perhaps, of the most abstract kind (as Misesian praxeology). All formal modelling imposes some constraints at some level in the model; otherwise, modelling is pointless. Kirzner's theory, however, may be taken to imply that we cannot be sure that any constraint that we have put into our model will not be contested by some alert entrepreneur, as it were. If all of economics should reflect the entrepreneurial quality of alertness, but it is impossible to (formally) model entrepreneurship, then formal modelling would appear to be excluded in economics.

However, another – and, we believe, more correct – interpretation is possible. More specifically, we read Kirzner's story as a methodological imperative that instructs the modelling economist to be alert to the possibility that the type and severity of the constraints he introduces in his modelling exercises may be utterly implausible in the face of the general quality of entrepreneurial alertness. It is a warning that the predictions of a model may not be borne out in reality because of entrepreneurial processes of discovery that take account of facts that were not known to the modeller. Thus, to use a pertinent example, a contract theorist shouldn't dogmatically insist there is one and only one solution, namely vertical integration, to bilateral trading relations involving complementary assets (cf. Hart 1995), since real world alert agents/entrepreneurs may come up with solutions that are as, or more, efficient than vertical integration (Aghion *et al.* 1994; Nöldeke and Schmidt 1995).[11] In general, there are often many possible contractual and institutional arrangements that may remedy interaction problems – some of which may be completely unknown to the modelling economist. In contrast, in contract theory there is often a one-to-one correspondence between problems and solutions in the sense that there is one, and only one, solution to a given interaction problem. Of course, this is a matter of suppressing so many margins that only one solution is possible. However, this also makes the application of the model to real world situations, where many solutions are often possible, problematic.

These considerations relate to the application and interpretation of economic models. Thus, one may interpret the instruction that entrepreneurship should be taken seriously as meaning that in constructing his economic model, the modeller should ask whether a certain constraint of the model is a plausible constraint on behavior, considering that entrepreneurship, in the sense of agents discovering new opportunities, is a quite prevalent phenomenon.[12]

This boils down to our second new institutionalist/Austrian criterion for proper isolation in economics: in economic theorizing, one should not suppress entrepreneurship when it may be critical to the understanding of the phenomenon.[13]

The criterion is not unproblematic. Thus, some may question whether entrepreneurship can really be included in a model. We do think that entrepreneurship can in fact be included in formal models (cf. also Littlechild 1986). For example, it is certainly possible to model situations where agents are initially ignorant (although the modeller isn't) but gradually discovers new facts (as in Littlechild 1979). However, our criterion is primarily directed towards the application and interpretation of models – and here it should be remembered that entrepreneurs discover things that may not have been known to the modeller, thus overturning the conclusions of the model.

In order to make more concrete what we take to be distinctive of new institutionalist and Austrian perspectives on what constitutes (il)legimitate isolation in economics, it may be helpful to provide a few examples of disputes that revolved around isolation and in which Austrian and new institutionalist economists were involved.

3 SUPPRESSING MARGINS AND ENTREPRENEURSHIP: EXAMPLES AND CLARIFICATION

Perhaps the best known example of the isolation procedures of suppressing margins and entrepreneurship is Keynesianism of the Hicks–Hansen–Modigliani type (which was once referred to as 'the neoclassical synthesis'). This type of macroeconomic modelling was designed to produce Keynesian results by introducing spanners in the works of an otherwise perfect 'classical' model. This was accomplished by assuming that money wages were rigid in the downwards direction (Leijonhufvud 1968). In fact, in the reading of Hutt (1939), Keynes produced his results by simply assuming away all optimizing and entrepreneurial behaviour on specific markets, namely labour markets. Similar charges were much later made against Keynesian economics by new classical economists. In the context of macroeconomic modelling they invoked the general heuristic principle of banishing as far as possible 'free parameters', that is, constraints or assumptions that had no obvious foundation in choice theory (Lucas 1981, 1987).

Other well-known examples concern the (mis)uses in economics of the public good nature of lighthouses, the externalities involved in decentralized production of apples and honey, and the collective goods of fisheries and other non-exclusive resources (Cowen 1988). For example, the traditional categorization in economics of lighthouses as pure public goods arguably stems from an unexamined assumption that the enforcement of property rights for this particular type of good would be prohibitively costly. In contrast, careful consideration of the full set of options available to suppliers of lighthouse services revealed that sufficiently low-cost means of enforcing (at least a significant subset of) the relevant property rights did in fact exist – and were historically employed by alert entrepreneurs (Coase 1988). The morale of this story is the by now well-known point that what are public goods, etc. is dependent upon the structure of property rights (Demsetz 1964, Cowen 1985) – but that structure is to a large extent defined by alert entrepreneurs through contractual innovations, innovations in enforcement methods, etc. Therefore, neglecting such entrepreneurship easily leads to erroneous conclusions. As Cheung (1969a: 65) observed, economists have had a tendency to take '. . .

assertions of fact for granted, accepting claims of deficient contractual arrangements without demanding evidence'.

Having provided some examples of how economists have made problematic theoretical isolations by suppressing margins and suppressing entrepreneurship, we shall now make a more careful attempt to clarify the meanings of these procedures. There are subtle differences between the two.[14] However, both refer to different ways of suppressing some costs and benefits that might be relevant to real-world decision makers, carried out for the purpose of making modelling tractable and typically also of producing certain outcomes from the model.

The procedure of 'suppressing margins' means that as part of modelling the constraints that the agent faces, the modeller stipulates (not necessarily giving any reasons) that the agent is prohibited from knowing or doing certain things which might not be inaccessible to real world decision makers. This is typically accomplished by choosing extreme values for some variables. For example, as the concept of asymmetric information is normally used in information economics, it means that the costs on the part of non-informed agents of obtaining information are effectively infinite – which they typically wouldn't be to real-world decision-makers. This means that some actions – such as acquiring more information about the actions of the agents – are prohibited *ex ante*, and a margin (how much information to gather?) that would otherwise be relevant to real-world decision-makers is suppressed. However, in contrast, the agent is informed, and typically perfectly informed (usually in a common knowledge sense), about all other variables, and is allowed to take all the remaining margins (which are all supposed to have been discovered already) fully into account.

Now, suppressing margins is not illegitimate per se; most economists engage in that practice.[15] For example, in his famous 'lemons' paper Akerlof (1970) clearly suppresses margins by assuming that buyers are completely prohibited from knowing the quality of any specific car. However, this doesn't mean that his story stops there. Actually, he points out that the very reason for conducting the analysis is to find out what may be the reason for *alternative* institutional solutions – and not just one specific solution – to the adverse selection problem, such as warranties, brand names and the like. Thus, one may suppress margins, provided room is left for the agents to invent around the problems caused by suppressed margins. As we see it, this open-end approach is characteristic of the work of, for example, Demsetz (1964, 1967), Cheung (1969a, b, 1983), and Barzel (1997). Margins are suppressed *in order to* understand how real-world agents may evolve various responses to interaction problems.

Not everybody takes such an approach. As we have seen, in macroeconomics and public policy debates, margins have been suppressed in order to justify certain solutions (i.e. some sort of public intervention) to presumed market failures, without inquiring into alternative institutional solutions.

Relatedly, modern contract theorists, such as Oliver Hart (1995), suppress margins in order to explain a *certain* institutional solution (such as a certain type of ownership pattern), without inquiring into alternative institutional solutions that may keep interaction problems at bay (e.g. alternative contractual solutions).[16] Per decision of the modeller, agents are not allowed to surpass the problems caused by suppressed margins by evolving new institutional solutions. This is an example of 'suppressing entrepreneurship'.

Whereas the suppression of margins refers to prohibiting the agent from knowing or doing certain things within a given interaction structure (typically by choosing extreme values for some variables), suppressing entrepreneurship rather refers to prohibiting the agents from going beyond given interaction structures in an attempt to remedy the problems caused by suppressed margins. Suppressing entrepreneurship implies that agents are not allowed to imagine and implement new institutional solutions to, for example, externality problems. Because of such restrictions, there may be value left in the public domain (Barzel 1997), that is to say, unexploited profit opportunities. However, agents are prohibited from capturing this value as a matter of modelling convention (or, lack of imagination on the part of the modelling economist). Entrepreneurship becomes suppressed.

4 THEORETICAL ISOLATION, MIT STYLE MODELLING, AND ITS PROBLEMS

4.1 Types of isolation

The procedures of 'suppressing margins and entrepreneurship' are particular instances of 'theoretical isolation', that is, the procedure under which '. . . a limited set of items is *assumed* to be isolated from the involvement or influence of the rest of the world' (Mäki 1999: 4, emphasis in original). As Mäki (1999) further clarifies, along one dimension theoretical isolation may be *vertical* (i.e. the particularities of items are abstracted away so that something resembling a universal emerges) and/or *horizontal* (i.e. isolation at a given level of abstraction). Along another dimension, it may be *internal* (i.e. the system is isolated from influences from within the system) and/or *external* (i.e. the system is isolated from items outside the system itself) (cf. also Bhaskar 1978).

Needless to say, all economic reasoning makes use of various types of isolations. For example, economists may apply partial equilibrium analysis (external isolation), suppress entrepreneurship (internal isolation), assume that contract drafting costs are zero (horisontal isolation), or claim that the essence of all economic organization is to align the incentives of the involved parties (vertical isolation). As these examples suggest, one isolates by *excluding*. What we have called 'suppressing margins' is a matter of exclusion; the analyst decides that for whatever reason, some margins are unimportant to the model and may be left out. Isolation may be brought about by 'idealizing assumptions' that explicitly mention an item, but choose extreme values for this item ($X = 0$ or $X =$ infinity or $X = 1$, depending on the scale). For example, isolation in economics often takes the form of working with 'on–off' models in which some variables are 'switched off' by assuming that their value is zero, while others are 'switched on'. Alternatively, isolation may be brought about by simply omitting an item without mentioning it (Mäki 1999). Isolation is clearly indispensable to economic analysis. Equally clearly, the sort of specific isolations that economists adopt are root causes of controversy in economics, as our earlier examples suggest. [17]

Although the idealizing assumptions involved in isolations are false statements about the world, they may be defended in different ways, often reflecting a mixture of ontological and more pragmatic considerations. For example, some isolations '. . . may be based on metaphysical considerations; they are made to exclude those aspects of the object that are expected to be ontically peripheral or inessential' (Mäki 1994: 153). Alternatively, isolations may be defended by pointing to the need for mathematical tractability. Conversely, specific isolations may be attacked on both ontological and pragmatic grounds; for example, it may be argued that a specific isolation excludes some ontically essential feature, or that it hasn't gone sufficiently far for the argument to be put in formal terms.

4.2 'No-Fat' MIT style theory

With respect to the issue of rationalizing and defending specific isolations, it is noteworthy that formal economists, including contract theorists, often view modelling that proceeds in formal, mathematical terms as realizing *both* the need for tractability *and* for capturing the essential aspects of a phenomenon. Eric Rasmussen (1994: 3) characterizes an influential instantiation of this approach as 'MIT-style theory', and explains that the:

> . . . heart of the approach is to discover the simplest assumptions needed to generate an interesting conclusion – the starkest, barest, model that has the desired result. This desired result is the answer to some relatively narrow question.

Thus, MIT style theorizing follows a two-step procedure, where the theorist first observes a stylized fact, and then finds a series of premises which together mathematically imply the observed stylized fact. As Camerer (1994: 208) observes, such '. . . [n]o-fat modelling with game theory has swept the economics profession', and contract theory is certainly no exception to this; it is in fact completely cast within the mold of MIT style theorizing. For example, the analyst observes some contracting practices and tailor-makes a game theoretic explanation that is as simple as possible. In practice this means that it involves numerous, often very far-reaching isolations that typically consist of making extreme idealizing assumptions with respect to the values of certain variables (e.g. $X = 0$ or $I = $ infinity). Such a 'stark and bare' model is usually a very stylized non-cooperative game theory model, where everything (information partitions, nature's move, etc.) is carefully laid down in the game's protocol. Modelling then means working 'backwards' from the *explanandum* phenomenon to its explaining causes in terms of such a 'stark and bare' model.

4.3 Problems with MIT style modelling

While MIT style theorizing is now arguably the dominant mode of discourse in formal economics, it is not completely uncontroversial (cf. also Camerer 1994). On the most obvious level, no-fat models only provide logically sufficient, and not necessary, premises for deriving an observed fact. Many other explanations may be possible. Closely related to this, explaining by means of no-fat models is, as it were, almost too easy, so that bad explanations are as easy to construct as good ones (Camerer 1994: 211).[18] Another well-known problem with game theoretic no-fat modelling is the sensibility of equilibria to a multitude of factors, such as information partitionings, the sequence of moves, the number of players and so on.

A somewhat different critique – more in line with the basic thrust of this paper – has to do with the character of the isolations that are *typically* performed in no-fat modelling. Although its proponents may argue that no-fat modelling is simply Occam's razor in operation, critics may counter that the liposuction sometimes goes too far, that is, the isolations *typically* involved in MIT style are simply too extreme.[19] Too much is excluded by means of extreme idealizing assumptions. Some of these objections bring us back to the discussion earlier in this section of how claims of what is essential (and inessential) influence theorizing.

Thus, it may be argued that because of their extreme idealizing assumptions, practitioners of MIT style theorizing exclude essential aspects of the economic problems facing real word decision-makers. For example, economists of more heterodox stripes – such as new institutionalists, evolutionary economists and Austrian economists – may balk at the idea that everything but for a few variables is common knowledge. From these perspectives, discovery, learning and coping with problems introduced by transaction costs constitute the essence of 'the economic problem'.

In our view, these differences reflect rival views of the complex interplay between reality and theorizing, rather than necessarily rival views of the nature of the world. Among other things, this involves different views of the starting points of theorizing in economics. Thus, practitioners of MIT style theorizing, including contract theorists, explicitly begin from extremely stylized settings, such as the full competitive model (Hart and Holmström 1987), and gradually introduce more and more relaxing assumptions. This 'de-isolation' typically proceeds in terms of the construction of a string of loosely connected models where each model highlights the effects of relaxing one or a very few assumptions (or of introducing a new explanatory variable), keeping everything else intact. Such an incremental change in the *explanans* is typically designed to allow the theorist to address a new *explanandum* phenomenon. [20]

In the following sections, we shall see how a very influential group of contemporary economists have started from an extreme model (competitive equilibrium), applied the MIT modelling style, and have produced models that are characterized by isolations that amount to suppressing margins and entrepreneurship.

5 CONTRACT THEORY

Contract theory is only a subset, albeit a large and significant one, of the modern economics of organization, which also includes, for example, transaction cost economics. However, because of the heterogeneity of the various streams in the modern economics of organization, we here concentrate on the relatively homogenous subset of contract theory.

Common to contract theories is that they are partial equilibrium models, examine small-scale interaction, focus on (explicit and implicit) contracting relations, use non-cooperative game theory, assume Bayesian behaviour, and use perfect Bayesian equilibria as the relevant solution concept. Although, contract theories are partial equilibrium theories, and although they emphasize bilateral aspects of transactions, they have a foundation in general equilibrium theory (and perhaps in its mechanism design ramifications), both historically and conceptually (Guesnerie 1992). In a sense, the Arrow–Debreu model is a contractual model with the specific property that it demonstrates the conditions that must obtain for all problems of organization to be trivial. The recognition in the 1960s that all Arrow–Debreu states of nature may not be observable (rather, verifiable) formed the basis for work on moral hazard (hence, incentive contracts), and the situation in which states of nature are known to agents, but not to the auctioneer, formed the basis for work on adverse selection (hence, revealing contracts).

It is therefore not surprising that modern contract theorists very explicitly see their work as '. . . a natural way to enrich and amend the idealized competitive model in an attempt to fit the evidence better' (Hart and Holmström 1987: 71). More specifically, analysis has usually started out from an *ex ante* competitive equilibrium setting, for the reason that this reduces '. . . market forces to simple constraints on expected utilities [which] greatly facilitates equilibrium analysis' (Hart and Holmström 1987: 74) of the contracting problem. For example, reservation utilities are given rather than endogeneous to the analysis. Given this, contracting can be reduced to an 'optimization' problem, whereas the introduction of, say, imperfect competition broadens the problem to one of 'equilibrium' analysis, that is, many more interdependent variables now have to be taken into account. [21] Given this overall characterization, a first rough classification is to distinguish between complete and incomplete contract theories. The former category includes principal–agent theories (Salanié 1997) and the latter one includes the new property rights theories (Hart 1995).[22] We here very briefly summarize these different modelling strategies.

Under complete contracting, the contracting agents can (costlessly) write a contract that describes their actions given all the future contingencies that may influence their contractual relation.[23] In this context, there may be failure to reach the first-best outcome because of asymmetric information and different risk-preferences,[24] but given these constraints there is a determinate preferred outcome, on which the parties will coordinate unproblematically. (In terms of the construction of the model, formulating the contracting problem within an optimization framework means that no scope can be left for coordination failures.)

Under incomplete contracting, in contrast, some contingencies are left out of contracts for whatever reasons, such as information costs, the limitations of natural language, etc. Or, while it may be possible for partners to agree on contract terms, these may not be enforceable by a third party, such as a court (i.e. are 'non-verifiable').[25] Since complete contingent contracts cannot be written, parties to a contract may find it necessary to renegotiate their contracts after the contract has been signed, either because they encounter states of nature about which the contract is silent or where the contract specifies inefficient terms. Thus, in this framework there is still transactional work to be done *ex post*, at least in some states of the world. In the Grossman–Hart–Moore version of this idea, it is assumed that the outcome of the renegotiation process can be foreseen at the time of drafting contracts and that the process does not involve costly bargaining – hence, will be efficient. Nevertheless, the very fact of the possibility of renegotiation may be sufficient to cause inefficient levels of investment in relation-specific assets.

This directs analytical attention to property rights, or more precisely residual control rights, that is, the rights to control the use of assets in states of nature that are not described in the contract. The interest then centers on which pattern of ownership rights leads to the most efficient outcome. This depends on the characteristics of the involved assets (e.g. whether they are complementary), on whose assets are most important to the joint surplus, and on who is most responsive to incentives, since ownership by one of the parties will attenuate the incentives of the other party. The bottom-line is that the efficient ownership arrangements primarily turn on the trade-off between incentives for the buyer and the seller.

The Grossman–Hart–Moore property rights approach has recently given rise to substantial debate within contract theory.[26] For example, it has been argued that property rights are not always necessary for reaching efficient outcomes, but that various mechanisms that do not imply a re-allocation of property rights and which are actually employed by real-world agents (say, options contracts) can handle the problems of unverifiable contract terms.

Thus, one comes back to the complete contracting (principal–agent) tradition (Maskin and Tirole 1999a, b; Tirole 1999). Relatedly, there has been some uneasiness about the supposedly less rigorous and more *ad hoc* type of modelling that characterizes the incomplete contracts literature relative to the principal–agent literature (Maskin and Tirole 1999a, b). Although these disputes surely centre around specific isolations, they are internal, highly technical, and do not involve a significant subset of the isolations actually made by contract theorists. In the following we shall take more of the outsider's view, and critically scrutinize what we consider to be key problematic isolations of contract theory.

6 SUPPRESSING MARGINS AND ENTREPRENEURSHIP IN CONTRACT THEORY

In this section we address specific methods of isolation in contract theory, concentrating on how margins and entrepreneurship are suppressed by means of extreme idealizing assumptions. As we shall see, most of the problematic isolations of contract theory are horizontal ones.[27] Moreover, the specific form many of these isolations take result in what may be called 'on–off' models, in which margins are either completely suppressed or completely open to agents (e.g. agents are either perfectly informed or not informed at all, property rights are either perfectly enforced or not enforced at all, contracts are either fully verifiable or completely non-verifiable, etc.). There is seldom anything in between these extreme possibilities. As we further argue, this results in models that provide often one-sided views of contractual arrangements, including the firm. Moreover, we suggest that contract theory models are often not robust, in the sense that their outcomes are extremely sensitive to the specific isolations that are adopted.[28]

6.1 Coordination, equilibrium and process

The essence of economic organization is usually taken to be to obtain some sort of coordination, for example, to align the plans of cooperating parties in the face of volatility. However, the coordination problems that are treated in contract theory are very narrow, at least when compared to the coordination problems that interest Austrians and new institutionalists. This relates to both what may be called the 'scope' and 'form' of coordination problems. With respect to the scope of coordination problems, contract theorists only consider incentive–conflict problems (whereas other type of coordination problems are possible, Foss 1999). With respect to the form of coordination problems, modern contract theory utilizes specific game theoretical (Bayesian) equilibrium concepts that involve very strong assumptions about agents' coordinative capabilities. Coordination takes place by means of pure ratiocination, and there is no mention of discovery, trial and error learning and the like.[29]

Thus, from an Austrian and new institutionalist perspective, contract theory makes questionable horizontal isolations with respect to the set of coordination problems that are considered. Contract theorists defend these specific isolations by arguing that non-incentive coordination problems have no bearing on issues of economic organization (Hart 1995) and that process aspects are 'unimportant subcomponents' of the model and can therefore be treated 'in a cursory way' (Rasmussen 1994: 3). For example, *ex post* bargaining processes may safely be 'blackboxed', as when theorists (e.g. Grossman and Hart 1986) simply assert that certain bargaining solutions (say, Nash) will obtain (Aghion *et al.* 1994, Kreps 1996). However, this may be very problematic when the conclusions of the model are not robust to alternative conceptualizations of the bargaining process, as seems to be the case in the new property rights approach.[30]

Furthermore, process issues and (other) issues of bounded rationality are hard to reasonably suppress to the extent that they crucially influence agents' choice of contractual forms, as Williamson (1996, 1998) has argued. In his work, there is more to integration than simply the concentration of ownership rights (as in the new property rights approach). For example, as his work on the multidivisional corporation illustrates, one advantage of organization in this view is that it can economize on bounded rationality by making members specialize in collecting and processing different types of information and that it allows for sequential, adaptive decision-making (Williamson 1985).

6.2 Isolations Relating to Knowledge and Rationality

Contract theory makes a number of strong horizontal isolations with respect to what is assumed about the knowledge that agents possess. For example, in the new property rights approach it is often assumed that although certain actions (say, investments) or objects may be fully *observable* by the contracting parties, they are not *verifiable* to a third party, such as a court; therefore, the contract is left incomplete. However, while it seems to be reasonable to assume that many things may be hard (i.e. costly) to verify to courts, why assume that some things are *completely* verifiable, whereas other things are *completely* unverifiable? The effect of this on–off approach is to suppress those ways in which contracting parties may try to make some actions or things more verifiable to courts.[31] Therefore, it is not considered either exactly *how much* verifiability can be allowed for in order to produce the predictions of the theory.

Such ignorance with respect to a few relevant variables contrasts with the strong cognitive powers that are in fact otherwise routinely ascribed to agents in contract theory. These powers are perhaps particularly striking and paradoxical in the context of the literature on contractual incompleteness (Grossman and Hart 1986, Hart 1995). Formal incomplete contract theorists sometimes flirt with bounded rationality (e.g. Hart 1995: 81), but they do not take it very seriously.[32] Not only are the agents in a contractual relation symmetrically and perfectly informed; they are also assumed to be able to foresee the pay-offs from their relation, even if they do not know at all the physical characteristics of the good they are trading and even if unforeseen contingencies occur.[33] Thus, the parties to a contract can correctly anticipate the distribution of utility – although they cannot describe the sources of that utility. This sort of inconsistency is arguably the result of extreme on–off models, where agents are perfectly informed about some things (e.g. the distribution of utilities in a relation) and completely ignorant about other things (e.g. the sources of the utility).

6.3 Transaction cost isolations

It is possible to distinguish between principal–agent and new property rights theories on the basis of the kind of horizontal isolations they make with respect to transaction costs.[34] Specifically, a distinction may be based on idealizing assumptions with respect what particular types of transaction costs are excluded. Thus, in principal–agent theories, the relevant transaction cost is the loss in welfare relative to the first-best that is caused by the cost of observing effort being infinitely large, while the costs of writing (complete!) contracts are taken to be zero. In new property rights theories, on the other hand, there are no monitoring costs (or other information costs), while the costs of writing complete contracts are infinitely large. Thus, the two theories are extreme mirror images with respect to the transaction costs they consider.

6.4 Property rights isolations

According to the new property rights perspective, ownership rather than contractual means may be solutions to problems caused by specific investments. More precisely, ownership should be associated with the residual right to decide over asset uses in those situations that are not covered by contract (hence, contracting is incomplete). The value of ownership derives from its being a bargaining chip in these situations, because it is common knowledge what is the value of (human and physical) assets in alternative (second-best) uses. The interest centers on finding those allocations of ownership that maximize surplus.

However, as we have argued in more detail elsewhere (Foss and Foss 2000a) many of the specific claims and implications that can be found in the new property rights approach are dependent on the suppression of some margins that would be relevant to real-world decision-makers. Most fundamentally new property rights theorists consistently do not make the important distinction between legal rights and economic rights. Barzel (1994: 394) provides a convenient summing-up of the economic concept of property rights:[35]

... as an individual's net valuation, in expected terms, of the ability to directly consume the services of the asset, or to consume it indirectly through exchange. A key word is *ability*: The definition is concerned not with what people are legally entitled to do but with what they believe they can do.

'Ability' thus refers to, among other things, the costs and benefits of monitoring and enforcing one's rights. Clearly, ability in this sense may exist in different degrees to different decision-makers. In fact, there is likely to be a continuum of abilities, as determined by the nature of the assets and the exercise of entrepreneurship in the development of enforcement technology, contractual solutions and so on.

The issue of a distribution of abilities does not arise in the new property rights approach, since ability is taken to be perfect or it is not existent at all, that is, isolation is accomplished by the idealizations of assuming that this particular variable is either zero or infinity. Specifically, residual rights of control (i.e. ownership rights) are supposed to be completely backed-up by the legal system, including the courts (thus resulting in full abilities). However, other rights (in the Barzel sense of these) are assumed to be completely outside the reach of the courts; otherwise there wouldn't be any hold-ups, inefficient investment, etc. It is therefore not recognized in the context of the new property rights theory that no property rights are fully enforceable, and that rights are enforceable in different degrees, for example, because of different monitoring abilities (Barzel 1997). Thus, important margins are supressed in the new property rights theory.

In fact, appropriation of rights will take place *whenever* there are costs of detecting appropriation, of taking precautionary measures against appropriation, and of verifying that appropriation has taken place to a third party. This means that solutions may change if one 'frees' some of the margins that are suppressed in the model. For example, elsewhere we begin from the setting normally considered in the new property rights approach – namely a bilateral contracting setting with unverifiable human capital investments and complementary physical assets – and opened a margin by allowing the contracting parties to choose how much *care* they want to exercise when they operate the physical assets in the relation (Foss and Foss 2000a). In this case, it may sometimes maximize joint surplus if the agent whose human capital investments matter *least* to joint surplus is given ownership rights. This is because giving him the ownership to the asset improves his incentives to treat it in a careful way, and thus eliminates the need for monitoring. The resources saved on reduced monitoring may swamp the loss from a hold-up.

6.5 Defending contract theory

In the preceding sections, we have criticized a number of specific contract theory idealizations on various grounds, for example, that they are contrary to how reasonable agents placed in similar circumstances would act and that their on–off nature means that contract theory models are not very robust. Many other, perhaps more general, critiques are possible, for example, that contract theory models make exorbitant demands on the cognitive powers of individuals (e.g. Kreps 1996) or even that they are flatly inconsistent in only admitting bounded rationality or transaction costs to enter the model with respect to select variables (e.g. Furubotn and Richter 1996). However, we here disregard the latter types of critique.

There is at least one defence against our charges that a contract theorist may adopt and which is both obvious and strong. This is to defend the specific idealizations adopted in a specific model by arguing that each model highlights the consequences of some transaction cost, and that the full *ensemble* of contract theory *models* – the *theory* – adds up to a good approximation to the different real-world implications of the existence of different types of transaction costs. For example, when confronted with a critique of the basic principal–agent model that effort cannot be observed by the principal, an agency theorist may adopt the defence that there are models of performance measurement or models in which information search is explicitly featured (e.g. Aghion and Tirole 1997). Thus, one should simply shift from a model with a completely uninformed principal to a model in which the principal is informed, for example, by a noisy signal. Taken together, these different agency models provide a good approximation to real world agency problems.

Strong as it is, there are nevertheless still problems left with this defence. On the obvious level, notice that the defence amounts to defending one model characterized by suppressed margins and entrepreneurship by pointing to the existence of another model that exhibits the same feature,[36] while the starting point of the whole critique was the problematic nature of suppressing margins and entrepreneurship. Perhaps a deeper problem, however, is that various partial contract theory models are not likely to be additive in the sense of the would be defender of contract theory. For example, the solution to contractual problems proposed within principal–agent theory may not be robust to the inclusion of assumptions from new property rights theory and *vice versa*. Thus, if contract drafting costs (a feature of new property rights models) are allowed into principal–agent models, it may well be that the costs of drafting the complete, second-best contractual solution to the principal–agent problem may be so large that they swamp the benefits of doing so, producing a different contractual outcome (Cheung 1969b). Or, more generally, various transaction costs are likely to be interdependent, so that, for example, there is an inverse relation between *ex ante* contract drafting costs and *ex post* enforcement costs. Such interdependency effects are likely to be reflected in contractual outcomes in non-trivial ways.[37] Therefore, the particular horizontal isolations with respect to transaction costs that are adopted in contract theory cannot easily be defended by arguing that, taken together, partial models provide the full picture.

7 CONCLUSION

In this paper, we have contrasted what we think is a basic worldview and a view of theorizing in economics that are shared by Austrians and new institutionalists with the modelling strategies pursued in modern contract theory. More specifically, we asserted that Austrians and new institutionalists begin from a view of the economy as fraught with ignorance and transaction costs, and ask how many and which isolations are necessary for grasping the essence of some phenomenon. Ignorance, bounded rationality and transaction costs should not be admitted into modelling in the piecemeal fashion of modern contract theorists. Although the role of extreme models, such as the competitive equilibrium model, is in no way prohibited by these economists, they are hardly seen as starting points for analysis per se; rather, they simply state the conditions that must obtain for a number of real world institutions to be of no significance.[38]

In contrast, modern contract theorists begin (historically and logically) from an extreme model, namely the competitive equilibrium model. Work in contract economics may thus broadly be described as 'de-isolating' this model in various ways, so as to bring it closer to reality (Hart and Holmström 1987). This type of work is often referred to as 'no-fat MIT style theory' (Rasmussen 1984), and is taken by its proponents to be rigorous and capable of grasping essential aspects of economic reality. As we have seen, however, the result of this modelling strategy is to produce 'on–off' models, in which margins are either completely suppressed or completely open to agents (e.g. agents are either perfectly informed or not informed at all, property rights are either perfectly enforced or not enforced at all, contracts are either fully verifiable or completely non-verifiable, etc.). There is seldom anything in-between these extreme possibilities, a result of the specific way in which contract theorists horizontally isolate.

This produces arbitrary, non-robust models that suppress margins and entrepreneurship and which provide often one-sided views of contractual arrangements, including the firm. For example, ownership is only seen as a matter of supplying agents with bargaining chips (Hart 1995). However, ownership may arise for many other reasons, some of them speculative. Thus, an agent may acquire ownership rights to some asset because ownership confers flexibility advantages in the face of transaction costs that have nothing to do with the hold-up threat. As Littlechild (1986: 35) argued, it may pay to buy, say, the field at the bottom of one's garden from one's neighbour, if one takes into account '. . . that he may discover some new uses for the field that I haven't yet thought of, but would find objectionable'. Or, an entrepreneur may acquire ownership rights to some asset, because the contract law prohibits him from realizing speculative gains (caused by movements in relative prices) from the unspecified quantity clauses of some long-term contract. However, in the context of modern contract theory, these possibilities are not considered.

Finally, let us repeat in perhaps more explicit terms that this paper should not be read as a call for the abandonment of formal work on economic organization. We are very impresssed by much of this work, and we do think that some contributions to contract theory are much less vulnerable to the critique that we have put forward in this paper than others. An example of a 'less vulnerable' contribution is Holmström and Milgrom (1994) which is a sophisticated attempt to keep many margins open and understand the complex interaction effects between different margins that produce different patterns of economic organization. However, we are worried about an approach where just any margin can be closed, although the particular margin may be crucial for understanding the phenomenon under consideration, and where this is seldom justified – arguably an unfortunate and unintended by-product of the increasingly widespread use of MIT style theory in the economics profession.

Kirsten Foss and Nicolai J. Foss
Copenhagen Business School
kf.ivs@cbs.dk/njf.ivs@cbs.dk

ACKNOWLEDGEMENT

The comments of Mark Blaug, Jerry Ellig, Matthias Klaes, Roger Koppl, Dick Langlois, Brian Loasby and Jack Vromen on an earlier version of this paper are gratefully acknowledged. In particular, we owe a great debt to Thráinn Eggertson, Peter Klein, Uskali Mäki and an anonymous reviewer for very useful comments, insights, corrections, etc. Of course, all remaining errors and obscurities are entirely our responsibility.

NOTES

1 Hart and Holmström (1987) and Salanié (1996) are excellent overviews of the field.
2 See also Brousseau and Fares (1998) for a splendid paper that makes much the same point, though not from a methodological point of view.
3 Although in a rather inclusive reading (Langlois 1986).
4 However, other perspectives and insights could also inform such a critique; see, for example, Peltzman's (1991) critique of new industrial organization theory from the position of the Chicago applied price theory tradition or Kreps' (1996) critique of contract theory from the perspective of behavioral game theory.
5 Important exceptions are Barzel (1987), Baumol (1993), Casson (1997) and Gifford (1999).
6 For example, Williamson (1998) now defends his basic notion that economic organization mostly reflects efficiency considerations by pointing to the alertness of businessmen (rather than to the selection argument that he has on earlier occasions invoked). Hence, his (1998: 18) quotation of the businessman Rudolf Spreckels: 'Whenever I see something badly done, or not done at all, I see an opportunity to make a fortune'.
7 In contrast, in contract theory the judge is often supposed to be boundedly rational while transacting agents are not (Hart 1990).

8   In fact, from an Austrian and new institutionalist point of view such strong symmetry would be an illegitimate idealization.

9   To give an example, in an article on consumer theory one does not have to justify the assumption that consumers do not steal from the grocery store. However, if one is concerned with the explanation of why customers are sometimes not allowed to engage in sorting activities, stealing may be a relevant margin to consider. Thus, it is not necessary to give an explicit argument for the omission of every possible choice variable that could have been included in the model. (Thanks to an anonymous reviewer for challenging us on this issue.)

10 It should be noted that Kirzner is generally careful to point out that this tendency is by no means automatic or perfect.

11 Also, the Folk Theorem for infinitely repeated games suggests that if agents put sufficient weight on future pay-offs, there are equilibria (which may be given an interpretation in terms of reputation capital) that sustain first-best outcomes despite the absence of integrated ownership.

12 Striking a hermeneutic chord, one may argue that the economist must put himself 'in the shoes' of the agents he models (O'Driscoll and Rizzo 1985; Koppl and Langlois 1991).

13 For example, when trying to understand price dynamics, it may be legitimate to suppress Schumpeterian institutional and technological entrepreneurship, but perhaps not Kirznerian entrepreneurship that aims at discovering possibilities of arbitrage.

14 For example, while the suppression of margins does not necessarily imply the suppression of entrepreneurship, the suppression of entrepreneurship must always involve the suppression of some margins.

15 Moreover, the procedure of suppressing margins is not one that is specific to, say, mainstream economists. For example, in evolutionary economics, where equilibrium is not necessarily a feature of the model, theorists often suppress margins by assuming that all behaviour is routinized (e.g. Nelson and Winter 1982). On the other hand, equilibrium may be a feature of a model in which virtually no margins are suppressed, as in cooperative game theory or the work of Yoram Barzel. However, in this case, there may be many equilibria.

16 Furthermore, to these economists it is completely legitimate to suppress *any* margin if it can somehow throw light on some contractual phenomenon.

17 Mäki (1999) is a study of the disputes surrounding transaction cost economics in these terms.

18 Others have made similar comments on related branches of modern economics. Thus, Peltzman (1991: 206) refers to the '. . . seeming inability of recent theory to lead to any powerful generalization. This is especially true in the area of game theory where this problem seems beyond remediation'. Modern contract theory is completely game theory-based.

19 Please note the qualifier 'typically.' We do not mean to imply that MIT style modelling, as least as characterized by Rasmussen (1994), *necessarily* implies problematic isolations, such as suppressing margins and suppressing entrepreneurship. However, since MIT style modelling usually implies the construction of 'on–off' models, where extreme values are assumed for a great many variables, the suppression of margins and entrepreneurship tend to go naturally with this kind of theorizing.

20 In contrast, new institutionalists and Austrians do not begin from extreme models in the same way. Perhaps we may say that whereas to the formal economist, economics progresses by means of incremental de-isolation relative to one well-defined model (i.e. the competitive equilibrium model), to the Austrian or new institutionalist economist one rather begins from the real world in its complexity and asks which and how many isolations are necessary for grasping the essence

of some phenomenon (Coase 1981), using extreme models as no more than reference points.

21 However, some contract theorists have constructed models that simultaneously determine employment contracts and labour market equilibrium (e.g. MacLeod and Malcomson 1989). Thus, it is not always the case that reservation utilities are treated as exogenous parameters. (Thanks to an anonymous reviewer for making us aware of this).

22 'New' to distinguish these theories from the 'older' property rights theories associated with Coase, Alchian, Demsetz *et al*. See Foss and Foss (2000a) for a comparison of the new and the old property rights theories.

23 However, although all contingencies can be specified, the court may not be able to verify some contingencies or outcomes. The parties may therefore not be able to condition performance on every relevant contingency. However, under complete contracting, all payments and actions can be specified *ex ante*. It is important not to confuse complete contracting with Arrow–Debreu contracting (sometimes called 'comprehensive' contracting). In the latter, every conceivable action and state of the world can be included in the contract *ex ante* and *all* contract terms are fully enforceable (in contrast to complete contracting).

24 'First-best' is what can be done when everything that matters to the parties to a contract can be made part of the contract, and the contract is fully enforceable. This is equivalent to what a fully informed hypothetical benevolent planner could achieve. Second-best is what an uninformed benevolent planner could achieve, subject to the same informational constraints as the uninformed agents in the model.

25 More precisely, incomplete contracting obtains if performance of the original terms of agreement leaves gains from trade unrealized *given* the information available to the parties to the contract at the time performance takes place (Masten 1998). Incomplete contracting implies that some actions and payments will have to be determined *ex post*. The difference between complete and incomplete contracting also has to do with the role of the court. In complete contracting theories, courts are assumed to enforce the original agreement, and ordering is efficacious, even if all information may not be available to the court. This is in contrast to the incomplete contracting approach where the incompleteness of contracts introduces opportunities for recontracting and where court enforcement of the original terms would leave gains from trade unrealized given the information available to courts at the time performance takes place.

26 Thus, it has been the subject of a recent Clarendon lecture (Hart 1995), a Walras–Bowley lecture (Tirole 1999) and a whole issue of the *Review of Economic Studies* (Vol. 66, no. 1, 1999).

27 Moreover, what we call 'suppressing entrepreneurship' is arguably an 'internal isolation'.

28 Which is a point that has also been raised by some contract theory insiders, for example, Maskin and Tirole (1999b), Aghion *et al.* (1994), and Nöldeke and Schmidt (1995).

29 Thus, agents are assumed to be able to coordinate on any desired game form and equilibrium there of, subject to constraints such as attitudes to risk, incentive trade-offs, bargaining power, and asymmetric information.

30 For example, Aghion *et al.* (1994) show that adopting a specification of the *ex post* bargaining (renegotiation) process that differs from that assumed by Grossman and Hart (1986) or Hart and Moore (1990) by allocating all bargaining power to one of the parties and specifying a default point if renegotiation breaks down completely eliminates the crucial underinvestment result. See also Nöldeke and Schmidt (1995), and Hermalin and Katz (1993).

31   It is quite hard to think of actions or things that are 100 per cent unverifiable. Hart (1995: 37–8) himself supplies the example of his own contract with Oxford University Press in which the quality level of the book is not specified, because, Hart asserts, that level is essentially unverifiable. But is it really? Why couldn't OUP or the court draw on expert witnesses, for example, Professor Hart's colleagues, for ascertaining the quality of the manuscript in a possible court case? For a critique of the 'observable but not verifiable' assumption that is so critical to incomplete contract theory, see Tirole (1998).

32   One notable exception is Anderlini and Felli (1994).

33   Of course, the motivation for this assumption is that otherwise the whole theory threatens to fall apart. As Moore (1992: 180) comments: 'If parties cannot foresee certain events, let alone anticipate how surplus would be divided in the event of renegotiation, then how is this likely to affect the size and nature of their specific investments?'. However, Maskin and Tirole (1999a) point out that there is a tension between the assumption of dynamic programming and the presence of transaction costs. If agents can in fact perform dynamic programming, then transaction costs (of describing actions or the nature of goods in advance) will not restrict the set of outcomes that contracts can implement.

34   However, it should be mentioned that formal contract theorists are rather reluctant to use the term 'transaction costs', presumably because it is considered too imprecise (or even irrelevant, see Maskin and Tirole 1999a). This is somewhat ironic, given that much early work on transaction costs took place in formal theory, namely general equilibrium theory (e.g. work on monetary economies, sequence economies, etc.) (see Klaes 1999 for a fine historical survey of the emergence of the concept of transaction costs).

35   Earlier, von Mises (1936: 27) pointed out that ownership refers to 'the power to use economic goods', that '... ownership is the *having* of the goods which the economic aims of men require', and that '... the economic significance of the legal *should have* lies only in the support it lends to the acquisition, the maintenance and the regaining of the natural *having*'.

36   Peltzman's (1991: 207) acerbic comment on game theoretic new industrial organization is tempting to quote here: '... the production of new models and tidying up of old ones seem to be the major goals of this research enterprise. The uninitiated observer faced with this long march of models soon begins groping for motivation to stay to the end of the parade'.

37   To be fair, it should be mentioned that contract theorists are not necessarily blind to this (cf. Holmström and Milgrom 1994). However, models that incorporate interdependency effects are very few. A good, though apparently somewhat controversial, discussion of some of the problems that interdependency raises for economic analysis can be found in Hicks (1979).

38   In a sense, they can of course still be starting points, namely by raising puzzles.

39   Hart and Holmström (1987: 105) noted the 'extreme sensitivity' of optimal incentive schemes to, for example, slight changes in the relation between actual performance and verifiable information. But the discovery of the unrobust nature of contract theory models goes back at least to Mirrlees (1974), a paper that prompted more than a decade of research on how the optimal contract depends on, for example, the specific form of the utility function.

REFERENCES

Aghion, Philippe, Dewatripont, Matthias and Rey, Patrick (1994) 'Renegotiation design with unverifiable information', *Econometrica* 62: 257–82.

Aghion, Philippe and Tirole, Jean (1997) 'Formal and real authority in organization', *Journal of Political Economy* 105: 1–29.

Akerlof, George A. (1970) 'The market for "lemons"', in G.A. Akerlof (ed.) *An Economic Theorist's Book of Tales*, Cambridge: Cambridge University Press.

Alchian, Armen A. (1965) 'Some economics of property rights', in A.A. Alchian (ed.) *Economic Forces at Work*, Indianapolis: Liberty Press.

Alchian, Armen A. and Demsetz, Harold (1972) 'Production, information costs, and economic organization', *American Economic Review* 62: 772–95.

Anderlini, Luca and Felli, Leonardo (1994) 'Incomplete written contracts: undescribable states of nature', *Quarterly Journal of Economics* 117: 1085–124.

Barzel, Yoram (1987) 'The entrepreneur's reward for self-policing', *Economic Inquiry* 25: 103–16.

Barzel, Yoram (1994) 'The capture of wealth by monopolists and the protection of property rights', *International Review of Law and Economics* 14: 393–409.

Barzel, Yoram (1997) *Economic Analysis of Property Rights*, 2nd edn, Cambridge: Cambridge University Press.

Baumol, William J. (1993) *Entrepreneurship, Management and the Structure of Pay-Offs*. Cambridge, MA: MIT Press.

Bhaskar, Roy (1978) *A Realist Theory of Science*, Brighton: Harverster-Wheatsheaf.

Brousseau, Eric and Fares, M'hand (1998) 'Incomplete contracts and governance structures,' unpublished manuscript.

Camerer, Colin (1994) 'Does strategy research need game theory?', in David J. Teece, Richard Rumelt and Dan Schendel (eds) (1994) *Fundamental Issues in Strategy*, Boston: Harvard Business School Press.

Casson, Mark (1997) *Information and Organization*, Oxford: Oxford University Press.

Cheung, Stephen S.N. (1969a) 'The structure of a contract and the theory of a non-exclusive resource', *Journal of Law and Economics* 10: 49–70.

Cheung, Stephen S.N. (1969b) 'Transaction costs, risk aversion and the choice of contractual arrangement', *Journal of Law and Economics* 12: 23–42.

Cheung, Stephen S.N. (1983) 'The contractual nature of the firm', *Journal of Law and Economics* 26: 1–22.

Coase, Ronald H. (1981) 'How should economists choose?,' in R.H. Coase (ed.) *Essays on Economics and Economists*, Chicago: University of Chicago Press.

Coase, Ronald H. (1988) *The Firm, the Market and the State*, Chicago: University of Chicago Press.

Cowen, Tyler (1985) 'Public goods definitions and their institutional context: a critique of public goods theory', *Review of Social Economy* 43: 53–63.

Cowen, Tyler (1988) *The Theory of Market Failure: A Critical Examination*, Fairfax: George Mason University Press.

Debreu, Gerard (1959) *Theory of Value*, New York: Wiley.

Demsetz, Harold (1964) 'The exchange and enforcement of property rights', in H. Demsetz (ed.) *Ownership, Control, and the Firm*, Oxford: Basil Blackwell.

Demsetz, Harold (1967) 'Toward a theory of property rights', in H. Demsetz (ed.) *Ownership, Control, and the Firm*, Oxford: Basil Blackwell.

Demsetz, Harold (1969) 'Information and efficiency: a different viewpoint,' in H. Demsetz (ed.) *Ownership, Control, and the Firm*, Oxford: Basil Blackwell.

Foss, Kirsten and Foss, Nicolai J. (2000a) 'Assets, attributes and ownership', forthcoming in the *International Journal of the Economics of Business*.

Foss, Kirsten and Foss, Nicolai J. (2000b) 'Economic organization and the trade-off between productive and destructive entrepreneurship', unpublished manuscript.

Foss, Nicolai J. (1994) 'Realism and evolutionary economics', *Journal of Social and Biological Systems* 17: 21–40.

Foss, Nicolai J. (1999) 'The use of knowledge in firms', *Journal of Institutional and*

Theoretical Economics 155: 458–86.

Furubotn, Erik and Richter, Rudolf (1997) *Institutions and Economic Theory*, Ann Arbor: Michigan University Press.

Gifford, Sharon (1999) 'Endogenous transaction costs', forthcoming in *American Economic Review*.

Grossman, Sanford, and Hart, Oliver (1986) 'The costs and benefits of ownership: a theory of lateral and vertical integration', *Journal of Political Economy* 94: 691–719.

Guesnerie, Roger (1992) 'The Arrow–Debreu paradigm faced with modern theories of contracting', in Lars Werin and Hans Wijkander (eds) *Contract Economics*, Oxford: Blackwell.

Hamminga, Bert and De Marchi, Neil B. (eds) (1994) *Idealization VI: Idealization in Economics*, Amsterdam: Rodopi.

Hart, Oliver. (1990) 'Is 'bounded rationality' an important element of a theory of institutions?', *Journal of Institutional and Theoretical Economics* 16: 696–702.

Hart, Oliver (1995) *Firms, Contracts and Financial Structure*, Oxford: Clarendon Press.

Hart, Oliver and Holmström, Bengt (1987) 'The theory of contracts', in Truman F. Bewley (ed.) *Advances in Economic Theory. Fifth World Congress*, Cambridge: Cambridge University Press.

Hart, Oliver and Moore, John (1990) 'Property rights and the nature of the firm', *Journal of Political Economy* 98: 1119–58.

Hart, Oliver and Moore, John (1999) 'Foundations of incomplete contracts', *Review of Economic Studies* 66: 115–38.

von Hayek, Friedrich A. (1937) 'Economics and knowledge', in F.A von Hayek (1948) *Individualism and Economic Order*, Chicago: University of Chicago Press.

von Hayek, Friedrich A. (1948) *Individualism and Economic Order*, Chicago: University of Chicago Press.

Hermalin, Benjamin and Katz, Michael L. (1993) 'Judicial modification of contracts between sophisticated parties: a more complete view of incomplete contracts and their breach', *Journal of Law, Economics, and Organization* 9: 230–55.

Hicks, John R. (1979) *Causality in Economics*, New York.

Holmström, Bengt and Milgrom, Paul (1994) 'The firm as an incentive system', *American Economic Review* 84: 972–91.

Hutt, William H. (1939) *The Theory of Idle Resources*, Indianapolis: Liberty Press.

Kirzner, Israel M. (1973) *Entrepreneurship and Competition*, Chicago: University of Chicago Press.

Kirzner, Israel M. (1997) 'Entrepreneurial discovery and the competitive market process: an Austrian approach', *Journal of Economic Literature* 35: 60–85.

Klaes, Matthias (1999) 'The birth of the concept of transaction costs: issues and controversies', unpublished manuscript.

Knight, Frank H. (1965) [1921] *Risk, Uncertainty and Profit*, New York: Augustus M. Kelley.

Koppl, Roger and Langlois, Richard N. (1991) 'Fritz Machlup and Marginalism: a reevaluation', *Methodus* 3: 86–102.

Kreps, David M. (1996) 'Markets and hierarchies and (mathematical) economic theory', *Industrial and Corporate Change* 5: 561–97.

Kyläheiko, Kalevi (1998) 'Making sense of technology: towards a synthesis between neoclassical and evolutionary approaches', *International Journal of Production Economics* 56–7: 319–32.

Langlois, Richard N. (1986) 'The new institutional economics', in R.N. Langlois (ed.) *Economics as a Process: Essays in the New Institutional Economics*, Cambridge: Cambridge University Press.

Leijonhufvud, Axel (1968) *On Keynesian Economics and the Economics of Keynes*, Oxford: Oxford University Press.

Littlechild, Stephen (1986) 'Three types of market process', in Richard N. Langlois (ed.) *Economics as a Process: Essays in the New Institutional Economics*, Cambridge: Cambridge University Press.

Littlechild, Stephen (1979) 'An entrepreneurial theory of games', *Metroeconomica* 31: 145–65.

Lucas, Robert E. (1981) *Studies in Business Cycle Theory*, Cambridge, MA: MIT Press.

Lucas, Robert E. (1987) *Models of Business Cycles*, Oxford: Basil Blackwell.

MacLeod, W. Bentley and Malcomson, James M. (1989) 'Implicit contracts, incentive compatibility, and involuntary unemployment', *Econometrica* 57: 447–80.

Maskin, Eric and Tirole, Jean (1999a) 'Unforeseen contingencies and incomplete contracts', *Review of Economic Studies* 66: 83–114.

Maskin, Eric and Tirole, Jean (1999b) 'Two remarks on the property-rights literature', *Review of Economic Studies* 66: 139–50.

Masten, Scott (1998) 'Contractual choice', forthcoming in Gerrit de Geest and Boudewijn Bouckaert (eds) *Encyclopedia of Law and Economics,* Aldershot: Edward Elgar.

Mirrlees, James (1974) 'Notes on welfare economics, information and uncertainty', in M. Balch, Donald McFadden and S. Wu (eds) *Essays on Economic Behavior Under Uncertainty,* Amsterdam: North-Holland.

von Mises, Ludwig (1949) *Human Action*, London: William Hodge.

Moore, John (1992) 'Comment', in Lars Werin and Hans Wijkander (eds) *Contract Economics*, Oxford: Blackwell.

Mäki, Uskali (1992) 'On the method of isolation in economics', in Craig Dilworth (ed.) *Intelligibility in Science*, Amsterdam: Rodopi.

Mäki, Uskali (1994) 'Isolation, idealization, and truth in economics', in Bert Hamminga and Neil B. de Marchi (eds) *Idealization VI: Idealization in Economics,* Amsterdam: Rodopi.

Mäki, Uskali (1998) 'Is Coase a realist?', *Philosophy of the Social Sciences* 28: 5–31.

Mäki, Uskali (1999) 'Theoretical isolation and explanatory progress: transaction cost economics and the dynamics of dispute', unpublished manuscript.

Nelson, Richard R. and Winter, Sidney G. (1982) *An Evolutionary Theory of Economic Change*, Cambridge, MA: Belknap Press.

Nöldeke, Georg and Schmidt, Klaus M. (1995) 'Option contracts and renegotiation: solution to the hold-up problem', *RAND Journal of Economics* 26: 163–79.

O'Driscoll, Gerald P. and Rizzo, Mario (1985) *The Economics of Time and Ignorance*, Oxford: Basil Blackwell.

Peltzman, Sam (1991) 'The handbook of industrial organization: a review article', *Journal of Political Economy* 99: 201–17.

Rasmussen, Eric (1994) *Games and Information*, Oxford: Basil Blackwell.

Salanié, Bertrand (1997) *Contract Economics,* Cambridge: MIT Press.

Shackle, George L.S. (1972) *Epistemics and Economics*, Cambridge: Cambridge University Press.

Shavell, Steven (1998) 'Contracts', in Peter Newman (ed.) *The New Palgrave Dictionary of Economics and the Law*, London: Macmillan.

Tirole, Jean (1999) 'Incomplete contracts: where do we stand?', *Econometrica* 67: 641–81.

Williamson, Oliver E. (1985) *The Economic Institutions of Capitalism*, New York: Free Press.

Williamson, Oliver E. (1996) *The Mechanisms of Governance*, Oxford: Oxford University Press.

Williamson, Oliver E. (1998) 'Human actors and economic organization', paper presented to the ISNIE conference, Paris, 17–19 September 1998.

Volume 14(1): 29–52
ISSN 1350–5084
Copyright © 2007 SAGE
(London, Thousand Oaks, CA
and New Delhi)

The Emerging Knowledge Governance Approach: Challenges and Characteristics

articles

Nicolai J. Foss

Norwegian School of Economics and Business Administration, Bergen, Norway and Copenhagen Business School, Denmark

Abstract. *The 'knowledge governance approach' is characterized as a distinctive, emerging approach that cuts across the fields of knowledge management, organization studies, strategy and human resource management. Knowledge governance is taken up with how the deployment of governance mechanisms influences knowledge processes, such as sharing, retaining and creating knowledge. It insists on clear micro (behavioural) foundations, adopts an economizing perspective, and examines the links between knowledge-based units of analysis with diverse characteristics and governance mechanisms with diverse capabilities of handling these transactions. Research issues that the knowledge governance approach illuminates are sketched.* **Key words.** *governance; knowledge management; organizational economics*

The purpose of this article is to characterize an emerging approach—the 'knowledge governance approach' (henceforth, the 'KGA')—in terms of how it differs from other parts of the knowledge-based literature, the problems it seeks to solve, and the methods and ideas it applies.[1] The approach may be briefly defined as a sustained attempt to uncover how knowledge transactions—which differ in their characteristics—and governance mechanisms—which differ with respect to how they handle

DOI: 10.1177/1350508407071859

http://org.sagepub.com

transactional problems—are matched, using economic efficiency as the explanatory principle. In terms of intellectual underpinning, the KGA largely takes its cues from organizational economics (particularly transaction cost economics), but also recognizes a need to go beyond this body of thought in terms of the treatment of motivation and cognition on the level of individuals (Grandori, 1997; Osterloh and Frey, 2000), how transactions are dimensionalized (Nickerson and Zenger, 2004), and the set of governance mechanisms that are considered (Grandori, 2001). Cutting thematically across the fields of knowledge management ('KM'), human resource management, organization theory and strategic management, the KGA starts from the hypothesis that knowledge processes (i.e. the creation, retention and sharing of knowledge; Argote, 1999) can be influenced and directed through the deployment of governance mechanisms, in particular the formal aspects of organization that can be manipulated by management, such as organization structure, job design, reward systems, information systems, standard operating procedures, accounting systems and other coordination mechanisms (Grandori, 2001). The KGA asserts that such governance mechanisms should be seen as critical antecedents of knowledge processes.

Philosophically, the KGA asserts the need to build micro-foundations based in individual action and interaction for organizational knowledge-based phenomena (knowledge sharing, organizational knowledge creation) (i.e. 'methodological individualism'; Coleman, 1990; Felin and Foss, 2005; von Hayek, 1955); it attempts to trace the specific mechanisms through which organization exerts its influence on knowledge processes ('mechanism-based explanation'; Hedström and Swedberg, 1996; Machamer et al., 2000); and it is unabashedly rational(istic) in its approach to explanation on the scientific domain and to organization design on the managerial domain (Williamson, 1996).

The article is structured as follows. I begin by locating the KGA in the overall 'knowledge movement', that is, the broad interest in the management of knowledge that has characterized many fields in business administration during the last decade. However, this movement is beset by some fundamental weaknesses, and the KGA has arisen as a response to these weaknesses. The article ends by giving a characterization of the KGA in terms of the problems it addresses and how it may solve these. Examples of existing research that may be seen as lying within the KGA are provided.

Why the Knowledge Governance Approach?

The Knowledge Movement

'Knowledge' has been all the rage for more than a decade in a number of fields in management studies (e.g. Eisenhardt and Santos, 2002; Grandori and Kogut, 2002). A 'knowledge movement' that cuts across traditionally separate disciplines in business administration has emerged. The strategy field has witnessed a proliferation of approaches that all place knowledge

The Emerging Knowledge Governance Approach
Nicolai J. Foss

centre stage (e.g. Grant, 1996; Kogut and Zander, 1996; Spender, 1996); the international business field is in the process of developing a view of the multinational corporation as a knowledge-based entity (Tallman, 2003); network ideas that stress connections between knowledge nodes, often based on sociological notions of network ties (Granovetter, 1973), are becoming increasingly influential (Kogut, 2000; Tsai, 2001, 2002; Tsai and Ghoshal, 1998); and, of course, KM has become not only a huge body of literature, but also a widespread organizational practice (Easterby-Smith and Lyles, 2003; Spender, 2005).

It is appropriate to characterize all this as a 'movement' because of the shared conviction that the management of knowledge of whatever kind has become a critical issue for competitive dynamics, international strategy, the building of resources, the boundaries of firms and many other issues. There is also agreement that it is meaningful to speak of different kinds of knowledge, each implying different management needs. And there seems to be an inbuilt pluralism to the knowledge movement, an agreement that no single established business administrative field or social science perspective is likely to carry us all the way towards a comprehensive understanding of the management of knowledge.

Those scholars who may be seen as working with the KGA are sympathetic fellow-travellers in the overall knowledge movement. However, the KGA stands out as a distinctive part of the knowledge movement because it points to a number of central problems that have not yet been satisfactorily addressed, and because there is a specific unity to the approach taken to solve such problems. Before the boundaries of this emerging approach can be identified, it is necessary to discuss the gaps in the extant literature that the KGA has arisen as a response to.

Research Gaps

As indicated the knowledge movement is broad and highly diverse in terms of research interests, underlying disciplines, research methods, results, philosophical underpinnings, etc. In fact, the knowledge management field alone is highly diverse. Nevertheless, there are a number of distinct shared research gaps in the knowledge movement that the KGA may be seen as reacting to. To get an idea of what these may be, consider the following two examples: (1) the governance of knowledge intensive firms (Starbuck, 1992) or 'human capital organizations' and (2) the importance of knowledge for competitive advantage. There are serious gaps in our understanding of these and the KGA may help close the gaps.

Governance of human capital organizations 'Human capital organizations' are organizations where a significantly larger part of value-added can be ascribed to human than to physical assets. They range from R & D-intensive manufacturing firms to professional services firms, and rely on scarce 'expert talent'. These changes with respect to an increasing human capital component of firms' productive inputs are often argued to take place in

31

tandem with an increase of the 'knowledge-content' in outputs, a stepping up of innovative activity, an increasing differentiation of demand, increasing globalization, and increasingly inexpensive networked computing—complementary changes that are taken to indicate the emergence of the 'knowledge economy' (Halal and Taylor, 1998) or at least a new paradigm of 'modern manufacturing' (Milgrom and Roberts, 1990).

Fundamental changes in economic organization are also implied by the increased prevalence of human capital organizations, as reflected in notions of the 'changing employment contract', 'new organizational forms', 'internal disaggregation', etc. In particular, many scholars have argued that the boundaries of firms are being radically transformed, not just because firms increasingly disaggregate (i.e. outsource, spin-off, etc.), but also because the very notion of firm boundaries is becoming increasingly problematic as (inalienable) human capital increasingly dominates (alienable) physical capital as the most important category of productive capital (see Foss, 2002).

As this suggests, the advent and increased prevalence of human capital organizations have profound implications for the deployment of governance mechanisms such as the allocation (and exercise) of authority and the design of reward systems. In fact, according to a viewpoint that has almost acquired the status of conventional wisdom, human capital organizations may be differentiated from 'traditional' firms in terms of governance mechanisms by relying less on direction through the exercise of authority, eschewing high-powered performance incentives and embracing 'culture' and 'clan' modes of organizational control (at least for the core group of employees) (e.g. Child and McGrath, 2001). Organizational control is exercised through very different mechanisms in the two kinds of firms.

However, Teece (2003) develops a completely contrary view. Teece explains how the organization of his own firm (Law and Economics Consulting Group, LECG), a professional services firm, is very much different from the above portrayal of how human capital organizations are administered and controlled. In particular, while indeed the traditional blunt authority-mechanism (supervision, order-giving) is 'extremely weak' in this firm, very high-powered performance incentives are used (instead). The two features are related, for by setting compensation for 'experts' '... purely as a certain percentage a of the expert's own individual bill-out rate times hours worked (as accepted by the client)' (Teece, 2003: 909), strong incentives are coupled with a small need for monitoring. Teece speculates that the specific organizational design of LECG (and there are other features in addition to those briefly mentioned here) '... may well portend the future for professional service organizations endeavouring to leverage top talent' (p. 914).

The point is, of course, not that Teece is right and those who argue differently are wrong or *vice versa*. Both may be right—for different kinds of human capital organizations or for different environments. The problem is

The Emerging Knowledge Governance Approach
Nicolai J. Foss

rather that we do not have a good theory that will allow us to discriminate between these alternative accounts in a clean manner. Such a theory would start from a knowledge-related unit of analysis and explain how the efficient deployment of governance mechanisms systematically varies when the unit of analysis varies, given assumptions about agents' knowledge and motivation and given assumptions about the principle (e.g. efficiency) that links the unit of analysis with alternative kinds of governance mechanisms (or combinations thereof).

Knowledge and competitive advantage Strategic management may well be the field in business administration (at least among the more traditional/ well-established fields) where knowledge-based approaches have been developed and applied with the greatest success (measured in terms of overall influence in a field) (e.g. Grant, 1996; Kogut, 2000; Kogut and Zander, 1992; Spender, 1996). Thus, the dominant resource-based view, while not logically committed to placing knowledge resources centre stage nevertheless often does exactly this. The underlying argument seems to be that knowledge resources empirically are particularly often the cause of competitive advantages and are particularly difficult to imitate. In particular, much interest has centred on knowledge constructs such as capabilities that are placed on the firm-level, as primary examples of value-creating and difficult to imitate resources. A key idea here is that differential firm performance can be traced to differential capabilities; successful firms control capabilities that result in more appropriable value-added than less successful firms. However, the explanatory stance typically taken in the resource/capabilities view is not satisfactory. There are two reasons for this.

First, the literature reasons directly from something placed on the firm-level (i.e. capabilities are antecedents) to something else that is also placed on the firm-level (e.g. competitive advantage). Aggregates are directly linked to (in fact, claimed to cause) other aggregates. This is known as 'methodological collectivism' (Coleman, 1990; von Hayek, 1955). In short, this stance is problematic because it suppresses the level of individual action and interaction. A recent attack on collectivism in strategy research has been launched by Lippman and Rumelt (2003). They point out that arguing that 'firms' (i.e. collective entities) earn a residual return called 'profits' is highly misleading. In particular, it obscures the complex process of appropriating value where the appropriation is not undertaken by firms (and certainly not by 'capabilities') but by the firm's stakeholders that come equipped with different bargaining powers. Thus, a 'collectivist' approach obscures important micro-mechanisms. In the present context, what is obscured is the issue of how knowledge that ultimately resides on the level of the individuals is somehow integrated through organizational means into organization-level capability, and how this integration results in knowledge being utilized in such a manner that competitive advantage becomes the result.

33

Organization 14(1)
Articles

Second, the collectivist capabilities perspective in strategy neglects organization—and does so at its peril. Although capabilities are often taken to be *organizational* processes that enable managers to carry out certain key tasks, organization itself seems almost conspicuous by its absence in most capabilities work. By 'organization' is here understood the formal and informal allocation of decision (or property) rights and the mechanisms that enforce such rights (Jones, 1983). This rights allocation and the accompanying enforcement mechanisms constitute the distribution of authority, the attributes of governance mechanisms, organizational structure and other aspects of formal organization, but clearly also relates to, for example, social ties and networks inside firms. An allocation of property rights is also an allocation of incentives (Barzel, 1997), including incentives to search for knowledge, share knowledge, accumulate human capital, leverage knowledge capital, etc. (Foss and Mahnke, 2003); moreover, property rights influence bargaining powers (Hart, 1995). For example, social ties and networks—much emphasized in KM research—are important for understanding the links between knowledge and superior returns, not just because of their potentially beneficial effects on returns, but also because such ties and networks grant legitimacy to the claims that employees may make on rents (Coff and Blyler, 2003). In turn, these appropriation issues matter to knowledge processes, because employee incentives to search for, share, create, and integrate knowledge are influenced by how much they can appropriate (Coff, 1999).

Causes of Research Gaps

There are probably many reasons why the above research gaps exist. The following discuss some of the major causes, concentrating on the missing micro-foundations in the knowledge movement and the neglect of governance mechanisms as antecedents of knowledge processes.

Missing micro-foundations Consider Figure 1 which builds on the work of sociologist James Coleman (1990).

The Figure makes a distinction between the macro-level and the micro-level. For example, it may be that the macro-level is organizational whilst the micro-level is that of individuals. As shown, there are links between macro-macro (Arrow 4) and macro-micro (Arrow 1), micro-micro (Arrow 2), and micro-macro (Arrow 3). The Figure also makes a distinction between what is to be explained (i.e. the *explanandum*) and its explanation (the *explanans*). Usually, the aim is to explain either a macro-level phenomenon (located in the upper right hand corner of Figure 1), such as a firm-level outcome, or a correlation between macro-phenomena (i.e. Arrow 4). In order to explain the analyst makes use of theoretical mechanisms implied by the arrows (Hedström and Swedberg, 1996; Machamer et al., 2000). Note that the arrows in Figure 1 are, from a theoretical perspective, empty boxes. They may be filled with different kinds of theoretical mechanisms, quite dependent on the choices of the analyst.

34

The Emerging Knowledge Governance Approach
Nicolai J. Foss

Figure 1. A General Model of Social Science Explanation

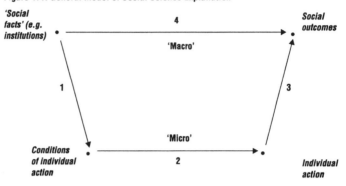

The Coleman diagram can be used to diagnose in a more precise manner some of the problematic features of extant work in the knowledge movement; see Figure 2.

Figure 2. Capabilities as Antecedent to Competitive Advantage

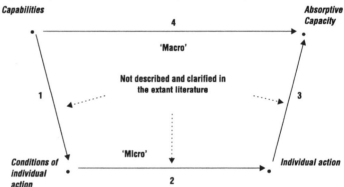

Consider again the strategic management manifestation of the knowledge movement, that is, the capabilities (or knowledge-based) view (e.g. Kogut and Zander, 1992, 1996). In terms of the diagram depicted in Figure 2, capabilities theorists usually posit a direct relation between capabilities and competitive advantage, that is, they make use of Arrow 4. However, Arrow 4 explanation can only be used under special circumstances and only as a shorthand way of representing more complex underlying behaviours. The reason is fundamentally ontological: there are no conceivable mechanisms that directly take us from the organization-level construct of capability to organization-level outcomes such as competitive advantage. A research gap in the capabilities view therefore concerns accounting for the impact on

35

Organization 14(1)
Articles

performance of capabilities in terms of other, more 'micro' mechanisms (Arrows 1, 2 and 3). There is, of course, a substantial KM dimension to this. For presumably firm-level capability is, among other things, a reflection of representations, beliefs, information, etc. that, ultimately, is held by individual employees and utilizing this knowledge in an optimal manner is a key KM task. Thus, talking of the need to manage capabilities for the purposes of achieving competitive advantage is simply shorthand for a KM task that inherently involves the micro-level of organizations.

Organizational antecedents The Coleman diagram is also useful for understanding the role that organizational antecedents play in the knowledge movement. Such antecedents may be thought of as being placed at the North-Eastern node in Figure 2 (i.e. substitute 'capabilities' with 'governance mechanisms'). The deployment of information systems, incentive schemes, allocations of decision rights and authority and so on directly impact on the conditions of individual action. Governance mechanisms are, of course, deployed in the belief that influencing the conditions of actions (the south-eastern node) in a certain manner will lead employees to take those decisions (the south-western node) that, when aggregated (Arrow 3), lead to favourable organizational outcomes (the north-western node in Figure 1). Thus, the attempt to better exploit certain knowledge assets through knowledge sharing (an organizational outcome) may be implemented by setting up reward systems for knowledge sharing (and knowledge searching), installing monitoring mechanisms that make sure that knowledge that is shared (and for which rewards are paid) is actually relevant knowledge and so on.

In general, the knowledge movement has a problem with organizational antecedents. To be sure, organization issues often do get mention in various discussions of knowledge processes within and between firms (e.g. Hamel, 1991; Hedlund, 1994; Lyles and Schwenk, 1992).[2] Special issues of journals have been devoted to the theme of the link between organization and knowledge processes [e.g. *Journal of International Business Studies*, 35(5), 2004; *Journal of Management Studies*, 38(7), 2001]. A recent (excellent) textbook on KM (Hislop, 2005) discusses communities of practice, boundary-spanning processes, power and conflict, ICT, culture and HRM issues, virtual organizations, MNC and knowledge-intensive firms, all in separate chapters. In sum, it would be factually incorrect to argue that the knowledge/organization link is a *neglected* one. However, some critical observations are still pertinent here.

First, it is characteristic that many contributions to the organization-knowledge link have a collective(ist) orientation in the sense that the analytical reduction indicated in Figures 1 and 2 is not performed. Instead, the explanation takes place solely on the collective level; for example, theorists discuss the role of 'communities of practice' (Brown and Duguid, 1998)— that is, collective entities —for organization-level knowledge. As a telling example, in none of the contributions to the *Journal of Management Studies*

The Emerging Knowledge Governance Approach
Nicolai J. Foss

special issue on KM do we find an explicit attempt to link organization and knowledge by means of mechanisms corresponding to Arrows 1, 2 and 3 in Figure 1.

Second, it is characteristic that 'organization' predominantly means 'informal organization', that is, networks, culture, communities of practice and the like, rather than formal governance mechanisms. The allocation of authority and decision rights, the provision of incentives, and the creation of organizational structure may be *invoked*—but they are seldom if ever *integrated* into the analysis. A good example of this tendency is recent work on knowledge sharing and innovation that takes Granovetter (1973) as the main theoretical foundation. For example, Tsai (2001) argues that if organizational units occupy a more central network position, they perform better in terms of innovation. Social networks facilitate new knowledge creation within organizations. Hansen (2002) develops a concept of 'knowledge networks' to explain why some business units are able to take advantage of knowledge that resides in other parts of the organization, while other units may not be. And so on. In almost all of this kind of work, there is a neglect of formal organization.[3] For example, the issue of incentive compatibility in situations where employers wish employee to expend effort on searching for and sharing knowledge, and how various kinds of rewards may (or may not) prompt the desired behaviours have been surprisingly neglected.

Organizational costs Foss and Mahnke (2003) note that the KM literature in particular, and arguably also the knowledge movement at large, are strangely innocent of notions of cost (save, of course, for mention of costs of setting up IT systems). In particular, organizational costs, they note, are almost universally ignored. Because of these neglects the question of whether knowledge sharing is always beneficial is seldom raised. Thus, maximum knowledge sharing is implicitly assumed to be desirable, although, of course, optimum knowledge sharing is never equal to maximum knowledge sharing.

Organizational alternatives Although the issue of organizational alternatives for knowledge processes (e.g. knowledge sharing) gets mention in the knowledge movement, alternatives are seldom confronted in terms of an economizing logic. The reason lies in the absence in the literature of an explicit cost calculus related to knowledge processes and the organization thereof. In the absence of any such (transaction) costs, decision-makers would immediately pick those knowledge-related activities that maximize value creation (Coase, 1960; Foss and Foss, 2005). Moreover, how these activities were organized would not matter for value creation (Coase, 1937).

However, in the presence of costs of, say, sharing knowledge the issue of organizational alternatives becomes pressing. For example, a relevant alternative to knowledge sharing may sometimes be more delegation of decision rights: if the problem is to make better use of existing knowledge, it can be better to allow the employees who hold this knowledge to make better use of it than to spread it to the rest of the organization. What is best

Organization 14(1)
Articles

depends on the net benefits associated with each alternative. However, such comparative assessments are virtually never performed.

The neglect of organizational costs is accompanied by a neglect of not only organizational alternatives, but also of formal organization. If only informal organization is considered, there is a tendency to become less normative. A concern with *formal* organization (as in the organization design literature; e.g. Mintzberg, 1979) is usually accompanied by an attempt to devise *efficient* organization; such a normative ambition appears to be much less prevalent when the concern is with informal organization.[4] The attempt to devise efficient organization involves a consideration of organizational alternatives that are evaluated relative to some yardstick, such as net benefits. Such a normative enterprise is a key component of the KGA.

What is the Knowledge Governance Approach Trying to Accomplish? Problems and Heuristics

Knowledge Governance Problems

The KGA identifies, grapples with, and solves problems that lie in the intersection of organization and knowledge processes, problems that for various reasons are hard to approach and solve within other knowledge-based approaches or where these approaches give a different solution than the KGA. In the following, examples of such problems are provided and discussed.

Motivation and knowledge processes The KGA stresses micro-foundations, implying that a starting point is taken in behavioural assumptions. In contrast, explicit behavioural assumptions are seldom made in knowledge-based contributions (but see Kogut and Zander, 1996). The choice of behavioural foundations is partly determined by the kind of questions to which answers are sought.

For example, Osterloh and Frey (2000) examine how knowledge transfer is influenced by organizational design. This research question is embedded in a broader discussion of how firms increasingly introduce market elements to exploit the advantages of price mechanisms, by making exchanges between departments or actors more explicit and enabling them to reward according to the contribution to a firm's profit. In order to theorize the mechanisms lying between organizational variables and organizational-level knowledge sharing, the authors begin by identifying a number of exchange hazards that beset internal knowledge transactions. They argue that the transfer of tacit knowledge cannot be accomplished by contracting, and that employees cannot be sanctioned for holding back tacit knowledge. Therefore, the management of individual motivation becomes central. Firms have access to mechanisms (that markets do not) to manage intrinsic motivation, such as participation which signifies agreement on common goals and raises employees' self-determination, thereby strengthening intrinsic motivation and personal relationships, which allows for establishing psychological

The Emerging Knowledge Governance Approach
Nicolai J. Foss

contracts based on emotional loyalties, which in turn raise the intrinsic motivation to cooperate. In contrast, the heavy-handed use of market-like incentives may destroy intrinsic motivation (i.e. the 'crowding effect'). To develop the argument the authors rely on psychological theories of individual motivation.

Like Osterloh and Frey, Foss (2003) argues that infusing hierarchies with market control in order to increase knowledge sharing and creation is inherently difficult. The argument in this article is that there is a fundamental incentive problem of establishing credible managerial commitments to not intervene in delegated decision-making (and heavy delegation is an integral part of 'internal hybrids'). The argument is illustrated with the case of the organizational transformations that took place in the 1990s in the world-leading hearing aids producer, Oticon. Frequent managerial meddling with decision rights that, in accordance with the official Oticon culture, had been delegated to employees led to a severe loss of motivation, and arguably caused the change to a more structured organization from the earlier extremely decentralized form. Thus, in order to understand the influence of organizational form on knowledge processes, this article, like Osterloh and Frey (2000) focuses on the level of individual employees and their motivation.

These two articles provide insights into the motivational aspects of conscious management efforts to influence knowledge processes by means of the deployment of governance mechanisms. However, one article is purely theoretical (Osterloh and Frey) while the other single-case-based (Foss). More systematic evidence needs to be assembled on these motivational dimensions of knowledge governance. In addition theoretical enquiry is needed into issues such as which kinds of incentives (and which incentive intensities) work best for which kind of knowledge processes. Conceivably, one kind of incentive may work for knowledge sharing but not for knowledge production. Or, only the strength of the incentives provided should differ. Or, the incentives may be exactly the same. Or, they may only work if combined with other kinds of incentives. In sum,

KGA Research Question 1

What is the impact of different kinds of (systems and strength of) incentives on knowledge sharing, integration and creation, taking into account the complex dynamics of motivation (e.g. the crowding effect)?

Deploying governance mechanisms to influence knowledge processes The issue of what governance mechanisms are chosen to steer knowledge sharing, integration and creation relates to organizational choice in a broad sense, that is, it includes choices between the two levels of analysis of governance structures[5] and organizational forms, that is, the specific combination of elements of governance mechanisms inside organizational forms. Consider the following examples of analyses that relate to these two levels of analysis.

Organization 14(1)
Articles

Nickerson and Zenger (2004) seek to explain how alternative organizational forms influence the efficient production of valuable knowledge. The unit of analysis for knowledge generation is a specific problem, whose value is determined by the values in the array of possible solutions and the cost of discovering a particularly valuable problem. The solution to complex problems is assumed to represent unique combinations or syntheses of existing knowledge. Problems differ according to their decomposability. Decomposable problems involve limited interaction, whereas non-decomposable problems involve extensive interaction. This has important implications for the type of searching for a solution. Directional search refers to classic trial and error search. It is efficient only for decomposable activities. Heuristic search refers to a group or team cognitively evaluating probable consequences of design choices.

Non-decomposable problems require individuals to share their specialized knowledge. The ability or motivation to share knowledge is impeded by two conditions: humans are cognitively constrained in the speed with which they learn and are prone to self-interest. The wide distribution of knowledge in conjunction with self-interest leads to two knowledge-related exchange hazards: knowledge appropriation and strategic knowledge accumulation. Consequently, efficiency considerations dictate the selection of an optimal governance mechanism and the provision of incentives. Three distinct governance structures and their suitability for problems with differing characteristics are examined: markets, authority-based hierarchies and consensus-based hierarchies. Briefly, markets are ideally suited when problems are decomposable and directional search is desired; consensus-based hierarchy creates high organizational costs and should only be adopted when the benefits for consensus are high, which is for problems that are highly complex and non-decomposable; finally, authority-based hierarchy is superior to markets in supporting heuristic search, but inferior in supporting directional search. The authors propose that authority based-hierarchies are best suitable for a range of problems that are moderately complex.

Osterloh and Frey (2000) and Foss (2003) examine the impact of organization form on knowledge processes, making a sharp distinction between firms and markets. The implicit argument is that 'discrete structural alternatives' such as firms and markets can be sharply distinguished because of strong complementarities between the constituent organizational elements (Milgrom and Roberts, 1990; Williamson, 1996). However, an open issue concerns how strong such complementarities are. A prevalent claim is that they tend to become less binding in the knowledge economy, as traditional organizational forms have difficulties efficiently organizing knowledge-transactions, giving rise to networks that mix firm and markets and cut across the boundaries of firms (Liebeskind et al., 1996).

Grandori (1997, 2001) analyses the various kinds of governance mechanisms that govern the transfer, sharing and integration of knowledge

The Emerging Knowledge Governance Approach
Nicolai J. Foss

between and within firms. Firms have enriched their knowledge management systems with explicit mechanisms to provide incentives for knowledge integration. Grandori (2001) argues that not only hierarchical and (what she calls) 'communitarian' mechanisms are usually applied, but also price-based (market-like) contracts and decentralized, but not identity-based mechanisms. She concludes that the portfolio of mechanisms that are effectively employable between firms to link nodes of specialized knowledge can hardly be distinguished from those mechanisms employable within firms. An implication of her discussion is a denial of the strong emphasis on organizational elements that can be found in large parts of organizational theory.

Grandori certainly has a point in suggesting that organizational theorists may too strongly have emphasized the theme of complementarity between 'governance mechanisms', and that too much emphasis (therefore) has been on 'discrete structural forms' of organization. She may also be right that the increasing importance of the sourcing, coordination and deployment of knowledge inputs in production makes complementarities between elements of governance mechanisms less strong. However, Grandori may also be wrong. Clearly, what is needed here is (again) more systematic empirical knowledge. However, more theoretical inquiry is similarly needed into how different combinations governance mechanisms may impact knowledge processes. Very little of this kind of design-oriented research exists (e.g. Siggelkow and Rivkin, 2005).[6]

KGA Research Question 2

What combinations of governance mechanisms are best suited for promoting knowledge sharing, integration, and creation within and between firms?[7]

Identifying knowledge-based hazards? Osterloh and Frey (2000), Grandori (2001) and Foss (2003) all more or less explicitly argue that knowledge processes have a number of salient features that set them apart from many 'ordinary' business processes (e.g. coordinating logistics, running an assembly line, making a contract with a supplier, etc.) and that the increasing importance of knowledge processes has an impact on which kinds of governance mechanisms can be deployed how and in which combinations. However, a deep and systematic analysis of what sets knowledge processes apart from ordinary business processes in terms of giving rise to organizational problems or hazards is largely missing from the literature.

This is highly problematic, as arguments concerning the deployment of administrative machinery to influence knowledge processes must ultimately be based on analysis of which kind of knowledge-related problems such deployment is supposed to solve. Moreover, existing claims may be contested. For example, Osterloh and Frey's arguments that the transfer of tacit knowledge cannot (at all?) be accomplished by contracting, and that employees cannot (at all?) be sanctioned for holding back tacit knowledge are questionable; for example, agreements can be made that a senior

41

Organization 14(1)
Articles

employee accepts a new employee as an apprentice and the outcome of the arrangement can to a certain extent be monitored. In sum, what is needed is a more thorough understanding of the organizational hazards that knowledge processes may give to and how these may be remedied by means of governance mechanisms (see also Buckley and Carter, 1996; Heimannn and Nickerson, 2002).

KGA Research Question 3

What are the peculiar organizational and exchange hazards of knowledge processes, and how does the deployment of governance mechanisms remedy such hazards?

While the above research questions are highly abstract (and, of course, do not exhaust the space of possible overall KGA research questions), they are: (1) fundamental; (2) unique to the KGA and (3) necessary to address in order to undertake more applied research. For example, hypothesis development relating to how multinational corporations leverage human resource management systems to promote knowledge sharing (Minbaeva et al., 2003), research into how governance mechanisms are deployed to knowledge-based strategic alliances (Heimeriks and Duyster, 2006; Mowery et al., 1996; Oxley, 1997) or the understanding of the governance of human capital organizations (Child and McGrath, 2001; Teece, 2003), the organizational antecedents to absorptive capacity (Janssen et al., 2006), the knowledge-based underpinnings of competitive advantage, the link between control of knowledge assets and the appropriation of surplus from relations (Coff, 1999; Coff and Blyler, 2003) and the provision of incentives to knowledge workers (Osterloh and Frey, 2000), are furthered to the extent that they are framed in ways that are akin to the above research questions and build on the answers that can be given to these questions.

Explanation in the Knowledge Governance Approach

In terms of Figure 1, the KGA identifies as its overall *explanandum* the relation between governance mechanisms and knowledge outcomes, recognizing that correlational analysis of the relation between these macro-entities and outcomes (i.e. Arrow 4 in Figure 1) is at best a starting point and that ultimately the relations need to be accounted for in terms of mechanisms that relate to Arrows 1, 2 and 3.

Microfoundations KGA explanation starts with the individual agent (even though it may be permissible to introduce more collective concepts, such as organization structure, in the analysis as shorthand). This implies modelling (i.e. making specific assumptions about) individual agents' preferences, knowledge, incentives, etc. This emphasis on individualistic foundations as an attempt to meet the lacunae left in the knowledge movement by the overriding emphasis on collective constructs. As Argote and Ingram (2000: 156) noted, to the extent that there has been progress in studying knowledge as

The Emerging Knowledge Governance Approach
Nicolai J. Foss

the basis of competitive advantage, '… it has been at the level of identifying consistencies in organizations' knowledge development paths and almost never at the level of human interactions that are the primary source of knowledge and knowledge transfer'. The knowledge governance approach attempts to address this 'primary source' by taking an explicitly individualistic approach. For example, the fundamental idea of Osterloh and Frey (2000) is understandable only if the analysis explicitly begins from individual motivation. More generally, the KGA asserts that many insights (including those that will emerge from addressing the research questions outlined above) cannot be reached *in lieu* of a starting point in individuals.

However, the question is, which micro-foundations? The general guideline is that this depends on the questions one tries to solve. Thus, economists have found that they have had to increasingly change the way they model individual cognition and motivation towards greater realism as they have moved from treating only market and macro-phenomena to also address contracts, organizations, networks, trust, and so. Moreover, a general rule is that the lower the level of analysis, the more fine-grained the description of the individual agent (Machlup, 1967). Because the KGA is intimately concerned with how the deployment of specific governance mechanisms impacts knowledge processes (i.e. a low level of analysis), rather specific assumptions need to be made about individual agents, and these assumptions must 'allow for' the phenomena to which an explanation is sought. Thus, assumptions that agents are always highly informed and docile will not assist the KGA.

While the KGA is sympathetic to the behavioural assumptions of transaction cost economics—that is, bounded rationality and opportunism (Williamson, 1996)—as these allow for the kind of organizational and exchange hazards that the KGA is concerned with, these behavioural assumptions may still be too coarse. Thus, 'bounded rationality' means many things and 'opportunism' may manifest itself in multiple ways. Moreover, bounded rationality and opportunism are not given, but can be influenced by governance mechanisms. Relatedly, a more sophisticated view of motivation (e.g. as in Osterloh and Frey, 2000) than is conventional in the economics of organization must be included in the KGA. Rather than merely representing the personal aesthetics of the present author, this reflects that a more nuanced view of motivation, one that is informed by advances in social psychology and organizational behaviour, seems necessary to capture the full complexity of the mechanisms that link governance mechanisms and knowledge processes (Cabrera et al., 2006; Grandori, 1997, 2001; Lindenberg, 2003; Osterloh and Frey, 2000).

Unit(s) of analysis It has been argued that the absence of a clear unit of analysis is a source of confusion in the knowledge movement at large (Williamson 1999). Is it routines (Nelson and Winter, 1982), or dynamic capabilities (Teece et al., 1997), or practices (Spender, 2005), or knowledge assets (Winter, 1987)? However, disciplines, fields, or approaches are not necessarily characterized

43

Organization 14(1)
Articles

by unique units of analysis. Thus, the existing diversity in the knowledge movement may simply reflect that different research problems are involved. Moreover, the emphasis on micro-foundations in the KGA does not dictate a specific unit of analysis, and is consistent with taking, for example, the 'problem' (Nickerson and Zenger, 2004) or the 'transaction' (Williamson, 1996) or a 'knowledge unit' (Simonin, 1999; Contractor and Ra, 2002) as the unit of analysis.[8] In general, what is the preferred unit of analysis should depend on the relevant research problems. The unit may differ depending on whether the focus is knowledge sharing or knowledge creation.

That being said, some units of analysis seem to be more generally applicable than others. Thus, Nickerson and Zenger (2004) construct a theory about the organization of knowledge creation, based on taking the problem as the unit of analysis. However, this seems primarily designed for understanding the governance of knowledge creation (i.e. solving problems by combining knowledge); it seems less well-suited for understanding knowledge sharing or integration.[9] The most generally applicable unit of analysis for the kind of problems that the KGA seeks to solve is the knowledge transaction, that is, the transfer of an identifiable 'piece' of knowledge from one actor to another one. Knowledge transactions are involved in knowledge sharing, integration, and creation. Note that taking the knowledge transaction as unit of analysis has the added benefit of linking up with organizational economics and an established framework for linking transactions to alternative kinds of organizing.

Dimensionalizing knowledge transactions However, the way of dimensionalizing transactions that has become dominant in organizational economics, namely the transaction cost economics triad of frequency/uncertainty/asset specificity, is at best incomplete for the purposes of treating knowledge transactions (see also Grandori, 2001; Heimannn and Nickerson, 2002; Nickerson and Zenger, 2004). It is not clear how dimensionalizing a knowledge transaction in these terms assist the understanding of, for example, knowledge sharing where transactional problems may be caused more by the degree of codification of the relevant knowledge than its 'uncertainty' (whatever that might mean in the specific context). The knowledge-based literature is unfortunately not entirely forthcoming with respect to dimensionalizing knowledge.[10]

An important exception is the Winter (1987) taxonomy, which has been the basis for much subsequent empirical work (e.g. Kogut and Zander, 1993; Simonin, 1999). Winter introduces the dimensions of tacitness versus explicitness, system-quality versus stand-alone, teachability versus non-teachability, and complexity versus non-complexity. Although these dimensions have usually been applied to more aggregate knowledge constructs (such as routines and capabilities) in the empirical literature, they can also be used to characterize knowledge transactions. Accordingly knowledge transactions can be dimensionalized in terms of the characteristics of the underlying knowledge. Clearly, there is no need to stop the process of dimensionalizing with the Winter taxonomy; other dimensions may be relevant.

The Emerging Knowledge Governance Approach
Nicolai J. Foss

For example, scholars working from a transaction cost economics perspective have suggested adding 'appropriability' as a relevant dimension (e.g. Oxley, 1997)[11] and Contractor and Ra (2002) suggest adding how 'novel' the knowledge is (knowledge with a higher degree of novelty is more costly to contract, absorb, assimilate, integrate, etc.). In the context of the KGA, the import of a dimensionalization of the unit of analysis is that the costs of sharing, integrating, and creating knowledge vary systematically with the relevant dimensions, and that the deployment of governance mechanisms to curb such costs should take this into account.

Organizational hazards Knowledge transactions give rise to organizational hazards and costs depending on how they score in terms of the above dimensions. Thus, in the context of sharing knowledge, knowledge transactions that are characterized by (explicitness, stand-alone, high teachability, non-complexity) are likely to be significantly less costly to administer than knowledge transactions with the opposite characteristics. Transactions (in the context of knowledge sharing) that involve knowledge that is new, tacit, has significant system-quality, is hard to teach, etc. are associated with cost of transmitting the knowledge from sender to receiver, (measurement) costs of ascertaining the extent to which knowledge has been shared, (monitoring) costs of inspecting input performance, and other well known organizational costs.

Knowledge governance As a positive approach the KGA shares a fundamental aim with the economics of organization: to examine how knowledge transactions—which differ in their characteristics—and governance mechanisms—which differs with respect to how it handles transactional problems—are matched, using economic efficiency as the explanatory principle and given behavioural assumptions (see Buckley and Carter, 1996; Grandori, 2001; Heimannn and Nickerson, 2002; Nickerson and Zenger, 2004; Williamson, 1996). As a practical and normative enterprise, knowledge governance means deploying governance mechanismses that mitigate costs of sharing, integrating and creating knowledge owing to the above characteristics of knowledge (Heimann and Nickerson 2002: 98). Knowledge governance therefore means deploying governance mechanisms so as to maximize the net benefits from processes of transferring, sharing and creating knowledge. This is similar to the transaction cost minimizing logic of transaction cost economics.

Consider some examples of such 'efficient alignment'. Knowledge sharing usually involves at least two activities, minding one's ordinary job and sharing knowledge with somebody else. When the relevant knowledge is tacit, it is usually costly to write it into a formal agreement (Osterloh and Frey, 2000). Providing high-powered incentives to the presumed knowledge sharer leads to a 'multi-tasking problem' (Holmström and Milgrom, 1991); the incentive is to concentrate effort on the measurable task and not on knowledge sharing which is costly to measure. Given tacitness, job-design and rewards are clearly related with respect to their impact on knowledge

45

sharing. A related problem may arise in the case where firms design production and development teams as partly overlapping in order to improve lead-time (Clark and Fujimoto, 1991). In this situation, it can be dangerous to use performance-based rewards because of the externalities between the activities of the two teams. Given the system-quality of knowledge in this case, task allocation and the definition of organizational units interact with reward systems in influencing the generation of knowledge. A third example concerns the use of delegation in the context of the sharing of knowledge. Given that tacitness increases the costs of making explicit agreements, delegation of the right to initiate, carry out, etc. knowledge sharing with colleagues seems to be an efficient alternative to instructing employees to share specific knowledge. In contrast, when knowledge is explicit, such delegation appears to be less necessary.

The crowning achievement of the KGA will be a discriminating alignment framework that can organize examples such as the above, bring out the unifying logic, and allow for predictions. Some inspired beginnings in this respect are Grandori (2001), Heimannn and Nickerson (2002) and Contractor and Ra (2002). At the present stage of development, what is arguably most needed, however, is empirical work that can assist in identifying knowledge-based hazards, ascertain how organizations deal with such hazards by deploying governance mechanisms, find out how these mechanisms are characteristically combined, and examine the performance implications of knowledge. Empirical work that grapples with these kind of issues has emerged within the last five years or so (e.g. Foss, 2003; Heimann and Nickerson, 2004; Hoetker and Mellewigt, 2006; Macher, 2006; Mayer and Argyres, 2004). The body of work is not large, but it is growing and may be taken as evidence of the fruitfulness of the KGA.

Conclusions: Defining the Knowledge Governance Approach

Pondering the issue of what 'knowledge approaches can contribute to organizational theory', Anna Grandori (in Grandori and Kogut, 2002: 225) observed that what can be contributed is '... a new "contingency" factor for understanding organizational arrangements ... Knowledge complexity, differentiation, and specialization, complementarity and interdependence are emerging as important contingencies affecting effective organization and governance solutions'. Grandori is indeed correct that an increasing number of papers in organizational theory, organizational economics, international business and strategic management incorporate new knowledge-based 'contingency factors'. However, the contention of this article is that one can go further and posit the existence of an emerging, distinctive approach—the 'knowledge governance approach' —that is taken up with theoretically grounding and empirically exploring the interplay between knowledge-based contingency factors and organization.

Accordingly, the purpose of the article has been to provide an identification of the KGA in terms of how it has arisen as a reaction to shortcomings in the

The Emerging Knowledge Governance Approach
Nicolai J. Foss

knowledge movement at large, the problems it seeks to solve and its approach to solving these problems. These three themes all centre on the issue of micro-foundations: the KGA is unique in accounting for the micro-level mechanisms that link governance mechanisms and knowledge processes. It is fundamentally because of this micro-emphasis that the KGA can uphold the explanation (beyond correlation) of how governance mechanisms can influence knowledge processes as a key research question. Similarly, it is this emphasis that lends credence to the design ambitions of the KGA: theories that explain and detail the mechanisms that mediate between instruments and outcomes are inherently more useful than theories that simply postulate a correlation (Coleman, 1990).

The emphasis on knowledge in a number of fields in business administration during the last two decades has been a major step forward. However, much of the relevant literature has been practice-driven and oriented towards prescriptions, and has had little or unclear disciplinary foundations. A hindrance for true application has been a certain explanatory naivety in much of this literature (e.g. the emphasis on ill-understood 'capabilities'). The KGA can be seen as an attempt to simultaneously meet the insistence on practical applicability of, for example, the KM field and the insistence of relative rigour that characterizes fields such as organizational design theory or organizational economics. In that respect, it marks a return to the ideals that animated the organizational design literature of the 1960s and 1980s, which certainly also touched on issues that are related to the KGA [e.g. the concern with how organizational structure impacts information processes, the notion of 'adhocracies' in Mintzberg (1979) which acknowledges organizations where human capital inputs are particularly important, etc.]. In order to successfully meet both ambitions, much more work is needed within the KGA. This article has sketched the kind of work that should be done to further the KGA.

Notes

I am grateful to participants at the 2005 EGOS Conference for comments on the talk that formed the basis of this article, to Andreas Scherer for urging me to put my thoughts in a written format, to Peter Abell, Teppo Felin and J.-C. Spender for very stimulating discussions on various occasions of fundamental issues that are treated in this article, and to four anonymous reviewers for truly excellent feedback. Thanks to Yvonne Borkelmann for research assistance.

1 The term 'knowledge governance' seems to have been first used by Grandori (1997).
2 The organization/knowledge-and-information link is certainly not a recent one either, as many writers have argued that organization is responsive to knowledge and information and that in turn organization may shape knowledge and information. Thus, on a fundamental level the information-processing emphasis in organization theory of the 1960s and 1970s illustrates the first causality, and earlier, von Hayek's (1945) famous argument concerning the need

47

Organization 14(1)
Articles

for decentralization when relevant knowledge is 'knowledge of time and circumstance' makes a similar point on an even more abstract level. Less abstractly, the innovation management literature has long stressed that such organizational issues as role definition, team composition, the distribution of authority, and communication efforts should be very much responsive to the nature of the development effort (e.g. Clark and Fujimoto, 1991).

3 An exception is Tsai (2002) who indicates that formal hierarchical structure, in the form of centralization, has a significant negative effect on knowledge sharing. In contrast, informal lateral relations, in the form of social interaction, have a significant positive effect on knowledge sharing.

4 This is hardly surprising, as many of the components of informal organization, such as culture, are semi-permanent traits of an organization that may be harder to change than organizational design variables such as the components of organizational structure, reward systems, etc. In the language of optimal control theory, informal organization variables are more like 'state variables' whereas formal organization variables are more like 'control variables'.

5 In the sense of Williamson (1996), that is, the choice between hierarchies, hybrids, and markets.

6 Some initial empirical investigations are Laursen and Foss (2003) who empirically examine the impact of new HRM systems on innovation, Minbaeva et al. (2003) who examine how HRM in the subsidiaries of multinational firms impact knowledge transfer within such firms and Foss (2003) who use a case study to argue that the combination of a strong authority mechanism (implying frequent managerial intervention) with a high degree of delegation and project-based organization is an inefficient one for the purpose of knowledge creation.

7 A derived research issue—too complicated and encompassing to treat in detail here—concerns the interaction of formal and informal elements of organization with respect to knowledge processes. For example, may formal reward systems for knowledge sharing be destructive of psychological contracts that encourage knowledge sharing? Some of this is touched upon in Osterloh and Frey (2000).

8 Although notions of 'firm-level' knowledge, such as 'capabilities', do not seem to have a clear foundation in individual action, and will be avoided in the KGA.

9 For example, in the case of knowledge sharing, the solution may be obvious (e.g. everybody should know X); however, the problem is inducing Jack to share X with Jill and other employees.

10 The many studies of inter-firm imitation and intra-firm knowledge transfer (e.g. Maritan and Brush, 2003) tend to develop dimensions of, say, capabilities in an inductive manner and the explicit or implicit dimensionalizations differ from study to study.

11 Appropriability is to some extent derivative of, e.g. the tacitness versus explicitness dimension, but not fully, as it also includes the legal framework surrounding the transaction.

References

Argote, Linda (1999) *Organizational Learning: Creating, Retaining and Transferring Knowledge*. Boston, MA: Kluwer.

The Emerging Knowledge Governance Approach
Nicolai J. Foss

Argote, Linda and Ingram, Paul (2000) 'Knowledge Transfer: A Basis for Competitive Advantage in Firms', *Organizational Behavior and Human Decision Processes* 82(1): 150–69.

Barzel, Yoram (1997) *Economic Analysis of Property Rights*. Cambridge: Cambridge University Press.

Brown, John S. and Duguid, Paul (1998) 'Organizing Knowledge', *California Management Review* 40(3): 90–111.

Buckley, Peter J. and Carter, Martin J. (1996) 'The Economics of Business Process Design: Motivation, Information, and Coordination Within the Firm', *International Journal of the Economics of Business* 33: 301–32.

Cabrera, A., Collins, W. C. and Salgado, J. F. (2006) 'Determinants of Organizational Engagement in Knowledge Sharing', *International Journal of Human Resource Management* 17: 245–64.

Child, John and McGrath, Rita (2001) 'Organizations Unfettered: Organizational Form in an Information Intensive Economy', *Academy of Management Journal* 44: 1135–48.

Clark, Kim B. and Fujimoto, T. (1991) *Product Development Performance: Strategy, Organisation and Management in the World Auto Industry*. Boston, MA: Harvard University Press.

Coase, Ronald H. (1937) 'The Nature of the Firm', *Economica* 4: 386–405.

Coase, Ronald H. (1960) 'The Problem of Social Cost', *Journal of Law and Economics* 3: 1–44.

Coff, Russell (1999) 'When Competitive Advantage Doesn't Lead to Performance: Resource-Based Theory and Stakeholder Bargaining Power', *Organization Science* 10: 119–33.

Coff, Russell and Blyler, M. (2003) 'Dynamic Capabilities, Social Capital, and Rent Appropriation: Ties that Split Pies', *Strategic Management Journal* 24: 677–86.

Coleman, James S. (1990) *Foundations of Social Theory*. Cambridge, MA: The Belknap Press of Harvard University Press.

Contractor, Farok J. and Ra, Wonchan (2002) 'How Knowledge Attributes Influence Alliance Governance Choices', *Journal of International Management* 8: 11–27.

Easterby-Smith, Mark and Lyles, Marjorie A., eds (2003) *Handbook of Organizational Learning and Knowledge Management*. Oxford: Blackwell Publishing.

Eisenhardt, Kathleen M. and Santos, Filipe M. (2002) 'Knowledge-Based View: A New Theory of Strategy?' in A. Pettigrew, H. Thomas and R. Whittington (eds) *Handbook of Strategy and Management*, pp. 139–64. London: Sage.

Felin, Teppo and Foss, Nicolai J (2005) 'Strategic Organization: A Field in Search of Micro-Foundations', *Strategic Organization* 3: 441–55.

Foss, Nicolai J. (2002) 'New Organizational Forms—Critical Perspectives', *International Journal of the Economics of Business* 9(1): 1.

Foss, Nicolai J. (2003) 'Selective Intervention and Internal Hybrids: Interpreting and Learning from the Rise and Decline of the Oticon Spaghetti Organization', *Organization Science* 14: 331–49.

Foss, Kirsten and Foss, Nicolai J. (2005) 'Value and Transaction Costs', *Strategic Management Journal* 26: 541–53.

Foss, Nicolai J. and Mahnke, Volker (2003) 'Knowledge Management: What Does Organizational Economics Contribute?', in Mark Easterby-Smith and Marjorie Lyles (eds) *Handbook of Knowledge Management*. Oxford: Basil Blackwell.

Grandori, Anna (1997) 'Governance Structures, Coordination Mechanisms and Cognitive Models', *Journal of Management and Governance* 1: 29–42.

Organization 14(1)
Articles

Grandori, Anna (2001) 'Neither Hierarchy nor Identity: Knowledge Governance Mechanisms and the Theory of the Firm', *Journal of Management and Governance* 5: 381–99.

Grandori, Anna and Kogut, Bruce (2002) 'Dialogue on Organization and Knowledge', *Organization Science* 13: 224–32.

Granovetter, Mark (1973) 'The Strength of Weak Ties', *American Journal of Sociology* 78: 1360–80.

Grant, Robert M. (1996) 'Towards a Knowledge-Based Theory of the Firm', *Strategic Management Journal* 17: 109–22.

Halal, William E. and Taylor, K. B. (1998) *Twenty-First Century Economics: Perspectives of Socioeconomics for a Changing World.* New York, NY: St. Martin's Press.

Hamel, Gary (1991) 'Competition for Competence and Inter-Partner Learning Within International Strategic Alliances', *Strategic Management Journal* 12: 83–103.

Hansen Morten T. (2002) 'Knowledge Networks: Explaining Effective Knowledge Sharing in Multiunit Companies', *Organization Science* 13: 232–48

Hart, Oliver (1995) *Firms, Contracts, and Financial Structure.* Oxford: Oxford University Press.

Hedlund, Gunnar (1994) 'A Model of Knowledge Management and the N-Form Corporation', *Strategic Management Journal* 15: 73–91.

Hedström, Peter and Swedberg, Richard (1996) 'Social Mechanisms', *Acta Sociologica* 39: 281–308.

Heimann, Bruce and Nickerson, Jack A. (2002) 'Towards Reconciling Transaction Cost Economics and the Knowledge-based View of the Firm: The Context of Interfirm Collaborations', *International Journal of the Economics of Business* 9: 97–116.

Heimann, Bruce and Nickerson, Jack A. (2004) 'Empirical Evidence Regarding the Tension Between Knowledge Sharing and Knowledge Expropriation in Collaborations', *Managerial and Decision Economics* 25: 401–20.

Heimeriks, Koen and Duysters, Geert (2006) 'Alliance Capability as Mediator Between Experience and Alliance Capability', *Journal of Management Studies* (forthcoming).

Hislop, David (2005) *Knowledge Management in Organizations.* Oxford: Oxford University Press.

Hoetker, Glenn and Mellewigt, Thomas (2006) 'Matching Alliance Governance to Alliance Content,' in Africa Ariño and Jeff Reuer (eds) *Strategic Alliances.* Basingstoke: Palgrave Macmillan.

Holmström, Bengt and Milgrom, Paul (1991) 'Multitask Principal-Agent Analyses: Incentive Contracts, Asset Ownership, and Job Design', *Journal of Law, Economics, and Organization* 7: 24–52.

Jansen Justin J.P, van den Bosch, Frans A. J. and Volberda, Henk W. (2006) 'Managing Potential and Realized Absorptive Capacity: How Do Organizational Antecedents Matter?', *Academy of Management Journal* 48: 999–1015.

Jones, Gareth R. (1983) 'Transaction Costs, Property Rights, and Organizational Culture: An Exchange Perspective', *Administrative Science Quarterly* 28: 454–67.

Kogut, Bruce and Zander, Udo (1992) 'Knowledge of the Firm, Combinative Capabilities, and the Replication of Technology', *Organization Science* 3: 383–97.

The Emerging Knowledge Governance Approach
Nicolai J. Foss

Kogut, Bruce and Zander, Udo (1993) 'Knowledge of the Firm and the Evolutionary Theory of the Multinational Corporation', *Journal of International Business Studies* 24: 625–45.

Kogut, Bruce and Zander, Udo (1996) 'What Firms Do? Coordination, Identity, and Learning', *Organization Science* 7: 502–18.

Kogut, Bruce (2000) 'The Network as Knowledge: Generative Rules and the Emergence of Structure', *Strategic Management Journal* 21: 405–25.

Laursen, Keld and Foss, Nicolai J. (2003) 'New HRM Practices, Complementarities, and the Impact on Innovation Performance', *Cambridge Journal of Economics* 27: 243–63.

Liebeskind, Julia P., Oliver, Amalya A., Zucker, Lynne and Brewer, Marilyn (1996) 'Social Networks, Learning, and Flexibility: Sourcing Scientific Knowledge Among New Biotechnology Firms', *Organization Science* 7: 428–43.

Lindenberg, Sigward (2003) 'The Cognitive Side of Governance', *Research in the Sociology of Organizations* 20: 47–76.

Lippman, Steven A. and Rumelt, Richard P. (2003) 'The Payments Perspective', *Strategic Management Journal* 24: 903–27.

Lyles, Marjorie A. and Schwenk, Charles R. (1992) 'Top Management Strategy and Organizational Knowledge', *Journal of Management Studies* 29: 155–74.

Machamer, P., Darden, L. and Craver, C. F. (2000) 'Thinking About Mechanisms', *Philosophy of Science* 67: 1–25.

Macher, Jeffrey. T. (2006) 'Technological Development and the Boundaries of the Firm', *Management Science* 52(6): 826–43.

Machlup, Fritz (1967) 'Theories of the Firm: Marginalist, Managerial and Behavioral', in Fritz Machlup (1978) *Essays on Economic Methodology*. New York, NY: Wiley.

Maritan, C. A. and Brush, T. H. (2003) 'Heterogeneity and Transferring Practices: Implementing Flow Manufacturing in Multiple Plants', *Strategic Management Journal* 24: 945–60.

Mayer, Kyle and Argyres, Nicholas (2004) 'Learning to Contract', *Organization Science* 15: 394–410.

Milgrom, Paul and Roberts, John (1990) 'The Economics of Modern Manufacturing: Technology, Strategy and Organization', *American Economic Review* 80: 511–28.

Minbaeva, Dana, Pedersen, Torben, Björkman, Ingemar, Fey, Carl and Park H.J. (2003) 'MNC Knowledge Transfer, Subsidiary Absorptive Capacity, and HRM', *Journal of International Business Studies* 34: 586–99.

Mintzberg, Henry (1979) *The Structuring of Organizations*. Englewood Cliffs, NJ: Prentice-Hall.

Mowery, David C., Oxley, Joanne and Silverman, Brian (1996) 'Strategic Alliances and Interfirm Knowledge Transfer', *Strategic Management Journal* 17: 77–91.

Nelson, Richard R. and Winter, Sidney G. (1982) *The Evolutionary Theory of the Firm*. Cambridge, MA: Harvard University Press.

Nickerson, Jackson and Zenger, Todd (2004) 'A Knowledge-Based Theory of the Firm: The Problem-Solving Perspective', *Organization Science* 15(6): 617–32.

Osterloh, Margit and Frey, Bruno (2000) 'Motivation, Knowledge Transfer and Organizational Form', *Organization Science* 11: 538–50.

Oxley, Joanne (1997) 'Appropriability Hazards and Governance in Strategic Alliances: A Transaction Cost Approach', *Journal of Law, Economics, and Organization* 13: 387–409.

51

Organization 14(1)
Articles

Siggelkow, Nicolaj and Rivkin, Jan W. (2005) 'Speed and Search: Designing Organizations for Turbulence and Complexity', *Organization Science* 16: 101–22.

Simonin, Bernard L. (1999) 'Transfer of Marketing Know-How in International Strategic Alliances', *Journal of International Business Studies* 30: 463–90.

Spender, J.-C. (1996) 'Making Knowledge the Basis of a Dynamic Theory of the Firm', *Strategic Management Journal* 17 (Winter special issue): 45–62.

Spender, J.-C. (2005) 'Review Article: An Essay of the State of Knowledge Management', *Prometheus* 23: 101–16.

Starbuck, William (1992) 'Learning by Knowledge-Intensive Firms', *Journal of Management Studies* 29: 713–41.

Tallman, Steven (2003) 'The Significance of Bruce Kogut's and Udo Zander's Article, 'Knowledge of the Firm and the Evolutionary Theory of the Multinational Morporation', *Journal of International Business Studies* 34: 495–97.

Teece, David J. (2003) 'Expert Talent and the Design of (Professional Services) Firms', *Industrial and Corporate Change* 12: 895–916.

Teece, David J., Pisano, Gary and Shuen, Amy (1997) 'Dynamic Capabilities and Strategic Management', *Strategic Management Journal* 18: 509–34.

Tsai, W. P. (2001) 'Knowledge Transfer in Intra-Organizational Networks', *Academy of Management Journal* 44: 996–1004.

Tsai, W. P. (2002) 'Organization Social Structure of "Coopetition" within a Multiunit Organization', *Science* 13: 179–90.

Tsai, W. P. and Ghoshal, S. (1998) 'Social Capital and Value Creation: The Role of Interfirm Networks', *Academy of Management Journal* 41: 464–76.

von Hayek, Friedrich A. (1945) 'The Use of Knowledge in Society', in *Individualism and Economic Order*. Chicago, IL: University of Chicago Press.

von Hayek, Friedrich A. (1955) *The Counter-Revolution of Science*. Chicago, IL: University of Chicago Press.

Williamson, Oliver E. (1996) *The Mechanisms of Governance*. Oxford: Oxford University Press.

Williamson, Oliver E. (1999) 'Strategy Research: Governance and Competence Perspectives', *Strategic Management Journal* 20: 1087–108.

Winter, Sidney G. (1987) 'Knowledge and Competence as Strategic Assets', in D. Teece (ed.) *The Competitive Challenge*, pp. 159–84. Cambridge, MA: Ballinger.

Nicolai J. Foss is Professor at Copenhagen Business School and the Norwegian School of Economics and Business Administration. He is Director of the Center for Strategic Management and Globalization at Copenhagen Business School. His research is mainly concerned with firm strategy and economic organization. He is particularly interested in the intersection between these two fields. His work has been published in *Journal of International Business Studies*, *Journal of Management and Governance*, *Journal of Management Studies*, *Organization Science*, *Strategic Management Journal*, *Strategic Organization* and other journals. **Address:** Department of Strategy and Management, Norwegian School of Economics and Business Administration, Breiviksveien 40; N-5045; Bergen, Norway, and Center for Strategic Management and Globalization, Copenhagen Business School, Porcelænshaven 24B, 2nd Floor, 2000 Frederiksberg; Denmark. [email: njf.smg@cbs.dk]

PART II

ECONOMIC ORGANIZATION

9

Int. J. of the *Economics* of *Business, Vol. 9, No. 1, 2002, pp. 9–35*

'Coase vs Hayek': Economic Organization and the Knowledge Economy

NICOLAI J. FOSS

ABSTRACT *Many writers argue that economic organization is undergoing major transformation in the emerging knowledge economy; authority relations are withering; legal and ownership-based definitions of the boundaries of firms are becoming irrelevant and there are increasingly few constraints on the set of feasible combinations of coordination mechanisms. The present paper critically deals with these claims, beginning from the basic idea that they may be analysed as turning on the implications for the Coasian firm of the Hayekian notion that the distributed knowledge is a strong constraint on the use of planned coordination. It argues that there are efficiency reasons for the existence of authority under Hayekian distributed knowledge; that the increasing importance of knowledge in production does not render legal and ownership-based notions of the boundaries of the firm irrelevant; and that coordination mechanisms will also cluster in certain, predictable combinations in the emerging knowledge economy. Thus, Coasian firm organization is consistent with Hayekian knowledge conditions.*

Key words: The knowledge economy; Authority; Firms' boundaries; Internal organization.

JEL classification: D23, L14, L22, D80.

1. Introduction

During the last decade, management academics have strongly stressed the role of organizational factors in the process of building knowledge-based strategies that will bring sustained competitive advantage.[1] Thus, it is typically argued that adopting 'new organizational forms' (Daft and Lewin, 1993) – that is, new ways of structuring internal organization and the boundaries of firms – is necessary for

I acknowledge discussion with, and helpful comments of, Mark Casson, Kirsten Foss, Bruno Frey, Anna Grandori, Geoff Hodgson, Margit Osterloh, Edwin Rühli, Ron Sanchez, seminar audiences at Universität Zürich, The Norwegian Business School, Bergen, Copenhagen Business School, Universität Freiburg, Université Caén, one reviewer and particularly Thorbjørn Knudsen. Errors remain my own.
Nicolai J. Foss, Department of Industrial Economics and Strategy, Copenhagen Business School, Howitzvej 60; 2000 Frederiksberg; Denmark; e-mail: njf.ivs@cbs.dk

International Journal of the Economics of Business
ISSN 1357-1516 print/ISSN 1466-1829 online © 2002 Taylor & Francis Ltd
http://www.tandf.co.uk/journals
DOI: 10.1080/13571510110102958

becoming the 'information age organizations' (Mendelsson and Pillai, 1999) that can build the 'dynamic capabilities' required for competing in the emerging 'knowledge economy.' Radical changes in the organization of economic activities are argued to take place in tandem with, and perhaps prompted by, changes in the composition of inputs toward knowledge inputs, an increase of the 'knowledge-content' of outputs, the declining importance of physical capital in production and the parallel and increasing importance of human capital, a stepping up of innovative activity, and increasingly inexpensive networked computing – that is, those changes that are increasingly taken to indicate the emergence of the knowledge economy (Halal and Taylor, 1998; Prusac, 1998; Tapscott, 1999; Munro, 2000).

There is growing, although still somewhat sparse, evidence that firms are, in fact, increasingly experimenting with new ways of structuring their governance of transactions, and that these changes have implications for profitability (Mendelsson and Pillai, 1999), productivity (Ichniowski *et al.*, 1996; Cappelli and Neumark, 2001), and innovation performance (Laursen 2002; Laursen and Foss, 2002). It seems that some of these changes are related to changes in the form of competitive activities, in firms' input requirements, and their use of information technologies (Rajan and Zingales, 1998). The still rather open questions are how, and how much, economic organization will be affected. Much more empirical work is needed to assess the validity of the sometimes rather far-reaching claims that are put forward by advocates of the radical decentralization of firms, empowerment schemes, and the like. However, it is certainly possible to engage in dialogue on a purely theoretical level with those who argue that economic organization is in the process of a radical transformation as a result of the emergence of the knowledge economy. To do so is the purpose of the present paper. Thus, I shall discuss the implications for the organization of economic activities of industries becoming increasingly 'knowledge-intensive,'[2] an increasing share of the workforce being constituted by 'knowledge workers,' commercially useful knowledge becoming increasingly distributed, etc., accepting, for the sake of argument, these alleged tendencies as facts. In generic theoretical terms, I discuss the implications for the Coasian firm of the Hayekian notion that the distributed and subjective character of economically relevant knowledge is a strongly binding constraint on the use of planned coordination. Hence, the title of the paper.

Understanding economic organization in the context of the emerging knowledge economy is an important challenge for a number of reasons. Strong claims are being made on the subject, particularly by management scholars and sociologists, and it is important to examine the validity and reach of those claims. So far, organizational economists have only given sporadic attention to these issues (e.g., Holmström and Roberts, 1998; Mendelsson and Pillai, 1999), although they go right to the heart of the crucial and perennial issues in the theory of economic organization. Thus, in many recent writings on economic organization in the knowledge economy, it is asserted that authority relations, the boundaries of firms and the way in which mechanisms for coordinating economic activities are linked will undergo significant change under the impact of the increasing importance of knowledge that is complex, controlled by specialists, and distributed in character. Although such claims clearly concern the central issues in the economics of organization, it is sometimes argued (e.g., Boisot, 1998; Helper *et al.*, 2000) that the economics of organization is incapable of framing and explaining issues of economic organization in the knowledge economy.[3]

The following arguments and positions are developed in the paper. Although it is a justified complaint that organizational economics so far has not seriously addressed economic organization in the context of the knowledge economy, organizational economics insights are extremely useful for framing the issues. Moreover, they help to temper – by making clear the limits of – more extreme claims about organization in the knowledge economy. Among such claims are that authority relations will strongly diminish in importance (Zucker, 1991); that ownership-based and legal definitions of the boundaries of firms will become increasingly irrelevant for understanding the organization of economic activities (Helper *et al.*, 2000); and that constraints on the space of feasible combinations of coordination mechanisms will be very significantly relaxed (Miles, *et al.* 1991; Tapscott, 1999).

This paper shows that even in the knowledge economy, authority relations will continue to exist as efficient coordination mechanisms, defining the boundaries of firms in terms of asset ownership is entirely meaningful, and relations of complementarity between coordination mechanisms will obtain, so that transactions will tend to cluster in discrete structural forms (i.e., governance structures). However, this does not mean that organizational economics can survive confrontation with the knowledge economy in a completely unchanged form. On the contrary, work needs to be done to better understand the impact of knowledge assets (cf. also Holmström and Roberts, 1998), distributed knowledge (Foss, 1999), and environmental complexity on organizational design.[4] In particular, organizational economists need to develop a more refined and realistic understanding of authority than the existing crude view which has been essentially unchanged since Coase (1937) and Simon (1951).

The design of the paper is as follows. I begin by clarifying the subject under discussion, isolating two assumptions on the role of knowledge in production and four propositions that concern how changes in authority relations, the boundaries of the firm and internal organization are driven by changes in the way in which knowledge enters into productive activities. Taken together, these assumptions and propositions are intended to capture the main thrust of recent claims about economic organization in the knowledge economy (section 2). The strategy in the remaining parts of the paper then is to examine whether the stated assumptions on the role of knowledge in production imply the propositions as these pertain to authority (sections 3 and, 4), the boundaries of the firm (section 5), and the combinability of coordination mechanisms (section 6).

2. Economic Organization in the Knowledge Economy: An Interpretation of Recent Debate

Some Recent Claims about Economic Organization in a Knowledge Economy

A number of different disciplines, fields and sub-fields are involved in the ongoing discussion of efficient organization in the context of the emerging knowledge economy. Still, a number of distinct shared themes are discernible. Thus, at the overall level, a consensus seems to be emerging that tasks and activities in the knowledge economy need to be coordinated in a manner that is very different from the management of traditional industrial manufacturing activities, with profound implications for the authority relation and the internal organization and boundaries of firms. This is seen as a response to the changing role of knowledge in production.

Thus, a typical line of argument begins from noting that because of the increasing importance in knowledge-intensive industries of combining diverse knowledge inputs, sourcing knowledge for this purpose, and keeping sourcing options open, networks between agents controlling critical knowledge increasingly become the relevant dimension for understanding the organization of economic activities (Powell, 1990; Zucker, 1991; Harryson, 2000). Such networks typically cut across the boundaries of the firm, at least to the extent that these are defined in terms of ownership.[5] The legal boundaries of the firm will only coincide with the boundaries of knowledge-based networks if considerations of appropriability, imposing a need for protecting knowledge, dominate considerations of sourcing knowledge from networks. More likely, however, the boundaries between markets and firms, as defined in legal and/or ownership terms, will fade into insignificance as generalized reciprocal knowledge exchange in communities of practice and other network forms, as well as hyper-competitive conditions, make knowledge protection issues less relevant.

Thus, according to this argument the (presumed) fact that knowledge is becoming more dispersed, and increasingly must be sourced outside of the firm as traditionally defined, has profound implications for our understanding of the *loci* of economic activities and the boundaries between these. An accompanying argument asserts that as knowledge becomes increasingly dispersed, authority also tends to shift to expert individuals who control important knowledge resources. This has two effects. First, to the extent that the agents controlling these resources are not employees or otherwise agents of the firm, this contributes to the blurring of the boundaries of the firm.[6] Second, to the extent that important knowledge assets are increasingly controlled by employees ('knowledge workers') themselves, authority relations are fading into insignificance. This is partly a result of the increased bargaining power on the part of knowledge workers (stemming from the control over critical knowledge assets) (Coff, 1999), and partly a result of the increasingly specialist nature of knowledge work (Hodgson, 1998a). The specialist nature of knowledge work implies that principals/employers become increasingly ignorant about the members of the set of actions that are open to specialist agents/employees, thus making the exercise of authority through direction increasingly inefficient. The combined effect of these tendencies is to wreck the economist's traditional authority and/or ownership-based criteria of what distinguishes market transactions from hierarchical transactions (Zingales, 2000). Thus, whether direction by means of order giving (Coase, 1937; Simon, 1951; Williamson, 1985; Demsetz, 1988) and backed up by the ownership of alienable assets (Hart and Moore, 1990) obtains or not is increasingly irrelevant for understanding the organization of economic activities in a knowledge economy (Grandori, 2002).

The emerging knowledge economy also influences the design of firms' internal organization, that is, their internal allocation of decision rights and their structuring of remuneration schemes. As Miles *et al.* (1997: 7) argue:

> Each major era in business history has featured a particular form of organization. Early hierarchical, vertically integrated organizations have largely given way to network organizations that link the assets and know-how of numerous upstream and downstream industry partners. A number of leading companies today are experimenting with a new way of organizing – the cellular form. Cellular organizations are built on the principles of entrepreneurship, self-organization, and member ownership.

In the future, cellular organizations will be used in situations requiring continuous learning and innovation.

By suggesting that radical internal hybrids, 'built on the principles of entrepreneurship, self-organization, and member ownership,' are emerging as stable organizational modes, such quotations suggest that mechanisms for coordinating economic activities are more combinable, and that the set of stable discrete governance structures is larger, than is conventionally assumed in much of organization theory and in the economics of organization (e.g., Coase, 1937; Williamson, 1996).[7] These new governance structures are increasingly referred to as 'new organizational forms' (Daft and Lewin, 1993; Zenger and Hesterly, 1997). To the extent that new organizational forms represent new ways of combining mechanisms that have traditionally been seen as characteristic of governance structures that are polar opposites, they also exemplify the fading boundaries between markets and firms (Helper *et al.*, 2000).

What Is Going On Here? Some Interpretive Assumptions and Propositions

It is first necessary to define those aspects of the knowledge economy that are most obviously relevant for an understanding of economic organization. Existing treatments emphasize phenomena, such as increased knowledge content of outputs and the composition of inputs, hyper-competition and therefore the paramount importance of learning, decreasing average corporate size, the importance of IT innovations, increasing differentiation of demand, increased general environmental complexity, increasing importance of networks for the transfer and production of knowledge, etc. (e.g., D'Aveni, 1994; Nonaka and Takeuchi, 1995; Grant, 1996; Miles *et al.*, 1997; Boisot, 1998; Matusik and Hill, 1998; Coombs and Metcalfe, 2000; Zingales, 2000).

Dealing with all of these as they impact on economic organization is a task of forbidding complexity. For *the purposes of understanding economic organization*, recent claims about the impact of the knowledge economy on economic organization may be usefully narrowed down to two basic assumptions about knowledge in production and four basic propositions about economic organization.[8] The assumptions are:

● *Assumption 1*: Knowledge that is sourced for productive purposes is becoming increasingly distributed (e.g., Coombs and Metcalfe, 2000).[9]
● *Assumption 2*: Knowledge assets controlled by individual agents ('knowledge workers') are becoming increasingly important in production in terms of contribution to value-added (e.g., Boisot, 1998).

For convenience, settings in which both Assumptions 1 and 2 hold true are characterized as 'Hayekian settings'.

The three following propositions about economic organization in the emerging knowledge economy focus the issues further:

● *Proposition 1*: Authority relations will become increasingly inefficient means of allocating resources and will therefore wither (e.g., Semler, 1989; Hodgson, 1998a).

- *Proposition 2*: The boundaries of firms blur because of the increasing importance of knowledge networks that transcend those boundaries. Thus, while formal legal and ownership-based definitions of the boundaries of the firm may be made, they will be increasingly irrelevant from an economic perspective (e.g., Badaracco, 1991; Zucker, 1991; Helper *et al.*, 2000).
- *Proposition 3*: Coordination mechanisms are combined in new, innovative ways (i.e., 'new organizational forms').[10] This suggests that efficiency does not require such mechanisms to be combined in discrete governance structures. Coordination mechanisms combine over a continuum, not in discrete chunks (e.g., Grandori, 1997, 2002).

Although these propositions are rather open-ended, they are open to theoretical treatment (and in principle to empirical test as well). So is the final proposition:

- *Proposition 4*: The effects described in Propositions 1, 2 and 3 are driven by changes in the way in which knowledge enters into the productive process, as described in Assumptions 1 and 2.

Proposition 4 is critically discussed in the following sections by examining whether the effects described in Propositions 1, 2 and 3 necessarily follow from Assumptions 1 and 2. I discuss the role (if any) of authority in Hayekian settings, examine the connections between authority and ownership, and finally discuss how authority and ownership constrain the malleability and combinability of coordination mechanisms.

3. The Knowledge Economy as a Challenge to Authority Relations

The Standard Economics View of Authority: Coase and Simon

It is conventional to date the birth of organizational economics to Ronald Coase's 1937 paper, 'The Nature of the Firm.' This is justified by Coase's stress on market failure caused by transaction costs as the starting point for any explanation of firms, and by his contractual approach, comparative institutionalism, and clear identification of the main explanatory requirements of a theory of the firm (i.e., explaining the existence, boundaries, and internal organization of firms).[11] Of particular interest here, Coase also founded the widespread practice of identifying the firm with the employment contract; indeed, he puts much emphasis on the flexibility afforded by incomplete employment contracts and the authority relation as the ultimate reason for the existence of firms.[12] Thus, as Langlois and Foss (1999) argue, Coase's explanation for the emergence of the firm is ultimately a coordination one. The firm is an institution that lowers the costs of qualitative coordination in a world of uncertainty.[13] The employment contract is explained in related terms, as '. . . one whereby the factor, for a certain remuneration (which may be fixed or fluctuating) agrees to obey the directions of an entrepreneur *within certain limits*. The essence of the power is that it should only state the limits to the powers of the entrepreneur. Within these limits, he can therefore direct the other factors of production' (idem.: 242).[14]

A later paper by Herbert Simon (1951) provided a formalization of Coase's notion of the employment relationship and a clarification of the notion of authority. The latter is defined as obtaining when a 'boss' is permitted by a 'worker' to select actions, $\mathbf{A}^O c\mathbf{A}$, where $\mathbf{A}$ is the set of the worker's possible behaviours. More or less authority is then simply defined as making the set $\mathbf{A}^O$ larger or smaller. The model is basically a multi-stages game in the context of an incomplete contract with *ex post* governance: In the first period, the prospective worker decides whether to accept employment or not. Then nature intervenes, uncertainty is resolved, and the costs and benefits associated with the various possible tasks are revealed. Finally, the boss directs the worker to a task. To the extent that the boss cares about his reputation, he will not direct the worker to undertake tasks that lie outside the latter's 'zone of acceptance,' and there may thus be an equilibrium in the three-stages game.[15]

To sum up, in the Coase-Simon view of authority, the action space is well-defined and known both to the boss and the worker; the boss observes those states of nature to which it is necessary to react (e.g., a realization of demand on the firm's product markets); he possesses the right to direct the worker, and the worker obeys the boss' instructions 'within limits.'

The Sources of Authority

The Coase-Simon view of authority raises a number of problems. One of these is well-established in the literature, and concerns the problem of what is ultimately the source of the employer's authority given that human assets are inalienable, so that slavery is usually not a viable arrangement. As will be discussed subsequently, there are other problems that only become apparent in what was earlier called 'Hayekian settings,' and which relate to the critique put forward by proponents of the knowledge economy of authority relations. However, since addressing these latter problems is made easier by an understanding of the more conventional problem concerning the sources of the employer's authority, we briefly consider this problem first.

The problem of the sources of employers' authority was famously initiated by Alchian and Demsetz's (1972) argument that it is not meaningful to assume that an employer can force an employee to do what the employer wants in the absence of coercion. An implication of this view is that the distinction between the authority-based and the price-based modes of allocation emphasized by Coase and Simon is superficial. One may perhaps talk about a nexus of contracts becoming more 'firm-like,' as continuity of association among input owners increases and/or residual claimancy becomes more concentrated, but it is not in general useful to talk about 'firms' as distinctive entities. In reality, they argue, there is no economic difference between 'firing' one's grocer and firing one's secretary.[16]

One response to this view is the Williamsonian one (Williamson, 1985, 1996) that there are in fact fundamental economic differences between firms and markets, because the law makes an explicit distinction between market transactions and employment transactions – a distinction that makes the incentives faced by the parties to the relevant transactions differ (Masten, 1991), and provides an economic role for authority (Vandenberghe and Siegers, 2000). However, the incomplete contracts approach of Oliver Hart and others (Grossman and Hart, 1986; Hart, 1995, 1996; Hart and Moore, 1990) provides a perspective that is not dependent on legal considerations of this kind. In one important respect this approach differs from all earlier treatments of authority: Whereas Weber, Coase, Barnard, Simon, etc. focus on direct authority over (non-alienable) human assets, the incomplete contracts literature rather explain authority over human assets as something that is *indirectly* acquired through authority (ownership) over alienable assets. Since use will be made of this kind of reasoning later, it is worth briefly examining it.

Contributors to the incomplete contract literature distinguish two basic types of decision rights ('property rights'), namely specific rights and residual rights. The latter are generic rights to make decisions in circumstances not spelled out in the contract, and imply the ability to exclude other agents from deciding on the use of certain assets. Residual control rights are conferred by legal ownership.[17] In contrast, specific rights are allocated through contract terms. If contracts were complete, all rights would be specific, and there would be no residual rights. Two kinds of assets are distinguished, namely alienable (i.e., non-human) and non-alienable (i.e., human) assets. Given this, the distinction between an independent contractor and an employee (i.e., between an inter-firm and an intra-firm transaction) now turns on who owns the non-alienable assets that an agent (whether independent or employee) utilizes in his work. An independent contractor owns his tools etc., while an employee does not. The importance of asset ownership derives from the fact that the willingness of an agent to undertake a *non-contractible* investment (say, exertion of effort or investment in human capital), which is specific to the asset, depends on who owns the asset.

As in Alchian and Demsetz, the parties to a relation – whether customer and grocer, or employer and employee – are seen as being in a bargaining situation, each having an outside option. Although the parties are assumed to always reach an efficient agreement, the division of the surplus from the relation will nevertheless depend on who owns the alienable assets in the relation, since the pattern of ownership will influence the parties' outside options. In this scheme '. . . an employer's authority is represented not by the ability to force an employee to do what s/he wants, but rather by the ability to obtain a substantial share of the *ex post* surplus from the relationship through the control of non-human assets' (Hart 1996: 379). Efficiency considerations then suggest that authority (i.e., ownership to the alienable assets) should be allocated to the agent who makes the most important (non-contractible) relation-specific investment. Thus, in an elegant manner Hart (and his colleagues) link together the issues of the boundaries of the firm (which are defined in terms of ownership of alienable assets) and authority.[18] Use will later be made of this argument. However, the problem of the sources of authority is not the only challenge to the notion of authority.

Knowledge-based Challenges to Authority

So far, the debate on authority in organizational economics has almost exclusively centred on providing responses to the Alchian and Demsetz (1972) challenge. However, these responses do not meet (at least directly) the arguments of those who claim that authority relations will wither in the emerging knowledge economy (i.e., Proposition 1). Recall the earlier argument that for the sake of analytical convenience we may think of this in terms of the decline in the efficiency and prevalence of authority relations being driven by the two basic assumptions about knowledge in productive activities. In other words, if we take seriously the presence of Hayekian settings, we should ask what happens to the standard economics view of authority.

(1) If the employer does not possess full knowledge of the employee's action set (i.e., the actions that he can take when uncertainty is resolved), so that the employee can take actions about which the employer has no knowledge? This

possibility is explicitly excluded in the Coase-Simon view of authority (Simon, 1951).

(2) If the employee is better informed than the employer with respect to how certain tasks should (optimally) be carried out? In the Coase-Simon view of authority there is an implicit assumption that the employer is at least as well informed, and presumably better, about the efficiency implications of alternative actions.[19]

One reason why so little attention has been devoted to these problems arguably is that they are not necessarily problems of 'asymmetric information' as this is understood in information economics (so that standard modeling tools are not easy to apply). In a typical asymmetric information problem, an uninformed agent knows what he is uninformed about (e.g., the precise quality of a car). However, this excludes ignorance (Kirzner, 1997; Foss, 1999). A possible interpretation of the claim that authority relations will be transformed, and likely wither, in the emerging knowledge economy is that such relations are breaking down under the impact of principals becoming increasingly uninformed about the actions open to agents (an effect of Assumption 1) and at the same time becoming increasingly reliant on the knowledge controlled by agents (i.e., Assumption 2).[20] These are the characteristics of Hayekian settings.

Distributed Knowledge, Delegated Rights, and Authority

Hayek may well have been the first economist to clearly frame the issue of how to make best use of distributed knowledge (1945: 77–8; see also Hayek, 1937). As he explained:

> The economic problem of society is . . . not merely a problem of how to allocate 'given' resources – if 'given' is taken to mean given to a single mind which deliberately solves the problem set by these 'data'. It is rather a problem of how to secure the best use of resources known to any of the members of society, for ends whose relative importance only these individuals know. Or, to put it briefly, it is a problem of the utilization of knowledge which is not given to anyone in its totality.

As the date of Hayek's paper suggests, the problem of making optimal use of distributed knowledge is, of course, not a novel one, only brought about by the emergence of the knowledge economy; rather, *any* complex social system confronts it (Hayek, 1964). However, proponents of the position that economic organization is undergoing a radical transformation as a result of the emergence of the knowledge economy implicitly assert that problems posed by Hayekian distributed knowledge have become increasingly pressing for firms (cf. Cowen and Parker, 1997). Thus, because of the increased importance of specialist workers, the increased knowledge-intensity of production, and the increasing need to combine knowledge from multiple, diverse sources (Coombs and Metcalfe, 2000), coping with the problem posed by Hayekian distributed knowledge has moved from being a problem for socialist planners to also being a problem confronted by managers of firms in capitalist economies.

Hayek's well-known point is that a market system (but not a socialist one) promotes a tendency towards allocating property rights to those who can make best use of them; a system with alienable property rights solves simultaneously both the assignment and the moral hazard problem. However, firms solve these problems differently. Thus, resources within firms are directed (to a larger extent than in markets), and motivation of employees is engineered (to larger extent than in markets). From a Hayekian perspective, firms would seem to be inherently disadvantaged relative to markets, for firms encounter a fundamental problem that markets do not, namely '. . . the problem which any attempt to bring order into complex human activities meets: the organizer must wish the individuals who are to cooperate to make use of knowledge that he himself does not possess' (Hayek, 1973: 49). The fact that firms do exist is *prima facie* evidence that they can somehow cope with the problem.[21]

One obvious way to handle the Hayekian knowledge-problem in firms is to suppress distributed knowledge as far as possible by discouraging local initiative, indoctrinating employees harshly, and operating with rigid routines and operating procedures.[22] The archetypal 'machine bureaucracy' fits this overall character-ization. However, to the extent that competition is increasingly knowledge-based, this is a self-defeating strategy, because suppressing distributed knowledge in this way also implies that beneficial explorative and innovative efforts are suppressed. Therefore, an often more attractive way to handle the presence of distributed knowledge inside is to delegate decision rights (cf. Hayek, 1945: 83–4; Galbraith, 1974: 31–4; Jensen and Meckling, 1992), balancing the resulting agency costs against the benefits from improved use of distributed knowledge.[23] An inter-pretation of internal hybrids, such as team organization, 'molecular forms,' and the like, is that these manifest attempts to delegate decision rights and structure reward schemes so that such optimal tradeoffs are reached (Jensen and Wruck, 1994; Zenger and Hesterly, 1997; Foss and Foss, 2002; Zenger, 2002).

While Hayekian distributed knowledge may be an important component in the understanding of internal hybrids, it does not answer the puzzle of why such hybrids are organized *inside* firms at all, being subject to the exercise of authority. Although remuneration schemes are often adjusted to complementary changes in the delegation of decision rights, implementing internal hybrids does, of course, not imply that employees become full residual claimants. Moreover, being overruled by formal hierarchical superiors may harm motivation (Aghion and Tirole, 1997; Frey, 1997). Thus, moving internal hybrids, such as teams, out of firms would seem to yield efficiency gains, because this will strengthen incentives.[24] In fact, spin-offs, carve-outs, and like practices may be explained in such terms, so we should ask why not all internal hybrids are spun-off. Adding to the puzzle is that authority in the Coase-Simon sense appears to play at best a very limited role under Hayekian dispersed knowledge. This is because the Coase-Simon notion of authority assumes that a directing principal is at least as knowledgeable about the relevant tasks as the agent being directed.

The ownership-based notion of authority developed by Hart also seems to play only a limited role under Hayekian distributed knowledge. There are at least two reasons for this, relating to Assumption 1 and Assumption 2, respectively. First, in Hart's framework *all* residual decision-making power is concentrated in the hands of the owner/manager, whereas in reality delegation often amounts to delegating at least some residual decision rights to hierarchical subordinates (e.g., division managers). Implicitly, the notion that, on the one hand, there are rights that may be clearly specified in a contract and allocated to another party, and that, on the other hand, there are rights that cannot at all be specified in a contract but can only be allocated to a single party through asset ownership, means that the only room left for delegation is that agents receive well-specified rights to carry out well-specified actions. However, this implies that if agents can take actions about which principals have no knowledge or are better informed about how certain actions should be carried out, the superior knowledge of agents cannot be utilized. A second reason why Hartian ownership-based authority may be irrelevant is that the assets that in Hart's scheme confer authority are physical assets (Hart, 1995). However, an important claim in recent debate on the knowledge economy is exactly that physical assets are of waning importance, and that knowledge assets controlled by knowledge workers are becoming more important (Myers, 1996; Boisot, 1998; Neef, 1998). Of course, the implication is that ownership over physical assets is an increasingly ineffective source of bargaining power and that, therefore, authority must wane as bargaining power increasingly becomes more symmetrically distributed.

Narrow and Broad Notions of Authority

Although there are reasons to expect authority to be a highly inefficient coordination mechanism under the conditions described by Assumptions 1 and 2, we do not observe the well-nigh complete breakdown of authority relations that this line of thinking may imply. One reason is the possibility of benefits of firm organization that offset the knowledge-related inefficiencies of authority, as mentioned earlier. Another reason is the simple one that there is a large distance between the real phenomenon of authority and our models of that phenomenon. In fact, both those who have criticized authority for being an increasingly inefficient coordination mechanism in the emerging knowledge economy and organizational economists may be criticized for working with a too narrow understanding of authority. For example, a representative of the first group, Anna Grandori (1997: 35) argues that

> . . . whatever its basis, authority is a feasible governance mechanism only if information and competence relevant to solving economic action problems can be transferred to and handled by a single actor, a positive "zone of acceptance" exists, the actions of other supervised actors are observable, and if the system is not as large as to incur an overwhelming communication channel overload and control losses.

This critique seems to be directed at the Coase-Simon view of authority, and is, as such, a valid criticism. The Coase-Simon view is (too) narrow, because it implies that the boss directs the worker's actions in detail, based on a complete knowledge of the worker's action set, and because it implicitly asserts that the boss is always at least as, or more, knowledgeable about what actions should optimally be carried out. To the extent that authority is understood only in this narrow sense, it is not difficult to argue that authority will become increasingly inefficient and therefore increasingly less prevalent as a coordination mechanism (i.e., Proposition 1).

However, as Simon (1991: 31) himself pointed out four decades after his initial paper on authority, '[a]uthority in organizations is not used exclusively, or even mainly, to command specific actions.' Instead, he explains, it is a command that takes the form of a result to be produced, a principle to be applied, or goal constraints, so that '[o]nly the end goal has been supplied by the command, and not the method of reaching it.' This notion of authority as commanding somebody to work towards a specified goal, for example, backed up by some superior bargaining power, is entirely consistent with Assumptions 1 and 2. Indeed, in most large decision rights are allocated by the top-management team and the board of directors to lower hierarchical levels, presumably in order to cope better with distributed knowledge (Jensen and Meckling, 1992). However, typically these rights are circumscribed. For example, the right to use an asset in certain ways may be delegated; however, it is understood that that right does not entail the right to use the asset in the service of a competitor firm (Holmström, 1999). Thus, decision rights are delegated in firms, but they are delegated as means to an end (Hayek, 1973); their use is monitored (Jensen and Meckling, 1992), and top-management reserves ultimate decision rights for itself (Baker *et al.*, 2000). This suggests that authority in the sense of direction and centralized decision-making – which does not necessarily require detailed knowledge about a subordinate's knowledge or available actions – may persist in Hayekian settings, including the emerging knowledge economy. The following section discusses this in greater detail.

4. Authority in Hayekian Settings

Hidden Knowledge

This section examines the role of authority, understood in the broad sense of directing somebody to carry out an activity so that some end goal is reached, under distributed knowledge. To increase concreteness, situations involving distributed knowledge are approximated by 'hidden knowledge' (Minkler, 1993) in principal-agent relations. That is, it will be assumed that the problem facing a principal is not just that she is uninformed about what state of nature has been revealed or of the realization of the agent's effort (i.e., hidden information), as in the standard agency paradigm. Rather, the agent's knowledge is superior to that of the principal with respect to certain production possibilities (i.e., hidden knowledge). The principal may be ignorant about some members of the set of possible actions open to the agent, or the agent may be better informed than the employer with respect to how certain tasks should (optimally) be carried out, or both. Given this, the issue is whether it is possible, under hidden knowledge, to make sense out of this notion of authority on grounds of efficiency. It turns out that it is indeed possible to explain the presence of authority in such a setting. The key factors that will be considered in the following are (1) the urgency of decisions, (2) decisive knowledge, and (3) monitoring, incentives, and externalities.

The Urgency of Making Decisions

While Hayek (1945) did much to identify the benefits of the price with respect to coping with the problems introduced by distributed knowledge and unexpected disturbances, he arguably neglected those situations where efficiency requires that adaptation be 'coordinated' rather than 'autonomous' (Williamson, 1996). Coordinated adaptation or action may be required when actions or activities are complementary (Milgrom and Roberts, 1990; Kirsten Foss, 2001). Coordination problems are examples of this. In game-theoretic parlance, these problems obtain when there is more than one equilibrium in pure strategies, such as in the choice of standards. Game theory demonstrates that even in extremely stylized and simple, but still decentralized, settings with players possessing perfect reasoning capabilities and common knowledge, they may still be unable to coordinate their independently taken actions or only coordinate these after costly trials and errors (for a review, Foss, 2001). Authority may be a least-cost response to such problems.

In order to isolate the costs and benefits of centralized and decentralized decision-making in a specific context, Bolton and Farrell (1990) study a coordination problem with private information in the setting of a natural monopoly market. The coordination problem concerns who should enter the market when costs are sunk and the size of costs is private information. Under decentralization, which is represented as a two-period incomplete information game of timing (sink costs/enter or wait another period), each firm is uncertain about whether the other firm will enter. However, the incentive to enter depends on a given firm's cost, low-cost firms being less worried that their rival will enter (and *vice versa*). If costs are sufficiently dispersed, the optimal outcome prevails, that is, the lowest-cost producer enters and preempts the rival(s). However, if costs are equal or are high for both, inefficiencies may obtain, since firms will then enter simultaneously (inefficient duplication) or will wait (inefficient delay).

Enter a central authority whose job is to nominate a firm for entry. In the spirit of Hayek, Bolton and Farrell assume that this central authority cannot possess knowledge about costs. In their model, the authority nominates the high cost producer half of the time, which is clearly inefficient. However, this cost of centralization should be compared against the costs of decentralization (delay and duplication). Bolton and Farrell show that ". . . the less important the private information that the planner lacks and the more essential coordination is, the more attractive the central planning solution is" (1990: 805). Moreover, the decentralized solution performs poorly if urgency is important. Centralization is assumed to not involve delay and is therefore, under this strong assumption, a good mechanism for dealing with emergencies, a conclusion they argue is consistent with the observed tendencies of firms to rely on centralized authority in cases of emergencies.[25]

The inefficiencies under decentralization (duplication, delay) that Bolton and Farrell point to may arguably be particularly relevant for much "knowledge-intensive" production. This is because much of this production is 'pooled' rather than 'sequential' or 'reciprocal' (in the terminology of Thompson, 1967). 'Pooled activities' involve relatively decentralized efforts aiming at a common end. Research-based organizations where much production takes place in decentralized project-groups is a clear example. In such organizations, a centralized authority may be necessary to give priority to certain projects rather than others, even though that authority is basically very ill informed about the projects (for an example, see Foss, 2000).

Decisive Knowledge

Even though hidden knowledge conditions obtain, the principal may still hold knowledge that is *decisive*. Information is (strongly) decisive when no further information is required in order to make a rational decision. Thus, although there may be uncertainty about certain aspects of the environment, resolving this uncertainty will not (significantly) alter the decision, because the variation in the uncertain factors, or the impact of their variation on the costs and benefits of alternative courses of action (or strategies) is so small that the rational decision maker would want (and expect) to take the same course of action whatever this additional information turned out to be. For example, if supply conditions (changing technologies and/or input prices) are more volatile than demand conditions (changing sales and/or tastes), it may pay to investigate supply before investigating demand. In fact, if supply volatility is considerably higher, it may be evident what the firm should do in terms of its output and pricing decisions without checking demand conditions. In both cases, information about supply is decisive (and more so in the latter case).

According to Casson (1994), decisiveness and the cost at which knowledge can be communicated explains the allocation of decision rights. In terms of the examples, if furthermore the decisive knowledge is costly to communicate, decisiveness and costly communication suggest that decision rights should be allocated towards to the production side of the firm. This is an instance of the more general principle that decision rights will tend to be concentrated in the hands of the individual who has access to the decisive information, and particularly so the more costly it is to communicate this information. Casson (1994) uses this reasoning to why firms are hierarchical and to address other aspects of organizational structure. The reasoning not only casts light over the allocation of authority, but also over why, under hidden knowledge, interacting parties may rationally choose an authority relation. When knowledge is hidden, but not decisive and the costs of an incorrect decision are (on average) less than the costs of trying to communicate the knowledge from agent to principal, directing the agent through an authority relation will be efficient. Also, the more decisive the principal's knowledge relative to the agent's, the more attractive will the authority relation be, all else equal. Authority will be less efficient, the greater the number of parties who hold decisive knowledge, and the lower the costs of communication. In such cases, partnerships may substitute for the authority relation.

Monitoring, Incentives and Externalities

Hidden knowledge would seem to introduce special problems for the use of monitoring mechanisms and incentive pay, as discussed in the mainstream agency literature (e.g., Holmström, 1979; Minkler, 1993; Aghion and Tirole, 1997; Foss, 1999; Foss and Foss, 2002). With respect to monitoring under hidden knowledge, Minkler (1993: 23) argues that '. . . if the worker knows more than the entrepreneur, it is pointless for the entrepreneur to monitor the worker.' In the extreme case, both the agent's type and actions may be fully observable by the principal but the latter may still not understand the full set of production possibilities open to the agent. If monitoring is not workable, the problem is to design a contract that allows the agent to use his superior knowledge *ex post*, and gives him the incentive to do so efficiently. This will amount to allocating decision rights as well as rights to residual income streams to the agent,[26] as in a partnership. Authority seems to be as 'pointless' as monitoring, since the exercise of authority would seem to involve some degree of monitoring (checking whether commands have been followed).

However, the fact that accurate input monitoring is compromised by hidden knowledge conditions does not mean that authority is also compromised. Although the principal may not fully understand the set of production possibilities open to the agent, he may still be able to form estimates of the level of output that can 'reasonably' be expected of the agent (Hart and Moore, 1990; Foss and Foss, 2002). The ability of a principal to exercise judgment and form conjectures of an agent's output even under hidden knowledge implies that authority, in the broad sense of directing somebody to carry out an activity so that some end goal is reached, may be entirely workable under hidden knowledge. The holder of authority can check whether the end goal was, in fact, reached, and can reward or sanction the agent accordingly. Thus, although the narrow (Coase-Simon) notion of authority may be compromised by hidden knowledge conditions, the broad notion of authority is not.

Recent work in agency theory (Holmström and Milgrom, 1991; Holmström, 1999; Prendergast, 1999) suggests that (loosely) the more we move towards multi-tasking, costly-to-measure activities, multiple types of agents, etc., the more likely is it that the principal will choose to rely on many different incentive instruments to influence the agent's behaviour. A key theme in much recent work on organization in the knowledge economy is that tasks are becoming increasingly complex and difficult to measure because of their increasing 'knowledge-content,' and that this in itself is a force that is destructive of authority relations (Hodgson, 1998a). However, rather than reducing the need for the exercise of authority, these changes imply a renewed role for authority. A key managerial task is to balance incentive instruments (Holmström, 1999), that is, design and maintain coherence between the various ways in which an employee may be motivated so that negative spill-over effects between these ways are minimized.[27] This managerial task will become increasingly important, as firms have to use multiple incentive instruments to motivate 'knowledge workers.' In a dynamic economy, maintaining coherence between such instruments may be a recurrent task. There may be economies of scale and learning economies in this task (Hermalin, 1999), suggesting that it be centralized in the hands of a central authority.

Summing Up

It has been argued that it is possible to give efficiency explanations of authority under conditions corresponding to Assumption 1, at least if authority is under-stood in the broad sense of commanding somebody to work towards a specified goal. Admittedly, the narrow (Coase-Simon) notion of authority at direction based on superior knowledge and aimed at the carrying of specific actions on the part of employees, is harder to align with distributed knowledge conditions. Thus, the limits of Proposition 1 have been clarified: the proposition at best applies to the narrow ('Coase-Simon') notion of authority. Moreover, some determinants of the use of authority have been isolated. Thus, the urgency of decisions, the extent of decisiveness, the need to balance different incentive instruments and scale activities in this activity are all forces that promote the use of authority, all else equal.[28]

The increasing prevalence of internal hybrids that go beyond traditional hierarchies with respect to how decision rights and reward schemes are structured (Zenger and Hesterly, 1997; Zenger, 2002) may be partly caused by the constraint represented by Assumption 1 becoming increasingly binding. Still, internal hybrids remain organized inside the firm, so that members of teams, self-organizing groups, and the like are still subject to the exercise of authority. A reason for this is that even under the conditions described by Assumption 1, there may be a need for authority. When there is such a need, it is often efficient to centralize ownership to alienable assets. This may be the case although Assumption 2 ('Knowledge assets controlled by individual agents ('knowledge workers') are becoming increasingly important in production in terms of contribution to value-added') also holds true, as will be argued in the following section.

5. Ownership and Firm Boundaries in Hayekian Settings

Ownership and Assets in the Knowledge Economy

Although the previous section argued that authority can exist under distributed knowledge, little was said there about the sources of authority. However, recall the earlier arguments that ownership may play a key role as a source of authority. The purpose of the present section is to go more into ownership issues – particularly the ownership of knowledge assets – and therefore the issue of the boundaries of the firm. One of the key characteristics of the knowledge economy is usually taken to be the increased importance in production of knowledge assets and the decreasing importance of physical assets (Boisot, 1998). A further argument is that this transformation will also transform economic organization, because knowledge assets have different implications for the boundaries of firms than physical assets (e.g., Powell, 1990; Zucker, 1991; Kogut and Zander, 1992; Boisot, 1998; Mahnke, 2002).[29]

The category of 'knowledge assets' is a broad one – encompassing individually held tacit knowledge, firm-level capabilities ('organizational knowledge'), patents, client lists, etc. – and, partly for this reason, difficult to analytically frame.[30] Different – albeit all somewhat underdeveloped – modeling strategies are available. One strategy is to stress problems of appropriability as a key determinant of the boundaries of the firm (Teece, 1987; Liebeskind, 1997). In this scheme, the boundaries of the firm reflect attempts to maximize the rent streams from the firm's valuable knowledge assets (rather than the hold-up problem). A second one is to stress that many knowledge assets are collective or public goods (e.g., capabilities or reputational assets) and that this creates free-rider problems, causing a need to delimit access to such goods (Holmström and Roberts, 1998; Osterloh *et al.*, 2002). A third strategy is to argue that knowledge assets in the form of differential capabilities give rise to communication costs and attempts to economize with such costs help determining the boundaries of the firm (Langlois, 1992; Monteverde, 1995). Finally, a fourth possibility is to rely on transaction cost economics and incomplete contracts theory arguments about the need to protect specialized assets and investments specific to such assets from rent-capture attempts (Rabin, 1993; Brynjolfsson, 1994; Putterman, 1995). Since the latter strategy is the one that most obviously connects to the theme of authority that has been pursued in so much of this paper, I briefly apply this approach.

Knowledge Assets and the Boundaries of the Firm

Following Brynjolfsson (1994), use will be made of the incomplete contracts modeling methodology of Hart and Moore (1990) to get an understanding of the implications of knowledge assets for the boundaries of the firm. This is a key issue, because asset ownership may, as argued earlier, provide the bargaining lever that backs up authority, and the concentration of decision rights that we call authority may have important efficiency implications, as already argued. Thus, this section connects the previous discussion of authority in a knowledge economy with the issue of the boundaries of the firm in such an economy. The emphasis is on supporting the claim made earlier that when there is a need for centralized coordination, efficiency considerations suggest a need for also concentrating asset ownership (Holmström, 1999; Hermalin, 1999).

The primary required change in the basic Hart and Moore framework is a more explicit introduction of knowledge assets (which may be alienable or non-alienable). In fact, we can dispense entirely with physical assets, and discuss a purely knowledge-based firm.[31] It is assumed that agents enter into productive relations with other agents but that synergies between agents occur only through the assets that they control (and not through the actions they take). Furthermore, although assets may influence the value of actions, the reverse is not true (Brynjolfsson, 1994: 433). This means that we can write the cost of agent i's action as $c(x_i)$ and the marginal value of i's actions when he is in a productive relation with other agents simply as $v_i(A)$, where A is the set of all assets owned by agents (and their actions can be suppressed).[32]

For simplicity, assume that two agents interact and that one of these, 'the entrepreneur,' owns a knowledge asset, K, that is 'inside his head' (e.g., an entrepreneurial idea) and the other agent, 'the scientist,' owns the only other asset in the relation, P, which we may assume to be a 'patent.' Both assets are necessary to the create value in the relation, and K and P are (strictly) complementary, so that the one is of value 0 without the other. It is prohibitively costly to communicate the knowledge embodied in K from the entrepreneur to the scientist, so K is effectively non-alienable, although the services of K may of course be traded. Moreover, it is not possible to write a comprehensive contract, governing the use of the assets in all contingencies. Given this, we may ask who should own the alienable asset, P, which – in terms of the Hart and Moore (1990) analysis – is tantamount to asking who should own the firm.

In this setting, if the entrepreneur makes an effort investment, x_e, that is, elaborates on his idea and creates extra value, the scientist can effect a hold-up on the entrepreneur, since the latter needs access to the patent to create value (and the contract is incomplete). Of course, the reverse also holds, so that if the scientist makes an effort investment, x_s, (e.g., a spin-off patent), the entrepreneur can hold-up the scientist by threathening to withdraw from the relation. Under the standard assumption of Nash bargaining, the entrepreneur and the scientist each realizes half of the extra value created as a result of their efforts. Because of the externality problem, each underinvests; specifically, each party invests to the point where the marginal cost of effort investment equals $\frac{1}{2}$ of the marginal value.[33] Suppose instead that the entrepreneur owns *both* the patent and the entrepreneurial idea. This will strengthen the entrepreneur's incentives (the scientist cannot hold him up anymore) and it will leave the scientist's incentives unaffected.[34] Obviously, this ownership arrangement should be chosen.

A conclusion at this stage is that it *is* possible to speak of the boundaries of the firm in terms of ownership (and therefore also in legal terms) – even in a situation where all assets are knowledge assets. However, this does not yet demonstrate the point made earlier, namely that concentration of coordination tasks produces a need for concentration of ownership. We can address this issue, however, by assuming that one of the agents has decisive information (in the sense of Casson, 1994). While efficiency may require that this agent should have decision rights amounting to authority, should he also be an owner?

Consider a 'knowledge-based' group of scientists where each scientist owns a patent, P_i. One of the scientists possesses decisive knowledge, C, and the other scientists communicate directly with him rather than with each other.[35] For example, this agent aggregates information from the messages of the other agents and issue directives. His knowledge is decisive in the sense that without it, all actions of the other agents produce zero value. The coordinator may improve on this decisive knowledge. Each agent needs access to his own patent and to C in order to be productive. Given this assumption (which means that we need only consider relations between any agent and the coordinator), we have the by now familiar under-investment problem for both the coordinator and the scientists.[36] If the coordinator is given ownership to all patents, things change: While the incentives of the scientists are not affected,[37] the incentives of the coordinator to invest in augmenting his decisive coordination knowledge are strengthened. Thus, this ownership arrangement should be chosen.

Summing Up

Although the framework that has been applied in this section is extremely stylized and in many ways quite limited (Holmström, 1999; Foss and Foss, 2001), it does provide an answer to Proposition 2. The reasoning shows, first, that it makes perfect sense to address ownership issues in terms of knowledge assets, and, second, that ownership to such assets may be important in situations where agents need to be provided with incentives (and where contracts are incomplete), and, third, that even though knowledge assets controlled by individual agents ('knowledge workers') are becoming increasingly important in production in terms of contribution to value-added (i.e., Assumption 2), it still does not follow from this alone that the boundaries of firms will blur. The economically important distinction is not between physical and knowledge assets, as it is often asserted (e.g., Boisot, 1998), but between alienable and inalienable assets, and many knowledge assets are perfect alienable. The implication is that to the extent that not all knowledge assets are inalienable, ownership-based (and therefore also legal) definitions of the boundaries of the firm will continue to be important. Finally, the discussion ties together the notions of authority and ownership in the context of knowledge-based production, since it suggests that when there is a need for centralized decision-making, it is often efficient to have this backed up by asset ownership. As will be argued in the following section, this has implications for the issue of the extent to which coordination mechanisms can be combined, that is, Proposition 3.

6. Organization Design in Hayekian Settings

The Malleability and Combinability of Coordination Mechanisms

So far, it has been argued that there is a tight connection between authority and ownership and that this connection will also be manifest in Hayekian settings. This raises the issue of whether there may be tight connections between organizational elements in general. In fact, the dominant perspective in much of organization theory and organizational economics has been that various coordination mechanisms indeed cluster in discrete, stable governance structures in predictable ways. The specific combinations are typically seen as being dependent upon the underlying technology, characteristics of the environment, such as exchange conditions, and the strategy of the firm (Thompson, 1967; Williamson, 1985, 1996; Nickerson and Zenger, 2000). The notion of complementarity has been put forward as an important element in the understanding of this (Holmström and Milgrom, 1994; Zenger, 2002).

In contrast to this, it has been argued that there are no compelling reasons why specific coordination mechanisms should necessarily cluster in a few ideal typical governance structures of the 'firm-hybrid-market' variety (particularly Grandori, 1997, 2002). In particular, advances in networked computing, management information systems, and methods of measuring performance have strongly expanded the set of feasible combinations of coordination mechanisms (Miles et al., 1997, 1998). 'Cellular' or 'molecular' forms, which are particularly suited to the requirements introduced by the knowledge economy, are examples. The fact that these forms – which much operate on market-like principles (Miles *et al.*, 1997; Cowen and Parker, 1997) – are still organized inside firms just serve to illustrate the malleable nature of coordination mechanisms. However, in the following, I argue – concentrating on firms' internal organization – that coordination mechanisms are not completely malleable, and that such mechanisms will cluster in discrete governance structures, also in the emerging knowledge economy.

Incentive Limits to the Use of Market Mechanisms

To an economist, the debate in the management and organization fields of 'combining coordination mechanisms' is mirrored by debates on combining market and hierarchy in the comparative systems and transfer pricing literatures. For example, in the context of comparative systems, Mises (1949: 709) long ago argued that there are inherent contradictions involved in 'playing market,' that is, trying to simulate a market inside a hierarchy. His arguments anticipated later incentive arguments, including the importance of credible commitment for incentives. Referring to various socialist schemes of his day that tried to preserve some market relations while eliminating capital and financial markets, Mises argued that these schemes would be unworkable. The concentration of ultimate decision-making rights and responsibilities, and therefore ownership, in the hands of a central planning board would dilute the incentives of managers. Thus, while planning authorities could delegate rights to make production and investment decisions to managers, these rights were likely to be used inefficiently. First, since managers couldn't be sure that they would not be overruled by the planning authorities, they were not likely to take a long view, notably in their investment decisions. Moreover, since managers were not the ultimate owners, they were not the full residual claimants of their decisions and, hence, would not make efficient decisions. Therefore, Mises declared, the attempt to 'play market' under socialism would lead to inefficiencies. In a related vein, the attempt to simulate markets in a firm hierarchy may lead to inefficiencies.

As later research has clarified, the problem may be handled if the planning authorities can credibly commit to a non-interference policy. However, doing so may be very hard, since reneging on a promise to delegate will in many cases be extremely tempting and those to whom rights are delegated anticipate this.[38]

Arguably, organizations that try to infuse their structures with organizational elements characteristic of the market are more prone to suffer from these commitment problems than firms with more traditional hierarchical structures. The reasons are that decision rights are more solidly established in a traditional hierarchy than in, say, a flat, project-based organization, and that a CEO who selectively intervenes in a hierarchical organization risk overruling the whole managerial hierarchy, whereas this is not a concern in a flat organization.

Implications

An implication is that mixing very different coordination mechanisms may lead to efficiency losses, and may not be sustainable for this reason.[39] The basic problem is that emulating market organization inside firms amounts to 'playing market.' Unlike independent agents in markets, corporate employees never possess ultimate decision rights. They are not full owners. This means that those who possess ultimate decision rights can always overrule employees. Thus, there are fundamental incentive limits to the extent to which market principles can be applied inside firms. These insights suggest that, contrary to Proposition 3, coordination mechanisms do cluster in certain predictable ways. In particular, there are incentive limits to the extent to which the introduction of coordination mechanisms characteristic of the market can be introduced in firms. Advances in measurement methods and networked computing may have eased the extent to which decision rights can be delegated inside a corporate hierarchy (Zenger and Hesterly, 1997). However, there are inherent tensions between authority (as backed up by ownership) and delegated rights which constrains the space of feasible combinations of coordination mechanisms. To the extent that authority persists in the knowledge economy, so will these limits.

7. Conclusions

Addressing economic organization in the context of the emerging knowledge economy is a task of almost forbidding complexity. It is also inherently speculative, suggesting to some that the use of scenario techniques is appropriate (Hodgson, 1998a) or that a multi-disciplinary approach is justified (Daft and Lewin, 1993). The present paper has taken a narrower approach, being founded on the notion that organizational economics is helpful for clarifying the central issues and for providing tentative answers. Admittedly, the richness of the recent literature on organization in the knowledge economy may have been sacrificed by the relative narrowness of the present approach. However it has the advantage of making issues of contention and the terms of the debate explicit, thus contributing a possible starting point for further empirical and theoretical work.

Thus, it has been argued that the recent literature on economic organization in the knowledge economy may be summarized in a handy way by means of two basic assumptions and four propositions. It was further asked: accepting that knowledge has become increasingly distributed and that knowledge assets are increasingly important in production, is it then true that authority relations will wither, that legal and ownership-based definitions of the boundaries will become unimportant, and that coordination mechanisms can be combined virtually at will? The answers to all these questions were negative – Coasian firm organization is consistent with Hayekian knowledge conditions; the knowledge economy will not mean that the authority-based firm with boundaries defined in terms of asset ownership will vanish. Moreover, the very existence of ownership-based authority implies that there are constraints on the space of feasible combinations of coordination mechanisms; firms and markets will continue to exist as clearly demarcated institutions (cf. also Hodgson, 2002).

Finally, a word about the strawman issue. Although it may be possible to find authors who present Propositions (1) to (4) in an extreme form, it may be countered that one can always dig up unimportant extremists, smash their arguments, and obtain an easy victory. Two responses are pertinent here. First, the proponents of Propositions (1) to (4) that have been cited are not unimportant extremists, but established and respected academics. Second, even if the statements contained in the Propositions are, perhaps, extreme, investigating them is still a worthwhile task. This is because such an activity helps establishing the boundaries of the discussion. For example, although it may be argued that nobody truly believes that all authority relations will disappear completely in the knowledge economy, we still need to know why authority relations will persist and how they will change. Thus, one result of the present discussion is the clarification of the conditions under which authority relations will exist when knowledge is distributed.

Notes

1. See, for example, Nonaka and Takeuchi (1995), Grant (1996), Myers (1996), Brown and Eisenhardt (1998), Day and Wendler (1998), Miles *et al.* (1997, 1998) for different perspectives on this overall idea. The pedigree of this goes back a long time, including, for example, Burns and Stalker (1961).
2. For empirical evidence, see Tomlinson (1999).
3. For example, Helper *et al.*, (2000: 443) argue that '. . . firms are increasingly engaging in collaborations with their suppliers, even as they are reducing the extent to which they are vertically integrated with those suppliers. This fact seems incompatible with traditional theories of the firm which argue that integration is necessary to avoid the potentials for hold-ups created when non-contractible investments are made.'
4. It is also true that organizational economics needs to develop a better understanding of particularly internal hybrids (Zenger 2002; Foss 2000a). Notably, transaction cost economics does not seriously treat internal hybrids.
5. The reasoning turning on the proposition that networks are particularly useful organizational arrangements for sourcing and transferring knowledge because they allegedly avoid the costs of pricing knowledge in a market or transferring it in a hierarchy (Powell, 1990: 304; Liebeskind *et al.*, 1995: 7).
6. As Zucker (1991: 164) argues: 'While bureaucratic authority is by definition located within the firm's boundaries, expert authority depends on the information resources available to an individual, and not on the authority of office. Thus, authority may be located within the organization . . . but when an external market source can provide information that leads to greater effectiveness, then authority tends to migrate into the market.'
7. See Grandori (1997, 2002) for a sophisticated argument that because both organization theory and organizational economics have put too much of an emphasis on discrete, stable, 'consistent' governance structures, and too little on more micro-analytic coordination mechanisms (e.g., price, norms, authority, teams, etc.), the number of ways in which such mechanisms may be combined has been strongly under-estimated.
8. The possible risk of constructing a strawman is admitted. This is discussed further in the Conclusion.
9. 'Distributed knowledge' is knowledge that is not possessed by any single mind and which may be private and tacit, but which it will nevertheless be necessary to somehow mobilize for the carrying out of a productive task (Hayek, 1945). Many writers have argued that such distributed knowledge is of increasing importance in an innovation-rich, knowledge-based economy (e.g., Ghoshal, Moran and Almeida-Costa, 1995; Hodgson, 1998a; Coombs and Metcalfe, 2000). Grant (1996: 378) argues that Hayekian distributed knowledge is crucial to the understanding of organizational capabilities: 'Although higher-level capabilities involve the integration of lower-level capabilities, such integration can only be achieved through integrating individual knowledge. This is precisely why higher-level capabilities are so difficult to perform.'
10. By the term 'coordination mechanisms' reference is made to a wide set of mechanisms for allocating resources, such as authority, prices, standard operating procedures, routines, contracts, goal setting, voting, etc. For an innovative overview, see Grandori (2002) and for some classic organization theory references, see Galbraith (1974) and Ven, Delbecg and Koenig (1976).
11. In other respects, however, Coase is not so obvious a precursor. For example, the emphasis in the modern economics of organization on incentive conflicts, including the hold-up problem (Williamson, 1985; Hart, 1995), as a main explanatory principle cannot be found in Coase's paper, as he has stressed himself (Coase, 1988).

12. 'It may be desired to make a long-term contract for the supply of some article or service,' Coase writes. 'Now, owing to the difficulty of forecasting, the longer the period of the contract is for the supply of the commodity or service, the less possible, and indeed, the less desirable it is for the person purchasing to specify what the other contracting party is expected to do. . . . Therefore, the service which is being provided is expressed in general terms, the exact details being left until a later date. . . . The details of what the supplier is expected to do is not stated in the contract but is decided later by the purchaser. When the direction of resources (within the limits of the contract) becomes dependent on the buyer in this way, that relationship which I term a "firm" may be obtained' (Coase, 1937: 242–3).

13. Apparently, some organization scholars disagree with this. Thus, Grandori (1997: 37) notes that it has been 'well-documented' in organization studies that '. . . authority is not very effective in managing uncertainty.' It will later be argued that this depends much on the context; for example, if strong interdependencies ('complementarities') between activities are involved, authority may be extremely effective for 'managing uncertainty.'

14. See Hodgson (1998b) for an interesting critical discussion of Coase's notions of authority and the employment contract.

15. In a recent contribution, Wernerfelt (1997) elaborates on these Coasian and Simonian premises. By portraying governance mechanisms as gameforms (spot contracting, price lists, hierarchy) chosen to regulate trade Wernerfelt makes precise Coase's idea that the choice of a governance mechanism is partly determined by the flexibility afforded by that mechanism and he extends Simon's analysis by explicitly comparing alternative mechanisms. Specifically, gameforms determine how players adapt to changes in the environment and communicate about these changes. Wernerfelt's conjecture is that these different gameforms will be systematically characterized by different levels of costs of making adaptations. For example, authority is simply an implicit contract which states that one of the parties should have the authority to tell the other what to do (as in Coase, 1937). This game-form requires less bargaining over prices than the market game-form, and is selected to save to on communication (adaptation) costs. The agreement to play by the least costly adaptation-mechanism is upheld by the parties' concern for reputation in a repeated game.

16. Note that this 'nexus of contracts' position is remarkably close to the position that in a knowledge-based economy, the firm/market boundary is unclear and the notion of authority elusive at best, although its conceptual basis is rather different.

17. For a critique of these aspects of the incomplete contract literature, see Foss and Foss (2001).

18. This is not to say that the Hart approach is entirely unproblematic as an approach to the employment contract or the firm. For example, the bargaining power possessed by a principal who owns the complementary physical assets in a relation may be exercised over an employee *or* it may be exercised over a legally independent party who just happens to have given up ownership of alienable assets to strengthen incentives (i.e., vertical quasi-integration) (Foss and Foss 2001). In other words, there is no one-to-one correspondence between the firm and the Hart understanding of the exercise of authority. In fact, as Bengt Holmström (1999: 87) has recently argued, the incomplete contracts literature '. . . is a theory about asset ownership by individuals rather than by firms.'

19. This is explicitly argued in Demsetz (1988) and Conner and Prahalad (1996).

20. Of course, there are many other reasons why economic organization may differ in the emerging knowledge economy. For example, to the extent that increased innovative activity is taken to be a hallmark of the knowledge economy (Brown and Eisenhardt, 1998; Coombs and Metcalfe, 2000), this may require changes in the distribution of decision rights and reward schemes in organizations. Such changes don't turn on the Hayekian problem of distributed knowledge *per se.*

21. And/or that there are offsetting benefits of firm organization, such as the superior ability of firms to organize transactions characterized by high levels of relation-specific investments (Williamson, 1985, 1996; Grossman and Hart, 1986; Hart and Moore, 1990).

22. Marglin (1974) tells such a story of the emergence of capitalist authority (although one whose Marxian pedigree makes it strongly differ from the Hayekian emphasis on dispersed knowledge): A thoroughgoing de-skilling of labour was required before capitalist relations could thriumph.

23. There is an argument that under Hayekian distributed knowledge, *de facto* delegation of rights *already* obtains. Thus, the formal right to decide need not confer effective control over decisions, as Aghion and Tirole (1997) point out with a bow to Max Weber. Real authority is already largely determined by the structure of information in the organization, including the distribution of Hayekian dispersed knowledge. Of course, agents who possess local knowledge may be subject to the exercise of authority by uninformed hierarchical superiors, but this is likely to harm incentives (cf. also Frey, 1997; Osterloh, Frost and Frey, 2002). In Aghion and Tirole (1997), an increase in the agent's real authority is assumed to lead to control losses from the point of view of the principal but also to promote initiative.

24. Some writers draw what appears to be the logical consequence of a Hayekian starting point, and flatly argue that only firms that explicitly emulate market organization to the largest possible extent can survive and prosper in the knowledge economy (Cowen and Parker, 1997). However, they fail to explain why firms should exist under these circumstances.

25. Although Bolton and Farrell do not note this, the example is vulnerable to the critique that the two firms may enter a court-enforceable contract that let entry depend on the flipping of a coin. However, in many realistic situations, particularly when urgency is involved, contracts may not be court-enforceable or the potential delay introduced by using the court system may be intolerable.

26. The precise arrangements may also involve the payment of a lump sum from the agent to principal (as in franchising relationships), and it will be shaped by the risk-preferences of the parties and whether liquidity constraints are present or not.

27. For example, if motivation is mainly secured by pecuniary means, this may harm other instruments, such as trying to motivate by fostering a culture that emphasizes trust and sharing.

28. These reasons also seem broadly consistent with organization theory work on authority in the context of flat hierarchies (where Hayekian distributed knowledge is particularly to exist). In a study of authority in newspaper publishing companies, Brass (1984) identified the determinants of authority as 'criticality' (i.e., decisive knowledge), 'centrality' (i.e., centralized decision rights because of economies of scale in certain tasks), and 'the friendship network.'

29. In fact, two of the flagbearers of modern formal contract economics, Holmström and Roberts (1998: 90), recently observed that 'Information and knowledge are at the heart of organizational design, because they result in contractual and incentive problems that challenge both markets and firms . . . In light of this, it surprising that leading economic theories . . . have paid almost no attention to the role of organizational knowledge.'

30. For example, it is not clear what it means to speak of ownership of firm-level capabilities. For a discussion of this and related issues, see Zingales (2000).

31. This is because the key issue is not whether assets are material or immaterial, but whether they are alienable or non-alienable.

32. One may wonder what has happened to the notion of Hayekian distributed knowledge in this setting (i.e., Assumption 1). However, although it is a necessary assumption that the agents can observe each others' marginal product values, they don't need to observe each others' specific actions or know the underlying knowledge. Thus, Hayekian distributed knowledge is consistent with the assumptions being made here.

33. The first-order conditions are given by $\frac{1}{2}v^e$ (K, P) + $\frac{1}{2}$ v^e (K) = c' (x_c) and $\frac{1}{2}$ v^s (K, P) + $\frac{1}{2}$ v^s (P) = c' (x_s). Since it has been assumed that the value of the assets outside the relation is zero, the second term in these two expressions equals zero.

34. This may be seen from inspecting the first order conditions when the entrepreneur owns both K and P: $\frac{1}{2}$ v^e (K, P) + $\frac{1}{2}$ v^e (K, P) = c' (x_c) and $\frac{1}{2}v^s$ (K, P) = c' (x_s).

35. This suggests that incentives are likely to be strengthened by spinning off employees who come up with idiosyncratic entrepreneurial ideas that are costly to communicate to the rest of the firm.

36. This is a strong assumption, but one that is made for analytical convenience. The main point simply is that there is a central agent whose centrality in the information network is crucial to the value-creating efforts of other agents.

37. For example, the first-order condition for any individual scientist is: $\frac{1}{2}$ v^i (P, C) + $\frac{1}{2}$ v^i (P) = c' (x_i), where the second term is zero.

38. The first-order condition for any individual scientist is now: $\frac{1}{2}v^i$ (P, C) = c' (x_i), which is the same as as the previous first-order condition.

39. Williamson (1996) refers to these two kinds of problems with his concept of the 'impossibility of (efficient) selective intervention.' The main problem is that incentives are diluted. This is because the option to intervene '. . . can be exercised both for good cause (to support expected net gains) and for bad (to support the subgoals of the intervenor)' (Williamson, 1996: 150–1). Promises to only intervene for good cause can never be credible, Williamson argues, because they are unenforcable.

40. See Foss (2000) for a specific empirical application of this logic, namely the attempt to introduce market relations in the internal organization of the Danish hearing aid producer, Oticon, and the later abandonment of this experiment.

References

Aghion, P. and Tirole, J., "Formal and Real Authority in Organization," *Journal of Political Economy*, 1997, 105, pp. 1–29.

Alchian, A.A. and Demsetz, H., "Production, Information Costs, and Economic Organization," (originally published in 1972), in Armen A. Alchian, ed,. *Economic Forces at Work*. Indianapolis: Liberty Press, 1977.

Badaracco, J.L., "The Boundaries of Firms," in Amitai Etzioni and Paul R. Lawrence, eds, *Socio-Economics: Toward a New Synthesis*. Armonk: M.E. Sharpe, 1991.

Baker, G., Gibbons, R. and Murphy, K.J., "Informal Authority in Organizations," *Journal of Law, Economics and Organization*, 1999, 15, pp. 56–73.

Baker, G., Gibbons, R. and Murphy, K.J., "Relational Contracts and the Theory of the Firm," unpublished manuscript, 2000.

Boisot, M., *Knowledge Assets: Securing Competitive Advantage in the Information Economy*. Oxford: Oxford University Press, 1998.

Bolton, P. and Farrell, J., "Decentralization, Duplication, and Delay," *Journal of Political Economy*, 1998, 98, pp. 803–26.

Brass, D.J., "Being in the Right Place: A Structural Analysis of Individual Influence in an Organization," *Administrative Science Quarterly*, 1984, 29, pp. 518–39.

Brown, S.L. and Eisenhardt, K.M., *Competing on the Edge: Strategy as Structured Chaos*. Boston: Harvard Business School Press, 1998.

Brynjolfsson, E., "Information Assets, Technology, and Organization," *Management Science*, 1994, 40, pp. 1645–62.

Burns, T. and Stalker, G.M., *The Management of Innovation*. London: Tavistock, 1961.

Cappelli, P. and Neumark, D., "Do 'High-Performance' Work Practices Improve Establishment-Level Outcomes?," *Industrial and Labor Relations Review*, 2001, 54(4), pp. 737–75.

Casson, M, "Why are Firms Hierarchical?," *International Journal of the Economics of Business*, 1994, 1, pp. 47–76.

Cheung, S.N.S., "The Contractual Nature of the Firm," *Journal of Law and Economics*, 1983, 26, pp. 1–22.

Coase, R.H., "The Nature of the Firm," originally published 1937, in Nicolai J. Foss, ed., *The Theory of the Firm: Critical Perspectives in Business and Management, Vol II*. London: Routledge, 1999.

Coff, R.W., "When Competitive Advantage Doesn't Lead to Performance: The Ressource-Based View and Shareholder Bargaining Power," *Organization Science*, 1999, 10, pp. 119–134.

Conner, K.R. and Prahalad, C.K., "A Resource-Based Theory of the Firm," *Organization Science*, 1996, 7, pp. 477–501.

Coombs, R. and Metcalfe, S., "Organizing for Innovation: Co-ordinating Distributed Innovation Capabilities," in Nicolai J. Foss and Volker Mahnke, eds., *Competence, Governance, and Entrepreneurship*. Oxford: Oxford University Press, 2000.

Cowen, T. and Parker, D., *Markets in the Firm: A Market Process Approach to Management*. London: The Institute of Economic Affairs, 1997.

Daft, R. and Lewin, A., "Where Are the Theories of the 'New' Organizational Forms?," *Organization Science*, 1993, 4, pp. i–iv.

D'Aveni, R., *Hypercompetition: The Dynamics of Strategic Maneuvering*. New York: Basic Books, 1994.

Demsetz, H., "The Theory of the Firm Revisited," *Journal of Law, Economics, and Organization*, 1988, 4, pp. 141–61.

Fama, E. and Jensen, M.C., "Separation of Ownership and Control," *Journal of Law and Economics*, 1983, 26, pp. 301–25.

Foss, K., "Organizing Technological Interdependencies: A Coordination Perspective on the Firm", *Industrial and Corporate Change*, 2001, 10, pp. 151–78.

Foss, K. and Foss, N.J., "Assets, Attributes and Ownership," *International Journal of the Economics of Business*, 2001, 8, pp. 19–37.

Foss, K. and Foss, N.J., "Economic Organization and the Trade-Offs Between Productive and Destructive Entrepreneurship," forthcoming in Nicolai J. Foss and Peter G. Klein, eds, Entrepreneurship and the Firm: Austrian Perspectives on Economic Organization, Aldershot: Edward Elgar, 2002.

Foss, N.J., "The Use of Knowledge in Firms", *Journal of Institutional and Theoretical Economics*, 1999, 155, pp. 458–86.

Foss, N.J. "Internal Disaggregation in Oticon: Interpreting and Learning from the Rise and Decline of the Spaghetti Organization," Working Paper, Department of Industrial Economics and Strategy, Copenhagen Business School, 2000.

Foss, N.J. "Leadership, Beliefs and Coordination," *Industrial and Corporate Change*, 10, 357–88.

Frey, B., *Not Just for the Money: An Economic Theory of Personal Motivation*. Cheltenham: Edward Elgar, 1997.

Galbraith, J.R. "Organization Design: An Information Processing View," *Interfaces*, 1974, 4(3), pp. 28–36.

Ghoshal, S., Moran, P. and Almeida-Costa, L., "The Essence of the Megacorporation: Shared Context, not Structural Hierarchy", Journal of Institutional and Theoretical Economics, 1995, 151, pp. 748–59.

Grandori, A., "Governance Structures, Coordination Mechanisms and Cognitive Models," *Journal of Management and Governance*, 1997, 1, pp. 29–42.

Grandori, A., *Organizations and Economic Behavior.* London: Routledge, 2002.

Grant, R.M., "Prospering in Dynamically-Competitive Environments: Organizational Capability as Knowledge Integration," *Organization Science*, 1996, 7, pp. 375–87.

Grossman, S. and Hart, O., "The Costs and Benefits of Ownership: A Theory of Vertical Integration," *Journal of Political Economy*, 1986, 94, pp. 691–719.

Halal, W.E. and Taylor, K.B., *Twenty-First Century Economics: Perspectives of Socioeconomics for a Changing World.* New York: St. Martin's Press, 1998.

Harryson, S.J., *Managing Know-Who Based Companies.* Cheltenham: Edward Elgar, 2000.

Hart, O., *Firms, Contracts, and Financial Structure.* Oxford: Oxford University Press, 1995.

Hart, O., 1996. "An Economist's View of Authority," *Rationality and Society* 8, pp. 371–86.

Hart, O. and Moore, J., "Property Rights and the Nature of the Firm," *Journal of Political Economy*, 1990, 98, pp. 1119–58.

Hayek, F.A.V., "Economics and Knowledge," originally published 1937 in *Individualism and Economic Order.* Chicago: University of Chicago Press, 1948.

Hayek, F.A.V., "The Use of Knowledge in Society," originally published 1945 in idem., *Individualism and Economic Order.* Chicago: University of Chicago Press, 1948.

Hayek, F.A.V., *Law, Legislation, and Liberty, Vol. 1: Rules and Order,* Chicago: University of Chicago Press, 1973.

Hayek, F.A.V., "The Theory of Complex Phenomena," in idem., *Studies in Philosophy, Economics, and Politics.* London: Routledge and Kegan Paul, 1978.

Helper, S., MacDuffie, J.P. and Sabel, C., "Pragmatic Collaborations: Advancing Knowledge While Controlling Opportunism," *Industrial and Corporate Change*, 2000, 9, pp. 443–87.

Hermalin, B., "The Firm as a Non-Economy: Some Comments on Holmstrom," *Journal of Law, Economics and Organization*, 1999, 15, pp. 103–5.

Hodgson, G., *Economics and Utopia.* London: Routledge, 1998a.

Hodgson, G., "The Coasean Tangle: The Nature of the Firm and the Problem of Historical Specificity," in S.G. Medema, ed., *Coasean Economics: Law and Economics and the New Institutional Economics.* Boston: Kluwer Academic Publishers, 1998b.

Hodgson, G. "The Legal Nature of the Firm and the Myth of the Firm-Market Dichotomy," *International Journal of the Economics of Business*, 2002, (this issue).

Holmström, B., "Moral Hazard and Observability," *Bell Journal of Economics*, 1979, 10, pp. 74–91.

Holmström, B., "The Firm as a Subeconomy," *Journal of Law, Economics, and Organization*, 1999, 15, pp. 74–102.

Holmström, B. and Milgrom, P., "Multitask Principal-Agent Analysis: Incentive Contracts, Asset Ownership and Job Design," *Journal of Law, Economics and Organization*, 1991, 7, pp. 24–54.

Holmström, B. and Milgrom, P., "The Firm as an Incentive System," *American Economic Review*, 1994, 84, pp. 972–91.

Holmström, B. and Roberts, J., "The Boundaries of the Firm Revisited," *Journal of Economic Perspectives*, 1998, 12, pp. 73–94.

Ichniowski, C., Kochan, T.A., Levine, D., Olson, C and Strauss, G., "What Works at Work: Overview and Assessment," *Industrial Relations* 1996, 35, pp. 299–333.

Jensen, M.C. and Meckling, W.H., "Specific and General Knowledge and Organizational Structure," in L. Werin and H. Wijkander, eds., *Contract Economics.* Oxford: Blackwell, 1992.

Jensen, M.C. and Wruck, K., "Science, Specific Knowledge and Total Quality Management," originally published 1994 in M.C. Jensen, ed., *Foundations of Organizational Strategy.* Cambridge: Harvard University Press, 1998.

Kirzner, I.M., "Entrepreneurial Discovery and the Competitive Market Process: An Austrian Approach," *Journal of Economic Literature*, 1997, 35, pp. 60–85.

Kogut, B. and Zauder, U., "Knowledge of the Firm, Combinative Capabilities, and the Raptication of Technology." *Organization Science* 1992, 3, pp. 383–97.

Langlois, R.N., "Transaction-Cost Economics in Real Time," *Industrial and Corporate Change*, 1992, 1, pp. 99–127.

Langlois, R.N. and Foss, Nicolai J., "Capabilities and Governance: the Rebirth of Production in the Theory of Economic Organization," *KYKLOS*, 1999, 52, pp. 201–18.

Laursen, K., "The Importance of Sectoral Differences in the Application of (Complementary) HRM Practices for Innovation Performance," *International Journal of the Economics of Business*, 2002 (this issue).

Laursen, K. and Foss, N.J., "New HRM Practices, Complementarities, and the Impact on Innovation Performance," *Cambridge Journal of Economics*, forthcoming 2002.

Liebeskind, J.P., "Keeping Organizational Secrets: Protective Institutional Mechanisms and their Costs," *Industrial and Corporate Change*, 1997, 6, pp. 623–63.

Liebeskind, J.P., Oliver, A.L., Zucker, L.G. and Brewer, M.B., *Social Networks, Learning, and Flexibility: Sourcing Scientific Knowledge in New Biotechnology Firms*. Cambridge: NBER Working Paper No. W5320, 1995.

Mahnke, V., *The Economic Organization of Intellectual Production*. Oxford: Oxford University Press, 2002.

Marglin, S.A., "What Do Bosses Do?," The Origins and Functions of Hierarchy in Capitalist Production," *Review of Radical Political Economy*, 1974, 6, pp. 33–60.

Masten, S., "A Legal Basis for the Firm," in O.E. Williamson and S.G. Winter, eds., *The Nature of the Firm: Origins, Evolution, and Development*. Oxford: Oxford University Press, 1991.

Matusik, S.F. and Hill, C.W.L., "The Utilization of Contingent Work, Knowledge Creation, and Competitive Advantage," *Academy of Management Review*, 1998, 23, pp. 680–97.

Mendelsson, H. and Pillai, R.R., "Information Age Organizations, Dynamics, and Performance," *Journal of Economic Behavior and Organization*, 1999, 38 pp. 253–81.

Meyer, C., "How the Right Measures Help Teams Excel," *Harvard Business Review*, May–June 1994, pp. 95–103.

Miles, R.E. and Snow, C.C., "Causes of Failure in Network Organizations," *California Management Review*, 1992, pp. 53–72.

Miles, R.E., Snow, C.C., Mathews, J.A., Miles, G. and Coleman, H.J., Jr., "Organizing in the Knowledge Age: Anticipating the Cellular Form," *Academy of Management Executive*, 1997, 11 pp. 7–20.

Miles, R.E., Miles, G. and Snow, Charles C., "Good for Practice: An Integrated Theory of the Value of Alternative Organizational Forms," in G. Hamel, C.K. Prahalad, H. Thomas and D. O'Neal, eds., *Strategic Flexibility: Managing in a Turbulent Environment*. New York: John Wiley, 1998.

Milgrom, P., "Employment Contracts, Influence Activities and Efficient Organization Design," *Journal of Political Economy*, 1988, 96, pp. 42–60.

Milgrom, P. and Roberts, J., "The Economics of Modern Manufacturing: Technology, Strategy and Organization," *American Economic Review*, 1990, 80, pp. 511–28.

Minkler, A.P., "Knowledge and Internal Organization," *Journal of Economic Behavior and Organization*, 1993, 21, pp. 17–30.

Mises, L.V., *Human Action*. London: William Hodge, 1949.

Monteverde, K., "Technical Dialog as an Incentive for Vertical Integration in the Semiconductor Industry," *Management Science*, 1995, 41, pp. 1624–38.

Munro, Don. "The Knowledge Economy," *Journal of Australian Political Economy*, 2000, 45, pp. 5–17.

Myers, P.S., ed., *Knowledge Management and Organizational Design*. Boston: Butterworth-Heinemann, 1996.

Neef, D., ed., *The Knowledge Economy*. Boston: Butterworth-Heinemann, 1998.

Nickerson, J. and Zenger, T., "Being Efficiently Fickle: A Dynamic Theory of Organizational Choice," unpublished manuscript, 2000.

Nonaka, I. and Takeuchi, I., *The Knowledge-Creating Company*. Oxford: Oxford University Press, 1995.

Osterloh, M., Frost, J. and Frey, B., "The Dynamics of Motivation in New Organizational Forms," *International Journal of the Economics of Business*, 2002, 9, this issue.

Powell, W., "Neither Market, Nor Hierarchy: Network Forms of Organization," *Research in Organizational Behavior*, 1990, 12, pp. 295–336.

Prendergast, C., "The Tenuous Tradeoff of Risk and Incentives," working paper, 1999.

Prusac, L., "Introduction to Series – Why Knowledge, Why Now?," in D. Neef, ed., *The Knowledge Economy*. Boston: Butterworth-Heinemann, 1998.

Putterman, L., "Markets, Hierarchies and Information: On a Paradox in the Economics of Organization," *Journal of Economic Behavior and Organization*, 1995, 26, pp. 373–90.

Rajan, R.G. and Zingales, L., "Power in a Theory of the Firm," *Quarterly Journal at Economics*, 1998, 113, pp. 387–432.

Semler, R., "Managing Without Managers," *Harvard Business Review*, Sept.–Oct. 1989, pp. 76–84.

Simon, H.A., "A Formal Theory of the Employment Relationship," in idem., *Models of Bounded Rationality*. Cambridge: MIT Press, 1982.

Simon, H.A., "Organizations and Markets," *Journal of Economic Perspectives*, 1991, 5, pp. 25–44.

Rabin, M., "Information and the Control of Productive Assets," *Journal of Law, Economics and Organization*, 1993, 9 pp. 51–76.

Tapscott, D., ed., *Creating Value in the Network Economy*. Boston: Harvard Business School Press, 1999.

Teece, D.J., "Profiting from Technological Innovation: Implications for Integration, Collaboration, Licensing and Public Policy," in *The Competitive Challenge*. Cambridge: Ballinger Publ. Comp, 1987, pp??

Thompson, J.D., *Organizations in Action*. New York: McGraw-Hill, 1967.

Tomlinson, M., "The Learning Economy and Embodied Knowledge Flows in Great Britain," *Journal of Evolutionary Economics*, 1999, 9, pp. 431–51.

Vandenberghe, A.-S. and Siegers, J., "Employees versus Independent Contractors for the Exchange of Labor Services: Authority as Distinguishing Characteristic?," Paper for the 17th Annual Conference on the European Association of Law and Economics, Gent, 14–16 September, 2000.

Ven, A.H. V.D., Delbecq, A.L. and Koenig, Jr., R., "Determinants of Coordination Modes Within Organizations," *American Sociological Review*, 1976, 41 (April), pp. 322–38.

Wernerfelt, B., "On the Nature and Scope of the Firm: An Adjustment Cost Theory," *Journal of Business*, 1997, 70, pp. 489–514.

Williamson, O.E., *Markets and Hierarchies*. New York: Free Press, 1975.

Williamson, O.E., *The Economic Institutions of Capitalism*. New York: The Free Press, 1985.

Williamson, O.E., *The Mechanisms of Governance*. Oxford: Oxford University Press, 1996.

Zenger, T., "Crafting Internal Hybrids: Complementarities, Common Change Initiatives, and the Team-Based Organization," *International Journal of the Economics of Business*, this issue, 2002.

Zenger, T. and Hesterly, W.S., "The Disaggregation of Corporations: Selective Intervention, High-Powered Incentives, and Molecular Units," *Organization Science*, 1997, 8 pp. 209–22.

Zingales, L., "In Search of New Foundations," *Journal of Finance*, forthcoming.

Zucker, L., "Markets for Bureaucratic Authority and Control: Information Quality in Professions and Services," *Research in the Sociology of Organizations*, 1991, 8, pp. 157–90.

[10]

Selective Intervention and Internal Hybrids: Interpreting and Learning from the Rise and Decline of the Oticon Spaghetti Organization

Nicolai J. Foss

LINK, Department of Industrial Economics and Strategy, Copenhagen Business School,
Solbjergvej 3; 2000 Frederiksberg, Denmark
njf.ivs@cbs.dk

Abstract

Infusing hierarchies with elements of market control has become a much-used way of simultaneously increasing entrepreneurialism and motivation in firms. However, this paper argues that such "internal hybrids," particularly in their radical forms, are inherently hard to successfully design and implement because of a fundamental incentive problem of establishing credible managerial commitments to not intervene in delegated decision making. This theme is developed and illustrated, using the case of the world-leading hearing aids producer, Oticon. In the beginning of the 1990s, Oticon became famous for its radical internal hybrid, the "spaghetti organization." Recent work has interpreted the spaghetti organization as a radical attempt to foster dynamic capabilities by organizational means, neglecting, however, that about a decade later the spaghetti organization has given way to a more traditional matrix organization. In contrast, an organizational economics interpretation of Oticon organizational changes is developed. This lens suggests that a strong liability of the spaghetti organization was the above incentive problem: Frequent managerial meddling with delegated rights led to a severe loss of motivation, and arguably caused the change to a more structured organization. Refutable implications are developed, and the discussion is broadened to more general issues of economic organization.

(*Internal Hybrids; Organizational Change; Delegation; Managerial Commitment Problems; New Organizational Forms*)

Introduction

In academic research as well as in managerial practice, the search for the sources of competitive advantage has increasingly centered on organization-related factors (e.g., Barney 1986, Kogut and Zander 1992, Mosakowski 1998, Nahapiet and Ghoshal 1999). Thus, it is argued that many firms radically change the way in which they structure their boundaries (e.g., Helper et al. 2000) as well as their internal organization (e.g., Miles

et al. 1997). They arguably do this in an attempt to foster the dynamic capabilities that are necessary for competing in the emerging knowledge economy. Fundamental advances in IT and measurement technologies have facilitated these changes (Zenger and Hesterly 1997), while equally fundamental developments in the organization and motives of capital markets as well as increasing internationalization are claimed to have made them necessary (Halal and Taylor 1998).

From an organizational economics perspective, these experiments with economic organization fall into the categories of either *external hybrids* (Williamson 1996) (that is, market exchanges infused with elements of hierarchical control), or *internal hybrids* (Zenger 2002) (that is, hierarchical forms infused with elements of market control). The aims of the experimental efforts are to reduce coordination costs, improve incentives, and help to clarify the nature of the businesses the firm is in, thereby improving entrepreneurial capabilities and the ability to produce, share, and reproduce knowledge (Grant 1996, Day and Wendler 1998, Miles et al. 1997, Mosakowski 1998). Although both internal and external hybrids are means to reach these aims, they would seem to be highly imperfect substitutes. For example, adopting an internal hybrid form has the benefit of involving fewer layoffs relative to adopting external hybrids. Also, spin-offs, carve-outs and the like are often legally complex operations, whereas adopting an internal hybrid may simply be a matter of managerial fiat. Further, management may fear that leaving too many activities in the hands of other firms will hollow out the corporation (Teece et al. 1994), or make it difficult to protect valuable knowledge (Liebeskind 1996). Given this, one may wonder why firms should ever make governance choices in favor of external hybrids. However, a main point of this paper is that internal hybrids are beset by distinct incentive costs that external hybrids tend to avoid, and

1047-7039/03/1403/0331$05.00
1526-5455 electronic ISSN

Organization Science © 2003 INFORMS
Vol. 14, No. 3, May–June 2003, pp. 331–349

that this may explain why external hybrids are chosen over internal hybrids.

Research on new organizational forms is an emerging field (Daft and Lewin 1993, Zenger and Hesterly 1997, Foss 2002), and rather little is known about the costs and benefits of these organizational forms.[1] This paper mixes empirical observation with theoretical reasoning, mostly drawn from organizational economics, in order to gain a better understanding of the organizational design problems of internal hybrids. The theoretical emphasis is on the (neglected) costs of internal hybrids, and in particular on motivational and commitment problems that derive from the delegation of decision rights. The root of such problems is that in firms, (delegated) decision rights are not owned; they are always loaned from the holder(s) of ultimate decision-making rights, namely the top management and/or the shareholders. Given this, a fundamental problem for top management/owners is to commit to real delegation and refrain from *selective intervention* (Williamson 1996) that harms motivation, and may reduce effort and investments in firm-specific human capital.

These ideas are developed and discussed empirically with reference to organizational changes that took place in the Danish electronics (primarily hearing aids) producer, Oticon A/S, beginning in 1991. Oticon became world famous for its radical delegation experiment. The "spaghetti organization," as it came to be called, was explicitly conceived of by its designers as an attempt to infuse the Oticon organization with strong elements of market control (Kolind 1990, Lyregaard 1993) and was seen as a hard-to-replicate source of knowledge-based competitive advantage (e.g., Gould 1994). In fact, a recent cottage industry has treated the Oticon experience as an outstanding example of the sustained benefits that radical project-based organizations may provide (e.g., Lovas and Ghoshal 2000, Ravasi and Verona 2000, Verona and Ravasi 1999). However, his literature fails to note that the spaghetti organization in its initial radical form does not exist anymore; it has been superseded by more structured administrative systems since around 1996. In the following, these organizational changes will be discussed from an organizational economics starting point. The approach followed with respect to understanding the nature of organizational changes in Oticon is a historical one that relies heavily on the large number of thick descriptions of Oticon that have been produced by a number of mainly Danish academics, journalists, and Oticon insiders throughout the 1990s (in particular, Lyregaard 1993; Poulsen 1993; Morsing 1995; Morsing and Eiberg 1998; Eskerod 1997,

1998; Jensen 1998). However, these sources were supplemented with semistructured interviews with the prime mover behind the spaghetti experiment, then-CEO, Lars Kolind, as well as the present Oticon HRM officer (both June 2000).

The paper begins by developing an organizational economics interpretation of the spaghetti organization (*The Spaghetti Organization: A Radical Internal Hybrid*). The spaghetti organization appears to have been a particularly well-crafted internal hybrid. Still, it gave way to a more traditional matrix structure. It is not plausible to ascribe this organizational change to outside contingencies or to dramatic changes in strategic intent. This suggests that the spaghetti organization may have been beset by organizational costs that came to dominate the benefit aspects, necessitating a change of administrative systems (*Spaghetti and Beyond*). The Oticon spaghetti experiment carries lessons for the design of internal hybrids. In particular, it directs attention to the incentive problems of delegating rights within a firm when top management keeps ultimate decision rights. Refutable propositions for the design of internal hybrids are derived (*Discussion: Implications for Internal Hybrids*).

It should be clear already at this stage that the following is an attempt to pursue *a specific interpretation* of the Oticon spaghetti episode. Organizational economics per se is hardly in an early stage of theory development anymore, given that early work goes back more than six decades (Coase 1937), and the last three decades have witnessed a flurry of work in this field. There is therefore little need for following a logic of grounded theory (Glaser and Strauss 1967). Moreover, organizational economics is a particularly appropriate tool of interpretation in the present context, because only this body of theory *simultaneously* frames internal hybrids theoretically, casts the analysis in the relevant comparative-institutional terms (e.g., allows comparison of external and internal hybrids), and frames the kind of incentive problems that will be central in the following analysis. For example, neither information processing or motivation theory can accomplish all this.[2]

In sum, the contributions of this paper are to (1) present a novel, and in key respects more encompassing, account and interpretation of a well-known organizational change case, exemplifying the interpretive usefulness of organizational economics in the process; (2) analyze the (neglected) costs of internal hybrids in terms of the problem of selective intervention, thus contributing to understanding the efficient design of such hybrids; and (3) argue that the analysis under (2) is also helpful for understanding broader issues of economic organization, such as the governance choice between internal and external hybrids.

The Spaghetti Organization: A Radical Internal Hybrid

Recent work has used the Oticon Spaghetti experiment for the purpose of developing notions of strategy making as "guided evolution" (Lovas and Ghoshal 2000), and to discuss how the deliberate introduction of "structural ambiguity" through the choice of loosely coupled administrative systems (Ravasi and Verona 2000) may help to build "organizational capabilities for continuous innovation" (Verona and Ravasi 1999). This literature places all of the emphasis on the benefit side (mostly innovation performance) of the spaghetti experiment and fails to note that (and explain why) the spaghetti organization has been largely abandoned. In contrast, this paper accounts for the costs of this particular internal hybrid in terms of organizational economics, and uses this account to explain the change from the spaghetti organization.

Oticon: Background

Founded in 1904 and based mainly in Denmark, Oticon (now William Demant Holding A/S) is a world leader in the hearing aids industry.[3] In the first part of the 1990s, Oticon became a famous and admired instance of radical organizational change. CEO Lars Kolind and his new organizational design became favorites of the press, consultants, and academics alike.[4] The new organization was cleverly marketed as the very embodiment of empowering project-and team-based organization. Moreover, it quickly demonstrated its innovative potential by re-vitalizing important, but "forgotten" development projects that, when implemented in the production of new hearing aids, produced significant financial results, essentially saving the firm from a threatening bankruptcy, as well as by turning out a number of new strong spin-off products. The background to the introduction of the spaghetti organization was the loss of competitive advantage that Oticon increasingly suffered during the 1980s as a result of increasingly strong competition (mainly from the United States). Also, a change in the technological paradigm (Dosi 1982) in the hearing aids industry was gradually taking place through the 1980s from "behind-the-ear" hearing aids to "in-the-ear" hearing aids (Lotz 1998). Oticon's success in the 1970s was founded on miniaturization capabilities. While these had been critical for competitive advantage in the "behind-the-ear" hearing aid paradigm, new technological capabilities in electronics which were not

under in-house control by Oticon were becoming crucially important in the emerging in-the-ear paradigm.

There is evidence (e.g., Poulsen 1993, Gould 1994, Morsing 1995) that at the end of the 1980s Oticon was locked into a competence trap that was reinforced by strong groupthink characterizing both the management team and the employees. A symptom of this was that the dominant opinion among managers and development personnel at Oticon was that the in-the-ear hearing aid would turn out to be a commercial fiasco. Moreover, in-the-ear hearing aids were not perceived to be Oticon turf, in terms of both technological and marketing capabilities (Poulsen 1993). The self-image of the company clearly was one of being a traditional industrial company with its strongest technological capabilities in miniaturization and specializing in mass-producing behind-the-ear hearing aids, developing the underlying technology incrementally. Administrative systems were organized traditionally with functional departments, the managers of which together constituted the senior executive group. When problems began to accumulate, various attempts were made to change the situation, which, however, were either too insignificant or did not survive political jockeying inside Oticon. In 1988, Lars Kolind assumed the position of new CEO, concentrated all decision-making power in his own hands, and implemented drastic cost-cutting measures. However, he also quickly realized that something else had to be done to cope with the decisive changes that were underway with respect to products and processes in the industry. More radical measures were needed with respect to the strategic orientation of the firm, the administrative systems that could back this up, and the technology that the firm sourced, leveraged, and developed.

Trying Spaghetti

The new, radical measures were first sketched in a six-page memo (Kolind 1990), which described a fundamental change of corporate vision and mission: The company should be defined broadly as a first-class service firm with products developed and fitted individually for customers, rather than narrowly, as a manufacturing company producing standard behind-the-ear hearing aids. A new organizational form, namely the "spaghetti organization" (called so in order to emphasize the point that it should be able to change rapidly, yet still possess coherence), would support this strategic reorientation. The new form should be explicitly "knowledge-based," that is, consisting of "...knowledge centres...connected by a multitude of links in a non-hierarchical structure" (Kolind 1994, pp. 28–29). Making the organization "anthropocentric," that is, designing jobs so that these would "... fit the individual person's capabilities and needs" (ibid., p. 31), was argued to provide the motivational support for this knowledge network. Furthermore, basing the network on "free market forces" (Lyregaard 1993) would make it capable of actually combining and recombining skills in a flexible manner, where skills and other resources would move to those (new) uses where they were most highly valued. Clearly, the aim was to construct a spontaneously working internal network that would work with only minimal intervention on the part of Kolind and other managers, that is, "essentially, a free market at work" (LaBarre 1996).

The new organizational form was primarily implemented in the Oticon headquarters (i.e., administration, research and development, and marketing). To symbolically underscore the fundamental transformation of Oticon, headquarters moved at 8 am on 8 August 1991 to a completely new location north of Copenhagen. In the new building, all desks were placed in huge, open office spaces, and employees did not have permanent desks, but would move depending on which projects they were working on. The number of formal titles was drastically reduced, resulting in a two-layered structure with Kolind and 10 managers representing the managerial team and the remaining part of the organization being organized into projects (Kolind 1994). Thus, the new organization represented a breakdown of the old functional department-based organization into an almost completely flat, project-based organization. Departments gave way to "Competence Centers" (e.g., in mechanical engineering, audiology, etc.) that broke with the boundaries imposed by the old departments. The "multijob" concept represented a notable break with the traditional division of labor in organizations. It was based on two key features: First, there were no restrictions on the number of projects that employees could voluntarily join, and, second, employees were actively encouraged (and in the beginning actually required) to develop and include skills outside of their existing skill portfolio.[5] The underlying notion was that this would increase the likelihood that project teams would consist of the right mix of complementary skills and knowledge, because of the increase in the scope of the knowledge controlled by each team member. Moreover, the multijob concept would ease knowledge transfer because of the increase in the overlap of knowledge domains that it would produce, as employees familiarized themselves with other employees' specialized fields.

These changes were accompanied by an extensive delegation of the rights to make decisions on resource allocation. Notably, employees would basically decide

themselves which projects they would join rather than being assigned to tasks and projects from "above." Project managers were free to manage projects in their preferred ways. Wage negotiations were decentralized, with project managers receiving the right to negotiate salaries.[6] Finally, although project teams were self-organizing and basically left to mind their own business once their projects were ratified, they were still required to meet with a "Projects and Products Committee" once every three months for ongoing project evaluation.

To meet the two potentially conflicting aims of making it possible for project teams to rapidly and flexibly combine the right skills, and achieving overall coherence between rather independently taken decisions, the new organization was founded on four fundamental ideas (Kolind 1994). First, as noted, the traditional functional department structure was eliminated in favor of a project organization that went considerably beyond the traditional matrix structure. While this served to increase flexibility, other measures were directed towards achieving organizational coherence. Thus, secondly, new information technology systems were designed and implemented to make it possible to coordinate plans and actions in this decentralized organization. Everybody was supposed to have full access to the same information. Third, the traditional concept of the office was abandoned, as already mentioned. Finally, Kolind worked hard to increase intrinsic motivation by developing a corporate value base that strongly stressed responsibility, personal development, and freedom. These fundamental organizing principles were backed up by other measures. For example, to increase motivation Kolind introduced an employee stock program, in which shop floor employees were invited to invest up to 6.000 Dkr (roughly 800 USD) and managers could invest up to 50.000 Dkr (roughly 7.500 USD). Although these investments may seem relatively small, in Kolind's view they were sufficiently large to significantly matter for the financial affairs of individual employees; therefore, they would have beneficial incentive effects. More than half of the employees made these investments.

The implementation of the spaghetti organization had quick and strong performance effects (Peters 1992, Poulsen 1993). Improved performance in terms of the use and production of knowledge was almost immediate, resulting in a string of remarkable innovations during the 1990s (Verona and Ravasi 1999, Ravasi and Verona 2000). Improved growth and financial performance followed somewhat later (see Table 1).[7]

With respect to improvements in the use of knowledge, the spaghetti organization allowed significant

NICOLAI J. FOSS *Selective Intervention and Internal Hybrids*

Table 1   Oticon Financial and Technological Performance

	1988	1989	1990	1991	1992	1993	1994	1995	1996	1997	1998	1999
Net rev. (mio. Dkr)	423.8	449.6	455.4	476.5	538.8	661.3	750.3	940.2	1,087.3	1,413.4	1,613.1	1,884.3
Profit mg. (%)	1.6	8	3.7	1.8	5.8	13.1	17.9	12.4	12.8	13.8	15.4	17.9
RoE (%)	−8.5	11.6	9.4	−1.5	7.2	37	37.9	25.9	24.3	30.6	35.7	53.8
Product innovation				Multifocus	Personic	Oticon 4 kids	Noah	Microfocus	Digifocus	Spin-off innovations of digifocus	Spin-off innovations of digifocus	Ergo swift digifocus II

Note. Sources: Ravasi and Verona (2000), Annual Reports of Oticon A/S, and William Demant Holding A/S.

shelved projects to be revitalized. For example, it was realized that Oticon already had embarked upon development projects for in-the-ear hearing aids as far back as 1979. These projects provided essential inputs into many of the product innovations that Oticon launched during the 1990s. Another effect of the spaghetti organization was that product development time was reduced by 50%. In 1993, half of Oticon's sales stemmed from products introduced in 1993, 1992, and 1991. A total of 15 new products had been introduced since the implementation of the new organization, whereas none had been introduced in the last years of the earlier organization.

A recurring theme in academic treatments of the Oticon spaghetti organization (Morsing 1995, Verona and Ravasi 1999, Ravasi and Verona 2000) is that an important cause of the observed increase in Oticon's innovativeness was the introduction of "structural ambiguity"—that is, the deliberate engineering of freedom and ambiguity in the role system and in the authority structure by means of the introduction of a radical project organization. This condition facilitated the efficient and speedy integration and production of knowledge, resulting in the observed improvement of Oticon innovativeness in the 1990s. This interpretation fails, however, to explain why the spaghetti organization was gradually abandoned from about 1996 in favor of a more traditional matrix organization. It also fails to account for the possible costs of the spaghetti organization. The following section presents a complementary interpretation, based mainly on organizational economics.

The Spaghetti Organization as an Internal Hybrid

A striking aspect of the spaghetti organization is the prevalence of the market metaphor in the commentaries on the new form by both insiders and outsiders (Peters 1992, Lyregaard 1993, LaBarre 1996).[8] The spaghetti organization may indeed be interpreted as a radical internal hybrid, because the organization was strongly infused with elements characteristic of market exchange (see Table 2). Although there was no attempt to price internal services in the spaghetti organization and Oticon

employees did not become legally independent suppliers of labor services, in many other relevant dimensions Oticon was more like a market than a traditional hierarchical firm. Thus, employees (particularly project leaders) were given many and quite far-reaching decision-making rights. Development projects could be initiated by, in principle, any employee, just like entrepreneurs in a market setting, although these projects had to pass not the market test, but the test of receiving approval from the Projects and Products Committee. Project groups were self-organizing in much the same way that, for example, partnerships are self-organizing. The setting of salaries was decentralized to project leaders, acting like independent entrepreneurs (*Business Intelligence* 1993). Incentives became more high-powered (i.e., efforts and rewards were more closely tied together) as performance

Table 2   Market Organization and the Spaghetti Simulation

Market Organization	The Spaghetti Organization
Allocation by means of pricing	Transfer prices not used
Legal independence between parties (contract law)	Employment contracts (employment law)
Freedom of contract	Approximated by delegating rights to suggest and join projects
High-powered incentives	Variable pay; initially based on objective input and output measures
Dispersed residual claimancy	Employee stock schemes
Dispersed decision rights	Very widespread delegation of rights
Dispersed ultimate decision rights (dispersed formal authority)	Concentrated ultimate decision rights (concentrated formal authority)
Resource allocation decentralized and strongly influenced by local entrepreneurship	Local entrepreneurship very strongly encouraged Projects approval easily obtained
Strong autonomous adaptation properties	Secured through extensive delegation of decision rights

pay was increasingly used and as the employee stock ownership program was introduced, thus mimicking the superior incentive properties of the market. Most hierarchical levels were eliminated and formal titles done away with, etc., mimicking the nonhierarchical nature of the market. In sum, market organization was indeed emulated in a number of dimensions.

As a general matter, the attraction of infusing hierarchical forms with elements of market control is that some of the basic advantages of the hierarchy, such as the superior ability to perform coordinated adaptation to disturbances (Williamson 1996), build specialized social capital (Nahapiet and Ghoshal 1999), and share knowledge (Osterloh and Frey 2000), can be combined with the superior incentive properties of the market (Williamson 1996) and its superior flexibility with respect to autonomous adaptation (Hayek 1945, Williamson 1996). Along similar lines, Kolind explicitly saw the spaghetti organization as combining the superior abilities of a hierarchy to build knowledge-sharing environments and foster a cooperative spirit with the flexibility and creativity of a market-like project organization (Kolind 1994).

The Structure of Rights in the Spaghetti Organization

Organizational economics suggests that understanding the costs and benefits of any organizational form requires examining the structure of decision and income rights in the relevant form (Fama and Jensen 1983; Jensen and Meckling 1992; Hart 1995; Williamson 1996; Barzel 1997; Baker et al. 1999, 2002; Holmström 1999). The benefits and the costs of the spaghetti organization can be comprehended through this lens. The remaining part of this section concentrates on the benefit side.

Centralized decision-making systems, particularly large ones, have well-known difficulties with respect to mobilizing and efficiently utilizing important "sticky" knowledge (von Hippel 1994) such as the precise characteristics of specific processes, employees, machines, or customer preferences (Jensen and Wruck 1994). They therefore often also have difficulties combining such knowledge into new products and processes (Laursen and Foss 2002). As Hayek (1945) explained, the main problem is that much of this knowledge is transitory, fleeting, and/or tacit, and therefore costly to articulate and transfer to a (corporate) center. Markets have advantages relative to pure hierarchies with respect to utilizing such knowledge, particularly when it is not required to utilize the relevant knowledge in conjunction with other knowledge sets (where a hierarchy may have comparative advantages).[10] Thus, markets economize on the costs

of transferring knowledge by allocating decision rights to those who possess the relevant knowledge, rather than the other way around (Hayek 1945, Jensen and Meckling 1992). Rights will move towards the agents who place the highest valuation on those rights. Since these agents become residual claimants, effective use will be made of the rights they acquire. From this perspective, internal hybrids are fundamentally attempts to mimic, inside the hierarchy, the decentralization of decision and income rights that characterizes the market in an attempt to improve the efficiency of processes of discovering, creating, and using knowledge.[10]

The spaghetti organization may be understood through this lens, that is, as a hybrid organizational design that aimed at improving the colocation of knowledge and rights through extensive delegation, and backed up this delegation of decision rights by giving employees more income rights. By giving project teams extensive decision rights, requiring that ideas for projects be made public, and ensuring that project teams possessed the necessary complementary skills for a particular marketing, research, or development task, the spaghetti organization stimulated a colocation of decision rights with knowledge. High-powered incentives were provided in an attempt to make sure that efficient use was made of those rights. This improved the use of existing knowledge (cf. the revitalization of "forgotten" projects) and eased the combination of knowledge in the production of new knowledge.

However, Oticon's use of "free market forces" (Lyregaard 1993) was fundamentally a simulation, because the allocation of decision rights in that organization (as in any firm) remained in important respects different from the allocation that characterizes market organization. In contrast to markets, firms cannot concentrate income rights (i.e., residual claimancy) and decision rights to the same extent, in the same hands. An agency problem results from this separation. Many of the elements of the spaghetti organization may be seen as responses to this fundamental agency problem, most obviously the increased use of high-powered incentives. Consider also the rights to allocate resources to a particular project. These may be broken down into groups of decision-making rights, namely rights to (1) initiate projects, (2) ratify projects, (3) implement projects, and (4) monitor and evaluate projects (cf. Fama and Jensen 1983). The efficiency of decision-making processes in project-based firms rests on the allocation and exercise of such rights. For reasons of efficiency, firms usually do not concentrate these rights in the same hands; rather, initiation and implementation rights may be controlled by one person (or team), while ratification and monitoring rights are controlled by other persons, usually hierarchical superiors.[11]

This allocation of decision rights was characteristic of the spaghetti organization. Whereas anybody could initiate a project, projects had to be evaluated by the Products and Projects Committee that was staffed by Kolind, the development manager, the marketing manager, and the support manager. The Committee either rejected or approved of the project. The only formal criteria for getting a project accepted were that the relevant project relate to the business areas of Oticon and yield a positive return over a three-year period and with a discount rate of 30%. Apparently, the Products and Projects Committee did not control the use of corporate resources by means of controlling the budgets of individual projects at the project ratification stage. In particular, the use of human resources—the main input category—across projects was not monitored. The rights to implement a project following approval included the right to hire employees in open competition with other projects (Eskerod 1998). Operating projects would meet every third month with the Products and Projects Committee, or a representative thereof, for project evaluation (i.e., monitoring).

The fact that the Projects and Products Committee could veto a project ex ante suggests that it was the real holder of power in Oticon. Frequent intervention on the part of the Committee ex post project approval confirms this (Eskerod 1998). Thus, it became increasingly clear that the Committee could at any time halt, change, or even close projects. This kind of intervention took place frequently. The Projects and Products Committee's exercise of their ultimate decision rights may be seen as simply reflecting the separation discussed above between decision management (i.e., initiation, implementation, and daily project management) and decision control (i.e., project evaluation and monitoring).[12] However, this separation does not logically imply the kind of ex post intervention that the Committee engaged in. For example, one may imagine that the relevant rights might be allocated so precisely and with so much foresight that there are no incentives to intervene ex post, as in the case of a very detailed contract between two legally independent firms. However, the way in which the Projects and Products Committee exercised their ultimate decision rights is more akin to reneging on a contract, perhaps even to performing a "hold-up" (Williamson 1996). Thus, the Committee effectively reneged in implicit contracts with the projects as the efforts of project became, in the eyes of the Committee, superfluous (e.g., because

of new technological developments), moved in unforeseen directions, or were revealed to have been founded on ill-conceived ideas. In turn, this exercise of ultimate control rights caused unforeseen incentive problems, as will be discussed later.

Organizational Complementarities

An interesting aspect of the spaghetti organization is that an explicit logic of complementarity was present in the reasoning of its main designer. Observed Kolind: "It was not strictly necessary to do all these things at the same time, but we opined that with a simultaneous implementation of the changes [in organizational elements]...they would reinforce each other" (in Mandag Morgen 1993, p. 17; my translation). Complementarities between elements of an organizational form exist when increasing the level of one element increases the marginal return from increasing the level of all remaining elements (Milgrom and Roberts 1990, Hemmer 1995, Zenger 2002). Loosely, when complementarity obtains, the dynamics of organizational elements imply that they move together. Changing one element in an isolated way is likely to set in motion (possibly unforeseen) processes of change in other elements because the system will grope towards an equilibrium where all elements have changed (Zenger 2002). The process of groping may be associated with serious inefficiencies. Therefore, organizational change initiatives should "get the complementarities right."

Apparently, the spaghetti organization did exactly this. Thus, the change in the rights structure of Oticon was such that decision rights changed in a way that was complementary to the change in income rights; specifically, widespread delegation of decision rights was accompanied by making incentives more high powered through performance pay and employee ownership. In turn, the change in incentives was backed up by complementary changes in measurement systems. Thus, a performance evaluation system was implemented in which employee performance was measured in three to eight different dimensions (depending on the type of employee) and pay was made dependent on these measures (Poulsen 1993).

Other initiatives may also seen to be complementary to the increase in the delegation of rights in the spaghetti organization. For example, the open office landscape and the strategically placed coffee bars and staircases were complementary to rights delegation in terms of utilizing and building knowledge because they helped foster the knowledge exchange that gave rise to new ideas for project teams. With respect to the moral hazard problem introduced by delegating rights, the new much-more information-rich environment was also complementary to this delegation, because it helped to build reputational effects (cf., Eskerod 1997, 1998) and eased mutual monitoring among employees, keeping agency problems at bay. Kolind's (1990) strong emphasis on building culture in the new organization may be seen in a similar light: Influencing preferences through the building of shared values became an important activity in the spaghetti organization, because its strong delegation of rights introduced both problems of coordinating independently made decisions (Miller 1992) and agency problems, problems that are reduced as preferences become more homogeneous. The complementary nature of these organizational elements also explains the speed and toughness with which Kolind managed the transition from the old organization.[13] This is because it is usually inefficient to change systems of complementary elements in an incremental manner; transition between such systems should normally be accomplished in a "big bang" manner (cf., Dewatripont and Roland 1995).

Spaghetti and Beyond

Retreating from Spaghetti
In his account of the spaghetti organization, Gould (1994, p. 470) noted that "...Lars Kolind's vision was the right one for Oticon. In any case, one thing was certain: there could be no turning back." However, beginning in 1996, a considerable "turning back" actually began: Oticon embarked upon a partial abandonment of the spaghetti organization and gradually adopted a more traditional matrix structure. In 1996, Oticon headquarters was divided into three "business teams" that are essentially new administrative layers. In addition to the business teams, a "Competence Center" was set up. This unit is in charge of all projects and their financing and of an operational group that controls administration, IT, logistics, sales, and exports. It is one of the successors to the now abandoned Projects and Products Committee. However, its style of managing projects is very different. In particular, care is taken to avoid the kind of intervention in already-approved-of projects that characterized the Products and Projects Committee. The team leaders and the head of the Competence Center comprise, together with the CEO, the "development group," which may be seen as a second successor to the Products and Projects Committee of the original spaghetti organization. The development group, which essentially is the senior executive group, is in charge of overall strategy making. It is also the unit from which most of the initiative with respect to starting new projects comes. Many of

the decision-making rights earlier held by project leaders have now been concentrated in the hands of the Competence Center, or the managers of the business teams. For example, project leaders' rights to negotiate salaries have been constrained. Project leaders are appointed by the Competence Center, so that the right to be a project leader is not something that one grabs, as under the spaghetti organization. Although the multijob concept is still present, the extreme forms that characterized the spaghetti organization are not.

To sum up, recent changes of administrative systems at Oticon have amounted to a break with the radical bottom-up approach that characterized the original spaghetti structure. Thus, although Oticon is still characterized by considerable decentralization and delegation of rights, many of the crucial elements of the spaghetti organization have been left.

Searching for Possible Causes of the Partial Failure of the Spaghetti Experiment
Although the spaghetti organization at first inspection seems to have been a particularly well-crafted internal hybrid, closer inspection may reveal design mistakes that caused its abandonment. An organizational economics perspective suggests that a number of candidates for design mistakes be discussed. They may be grouped into problems of allocating competence, eliminating tournaments, sacrificing specialization advantages, coordination, knowledge sharing, and influence activities.[14] They are discussed in the following.

Allocating Competence. Demsetz (1988) and Casson (1994) argue that firms are hierarchical because this is an efficient way of utilizing different yet complementary knowledge; direction may be less costly than instruction or joint decision making. When this is the case, those with more decisive knowledge should direct those with less decisive knowledge. Thus, the hierarchy is an efficient method of allocating competence. The spaghetti organization eliminated most hierarchical levels. Thus, the extent to which hierarchy could be used as a sorting mechanism for allocating skills was much smaller in the spaghetti organization. For example, the delegation of project initiation rights implied that competent and less competent employees had the same rights to initiate projects and get a hearing before the Projects and Products Committee. Knowledge-based inefficiencies may have resulted that may have been avoided in a traditional hierarchy.

However, this explanation implicitly asserts that managers are, on average, more knowledgeable with respect to what actions subordinate employees should optimally

338

take than these employees are themselves. If this is not the case, bottom-up selection processes may sort better than hierarchical processes. In fact, the spaghetti organization was (at least in the official rhetoric) very much founded on the notion that bottom-up processes would select more efficiently than hierarchical processes. Hierarchical superiors may be more knowledgeable about which actions should be optimally taken by subordinates when there are strong complementarities between the actions of subordinates, and hierarchical superiors possess superior information about these complementarities and/or they possess private information about which states of the world have been realized (Foss and Foss 2002). To be sure, complementarities between subordinates' actions and knowledge sets obtained in the spaghetti organization. However, the purpose of the spontaneous, marketlike, bottom-up processes was exactly to discover and utilize such complementarities—something that the earlier hierarchical organization had not been capable of. Thus, it seems unlikely that abolishing the hierarchy in Oticon led to serious inefficiencies related to the allocation of competence.

Eliminating Tournaments. From an incentive perspective, the extremely flat spaghetti organization implied that one particular incentive instrument was no longer available to the organization: Hierarchical job ladders could no longer function as incentive mechanisms in their own rights because the spaghetti organization essentially abolished what agency theorists call "tournaments" between managers (Lazear 1995). Promotion was no longer a "prize" that could be obtained through expending effort. However, while the spaghetti organization may have eliminated this particular incentive instrument, it introduced a number of new incentive instruments, such as performance pay. From the point of view of individual employees, these new instruments may have had stronger motivational effects than tournaments because they were less open to political manipulation. Thus, the sacrifice of tournaments as an incentive instrument may not have been a major problem.

Sacrificing Specialization Advantages. A key component of the spaghetti organization was the multijob concept which implied that each employee was (1) encouraged to develop skills outside her present skill portfolio and (2) free to join projects as she saw fit. Much work on Oticon has treated the multijob concept as a strong stimulus to knowledge exchange and integration (e.g., Verona and Ravasi 1999, Ravasi and Verona 2000), presumably quite rightly so. However, the concept may also have introduced distinct costs, most obviously the sacrifice of specialization advantages that it

would seem to imply. However, there are indications that this was actually not the case. For example, an Oticon engineer may have been encouraged to develop English writing skills, which would place him in a better position to undertake technical translation relevant to his project, and do so in a more informed way than a professional translator would be capable of. Thus, this aspect of the multijob concept may have led to beneficial exploitation of complementarities between different skills.

Problems of Coordination. However, there is strong evidence that the second part of the multijob concept, the freedom to join projects, had significant costs.[15] Nobody kept track of the total time that employees spent on projects.[16] Moreover, project leaders were free to try to attract those who worked on competing projects, and in many cases they succeeded in doing so. This was a consequence of the explicit aim to emulate the market, but the effect was that it was hard to commit employees to projects and to ensure an efficient allocation of attention to projects (Gifford 1992). This led to severe coordination problems because project leaders had no guarantee that they could actually carry a project to its end. Moreover, many employees joined more projects than their time resources possibly allowed for, creating problems of coordinating schedules and work hours. The Products and Projects Committee had no routines for dealing with these problems. Apparently, reputation mechanisms were not sufficient for coping with them either. It would perhaps seem that these problems could have been reduced by simply prohibiting employees from working on more than, say, two projects that could not add up to more than 100% of the employee's total work hours.[17] Establishing such controls in the original spaghetti organization would, however, have run against the official rhetoric of autonomy, empowerment, and delegation. Alternatively, monitoring systems might have been refined to control dimensions of employee behavior that related to their attention and work allocation across the projects in which they participated, so as to reduce coordination problems. However, the very elaborate monitoring system that was implemented together with the spaghetti organization and that involved the construction of objective measures on half a dozen aspects of employee behavior (Poulsen 1993) appears to have been quickly and tacitly shelved and substituted with a simpler system that relied much more on subjective performance assessment (Business Intelligence 1993). This suggests that the problem with monitoring systems under the original spaghetti organization rather was that they were already too complex and costly to administer in practice.

Problems of Knowledge Sharing. The multijob concept promoted knowledge sharing and, in turn, knowledge creation. However, there is evidence (Eskerod 1997, 1998) that knowledge sharing was not always spontaneous and uninhibited. In fact, in some cases, knowledge tended to be held back within projects, because of the widespread and correct perception that projects were essentially in competition over corporate resources. Thus, by stressing so strongly a marketlike competitive ethos and by making incentive systems more "high-powered" (Williamson 1996) than they had been under the old organization, the spaghetti organization to some extent worked against its stated purposes. The organization's measurement and reward systems apparently could not fully cope with these problems. It may be questioned how significant this problem was. The impressive innovation record of Oticon in the 1990s indicates that the firm's creation of knowledge may not have been significantly harmed by the competitive relations existing within the spaghetti organization. Still, the relevant question is whether the knowledge-sharing environment could have been better designed. Knowledge sharing is not necessarily best stimulated by a kind of project organization that simulates competitive markets. To the extent that knowledge sharing is a hard-to-measure performance variable, employees are likely to put less of an emphasis on this (Holmström and Milgrom 1991). Upon realizing this, resorting to lower-powered incentives is likely (Holmström 1999). This corresponds to what has happened in Oticon. Although the performance measurement systems in Oticon now includes attempts to measure employees' contribution to knowledge sharing, it is also the case that the strong competitive ethos which characterized the spaghetti organization has been significantly dampened in the successor form.

Influence Activities. Influence activities are activities that subordinates engage in when they influence hierarchical superiors to make decisions that are in their own interests, rather than in the organization's (Milgrom 1988, Argyres and Mui 2000). Resources expended on influence activities are, from the point of view of the organization, waste. It is arguable that it is relatively more difficult under an organization such as the spaghetti organization to protect against influence activities. This is because everybody has, in principle, direct access to the management team. A comparative advantage of the traditional, hierarchical, and rule-governed organization is exactly that it may be better at protecting itself against influence activities because access to those who hold ultimate decision rights is more difficult. In fact, the spaghetti organization which actively stimulated competition between project groups for the approval of the only

relevant "hierarchical superior" left, namely the Projects and Products Committee, did produce such influence activities (Eskerod 1998). In contrast, under the hierarchical form existing prior to the spaghetti organization, such activities had been much less prevalent because of the aloof management style of the old management (Poulsen 1993). Personal relations to those who staffed the Committee became paramount for having a project ratified by the Committee. As Eskerod (1998, p. 80) observed:

> Part of being a project group may be lobbying in the PPC trying to obtain a high priority status by influencing the PPC members. The reason for doing this is that a high priority project is regarded as a very attractive place for the employees, because the management sees this project as important.

It is, however, not clear from the existing empirical studies of the spaghetti organization that this was perceived of as a serious problem in the organization—for example, whether it resulted in obviously unimportant projects being approved of by the Committee. Rather, it was taken as an unavoidable, and relatively small, cost of the spaghetti organization.[18]

To sum up, the search for the causes of the partial abandonment of the spaghetti organization so far seems to lead only to inefficiencies stemming from the lack of well-functioning project management routines on the part of Products and Projects Committee being a serious problem. However, handling this problem did not necessarily require a major organizational change. Still, the many possible small liabilities of the spaghetti organization (problems of knowledge being held back in projects, influence activities, etc.) may together have added up to significant costs that could be reduced by adopting a more structured organizational form (Børsens Nyhedsmagasin 1999, interview with Henrik Holck on June 2000). Moreover, there is one fundamental problem left that was clearly present in the spaghetti organization, and which is a strong candidate for explaining the abandonment of that organizational form.

The Problem of Selective Intervention

Although infusing hierarchical forms with elements of market control seems attractive, crafting and implementing such internal hybrids is a highly complicated problem. One reason is a fundamental incentive problem that plagues all hierarchies, but is arguably particularly prevalent in the kind of very flat organizations of which the Oticon spaghetti organization is an example. An early statement of the nature of this problem can be found in the comparative systems literature in economics, that is, the literature taken up with the economic differences between capitalist and socialist systems. Thus, Mises (1949, p. 709) argued that there are fundamental problems involved in "playing market" inside hierarchies.[19] Specifically, schemes for a socialist market economy would not work because the concentration of ultimate decision-making rights and responsibilities (i.e., ownership) in the hands of a central planning board would dilute the incentives of managers. Thus, while planning authorities could delegate rights to make production and investment decisions to managers, these rights would be inefficiently used. First, because managers could always be overruled by the planning authorities, they were not likely to take a long view, notably in their investment decisions. Second, because managers were not the ultimate owners, they were not the full residual claimants of their decisions and, hence, would not make efficient decisions.

Later research has clarified that (1) handling the problem requires that the planning authorities can credibly commit to a noninterference policy, and (2) the problem goes beyond the comparative systems context. It is latent (or manifest) in all relations between "rulers" and "ruled" (North 1990, Miller 1992, Williamson 1996, Foss and Foss 2002). The problem arises from the fact that it is hard for the ruler to commit to a noninterference policy because reneging on a promise to delegate will in many cases be extremely tempting, and those to whom rights are delegated will anticipate this. Loss of motivation results. The problem is not unknown in organizational studies, (e.g., Vancil and Buddrus 1979, p. 65). In particular, Williamson's (1996) concept of the "impossibility of selective intervention" is highly relevant. He describes it as

> ...a variant on the theme, "Why aren't more degrees of freedom always better than less?" In the context of firm and market organization, the puzzle is, "Why can't a large firm do everything that a collection of small firms can and more." By merely replicating the market the firm can do no worse than the market. And if the firm can intervene selectively (namely, intervene always but only when expected net gains can be projected), then the firm will sometimes do better. Taken together, the firm will do at least as well as, and will sometimes do better than, the market (1996, p. 150).

Williamson directly argues that (efficient) selective intervention of this kind is "impossible." Incentives are diluted, because the option to intervene "...can be exercised both for good cause (to support expected net gains) and for bad (to support the subgoals of the intervenor)" (Williamson 1996, pp. 150–151). Promises to only intervene for good cause can never be credible, Williamson argues, because they are not enforceable

in a court of law. The wider implication of this reasoning is that because decision rights cannot be delegated in a court-enforceable manner inside firms (i.e., are not contractible), authority can only reside at the top. Authority cannot be delegated, even informally, because any attempt to do this will run into the problem of the impossibility of selective intervention. One would therefore expect to see little use of delegation. Given that delegation is clearly a viable and widespread organizational practice, this suggests that this implication is going too far.

In fact, it is conceivable that the "intervenor" may credibly commit to not intervene in such a way that the "subgoals of the intervenor" are promoted. The logic may be stated in the following way (cf. Baker et al. 1999). Assume that a subordinate initiates a project.[20] Assume further that the manager has information that is necessary to perform an assessment of the project, but that he decides upfront to ratify *any* project that the subordinate proposes. Effectively, this amounts to full informal delegation of the rights to initiate and ratify projects—"informal," because the formal right to ratify is still in the hands of the manager and because that right cannot be allocated to the subordinate through a court-enforceable contract (cf. Williamson 1996). Because the subordinate values being given freedom—she is partly a residual claimant to the outcomes of his activities—this will induce more effort in searching for new projects (Aghion and Tirole 1997, Foss and Foss 2002). To the organization, the expected benefits of these increased efforts may be larger than the expected costs from the bad projects that the manager has to ratify. However, a problem arises when the manager has information about the state of a project ("bad" or "good"), because he may then be tempted to renege on a promise to delegate decision authority, that is, intervene in a "selective" manner. If he overrules the subordinate, the latter will lose trust in him, holding back on effort. Clearly, in such a game a number of equilibria, each one characterized by different combinations of employee trust and managerial intervention, are feasible. What determines the particular equilibrium that will emerge is the discount rate of the manager, the specific trigger strategy followed by the subordinate (e.g., will he lose trust in the manager for all future periods if he is overruled, or will he be more forebearing?), and how much the manager values his reputation for not reneging relative to the benefits of reneging on a bad project (Baker et al. 1999).

All of the above build on standard economics assumptions on motivation and cognition: Employees are motivated solely by being able to share in the outcomes of their activities, and managerial intervention decreases motivation because it means that the expected gain of putting effort into a project diminishes. Including richer motivational and cognitive concerns aggravates the problem of selective intervention. As argued in an extensive literature in psychology (summarized in Frey 1997), people are also likely to be intrinsically motivated. Such motivation may be sustained by psychological contracts that involve loyalties and emotional ties (Brockner et al. 1992, Robinson and Morrison 1995, Osterloh and Frey 2000, p. 541). Managerial intervention, particularly when it is perceived to be essentially arbitrary, may break such contracts and harms intrinsic motivation (Robinson and Rousseau 1994). Other parts of psychological research (summarized in Bazerman 1994) suggest other ways in which the problem of selective intervention may be aggravated in practice. Thus, robust findings in experimental psychology show the presence of a systematic overconfidence bias in judgment; that is, people tend to trust their own judgments more than is "objectively" warranted. Managers are not exceptions to this bias, perhaps quite the contrary. The presence of the overconfidence bias in the judgments that underlie managerial decision making is likely to aggravate the problem of selective intervention, because it produces additional meddling in subordinates' decisions (Nickerson and Zenger 2001, p. 15).

Selective Intervention in Oticon
It is arguable that the main reason that the spaghetti organization was changed into a more hierarchical organization has to do with the kind of incentive and motivational problems described above. The official Oticon rhetoric, stressing bottom-up processes in a flexible, marketlike, and essentially self-organizing system with substantial autonomy and a management team (i.e., the Projects and Products Committee) that acted as little more than facilitator (Kolind 1990, Lyregaard 1993), became increasingly at odds with the frequent selective intervention that was undertaken by the Projects and Products Committee.[21] The need for selective intervention was rationalized by an external observer in the following terms:

> ...PPC [the Products and Projects Committee] does not make general written plans, which are accessible to the rest of the organization...if this were done, plans would have to be adjusted or remade in an ever-continuing process, because the old plans had become outdated (Eskerod 1998, p. 80).

This entirely ad hoc approach was taken by the Products and Projects Committee to be an unavoidable feature of a flexible, project-oriented organization (Eskerod

1998, p. 89). However, it was also a direct signal to employees that the "contract" between any project and the Products and Projects Committee was very incomplete (Williamson 1996), and that the Committee might at any time exercise its ultimate control rights for the purpose of intervening in projects. This produced diluted incentives and badly harmed motivation (as documented at length by Eskerod 1997, 1998). Accumulating frustration finally resulted in a major meeting in 1995, which marked the beginning of the retreat from the spaghetti organization. At the meeting employees dramatically expressed their concerns about the contrast between on the one hand, the Oticon value base, including the strong rhetoric of delegation, and on the other hand, the way in which the company was actually managed. Frustration that projects were interrupted in seemingly arbitrary ways and that the organization was far better at generating projects than at completing them was explicitly voiced.

The preceding discussion suggests that a fundamental problem in the spaghetti organization was that Kolind and the Products and Projects Committee never committed to a policy of not intervening selectively; neither, apparently, did they intend to do so or even see any rationale in it. Kolind's view appears to have been that in important respects and in many situations, he and the Products and Projects Committee would possess accurate knowledge about the true commercial and technical possibilities of a given project, and that efficient utilization of corporate resources dictated intervening in, and sometimes closing down, projects. However, that view clashed on a basic level with the rhetoric of widespread delegation of decision rights, leading to the demise of the spaghetti organization and the adoption of the present more-structured matrix organization.

In principle, Kolind and the Products and Projects Committee could have committed to a policy of noninterference from the beginning, rather than acting on the belief that organizational flexibility required that they selectively intervene in projects. Conceivably, this might have made this radical internal hybrid viable. However, even if Kolind and the Products and Projects Committee had announced initially that they would refrain from selective intervention, there are reasons why this commitment may not have been sustainable in the longer run. Thus, it was increasingly clear that the elaborate system of measures that was initially installed was inadequate. It did not capture important dimensions of behavior (e.g., employees' contribution to knowledge sharing) and it may have contributed to some projects holding back knowledge. Rather than trying to refine the system further, it was abandoned.[22] However, the implication was that management could no longer take place solely through incentives (following initial ratification of projects). The employee stock ownership program was arguably not sufficiently high powered to truly motivate, and did not confer sufficient decision rights to halt the practice of selective intervention to employees. The implication was that Kolind and the Products and Projects Committee had to engage in much more monitoring of the projects. Doing this without compromising team autonomy and harming motivation was unlikely.

The New Organization

A notable feature of the present Oticon organization lies in its much more consistent approach towards projects. Organizational expectations are that priorities do not change in the rapid and erratic manner that characterized the original spaghetti organization, and that employees can be much more sure that the projects they are working on are taken all the way to the end. In the new organization, projects are rarely stopped or abandoned, and there is an explicitly stated policy of sticking to ratified projects. Two reasons are given for this. First, projects are more carefully examined with respect to technical feasibility and commercial implications. An aspect of this is that the Competence Center now much more actively puts forward project ideas and contacts potential project leaders, rather than relying on the bottom-up approach that characterized the original spaghetti organization. Thus, hierarchical selection has to some extent substituted for selection performed by bottom-up processes. Second, the wish to avoid harming motivation (i.e., diluting incentives) by overruling ongoing projects is strongly stressed. The management team has openly announced this policy, and has made it credible by (1) consistently sticking to it and (2) researching project ideas carefully ex ante so that employees' perceived probability that intervention will occur is low. Some reasons why a more traditional hierarchy may be better at making such commitment credible is discussed in the following section.

Discussion: Implications for Internal Hybrids

Proponents of internal hybrids argue that their advantage lies in the ability to integrate the virtues of more conventional organizational forms (Miles et al. 1997). Specifically, internal hybrids combine the ability to achieve efficiencies through specialization that characterizes the functional form with the relative independence that can be granted in a divisional form, and the ability to transfer resources and capabilities across division and business unit boundaries that characterize the matrix organization (e.g., Miles and Snow 1992). The designers of the Oticon spaghetti organization invoked strikingly similar arguments (Kolind 1990, 1994; Lyregaard 1993). This suggests that broader lessons with respect to the efficient design of internal hybrids may emerge from the Oticon experience.

Getting Complementarities Right

A basic proposition in much of organization theory is that for reasons of efficiency, organizational forms are aligned with environmental conditions, strategies, and exchange conditions in a systematic and discriminating manner (Thompson 1967, Meyer et al. 1993, Williamson 1996, Nickerson and Zenger 2000). Thus, Zenger (2002, p. 80) argues that many attempts to infuse hierarchies with elements of market control break with this basic proposition and often "...violate patterns of complementarity that support traditional hierarchy as an organizational form." For example, managers implement new structures without new performance measures and new pay systems, or they implement new pay systems without developing new performance measures. This results in unstable, possibly inefficient, hybrid forms. In contrast, viable internal hybrids are characterized by organizational elements clustering in certain characteristic, complementary combinations, just as in the case of markets and hierarchies (Williamson 1996).

Did the spaghetti organization get the complementarities between organizational elements right? On first inspection, it did, as has been argued. However, closer inspection reveals a somewhat different picture. Thus, it may be argued that Oticon did not get the organizational complementarities exactly right, because the kind of radical internal hybrid that was adopted requires that projects be managed almost exclusively through the provision of incentives and ownership (Miles et al. 1997, Zenger 2002). The performance measurement systems in the spaghetti organization were not adequate to support precise performance evaluation. Some relevant performance dimensions (e.g., contribution to knowledge sharing) were not measured at all. Also, the incentive effects of the employee stock ownership program appear to have been limited. Thus, remuneration schemes may not have rested on sufficiently precise and encompassing measures and were not sufficiently high powered to complement the widespread delegation of decision rights in the organization. This fostered a need for selective intervention on the part of Kolind and the Products and Projects Committee that went beyond what would have been necessary with better measures of employee performance, and which had the unintended effect that motivation was seriously harmed. This reasoning suggests the following proposition:

PROPOSITION 1. *Internal hybrids that violate patterns of complementarity characteristic of this organizational form will be subject to more problems of selective intervention than hybrid forms that get the complementarities right.*

A corollary to this proposition is that advances in measurement methods will result in less selective intervention because the measurement of performance is improved so that the moral hazard stemming from the delegation of rights is reduced.

Problems of Intervention and Organizational Form

The motivational and incentive problems that may emerge from managerial selective intervention are not independent of organizational structure, notably, the number of hierarchical layers in the organization, and therefore the distribution of information and authority in a firm. Arguably, organizations that adopt internal hybrids that amount to drastically reducing the number of hierarchical layers, such as Oticon's spaghetti experiment, are more prone to the problem than more traditional hierarchical firms. There are (at least) three reasons for this.

First, decision rights are more solidly established in a traditional hierarchy, which is associated with well-defined, distinct positions than in a flat, project-based organization where decision rights are more fleeting. Organizational expectations that certain positions come with certain decision rights are very well established, and potentially costly for a top manager to break with through selective intervention. The same kind of organizational expectations are not likely to be established in a flat, project-based organization. Second, a top manager who selectively intervenes in a hierarchical organization risks overruling the *whole* managerial hierarchy (all those below him), whereas this may be a smaller concern in a flat organization where the CEO may only harm motivation in a specific project team if he overrules that team. Third, information-processing perspectives (Thompson 1967, Galbraith 1974) suggest that the hierarchy is not just a structure of authority, but also one of information. The informational distance between projects and top manager may be increased by having a multilayered hierarchy. This implies that the top manager knows that he is in key dimensions ignorant about the project (Aghion and Tirole 1997). In this case, his incentives to selectively intervene will be small. The preceding arguments suggest the following proposition:

PROPOSITION 2. *An internal hybrid form that is organized within a firm with few hierarchical layers will be associated with larger efficiency losses caused by problems of selective intervention than an internal hybrid form that is organized within a firm with more hierarchical layers.*

Problems of Intervention and the External Environment

A key reason why the Products and Projects Committee considered that frequent selective intervention was necessary had to do with the impossibility of making detailed plans for future business development in an industry where unforeseen contingencies (e.g., new technologies) often occurred. This suggests a third proposition:

PROPOSITION 3. *There will be more selective intervention in internal hybrid forms that operate in turbulent industries than in internal hybrid forms that operate in tranquil industries.*

This proposition may be taken to be the other side of the coin of the transaction cost argument that *external* hybrids are unstable in "dynamic" industries (Williamson 1996) because in such industries unexpected contingencies that may give rise to holdups are more likely. Along similar lines, the argument underlying Proposition 3 is that in dynamic industries, the implicit contract between teams/projects and management in *internal* hybrids is likely to be relatively more incomplete than in more tranquil industries. Therefore, management is likely to engage in more selective intervention in an attempt to influence how projects react to unexpected contingencies.

Internal and External Hybrids and Internal and External Markets

The problem of selective intervention casts a novel light over governance choices between internal and external hybrids and internal and external markets (Poppo 1995). These organizational forms may be seen as rather close substitutes. For example, they may be adopted in order to better exploit local knowledge (Cowen and Parker 1997), or to strengthen incentives, because they make agents residual claimants to a higher degree than is the case in traditional hierarchies. However, whereas internal hybrids/internal markets may suffer from problems stemming from selective intervention, external hybrids/external markets do not suffer from these. Of course, external hybrids and markets may suffer from inefficiencies caused by holdup problems when specific assets are deployed. However, creating competition between suppliers, investing in hostages, having some tapered integration, etc., may strongly reduce problems related to holdup. The legal system also constrains the holdup possibility, however imperfectly. In contrast, a solution to the problem of avoiding harmful selective intervention cannot rely on market forces or court-enforceable contracts. The implication is that, on average, external markets and external hybrids are likely to have incentive properties that are superior to those of internal markets and internal hybrids, so that there will be (transaction and production) cost penalties associated with the use of the latter. This results in the following proposition:

PROPOSITION 4. *Firms that choose external hybrids (markets) over internal hybrids (markets) will have a cost performance that is superior to those that choose internal hybrids (markets) over external hybrids (markets).*

This reasoning may be seen as a variation of a familiar theme of transaction cost economics (Williamson 1996), namely that vertical integration be considered the option of last resort.

Managing Commitment to Not Selectively Intervene
While theory suggests that the problem of committing to not selectively intervene is a tough one, we do seem to observe a substantial amount of delegation in real-world firms. This indicates that it is possible to credibly commit to nonintervention. There are two fundamental methods that managers may use for this purpose. Both essentially tie the hands of a would-be intervenor.

The first one is to commit oneself to being (rationally) ignorant. Thus, a manager may choose not to be informed about a number of critical dimensions in projects. In very hierarchical organizations this may be easy to accomplish because of the large informational distance between topmanagement and projects. A second approach proceeds by managers making it harmful to themselves to selectively intervene. Open announcement of a nonintervention policy, making such policy recorded in company documents, working to install it in corporate culture, etc., all contribute to meeting this aim because it makes the possible clash between the communicated values and managerial interventionist practice extremely sharp, and makes very obvious the break of the explicitly stated psychological contract (Brockner et al. 1992).

The Spaghetti Organization as a Modulation Between Stable Organizational Forms
Although organizational forms that break with a logic of complementarity may incur penalties in terms of static efficiency (i.e., economizing with transaction costs and

costs of production), they may still conceivably yield benefits in terms of dynamic efficiency (i.e., innovativeness). Calls for "chaotic" organization (Peters 1992) often implicitly make such arguments. Organization design needs to consider both types of efficiencies (Ghemawat and Ricart i Costa 1993). An implication is that in an intertemporal perspective, choosing "consistent" configurations of organizational elements may not necessarily maximize the value of the firm. An ingenious argument of this kind has been developed by Nickerson and Zenger (2000). They suggest that considerations of efficiency may require modulating between discrete organizational forms—such as the old hierarchical Oticon organization and the postspaghetti matrix structure—even in response to a *stable* set of environmental conditions. This is because the steady-state functionality delivered by a discrete organizational form may itself be discrete, and the desired functionality may lie in-between those delivered by the discrete organizational forms. Efficiency gains may then be obtained by modulating between the forms.

If indeed the Oticon spaghetti organization may have incurred inefficiencies with respect to the organization of its administrative systems, it is hard to dispute that it was also a quite innovative organization (cf. Table 1). These benefits may likely have overwhelmed the organizational costs. Although the spaghetti organization was not stable in the presence of the problem of selective intervention, it would still have made sense to choose this form, even if the designers had known it to be inherently unstable. In fact, much of the early discussion of the spaghetti organization made reference to the need to try something entirely new and admittedly chaotic, for the purpose of drastically shaking up the original, bureaucratic organization (Kolind 1990, Peters 1992, Poulsen 1993). This is consistent with Nickerson and Zenger's theory: The spaghetti organization may indeed be an example of modulating between the stable organizational form of the traditional, prespaghetti hierarchy, and the stable matrix organization *post* the spaghetti. What lends credence to this interpretation is that although the hearing aids industry was technologically quite dynamic in the relevant period (Lotz 1998), it is not possible to identify environmental changes that might have caused the organizational change away from the spaghetti.

Firms and Markets
The present discussion casts light over the classical issue of what the fundamental differences are between firms and markets, and supports the original Coasian position that the key difference is that markets do not rely on resource allocation by means of authority, whereas

firms do (Coase 1937). "Authority" is a problematic word because it is often invested with a too-narrow meaning, for example, detailed direction and supervision (Foss and Foss 2002). Ultimately, the meaning of having authority is that one can restrict the decisions of one's subordinate, overrule him, and perhaps fire him. This means that although decision rights may be delegated, we can still trace the chain of authority in a firm, and we will always realize that ultimate decision-making power resides at the top. As this paper has illustrated, all subordinates' decision rights "are loaned, not owned" (Baker et al. 1999, p. 56). Fundamentally, it can never be otherwise. This is because ultimate decision-making rights can only be transferred from bosses to subordinates in one way, namely by transferring ownership (Hart 1995). However, transferring ownership amounts to spinning-off the person to whom ownership is given. It means creating a new firm. It is this fundamental difference in how ownership is allocated that underlies the problem of selective intervention. The analysis in this paper thus makes direct contact with important modern theories of economic organization (Hart 1995, Williamson 1996, Baker et al. 2002) that stress the importance of ownership for the understanding of the nature of firms and firm boundaries.

Conclusions

To many firms, the adoption of new, hybrid organizational forms is increasingly seen as imperative. However, rather little theoretical and empirical research has treated particularly internal hybrids. This paper has examined a specific experiment with adopting and later strongly modifying a radical internal hybrid in an attempt to identify some possible liabilities of the adoption of such organizational forms. In particular, the focus has been on motivational problems that may be caused by problems of committing to refraining from harmful selective intervention. A main argument was that problems of selective intervention are particularly prevalent in organizations that adopt radical internal hybrids. In contrast, firms with more traditional hierarchical structures better shield themselves from these problems. Managers may commit to nonintervention by means of rationally choosing to be ignorant or by making it harmful to themselves to selectively intervene. Finally, the problem of selective intervention is a prime candidate for understanding the incentive liabilities of hierarchies and internal hybrids vis-à-vis markets or external hybrids.

Although this paper has thus exemplified the interpretive power of organizational economics, admittedly organizational economics only tells a part of the story. From an organizational economics perspective, the spaghetti organization represented a matrix of rights and incentives that are helpful for understanding its liabilities and how these liabilities gave rise to certain organizational dynamics (i.e., the partial abandonment of the spaghetti organization). However, it may indeed also be understood in terms of an attempt to, for example, foster dynamic capabilities (Ravasi and Verona 2000), a perspective that lies outside of organizational economics. Thus, the full story of the Oticon spaghetti experiment requires that more than one perspective be considered. Relatedly, the paper has suggested that organizational economics should consider to a fuller extent psychological insights in motivation and in cognition. While it is possible to tell stories of managerial commitment, selective intervention, and stifled incentives based only on organizational economics, there is little reason to be so narrow. A vast literature on procedural justice in organization, psychological contracts, and (biased) cognition exists, the insights of which may be combined with organizational economics insights in order to further the understanding of problems of managerial commitment, including problems of selective intervention (cf. also Miller 1992, Lindenberg 2000).

Acknowledgments

The author acknowledges discussion with, and helpful comments from, Kirsten Foss, Robert Gibbons, Anna Grandori, Henrik Holck, Lars Kolind, Kristian Kreiner, Peter Lotz, Volker Mahnke, Peter Maskell, Mette Morsing, two anonymous reviewers, and Senior Editor Axel von Werder, as well as seminar audiences at Copenhagen Business School, the Universität Freiburg, Norges Handelshøyskole, and the University of Pisa on earlier drafts of this paper. All mistakes, errors of interpretation, etc. are solely the responsibility of the author.

Endnotes

[1] Zenger (2002) argues that much more work exists on external hybrids than on internal hybrids, investigation of the latter being largely confined to work on the multidivisional form. And Poppo (1995, p. 1.845) points out that "[e]mpirical work that examines the differences between internal and external markets are rare.... Theory in this area is also limited."

[2] However, a main purpose of conducting analysis of single cases often is to be able to pose competing explanations for the same set of events (and perhaps to indicate how these explanations may be applied to other situations) (Yin 1989). Moreover, basic considerations of internal validity dictate that alternative explanations be considered. However, while I shall indeed make reference to and discuss other possible explanations of some of the relevant events (e.g., ideas from motivation theory and information processing theory), the main emphasis is on developing one specific interpretation. While an eclectic, multiple-perspective approach may be superior in the abstract, more insight may arguably be provided in the concrete by pursuing, in a relatively narrow fashion, one specific interpretation and explore the limits of this interpretation.

NICOLAI J. FOSS *Selective Intervention and Internal Hybrids*

[3] See Lotz (1998) for a careful analysis of the hearing aids industry, with particular emphasis on patterns of innovation. The history of Oticon prior to the introduction of the spaghetti organization is extensively covered in Poulsen (1993) and Morsing (1995), and, more briefly, in Gould (1994) and Lovas and Ghoshal (2000, pp. 877–878).

[4] The Oticon case is reportedly the best-selling IMD case (Gould 1994) ever (Børsens Nyhedsmagasin 8 November, 1999). Kolind's dramatic and symbol-laden way of implementing the spaghetti organization, as well as the form itself, are still being given extensive treatment in management textbooks (e.g., Boddy and Paton 1998).

[5] As Kolind explained to Gould (1994, p. 465): "We quickly agreed that all employees would have a portfolio of jobs, and we were tough; we said at least three jobs, with the main one in their profession or using their greatest competence, and the other two in outside areas. This concept really expands an organization's resources: engineers are doing marketing, marketing people manage development projects, and financial people help with product development."

[6] Although the variance on the distribution of salaries was increased as a result of the new reward schemes, average salaries do not appear to have changed. In fact, average Oticon salaries have been, and still are, comparatively low, particularly for software developers. Intrinsic motivation is a key aspect of Oticon motivation system, and is seen as complementary to (rather than substituting for) extrinsic motivation. On intrinsic and extrinsic motivation, and its implications for organizational theory, see Frey (1997) and Osterloh and Frey (2000).

[7] Oticon's growth in the 1990s largely represented growth of market share, because the size of the market for hearing aids stagnated in that decade.

[8] Much recent management literature has suggested that firms in volatile elements need to emulate markets to the largest possible extent (e.g., Halal et al. 1993, Cowen and Parker 1997).

[9] For a full comparative analysis, see Nickerson and Zenger (2001).

[10] The possibility that external hybrids or market contracting may be alternatives to internal hybrids never seems to have been considered in Oticon. Thus, that incentives may be strengthened by relying on the *real* market (rather than the simulated internal one) through spinning-off functions and departments (Aron 1991) does not appear to have been seen as a serious alternative to internal disaggregation.

[11] Exceptions may occur when giving subordinates more extensive rights (e.g., a package of initiation, ratification, and implementation rights) strengthens employee incentives (see Aghion and Tirole 1997, Baker et al. 1999, and Foss and Foss 2002 for analyses of this).

[12] For example, it could reflect attempts to curb moral hazard in project teams. However, the increased use of high-powered incentives and more widespread employee ownership were designed to remedy problems of moral hazard.

[13] The change was assisted by the symbolic acts undertaken by Kolind, which helped to signal his commitment to the change (Hermalin 1998). For example, Kolind invested 25 million Dkr (approximately 4 million USD) of his own funds in the firm.

[14] In addition, a motivation theory perspective would suggest that while employees' lower-level needs were not sufficiently satisfied (low income, uncertainty due to the reorganization and layoffs), management already tried to address their higher-level needs (more comprehensive tasks, more responsibility). Thanks to an anonymous reviewer for this point.

[15] Eskerod (1997, 1998) in particular documents this. My later interview with the chief HRM officer strongly confirmed Eskerod's finding that the multijob concept had severe costs in terms of problems of coordination and frustrating employees.

[16] And neither would this have been possible, as nobody in Oticon, not even the Projects and Products Committee, kept track of the total number of development projects. Records were only kept of the 10–20 major projects. An estimate is that under the spaghetti organization, an average of 70 projects were continously running (Eskerod 1998, p. 80).

[17] In fact, the more structured project organization gradually implemented from 1996 has established controls that secure that the coordination and time-allocation problems that beset the original spaghetti organization are kept at bay.

[18] Interview with HRM manager Henrik Holck.

[19] Somewhat later, the literature on internal transfer prices revealed the existence of various incentive problems that may beset this organizational practice (e.g., Holmström and Tirole 1991).

[20] This should be understood in a broad sense: A "project" may refer to many different types of decisions or clusters of decisions.

[21] See Simons (2002) for a highly pertinent discussion of employees' perception of the fit between managers' words and actions and the motivational consequences of this perception.

[22] Since behavior was apparently difficult to measure, a more output-based system could have been tried (Prendergast 1999), for example, contracts that specified rewards for specific accomplishments (e.g., a system that rewarded according to milestones in a development project). However, it is doubtful whether such a contract could actually be made court enforceable. A managerial commitment problem would again result.

References

Aghion, Philippe, Jean Tirole. 1997. Formal and real authority in organization. *J. Political Econom.* **105** 1–29.

Argyres, Nicholas, Vai-Lam Mui. 2000. Rules of engagement, informal leaders, and the political economy of organizational dissent. Unpublished paper.

Aron, Debra J. 1991. Using the capital market as a monitor: Corporate spin-offs in an agency framework. *RAND J. Econom.* **22** 505–518.

Baker, George, Robert Gibbons, Kevin J. Murphy. 1999. Informal authority in organizations. *J. Law, Econom. Organ.* **15** 56–73.

———, ———, ———. 2002. Relational contracts and the theory of the firm. *Quart. J. Econom.* **117** 39–83.

Barney, Jay B. 1986. Organizational culture: Can it be a source of sustained competitive advantage? *Acad. Management Rev.* **11** 656–665.

Baron, James N., David M. Kreps. 1999. Consistent human resource practices. *California Management Rev.* **41** 29–53.

Barzel, Yoram. 1997. *Economic Analysis of Property Rights.* Cambridge University Press, Cambridge, MA.

Bazerman, Max H. 1994. *Judgment in Managerial Decision Making.* Wiley, New York.

Boddy, David, Robert Paton. 1998. *Management: An Introduction.* Prentice Hall, London, U.K.

NICOLAI J. FOSS *Selective Intervention and Internal Hybrids*

Børsens Nyhedsmagasin. 1991. For Gud, Schrøder og Oticon. (1 Marts).

———. 1999. Opgør med Kolinds kaos. (8 November) 14–22.

Brockner, J., T. Tyler, R. Cooper-Schneider. 1992. The influence of prior commitment to an institution on reactions to perceived unfairness: The higher they are, the harder they fall. *Admin. Sci. Quart.* **37** 241–261.

Business Intelligence. 1993. A non-traditional performance and process measurement system. Mette Morsing, Kristian Eiberg, eds. *Managing the Unmanageable for a Decade.* Oticon, Hellerup, Denmark.

Casson, Mark. 1994. Why are firms hierarchical? *Internat. J. Econom. Bus.* **1** 47–76.

Coase, Ronald H. 1937. The nature of the firm. *Economica* (N.S.) **4** 386–405.

Cowen, Tyler, David Parker 1997. *Markets in the Firm: A Market Process Approach to Management.* The Institute of Economic Affairs, London, U.K.

Daft, Richard L., Arie Lewin. 1993. Where are the theories for the "new" organizational forms? An editorial essay. *Organ. Sci.* **4** i–iv.

Day, Jonathan, Jim Wendler. 1998. The new economics of organization. *McKinsey Quart.* **23** 4–18.

Demsetz, Harold. 1988. The theory of the firm revisited. *J. Law, Econom. Organ.* **4** 141–161.

Dewatripont, Matthias, G. Roland. 1995. The design of reform packages under uncertainty. *Amer. Econom. Rev.* **85** 1207–1223.

Dosi, Giovanni. 1982. Technological paradigms and technological trajectories. *Res. Policy* **11** 147–162.

Eskerod, Pernille. 1997. *Nye perspektiver på fordeling af menneskelige ressourcer i et projektorganiseret multiprojekt-miljø.* Ph.D. thesis, Handelshøjskole Syd, Sønderborg.

———. 1998. Organising by projects: Experiences from Oticon's product development function. Mette Morsing, Kristian Eiberg, eds. *Managing the Unmanageable for a Decade.* Oticon, Hellerup, Denmark.

Fama, Eugene, Michael C. Jensen. 1983. Separation of ownership and control. *J. Law and Econom.* **26** 301–325.

Foss, Nicolai J. 2002. "Coase vs Hayek" Economic organization and the knowledge economy. *Intern. J. Econom. Bus.* **9** 9–36.

———, Kirsten Foss. 2002. Authority and discretion: Tensions, credible delegation, and implications for new organizational forms. Downloadable from http://www.cbs.dk/link/papers

Frey, Bruno. 1997. *Not Just for the Money.* Edward Elgar, Aldershot, U.K.

Galbraith, Jay R. 1974. Organization design: An information processing view. *Interfaces* **4** 28–36.

Ghemawat, Pankaj, Joan E. Ricart i Costa. 1993. The organizational tension between static and dynamic efficiency. *Strategic Management J.* **14** 59–73.

Gifford, Sharon. 1992. Allocation of entrepreneurial attention. *J. Econom. Behavior and Organ.* **19** 265–284.

Glaser, B., A. Strauss. 1967. *The Discovery of Grounded Theory.* Aldine, Chicago, IL.

Gould, R. Morgan. 1994. Revolution at Oticon A/S: The spaghetti organization. Soumitra Dutta, Jean-Francois Manzoni, eds. 1999. *Process Re-engineering, Organizational Change and Performance Improvement.* McGraw-Hill, London, U.K.

Grant, Robert M. 1996. Prospering in dynamically-competitive environments: Organizational capability as knowledge integration. *Organ. Sci.* **7** 375–387.

Halal, William E., K. B. Taylor. 1998. *Twenty-First Century Economics: Perspectives of Socioeconomics for a Changing World.* St. Martin's Press, New York.

———, Ali Geranmayeh, John Pourdehnad. 1993. *Internal Markets: Bringing the Power of Free Enterprise Inside Your Organization.* Wiley, New York.

Hart, Oliver. 1995. *Firms, Contracts and Financial Structure.* Clarendon Press, Oxford, U.K.

Hayek, Friedrich A. von. 1945. The use of knowledge in society. in idem. 1948. *Individualism and Economic Order.* University of Chicago Press, Chicago, IL.

Helper, Susan, John Paul MacDuffie, Charles Sabel. 2000. Pragmatic collaborations: Advancing knowledge while controlling opportunism. *Indust. and Corporate Change* **9** 443–487.

Hemmer, Thomas. 1995. On the interrelation between production technology, job design, and incentives. *J. Accounting and Econom.* **19** 209–245.

Hermalin, Benjamin. 1998. Toward an economic theory of leadership: Leading by example. *Amer. Econom. Rev.* **88** 1188–1206.

Holmström, Bengt. 1999. The firm as a subeconomy. *J. Law, Econom. Organ.* **15** 74–102.

———, Paul Milgrom. 1991. Multitask principal-agent analyses: Incentive contracts, asset ownership, and job design. *J. Law, Econom. Organ.* **7** 24–52.

———, Joan Ricart i Costa. 1986. Managerial incentives and capital management. *Quart. J. Econom.* **101** 835–860.

———, Jean Tirole. 1991. Transfer pricing and organizational form. *J. Law, Econom. Organ.* **7** 201–228.

Jensen, Frank Dybdal. 1998. *Værdibaseret Ledelse—styring mellem regler og visioner.* Jurist- og Økonomforbundets Forlag, Copenhagen, Denmark.

Jensen, Michael C., William H. Meckling. 1992. Specific and general knowledge and organizational structure. Lars Werin, Hans Wijkander, eds. 1992. *Contract Economics.* Blackwell, Oxford, U.K.

———, Karen Wruck. 1998. Science, specific knowledge and total quality management. Michael C. Jensen, ed. *Foundations of Organizational Strategy.* Harvard University Press, Cambridge, MA.

Kogut, Bruce, Udo Zander. 1992. Knowledge of the firm, combinative capabilities, and the replication of technology. *Organ. Sci.* **3** 387–397.

Kolind, Lars. 1990. Think the unthinkable. Mette Morsing, Kristian Eiberg, eds. 1998. *Managing the Unmanageable For a Decade.* Oticon, Hellerup, Denmark.

———. 1994. The knowledge-based enterprise. Mette Morsing, Kristian Eiberg, eds. 1998. *Managing the Unmanageable for a Decade.* Oticon, Hellerup, Denmark.

LaBarre, Polly. 1996. This organization is dis-organization. Wysiwyg// 93/http://fastcompany.com/online/03/oticon.html

Laursen, Keld, Nicolai J. Foss. 2002. New HRM practices, complementarities, and the impact on innovation performance. *Cambridge J. Econom.* Forthcoming.

Lazear, Edward. 1995. *Personnel Economics*. MIT Press, Cambridge, MA.

Liebeskind, Julia Porter. 1996. Knowledge, strategy and the theory of the firm. *Strategic Management J.* **17** 441–452.

Lindenberg, Siegwart. 2000. It takes both trust and lack of mistrust: The workings of cooperation and relational signaling in contractual relationships. *J. Management and Governance* **4** 11–33.

Lotz, Peter. 1998. The paradox of high R&D and industry stability: Technology and structural dynamics in the global hearing instruments industry. *Indust. Innovation* **5** 113–137.

Lovas, Bjorn, Sumantra Ghoshal. 2000. Strategy as guided evolution. *Strategic Management J.* **21** 875–896.

Lyregaard, Poul-Erik. 1993. Oticon: Erfaringer og faldgruber. Steen Hildebrandt, Leif H. Alken, eds. *På vej mod helhedssyn i ledelse*. Ankerhus.

Mandag Morgen. 1991. Oticon satser dristigt, men resultaterne mangler. (15 Feb.) 15–18.

Meyer, Alan D., Anne S. Tsui, C.R. Hinings. Configurational approaches to organizational analysis. *Acad. Management J.* **36** 1175–1195.

Miles, Raymond E., Charles C. Snow. 1992. Causes of failure in network organizations. *California Management Rev.* **35** 53–72.

——, ——, John A. Mathews, Grant Miles, Henry J. Coleman, Jr. 1997. Organizing in the knowledge age: Anticipating the cellular form. *Acad. Management Executive* **11** 7–20.

Milgrom, Paul. 1988. Employment contracts, influence activities and efficient organization design. *J. Political Econom.* **96** 42–60.

——, John Roberts. 1990. The economics of modern manufacturing: technology, strategy and organization. *Amer. Econom. Rev.* **80** 511–528.

Miller, Gary. 1992. *Managerial Dilemmas*. Cambridge University Press, Cambridge, MA.

Morsing, Mette. 1995. *Omstigning til Paradis? Oticon i processen fra hierarki til spaghetti*. Copenhagen Business School Press, Copenhagen, Denmark.

——, Kristian Eiberg, eds. 1998. *Managing the Unmanageable for a Decade*. Oticon, Hellerup, Denmark.

Mosakowski, Elaine. 1998. Entrepreneurial resources, organizational choices, and competitive outcomes. *Organ. Sci.* **9** 625–643.

Nahapiet, Janine, Sumantra Ghoshal. 1999. Social capital, intellectual capital, and the organizational advantage. *Acad. Management Rev.* **23** 242–266.

Nickerson, Jackson, Todd Zenger. 2000. Being efficiently fickle: A dynamic theory of organizational choice. Unpublished paper, David Eccles School of Business, University of Utah.

——, ——. 2001. A knowledge-based theory of governance choice: A problem-solving approach. Unpublished paper, David Eccles School of Business, University of Utah.

North, Douglass C. 1990. *Institutions, Institutional Change, and Economic Performance*. Cambridge University Press, Cambridge, MA.

Osterloh, Margit, Bruno Frey. 2000. Motivation, knowledge transfer and organizational form. *Organ. Sci.* **11** 538–550.

Peters, Tom. 1992. *Liberation Management*. Alfred A. Knopf, New York.

Poppo, Laura. 1995. Influence activities and strategic coordination: Two distinctions of internal and external markets. *Management Sci.* **41** 1845–1859.

Poulsen, Per Thygesen. 1993. *Tænk det utænkelige—revolutionen i Oticon*. Schultz, Copenhagen, Denmark.

Prendergast, Canice. 1999. The provision of incentives in firms. *J. Econom. Literature* **37** 7–63.

Ravasi, Davide, Gianmario Verona. 2000. Organizing the process of knowledge integration: The benefits of structural ambiguity. *Scandinavian J. Management*. Forthcoming.

Robinson, S. L., E. W. Morrison. 1995. Organizational citizenship behaviour: A psychological contract perspective. *J. Organ. Behaviour* **16** 289–298.

——, Denise M. Rousseau. 1994. Violating the psychological contract: Not the exception but the norm. *J. Organ. Behaviour* **15** 245–259.

Simons, Tony. 2002. Behavioral integrity: The perceived alignment between managers' words and deeds as a research focus. *Organ. Sci.* **13** 18–35.

Teece, David J., Giovanni Dosi, Richard P. Rumelt, Sidney G. Winter. 1994. Understanding corporate coherence: Theory and evidence. *J. Econom. Behavior and Organ.* **23** 1–30.

Thompson, James D. 1967. *Organizations in Action*. McGraw-Hill, New York.

Vancil, Robert, Lee E. Buddrus. 1979. *Decentralization: Managerial Ambiguity by Design*. Irwin, Homewood, IL.

Verona, Gianmario, Davide Ravasi. 1999. Organizational capabilities for continuous innovation. Unpublished paper, Bocconi University.

von Hippel, Eric. 1994. "Sticky information" and the locus of problem solving: Implications for innovation. *Management Sci.* **40** 429–439.

von Mises, Ludwig. 1949. *Human Action*. Fox and Wilkes, San Francisco, CA.

Williamson, Oliver E. 1996. *The Mechanisms of Governance*. Oxford University Press, Oxford, U.K.

Yin, Robert K. 1989. *Case Study Research: Design and Methods*. Sage, London, U.K.

Zenger, Todd. 2002. Crafting internal hybrids: Complementarities, common change initiatives, and the team-based organization. *Intern. J. Econom. Bus.* Forthcoming.

——, William S. Hesterly. 1997. The disaggregation of corporations: Selective intervention, high-powered incentives, and molecular units. *Organ. Sci.* **8** 209–222.

Zucker, Lynne. 1991. Markets for bureaucratic authority and control: Information quality in professions and services. *Res. Sociology of Organ.* **8** 157–190.

[11]

Cambridge Journal of Economics 2006, **30**, 797–818
doi:10.1093/cje/bei107
Advance Access publication 8 February, 2006

'Tying the manager's hands': constraining opportunistic managerial intervention

Kirsten Foss, Nicolai J. Foss and Xosé H. Vázquez*

We discuss and examine empirically a firm-level equivalent of the ancient problem of 'tying the King's hands', namely how to avoid managerial intervention that is undertaken to reap private benefits but is harmful to overall value creation, that is, 'managerial opportunism'. The link from managerial intervention to firm-level value-creation is moderated by employee motivation. Thus, intervention in the form of managers overruling employees or reneging on delegation may demotivate employees, particularly when the intervention is perceived as being unfair, undertaken for personal gain, etc. We argue that a number of mechanisms, such as managers staking their personal reputation, employees controlling important assets, strong trade unions, etc. may function as constraints on managerial proclivities to intervene, thus reducing the problem of managerial opportunism. We derive four hypotheses from these ideas, and test them, using path-analysis, on a rich dataset, based on 329 firms in the Spanish food and electric/electronic industries.

Key words: Delegation of discretion, Employee motivation, Firm performance, Managerial intervention
JEL classifications: M12, M21, M54

1. Introduction

In this paper, we frame and examine empirically a firm-level equivalent to the ancient problem of 'tying the King's hands' (Root, 1989). A key theme in much work on the theory of the firm (e.g., Coase, 1937; Malmgren, 1961; Casson, 1994; Williamson, 1996; Foss, 1997; Wernerfelt, 1997) is that the exercise of managerial authority in response to changes in the environment provides a reason why firms exist. Thus, the implicit thrust of most of this work is that managerial intervention is always beneficial.[1] However, in actuality,

Manuscript received 6 October 2003; final version received 18 July 2005.
Address for correspondence: Center of Strategic Management and Globalisation, Copenhagen Business School, Porcelænshaven 24; 2000 Frederiksberg, Denmark; email: kf.smg@cbs.dk

*Copenhagen Business School (Kirsten Foss and Nicolai J Foss) and Universidade de Vigo (Xosé H. Vázquez). The comments of Sven Haugland, Thorbjørn Knudsen, Keld Laursen, Torben Pedersen, Frank Stephen and Xosé M. García-Vázquez are gratefully acknowledged. The field survey has benefited from financial support from SXID, a Research Unit of the Galician Government, through grant PROY99-10, and from CICYT, an agency of the Spanish Government through grant SEC2002-04471-C02-02.

[1] Only a handful of contributions have explicitly considered the opposite possibility (Dow, 1987; Kreps, 1990). For example, Dow explicitly discusses 'managerial opportunism'. Of course, in a broad sense, 'managerial opportunism' is not neglected, as it plays (in the form of managers' moral hazard) a major role in the fields of corporate finance and corporate governance (e.g., Noe and Rebello, 1996). However, we are taken up with managerial opportunism relative to employees (rather than shareholders), and this is clearly a neglected issue.

© The Author 2006. Published by Oxford University Press on behalf of the Cambridge Political Economy Society. All rights reserved.

209

798   K. Foss, N. J. Foss and X. H. Vázquez

managerial intervention will typically override existing instructions of employees. Moreover, in firms where employees are given considerable discretion, managerial intervention may amount to overruling decisions that employees have made on the basis of decision rights that have been delegated to them. This suggests that employee utility may be harmed by managerial intervention, and that net losses from such intervention are conceivable.

As Oliver Williamson (1996, pp. 150–1) points out, the option to intervene 'can be exercised both for good cause (to support expected net gains) and for bad (to support the subgoals of the intervenor)'. The reason why not all managerial intervention is with good cause is that it may be difficult to verify the nature of the cause. Moreover, promises to intervene only with good cause are hard to make credible, as they are not enforceable in a court of law, so that a problem of '*credibly* [promising] to respect autonomy save for those cases where expected net gains to intervention can be projected' (Williamson, 1993, p. 104) remains. An important puzzle therefore concerns how managerial intervention for a good cause (i.e., value-increasing intervention) may be promoted, while avoiding intervention for a bad cause (i.e., value-destroying intervention).[1]

The contribution of the present work to the understanding of this problem lies in examining the forces that may constrain intervention for a bad cause. Our key point of departure is transaction cost economics. Like Williamson (1996), we are concerned with the incentive aspects of internal organisation.[2] However, we also rely on other streams of research in organisational economics (e.g., Milgrom, 1988; Jensen and Meckling, 1992; Bijl, 1996; Milgrom and Roberts, 1996; Aghion and Tirole, 1997; Baker et al., 2002), particularly transaction cost economics (Williamson, 1993, 1996). Moreover, in order to lend further support for our arguments, we also draw on ideas about psychological contracts in organisations (Argyris, 1960; Rousseau, 1989; Coyle-Shapiro and Kessler, 2000; Tepper and Taylor, 2003), extrinsic and intrinsic motivation (Osterloh and Frey, 2000), and psychological research on decision-making (e.g., Bazerman, 1994). This eclecticism is motivated by two observations: First, the theory of hierarchical failure in organisational economics is substantially less developed than the theory of market failure. Theory development is required, and a certain measure of eclecticism is usually warranted in the early stages of theoretical development. Second, with respect to understanding behaviour and decision-making in organisations, organisational economics is arguably too narrow an approach (cf., Baron and Kreps, 1999). It has next to nothing to say about a host of psychological and sociological issues, some of which are important to understanding the limits to internal organisation.

Our argument begins from the observation that most firms rely on the use of both managerial authority and employee discretion, that is, the ability of employees to control resources including their own human capital.[3] While authority is needed, for example, to manage residual interdependencies, discretion may be rationally delegated to employees to

---

[1] Milgrom and Roberts (1996, p. 168) argue that 'the very existence of centralised authority is incompatible with a thorough going policy of efficient selective intervention. The authority to intervene inevitably implies the authority to intervene inefficiently'. While we agree that 'first-best intervention' is strictly impossible, 'second-best intervention' is feasible.

[2] While we do not explicitly make use of the standard transaction cost economics terminology of hold-up and asset specificity (mainly because this terminology has been developed for the analysis of market, rather than organisational, failure), there are nevertheless strong overlaps. Thus, the reneging of internal, implicit contracts that we address are akin to hold-up in market settings, and gives rise to similar incentive effects (i.e., inefficient investments).

[3] Evidently, this is not the case of one-person firms. Moreover, in some partnerships and co-operatives the distinction between managerial authority and employee discretion does not come into force.

the extent that it stimulates motivation and fosters local learning and the use of local knowledge. A considerable body of work in organisational economics has addressed issues that relate to the distinction between authority and delegation, such as the optimal span of control (Williamson, 1970), the design of information structures (Galbraith, 1974), and optimal delegation given the moral hazard problem (Jensen and Meckling, 1992; Armstrong, 1994; Aghion and Tirole, 1997).

In such treatments, authority is a matter of control and the giving of orders. Managers may, of course, make mistakes (e.g., Coase, 1937; Williamson, 1970), but managerial action is usually seen as beneficial. Other issues that are implied by the distinction between authority and discretion have been given less attention, notably how the exercise of authority may harm motivation, diminishing the beneficial effects of discretion.[1] From this perspective, a basic problem in organisational design is that beneficial delegation is hard to sustain under the property rights structure characterising the firm in which delegated decision rights are always 'loaned, not owned' (Baker *et al.*, 1999). Those who hold ultimate decision rights (i.e., authority) may use these to renege on delegation and/or overrule decisions made on the basis of delegated rights. This harms employee motivation and may have negative firm-level effects when employees put in less effort and/or undertake less investment in specific human capital. However, various mechanisms, such as implicit contracts (Kreps, 1990; Baker *et al.*, 1999), explicit credible commitments (Brockner *et al.*, 1992; Moe, 1997), or organisational structure (Aghion and Tirole, 1997) may reduce the incidence and severity of harmful managerial interventions.

The paper is organised as follows. We go beyond the usual economics treatment of authority as the picking of well-defined actions from an employee's action set (cf., Coase, 1937; Simon, 1951) and argue that authority also includes the power to delegate and constrain discretion, as well as the ability to veto subordinates' decisions. In this understanding, efficient exercise of authority obtains when discretion is delegated to employees so that the costs and benefits of delegation are equal on the margin. However, motivational problems may arise when managers exercise authority by reneging on the delegation of discretion or overruling employees. It is often in an organisation's interest to avoid such managerial intervention. In fact, there are various mechanisms that may credibly constrain the flexibility of managers to intervene opportunistically. Some of these are external to the firm (e.g., tight labour and capital markets, strong labour unions), and some are internal to the firm, such as credible commitments undertaken by managers themselves (e.g., managers staking personal reputations). A number of hypotheses are derived and tested on data from the Spanish electronics and food industries.

2. Managerial opportunism, delegation and employee motivation

2.1 Authority and delegation of discretion

Simon (1951) provides a classic notion of authority, one that has arguably been dominant in economics. Authority is defined as the situation in which a 'boss' is permitted by a 'worker' to select actions, $A^0 \subset A$, where A is the set of the worker's possible behaviours. For the worker to accept the assignment, it must lie within his 'zone of acceptance'. A limitation of Simon's notion of authority is that it seems to be based on the boss having all

---

[1] However, see Aghion and Tirole (1997) and Baker *et al.* (1999, 2002) for organisational economics work that has a bearing on these issues.

800   K. Foss, N. J. Foss and X. H. Vázquez

the information, the worker being merely a passive instrument who reacts to instructions based on this information. This is a notion that does not square easily with the increasing importance of partly self-managing knowledge-workers in modern production (e.g., Purser, 1998).

Simon (1991, p. 31) himself later noted that authority may be understood more broadly, namely as a command that takes the form of a result to be produced, a principle to be applied, or goal constraints, so that '[o]nly the end goal has been supplied by the command, and not the method of reaching it'. However, even this is arguably too narrow. Usually, some aspects of 'the method of reaching' an end goal are specified, so that employees are seldom granted full discretion. Indeed, a function of authority is the placing of restrictions on the decision rights that are granted to employees with respect to *how* they reach an end goal (Milgrom, 1988; Barzel, 1997; Holmström, 1999). This function of authority is exercised in order to avoid the costs associated with unwanted externalities that may arise from employee discretion, such as moral hazard, coordination failures (e.g., scheduling problems, duplicative efforts, cannibalisation of product markets, etc.).

Discretion may be defined as the ability of an agent to exercise control over an asset (Barzel, 1997). Managers may formally delegate discretion to employees for various reasons. For example, if an employee is better informed than the manager with respect to how certain tasks should be carried out, and this knowledge is costly to communicate (Casson, 1994; Melumad *et al.*, 1995), efficient co-location of decision-making rights and knowledge requires that the employee is given discretion with respect to how to use his/her expertise in problem solving (Jensen and Meckling, 1992). Also, delegation may be undertaken for motivational rather than knowledge-based reasons. Thus, literatures in social psychology (probably beginning with Roethlisberger *et al.*, 1939), as well as the more managerial literature on 'empowerment' (Conger and Kanungo, 1988; Thomas and Velthouse, 1990; Gal-Or and Amit, 1998), suggest that increasing the delegation of discretion to employees often 'raises the perceived self-determination of employees and therewith strengthens intrinsic motivation' (Osterloh and Frey, 2000, p. 543). In turn, this may lead to an increase in creativity in the pursuit of goals.[1] Expert knowledge is better utilised and learning is fostered (Mudambi *et al.*, 2003). In contrast, *decreasing* the level of delegated discretion may crowd out intrinsic motivation, particularly when this frustrates the employee's 'beliefs regarding the terms and conditions of the reciprocal exchange agreement' (Rousseau 1989, p. 23). These arguments suggest the following hypothesis:[2]

Hypotheses 1: *Employee motivation depends positively on the degree of delegation of discretion.*

---

[1] Some reservations and potential critiques should be noted at this point. First, it is conceivable that discretion may harm motivation if employees do not have the knowledge or personality to command such discretion. Second, employees may feel uncomfortable with increased discretion because it may imply responsibilities without additional pay or benefits. In short, employees need to have not just the opportunity, but also the ability and incentive to engage in self-management (cf., Mowday *et al.*, 1982). We hypothesize, however, that on the aggregate (firm) level, the positive motivational effects of increased delegation dominate the negative ones, and that opportunity to engage in self-management is at least to some extent matched by a corresponding ability to do so.

[2] Assuming a linear relation between delegation and motivation is clearly not uncontroversial. Thus, it may be argued that the relation hypothesised in Hypothesis 1 is concave rather than linear. For example, beyond a certain threshold, more delegation of discretion may harm motivation. We therefore tested whether the inclusion of the squared variable for delegation improves the goodness of fit and provides a significant coefficient. However, it turns out that the coefficients are not significant and that, although the absolute and incremental goodness of fit increases slightly, the parsimonious goodness of fit decreases considerably. We therefore opted for not including this squared variable.

2.2 Optimum delegation

The motivational effects of increased delegation arguably give rise to improved employee productivity. Partial evidence for this is the finding that giving R&D personnel the right to share research findings with others and to publish such findings increase R&D productivity (McMillan *et al.*, 2000; Mudambi *et al.*, 2003). In turn, increased employee productivity causes firm performance to improve. Thus, delegation is associated with various firm-level benefits.[1]

With respect to the *costs* of delegation, these are treated in the rich agency literature on optimum delegation (e.g., Jensen and Meckling, 1992; Armstrong, 1994; Aghion and Tirole, 1997; Gal-Or and Amit, 1998). A general conclusion is that delegation creates opportunities for employees to collect informational rents and/or engage in morally hazardous activities. Roughly, optimum delegation obtains when the incremental gain from making use of expert knowledge equals the incremental costs from loss of control. The cost caused by control loss is ultimately rooted in the differing preferences of managers and employees in the relevant hierarchy and the costs of monitoring relevant aspects of the employee's activities.

Although the agency approach is useful for framing the cost aspects of delegation, it has certain limitations. First, it builds on an assumption of complete contracting, which makes it hard to provide a rationale for authority (Hart, 1995), except in the limited sense of monitoring. Second, it abstracts from those costs of delegation that are not the result of moral hazard, but rather of mistakes, sub-goal optimisation, duplicative efforts, wrong timing of decisions and erroneous co-location of knowledge and decision rights made by entirely well-intentioned employees (cf., Hendry, 2002), and which may be reduced by means of the exercise of authority.

The trade-off associated with the optimum level of delegation involves numerous variables that may all change over time. Given this, a key management task arguably is to exercise authority in such a way that the organisation gropes towards optimum delegation, and to track the optimum level of delegation in the face of changing contingencies. Placing authority and discretion in separate analytical boxes is, therefore, a somewhat questionable procedure. This is also the case because the interdependence between authority and discretion gives rise to distinct motivational and incentive problems when employees expect that they may be overruled by managers or these may renege on delegation.

2.3 Managerial intervention and changes in delegation

As discussed earlier, there are both positive and negative implications for organisations in delegating discretion to employees. Thus, firms confront a basic trade-off in the choice of delegation. Once implemented, and in the absence of managerial intervention, optimum delegation will continue as long as contingencies, such as technology, tastes, competitive conditions etc. remain stable. Given this, (optimum) delegation may (in fact, should) change as a response to changed external contingencies (Lawrence and Lorsch, 1967; Casson, 1994).

---

[1] There are more direct reasons why delegation may improve firm performance. Thus, employees may be better informed than managers with respect to how certain tasks should be carried out (Jensen and Meckling, 1992). If such knowledge is costly to communicate, efficient co-location of decision-making rights and knowledge then requires that employees are delegated discretion with respect to how they use their expertise in problem solving (Casson, 1994; Melumad *et al.*, 1995). Furthermore, it is arguable that delegating discretion to employees will not only lead to a better use of existing knowledge, but also to the discovery of new knowledge that would not have been discovered in the absence of delegation (Miles *et al.*, 1997).

802   K. Foss, N. J. Foss and X. H. Vázquez

Because complex interdependencies still exist under delegated discretion, major changes in contingencies are likely to change the optimum degree of delegation.[1] Many contingencies cannot be foreseen, or it is too costly to try to do so (Malmgren, 1961; Williamson, 1996). Even if they can be foreseen, their impact on the preferred level of delegation may be difficult to specify *ex ante*. This amounts to a need for *ex post* decision-making (Coase, 1937; Malmgren, 1961; Williamson, 1996). While such decision-making can be arranged in a number of different ways, centralised decision-making in the form of authority becomes a preferable mechanism of coordination when those who may hold authority have a superior understanding of how contingencies influence interdependencies and the preferred degree of delegation (cf., Demsetz, 1991; Casson, 1994). The assumptions that (1) managers usually hold such knowledge and (2) will act on it in a manner that is beneficial to the firm has been made implicitly as a matter of routine in the theory of the firm literature. The latter assumption is closely related to the neglect in most of this literature of managers' opportunism.

Williamson's (1996) distinction between intervention for a good cause and intervention for a bad cause does much to dispel the above naïve assumptions. Thus, the notion of intervention for a bad cause explicitly introduces managerial opportunism, and therefore suggests that there are costs as well as benefits to managerial authority. One particular manifestation of such managerial opportunism is reneging on delegation and/or overruling employee decisions made on the basis of delegated discretion. This is akin to the way that opportunism is usually treated in the transaction cost economics literature, because there it is conventionally portrayed in terms of contractual renegotiation or breach of contract. Reneging on delegation or overruling employees can similarly be understood in terms of reneging on (non-written) contracts with employees or breaching such contracts. Such actions affect employee motivation.

2.4 Managerial opportunism and employee motivation

As a huge organisational behaviour literature suggests, employee motivation may be badly harmed by managerial intervention, particularly when such intervention is perceived as being undertaken for bad reasons. The reasons why employee motivation can be harmed by managerial intervention may be usefully classified as relating to intrinsic and extrinsic motivation (Deci, 1975), respectively.

Thus, managers may delegate discretion because they want to exploit and stimulate *intrinsic* motivation. It has been argued that certain activities (e.g., certain types of sharing behaviour and creativity) are best undertaken by employees who are intrinsically motivated (e.g., Baron and Kreps, 1999; Osterloh and Frey, 2000). Reneging on delegation or overruling employees may reduce intrinsic motivation because it reduces employees' room to manoeuvre and their self-determination (Baron and Kreps, 1999). *Extrinsic* motivation is relevant to the extent that delegation of discretion makes it possible for the employee to tie efforts and rewards more closely together. Reducing the delegation of discretion under these circumstances may reduce motivation for three reasons. First, it becomes more difficult to reach the performance goal for which rewards are paid. An example is closing

[1] For example, changes in the firm's overall strategy may require the building-up of a new product platform. Such new technologies typically require the delegation of more discretion to designers and engineers in order to stimulate exploration through wide bandwidth communication channels. Or, a change in the competitive conditions, such as an impending price war, may dictate that discretion be diminished in order to curb slack and reduce costs.

down an ongoing project in which employees have a direct financial stake. Second, reaping private benefits may become more difficult, for example, because on-the-job-consumption is constrained. Third, sunk cost investments in human capital may be less valuable, because the reduction in delegation of discretion implies that certain activities cannot be pursued to the same extent any more.

Cognitive forces may interact with motivational forces to reinforce the destructive consequences on employee motivation of managerial intervention. Thus, Heath *et al.* (1993) argue that, in an employee relationship, employees develop implicit and explicit expectations about the contract governing the relationship, and particularly about the benefits that they believe they deserve under the implicit contract, that is, their 'entitlements'. Such expectations may be represented by 'status quo' points, that is, what employees believe are their entitlements. The discretion that is delegated to employees may become part of their perceived entitlements, and negative motivational consequences follow from managerial intervention that interferes with these entitlements. Other areas of psychological research point to the phenomenon of loss aversion, that is, a loss relative to a status quo point is seen as more undesirable than a gain relative to the same point is seen as desirable. This means that employees will develop a bias against changing the level of discretion in a downwards direction, and that they can be expected to resist such changes, as well as suffer a loss of motivation if the change is, in fact, forced upon them.

A substantial body of work in organisational behaviour on psychological contracts speaks directly to the issues under consideration here. Thus, this kind of work suggests that managerial intervention that is perceived by employees as being unfair, arbitrary and in other ways breaks with what is perceived as established psychological or implicit contracts (i.e., it is opportunistic), it is very likely to harm motivation (Rousseau, 1989; Rousseau and Parks, 1992).[1] Rousseau and Parks (1992, pp. 36) state that 'contract violation erodes trust [and] undermines the employment relationship yielding lower employee contributions (e.g. performance and attendance) and lower employer investments (e.g. retention, promotion)'. In particular, organisational citizenship behaviour—that is, employee behaviour that promotes organisational efficiency but is not (perhaps, cannot be) explicitly recognised by an organisation's reward system—may suffer from opportunistic managerial intervention (Robinson and Morrison, 1995). Empirical work has reached similar conclusions (Robinson, 1996; Foss, 2003). The above reasoning is summed up in the following hypothesis:

Hypotheses 2: *Employee motivation varies negatively with opportunistic managerial intervention.*

For the firm, this is a problem to the extent that loss of motivation leads to employees cutting back on effort, and on firm-specific investments in human capital.[2] This implies the following hypothesis:

Hypotheses 3: *Overall firm performance varies negatively with opportunistic managerial intervention.*

---

[1] Note that this literature is not entirely uncontroversial. For example, see Guest (1998) for a sustained critique.

[2] Of course, loss of motivation may not automatically lead to, for example, less effort supply, if monitoring systems or extrinsic motivation can substitute for the loss of motivation caused by opportunistic managerial intervention.

2.5 Why opportunistic managerial intervention?

It is not immediately apparent why managers should ever intervene in such a manner. According to Hypothesis 3, opportunistic managerial intervention destroys value. In addition to managerial irrationality, there are two reasons for why this may happen, despite being obviously inefficient.

First, managers may derive a private benefit (in whatever form) from managerial intervention that destroys value. For example, managers who are up for promotion may derive private benefits from imposing restrictions to cut strongly the costs of the slack and externalities that are associated with a high level of delegation of discretion. For this to work as an equilibrium strategy, it is necessary that the manager is not punished for intervening in a value-destroying manner, for example, because his behaviour is simply not noticed by those who are in a position to punish him. This may be the case when the organisational costs arrive after only a significant delay, or if it is very difficult to trace organisational costs to the managers' behaviour.

A second reason relates to the familiar problem in the political economy of time inconsistency (Kydland and Prescott, 1977; Weingast and Marshall, 1988). For example, governments have an incentive to promise *initially* not to confiscate (too much of) the wealth created by entrepreneurs in order to strengthen their incentives actually to undertake investments, and *then*, in some later period, deviate from this promise and confiscate substantial portions of the created wealth. In the context of delegation, an analogous behaviour may consist in, first, promising substantial discretion. When employees, enthused about their new extended discretion, come up with profit-improving ideas about how to improve products, processes, etc., managers may harvest these, decide that the organisation already has its hands full with implementing these ideas, and that the level of delegated discretion may be usefully reduced in order to save costs.[1] However, the political economy literature referred to above also suggests that these problems may be checked by various institutions and mechanisms.

2.6 Credible delegation

The political economy concept of credible commitment (see also Williamson, 1996) implies that it is often in an organisation's long-term interest to avoid later period actions that break promises (here with respect to delegation), thereby harming organisational members, and that avoiding such behaviour may be accomplished by constraining the flexibility of managers in such a manner that the initial promise becomes credible (Kydland and Prescott, 1977; Weingast and Marshall, 1988). In the present context, there are two categories of mechanisms that contribute to making promises to not engage in opportunistic managerial intervention credible, namely what may be called *internal* and *external* mechanisms.

With respect to *internal* mechanisms, managers may *stake their personal reputations* (Miller, 1992; Argyris and Mui, 1999), for example, through symbolic and communicative acts (e.g., announcing in large-scale company gatherings one's firm commitment to certain policies and values (Brockner *et al.*, 1992). This suggests the following hypothesis:

Hypotheses 4a: *Opportunistic managerial intervention varies negatively with the strength of managers' personal reputations for pursuing a 'fair' policy in dealing with employees.*

---

[1] This may help explain why organisations often 'vacillate' between loose and hierarchical structures (Nickerson and Zenger, 2004).

Reputation effects are far from perfect with respect to constraining opportunistic behaviours (Williamson, 1996). This also holds for reputation effects inside the hierarchy. For example, managers change jobs and may not carry their reputation with them. Corporate cultures are longer lasting than personal reputations and serve to enforce implicit contracts in situations where personal reputations fail (Kreps, 1990):

Hypotheses 4b: *Opportunistic managerial intervention varies negatively with the extent to which corporate culture implies expectations that managers will pursue a 'fair' or 'hands off' policy in dealing with employees.*

Hierarchical structure also plays a role in constraining managerial opportunistic intervention. Thus, Milgrom (1988) argues that employee rent-seeking that aims at influencing hierarchical superiors to intervene selectively to the benefit of the rent-seeking employees will be constrained by rigid, hierarchical structures which makes such rent-seeking more costly. Also, upper and lower-level managers may differ in their preferences for intervention; for example, lower-level managers may derive a private benefit from overruling, whereas upper-level managers do not (Aghion and Tirole, 1997).

A third reason why hierarchical structure may constrain opportunistic managerial intervention (in fact, all managerial intervention) is that the hierarchy is not just a structure of authority, but also one of information (Thompson, 1967; Galbraith, 1974). Thus, there will be an informational distance between those possessing authority and those to whom discretion has been delegated. The size of this informational distance influences the basis for exercising judgment with respect to decisions whether to overrule employees or not. All else being equal, the more hierarchical layers that information has to pass through before reaching the level exercising authority, the less adequate is this basis likely to be. Moreover, even though there may be few hierarchical layers, managerial task descriptions may be such that managers will essentially be overloaded if they insist on being sufficiently informed to be in a position to overrule. If the manager realises that because of information overload, he is not in a position to decide rationally whether to overrule or not, he should not overrule (Aghion and Tirole, 1997). Thus, this reasoning predicts that overruling of employees is less likely to occur in organisations with large informational distances and/or managers that are heavily burdened with information:

Hypotheses 4c: *Opportunistic managerial intervention varies negatively with the informational distance in the corporate hierarchy.*

Some employees or groups of employees may be particularly costly for management to overrule, because they control critical resources, notably their own human capital. For example, Henry Ford II and the rest of the Ford top management team tolerated the open disagreement with official Ford strategy expressed by Lee Iacocca and his clique of loyal managers, because of the marketing skills exercised by Iacocca and his men (Halberstam, 1986). Overruling such employees means that they may cut back on the supply of their essential services and may refrain from augmenting their valuable human capital. This suggests the following hypothesis:

Hypotheses 4d: *Opportunistic managerial intervention varies negatively with the degree of human capital specificity.*

Employees with strongly specialised, important human capital may possess considerable bargaining power and influence (Rajan and Zingales, 1998). However, such influence may also be secured through other means, such as extensive employee ownership of the firm.

806   K. Foss, N. J. Foss and X. H. Vázquez

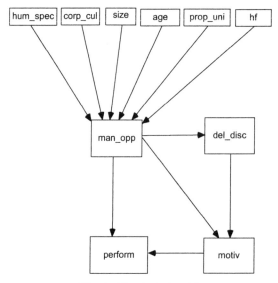

Fig. 1. *Hypothesised model*

This means that employee interests may be more strongly reflected in corporate decision-making, implying that, in such firms, opportunistic managerial intervention may be less prevalent:

Hypotheses 4e: *Opportunistic managerial intervention varies negatively with the degree to which employee interests are represented in corporate decision-making.*

With respect to *external* mechanisms that may enforce delegated discretion, a clear example is *strong trade unions or professional associations*. Their influence may imply that certain rights are so strongly protected (i.e., they are outside the 'zone of acceptance', Simon, 1951) that management cannot realistically change these (Argyris and Liebeskind, 1999).

Hypotheses 4f: *Opportunistic managerial intervention varies negatively with the degree of unionisation and the strength of unions and professional associations.*

Figure 1 shows the model summarising all these hypotheses. In the following section we present our dataset, the methods we have applied, and the results.

3. Data, variables and results

3.1 Data collection

Data were collected by mail questionnaire after an initial pilot testing of the instrument. The sample population is composed of all firms in the Spanish food and electric/electronic industries (SIC 20 and SIC 36) with a turnover of 3 million euros or more in the year 2000. The choice of these two very different industries was based on the need to obtain enough firm diversity while maintaining survey costs at reasonable levels. Concerning the size of firms, it is useful to note that the kind of information required for this study is not usually available for smaller firms or if it is, the results are often rather obvious. Moreover, the greater the size of the firm, the more experience it has, and the higher the competence of the survey participant regarding the concepts included in the questionnaire; this obviously affects the reliability of the responses by making the answers more rigorous.

Following these criteria, the population of the study was drawn from the directory, *DB Marketing: 700.000 empresas españolas*. This directory is updated on an annual basis by the international management consultancy, Dun & Bradstreet. From this database we identified 3,040 firms that met the conditions described above. We mailed an initial questionnaire with a customised letter addressed to the production manager in each firm. Thirty-six questionnaires were returned, either because the address was wrong or the firm had ceased its activity. Furthermore, not all the remaining questionnaires were valid: Missing values and the unfeasibility of identifying the firm to which some of the questionnaires belonged resulted in the final sample being composed of 329 firms (11% of the total population). Assuming the worst scenario for a binary variable, where $[p = q = 50\%]$, and imposing a confidence level of 95%, these figures represent a sampling error of ±5.09%.

3.2 Variables

Table 1 contains a brief description of the variables which we can group in two sets. The first stems from the Spanish directory of firms mentioned above (hierarchical form, performance, size and age of the firm), and from direct figures provided by the respondents (human specificity and propensity to unionize). Although the details appear in Table 1, it is relevant to note that size and age have been categorised after noticing that differences in firm behaviour are much more evident comparing the groups which were finally identified. Moreover, of all the possible measures for firm performance, we opted for one which is closely linked to workers' productivity: value added divided by the number of workers.

Second, given their conceptual complexity, we tried to measure delegation, motivation, managerial opportunism and corporate culture through the linear combination of several items. This process followed two steps. First of all, and based on the extant literature (Mowday *et al.*, 1982; Dewar *et al.*, 1980; Lawrence and Lorsch, 1967; Pugh and Hickson, 1976; Willman, 1983; Dow, 1987; Grimshaw and Rubery, 1998; Kotter and Heskett, 1992), a list of indicators for each variable was presented to a group of three production managers and two operators from diverse firms. They were asked to discuss how representative each indicator was of the corresponding construct and to propose others that were not in the original list. They concluded with a different number of indicators for each variable that, in their view, reasonably reflected what the variable tried to grasp. In a second stage, these indicators were tested in 20 interviews, together with the rest of the items of the questionnaire. We finally chose those for each variable that provided not only the highest Cronbach's α, but also a first component—through Principal Component Analysis—that could explain more than 50% of the variance of the items.

This process turned out to be satisfactory, although obviously not perfect. In the case of corporate culture and managerial opportunism, several indicators had to be pulled out in order to get a better reliability of the scale (Cronbach's α should be above 0,7 for a non-exploratory analysis; cf., Nunnally, 1978). For motivation and delegation of discretion, our initial measures based on the literature (Mowday *et al.*, 1982; Dewar *et al.*, 1980,

Table 1. *Description of the variables*

	Denomination and abbreviation	Description
X_1	Delegation of discretion (del_disc)	Degree of delegation to adapt to eventual modifications on the production line that affect several work stations (five levels).
X_2	Managerial opportunism (man_opp)	Propensity of a principal to impose orders exceeding the previously agreed limits to other agents who do not have to be consulted. Construct built up with Principal Component Analysis.
X_3	Hierarchical form (hf)	Two values: 1 for capitalist firms and 2 for worker-owned enterprises (most of the latter belong to the Mondragon cooperative).
X_4	Human specificity (hum_spec)	Difference between the time that a new worker with no experience in the industry spends until he/she reaches the normal productivity of his/her mates, and the time that a new worker who does have experience in the industry spends until she reaches that normal productivity (five levels).
X_5	Propensity to unionise (prop_uni)	Percentage of unionised workers within the firm.
X_6	Age (age)	Three values: 1 for firms that have been in existence for 10 years or less; 2 for firms between 11 and 30 years, and 3 for firms with more than 31 years.
X_7	Corporate culture (corp_cul)	Equivalent to the intensity of socialization: extent to which certain norms and values are widely shared and intensely held throughout the organisation. Construct built up with Principal Component Analysis.
X_8	Size (size)	Two values: 1 for SMEs with fewer than 100 operators; 2 for the rest.
X_9	Motivation (motiv)	Degree to which workers' commitment encourages them to do their best (five point Likert-type scale).
X_{10}	Performance (perform)	Value added divided by number of operators

respectively) did not offer a first component that could explain more than 50% of the variance of the items, so we decided to stick to just one item. Once the indicators were chosen for each construct and data were available, Principal Component Analysis was applied for corporate culture and managerial opportunism in order to get a single value. For strictly operational reasons (particularly to search for an easier interpretation of absolute figures), the latent variables were subsequently transformed to make them start with 1. Table 2 shows the main figures.

Finally, some of the variables referred to in the above hypotheses were not measured directly. This is the case for the 'strength of managers' personal reputations' construct. We proxy this construct with the age of the firm variable, based on the argument that young firms have higher expected mortality, which implies that the value of a manager's reputation in such a firm is smaller than in an older firm with a lower expected mortality. Also, we did not measure the construct 'informational distance in the corporate hierarchy' directly (H4c). We proxy this construct with the size variable, because it is reasonable to expect a positive relation between the size of a firm and the depth of its corporate hierarchy. Lastly, the variable 'degree to which employee interests are represented in corporate

Table 2. *Summary of items retained in each construct built up with principal component analysis*

Var	items in the variable	Factor loading	KMO index	Variance explained (%)	Cronbach's α
Managerial opportunism	Please indicate to what extent you agree with the following statements (1 being 'strongly disagree' and 5 'strongly agree'):		0.72	57.37	0.74
	1. If we paid overtime strictly, the firm would not be sustainable	0.849			
	2. Some operators cannot always use up their holidays because of production needs	0.782			
	3. Flexibility and cost-saving requirements foster the use of short-term contracts even for long term employment relationships	0.684			
	4. Operators believe that managers press them excessively	0.704			
Corporate culture	Please, indicate to what extent you agree with the following statements (1 being 'strongly disagree' and 5 'strongly agree'):		0.72	76.06	0.84
	1. Our operators know the history of the firm and its most important achievements	0.883			
	2. Our workers are acquainted with the firm's short- and long-term objectives	0.884			
	3. Working in our firm makes our workers experience a sense of pride	0.889			

decision-making' (H4e) has been measured by the hierarchical form of the firm, which distinguishes between capitalist and worker-owned firms.

3.3 Empirical results and discussion

Table 3 shows the means, standard deviations and correlations for the variables. Two initial important insights have to do with the rather low level of delegation of discretion that we can find in our study, whereas managerial opportunism achieves a high figure. Moreover, both are negatively correlated. Regarding their association with other variables, on the one hand, a high delegation of discretion is strongly related to a strong corporate culture, workforce motivation and labour productivity. On the other hand, managerial opportunism appears to be associated with little human specificity involved in the labour transaction, low motivation and corporate culture, and is especially relevant in SMEs and capitalist firms when compared with large corporations and worker-owned enterprises, respectively.

Since the object of our investigation has to do with the *interaction* among managerial opportunism, motivation and performance, we have developed a path analysis, which is

Table 3. *Descriptive statistics and correlations*

	Min.	Max.	Mean	St. dev.	1	2	3	4	5	6	7	8	9	10
1 del_disc	1	5	1.81	1.15	1									
2 man_opp	1	5.35	3.46	1	-0.24***	1								
3 hf	1	2	—	—	0.19***	-0.44***	1							
4 hum_spec	1	5	2.48	0.972	0.16***	-0.36***	0.020	1						
5 prop_uni	0	100	31.89	26.44	.075	-0.127**	-0.42***	0.076	1					
6 age	1	3	2.06	0.69	0.048	-0.22***	-0.1*	0.062	0.43***	1				
7 corp_cul	1	5.54	3.56	1	0.51***	-0.26***	-0.26***	0.26***	-0.139**	-0.088	1			
8 size	1	2	—	—	0.081	-0.26***	-0.042	0.029	0.23***	0.31***	-0.001	1		
9 motiv	1	4	2.35	0.925	0.37***	-0.41***	0.37***	0.24***	-0.11**	-0.017	0.73***	-0.02	1	
10 perform	-10.6	98.9	11.2	10.45	0.26***	-0.33***	0.31***	0.264***	-0.09*	-0.034	0.42***	0.071	0.51***	1

aPearson correlations for pairs of continuous variables and Spearman correlations when one or the two of them are ordinal or categorical.
*Significant at 10% level. **Significant at 5% level. ***Significant at 1% level.

commonly used in organisational analyses. Compared with conventional multivariate techniques, this procedure allows us to design a model with various levels of dependency. Also, since it takes into account the correlations among the exogenous variables when calculating the regression coefficients, we can avoid spurious relations and lessen multicollinearity problems. Finally, we can at the same time calculate the estimators and the measurement errors, so the literature (Bollen, 1989; Bollen and Long, 1993) suggests that results are statistically more robust than with conventional regressions.

It is worth noting that the model is probably far from being exhaustive in terms of including all potentially relevant independent variables. Rather, it does seem to be the best one that our insights allowed us to construct prior to this research, while sticking at the same time to the 'keep it simple' rule. We have actually tried to include the least possible number of variables and relations to address the problem exposed in the theoretical section. Notice that we do not mean to explain motivation, delegation of discretion, performance—we just try to show there is a particular relation between them. Thus, our aim is not only to verify or refute each one of the above hypotheses separately, but also to test whether their interaction is statistically significant.[1]

As noted above, Figure 1 presents the path diagram with the relations that our propositions suggest. Consider motivation, and observe that the arrows represent its dependency on the level of delegation of discretion (H1) and the degree of managerial opportunism (H2). In addition, despite firm performance obviously depending on many other variables, Hypothesis 3 emphasises that it will be at least affected by managerial opportunism. We controlled for industry also in the equation with performance as dependent variable. We decided to include in the model only the independent variables, however, for the sake of simplicity. The reason is that the estimators and the goodness of fit of the model did not suffer any important change. We also checked whether the relative influence of each independent variable measured by its standardised coefficient was modified, but they were not. Concerning the endogenous variables and starting with opportunistic managerial intervention, observe that, as suggested by Hypothesis 5, it varies negatively with the strength of managers' personal reputation—age—(H4a); corporate culture (H4b); corporate hierarchy—size—(H4c); the level of expert knowledge involved in the labour transactions (H4d); workers' participation in corporate decision making—hierarchical form—(H4e); and the degree of unionisation (H4f).

Finally, there are two second-order relations which do not appear explicitly in our set of hypotheses because they have already been well established in previous literature. The relation between motivation and performance has been discussed in seminal works such as McClelland (1955), Herzberg *et al.* (1959) or Vroom (1964), whereas the link between managerial opportunism and delegation of discretion is based on Simon (1951), Willman (1983), Dow (1987) or Kreps (1990). The argument is that, no matter how short-termed decisions might be (for instance working overtime, changing shifts, assuming new tasks, etc.), delegating discretion restricts the ability of managers to go beyond the *ex ante* agreed

---

[1] Construct building (managerial opportunism and corporate culture) could also be implemented in the same model. We chose to do it separately because we have checked that results do not change, and the final model is thus much simpler. Furthermore, motivation is treated as a continuous dependent variable, because the consequences of assuming data are interval when in fact they are ordinal are so small that the gain in statistical elegance and power justifies the possible distortion. Finally, there are dozens of measures of the goodness of fit (GF) for this kind of models (Bentler and Bonnet, 1980; Bollen and Long, 1993). The measures used here are the ones which appear to be more widespread in the empirical literature and in the specific software packages design for this tool (EQS, LISREL, AMOS, etc.).

'zone of acceptance'. Therefore, delegation cannot be credibly sustained in firms where managerial opportunism is high. The model takes, consequently, the following form:

$$man\_opp = \alpha_1 + \beta_{14}hum\_spec + \beta_{17}corp\_cul + \beta_{18}size$$
$$+ \beta_{16}age + \beta_{15}prop\_uni + \beta_{13}hf + e_1 \tag{1}$$

$$perform = \alpha_2 + \beta_{22}man\_opp + \beta_{29}motiv + \beta_{21}del\_disc + e_2 \tag{2}$$

$$motiv = \alpha_3 + \beta_{32}man\_opp + \beta_{31}del\_disc + e_3 \tag{3}$$

$$del\_disc = \alpha_4 + \beta_{42}man\_opp + e_4 \tag{4}$$

The path coefficients (the βs) are the main object of our estimation. They represent the beta weights obtained from a set of multiple regressions on the posited relationships within the model. In this case, given the absence of multivariate normality and the size of the sample, the method of estimation has been based on the Maximum Likelihood criterion with a bootstrap of 200 sub-samples (each coefficient represents the mean of the estimator for the 200 sub-samples). The results are shown in Table 4.

The path coefficient reflecting the influence of corporate culture on managerial opportunism does not seem to be significant (although Table 3 shows both are correlated). Our argument was that corporate cultures are longer lasting than personal reputations and serve to enforce implicit contracts in situations where personal reputations fail. Measurement errors notwithstanding, nevertheless, the problem could reside in the relation between the external and internal labour markets (Vázquez, 2004): the firm's reputation is less important for attracting good workers when the rate of unemployment is high, as is the case in Spain (11% in 2004). In other words, if alternative jobs opportunities are scarce, the need to enforce implicit contracts becomes more elastic, even in those firms with the best reputation. All the goodness of fit measures would increase if we respecified the model without the relation corporate culture/managerial opportunism.

Table 4. *Maximum likelihood estimation*[a]

Dep. var./indep. var.	Standardised coefficients	Non-standard. coefficients	Standard error	*t* value
man_opp/corp_cul	−0.035	−0.035	0.046	−0.760
man_opp/size	−0.160	−0.367	0.102	−3.592
man_opp/age	−0.115	−0.164	0.068	−2.416
man_opp/hf	−0.517	−1.644	0.153	−10.739
man_opp/hum_spec	−0.312	−0.318	0.044	−7.263
man_opp/prop_uni	−0.200	−0.008	0.002	−3.938
del_disc/man_opp	−0.238	−0.277	0.062	−4.445
motiv/man_opp	−0.341	−0.341	0.049	−6.938
motiv/del_disc	0.298	0.257	0.042	6.077
perform/motiv	0.369	4.661	0.676	6.896
perform/man_opp	−0.179	−2.258	0.676	−3.340

[a]$\chi^2/DF = 3.9$; goodness of fit index (GFI) $= 0.88$; root mean square error of approximation (RMSEA) $= 0.09$; adjusted goodness of fit index (AGFI) $= 0.838$; parsimonious goodness of fit index (PGFI) $= 0.841$.

Data suggest, therefore, that when compared with smaller, younger and capitalist firms, the level of opportunistic managerial intervention becomes lower in large corporations, older firms and cooperatives, respectively. Additionally, the propensity of managers to behave opportunistically also seems higher in firms with low specific human assets and with a low level of union affiliation. These findings confirm Hypotheses 4a, 4c, 4d, 4e and 4f, which state a negative relation between opportunistic managerial intervention and, respectively, managers' personal reputations (proxied by age), the informational distance in the corporate hierarchy (proxied by size), the level of human capital specificity, the degree to which employee interests are represented in corporate decision-making (proxied by hierarchical form), and finally, the strength of unions and professional associations (proxied by union affiliation).

Moreover, the standardised coefficients convey information for assessing the relative influence that each one of the independent variables exerts on managerial opportunism. Thus, not surprisingly, the hierarchical form of the firm seems to be the main mechanism that helps to avoid opportunistic intervention by managers; that is, the higher the degree to which employee interests are represented in corporate decision-making, the more difficult it is for managers to implement opportunistic interventions. In fact, it is even more important than the bargaining power stemming from local and specific knowledge or from the strength of unions in the firm. In turn, size and age of the firm apparently explain a lower percentage of the variance of managerial opportunism.

Regarding motivation, the results show that employees seem to be more motivated in firms with a higher delegation of discretion. In addition, as the level of managerial opportunism increases, workforce motivation clearly goes down. And, finally, there is a significant indirect effect of managerial opportunistic intervention on motivation through delegation of discretion. This evidence confirms Hypotheses 1 and 2, linking employee motivation to the level of delegation and the intensity of managerial opportunism.

With respect to firm performance, observe that Table 4 also reflects two additional important facts: first, it confirms Hypothesis 3, which suggests direct influence of managerial opportunistic intervention on firm performance. It is still to be proved, however, that this negative effect would still be maintained if firm performance were measured with financial ratios, and not with a ratio reflecting productivity concerns (other financial ratios were used but no conclusive results were obtained). The reason is that managers could behave opportunistically in order to earn more money, even if this entailed a decrease in overall productivity. For instance, if the firm makes its operators work overtime with no compensation at all, profits could increase despite its workers becoming less productive (because they might reciprocate by being more opportunistic, raising conflict in the firm or just because they might be more tired). Furthermore, the results in Table 4 also verify the relevant indirect effects that both managerial opportunism and delegation of discretion have on workers' productivity: whereas delegation of discretion exerts an indirect effect through motivation (Hypothesis 1), managerial opportunism modifies workers' performance by harming motivation (Hypothesis 2) and delegation of discretion (second-order relation).

4. Concluding discussion

In this final section, we sum up how we have contributed to existing theory, discuss limitations of the study and suggest implications for future research.

814   K. Foss, N. J. Foss and X. H. Vázquez

4.1 Contribution to established literature

Most firms make use of both authority and delegated discretion. However, the main point in this paper is that this gives rise to a latent conflict, one which may become manifest when managers overrule employees or renege on the discretion they have delegated. In turn, this may have negative motivational consequences and may harm firm performance. Ultimately, the problem arises because 'contracts' to delegate discretion are not enforceable in a court of law. Credible delegation may therefore be hard to sustain. However, we have pointed to and analysed how various mechanisms may make delegation credible.

Although the clash of authority and employee motivation is not entirely neglected in the theory of the firm literature *per se* (e.g. Miller, 1992; Aghion and Tirole, 1997; Baker *et al.*, 1999; Falaschetti, 2002), it is still fair to say that they have been given relatively little attention in this body of work. One manifestation of this is that the economics of organisation analyses of 'opportunism' have almost exclusively dealt with employee opportunism (Williamson, 1996), employer opportunism being largely neglected (cf., Dow, 1987). The basic idea that we have elaborated in this paper may be argued to be present already in Milgrom's (1988) argument that organisational form partly reflects an attempt to cope with employee rent-seeking and the inefficient selective intervention that may result from such rent-seeking. Also, a number of recent organisational economics contributions clearly go quite some way towards understanding the incentive liabilities of centralised authority (e.g., Milgrom and Roberts, 1996; Aghion and Tirole, 1997; Baker *et al.*, 1999). However, this remains an under-researched area in the economics of organisation literature, particularly given the apparently high incidence of managerial opportunism (cf., Coyle-Shapiro and Kessler, 2000). For this reason, interest in the mechanisms that can constrain harmful managerial intervention has also been rather scant.[1]

The problem of loss of employee motivation because of opportunistic managerial intervention is closely related to a key problem in the theory of the firm, namely what Williamson (1996, p. 150) calls the 'impossibility of selective intervention'. This is the 'puzzle' of 'Why can't a large firm do everything that a collection of small firms can and more?' Thus, a large firm could replicate the market and only intervene selectively when there would be expected net gains from this, so that 'the firm will do at least as well as, and will sometimes do better than, the market'. However, Williamson points out that such selective intervention is 'impossible'. Incentives are diluted, because the option to intervene 'can be exercised both for good cause (to support expected net gains) and for bad (to support the subgoals of the intervenor)' (Williamson, 1996, pp. 150–1), and employees know this. Promises to intervene only for a good cause can never be credible, Williamson argues, because they are not enforceable in a court of law. A fundamental problem—in theory as well as managerial practice—is therefore how to maximise managerial intervention for a good cause, while avoiding intervention for a bad cause. Our discussion goes some way to address how various mechanisms contribute to avoiding intervention for a bad cause.

---

[1] This is also the case of the organisational behaviour literature. This literature does not explicitly frame the issues in rational choice terms. Still, it is considerably more detailed with respect to analysing the actual contents of psychological (implicit) contracts between those who hold discretionary authority and those who do not and the psychological mechanisms that are at work in the case of perceived contract breach. We have mainly used this literature to provide support for some parts of our hypothesis development. However, we conjecture that the organisational behaviour literature in this field and the relevant organisational economics literature may well enter a fruitful liaison.

4.2 Limitations

A number of inherent limitations of the dataset imply that our analysis is far from perfect. First, as in most studies, some of our proxies reflect a certain roughness derived from data availability and reliability. Since their validity has been justified on theoretical as well as on empirical grounds, we think that they nevertheless represent and capture reasonably the theoretical constructs they proxy.

Second, the limitations of the dataset have constrained our theoretical framework. For example, we argue that employee motivation positively depends on the degree of delegation. The link between delegation (or 'task autonomy') and motivation has long been recognised in social psychology (e.g., Roethlisberger *et al.*, 1939). It has also long been recognised that for delegation to be effective, employees need to have not only the opportunity but also the incentive and the ability to engage in self-management. We have argued that reductions in delegation, at least when these are perceived as reflecting managerial opportunism, lead employees to reduce effort and human capital investment. This *may* lead to a confusion of cause and effect. For example, it is conceivable that cutting back on delegation is a result of finding out that employees lack the skills that are necessary to engage in self-management.

Third, more generally, much of our reasoning admittedly proceeds in dynamic terms— for example, we make references to breaking psychological contracts—that do not correspond directly to the measures that we use (e.g., we do not measure the incidence of broken contracts) and the cross-sectional nature of the study.

4.3 Implications for future research

Future research may well start from some of the above limitations. Thus, panel data need to be collected so as to correspond better to the dynamic nature of the argument. Also, it would be desirable if data allowed for cross-country comparisons. Otherwise, we cannot rule out the possibility of a country bias in our results.

Our study also suggests a number of avenues for further theoretical research. An obvious route is to formalise our verbal argument. More substantively, there are theoretical implications that await further development. One such implication is that the problem of reducing opportunistic managerial intervention may differ *systematically* across firms, depending on the details of their internal structure, so that some organisational forms are systematically more heavily burdened with problems of opportunistic managerial intervention. Another implication is that the discussion in this paper relates to the classic issue of the determinants of the boundaries of the firm. Thus, a fundamental premise of the analysis in this paper is that, in firms, delegated decision rights are loaned, not owned (Baker *et al.*, 1999). Ultimate decision-making rights can only be transferred from bosses to subordinates by transferring ownership (i.e., creating a new firm). The problem of sustaining credible delegation stems from this basic difference in ownership. The analysis in this paper thus makes direct contact with those modern theories of economic organisation (Hart, 1995; Williamson, 1996) that stress the importance of ownership for understanding the boundaries of the firm. Finally, we have pointed to the desirability of integrating organisational behaviour perspectives on psychological contracts more fully with organisational economics ideas, in order to get a fuller and more relevant understanding of the workings and implications of psychological and implicit contracts. Both fields stand to benefit from such an exercise (Gibbons, 1999).

816   K. Foss, N. J. Foss and X. H. Vázquez

Bibliography

Aghion, P. and Tirole, J. 1997. Formal and real authority in organization, *Journal of Political Economy*, vol. 105, no. 1, 1–29

Argyris, C. 1960. *Understanding Organizational Behaviour*, Homewood, IL, Dorsey Press

Argyris, N. and Liebeskind, J. P. 1999. Contractual commitments, bargaining power, and governance inseparability: incorporating history into transaction cost theory, *Academy of Management Review*, vol. 24, no. 1, 49–63

Argyris, N. and Mui, V-L. 1999. 'A Political-Economic Approach to Organizational Dissent', Working Paper

Armstrong, M. 1994. 'Delegation and Discretion'. Discussion Paper in Economics and Econometrics, Department of Economics, University of Southampton

Baker, G., Gibbons, R. and Murphy, K. J. 2002. Relational contracts and the theory of the firm, *Quarterly Journal of Economics*, vol. 117, no.1, 39–83

Baker, G., Gibbons, R. and Murphy, K. J. 1999. Informal authority in organizations, *Journal of Law, Economics and Organization*, vol. 15, no. 1, 56–73

Baron, J. M. and Kreps, D. N. 1999. *Strategic Human Resource Management*, New York, Wiley

Barzel, Y. 1997. *Economic Analysis of Property Rights*. 2nd edn, Cambridge, Cambridge University Press

Bazerman, M. H. 1994. *Judgment in Managerial Decision Making*, New York, Wiley

Bentler, P. M. and Bonnet, D. G. 1980. Significance tests and goodness of fit in the analysis of covariance structures, *Psychological Bulleting*, vol. 88, no. 3, 588–606

Bijl, P. W. J. de. 1996. Delegation of responsibility in organizations, 'Essays in Industrial Organization and Management Strategy', ch. 4, PhD Thesis, Tilburg University

Bollen, K. 1989. *Structural Equations With Latent Variables*, New York, John Wiley

Bollen, K. and Long, S. 1993. *Testing Structural Equations Models*, Thousand Oaks, CA, Sage

Brockner, J., Tyler, T. R. and Cooper-Schneider, R. 1992, The influence of prior commitment to an institution on reactions to perceived infairness: the higher they are, the harder they fall, *Administrative Science Quarterly*, vol. 37, no. 2, 241–61

Casson, M. 1994. Why are firms hierarchical?, *International Journal of the Economics of Business*, vol. 1, no. 1, 47–76

Coase, R. H. 1937. The nature of the firm, in Foss, N. J. (ed.) 1999. *The Theory of the Firm: Critical Perspectives in Business and Management*, Vol. II, London, Routledge

Conger, J. and Kanungo, R. 1988. The empowerment process: integrating theory and practice, *Academy of Management Review*, vol. 13, no. 3, 471–82

Coyle-Shapiro, J. and Kessler, I. 2000. Consequences of the psychological contract for the employment contract: a large-scale survey, *Journal of Management Studies*, vol. 37, no. 7, 903–30

Deci, E. 1975. *Intrinsic Motivation*, New York and London, Plenum Press

Demsetz, H. 1991. The theory of the firm revisited, in Williamson, O. E. and Winter, S. G. (eds) 1993. *The Nature of the Firm*, Oxford, Blackwell

Dewar, R. D., Whetten, D. A. and Boje, D. 1980. Examination of the reliability and validity of the Aiken and Hage Scales of Centralization, *Administrative Science Quarterly*, vol. 25, no. 1, 120–8

Dow, G. K. 1987. The function of authority in transaction cost economics, *Journal of Economic Behaviour and Organization*, vol. 8, no. 1, 13–38

Falaschetti, D. 2002. Golden parachutes: credible commitments or evidence of shirking?, *Journal of Corporate Finance*, vol. 8, no. 2, 159–78

Foss, N. J. 2003. Selective intervention and internal hybrids: interpreting and learning from the rise and decline of the oticon spaghetti organization, *Organization Science*, vol. 14, no. 3, 331–49

Galbraith, J. R. 1974. Organization design: an information processing View, *Interfaces*, vol. 4, no. 3, 28–36

Gal-Or, E. and Amit, R. 1998. Does empowerment lead to higher quality and profitability?, *Journal of Economic Behaviour and Organization*, vol. 36, no. 4, 411–31

Gibbons, R. 1999. Taking Coase seriously, *Administrative Science Quarterly*, vol. 44, no. 1, 145–57

Grimshaw, D. and Rubery, J. 1998. Integrating the internal and external labour markets, *Cambridge Journal of Economics*, vol. 22, no. 2, 199–220

Guest, D, 1998. Is the psychological contract worth taking seriously, *Journal of Organizational Behaviour*, vol. 19, no. 7, 649–64

Halberstam, D. 1986. *The Reckoning*, New York, Avon Books

Hart, O. 1995. *Firms, Contracts, and Financial Structure*, Oxford, Oxford University Press

Heath, C., Knez, M. and Camerer, C. 1993. The strategic management of the entitlement process in the employment relationship, *Strategic Management Journal*, vol. 14, no. 8, 75–93

Hendry, J. 2002. The principal's other problem: honest incompetence and the specification of objectives, *Academy of Management Review*, vol. 27, no. 1, 98–113

Herzberg, F., Mausner, B. and Snyderman, B. 1959. *The motivation to work*, New York, John Wiley

Holmström, B. 1999. The firm as a subeconomy, *Journal of Law, Economics, and Organization*, vol. 15, no. 1, 74–102

Jensen, M. C. and Meckling, W. H. 1992. Specific and general knowledge and organizational structure, in Werin, L. and Wijkander, H. (eds), *Contract Economics*, Oxford, Blackwell

Kotter, J. P. and Heskett, J. L. 1992. *Corporate Culture and Performance*, New York, Free Press

Kreps, D. M. 1990. Corporate culture and economic theory, in Alt, J. G. and Shepsle, K. (eds), *Perspectives on Positive Political Economy*, Cambridge, Cambridge University Press

Kydland, F. E. and Prescott, E. C. 1977. Rules rather than discretion: the inconsistency of optimal plans, *Journal of Political Economy*, vol. 85, no. 3, 473–90

Lawrence, P. and Lorsch, J. 1967. *Organization and Environment*, Cambridge, MA, Harvard Business School

Malmgren, H. B. 1961. Information, expectations, and the theory of the firm, *Quarterly Journal of Economics*, vol. 75, no. 3, 399–421

McClelland, D. C. 1955. *Studies in Motivation*, New York, Appleton-Century-Crofts

McMillan, G. S., Hamilton, R. D. and Deeds, D. L. 2000. Firm management of scientific information: an empirical update, *R&D Management*, vol. 30, no. 2, 177–82

Melumad, N. D., Mookherjee, D. and Reichelstein, S. 1995. Hierarchical decentralization of incentive contracts, *RAND Journal of Economics*, vol. 26, no. 4, 654–72

Miles, R. E., Snow, C. C., Mathews, J. A., Miles, G. and Coleman, H. J. Jr 1997. Organizing in the knowledge age: anticipating the cellular form, *Academy of Management Executive*, vol. 11, no. 4, 7–20

Milgrom, P. and Roberts, J. 1996. Bargaining costs, influence costs and the organization of economic activity, in Putterman, J. and Kroszner, R. eds. *The Economic Nature of the Firm*, Cambridge, Cambridge University Press

Milgrom, P. R. 1988. Employment contracts, influence activities, and efficient organizational design, *Journal of Political Economy*, vol. 96, no. 1, 42–60

Miller, G. 1992. *Managerial Dilemmas*, Cambridge, Cambridge University Press

Moe, T. 1997. A positive theory of public bureaucracy, in Mueller, D. C. (ed.), *Perspectives in Public Choice: A Handbook*, New York, Cambridge University Press

Mowday, R. T., Steers, R. M. and Porter, L. W. 1982. *Employee-Organization Linkages: The Psychology of Commitment, Absenteeism and Turnover*, New York, Academic Press

Mudambi, R., Mudambi, S. M. and Navarra, P. 2003. 'How to Motivate Knowledge Workers: An Empirical Investigation of Motivation Crowding Theory', Temple University, Discussion Paper 716-03, The Fox School of Business and Management

Nickerson, J. and Zenger, T. 2004. A knowledge-based theory of the firm: the problem-solving perspective, *Organization Science*, vol. 15, no. 6, 617–32

Noe, T. H. and Rebello, M. J. 1996. Asymmetric information, managerial opportunism, financing, and payout policies, *Journal of Finance*, vol. 51, no. 2, 637–60

Nunnally, J. C. 1978. *Psychometric Theory*, New York, McGraw-Hill

Osterloh, M. and Frey, B. S. 2000. Motivation, knowledge transfer and organizational form, *Organization Science*, vol. 11, no. 5, 538–50

Pugh, D. S. and Hickson, D. J. 1976. *Organizational Structure in its Context: The Aston Programme I*, Farmborough, Saxon House/Lexington Books

Purser, R. 1998. *The Self-Managing Organization*, New York, The Free Press

Rajan, R. G. and Zingales, L. 1998. Power in a theory of the firm, *Quarterly Journal of Economics*, vol. 113, no. 2, 387–432

818   K. Foss, N. J. Foss and X. H. Vázquez

Robinson, S. L. 1996. Trust and breach of the psychological contract, *Administrative Science Quarterly*, vol. 41, no. 4, 574–99

Robinson, S. L. and Morrison, E. W. 1995. Psychological contracts and OCB: the effects of unfulfilled obligations on civic virtue behaviour, *Journal of Organizational Behaviour*, vol. 16, no. 3, 289–98

Roethlisberger, F. J., Wright, H. A. and Dickson, W. J. 1939. *Management and the Worker*, Cambridge, MA, Harvard University Press

Root, H. 1989. Tying the king's hands: royal fiscal policy during the old regime, *Rationality and Society*, vol. 1, no. 2, 240–59

Rousseau, D. M. 1989. Psychological and implied contracts in organizations, *Employee Responsibilities and Rights Journal*, vol. 2, no. 2, 121–39

Rousseau, D. M. and Parks, J. M. 1992. The contracts of individuals and organizations, in Staw, B. M. and Cummings, L. L. (eds), *Research in Organizational Behavior 15*, Greenwich, JAI Press

Simon, H. A. 1951. A formal theory of the employment relationship, in *Models of Bounded Rationality*, Cambridge, MIT Press, 1982

Simon, H. A. 1991. Organizations and markets, *Journal of Economic Perspectives*, vol. 5, no. 2, 25–44

Tepper, B. J. and Taylor, E. C. 2003. Relationships among supervisors and subordinates, procedural justice perceptions and organizational citizenship behaviours, *Academy of Management Journal*, vol. 46, no. 1, 97–105

Thomas, K. W. and Velthouse, B. A. 1990. Cognitive elements of empowerment: an interpretive model and intrinsic task motivation, *Academy of Management Review*, vol. 15, no. 4, 666–81

Thompson, J. D. 1967. *Organizations in Action*, New York, McGraw-Hill

Vázquez, X. H. 2004. Allocation of decision rights on the shop floor: a perspective from transaction cost economics and organization theory, *Organization Science*, vol. 15, no. 4, 463–80

Vroom, V. H. 1964. *Work and Motivation*, New York, John Wiley

Weingast, B. R. and Marshall, W. J. 1988. The industrial organization of congress: or, why legislators, like firms, are not organized as markets, *Journal of Political Economy*, vol. 96, no. 1, 132–63

Wernerfelt, B. 1997. On the nature and scope of the firm: an adjustment cost theory, *Journal of Business*, vol. 17, 489–514

Williamson, O. E. 1970. *Corporate Control and Business Behaviour An Inquiry into the Effects of Organization form on Enterprise Behaviour*, Englewood Cliffs, NJ, Prentice Hall

Williamson, O. E. 1993. Transaction cost economics meets posnerian law and economics, *Journal of Institutional and Theoretical Economics*, vol. 149, no. 1, 99–118

Williamson, O. E. 1996. *The Mechanisms of Governance*, Oxford, Oxford University Press

Willman, P. 1983. The organisational failures framework and industrial sociology, in Francis, A., Turk, J. and Willman, P. (eds), *Power, Efficiency and Institutions*, London, Heinemann

12

ELSEVIER

Journal of Economic Behavior & Organization
Vol. 58 (2005) 246–276

JOURNAL OF
Economic Behavior
& Organization

www.elsevier.com/locate/econbase

Performance pay, delegation and multitasking under uncertainty and innovativeness: An empirical investigation

Nicolai J. Foss [a], Keld Laursen [b],*

[a] Center for Strategic Management and Globalization, Copenhagen Business School,
Porcelainshaven 24, 2000 Frederiksberg, Denmark
[b] Department of Industrial Economics and Strategy, Copenhagen Business School,
Solbjergvej 3, 2000 Frederiksberg, Denmark

Received 10 February 2003; accepted 31 March 2004
Available online 1 September 2005

Abstract

It has been recently noted that the trade-off between risk and incentives that agency theory predicts turns out to be rather weak. We examine predictions from agency theory on the basis of data from a data set encompassing close to 1000 Danish firms. We find that the relation between performance pay and environmental uncertainty is indeed weak. We examine the relation between delegation and environmental uncertainty, and find that this relation is confirmed. We also examine the multi-tasking agency hypothesis that as risk increases, the flexibility of agents is restricted. We fail to find support for this hypothesis.
© 2005 Elsevier B.V. All rights reserved.

JEL classification: C35; L23

Keywords: Uncertainty; Pay-for-performance; Delegation; Innovation; Competition

* Corresponding author. Tel.: +45 38152565; fax: +45 38152540.
E-mail address: kl.ivs@cbs.dk (K. Laursen).

N.J. Foss, K. Laursen / J. of Economic Behavior & Org. 58 (2005) 246–276   247

1. Introduction

Empirical work in agency theory is relatively scant, at least when compared to the abundance of theoretical papers that have appeared since the mid-1970s (Masten and Saussier, 2002), and to the rather large and cumulative body of empirical work in related areas, notably transaction cost economics (Shelanski and Klein, 1995). Moreover, the existing empirical evidence is somewhat inconclusive with respect to a number of the key predictions of the agency model. Although the reach of agency theory is considerably wider, the dominant portion of the extant empirical work has been taken up with examining the nature of the trade-off between risk and incentives and the implications thereof for contractual design, including the design of organizations and institutions. However, as Prendergast (1999, 2002) notes, the empirical relation between risk and incentives appears to be "tenuous." Moreover, many, perhaps most, other predictions from agency theory have not been subjected to empirical scrutiny. For example, multi-tasking agency theory (Holmström and Milgrom, 1991) predicts that an agent's flexibility (i.e., the number of tasks that he/she is allowed to engage in) will be restricted, the less reliable the performance measures for his/her main tasks become. Increasing environmental uncertainty will reduce the reliability of performance measures, leading to restrictions of agents' flexibility. This prediction has, to our knowledge, never been tested.[1]

In this paper, we undertake to examine the risk-incentives trade-off and related ideas from agency theory on the basis of data from a data set encompassing close to 1000 Danish firms. We find that the relation between the use of performance pay in these firms and the uncertainty they confront (which is one way to test the risk/incentives tradeoff) is indeed "tenuous". We then suggest, in line with, for example, Jensen and Meckling (1992), Mendelson and Pillai (1999) and Prendergast (2002), that this may be caused by the widespread use of delegation. Indeed, the paper may be read as (we believe) the first empirical test of Prendergast (2002). Thus, drawing on the Prendergast paper, we argue that an effect of delegation is breaking the simple relation between risks and incentives. We examine indications that suggest that firms that are more prone to use delegation of decision rights in their internal organization are also those firms that face a more uncertain environment than the rest of the population. We argue that this constitutes an indirect confirmation of the hypothesis. We also go beyond Prendergast (2002) by examining the multitasking agency hypothesis that as risk increases, the flexibility of agents is restricted (Holmström and Milgrom, 1991). We fail to find support for this hypothesis. We suggest that the reason for this finding is also related to the issue of delegation.

---

[1] At least explicitly. Holmström and Milgrom (1991) invoke earlier work by Anderson (1985) and Anderson and Schmittlein (1984) as indirectly yielding empirical support for their multitask agency model. Baker and Hubbard (2003) include multi-tasking considerations in their empirical analysis; however, their main interest is how multi-tasking considerations influence the boundaries of the firm rather than job-design per se.

2. Theory and hypotheses

2.1. Basic agency theory

We here briefly and simply restate the basics of the agency model (following the now standard model of Holmström and Milgrom, 1991). Consider a "task" with output x, that depends on the agent's effort, e, and a normal error term, ε, which has mean, μ and variance, σ^2, so that $x = e + \varepsilon$. μ, σ^2 and x are common knowledge for the agent and principal. e is unobservable to the principal, and σ^2 is uncontrollable for the agent. x is verifiable so that contracts, $s(x)$, specifying the payment from principal to agent can be (costlessly) written. The agent's preferences may be described by the exponential utility function, $-\exp[-r(s(x) - c(e))]$, where r is the coefficient of risk aversion and $c(e)$ is the agent's cost function.

In the standard formulation, the principal's problem is to choose s so that the agent puts effort forward and is not overly burdened with risk. Under certain assumptions (stated in Holmström and Milgrom, 1987), the second-best contract takes a linear form, $s(x) = \alpha x + \beta$, where α is a measure of how "high-powered" incentives are and β is simply an income transfer from the principal to the agent (which serves to satisfy the participation constraint). Maximizing the certainty equivalent of joint surplus, which is $u + \mu - 1/2r\alpha^2 \sigma^2 - c(e)$, subject to the agent's first-order condition, $c'(e) = \alpha$, yields the best choice of α. Holmström (1989) gives the example of assuming $c(e) = 1/2ke^2$, which yields $\alpha = (1 + kr\sigma^2)^{-1}$. Inspection of this expression reveals that the agent receives a higher share, the lower his/her aversion to risk is and vice versa (α, the "piece rate," and r, the coefficient of risk aversion, varies inversely), and that incentives (α) and variance (σ^2) also varies inversely. This is the tradeoff between risk-sharing and provision of incentives to supply effort.

The standard model may be extended in various ways, notably by introducing monitoring considerations. In the above setting, higher risk leads to more monitoring because higher risk leads to a fall in α, which in turn reduces effort, prompting an increase in monitoring. The provision of incentives may also be influenced by changing the agent's opportunity costs, that is, controlling which other activities he/she can engage in, for how long time and so on. Intuitively, the less restricted an agent is (that is, the more discretion he/she has with respect to his/her choice of which activities to engage in and for how long), the more costly it is to induce him to work on a specific project. Consequently, the costs of providing incentives may be reduced by restricting the set of activities that an agent is allowed to work on (Holmström and Milgrom, 1990). The costs of measuring the agent's performance in the various activities play a key role for how much the agent will be restricted, as clarified by Holmström and Milgrom (1991). A key prediction from their multitask-agency model is that the more costly it is to measure the agent's performance in his/her main activities, the more his/her flexibility will be restricted. Since risk and measurement cost can reasonably be assumed to correlate directly, this reasoning would seem to predict that as risk increases, the agent would tend to become increasingly constrained. An interpretation is that activities will tend to be clustered in those activities that are easily measurable, and those that are not; different kinds of incentives will be provided for each.

N.J. Foss, K. Laursen / J. of Economic Behavior & Org. 58 (2005) 246–276   249

2.2. Empirical work

In agency theory, environmental uncertainty has the effect of adding observation error to performance measures (i.e., increase measurement cost) (Holmström, 1979; Holmström and Milgrom, 1991; Prendergast, 2002). This increases the risk that is imposed on agents. Hence, the testable prediction is that risk and performance pay correlate negatively. However, as Prendergast (2002) documents at length, this prediction has not fared quite well in the face of the empirical evidence. Specifically, he considers the empirical evidence for the four classes of occupation of executives, sharecroppers, franchisees and sales force workers. In the case of executive compensation, the evidence is "inconclusive," although there is weak evidence for relative performance evaluation, an implication of the risk/incentives tradeoff. For sharecroppers, the fraction that they retain turns out to be increasing in the noisiness of financial returns that is directly counter to the agency prediction. Evidence from studies of franchising suggest that the choice of whether to keep outlets in-house or franchise them is influenced by uncertainty in a direction opposite to the prediction of agency theory; that is, the probability of choosing franchising is positively influenced by environmental uncertainty. The evidence on sales force integration is inconclusive. In sum, the empirical evidence would, on balance, seem to indicate that uncertainty and incentives are positively, rather than negatively, related. This contradicts the basic agency model.[2]

2.3. Resolving the uncertainty/performance relation

A strong candidate for explaining why the basic agency prediction seems to be falsified in the light of the empirical evidence is that basic agency theory fails to consider many of the benefits of delegation (Foss and Foss, 2002). Indeed, in the basic story, the *only* benefit of delegation seems to be economizing with the opportunity costs of the principal's time. If these were low or zero, the principal would carry out the task himself, particularly since differences in knowledge about how to carry out the task optimally do not seem to exist in the basic agency model.

In actuality, of course, much knowledge about how to carry out the task optimally resides with the agent and may be too costly to transfer to corporate headquarters (or other managerial layers) because of problems of eliciting the correct information or because the relevant knowledge is of a highly "impacted," tacit or complex, kind. Agents then have "real authority," in the sense of Aghion and Tirole (1997). In this situation, delegation co-locates decision rights with this knowledge. The attendant moral hazard problem may accordingly be reduced by using more output-based contracts. Organizational structure and reward mechanisms arguably reflects the relevant tradeoff (Jensen and Meckling). Thus, the choice of how to remunerate agents is one that is complementary to a host of other issues of organizational design (Holmström, 1999).

---

[2] Another possible explanation for the lack of empirical confirmation of the agency prediction is an "endogenous matching" problem (Ackerberg and Botticini, 2002). For instance, principal-agent matching may emerge when risk-loving or risk-neutral agents are attracted to more risky activities. Since agent's risk aversion is only imperfectly controlled for in most econometric studies, the associated endogeneity problem may cause misleading results.

As Prendergast (2002) points out, this kind of reasoning may help explain why we may, in fact, expect a positive relation between uncertainty and incentives; thus, as he notes, "uncertain environments result in the delegation of responsibilities, which in turn generates incentive pay based on output" (Prendergast, 2002, p. 1072). Thus, in stable environments, direct order-giving and input monitoring will be employed by the principal. In more uncertain environments, the principal may still be able to monitor the agent's activities, but will have less of an idea of which activities the agent should optimally work on and how these activities should be balanced. Information about these issues may reside with the agent rather than with the principal. In this situation, principals likely respond by offering output-based performance contracts (Barzel, 1997).

Clearly, we should expect the incidence and strength of the relation between environmental uncertainty and performance pay to be firm or industry dependent. There are a priori grounds for suspecting that it may be stronger in "high-tech"/"high knowledge-intensive", "dynamic" and "turbulent," firms and industries, as well those that are unregulated and/or facing global competition, than in the more traditional ones or in those that are regulated or do not facing global competition. We base this expectation on several arguments based on the observation that the use of delegation is likely to be more prevalent in the former kind of industries than in the latter (Mendelson and Pillai, 1999).

First, in industries that are low in knowledge intensity, managers are more likely to understand tasks, and there is, therefore, less asymmetrical information. Hence, the need for delegation and pay-for-performance is smaller, even under uncertainty. Second, given that firms in industries that are low in knowledge intensity on an average have a low-skilled workforce, it may be more difficult to delegate responsibility in such industries since such delegation likely requires a certain level of skills. Finally, in high knowledge-intensive industries, it may be that there is simply more "local" expert knowledge and, accordingly, that managers are forced to delegate responsibility more than in low knowledge-intensive industries, even when facing the same level of uncertainty.

Delegation has a role to play when it comes to multitasking environments as well. Notably, organizational practices such as planned job rotation and quality circles introduce multitasking environments. However, firms and industries in which multitasking is likely to be prevalent are also the firms and industries for which uncertainty is already high, relatively more output-based pay being used in response. Multitasking aggravates this since it adds to the difficulty of accurately measuring input performance and makes it even more attractive to substitute output-based pay for direct monitoring and other ways of restricting the agent. This contradicts the Holmstrom and Milgrom hypothesis that increasing risk under multitasking leads to restriction of the number of activities that an agent is allowed to work on: given that output-based pay is preferred under these circumstances, there is little reason to implement such restrictions. On the contrary, "dynamic" firms often stimulate multitasking for reasons of knowledge-integration and sharing.

2.4. Resolving hypotheses

A number of hypotheses may be derived from the above discussion. The first one is that as a general matter, the uncertainty/incentive relation is a positive one. Prendergast (2002) lists the relevant empirical evidence for this and develops a formal model that yields

N.J. Foss, K. Laursen / J. of Economic Behavior & Org. 58 (2005) 246–276   251

this relation. The evidence invoked by Prendergast is derived from rather different kinds of occupations (and underlying industries), making it relevant to consider whether the relation may in fact be a general one. Thus, we suggest that

Hypothesis 1.   There is an overall positive and significant relation between environmental uncertainty and the use of performance pay.

The underlying "mechanism" driving the positive relation between uncertainty and incentives is, as it been argued, delegation. An implication of this argument, explicitly stated in Prendergast (2002), is that if indeed delegation is the correct explanation for the positive relationship between uncertainty and performance pay, then after controlling for delegation we should see no relationship between uncertainty and performance pay. Thus, based on the above, we would expect the following hypotheses to hold true:

Hypothesis 2a.   Delegation and environmental uncertainty are positively correlated.

Hypothesis 2b.   After controlling for delegation, there will be no relationship between uncertainty and performance pay.

Moreover, we would expect the strength of the correlation between environmental uncertainty and the use of performance pay to vary between firms belonging to different industries. In other words, not only do we expect the level of adoption of pay-for-performance to increase as a function of environmental (industry) uncertainty as stated in Hypothesis 1, we also expect the effectiveness of uncertainty as a predictor of pay-for-performance to be lower in less "dynamic" sectors of the economy:

Hypothesis 3.   The strength of the correlation between environmental uncertainty and the use of performance pay is sector dependent, so that the correlation within more "dynamic" sectors is stronger than in less "dynamic" sectors.

Finally, we submit that contrary to the predictions from multitasking agency theory, firms in "dynamic," high-uncertainty industries, far from refraining from the use of multitasking, will actually use multitasking more frequently:

Hypothesis 4.   Firms that are placed in environments characterized by high uncertainty will restrict the activities that their employees can engage in less than those that are placed in low uncertainty environments.

We examine these hypotheses empirically in the remainder of the paper.[3]

---

[3] Our hypotheses relate to issues of complementarity among organizational elements since we argue that high-powered performance incentives are complementary to delegation. We try to deal with this in various ways in the empirical section of this paper.

3. Empirical analysis

3.1. Measures

While the use of pay-for-performance, delegation of responsibility and multitasking can be approximated relatively well by the use of questionnaires (see, for instance, Capelli and Neumark, 2001; Laursen and Foss, 2003; Mendelson and Pillai, 1999; Vinding, 2006) or by observing contracts, the measurement of uncertainty is a more difficult endeavor.[4] In the empirical agency literature various measures has been used to gauge the level of uncertainty facing the relevant agent. In the sub-section on "Empirical Work" in Section 2 of this paper, we briefly mentioned the four types of occupation considered in the empirical agency literature (executives, sharecroppers, franchisees and salesforce workers). In some of this literature, the measure of environmental uncertainty is idiosyncratic/specific to the activity in question. Such an idiosyncratic measure has been used in the case of (for instance) the analysis of franchising decisions, where the average proportion of discontinued outlets in the franchising sector in which the franchisor operates has been adopted (Lafontaine, 1992). Another example of a specific measure is the number of calls it takes to close a sale, averaged across the salespeople at the responding firm (Coughlan and Narasimhan, 1992).[5] For the analysis of sharecroppers, the coefficient of variation of yield has been used (Allen and Lueck, 1992). In addition to the specific measures of uncertainty, variation over time of aggregate sales data has been applied in some studies (Martin, 1988; Norton, 1987) as well as survey-based data assessing the stability in sales and forecasting accuracy (John and Weitz, 1989). In the literature on executive pay, the most commonly used proxy for risk or uncertainty is variation in returns (see, for instance, Bushman et al., 1996; Lambert and Larker, 1987; Sloan, 1992). It should be pointed out, however, that since managers are to some extent capable of controlling variations in sales, stock returns or profitability, not all of the variance will reflect uncertainty (Bushman et al., 1996; Lafontaine, 1992).

We here consider three measures of uncertainty, namely (i) the extent to which firms are innovative, (ii) the perceived increase in the level of competition and (iii) within industry variance in profitability. We include different measures reflecting uncertainty since all such measures are imperfect. With respect to innovative activity as a measure of uncertainty, it is well known that innovation involves the lack of knowledge about the precise cost and outcomes of different alternatives in addition to lack of knowledge of what the alternatives are (Freeman and Soete, 1997; Nelson and Winter, 1982). However, it may be argued that innovation is an uncertain activity in the rare event of major "breakthroughs," while more pedestrian incremental innovation in terms of smaller improvements is in fact routinized and hence reasonably predictable. Empirical evidence has shown (Mansfield et al., 1977) that even when the fundamental knowledge base and the expected directions of advance are fairly well known, it is still often the case that firms must first engage in exploratory research,

---

[4] However, note that our measure of performance pay only concerns the percentage of employees that are given performance pay. Thus, the view of the individual employees regarding high-powered incentives is, strictly speaking, not captured by this measure.

[5] The argument is that the longer it takes to close a sale, the more important is sales efforts and the less important is environmental uncertainty (Coughlan and Narasimhan, 1992, p. 106).

N.J. Foss, K. Laursen / J. of Economic Behavior & Org. 58 (2005) 246–276   253

development and design before the outcome will be known, what some manageable result will cost, or even whether useful results will emerge. As Dosi (1988, p. 1034) argues "even in the case of "normal" technical search (as opposed to the "extraordinary" exploration associated with the quest for new paradigms) strong uncertainty is present." Since innovation is not important to all firms and since it only partially reflects environmental uncertainty, we include the two other measures. With regard to the (increased) level of competition, the idea is that if the level of competition increases, the selection environment of the firm becomes tougher and the room for managerial slack becomes smaller. Hence, if the level of competition increases, the firm will become more dependent on the (uncertain) actions of the competitors.[6] The final measure is the more conventional measure of uncertainty used in the existing literature, namely within-firm/industry variance in profitability.

3.2. The empirical model

Based on the discussion above, the probability of observing a certain organizational practice may be specified as follows:

$$o = f(\beta_1 z, \beta_2 x). \tag{1}$$

Here, o is the probability of adopting an organizational practice to a certain extent within the firm, β_1 and β_2 are parameter vectors and z is a set of (exogenous) determinants of the application of certain organizational practices related to environmental uncertainty, while x is a set of other variables explaining the adoption of a certain organizational practice across business firms. The model may be made operational in the following way:

$$\text{Prob}(O_i = 0 \dots j) = \chi \text{SECT}_i + \alpha \text{LOGSIZE}_i + \varphi \text{SUBSID}_i$$
$$+ \eta \text{INNO} + \psi \text{COMP}_i + \omega \text{PROFITVAR} + \varepsilon_i, \tag{2}$$

where $\text{Prob}(O_i = 0, \dots, j)$ expresses the firms' probability of adopting a given organizational practice (such as pay-for-performance or delegation of responsibility) to a certain degree within the firm ("0" = no use, "1" = less than 25 percent of the workforce involved, "2" = 25–50 percent of the workforce and "3" = more than 50 percent of the workforce involved). We control for firm size by including a continuous variable measuring the number of employees in each firm expressed in logs (LOGSIZE). Moreover, we control for sectoral affiliation (SECT) by including three sector categories (see the paragraph below for a description). Finally, we control for whether or not the firm is a subsidiary of a larger firm (SUBSID), since decisions on the adoption of organizational practices may (at least partly) be decided at the level of the headquarter. The three measures of uncertainty include the level of novelty of the innovations produced by the firm in question (INNOF, INNOC, INNOW) and the firm's perceived change in the level of competition (COMP) and the within-firm/industry variance in profitability (PROFITVAR). The measure of innovation

---

[6] Note, however, that the relation between uncertainty and competition may not be monotonic. Moving from monopoly to oligopoly, things depend increasingly on the uncertain actions of competitors. However, continuing from oligopoly towards perfect competition, the actions of competitors matter less and less, so increased competition at some point may indicate less uncertainty. Thanks to an anonymous reviewer for pointing this out.

Table 1
Descriptive statistics for a set of DISKO variables ($N = 993$)

		Number of firms	Percent of sample
Industry affiliation	Low-KI	390	39.3
	Medium-KI	366	36.9
	High-KI	237	23.9
Number of employees	31–100	312	31.4
(SIZE[a])	101–200	203	20.4
	>200	478	48.1
Subsidiary	No	409	41.2
(SUBSID)	Yes	584	58.8
Competition	Strongly decreased	1	0.1
(COMP)	Somewhat decreased	10	1.0
	Unchanged	194	19.5
	Somewhat increased	339	34.1
	Strongly increased	449	45.2
Product innovation	No innovation	391	39.4
(INNOF)	Innovation new to the firm	434	43.7
(INNOC)	Innovation new to the country	89	9.0
(INNOW)	Innovation new to the world	79	8.0
Pay-for-performance	Not used	525	52.9
(PPAY)	<25 percent of the workforce	194	19.5
	25–50 percent of the workforce	79	8.0
	>50 percent of the workforce	195	19.6
Delegation	Not used	103	10.4
(DR)	<25 percent of the workforce	240	24.2
	25–50 percent of the workforce	265	26.7
	>50 percent of the workforce	385	38.8
Quality circles	Not used	522	52.6
(QC)	<25 percent of the workforce	264	26.6
	25–50 percent of the workforce	111	11.2
	>50 percent of the workforce	96	9.7
Planned job rotation	Not used	550	55.4
(PJR)	<25 percent of the workforce	288	29.0
	25–50 percent of the workforce	93	9.4
	>50 percent of the workforce	62	6.2

[a] *Note:* The variable used in the subsequent regressions is continuous.

is split into three different variables, INNOF, INNOC and INNOW, all reflecting product innovations to various degrees of novelty. INNOF reflects the launch of innovations new to the firm, INNOC reflects innovations new to the country, and INNOW reflects the launch of innovations new to the world. All three variables take the value of "0" if no such innovation was introduced in the given period and the value of "1" if an innovation of a certain degree of novelty was introduced. For the possible values of COMP variables, see Table 1 below. The calculation of PROFITVAR is based on register data from Statistics

N.J. Foss, K. Laursen / J. of Economic Behavior & Org. 58 (2005) 246–276   255

Denmark. The basis of the variable is firm profitability measured as firm profits divided by firm value added. The firms in the sample have been classified according to industry at the level of 83 industries by Statistics Denmark (see Appendix D to this paper).[7] However, given the fact that there are few firms in some industries, the industries have been aggregated up to a total of seventy industries in the cases where this seemed meaningful (see Appendix E for details of the aggregation). Since relatively complete data are available for the years 1992–1994, all firms with non-missing profit data for all of the 3 years are included in the analysis (in order to get a balanced panel). The number of firms with non-missing profit data are 1610 firms,[8] and hence we have 4830 observations on which to base the variance-in-profits variable. Based on those observations, the within-firm/industry (70 industries) variance is calculated, resulting in the PROFITVAR variable.[9] It follows from the hypotheses stated in Section 2 that we expect positive signs for the "uncertainty" variables.

The sectoral classification is key to Hypothesis 3 of this paper since we claim that firms in more "dynamic" sectors use performance pay to a larger extent than those in less "dynamic" sectors" for given levels of uncertainty (measured as innovation or increase in the level of competition). Details of the sectoral classification applied may be found in Appendices C and D to this paper. Firm types with the strongest internal capacity to develop new products and services are assumed to belong to "high knowledge-intensive industries" (see Appendix C and Laursen, 2002). Firms in such industries are producing specialized machinery and instrumentation, chemicals and pharmaceuticals and Information and Communication Technology (ICT) services, the latter including banking, accounting, consultancies, advertising, etc. Industries associated with the lowest capacity to develop new products and services internally ("low knowledge-intensity industries") are assumed to be the construction industry, retailing, cleaning and to some extent supplier dominated manufacturing industries (furniture, textiles, pulp, paper and paper products and so on). Scale-intensive manufacturing industries (bulk materials and assembly) and firms in the wholesale trade industry may be considered to be intermediate in relation to knowledge-intensity ("medium knowledge-intensity industries"). Based on this sectoral classification, we estimate the following model in order to test Hypothesis 3:

$$\text{Prob}(O_i = 0 \ldots j) = \chi_s \text{SECT}_i + \alpha_s \text{LOGSIZE}_i + \varphi_s \text{SUBSID}_i$$
$$+ \eta_s \text{INNO} + \psi_s \text{COMP}_i + \omega_s \text{PROFITVAR} + \varepsilon_i, \quad (3)$$

where the notation is the same as in Eq. (2). Footsign s indicates that the parameter is allowed to vary depending on to which sector each firm belongs.

---

[7] The appendices are available at the Journal's website (…).

[8] Note that in the calculation of the within-firm/industry variance in profits, we use all the possible observations available in the dataset. This contrasts to the econometric estimations to be found later in this paper, where we include the firms with more than 30 employees only (993 firms).

[9] It can been observed from Appendix E, that there are two industries still (research and development and legal activities) in each of which there is only one firm present with non-missing profit data for all of the 3 years. However, in the estimations it does not matter significantly for the results whether or not these two industries are included in the analysis.

3.3. The data

The main source of data for this paper is the DISKO database. The database is based on a questionnaire that aims at tracing the relationship between technical and organizational innovation in a way that permits an analysis of new principles for work organization and their implications for the use and development of the employee's qualifications in firms in the Danish private business sector. The survey was carried out by the DISKO project at Aalborg University (DK) in 1996. The questionnaire was submitted to a national sample of 4000 firms selected among manufacturing firms with at least 20 full-time employees and non-manufacturing firms with at least 10 full-time employees. Furthermore, all Danish firms with at least 100 employees were included in the sample, corresponding to 913 firms. The resulting numbers of respondents are 684 manufacturing and 1216 non-manufacturing firms, corresponding to response rates of 52 percent and 45 percent, respectively. The response rate within manufacturing industries ranges from 41 to 62 percent (across 7 industries), while the response rate within service industries ranges from 42 to 57 percent (across 10 industries). Accordingly, it is concluded that there are no serious industry response biases in the data. For both service and manufacturing firms there is, however, a bias in the sense that larger firms were slightly more prone to answer the questionnaire. In manufacturing the response rate was 58 percent among firms in the largest size category (>100 employees), while the corresponding figure in services was 55 percent. However, the problem is to some extent alleviated in this paper since we use the firms with at least 30 employees only (see below).

The first descriptive analysis of the survey can be found in Lund and Gjerding (1996) and in Gjerding (1997). The database is held by Statistics Denmark, and the data on the firms in the database can be linked to regular register data that are also held by Statistics Denmark. For the purposes of the present paper, data have been obtained on the size and profitability of the firms in the sample from regular register data. The choice was made to work only with firms with more than 30 employees since we are dealing with the application of *formal* work practices, practices that are simply less meaningful for smaller companies (why use delegation if the firm is not larger than a typical work team?).[10] By retaining only firms in the sample that are larger than 30 employees, we end up with a total of 993 firms.

Table 1 displays descriptive statistics for the variables that are used in this paper. Appendix B can be inspected for a description of the questions from the survey on the basis of which the variables have been constructed. Only about 10 percent of the firms do not use delegation of responsibility (10.4 percent) to varying degrees, while just about half of the firms in the sample apply pay-for-performance (52.9 percent). Also about half of the firms report use of quality circles (47.4) and planned job rotation (44.6). Most firms (79.3 percent) indicate that the level of competition has increased over recent years. While it is clearly observed that the perceived level of competition is highly skewed, it is also evident that the perceived increased level of competition varies in degree. The sample includes 391 non-innovators, 434 firms that produced products/services that were new only to the firm itself, 89 firms that produced products/services that were new to the national market, while 79 firms introduced products/services that were new to the world.

---

[10] In fact, including the entire sample does not change our results in any important way. The results using the entire sample can be obtained from the authors upon request.

N.J. Foss, K. Laursen / J. of Economic Behavior & Org. 58 (2005) 246–276   257

3.4. Estimation

Since the dependent variables are discrete and inherently ordered multinomial choice variables, the ordered probit model is applied as the main means of estimation (for an exposition of ordered probit models, see Greene, 2000, pp. 875–879). However, the decision to adopt various work practices is likely to involve interdependency; for instance, we have argued that uncertainty gives rise to adoption of delegation of responsibility, which in turn gives rise to pay-for-performance. Hence, the two adoption decision equations are connected. Nevertheless, if we assume independence between the error terms in these two equations and further assume that errors are normally distributed, the equations can be estimated one by one. However, if the error terms in the two equations are not independent, estimates obtained via the ordered probit procedure are inconsistent, and joint estimation is required. One possible approach is to estimate a bivariate probit model (see Greene, pp. 849–856). However, this means that we have to reduce our dependent variables to binary (zero/one) variables. Another possibility is the estimation of a system of simultaneous equations. If the two decisions are simultaneously determined, this is a superior approach since we can then, in principle, obtain efficient, consistent and unbiased estimates of the coefficients in our model. However, it is also an approach that is computationally difficult (possibly impossible) with two ordered multinomial-choice equations.[11]

Given these difficulties, we have as a starting point estimated the models separately, although the requirements for using this approach are very strict. However, in order to check the robustness of our results, we have also estimated two of the models as full information maximum likelihood (FIML) bivariate probit models by collapsing our dependent variables into binary variables so that "0" becomes no adoption and "1" becomes adoption to any degree; in other words, when the original dependent variables take the values of "2" or "3," they are recoded to take the value of "1." By following this procedure we explicitly model the fact that the adoption procedures of delegation and pay-for-performance are connected. Using this method, however, we make the simplifying assumption that the decision regarding the adoption of delegation is made *before* the decision concerning adoption of pay-for-performance.

Tables 2 and 3 contain the estimations relevant to Hypotheses 1, 2a and 2b, while the estimations relevant to Hypothesis 3 can be found in Table 4. The results regarding Hypothesis 4 can be found in Table 5. The null hypothesis that the slopes of the explanatory variables are zero is strongly rejected by the likelihood ratio test for all of the estimated models found in Tables 2–5. We also need to report the marginal effects corresponding to the coefficients in Tables 2–5 in order to make meaningful interpretations of the coefficients (Greene, pp. 877–878). The marginal effects are found in Tables A.2–A.9 in Appendix A.

Model (i), in Table 2, tests Hypothesis 1 using the single equation ordered probit model ("*There is an overall positive and significant relation between environmental uncertainty and the use of performance pay*"). With respect to our control variables, it can be seen from

---

[11] Although estimating models with categorical dependent variables in a set of *simultaneous* equations is a task to be solved still, the issue of dependence between equations with categorical dependent variables has been dealt with by Mayer et al. (2004, pp. 1076–1077) using a two-step estimation procedure. Unfortunately, this approach requires specific regularities in the data.

N.J. Foss, K. Laursen / J. of Economic Behavior & Org. 58 (2005) 246–276

Table 2
Ordered probit estimation explaining the adoption of delegation and pay-for-performance (N = 993)

Independent variables	Dependent variables							
	Model (i) pay-for-performance (PPAY)		Model (ii) delegation of responsibility (DR)		Model (iii) pay-for-performance (PPAY)		Model (iv) pay-for-performance (PPAY) × delegation of responsibility (DR)	
	Estimate	p-Value	Estimate	p-Value	Estimate	p-Value	Estimate	p-Value
CONSTANT	-0.980	0.000	0.225	0.308	-1.205	0.000	-1.127	0.000
LOW_KI	Benchmark							
MEDIUM_KI	0.048	0.581	0.172	0.038	0.020	0.815	0.020	0.824
HIGH_KI	-0.046	0.640	0.236	0.013	-0.087	0.383	-0.018	0.855
LOGSIZE	0.125	0.002	0.105	0.009	0.109	0.008	0.128	0.002
SUBSID	0.152	0.054	0.077	0.317	0.142	0.074	0.182	0.023
INNOF	0.212	0.013	0.219	0.006	0.178	0.037	0.264	0.002
INNOC	0.262	0.062	-0.016	0.911	0.263	0.065	0.318	0.024
INNOW	0.477	0.002	0.217	0.117	0.446	0.003	0.503	0.001
COMP	-0.017	0.728	0.075	0.092	-0.026	0.601	-0.010	0.837
PROFITVAR	3.049	0.000	1.477	0.293	2.841	0.000	2.879	0.000
DELEGATION (DR)					0.194	0.000		
Log likelihood	-1144.73		-1265.37		-1131.67		-1396.27	
Restricted log likelihood	-1168.76		-1289.07		-1168.76		-1424.42	
Likelihood ratio test	0.000		0.000		0.000		0.000	

Note: The marginal effects corresponding to the coefficients found in this table are reported in Tables A.2–A.5 (Appendix A).

Table 3
FIML estimates of a bivariate probit model explaining the adoption of delegation and pay-for-performance
($N = 993$)

Independent variables	Dependent variable			
	Model (i) delegation of responsibility (DR)		Model (ii) pay-for-performance (PPAY)	
	Estimate	p-Value	Estimate	p-Value
CONSTANT	−0.160	0.636	−2.079	0.000
LOW_KI	Benchmark			
MEDIUM_KI	0.115	0.387	−0.018	0.850
HIGH_KI	0.115	0.455	−0.168	0.117
LOGSIZE	0.151	0.024	0.080	0.097
SUBSID	0.167	0.184	0.148	0.113
INNOF	0.348	0.007	0.134	0.192
INNOC	0.047	0.820	0.284	0.062
INNOW	0.159	0.492	0.491	0.005
COMP	0.076	0.261	−0.034	0.530
PROFITVAR	4.931	0.051	1.483	0.149
DELEGATION (DR)			1.689	0.000
Log likelihood		−965.140		
Likelihood ratio test		0.000		

Note: The marginal effects corresponding to the coefficients found in this table are reported in Table A.6 (Appendix A).

the estimation of model (i) that being a large firm increases the probability of adopting pay-for-performance. This conclusion can be made based on the fact that the parameter for LOGEMP is positive and significant, and moreover, the marginal effect for the LOGEMP variable is negative (see Table A.2 (Appendix A)) only in the case of no use (PPAY = 0), while the marginal effects are positive at all levels of use of performance pay (PPAY = 1–3). It can also be noted that the marginal effect is particularly large in the case of PPAY = 3. In other words, a one percent increase in size increases the probability of adopting pay-for-performance to a low degree (involving <25 percent of the workforce) by 0.9 percent, while the probability of adopting pay-for-performance to a medium degree (involving 25–50 percent of the workforce) is increased by 0.7 percent and the probability of adopting pay-for-performance to a high degree (involving >50 percent of the workforce) increases by 3.4 percent as a result of a 1 percent increase in size. Moreover, based on the estimations found in Table 2 and Appendix Table A.2 it can be seen that being a subsidiary increases the probability of adopting pay-for-performance to an increasing degree.

Of our three uncertainty measures, the parameter for increased level of competition is insignificant. In contrast, all parameters for the innovation variables (INNOF, INNOC, INNOW) are significant, and the marginal effect is negative only in the case of no use of pay-for-performance. The effect is by far strongest in the case of PPAY = 3 (>50 percent of the workforce involved). As would be expected, given that higher degrees of novelty are associated with higher degrees of uncertainty, the parameter increases in size as a function of the degree of novelty of the innovation. Moreover, the parameter for PROFITVAR is very significant and has the right sign, according to Hypothesis 1. Also in this case, the marginal

Table 4
Probit estimation explaining the adoption of pay-for-performance, sectoral estimation ($N = 993$)

	Estimate	p-Value
CONSTANT		
Low-KI	−0.764	0.047
Medium-KI	−0.602	0.109
High-KI	−1.961	0.000
LOGSIZE		
Low-KI	0.045	0.524
Medium-KI	0.128	0.033
High-KI	0.184	0.061
SUBSID		
Low-KI	0.275	0.034
Medium-KI	0.021	0.872
High-KI	0.201	0.228
INNOF		
Low-KI	0.240	0.078
Medium-KI	0.320	0.020
High-KI	0.020	0.918
INNOC		
Low-KI	0.336	0.208
Medium-KI	0.033	0.892
High-KI	0.460	0.055
INNOW		
Low-KI	0.240	0.411
Medium-KI	0.478	0.033
High-KI	0.685	0.027
COMP		
Low-KI	0.029	0.693
Medium-KI	−0.150	0.069
High-KI	0.104	0.317
PROFITVAR		
Low-KI	1.099	0.385
Medium-KI	6.739	0.019
High-KI	8.861	0.012
Log likelihood	−1134.3	
Restricted log likelihood	−1168.8	
Likelihood ratio test	0.000	

Note: The marginal effects corresponding to the coefficients found in this table are reported in Table A.7 (Appendix A).

effect is negative only in the case of no use of pay-for-performance (PPAY = 0). Here, the effect is strongly negative, while the effect is strongly positive in the case of PPAY = 3. In sum, we find rather strong support for Hypothesis 1.

Model (ii) in Table 2 examines Hypothesis 2a ("Delegation and environmental uncertainty are positively correlated") using the single equation ordered probit model. In this case, LOGSIZE is significant, but the relevant marginal effects (see Table A.3 (Appendix

Table 5
Ordered probit estimation explaining the adoption of quality circles and planned job rotation ($N = 993$)

Independent variables	Dependent variables			
	Model (i) Quality circles (QC)		Model (ii) Planned job rotation (PJR)	
	Estimate	p-Value	Estimate	p-Value
CONSTANT	−1.133	0.000	−1.456	0.000
LOW_KI	Benchmark			
MEDIUM_KI	0.006	0.943	0.119	0.168
HIGH_KI	0.226	0.021	0.021	0.832
LOGSIZE	0.140	0.001	0.166	0.000
SUBSID	0.203	0.014	0.066	0.414
INNOF	0.293	0.001	0.248	0.004
INNOC	0.250	0.057	0.286	0.035
INNOW	0.184	0.202	0.412	0.004
COMP	0.005	0.908	0.070	0.136
PROFITVAR	1.152	0.314	1.108	0.362
Log likelihood	−1122.42		−1045.62	
Restricted log likelihood	−1152.94		−1073.64	
Likelihood ratio test	0.000		0.000	

Note: The marginal effects corresponding to the coefficients found in this table are reported in Tables A.8 and A.9 (Appendix A).

A)) are only positive in the case of DR = 3. That is, firms affiliated with a larger firm are only more prone to adopt delegation of responsibility when more than 50 percent of the employees are involved. In fact, the marginal effect is high and negative if less than 25 percent of the workforce is involved. The parameter for INNOF is significant at the 1 percent level, and again, the marginal effect is only positive for what concerns PPAY = 3 (>50 percent of the workforce involved). Another measure that reflects uncertainty, COMP, is significant at the 10 percent level, but once more the marginal effect is positive only for what concerns PPAY = 3. In other words, firms facing tougher competition are more likely to adopt delegation of responsibility only when more than 50 percent of the employees are involved in the delegation. The parameter for PROFITVAR is not significant. To conclude on Hypothesis 2a, it can be said that the hypothesis finds support to the extent that if firms face more competitive environments and/or they have introduced a product new to the firm, then they are more likely to use delegation of responsibility, conditional on whether delegation involves the majority of the workforce.

Model (iii) in Table 2 examines Hypothesis 2b ("*After controlling for delegation, there will be no relationship between uncertainty and performance pay*"). The hypothesis is not supported by the single equation ordered probit estimations since the parameters for the innovation and PROVITVAR variables remain significant. However, we do get an indication that adoption decisions concerning work practices involving delegation and pay-for-performance are related and perhaps complementary, given the strongly significant parameter for DR. Nevertheless, even when we have accounted for delegation, the results of the single equation ordered probit estimations indicate that uncertainty induces adoption of work practices involving pay-for-performance. However, we have no way of precisely asserting whether this result is due to the fact that our measures are only imperfect measures of uncertainty, whether there is some other mechanism linking uncertainty and delegation as well, or whether the result is due to the estimation technique, which requires very strict assumptions to hold true.

Although this paper is not a direct test of complementarity effects, our hypotheses do relate to issues of complementarity among organizational elements (as noted earlier) since we argue that high-powered performance incentives are complementary to delegation. Athey and Stern (1998) discuss the challenges of empirically identifying complementarities in organization form, noting how difficult it is to argue that practice A is complementary to characteristic B even if A and B usually appear jointly in organizations. However, Athey and Stern show that when we have adoption of (two) complementary work-practices on the right-hand side and some performance measure on the left-hand side, we can gauge complementarity effects by examining the influence of the interaction term between the two practices on the dependent variable. However, in this paper we have the complementary work-practices on the left-hand side, and accordingly, we cannot use interaction terms in the same fashion as suggested by Athey and Stern. Nevertheless, we include the interaction term as a dependent variable, reflecting joint implementation of delegation of responsibility and pay-for-performance in model (iv) of Table 2. The results show joint implementation of delegation of responsibility, and pay-for-performance is indeed related to two of our measures of uncertainty, innovation and firm/industry variance in profits, thus giving further support to Hypotheses 1 and 2a.

Another way of dealing with the issue of joint implementation of the two work practices is to estimate the model as a binary, bivariate probit with delegation as an endogenous variable, as mentioned in the introduction to this section of the paper. The estimations of this model allow for dependence in the estimation of the two practices, delegation and pay-for-performance, although it has to be acknowledged that the downside of using this procedure is the loss of information accruing due to the transformation of the dependent variables from ordered variables, with four possible outcomes, down to binary variables. Nevertheless, the results of the estimations using this procedure can be found in Table 3.

First, we confirm the finding that the firm/industry variance in the profits measure (PROFITVAR) is significant in explaining the adoption of delegation of responsibility. This is consistent with Hypothesis 2a of this paper. Moreover, when we control for delegation, PROFITVAR is no longer significant in explaining the adoption of pay-for-performance. This is consistent with Hypothesis 2b of this paper, a hypothesis that could not be confirmed when using the ordered probit model. It can be noted that using a single equation binomial probit model (these results not shown for reasons of space), the parameter for PROFITVAR is significant in explaining the adoption of pay-for-performance, a result which is consistent with Hypothesis 1.[12]

---

[12] It should be noted, however, that when delegation is entered in the pay-for-performance equation while using the binomial single equation estimation procedure, PROFITVAR becomes insignificant as well ($p = 0.101$). Hence, at least some of the explanation for the difference between the results using the ordered probit model and the bivariate probit model (allowing for dependence between the equations) has to do with the fact that the variables have been transformed to binary ones.

N.J. Foss, K. Laursen / J. of Economic Behavior & Org. 58 (2005) 246–276   263

Hypothesis 3 ("The strength of the correlation between environmental uncertainty and the use of performance pay is sector dependent, so that the correlation within more "dynamic" sectors is stronger than in less "dynamic" sectors") is put under scrutiny in Table 4, where the parameters are allowed to differ for each variable according to whether the firms belong to low, medium, or high knowledge-intensive sectors. LOGSIZE is again significant, but now only for medium and high knowledge-intensive firms. Being a subsidiary of a larger firm increases the probability of adopting pay-for performance for what concerns low knowledge-intensive sectors, whereas the parameter is insignificant with respect to medium and high knowledge-intensive firms. The marginal effects are particularly strong for PPAY = 3 (>50 percent of the workforce involved) for low knowledge-intensive sectors (see Table A.7 (Appendix A)).

Again, as when a common parameter was assumed, COMP is insignificant and even negative in the case of medium knowledge-intensive firms. However, the second set of variables reflecting uncertainty (the innovation variables) are significant for low knowledge-intensive firms only in the case of the lowest degree of novelty (INNOF), while the innovation variables are significant for high knowledge-intensive firms in the case of the cases of medium (INNOC) and high (INNOW) degrees of novelty (the marginal effects are negative only in the case of no use of PPAY for all significant variables). This finding is in accordance with the hypothesis. When it comes to the profit-variance measure (PROFITVAR), we find that the results are strongly consistent with Hypothesis 3 of this paper since the parameter is significant in the case of medium and high knowledge-intensive firms. Moreover, the parameter is larger for high knowledge-intensive firms than for medium knowledge-intensive firms. For both of the two significant types of firms, the interpretation of the parameters is straightforward since the marginal effects are negative only in the case of no use of PPAY. Overall, the findings give strong support to Hypothesis 3.

With respect to Hypothesis 4 ("Firms that are placed in environments characterized by high uncertainty will restrict the activities that their employees can engage in less than those that are placed in low uncertainty environments"), we apply two measures of "multitasking." The first has to do with the use of "quality circles" (QC), while the second has to do with the application of "planned job rotation." In both cases we argue that the two work practices allow for more multitasking and hence restrict the employees less. The relevant estimations can be found in Table 5. In the two models, the marginal effects for all variables (except for the three intercepts) are negative (see Tables A.8 and A.9 (Appendix A)) only in the case of no use (QC, PJR = 0), while the marginal effects are positive in the case of at all levels of adoption (QC, PJR = 1–3). SIZE is positive and significant for what concerns both QC and PJR. Hence, larger firms seem more likely to adopt quality circles and planned job rotation.

Innovations at all levels of novelty (INNOF, INNOC, INNOW) are positive and significant in both models as well, implying that firms with the ability to produce (uncertain) innovations are more prone to adopt QC and PJR. The other proxy for uncertainty, COMP, is insignificant in affecting both the likelihood of adopting planned job rotation and of quality circles, although for planned job rotation, the variable is not strongly insignificant. PROFITVAR has no explanatory power, although the parameter is non-negative, in contrast to the prediction of the standard agency multitasking model. In sum, the evidence is somewhat supportive of Hypothesis 4.

264   N.J. Foss, K. Laursen / J. of Economic Behavior & Org. 58 (2005) 246–276

4. Concluding discussion

This paper began by observing the seemingly tenuous tradeoff between risk and uncertainty. We then went on to suggest (in line with other authors) that this might be caused by the widespread use of delegation of decision rights. Moreover, we argued firms should restrict their employees less when faced with a more uncertain environment. This prediction is in contrast to the prediction of the standard agency theory. Subsequently, we made an attempt to shed light on these matters empirically, as empirical research on these matters may be characterized as relatively scant. It was further argued that firms' ability to produce innovations of an increasing degree of novelty and firms' perceived change in competition regime, as well as with-in industry variations in profitability, might serve as (imperfect) measures of environmental uncertainty.

The evidence was found to be consistent with the hypothesis stating that there is an overall positive and significant relation between environmental uncertainty and the use of performance pay in the sense that the likelihood of adopting pay-for-performance increases with firms' ability to produce product innovations, in particular when the majority of the workforce is involved in the pay-for-performance schemes. However, not only did we conjecture that there is an overall positive and significant relation between environmental uncertainty and the use of pay-for-performance, we also added the prediction that the strength of the correlation between environmental uncertainty and the use of performance pay is sector dependent so that firms in more "dynamic" sectors are more likely to use performance pay than those in less "dynamic" sectors, given a certain level of uncertainty. It was concluded that if firms produce innovations to an increasing degree of novelty, they are much more likely to adopt pay-for-performance involving the majority of the workforce and that this relationship was found to be the strongest for firms affiliated to high knowledge-intensity sectors. Moreover, we found that the relationship between the level of adoption of pay-for-performance schemes and uncertainty, measured as within-firm/industry variance in profits, becomes increasingly strong when the level of knowledge-intensity increases.

With respect to the hypothesis claiming that delegation and environmental uncertainty are positively correlated, we found support for this claim to the extent that if firms face more uncertain environments, then they are more likely to use delegation of responsibility, conditional on the observation that delegation involves the majority of the workforce. Although the parameter for the measure of within-firm/industry variance in profitability turned out not to be significant (albeit positive) in explaining the use of delegation in firms, when using the ordered probit model, the opposite prediction from standard agency theory (a negative relation) found no support in the available evidence. Moreover, when using the bivariate estimation technique, within-firm/industry variance in profitability was found to be a predictor of delegation. However, it should be noted that since an econometric technique for estimation of simultaneous equations while allowing for ordered discrete data does not yet exist, this question is not yet definitely resolved.

We also examined the specific multitasking agency hypothesis (the Holmström–Milgrom hypothesis) which states that as risk increases, the flexibility of agents is restricted. We found no evidence of such a relationship. First, we found that the parameter for

N.J. Foss, K. Laursen / J. of Economic Behavior & Org. 58 (2005) 246–276   265

within-firm/industry variance in profitability was positive (although not significant). Second, we found some evidence consistent with the view that firms that are placed in environments characterized by high uncertainty will restrict the activities that their employees can engage in *less* than those that are placed in low uncertainty environments. In this context, we found that firms with the ability to produce (uncertain) innovations are more prone to adopt quality circles and planned job rotation. Moreover, we found the final proxy for uncertainty, an increased level of competition, to affect positively the likelihood of adopting planned job rotation. Multitasking adds to the difficulty of accurately measuring input performance and makes it more attractive to substitute output-based pay for direct monitoring and other ways of restricting the agent. Given that output-based pay is preferred under these circumstances, there is little reason to implement such restrictions. On the contrary, we conjecture that "dynamic" firms often stimulate multitasking for reasons of knowledge-integration and sharing.

In closing, we touch on a problem of a deep methodological nature that points to the necessity of future empirical work on the issues treated herein. Our reasoning has essentially assumed that all firms in the sample are optimally organized, which then allows us to draw inferences about the proper relationship between underlying attributes and organizational characteristics (e.g., delegation) simply by observing what firms actually do. However, suppose some firms are doing it right while others are doing it wrong and that evolutionary market processes are not sufficiently strong or are still going on, so that inefficient firms have not been weeded out. The fact that we observe a particular attribute–characteristics pair will then not tell us much about the optimality of that pair. One possible answer to this problem is to take more of a process approach. For example, a priori reasoning may suggest that certain firms are "appropriately" aligned (in terms of underlying attributes and organizational characteristics), and the analyst may then examine their performance *over time*. Do appropriately organized firms do better over time than inappropriately organized firms? If not, this is indication that either a priori theorizing is faulty or market processes do not work efficiently. Future work will take such an approach to the issues treated here.

Acknowledgments

The comments of in particular Peter G. Klein but also of Nicholas Argyres, Stéphane Saussier, Brian Silverman and two anonymous referees of this journal on earlier versions of this paper are gratefully acknowledged. In addition, we wish to thank the participants in the DISKO project at Aalborg University for allowing us to use the data applied in this paper. The usual disclaimer applies.

Appendix A

See Tables A.1–A.9 .

Table A.1
Distribution of the degree of innovativeness, across low, medium and high knowledge-intensive industries

	NOINNO	INNOF	INNOC	INNOW
Low knowledge-intensive	63.6	29.8	4.0	2.6
Medium knowledge-intensity	37.5	47.8	7.3	7.3
High knowledge-intensity	28.4	47.9	13.2	10.5
Total sample	49.2	38.6	6.7	5.5

Table A.2
Marginal effects from probit estimations, adoption of pay-for-performance of across 993 Danish firms

	PPAY = 0	PPAY = 1	PPAY = 2	PPAY = 3
CONSTANT	0.390	−0.067	−0.059	−0.265
MEDIUM_KI	−0.019	0.003	0.003	0.013
HIGH_KI	0.019	−0.003	−0.003	−0.013
LOGSIZE	−0.050	0.009	0.007	0.034
SUBSID	−0.061	0.010	0.009	0.041
INNOF	−0.084	0.014	0.013	0.057
INNOC	−0.104	0.018	0.016	0.071
INNOW	−0.190	0.032	0.028	0.129
COMP	0.007	−0.001	−0.001	−0.005
PROFITVAR	−1.213	0.207	0.182	0.823

Table A.3
Marginal effects from probit estimations, adoption of delegation of responsibility across 993 Danish firms

	DR = 0	DR = 1	DR = 2	DR = 3
CONSTANT	−0.039	−0.044	−0.003	0.086
MEDIUM_KI	−0.030	−0.034	−0.003	0.066
HIGH_KI	−0.041	−0.046	−0.003	0.090
LOGSIZE	−0.018	−0.021	−0.002	0.040
SUBSID	−0.013	−0.015	−0.001	0.030
INNOF	−0.038	−0.043	−0.003	0.084
INNOC	0.003	0.003	0.000	−0.006
INNOW	−0.037	−0.043	−0.003	0.083
COMP	−0.013	−0.015	−0.001	0.029
PROFITVAR	−0.254	−0.289	−0.022	0.564

Table A.4
Marginal effects from probit estimations, adoption of pay-for-performance of across 993 Danish firms (Including delegation as an explanatory variable)

	PPAY = 0	PPAY = 1	PPAY = 2	PPAY = 3
CONSTANT	0.479	−0.085	−0.074	−0.321
MEDIUM_KI	−0.008	0.001	0.001	0.005
HIGH_KI	0.035	−0.006	−0.005	−0.023
LOGSIZE	−0.043	0.008	0.007	0.029
SUBSID	−0.056	0.010	0.009	0.038
INNOF	−0.071	0.013	0.011	0.047

N.J. Foss, K. Laursen / J. of Economic Behavior & Org. 58 (2005) 246–276   267

Table A.4 (*Continued*)

	PPAY = 0	PPAY = 1	PPAY = 2	PPAY = 3
INNOC	−0.105	0.019	0.016	0.070
INNOW	−0.177	0.032	0.027	0.119
COMP	0.010	−0.002	−0.002	−0.007
PROFITVAR	−1.130	0.201	0.174	0.756
DR	−0.077	0.014	0.012	0.052

Table A.5

Marginal effects from probit estimations, interaction between pay-for-performance and delegation of responsibility, across 993 Danish firms

	PFPDR = 0	PFPDR = 1	PFPDR = 2	PFPDR = 3	PFPDR = 4	PFPDR = 5	PFPDR = 6
CONSTANT	0.445	−0.011	−0.033	−0.088	−0.021	−0.104	−0.188
MEDIUM_KI	−0.008	0.000	0.001	0.002	0.000	0.002	0.003
HIGH_KI	0.007	0.000	−0.001	−0.001	0.000	−0.002	−0.003
LOGSIZE	−0.051	0.001	0.004	0.010	0.002	0.012	0.021
SUBSID	−0.072	0.002	0.005	0.014	0.004	0.017	0.030
INNOF	−0.104	0.003	0.008	0.021	0.005	0.024	0.044
INNOC	−0.125	0.003	0.009	0.025	0.006	0.029	0.053
INNOW	−0.199	0.005	0.015	0.039	0.010	0.046	0.084
COMP	0.004	0.000	0.000	−0.001	0.000	−0.001	−0.002
PROFITVAR	−1.136	0.028	0.085	0.224	0.055	0.265	0.480

Table A.6

Marginal effects from bivariate probit estimations, adoption of delegation and pay-for-performance across 993 Danish firms

	DR	PPAY
CONSTANT	−0.049	−1.440
MEDIUM_KI	0.035	−0.012
HIGH_KI	0.035	−0.116
LOGSIZE	0.046	0.055
SUBSID	0.051	0.102
INNOF	0.106	0.093
INNOC	0.015	0.197
INNOW	0.049	0.340
COMP	0.023	−0.024
PROFITVAR	1.506	1.027
DR		1.170

Table A.7

Marginal effects from probit estimation with sector-specific slopes, adoption of pay-for-performance across 993 Danish firms

	PPAY = 0	PPAY = 1	PPAY = 2	PPAY = 3
CONSTANT				
Low-KI	0.304	−0.053	−0.047	−0.204
Medium-KI	0.240	−0.042	−0.037	−0.161
High-KI	0.780	−0.136	−0.120	−0.524

Table A.7 (*Continued*)

	PPAY = 0	PPAY = 1	PPAY = 2	PPAY = 3
LOGSIZE				
Low-KI	−0.018	0.003	0.003	0.012
Medium-KI	−0.051	0.009	0.008	0.034
High-KI	−0.073	0.013	0.011	0.049
SUBSID				
Low-KI	−0.109	0.019	0.017	0.073
Medium-KI	−0.009	0.002	0.001	0.006
High-KI	−0.080	0.014	0.012	0.054
INNOF				
Low-KI	−0.096	0.017	0.015	0.064
Medium-KI	−0.127	0.022	0.020	0.086
High-KI	−0.008	0.001	0.001	0.005
INNOC				
Low-KI	−0.134	0.023	0.021	0.090
Medium-KI	−0.013	0.002	0.002	0.009
High-KI	−0.183	0.032	0.028	0.123
INNOW				
Low-KI	−0.095	0.017	0.015	0.064
Medium-KI	−0.190	0.033	0.029	0.128
High-KI	−0.273	0.048	0.042	0.183
COMP				
Low-KI	−0.012	0.002	0.002	0.008
Medium-KI	0.060	−0.010	−0.009	−0.040
High-KI	−0.042	0.007	0.006	0.028
PROFITVAR				
Low-KI	−0.437	0.076	0.067	0.294
Medium-KI	−2.681	0.468	0.412	1.801
High-KI	−3.525	0.615	0.541	2.368

Table A.8
Marginal effects from probit estimations, adoption of quality circles of across 993 Danish firms

	QC = 0	QC = 1	QC = 2	QC = 3
CONSTANT	0.451	−0.135	−0.135	−0.181
MEDIUM_KI	−0.003	0.001	0.001	0.001
HIGH_KI	−0.090	0.027	0.027	0.036
LOGSIZE	−0.056	0.017	0.017	0.022
SUBSID	−0.081	0.024	0.024	0.032
INNOF	−0.117	0.035	0.035	0.047
INNOC	−0.100	0.030	0.030	0.040
INNOW	−0.073	0.022	0.022	0.029
COMP	−0.002	0.001	0.001	0.001
PROFITVAR	−0.459	0.138	0.137	0.184

N.J. Foss, K. Laursen / J. of Economic Behavior & Org. 58 (2005) 246–276   269

Table A.9
Marginal effects from probit estimations, adoption of planned job rotation across 993 Danish firms

	PJR = 0	PLJ = 1	PLJ = 2	PLJ = 3
CONSTANT	0.575	−0.241	−0.169	−0.166
MEDIUM_KI	−0.047	0.020	0.014	0.014
HIGH_KI	−0.008	0.004	0.003	0.002
LOGSIZE	−0.066	0.028	0.019	0.019
SUBSID	−0.026	0.011	0.008	0.008
INNOF	−0.098	0.041	0.029	0.028
INNOC	−0.113	0.047	0.033	0.033
INNOW	−0.163	0.068	0.048	0.047
COMP	−0.028	0.012	0.008	0.008
PROFITVAR	−0.437	0.183	0.128	0.126

Appendix B. The questions from the DISKO survey that are used in this paper

1. How large a share of the firm's workforce is involved in following ways of organizing work? (none, <25 percent, 25–50 percent, >50 percent, corresponding to a 4 point Likert scale)
   a. Delegation of responsibility [DR].
   b. Performance pay (not piece work) [PPAY].
   c. Quality circles [QC].
   d. Planned job rotation PLJ].
2. Has the firm introduced new products/services during the period 1993–1995 when excepting minor improvements of existing products? (yes/no)

If the respondent answered yes to this question he/she was asked whether similar products/services could be found …

a. … on the Danish market (yes/no);
b. … on the world market (yes/no).

If the respondent answered that a similar product could be found both on the Danish market and on the world market, the first innovation variable (INNOF) was coded with the value of 1 ("new to the firm"); otherwise it was coded with the value of 0. If respondent answered that a similar product could be found on the world market, but not on the Danish market, the second innovation variable (INNOC) was coded with the value of 1 ("new to the country"); otherwise it was coded with the value of 0. If the respondent answered that a similar product could neither be found on the Danish market, nor on the world market, the third innovation variable (INNOW) was coded with the value of 1 ("new to the world"); otherwise it was coded with the value of 0.

3. To which extent has competition from other firms changed during recent years?
   a. Strongly decreased.
   b. Somewhat decreased.
   c. Unchanged.
   d. Somewhat increased.
   e. Strongly increased.

If the respondent answered "strongly decreased", the variable was coded with the value of 0, while the variable was coded with the value of 4 in the case where respondent answered "strongly increased".

Appendix C. The sectoral classification applied in the present paper

The starting point for our classification of firms into low-, medium- and high knowledge-intensive industries is the Pavitt taxonomy. Pavitt (1984) identifies differences in the importance of different sources of innovation according to which broad sector the individual firm belongs. The Pavitt taxonomy, based on grouping firms according to their principal activity, emerged out of a statistical analysis of more than 2000 post-war innovations in Britain. The underlying explanatory variables are the sources of technology, the nature of users' needs and firms' means of appropriation. Based on this, four overall types of firms were identified, namely supplier dominated firms, scale-intensive firms, specialised suppliers and science-based firms. *Supplier dominated* firms are typically small. Most technology comes from suppliers of equipment and material. *Scale intensive* firms are found in bulk materials and assembly. Their internal sources of technology are production engineering and R&D departments. External sources of technology include mainly interactive learning with specialised suppliers, but also inputs from science-based firms are of some importance. *Specialised suppliers* are small firms that are producers of production equipment and control instrumentation. Their internal sources of technology are design and development. External sources are users (science-based and scale-intensive firms). *Science-based firms* are found in the chemical and electronic sectors. Their main internal sources of technology are internal R&D and production engineering. Important external sources of technology include universities, but also specialised suppliers. In the present paper we considers supplier-dominated industries to be "low knowledge-intensity" industries, while scale intensive industries are considered to be "medium knowledge-intensity" industries. Science based and specialised supplier industries are considered to be "high knowledge-intensity" industries.

In the 1984 version of the Pavitt taxonomy, all service firms were considered to be supplier dominated (i.e. "low knowledge-intensity" industries). However, later on Pavitt (1990) acknowledged that some service firms had become increasingly innovative, including business services and financial services. Hence, we have classified firms in these industries as "high knowledge-intensity" industries. Moreover, we found in our sample that firms in the wholesale industries appear to produce a substantial amount of innovation since 63 percent of firms in these industries report that they have introduced an innovation over the period in question. Hence, rather than following the Pavitt taxonomy and classifying these industries as "low knowledge-intensity," we decided to classify them as "medium knowledge-intensity" industries. Finally, we follow Pavitt (1984) and consider the rest of the services industries to be supplier dominated (i.e. "low knowledge-intensity" industries). For a detailed assignment of all industries into our three sectors, see Appendix D to this paper. From Table A.1 (Appendix A) it can be seen that the high-knowledge-intensive firms are indeed the most innovative firms since 71.6 percent of firms in these industries reported that they are innovative to some degree. 62.5 percent of the firms in medium knowledge-

N.J. Foss, K. Laursen / J. of Economic Behavior & Org. 58 (2005) 246–276   271

intensity industries are innovative while only 36.4 percent of low knowledge-intensive industries are innovative.

Appendix D. The assignment of industries/firms into three sectoral categories

No.	Industry	Sector
1	Production, etc. of meat and meat products	Med-KI
2	Manufacture of dairy products	Med-KI
3	Manufacture of other food products	Med-KI
4	Manufacture of beverages	Med-KI
5	Manufacture of tobacco products	Med-KI
6	Manufacture of textiles and textile products	Low-KI
7	Manufacture of wearing apparel; dressing, etc. of fur	Low-KI
8	Manufacture of leather and leather products	Low-KI
9	Manufacture of wood and wood products	Low-KI
10	Manufacture of pulp, paper and paper products	Low-KI
11	Publishing of newspapers	Low-KI
12	Publishing activities, excl. newspapers	Low-KI
13	Printing activities, etc.	Low-KI
14	Manufacture of refined petroleum products, etc.	Med-KI
15	Manufacture of chemical raw materials	High-KI
16	Manufacture of paints, soap, cosmetics, etc.	Med-KI
17	Manufacture of pharmaceuticals, etc.	High-KI
18	Manufacture of plastics and synthetic rubber	Med-KI
19	Manufacture of glass and ceramic goods, etc.	Low-KI
20	Manufacture of cement, bricks, concrete ind., etc.	Med-KI
21	Manufacture of basic metals	Med-KI
22	Manufacture construction materials of metal, etc.	Med-KI
23	Manufacture of hand tools, metal packaging, etc.	Low-KI
24	Manufacture of marine engines, compressors, etc.	High-KI
25	Manufacture of other general purpose machinery	High-KI
26	Manufacture of agricultural and forestry machinery	High-KI
27	Manufacture of machinery for industries, etc.	High-KI
28	Manufacture of domestic appliances n.e.c.	Med-KI
29	Manufacture of office machinery and computers	High-KI
30	Manufacture of radio and communication equipment, etc.	High-KI
31	Manufacture of medical and optical instruments, etc.	High-KI
32	Building and repairing of ships and boats	Med-KI
33	Manufacture of transport equipment excl. ships, etc.	Med-KI
34	Manufacture of furniture	Low-KI
35	Manufacture of toys, gold and silver articles, etc.	Low-KI
36	General contractors	Low-KI
37	Bricklaying	Low-KI
38	Installation of electrical wiring and fittings	Low-KI
39	Plumbing	Low-KI
40	Joinery installation	Low-KI
41	Painting and glazing	Low-KI
42	Other construction works	Low-KI
43	Sale of motor vehicles, motorcycles, etc.	Low-KI
44	Maintenance and repair of motor vehicles	Low-KI
45	Service stations	Low-KI

Appendix D (*Continued*)

No.	Industry	Sector
46	Ws. of agricultural raw materials, live animals	Med-KI
47	Ws. of food, beverages and tobacco	Med-KI
48	Ws. of household goods	Med-KI
49	Ws. of wood and construction materials	Med-KI
50	Ws. of other raw mat. and semimanufactures	Med-KI
51	Ws. of machinery, equipment and supplies	Med-KI
52	Commission trade and other wholesale trade	Med-KI
53	Re. sale of food in non-specialised stores	Low-KI
54	Re. sale of food in specialised stores	Low-KI
55	Department stores	Low-KI
56	Retail sale of phar. goods, cosmetic art., etc.	Low-KI
57	Re. sale of clothing, footwear, etc.	Low-KI
58	Re. sale of furniture, household appliances	Low-KI
59	Re. sale in other specialised stores	Low-KI
60	Repair of personal and household goods	Low-KI
61	Hotels, etc.	Low-KI
62	Restaurants, etc.	Low-KI
63	Transport via railways and buses	Low-KI
64	Taxi operation and coach services	Low-KI
65	Freight transport by road and via pipelines	Low-KI
66	Water transport	Low-KI
67	Air transport	Low-KI
68	Cargo handling, harbours, etc.; travel agencies	Low-KI
69	Monetary intermediation	High-KI
70	Other financial intermediation	High-KI
71	Insurance and pension funding	High-KI
72	Activities auxiliary to financial intermediates	High-KI
73	Letting of own property	Low-KI
74	Real estate agents, etc.	Low-KI
75	Renting of machinery and equipment, etc.	Low-KI
76	Computer and related activity	High-KI
77	Research and development	High-KI
78	Legal activities	High-KI
79	Accounting, book-keeping and auditing activities	High-KI
80	Consulting engineers, architects, etc.	High-KI
81	Advertising	High-KI
82	Building-cleaning activities	Low-KI
83	Other business services	High-KI

Note: Low-KI, low knowledge-intensity sectors; Med-KI, medium knowledge-intensity sectors; High-KI, high knowledge-intensity sectors.

Appendix E. The assignment of industries/firms into profit variance categories

No.	Industry	N	Variance
V1	Production etc. of meat and meat products (i1)	30	0.024
V2	Manufacture of dairy products (i2)	27	0.047
V3	Manufacture of other food products (i3)	129	0.043
	Manufacture of tobacco products (i5)		

N.J. Foss, K. Laursen / J. of Economic Behavior & Org. 58 (2005) 246–276   273

Appendix E (*Continued*)

No.	Industry	N	Variance
V4	Manufacture of beverages (i4)	15	0.011
V5	Manufacture of textiles and textile products (i6)	69	0.042
V6	Manufacture of wearing apparel; dressing, etc. of fur (i7)	48	0.070
	Manufacture of leather and leather products (i8)		
V7	Manufacture of wood and wood products (i9)	75	0.022
V8	Manufacture of pulp, paper and paper products (i10)	66	0.085
V9	Publishing of newspapers (i11)	42	0.006
	Publishing activities, excl. newspapers (i12)		
V10	Printing activities, etc. (i13)	75	0.065
V11	Manufacture of refined petroleum products, etc. (i14)	24	0.030
	Manufacture of chemical raw materials (i15)		
V12	Manufacture of paints, soap, cosmetics, etc. (i16)	63	0.036
V13	Manufacture of pharmaceuticals, etc. (i17)	27	0.035
V14	Manufacture of plastics and synthetic rubber (i18)	135	0.023
V15	Manufacture of glass and ceramic goods, etc. (i19)	81	0.024
	Manufacture of cement, bricks, concrete ind., etc. (i20)		
V16	Manufacture of basic metals (i21)	69	0.045
V17	Manufacture construction materials of metal, etc. (i22)	84	0.018
V18	Manufacture of hand tools, metal packaging, etc. (i23)	102	0.030
V19	Manufacture of marine engines, compressors, etc. (i)24	54	0.033
V20	Manufacture of other general purpose machinery (i)25	105	0.057
V21	Manufacture of agricultural and forestry machinery (i26)	27	0.082
V22	Manufacture of machinery for industries, etc. (i27)	108	0.019
V23	Manufacture of domestic appliances n.e.c. (i28)	30	0.036
V24	Manufacture of office machinery and computers (i29)	84	0.068
V25	Manufacture of radio and communication equipment, etc. (i30)	51	0.060
V26	Manufacture of medical and optical instruments, etc. (i31)	90	0.045
V27	Building and repairing of ships and boats (i32)	24	0.101
V28	Manufacture of transport equipment excl. ships, etc. (i33)	60	0.091
V29	Manufacture of furniture (i34)	156	0.022
V30	Manufacture of toys, gold and silver articles, etc. (i35)	36	0.017
V31	General contractors (i36)	177	0.030
V32	Bricklaying (i37)	36	0.019
V33	Install. of electrical wiring and fittings (i38)	114	0.014
V34	Plumbing (i39)	66	0.008
V35	Joinery installation (i40)	84	0.015
V36	Painting and glazing (i41)	66	0.018
V37	Other construction works (i42)	33	0.010
V38	Sale of motor vehicles, motorcycles, etc. (i43)	243	0.061
V39	Maintenance and repair of motor vehicles (i44)	51	0.008
	Service stations (i45)		
V40	Ws. of agricul. raw materials, live animals (i46)	48	0.026
V41	Ws. of food, beverages and tobacco (i47)	96	0.065
V42	Ws. of household goods (i48)	150	0.037
V43	Ws. of wood and construction materials (i49)	51	0.051
V44	Ws. of other raw mat. and semimanufactures (i50)	87	0.034
V45	Ws. of machinery, equipment and supplies (i51)	336	0.049
V46	Commission trade and other wholesale trade (i52)	24	0.015
V47	Re. sale of food in non-specialised stores (i53)	63	0.032
	Department stores (i55)		

Appendix E (*Continued*)

No.	Industry	N	Variance
V48	Re. sale of food in specialised stores (i54)	15	0.004
V49	Retail sale of phar. goods, cosmetic art., etc. (i56)	120	0.007
V50	Re. sale of clothing, footwear, etc. (i57)	78	0.029
V51	Re. sale of furniture, household appliances (i58) Repair of personal and household goods (i60)	90	0.019
V52	Re. sale in other specialised stores (i59)	51	0.018
V53	Hotels, etc. (i61)	63	0.086
V54	Restaurants, etc. (i62)	39	0.010
V55	Transport via railways and buses (i63)	18	0.015
V56	Taxi operation and coach services (i64)	30	0.003
V57	Freight transport by road and via pipelines (i65)	165	0.008
V58	Water transport (i66) Air transport (i67)	15	0.107
V59	Cargo handling, harbours, etc.; travel agencies (i68)	96	0.028
V60	Monetary intermediation (i69) Other financial intermediation (i70) Insurance and pension funding (i71) Activities auxiliary to financial intermediates (i72)	15	0.089
V61	Letting of own property (i73) Real estate agents, etc. (i74)	18	0.012
V62	Renting of machinery and equipment, etc. (i75)	18	0.633
V63	Computer and related activity (i76)	69	0.023
V64	Research and development (i77)	3	0.025
V65	Legal activities (i78)	3	0.000
V66	Accounting, book-keeping and auditing activities (i79)	33	0.003
V67	Consulting engineers, architects, etc. (i80)	90	0.019
V68	Advertising (i81)	18	0.006
V69	Building-cleaning activities (i82)	45	0.007
V70	Other business services (i83)	27	0.079

Note: The numbers in brackets (i1, ..., i70) refers to the industry number in Table A.2 (Appendix A).

References

Ackerberg, D.A., Botticini, M., 2002. Endogenous matching and the empirical determinants of contract form. Journal of Political Economy 110, 564–591.

Aghion, P., Tirole, J., 1997. Formal and real authority in organization. Journal of Political Economy, 1–29.

Allen, D.W., Lueck, D., 1992. Contract choice in modern agriculture: crop-share versus cash rent. Journal of Law and Economics 35, 397–426.

Anderson, E., 1985. The salesperson as an outside agent or employee: a transaction cost analysis. Management Science 4, 234–254.

Anderson, E., Schmittlein, D., 1984. Integration of the salesforce: an empirical examination. RAND Journal of Economics 15, 385–395.

Athey, S., Stern, S., 1998. An empirical framework for testing theories about complementarity in organizational design. NBER Working Paper 6600.

Baker, G.P., Hubbard, T.N., 2003. Make versus buy in trucking: asset ownership, job design, and information. American Economic Review 93, 551–572.

Barzel, Y., 1997. Economic Analysis of Property Rights. Cambridge University Press, Cambridge.

N.J. Foss, K. Laursen / J. of Economic Behavior & Org. 58 (2005) 246–276   275

Bushman, R.M., Indjejikian, R.J., Smith, A., 1996. CEO compensation: the role of individual performance evaluation. Journal of Accounting and Economics 21, 161–193.

Capelli, P., Neumark, D., 2001. Do "high-performance" work practices improve establishment-level outcomes? Industrial and Labor Relations Review 54, 737–775.

Coughlan, A.T., Narasimhan, C., 1992. An empirical analysis of sales-force compensation plans. Journal of Business 65, 93–121.

Dosi, G., 1988. Sources, procedures and microeconomic effects of innovation. Journal of Economic Literature 26, 1120–1171.

Foss, K., Foss, N.J., 2002. Authority and discretion: tradeoffs, credible commitment, and implications for new organizational forms. LINK Working paper 02-16, Department of Industrial Economics and Strategy, Copenhagen Business School.

Freeman, C., Soete, L.L.G., 1997. The Economics of Industrial Innovation. Pinter, London.

Gjerding, A.N. (Ed.), 1997. Den Fleksible Virksomhed: Omstillingspres og Fornyelse i Dansk Erhvervsliv. DISKO-Projektet: Rapport nr. 1. Copenhagen: Erhvervsudviklingsrådet.

Greene, W.H., 2000. Econometric Analysis. Prentice-Hall, Upper Saddle River, New Jersey.

Holmström, B., 1979. Moral hazard and observability. Bell Journal of Economics 10, 74–91.

Holmström, B., 1989. Agency costs and innovation. Journal of Economic Behavior and Organization 12, 305–327.

Holmström, B., 1999. The firm as a subeconomy. The Journal of Law, Economics & Organization 15, 74–102.

Holmström, B., Milgrom, P., 1987. Aggregation and linearity in the provision of intertemporal incentives. Econometrica 55, 303–328.

Holmström, B., Milgrom, P., 1990. Regulating trade among agents. Journal of Institutional and Theoretical Economics 146, 85–105.

Holmström, B., Milgrom, P., 1991. Multitask principal-agent analyses: incentive contracts, asset ownership, and job design. Journal of Law, Economics, and Organization 7, 24–52.

Jensen, M.C., Meckling, W.H., 1992. Specific and general knowledge and organizational structure. In: Werin, L., Wijkander, H. (Eds.), Contract Economics. Blackwell, Oxford, pp. 251–274.

John, G., Weitz, B., 1989. Salesforce compensation: an empirical investigation of factors related to use of salary versus incentive compensation. Journal of Marketing Research 26, 1–14.

Lafontaine, F., 1992. Agency theory and franchising. RAND Journal of Economics 23, 263–283.

Lambert, R., Larker, D., 1987. An analysis of the use of accounting and market measures of performance in executive compensation contracts. Journal of Accounting Research 25, 85–125.

Laursen, K., 2002. The importance of sectoral differences in the application of complementary HRM practices for innovation performance. International Journal of the Economics of Business 9, 139–156.

Laursen, K., Foss, N., 2003. New human resource management practices, complementarities, and the impact on innovation performance. Cambridge Journal of Economics 27, 243–263.

Lund, R., Gjerding, A.N., 1996. The flexible company innovation, work organisation and human resource management. DRUID Working Paper 96-17, IKE Group, Department of Business Studies, Aalborg University.

Mansfield, E., Rapoport, J., Romero, A., Villani, S., Husic, F., Wagner, S., 1977. The Production and Application of Industrial Technology. Norton, New York.

Martin, R.E., 1988. Franchising and risk management. American Economic Review 78, 954–968.

Masten, S., Saussier, S., 2002. Econometrics of contracts: an assessment of developments in the empirical literature on contracting. In: Brousseau, E., Glachant, J.-M. (Eds.), The Economics of Contracts. Cambridge University Press, Cambridge, pp. 273–292.

Mayer, K.J., Nickerson, J.A., Owan, H., 2004. Are supply and plant inspections complements or substitutes? A strategic and operational assessment of inspection practices in biotechnology. Management Science 50, 1064–1081.

Mendelson, H., Pillai, R.R., 1999. Information age organizations, dynamics, and performance. Journal of Economic Behavior and Organization 38, 253–281.

Nelson, R.R., Winter, S., 1982. An Evolutionary Theory of Economic Change. Harvard University Press, Cambridge, Massachusetts.

Norton, S.W., 1987. An empirical look at franchising as an organizational form. Journal of Business 61, 197–217.

Pavitt, K.L.R., 1984. Sectoral patterns of technical change: towards a taxonomy and a theory. Research Policy 13, 343–373.

Pavitt, K.L.R., 1990. What we know about the strategic management of technology. California Management Review 32, 17–26.

Prendergast, C., 1999. The provision of incentives in firms. Journal of Economic Literature 37, 7–63.

Prendergast, C., 2002. The tenuous tradeoff between risk and incentives. Journal of Political Economy 110, 1071–1102.

Shelanski, H., Klein, P.G., 1995. Empirical research in transaction cost economics: a review and assessment, Journal of Law. Economics and Organization 11, 335–361.

Sloan, R.G., 1992. Accounting earnings and top executive compensation. Journal of Accounting and Economics 16, 55–100.

Vinding, A.L., 2006. Absorptive capacity and innovative performance: a human capital approach. The Economics of Innovation and New Technology 15, in press.

PART III

PROPERTY RIGHTS
AND ENTREPRENEURSHIP

13

Int. J. of the *Economics* of *Business, Vol. 8, No. 1, 2001, pp. 19–37*

Assets, Attributes and Ownership

KIRSTEN FOSS and NICOLAI FOSS

ABSTRACT   *The notion of full asset ownership is important in economics, for example, in recent work on the boundaries of the firm. Much of this work has been taken up with the issue why it matters who owns an asset. However, recognizing that assets have multiple attributes, and that these may be subject to capture in a world of positive measurement and enforcement costs, implies that the notion of full asset ownership is problematic. New property rights theorists sidestep these issues by implicitly assuming that residual rights of control are perfectly enforced (i.e. full asset ownership obtains). We discuss the notion of property rights and ownership in a setting characterized by positive costs of enforcement, and suggest that in such a setting, the new property rights model is a part of a more overarching perspective, which also includes older contributions to property rights economics.*

Key words: Ownership; Property rights; Economic organization

JEL classifications: D23, D80, L22.

1. Introduction

Considered from an economic point of view, what does it mean to own an asset? Until the publication of Coase (1960), this issue did not receive much attention from economists. However, the 1960s and 1970s witnessed intensive debate on aspects of the issue of asset ownership within what we here call 'the old property rights approach' (henceforth, the 'OPRA') (Alchian, 1977; Demsetz, 1988b; Barzel, 1997). Much of this work was taken up with identifying differences between alternative systems of property rights as alternative ownership arrangements (collective *vs.* private ownership). However, the economic meaning of asset ownership was never precisely pinned down in this literature (as outlined in Section 2).

Instead, attention has since the mid-1980s turned to the related issue of why it matters *who* owns an asset – the key concern of what is here called 'the new property

We are grateful to Yoram Barzel, Eric Brousseau, Jerome Davis, Thorbjørn Knudsen, Henrik Lando, Peter Møllgaard, Thomas Riis and two anonymous reviewers for comments on earlier drafts of this paper. Of course, all errors and obscurities are entirely our responsibility.
Kirsten Foss and Nicolai Foss, Department of Industrial Economics and Strategy, Copenhagen Business School, Howitzvej 60, DK–2000 Copenhagen F, Denmark; e-mail: kf.ivs@cbs.dk and nf.ivs@cbs.dk.

International Journal of the Economics of Business
ISSN 1357-1516 print/ISSN 1466-1829 online © 2001 Taylor & Francis Ltd
http://www.tandf.co.uk/journals
DOI: 10.1080/13571510110037555

rights approach' (henceforth, the 'NPRA') (Grossman and Hart, 1986; Hart, 1995) (see Section 3). However, as we shall argue in this paper, understanding the issue of 'why it matters who owns an asset' is made problematic by the fact that the very meaning of asset ownership is still not fully clear. More specifically, we argue that there are suppressed issues in the NPRA that relate to the meanings and functions of asset ownership. In our view, the NPRA builds on somewhat extreme assumptions, for example, that ownership is perfectly and costlessly enforceable.[1] Thus, the issue of the meaning of asset ownership under less than costless enforcement is suppressed.

Characterizing approaches as 'new' and 'old' may invoke an image of unbroken and unambiguous scientific advance. As already indicated, we consider this view false with respect to the specific approaches under consideration here. Seemingly, the NPRA has been able to resolve a number of unresolved problems that beset the OPRA, such as the central issue of what it means to own an asset. The notion of residual rights of control in the NPRA seems to offer a clear-cut answer to this. However, we shall argue that this notion amounts to side-stepping a number of important issues that the OPRA wrestled with. Among these are the problems posed for the notion of ownership of multi-attribute assets, the composite nature of ownership with respect to rights, and the distinction between the formal (legally defined) structure of ownership and the real structure, as defined partly by agents' capture of property rights. A critique informed by OPRA thus reveals the partial nature of NPRA (see Section 4). For example, we shall point out that with a broader and more realistic notion of residual rights of control one may obtain other results with respect to ownership patterns than those obtained in the NPRA. We show this by means of a simple example (Section 5). Moreover, we argue that with such a broader understanding of control rights, certain phenomena that are hard to address within the NPRA become explainable. For example, we argue that whereas the NPRA has difficulties in explaining the rationale of the employment contract (and therefore also the distinction between vertical integration and quasi-vertical integration), a broader notion of residual rights makes this possible.

Perhaps because of the absence of interaction among OPRA and NPRA writers,[2] these points have, to our knowledge, not been developed in the earlier literature. There are, however, similarities to other contributions, notably Aghion and Tirole (1997) and Holmström and Milgrom (1991, 1994). Like these writers, our aim is integrative. Thus, we are interested in making the notion of ownership more precise as well as more encompassing in order to identify more clearly the implications of ownership for economic organization.

2. Ownership and Property Rights in the 'Old' Property Rights Approach

Property Rights in Coase (1960)

The pioneering paper on the economics of property rights is conventionally and justifiably taken to be Coase (1960). In this paper, Coase examines the economic implications of the allocation of legally delineated rights (liability rights) to a subset of the total uses of an asset, namely those that have external effects on the value of other agents' abilities to exercise their use rights over assets. As a part of his critique of the Pigovian tradition in welfare economics (see Demsetz, 1996), Coase (1960: 155) notes that a reason for the failure of this tradition to come to grips fully with the externality issue lies in its 'faulty concept of a factor of production', which –

according to Coase – should be thought of, not as a physical entity but as a right to perform certain actions. These rights are property rights. Given this, private ownership is defined as the possession of 'the right to carry out a circumscribed list of actions' (*idem.*), that is, private ownership of an asset is the possession of a vector of rights to use that asset.[3] The vector of rights is circumscribed partly by legal or governmental restrictions, partly by the ability of the holder to exclude other agents from the specific uses defined by the rights. Thus, in Coase's view, ownership does not provide the owner with exclusive rights to assets, only to certain uses of the asset.

However, ownership *per se* does not appear to be what primarily interests Coase; his major concern is the allocation of use rights. In principle, this allocation is conceptually separate from the issue of ownership, since one can imagine that all possible uses (including future ones) of assets are known and can be contracted for. Thus, one can conceptually analyse the allocation of use rights without involving the notion of ownership at all, as in complete contracting theories (e.g. agency theory). Coase does not use this construct, though, but rather the zero transaction cost setting underlying the Coase theorem. In this setting, the concept of ownership and the issue of who owns an asset are truly insignificant. Even when Coase relaxes the strict zero transaction cost assumption, his interest lies more in understanding the allocative consequences of different legal delimitations of use rights than in ownership issues. Thus, a major problem left unaddressed by Coase is how much one needs to 'relax' the assumptions underlying the Coase theorem to produce a role for ownership.

Ownership in the 'Old' Property Rights Approach

Coase's paper gave rise to a spate of work on property rights and ownership (e.g. Alchian, 1977; Demsetz, 1988a,b; Alchian and Demsetz, 1972; Barzel, 1982, 1987, 1994, 1997, 1999; Cheung, 1969, 1983; Umbeck, 1981), that is, the OPRA. In retrospect, it is possible to see much of this work as concentrating on clarifying issues relating to ownership that Coase had not mentioned or had left as puzzles in the 1960 paper. These issues concern the meaning of ownership, the relationship between property rights and ownership, and the importance of legal considerations for understanding ownership.

Recall that Coase had simply thought of ownership as the possession of some vector of use rights over an asset. In itself, this raises questions such as: how much exclusivity over uses of assets is required before one qualifies as 'owner'? Moreover, Coase's understanding left unresolved the role played by other types of economic rights than use rights – such as income rights or rights to alienate the asset – in the understanding of ownership. What economic considerations determine the concentration of these types of rights in the hand of one person? Finally, what is the role played by legal considerations in the understanding of ownership; for example, is it possible (and/or desirable) completely to divorce economic and legal notions of ownership?

The OPRA literature of the 1960s and 1970s[4] only partially succeeded in giving answers to the puzzles left by Coase. Common to the various contributions to the OPRA is the overall conceptualization of property rights as social relations pertaining to the use of scarce resources and supported (enforced) by the formal laws, mores and customs of a social system (Alchian, 1977; Demsetz, 1988b) as well as by private enforcement (Umbeck, 1981; Barzel, 1997). Furthermore, the literature developed a more refined categorization of property rights, for example, introducing distinctions between use rights, income rights, rights to exclude and rights to alienate assets. Given this, the concept of ownership becomes linked to the possession of different types of property rights, so that ownership also becomes contingent on the factors that regulate the interaction among agents with respect to scarce resources and is typically used when property rights are bundled (Alchian, 1977).

However, there is still much vagueness in the OPRA literature about what truly distinguishes an owner from a non-owner. There are two main manifestations of this vagueness. The first one is ambiguity with respect to which bundles of rights one has to possess in order to be identified as owner. The second one is an ambiguity with respect to the extent to which ownership is defined by the recognition of others of a claim to ownership, that is, the extent to which exclusivity is based on a (explicit or implicit) recognition by other parties of the property rights of the owner or by the owner's own ability to maintain exclusivity.

With respect to the first type of ambiguity, it is notable that ownership tends to be defined depending on the analytical purpose. For example, Demsetz and Alchian both put much emphasis on the rights to exclude and alienate as the relevant criteria of private ownership in their work on systems of property rights, and see owners as those agents who can exercise these rights (Alchian, 1977; Demsetz, 1988b). However, they slightly change these latter criteria when they analyse the organization of the firm and corporate governance, where owners become defined as those possessing control rights (Demsetz, 1988b) or residual income rights (Alchian and Demsetz, 1972). With respect to the second ambiguity, the OPRA literature is confused on the issue of how many rights must be exclusive in order for ownership to obtain and what are the determinants of exclusivity of rights. For example, does ownership mean that the owner can exclude others from *any* use of his asset (as in Alchian, 1977), or does ownership allow for some sharing of use rights (as in Coase, 1960)?

Strategies for Dealing with the Ambiguities of Ownership

Such ambiguities have often been recognized by OPRA writers themselves. 'The meaning of full private ownership . . . is vague', Demsetz (1988c: 19) notes, although he thinks that '. . . certain rights of action loom more important than others. Exclusivity and alienabiliy are among them'. Given the complexity and ambiguity surrounding the economic notion of ownership, several strategies of clarification appear to have been explored by OPRA writers.

One is to drop the concept entirely for purposes of economic analysis (while recognizing that the concept makes perfect legal sense), and instead concentrate exclusively on property rights. This seems to be reflected in Coase's (1960) reluctance to use the concept of ownership. However, this strategy arguably runs into problems in the face of unforeseen uses of assets. In this case, there is a need for an institution that allocates these use rights. In fact, this institution is normally called private ownership.

A second strategy is to adopt a working definition of ownership as always comprising a certain minimum bundle of property rights, irrespective of time, place and institutions.[5] For example, one may argue that ownership is fundamentally defined by exclusivity and alienability. An obvious problem with this strategy is that, for example, it is unclear what is meant by exclusivity independently of institutional and historical considerations.

A third strategy, therefore, is to identify ownership with claims to exclusivity that are privately enforced and/or are enforced by various legal and non-legal institutions. This strategy, which may be associated with Umbeck (1981), makes ownership contingent on what is historically seen as constituting a recognized claim. More specifically, '. . . the abilities of individuals, or groups of individuals, to forcefully maintain exclusivity' (Umbeck, 1981: 39) are different across spatio-temporal and institutional characteristics, since they turn on positions of power and the ability to exercise force. Thus, ownership essentially becomes an expectation that an agent holds with respect to his ability to use certain resources. This view makes it clear that answering the question 'why it matters who owns an asset' must be heavily dependent upon the concrete institutions and allocations of force that define and enforce the rights of the owner – an insight that we shall make extensive use of in the following.

Barzel on Attributes and Assets

A particularly interesting OPRA contribution is represented by the work of Barzel (1982, 1987, 1994, 1997, 1999). Barzel's work is particularly useful with respect to the problematic issue of 'why it matters who owns an asset'. His central contribution, which we shall make use of in the following, is to introduce the notion of multi-attribute assets and to argue that it is more fruitful to focus on the ownership of attributes rather than of assets. Attributes are characteristics and possible uses of assets.[6] To Barzel, it is crucial that ownership in the *economic* sense pertains to the attributes of assets rather than to the assets themselves. There are two reasons for this.

The first one is that most assets have so many attributes – of which many may not be specified – that the notion of ownership of assets is vague.[7] This also explains why Barzel makes a categorical distinction between legal and economic notions of ownership. Whereas the former refers to a legally recognized holding of a title to an asset, the latter refers to those property rights over the attributes of an asset that are controlled by an agent. Nevertheless the concept of asset must remain important in economic analysis (and not just in property law). This is because it is often assets rather than attributes that are priced (because of measurement costs). Agents then may have different degrees of control over attributes of assets and thus more or less secure economic rights over the asset. Barzel (1994: 394; *emphasis in original*) explains economic rights as

> . . . an individual's net valuation, in expected terms, of the ability to directly consume the services of the asset, or to consume it indirectly through exchange. A key word is *ability.* The definition is concerned not with what people are legally entitled to do but with what they believe they can do.

However, the expected valuation of an asset depends on the attributes of the asset that one holds property rights over, so that attributes remain the fundamental unit of analysis.

The second reason for focusing on attributes rather than on assets is that Barzel's central concern is to determine the structure of ownership that will maximize the value of an asset when there are high measurement costs. High measurement costs imply that it will be efficient to leave some attributes unspecified. Allocation of ownership to such attributes takes place by means of capture. Those unspecified attributes that are captured become subject to control by agents, whereby 'control' means '. . . one's freedom to manipulate the particular unspecified attribute without making marginal payments to others' (Barzel, 1999: 5–6). The efficient pattern of ownership over the attributes of an asset is the one that minimizes uncompensated exploitation of attributes – which is a sophisticated restatement of the Coase's (1960) concern with the internalization of externalities. Relatedly, Barzel, like Coase, stresses that ownership – whether to attributes of assets or to assets themselves – is seldom fully exclusive. The refinement introduced by Barzel relative to Coase consists in adding the notion of measurement costs which explains the presence of unspecified attributes, attempts to capture these, and the institutions that constrain capture.

Although a focus on the multiple attributes of assets rather than on the assets themselves is an extremely helpful perspective, which we shall make use of later, it may be necessary to warn against completely neglecting transactions relating to assets (rather than to attributes). This is because the legal system and jurisprudence distinguishes between the law relating to contract and the law relating to ownership of assets. Moreover, the law relating to ownership is more than simply part of a low-cost enforcement institution; it is also a 'standard contract' that reduces information and communication costs and has allocative consequences for this reason. Moreover, legal ownership may also be perceived of as a property rights system in the sense that it is a low-cost way of allocating hitherto undiscovered uses of assets. For example, giving somebody legal ownership implies that he holds the legal right to future (as yet undiscovered) attributes of the asset, in the sense that the courts will not interfere with the use of the asset by the party identified as the owner.[8] As we shall see, this is a crucial point in the NPRA.

3. Ownership and Property Rights in the New Property Rights Approach

In the same way that the emergence of OPRA may conveniently and justifiably be dated to the publication of Coase (1960), the emergence of NPRA can be dated, just as conveniently and justifiably, to the publication of Grossman and Hart (1986). The approach outlined in that paper has swept economics and it is not too much off the mark to say that it defines the way the modern formal economist thinks about ownership and property rights.[9] In the following, we shall mostly refer to and rely on Hart's (1995) recent authoritative and widely cited statement of the fundamentals of the NPRA.[10]

Answers to Coase's Puzzles in the New Property Rights Approach

Recall that Coase (1960) had left unaddressed a number of issues concerning the meaning of ownership, the relationship between property rights and owner-ship, and the importance of legal considerations for understanding ownership. The OPRA was only partially successful in constructing a unified and consistent approach to these issues. There are many reasons for this limited success, such as a verbal style of theorizing, the lack of one well-defined problem that could structure analysis towards a more consistent approach, and a willingness to let definitions depend on the analytical purpose at hand. In contrast, the NPRA is explicitly formal, most of the analysis has centred on the problem of vertical integration and it has, because of its formal nature, adopted (seemingly) unambiguous definitions. This has allowed its proponents to state straightforward answers to the puzzles left by Coase.

With respect to the meaning of ownership and how it relates to property rights, the central idea in NPRA is the distinction between specific rights of control and residual rights of control. The former can be delineated and directly allocated through contractual means, whereas the latter is obtained through the legal ownership of assets and implies the '. . . right to decide usages of the asset in uncontracted-for contingencies' (Hart 1996: 371). However, residual rights to control encompass not only the rights to use assets, but also to '. . . decide when or even whether to sell the asset' (Hart, 1995: 65). In NPRA, ownership is defined as the legally enforced possession of an asset. The economic importance of ownership stems from the owner's ability to exercise residual rights of control over the assets. This economic conception is thus explicitly derived from the juristic conception.[11] In other words, the function of ownership is to allocate residual rights of control. Thus, the meaning of ownership, and its relation to property rights and the legal system are addressed in a straightforward manner.

As we shall later argue, however, reflection and evidence suggest that the notion of residual rights of control is not so unambiguous after all; in actuality, the specific meaning that NPRA writers attach to the concept is strongly dependent on background institutions, notably the ability to enforce ownership costlessly. This has implications for the economic understanding of the allocation of ownership, as we shall later show. Also, the limitations of the NPRA with respect to explaining legal ownership should be clearly understood. The NPRA is not a law and economics theory of the legal institution of ownership *per se*, but rather a theory of the efficient allocation of ownership. Before we enter into a more sustained critical discussion of the NPRA, we need more fully to characterize the NPRA.

Complete and Incomplete Contracts and Economic Organization

A crucial distinction in the NPRA is the distinction between complete and incomplete contracts, a distinction that was never made explicit in the OPRA.[12] To make clear the importance of this distinction has been one of the major analytical strengths of the NPRA. In the literature, two causes of contractual incompleteness are emphasized. One is a bounded rationality interpretation, according to which some future states cannot be anticipated, although the agents may hold a probability distribution over the pay-offs from their relation (Grossman and Hart, 1986).[13] Alternatively, all states are in fact anticipated, but for some reason agents are unable to specify their plans or the nature of these states in such a way that a court can ascertain whether a certain plan was carried out or a state materialized. The contract is left incomplete for this reason (Hart and Moore, 1990).

According to NPRA writers, incompleteness of contracts makes it possible to understand the economic function of ownership. The argument is that if one accepts that ownership confers residual rights to control, it must follow that it is only possible to understand the economic consequences of ownership under incomplete contracting,[14] for the basic reason that residual rights of control are only defined when this kind of contracting obtains.[15] In the terminology that we use here, these control rights refer to the holder's ability to manipulate unspecified attributes *in the future* without making marginal payments to others. Note, however, that there is no mention in the NPRA of the holder's ability to manipulate unspecified attributes without making marginal payments to others in a setting where all – present and future – contingencies and attributes are known, but where there may be costs of measurement and enforcement (as in Demsetz, 1988c; Holmström and Milgrom, 1991; Barzel, 1999). We shall later focus on this possibility by means of an example.

The implication of the NPRA reasoning is that theories that are based on a complete contract logic, such as formal agency theory, cannot explain either the allocation of ownership over asset, or the owner of an asset.[16] An important further implication is that these theories cannot address the issue of the boundaries of the firm, the main issue of concern of the NPRA. In contrast, Hart argues that the NPRA can unambigiously define *the* owner of an asset. This is particularly important for the analysis of the boundaries of the firm.

The Basic NPRA Set-up

Historically and conceptually, the NPRA has been developed in the context of the theory of the firm, more precisely the analysis of the vertical boundaries of the firm (Grossman and Hart, 1986; Demsetz, 1998). Applied to firms, the approach begins from the idea that ownership of non-human assets is what defines the firm. Thus if two different assets are owned by one person, we are dealing with one firm, whereas if the same two assets are owned by different persons, we are dealing with two different firms. The assets that are relevant here are non-human assets, since human assets are non-alienable. The importance of non-human assets derives from their (potential) function as bargaining levers in situations that are not covered by contract. This may be crucially important in situations where the parties have invested in specific assets – notably, investments in the parties' own human capital – and these assets are complementary to specific non-human assets. Crucially, the parties' investments in human assets are assumed to be non-contractible.

All bargaining that follows after the parties have made their investments in human assets is assumed to be efficient (in contrast to, e.g. Williamson, 1985). Therefore, the model revolves around the effect of ownership of non-human assets on the incentives to invest in human assets. Specifically, bargaining determines the allocation of returns from investments, so that each party gets his opportunity cost plus a share (they are assumed to share 50:50) of the (verifiable) profit stream. Since in this set-up individual returns will differ from social returns, and agents are sufficiently far-sighted to foresee this, investments will be inefficient. It is possible to influence the investment of one of the parties positively by reallocating ownership rights to non-human assets. A reallocation of ownership of physical assets alters the parties' opportunity costs of non-cooperation (the status quo point) after the specific investments have been made, and thus the expected payoffs from the investments.[17] However, this comes only at the cost of reducing one of the parties' investment incentives (excepting the situation in which the parties' marginal costs of investment are equal). This trade-off determines allocation of ownership and hence the efficient boundaries of the firm. Thus, the central issue is why it matters who owns an asset or a bundle of assets. Underlying this is that it is possible unambiguously to identify *the* owner of an asset.

4. Some Problems in the New Property Rights Approach

In this section, we shall argue that the NPRA claim of being able unambiguously to identify *the* owner of an asset is strongly dependent on the specific analytical set-up adopted by most NPRA writers.[18] This set-up is characterized by an implicit assumption of zero cost enforcement of ownership (i.e. residual rights of control) and thus full exclusivity in the use of assets. In other words, the NPRA implicitly black-boxes part of the institutional environment (Brousseau and Fares, 1998). In more realistic settings, characterized by positive costs of enforcement, measurement costs and multi-attribute assets (but not necessarily asymmetric information among the contractual parties), it may be more problematic to single out *an* owner of an asset. As we shall point out, the rather extreme set-ups that characterize most NPRA models also account for their inability to discriminate between a number of ownership arrangements, such as vertical quasi-integration and vertical integration.

The Notion of Residual Rights of Control

At first glance the NPRA notion of residual rights of control appears to be a conceptual sword that cuts through the Gordian knot of the meaning of ownership in the literature. However, on closer inspection the concept turns out not to be completely unambiguous. We here discuss whether residual rights of control unambiguously identify an owner. We shall argue that this depends on the divisibility and enforceability of these rights. Consider the divisibility issue first.

In a discussion of the connection between ownership, residual control rights and residual income rights, Hart (1995: 63–66) notes that the latter is '. . . not a very robust or interesting theoretical concept' (1995: 64).[19] The reason given is that residual income rights are not well defined since they can easily be divided which residual control rights cannot 'in the same way' (p. 64n). It is not clear what he has in mind here, but presumably Hart means that it is non-sensical to allocate residual rights of control *ex ante* between parties. For example, it does not make sense to *ex ante* allocate 80% of the residual rights control to one party (which of course is possible in the case of residual income rights).

However, this view neglects that assets have many attributes – and formal control over such attributes may be divided. For example, one may imagine joint ownership of a taxicab, where one chauffeur drives it on Monday to Wednesday (one attribute), and the other one drives it from Wednesday to Sunday (another attribute), both having full rights to the use of the asset within certain pre-negotiated contractual stipulations. Timesharing of condominiums is another quite prevalent phenomenon that also illustrates the division of control over attributes. Based on this alone, it is not easy to say who is the 'true' owner.

However, Hart has a way out. He admits that residual rights of control are in fact divisible, for example, when he talks about 'forms of intermediate ownership' (p. 61).[20] But he is quick to add that included in the notion of residual rights to control are also the rights to veto the use of an asset and to alienate that asset – and *these* rights are not divisible. In the context of the example above, one of the taxi drivers has thus got to be the ultimate owner. Even this will not do, however, as Hart's own work on co-operatives indicates (Hart and Moore, 1994). In a co-operative (or partnership), control is exercised by means of majority rule. But this implies that no single agent or group of agents can have a veto. In turn this means that if ownership is in fact identical to the right to veto, the ownership of a co-operative may be completely fleeting.

A final problem concerns the claim in the NPRA that residual rights of control are only indirectly tradable through the exchange of ownership titles. But this may not be the case in certain contexts (cf. also Demsetz, 1998). For example, leasing on a long-term basis may effectively be identical to obtaining ownership, particularly if the leasing arrangement lasts through the economic lifetime of the asset (Wiggins, 1991: 610n) or if the arrangement comes with a first-buy clause.

Asymmetric Treatment of Enforcement

In a number of contributions to the OPRA, there is an explicit distinction between the legal formal title to assets and the economic rights to those assets (e.g. Coase, 1960; Alchian, 1977; Barzel, 1997). In the presence of costs of measurement and enforcement, this distinction is important for *any* asset, whether human capital assets or non-human capital assets. While there is thus a symmetric treatment of the two-asset categories in the OPRA, the treatment in NPRA is asymmetric. This is because ownership to, and contracts over, physical assets are supposed to be fully and costlessly enforced by the legal system, whereas contracts involving investments in human capital are assumed to be completely unenforceable because of an asserted non-verifiability. Thus, in the NPRA approach there is only one clearly identified possibility of capture, namely with respect to capturing other parties' investments in their own human capital. However, in actuality there are other capture possibilities – because of the simultaneous presence of high costs of enforcement and multi-attribute assets – but these are assumed away in the NPRA by the assumption of costless enforcement.

Some Empirical Anomalies

The neglect in the NPRA of the multi-attribute nature of assets and of positive measurement and enforcement costs means that the NPRA has difficulties coming to grips with a number of real-world phenomena. Among these is the difference between quasi-vertical integration and full integration, a distinction that relates to the understanding of the employment contract.

Quasi-vertical integration is the ownership arrangement of one firm owning a number of the specific assets used by, for example, its supplier. Under *full integration* the manager of the supplier is turned into an employee of the firm. However, the economic rationales behind these two ownership arrangements are hard to distinguish in the NPRA. Note that quasi-vertical integration may be seen as an attempt to protect against hold-up on the part of the supplier – that is, exactly what vertical integration is supposed to do. Moreover, note that on the NPRA logic (Hart and Moore, 1990; Hart, 1995, 1996), the manager–owner of the supplier firm in a quasi-vertical integration relation has decreased incentives to invest in his human capital, *exactly* as if he had been turned into an employee of the firm. The relative bargaining positions of the parties with respect to sharing the joint surplus from their relation would appear to be the same under the two arrangements (*ceteris paribus*).

As this indicates, it is difficult to explain *the employment contract* using the NPRA; in fact, the existence of that contract is simply taken for granted in the NPRA. Hart (1995: 71) refers to the idea that a benefit of the employment contract is that carrying out activities within a firm means that information may be exchanged more readily. The reason, Hart speculates, is that the employer's control over assets gives him bargaining power over the employee, which implies that the employee may have an incentive to establish himself as reliable, hence, valuable to the employer and thus possibly increasing his future wage. However, one may counter that quasi-vertical integration may accomplish exactly the same, since ownership of the specific assets of another firm would have the same effect on information revelation. The NPRA approach may explain authority, but it does not explain the employment contract.

The inability of the NPRA to come to grips with these phenomena has to do with its neglect of the multi-attribute nature of assets in a setting with measurement and enforcement cost (where the latter depends on the institutional environment). In such a setting, an agent may engage in capture of unspecified attributes of assets that goes beyond the types of capture investigated by the NPRA, namely under-investment in human capital or hold-up. Making telephone calls to friends in far-away countries, using company cars for holiday trips, withholding effort, inefficiently using or maintaining assets, etc., are all examples of capture that cannot easily be pressed into the NPRA categories of hold-up or under-investment in human capital. However, such activities may be essential for discriminating between vertical integration and quasi-vertical integration, that is, explaining the employment contract.

It may be argued that invoking these examples means switching to an asymmetric information (agency) setting. This need not be the case, however. Even in a symmetrical information setting capture will take place, since even here resources will have to be expended on verifying actions to third parties or estimating economic consequences of capture that are unknown to all parties. Minimizing resources expended on preventing capture (i.e. measurement and enforcement costs) requires that measurement takes place at minimum cost. This may, however, depend on whether measurement takes place within the frame of an employment contract or within the frame of a contract between independent parties. The employment contract confers to the employer the right to monitor and sanction the employee in ways that for legal reasons cannot be applied to an independent contractor. This means that the employer is in a better position to choose where and when to monitor the exercise of capture. Thus, the employment contract will be chosen when it minimizes the costs of measuring capture.[21] However, this conclusion can only be reached if explicit allowance is made for that part of the institutional environment that regulates the employment relation.

Costs of measuring are likely to be some positive function of the number of attributes of the relevant assets, given a certain measurement technology. Multi-attribute assets tend to imply the presence of many margins of substitution (Demsetz, 1988c; Barzel, 1997), some of which may not be specified *ex ante* by the contractors. In a broader context, Demsetz (1988c: 18) points out that '[t]he general conclusion is that constraining the ability of persons to exercise specific rights of ownership causes them to rely in greater degree on substitute margins in their attempt to maximize utility'. Applied to the issue of the choice between vertical integration and quasi-integration, this implies that multi-attribute assets tend to produce a bias towards the employment contract (cf. also Holmström and Milgrom, 1991, 1994). This is due to the adaptability advantage of the employment contract. An employer's constraining of an employee's abilities to exercise control in some directions is likely to result in the employee substituting towards hitherto unspecified margins. The employment contract allows for adaptive handling of such behaviour.[22]

An interpretation of the above reasoning is that making room for agents' capture of property rights over unspecified attributes in a setting characterized by multi-attribute assets and positive costs of measurement and enforcement adds to the explanatory power of the NPRA framework. We pursue this further in the following section.

5. Towards a Broader Understanding of Ownership Patterns

In the preceding pages, we have implicitly extended the notion of residual rights of control. In the NPRA, these are rights to decide usages of assets in future, uncontracted-for contingencies, and are derived from the legal ownership of assets. The rights of ownership of these assets are perfectly enforced. As we have pointed out, assuming perfect enforcement is tantamount to making the notion of asset ownership completely dependent on a specific, and – we think – unrealistic institutional set-up.

However, a more realistic setting characterized by less than perfect enforcement, multi-attribute assets and measurement costs must imply a broader notion of residual rights of control. This is because in such a setting a number of attributes of assets are rationally left unspecified and possibly also unenforced. Hence, they will be subject to capture attempts, that is, attempts at being able to acquire and manipulate the services of various attributes without compensating others on the margin. Such capture may well go beyond the type of capture treated in the NPRA where capture only relates to the hold-up problem. In a more realistic setting, minimizing the costs due to capture may help determine ownership patterns in a way that is at variance with the NPRA. In the latter, the costs of capture are only represented by inefficient investments. However, there are other costs of capture, such as dissipation of wealth (Barzel, 1997). In the following example, we construct a stylized setting, in which these costs are also included and help determine ownership patterns.

An Example

Consider a person, N, who considers whether to make a specific and non-contractible investment in his human capital (repair skills) that makes his costs of repairing three specific but identical cars lower than the prevailing market price of car repair.[23] There are three potential drivers, A, B and C of the specific cars. Moreover, we assume that N's investment is complementary to the human capital investments undertaken by A, B and C in such a way that N prefers to have the investing drivers as customers and the investing drivers prefer to have N repairing the cars.[24] Thus, there are potential gains from trade. We also assume that N's marginal investment costs are much greater than the costs of A, B and C.

This example stays close to the basic NPRA set-up and, according to NPRA logic, efficiency dictates that, in the example, ownership should be allocated in such a way that N assumes ownership of the cars. Otherwise he will be held up by the owner(s) of the cars in the sense that they will share the rents on N's investments in accordance with the Nash bargaining solution. However, we shall argue that a different ownership pattern may result if provision is made for the possibility that A, B and C can capture unspecified valued attributes of the cars when N cannot perfectly verify such capture.

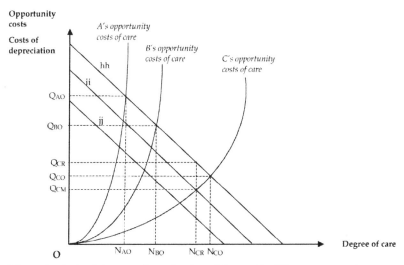

Figure 1. Optimal degrees of care for three drivers with different opportunity costs.

The efficient rationing of the use of durable assets, such as the three cars, requires not only that they are paid their marginal products, but also that they are paid for use-induced depreciation. Use-induced depreciation may take place with respect to a number of attributes of the car. N has two options of recovering use-induced depreciation, namely: (1) to charge an *ex ante* price that is independent of the actual (*ex post*) depreciation; or (2) to negotiate *ex post* a charge reflecting the depreciation. The problem with the first option is that of moral hazard, while the problem with the second option is one of strategic behaviour under bargaining. Remedying both problems requires costly verification of the actual depreciation.[25]

Assume, realistically, that it is costly to verify the depreciation of cars after they have been used.[26] This implies that an owner who rents out the cars will confront costs that can be avoided by the owner/driver. Because of his opportunity costs of time, an owner who rents out cars will rationally choose not to verify the depreciation of some attributes. Hence, he will not price these. Assume also that it is less costly to drive carelessly than to drive carefully, because careless driving reduces driving time. This means that while an owner/driver must trade off time against depreciation and safety, the renter/driver must only trade off time against safety.[27]

We shall here concentrate on the situation where N is owner and A, B and C are renter/drivers, and examine whether this ownership pattern is efficient. Consider Figure 1.

The figure shows the different opportunity cost schedules of the three drivers. Driver A has the highest opportunity costs of careful driving while driver C has the lowest opportunity costs of careful driving. Also shown in the figure are three cost lines. The *hh* line corresponds to the cost-schedule confronted by a hypothetical owner/driver if N has not invested in his human capital or if the owner/driver drives a non-specific car. This schedule reflects the market price for repair services for different degrees of care. For example, if driver A exercises the degree of care corresponding to N_{AO}, he will impose a depreciation on the car that can be measured by the costs of remedying that depreciation through repairing the car by others than N (i.e. Q_{AO}). The opportunity cost schedules of A, B and C as owner/drivers cross this schedule at the points (Q_{AO}, N_{AO}), (Q_{BO}, N_{BO}) and (Q_{CO}, N_{CO}). These points represent A, B and C's optimal trade-offs between the degree of care they exercise and the costs of depreciation.

The cost line, jj corresponds to the cost schedule of repairing specific cars that N confronts after having made a specific investment in his human capital and with A, B and C as customers. It is closer to the origin than the hh line, because the investment reduces N's cost of repairing the specific cars. For a given degree of care, the vertical distance between the hh line and the jj line represents the rents from N's human capital investment if N were an owner and if there were no costs of verifying depreciation. This corresponds to the basic set-up in NPRA (e.g. Hart, 1995). However, when he rents out the cars, he will not perfectly verify depreciation and this decreases the rents he can appropriate. This is different relative to the basic NPRA set-up.

The cost line, ii represents the market price of repairing the depreciation N chooses to detect. For high degrees of care, he will choose to verify most of the depreciation. The vertical distance between the ii and the hh line indicates (for any degree of care) the amount of rent from N's human capital investment that the driver/renter captures. The driver/renter can capture this rent because N chooses not to verify the depreciation of certain attributes.[28] The vertical distance between the ii and jj lines indicates (for any degree of care) the rent on N's own human capital investment that he can capture as an owner when renting out the cars. We make the strong assumption that this line also shows the division of rents between N and A, B and C, respectively, if they are owners of the specific cars. That is, it shows A, B and C's abilities to hold-up N for half of the rents on specific investment (for each repair service). This also corresponds to the basic NPRA set-up. Given this set-up, what is the optimal ownership pattern? In particular, will N rationally choose to own all specific cars. In passing, we note that according to NPRA logic, he should own them all.

Consider Figure 1 again. N wishes to extract the maximum rents from his investment. His incentives to invest is influenced by how much rent he can extract, as in the NPRA. This means that he wishes the rental price of cars to reflect as much as possible the costs of depreciation. However, the price cannot exceed the opportunity cost to an owner/driver of owning a non-specific car, that is, Q_{AO}, Q_{BO} and Q_{CO} in Figure 1 (where A, B and C are indifferent between owning a non-specific car and renting a specific car). However, N cannot reach these three points because of the costs of verifying depreciation, and will accordingly charge for the depreciation at points that lie below these points.

To find out what are the consequences of his inability to perfectly measure depreciation, consider driver/renter C in Figure 1. In a first-best world of zero costs of verification, total rents accruing to N would be equal to the vertical distance between hh and ii, measured at N_{CO} that is, the difference between the market cost of repair and N's cost of repair. However, given non-zero costs of verification, N will charge C a rental price that reflects the market price of repairing the *verified* depreciation (Q_{CM}). Given this, C will adjust his exercise of care accordingly (i.e. choose N_{CR}). This set of choices will induce a sharing of rents equal to that obtaining if C owns the specific car. Quite similar operations may be performed with respect to driver A and C.

Recall from Figure 1 that Q_{CO} is the charge that leaves C indifferent between being an owner and being a renter, when he is paying the full marginal costs for the depreciation he imposes on the car. Thus, if C is a renter, N can at most choose a mark-up on the rental services amounting to $Q_{CO}-Q_{CM}$. This mark-up may reflect both measurement costs and N's attempt to extract more rents of the driver/renters.

As the opportunity-cost schedules of the drives are drawn in Figure 1, N can impose a higher mark-up on B and an even higher one on A, leaving them indifferent between being an owner of a non-specific car and being a renter of a specific car. N's optimization problem is to choose the mark-up that maximizes the rent he extracts from all drivers. If N chooses a too high a mark-up, he will induce one or more of the drivers to switch to non-specific cars, making him loose rents on repair services. Therefore, it will be efficient for N to let these drivers own a specific car, continue to repair their cars and allow them to extract half of the rents on his investment.[29] An equilibrium may then exist in which A and B are renter/drivers and C is an owner/driver. This is because A and B's gains from not being fully marginally charged for the depreciation they impose on the car they drive is not overwhelmed by the mark-up.

Implications and Discussion

The above example has shown that capture, costly measurement (verification) and different types of individuals (A, B and C) may explain who owns an asset. Moreover, although the example stays very close to the basic NPRA set-up, it tells a story that contradicts the NPRA prediction that an individual who undertakes a human asset investment that is specific to some physical assets should also be the owner of those assets. In the example, ownership may thus fall in the hands of C rather than N, not in order to create threat points under *ex post* bargaining and avoid inefficient (i.e. third-best) investments, but in order to avoid a mark-up. Ultimately, the mark-up arises as a consequence of the driver/renters' capture of unspecified use rights over the car. This leads to depreciation of the cars, costly attempts to verify this depreciation on the part of N, and a mark-up that is uniform over the driver/renters because of N's costs of verifying depreciation.

Note that in the example there is a link between the economic function of ownership and the legal system. This link is established through the notion of costly verification, although in a way that differs from the NPRA. Costly verification influences who owns an asset, not because it creates a hold-up problem (as in the NPRA), but because it makes it costly to charge a correct marginal price of rental services.

Although ownership is structured to minimize capture, the example thus suggests that this structuring can take place in ways that differ from the NPRA model. In turn this suggests that the NPRA model is a special case of a more encompassing model of ownership – yet to be fully formally developed – in which the notion of capture of unspecified attributes also include those that are left unspecified due to measurement costs. To illustrate the partial nature of the basic NPRA set-up, NPRA conclusions may be derived from the basic setting of the above example. Recall that NPRA reasoning would lead to the conclusion that N should own all cars. In the context of the example, this requires that an incentive contract is made between the owner and the renters of the cars. The contract makes the charge contingent on the verified depreciation. Moreover, the verification of all attributes has to be sufficiently precisely so that an agent has a sufficient belief that he will be charged a correct rent. Otherwise, some of the renter/drivers may still prefer to be owners.

In their multi-task agency models, Holmström and Milgrom (1991, 1994) arrive at conclusions that are somewhat related to the ones above. What they call 'multi-tasking' is thus one representation of the multi-attribute nature of many assets. Relatedly, they also stress measurement costs. However, in contrast to this paper, they assume risk-aversion on the part of agents and asymmetric information. We only assume risk-neutrality and a certain degree of non-verifiability. Most importantly, however, in the Holmström and Milgrom models, capture is seen as function of measurement errors on signals on effort whereas in our example, capture is a function of purposefully leaving certain attributes unspecified. This means that in our example an incentive contract will not diminish the amount of capture.

6. Conclusion

The notion of asset ownership is one of the most vexing ones in economics. This is partly because the notion is highly context-specific and hard to discuss in isolation from legal considerations (Demsetz, 1998). This has produced a certain amount of confusion. On this background, it is hardly surprising that the NPRA has emerged as a dominant approach to the study of ownership and the economics of organization. It is seen (and advertised) as a clear formal approach that unambiguously defines the notion of asset ownership and builds a theory of economic organization on that basis.

However, in this paper, we have argued that the clarity of the NPRA is acquired at the cost of narrowness and a certain lack of explanatory power – a critique that we have developed by viewing NPRA ideas through a lens provided by the OPRA. Specifically, we have argued that the NPRA conceptualization of ownership as fully enforceable residual rights of control is too narrow with respect to identifying the nature and function of ownership. The NPRA neglects the difference between the legally defined structure of ownership (the holding of titles to assets) and the structure of ownership over attributes of assets that emerges from agents' capture. This also means that ownership only partakes of the role of a bargaining chip in situations of bilateral monopoly and the role played by ownership of minimizing the costs of capture is only partially reflected in the NPRA.

A possible implication is that, in spite of its clarity and elegance, the NPRA is not an unambiguous scientific advance over the OPRA. Another implication is that there is room for cross-fertilization between the OPRA and the NPRA.

Notes

1. The methodological aspects of this are treated in greater detail in Brousseau and Fares (1998) and Foss and Foss (2000).
2. Werin and Wijkander (1992) appear to be the sole exception.
3. In the following, we shall simply treat 'private ownership' and 'ownership' as synonymous, unless otherwise stated.
4. Furubotn and Pejovich (1972) is a classical overview of the early research.
5. The economic reason for the existence of such a bundle can be found in the existence of transaction costs which imply that '. . . the partitioned rights will be re-aggregated into more convenient clusters of rights' (Alchian, 1977: 134).

6. Thus, although Barzel does not mention this, the notion of 'attributes' also covers contingent goods, such as the use of an umbrella at noon on 16 April 2001 in Cambridge if it rains.

7. This is related to Demsetz's point that the notion of 'full private ownership' over assets is 'vague', and his argument that '[i]n one sense, it must always remain so, for there is an infinity of potential rights of actions that can be owned . . . It is impossible to describe the complete set of rights that are potentially ownable' (Demsetz, 1988c: 19).

8. Thanks to Thomas Riis and an anonymous reviewer for stressing this point.

9. In addition to the issues traditionally considered in the theory of the firm – such as the boundaries of the firm – the NPRA has been applied to, for example, corporate finance (Hart, 1995), corporate governance, the organization of production in public versus private firms, and the boundaries of knowledge-intensive firms (Brynjolfsson, 1994). Moreover, the approach is continuously being refined (notably Rabin, 1993; Farrell and Gibbons, 1995; Nöldeke and Schmidt, 1995; Hart and Moore, 1998; Rajan and Zingales, 1998), and extended, for example, combined with ideas from principal–agent theory (Holmström and Milgrom, 1991, 1994).

10. To the best of our knowledge and understanding, our points also apply to more formal statements of the NPRA, such as Grossman and Hart (1986), Hart and Moore (1990, 1994, 1998), Rajan and Zingales (1998).

11. In support of this, the noted American legal scholar and judge, Oliver Wendell Holmes is quoted (in Hart, 1995: 30n): 'But what are the rights of ownership? They are substantially the same as those incident to possession. Within the limits prescribed by policy, the owner is allowed to exercise his natural powers over the subject-matter uninterfered with, and is more or less protected in excluding other people from such interference. The owner is allowed to exclude all, and is accountable to no one.'

12. Although Coase (1937) had of course focused on incomplete contracts.

13. For a critique of this, see Kreps (1996).

14. However, this does not mean that ownership as a legal category cannot exist under complete contracting.

15. Incomplete contracting implies that some actions and payments will have to be determined *ex post*. The difference between complete and incomplete contracting also has to do with the role of the court. In complete contracting theories, courts are assumed to enforce the original agreement, and ordering is efficacious, even if all information may not be available to the court. This is in contrast to the incomplete contracting approach where the incompleteness of contracts introduces opportunities for recontracting and where court enforcement of the original terms would leave gains from trade unrealized given the information available to courts at the time performance takes place.

16. Complete contracting obtains when contracts are such that they have '. . . the relevant decisions (transfer, trade, etc.) depend on all verifiable variables, including possible announcements by the parties (concerning their valuation, costs, etc.)' (Tirole, 1988: 29n). In such a contracting regime, there will be no need for residual rights of control. Thus, Hart (1995: 5) argues that '. . .[i]f contracting costs are zero, we can sign a rental agreement that is as effective as a change in ownership. In particular, the rental contract can specify exactly what I can do with the machine, when I can have access to it, what happens if the machine breaks down, what rights you have to use the machine, and so on. Given this, however, it is unclear why changes in asset ownership ever need take place.' Note how this quotation indicates that the NPRA is really a theory of the allocation of ownership in a setting where ownership is a perfectly well-defined concept. This may be contrasted with the analysis of the emergence of the institution of ownership in, for example, Umbeck (1981).

17. However, there are certain problems of defining all relevant opportunity costs in an incomplete contract world. Contractual incompleteness may be due to high costs of specifying and verifying certain uses of assets, the lack of ability to foresee all possible uses of assets, or the lack of ability to foresee all future contingencies. In the two latter cases, the opportunity cost of non-corporation may be ill-defined, simply because future contingencies may change what are the best alternative uses of assets and these contingencies may not be foreseen. Thus, opportunity costs may change as new opportunities or contingencies become apparent and change the bargaining power of the parties and the value to the parties of ownership over assets. However, this is not part of the NPRA approach.

18. In his review of Hart (1995), Demsetz (1998: 449; emphasis in original) also notes that 'Hart writes as though he thinks that *asset* ownership is an unambiguous concept'.

19. Hart's specific reasoning on this is not easy to follow, however. He argues that '[g]iven that profit-sharing contracts are not in principle costly to write if profits are verifiable (and it is unclear how residual income is to be allocated if profits are not verifiable), the conclusion is that residual income may not be a very robust or interesting theoretical concept' (1995: 63–64). This would seem to be a *non sequitur*.

20. In this connection he refers to delegation (citing Aghion and Tirole, 1997).
21. This can be interpreted in an agency theory framework (Holmstrom and Milgrom, 1991, 1994) as a reduction in the error in the signals of effort that agents produce in different tasks due to more effective monitoring in employment relationships.
22. This is not to say that this is in any way the full explanation of the employment contract. Other considerations, such as bargaining and communication costs, are also relevant.
23. For example, we may assume that *N* specializes in repairing racing cars. However, he still preserves outside options, since he can continue to repair ordinary cars, although his productivity in these options is not improved. Thus, his threat points is unchanged by his human capital investment.
24. *A, B* and *C* still preserve the option of driving non-specific cars or have their specific cars repaired by another mechanic than *N*, but their utility from these outside options is not improved by their human capital investments. Thus, their threat points are unchanged by their human capital investments. To simplify the example, we also assume that *A, B* and *C*'s marginal benefits of investing in their human capital are equal.
25. We abstract from reputation effects and effects from repeated interaction. For example, one may assume that only *A, B* and *C* can drive the cars and that the model is a finite horizon one.
26. We regard costs of verifying performance and contractual compliance as part of measurement costs.
27. Thanks to an anonymous reviewer for pointing this out.
28. We simplify by assuming that the distance between *hh* and *ii* is the same for any degree of care (and therefore for both driver/renters). A possible interpretation is that certain attributes are inherently more difficult to verify than others and therefore will be left unverified for any degree of care (and type of driver/renter). A possible (self-experienced) example concerns minor scratches on rental cars in Palermo, Sicily, where rental firms apparently expect any car to be harmed in this way, making verifiability particularly costly. One is thus not charged for minor scratches.
29. We assume that wealth constraints are absent.

References

Aghion, P. and Tirole, J., "Formal and Real Authority in Organization," *Journal of Political Economy*, 1997, 105, pp. 1–29.
Alchian, A.A., "Some Economics of Property Rights," in A.A. Alchian, *Economic Forces at Work*, Indianapolis: Liberty Press, 1977 [paper originally published 1965].
Alchian, A.A. and Demsetz, H., "Production, Information Costs, and Economic Organization," *American Economic Review*, 1972, 62, pp. 772–95.
Barzel, Y., "Measurement Costs and the Organization of Markets," *Journal of Law and Economics*, 1982, 25, pp. 27–48.
Barzel, Y., "The Entrepreneur's Reward for Self-Policing," *Economic Inquiry*, 1987, 25, pp. 103–16.
Barzel, Y., "The Capture of Wealth by Monopolists and the Protection of Property Rights," *International Review of Law and Economics*, 1994, 14, pp. 393–409.
Barzel, Y., *Economic Analysis of Property Rights*, 2nd edn. Cambridge: Cambridge University Press, 1997.
Barzel, Y., "Transaction Costs and Contract Choice," unpublished manuscript, 1999.
Brousseau, E. and Fares, M., "Incomplete Contracts and Governance Structures," unpublished manuscript, 1998.
Brynjolfsson, E., "Information Assets, Technology, and Organization," *Management Science*, 1994, 40, pp. 1645–62.
Cheung, S.N.S., "Transaction Costs, Risk Aversion, and the Choice of Contractual Arrangements," *Journal of Law and Economics*, 1969, 12, pp. 23–42.
Cheung, S.S.N., "The Contractual Nature of the Firm," *Journal of Law and Economics*, 1983, 26, pp. 1–22.
Coase, R. H., "The Nature of the Firm," *Economica*, 1937, 4, pp. 386–405.
Coase, R.H., "The Problem of Social Cost," *Journal of Law and Economics*, 1960, 3, pp. 1–44.
Demsetz, H., "The Exchange and Enforcement of Property Rights," in H. Demsetz, *Ownership, Control, and the Firm.* Oxford: Basil Blackwell, 1988a [paper originally published in 1964].
Demsetz, H., "Toward a Theory of Property Rights," in H. Demsetz, *Ownership, Control, and the Firm.* Oxford: Basil Blackwell, 1988b [paper originally published in 1967].
Demsetz, H., "A Framework for the Study of Ownership," in H. Demsetz, *Ownership, Control, and the Firm.* Oxford: Basil Blackwell, 1988c.

Demsetz, H., "The Core Disagreement Between Pigou, the Profession, and Coase in the Analyses of the Externality Question," *European Journal of Political Economy*, 1996, 12, pp. 565–80.

Demsetz, H., "Review: Oliver Hart, "Firms, Contracts, and Financial Structure'," *Journal of Political Economy*, 1998, 106, pp. 446–52.

Foss, K. and Foss, N., "Theoretical Isolation in Contract Economics," *Journal of Economic Methodology*, 2000, 7, pp. 313–39.

Furubotn, E.G. and Pejovich, S., "Property Rights and Economic Theory: A Survey of Recent Literature," *Journal of Economic Literature*, 1972, 10, pp. 1137–62.

Grossman, S. and Hart, O., "The Costs and Benefits of Ownership: A Theory of Lateral and Vertical Integration," *Journal of Political Economy*, 1986, 94, pp. 691–719.

Hart, O., *Firms, Contracts and Financial Structure*. Oxford: Clarendon Press, 1995.

Hart, O., "An Economist's View of Authority," *Rationality and Society*, 1996, 8, pp. 371–86.

Hart, O. and Moore, J., "Property Rights and the Nature of the Firm," *Journal of Political Economy*, 1990, 98, pp. 1119–58.

Hart, O. and Moore, J., "The Governance of Exchanges: Members' Cooperatives Versus Outside Ownership," Mimeo, Harvard University, 1994.

Hart, O. and Moore, J., "Foundations of Incomplete Contracts," Working paper, Department of Economics, Harvard University, 1998.

Holmström, B. and Milgrom, P., "Multitask Principal–Agent Analyses: Incentive Contracts, Asset Ownership, and Job Design," *Journal of Law, Economics, and Organization*, 1991, 7, pp. 24–52.

Holmström, B. and Milgrom, P., "The Firm as an Incentive System," *American Economic Review*, 1994, 84, pp. 972–91.

Kreps, D.M., "Markets and Hierarchies and (Mathematical) Economic Theory," *Industrial and Corporate Change*, 1996, 5, pp. 561–96.

Nöldeke, G. and Schmidt, K.M., "Option Contracts and Renegotiation: A Solution to the Hold-Up Problem," *Rand Journal of Economics*, 1995, 26, pp. 163–79.

Rabin, M., "Information and the Control of Productive Assets," *Journal of Law, Economics, and Organization*, 1993, 9, pp. 51–76.

Rajan, R.G. and Zingales, L., "Power in a Theory of the Firm," *Quarterly Journal of Economics*, 1998, 112, pp. 387–432.

Tirole, J., *The Theory of Industrial Organization*. Cambridge, MA: MIT Press, 1988.

Umbeck, J., "Might Makes Rights: A Theory of the Formation and Initial Distribution of Property Rights," *Economic Inquiry*, 1981, 19, pp. 38–59.

Werin, L. and Wijkander, H., eds, *Contract Economics*. Oxford: Blackwell, 1992.

Wiggins, S.N., "The Economics of the Firm and Contracts: A Selective Survey," *Journal of Institutional and Theoretical Economics*, 1991, 147, pp. 603–61.

Williamson, O.E., *The Economic Institutions of Capitalism*. New York: The Free Press, 1985.

[14]

Strategic Management Journal
Strat. Mgmt. J., **26**: 541–553 (2005)
Published online in Wiley InterScience (www.interscience.wiley.com). DOI: 10.1002/smj.465

RESOURCES AND TRANSACTION COSTS: HOW PROPERTY RIGHTS ECONOMICS FURTHERS THE RESOURCE-BASED VIEW

KIRSTEN FOSS[1]* and NICOLAI J. FOSS[2]
[1] *Copenhagen Business School, Frederiksberg, Denmark*
[2] *Copenhagen Business School, Copenhagen, Denmark; and Norwegian School of Economics and Business Administration, Bergen, Norway*

Property rights economics furthers the resource-based view of strategic management in a number of ways. First, resources are conceptualized as being composed of multiple attributes for which property rights may be held. Second, a resource owner's ability to create, appropriate, and sustain value from resources depends on the property rights that he or she holds and on the transaction costs of exchanging, defining, and protecting them. While transaction costs are a major source of value dissipation, reducing such dissipation may create value. Implications for the RBV analysis of sustained competitive advantage are derived. Copyright © 2005 John Wiley & Sons, Ltd.

INTRODUCTION

According to Nobel Prize winner, Ronald Coase (1992: 716):

> [b]usinessmen in deciding on their ways of doing business and on what to produce have to take into account transaction costs ... In fact, a large part of what we think of as economic activity is designed to accomplish what high transaction costs would otherwise prevent.

For example, consider the DeBeers diamond cartel and the practice they have adopted for organizing sales. A customer informs DeBeers of her wishes for a specific number and quality of stones. DeBeers then offers the customer a packet of stones—a 'sight'—that roughly corresponds to the customer's wishes. The sight is offered on a 'take-it-or-leave-us' basis, where refusal to take the sight means that DeBeers refuses to deal with

Keywords: transaction costs; property rights; resource value
* Correspondence to: Kirsten Foss. Department of International Economics and Management, Copenhagen Business School, Porcelaenshaven 24, 2000 Frederiksberg, Denmark.
E-mail: kf.int@cbs.dk

the customer any more. The price is calculated based on the overall characteristics of the stones and no negotiation over the price is allowed.

Does this strategy reflect raw market power on the part of a player that controls 80 percent of the world market for raw diamonds? Property rights economists have argued that it does not (Barzel, 1982; Kenney and Klein, 1983). Rather, this is a practice that maximizes created value in firm–customer relations by reducing the costs customers otherwise would have expended on sorting and negotiating, and it arguably exists for this reason (it would be superfluous in a zero transaction cost world). DeBeers sorts the product, but only in a coarse manner. The 'take-it-or-leave-us' practice and the non-negotiable price mean that negotiation costs are effectively eliminated. As only minimum resources (i.e., transaction costs) are spent on sorting and negotiating, DeBeers' practice maximizes the total created value that the parties to the transaction can split. Similar practices can be observed in many other industries, such as the prepackaging of fruit and vegetables in grocery stores, or block booking in the movie industry (Barzel, 1982, 1997; Kenney and Klein, 1983).

Received 26 February 2002
Final revision received 22 December 2004

Strategic management research has paid little attention to transaction cost-reducing practices. However, their theoretical explanation has important implications for strategic management and, in particular, the resource-based view (the 'RBV') (Barney, 1991; Peteraf, 1993). First, transaction costs and value *creation* appear to be linked. Sorting costs, which are part of transaction costs, reduce created value in an exchange. However, certain sales practices may reduce transaction costs, increasing created value. In other words, they 'accomplish what high transaction costs would otherwise prevent.' Second, transaction costs and value *appropriation* appear to be linked. Suppose DeBeers posts prices that reflect the mean quality of the diamonds in a given sight. If DeBeers then allows customers to sort between the diamonds in a sight, customers will only pick high-quality stones. DeBeers' sales practice raises customers' (transaction) costs of sorting to infinity, allowing DeBeers to maximize the share of created value that it can appropriate from its resources.[1]

This paper explores the relations between transaction costs, and value creation and appropriation, relating the discussion to the RBV. In the process, we proffer concepts that are new to strategic management. Specially, we focus our arguments using the *economics of property rights* (EPR) (e.g., Coase, 1988; Alchian, 1977; Demsetz, 1988; Eggertson, 1990; Barzel, 1997). Property rights to resource attributes consist of the rights to use, consume, obtain income from, and alienate these attributes. Property rights are important to strategy because a resource owner's ability to create, appropriate, and sustain value from resources partly depends on the property rights that he or she holds and how well they are protected. In turn, transaction costs—the costs of exchanging, protecting, and capturing property rights—are important to strategy because they influence the value that a resource owner can appropriate. This conceptualization unifies the theoretical constructs of resources, property rights, transaction costs, value creation and appropriation.

Our contribution to clarifying the micro-foundations of the RBV is related to Lippman and Rumelt's (2003a, 2003b) recent attempt to construct a cooperative game theory foundation for the RBV. They point out that prices and, therefore,

the share of created value that is appropriated by a particular resource owner are bargaining outcomes, and they perceive value creation as mainly driven by search for new uses of resources. We broadly agree with this view. However, unlike Lippman and Rumelt we stress the crucial importance of transaction costs for value creation and appropriation. Our explicit focus on transaction costs helps explain how value can be created by reducing transaction costs and brings attention to ways of appropriating created value beyond bargaining. The sales strategy of DeBeers illustrates a means of increasing the value appropriated from customers. DeBeers raises the value it can impute to its bundle of resources solely by reducing overall transaction costs—without altering its bargaining power.

The design of the paper is as follows. We begin by applying the basic tenets of EPR to the notion of a resource. This leads to an understanding of resources as bundles of property rights to resource attributes, which in turn provides insight into value creation and value appropriation. The value that a resource owner can create and appropriate depends not only on the use, scarcity, and outside options of the resource (Barney, 1991; Lippman and Rumelt, 2003a), but also on the transaction costs of trading and protecting the property rights to the attributes that make up the resource. Further implications of EPR for the RBV are then developed by first examining value creation and appropriation in a setting where transaction costs are zero (Coase, 1988), and then tracing the implications for value creation and appropriation when transaction costs are added. The questions we address and seek to answer through this exercise are: How do transaction costs influence value creation and appropriation? What insights into opportunities for value creation and appropriation are gained through a focus on transaction costs? We relate EPR to the key RBV model (Barney, 1991; Peteraf, 1993). Finally, avenues for future work are discussed.

REFINING RESOURCE ANALYSIS: PROPERTY RIGHTS AND RESOURCE VALUE

Applying property rights economics to strategic management

The EPR has only been explicitly applied to the strategic management field in a few previous papers (Mahoney, 1992; Foss and Foss, 2000; Kim

---

[1] In fact, the sales practice may itself be a valuable resource for DeBeers.

and Mahoney, 2002; Foss, 2003), although property rights notions appear in analyses of the strategic implications of intellectual property issues (i.e., Teece, 1988; Argyres and Liebeskind, 1998; Oxley, 1999). However, EPR goes far beyond issues of intellectual property. We therefore turn to the fundamentals of the EPR, particularly as these relate to resources and resource value.[2]

Units of analysis

The EPR stresses that transactions involve the exchange of property rights rather than the exchange of goods per se (Coase, 1988). Hence, the unit of analysis is the individual property right. Although the units of analysis of EPR and the RBV differ, the EPR view agrees with the RBV position that resources matter for the analysis of sustained competitive advantage. However, the EPR *refines* the RBV understanding of resources, and how they create and appropriate value.

Different definitions of 'resources' are provided in the literature (see Wernerfelt, 1984; Barney, 1991; Grant, 1991). However, they all tend to see resources as 'elementary particles'—irreducible units. Resources are often better thought of as 'molecules' that are composed of bundles of rights to attributes. 'Attributes' consist of the different functionalities and services (Penrose, 1959) that assets can supply. Property rights are held to such attributes (Barzel, 1997) and consist of the right to consume, obtain income from, and alienate these attributes (Alchian, 1977). For example, a hi-fi system can play different kinds of music, with different levels of bass or treble at different volumes. All of these functionalities are attributes over which the owner holds property rights. However, the hi-fi's ability to play extremely loud music may not be realized if the law or neighborhood norms prevent this service. The relevant use rights are then constrained. Strategic assets, such as brand names, may also have multiple attributes, some of which may be similarly constrained. An owner of a brand name can decide in which contexts she wishes to deploy the brand name. However, her use rights may still be constrained, for example, if she is prohibited from using the brand name as a domain name on the Internet. How property rights are constrained by the law, agreements, or norms

influences how much value a resource owner can create and appropriate from the resource.[3]

Resources as bundles of property rights

These examples suggest that it is useful to think of resources as *bundles of property rights to attributes*. The resource is an important aggregation of the unit of analysis (the individual property right), because resources are traded or accumulated more often than individual property rights over attributes. The way in which attributes are bundled in goods often reflects production costs and technical constraints. However, transaction costs also play an important role.[4] Attributes are usually traded in bundles to economize the costs of specifying and trading individual resource attributes (Foss and Foss, 2001). Firms often acquire the entire bundle of property rights to a resource, such as a production facility, to avoid the costs of specifying and trading only those attributes that are of economic interest to the firm. However, such transaction costs hinder the resource owner in realizing the full potential value of the resource, because some attributes that are not used by the current owner are not traded (e.g., production time may be costly to trade). If the relevant transaction costs are somehow reduced so that such attributes can be specified and traded, the resource owner may appropriate more value from the resource.

Thinking of resources in terms of property rights to valued attributes implies that resources are not given, but are the *outcomes* of processes of economizing with transaction costs. Obvious examples are those resources that only exist *because* of transaction costs, such as contracts, and the DeBeers sales practice.[5] Seemingly identical resources may

---

[2] Only those aspects that are relevant to the RBV are discussed here. See Eggertson (1990) for a comprehensive presentation.

[3] This adds a property rights dimension to Penrose's (1959) distinction between resources and the services they yield. The services that a firm can derive from its resources (i.e., the fungibility of the resources) are not only constrained by path dependencies, the functionalities of the resource, and managerial imagination (Penrose, 1959), but also by the transaction costs of realizing the economic potential of the property rights and by the way in which those property rights are constrained.

[4] Relevant transaction costs are costs of drafting contracts (i.e., contracts become incomplete), costs of monitoring (which make moral hazard viable), measuring attributes (which induces adverse selection), and costs of protecting against entry and imitation (which reduce property rights to income streams from controlling certain market shares and resources).

[5] For example, whether goods such as copying machines and servicing agreements are sold as a combined good (i.e., a 'tying arrangement') depends on the costs to the seller or lessor of

be economically different when they are controlled by firms that are not equally capable of protecting the relevant resource attributes. For example, the 'same' kind of employees, employed in different firms with different incentive systems, will engage in different morally hazardous activities. From an economic standpoint, they are different resources and will be paid differently.

Resource value and transaction costs

Another implication of the property rights view of resources is that transaction costs influence the value that a resource owner can create and appropriate. The resource value that an owner can create depends on the bundle of property rights that she holds for the attributes of the resource, the constraints imposed on these property rights, *and* the costs of trading them. The value that a resource owner can appropriate also depends on transaction costs. Value appropriation presupposes that the owner can *exclude* non-owners from using or destroying attributes to which he holds property rights. While the resource owner has the legal right to exclude non-owners from using and obtaining value from his resources, he may still find it too costly to exclude non-owners from *all* possible uses of the resource. In effect, he cedes the relevant rights (Barzel, 1997). Similarly, given costs of protecting property rights over attributes, owners often choose to control the relevant property rights to varying degrees, an aspect reflected in the value that a resource owner can appropriate. For example, in a franchise chain the value of a brand name to the franchisor will be eroded (Dierickx and Cool, 1989) when it is too costly to the franchisor to exclude franchisees from using the name to sell low-quality products.

When resources are conceived of as bundles of property rights, the potential value that a resource owner can create and appropriate does not only depend on supply and demand conditions for the entire bundle of property rights, but also on how this bundle is constrained, the transaction costs involved in realizing the value of individual property rights, and the transaction costs of controlling the property rights to the attributes that constitute the resource. *Attempts to maximize resource value must take such transaction costs into account.*

monitoring the impact of non-standard servicing on the machine (Elzinga and Mills, 2001).

Controlling property rights: The capture and protection of property rights

An important part of transaction costs are the costs of using legal and/or private means of protection. Positive transaction costs imply that most property rights are not fully protected and can be subject to capture efforts (henceforth, 'capture'). By 'capture' we mean resource-consuming activities to appropriate value from other strategizers *without compensating them.*[6] Moral hazard, adverse selection, and hold-up are familiar examples of capture. While capture is different from exchange, it may take place in exchange relations. For example, two parties to a transaction agree on a price for a resource with certain attributes, such as a certain quality level); however, the supplier may deliver a resource of poorer quality. Such moral hazard on the part of the supplier amounts to capturing (some) valued resource attributes from the buyer (Chi, 1994).[7]

Given this definition of capture, 'protection efforts' (henceforth, 'protection') can be defined as the resource-consuming activities that strategizers undertake to reduce other strategizers' incentives to capture property rights. Since capture takes many forms, the notion of protection in EPR goes significantly beyond making and keeping resources costly to imitate or substitute (Teece, 1988; Barney, 1991). In addition to such protection strategies, property rights may be protected by choosing governance structures in order to reduce capture in the form of moral hazard or hold-up (Mahoney, 1992; Chi, 1994; Hart, 1995; Williamson, 1996), by using the legal system, by establishing private orderings (Williamson, 1996), deterring entry (Tirole, 1988), by writing contracts, and by adopting sales strategies to hinder adverse sorting (as in the DeBeers example) (Barzel, 1982; Kenney and Klein, 1983). The RBV mainly considers a subset of these protection activities, namely protecting against imitation, but stands to gain from considering a broader set than it presently does.

To illustrate, consider an insurance company that is the first to market a particular kind of

[6] Thus, capture creates what economists call 'externalities.'
[7] There is also a dimension of capture to competition. Competitive imitation and substitution, as well as competition in terms of quality, technology, and price, may be seen as capture because these competitive activities reduce the value that a resource owner can appropriate without compensating the owner of that resource (Barzel, 1994; Foss, 2003).

accident insurance concept, which in turn comes heavily into demand. The product can be fully protected from imitation using legal means. Moreover, assume that suppliers and customers can only bargain for a small part of the value created by the new concept. Given all this, the insurance company would seem to implement '. . . a value creating strategy not simultaneously being implemented by any current or potential competitors and . . . these other firms are unable to duplicate the benefits of this strategy' (Barney, 1991: 102). In other words, the company seems to have realized a sustained competitive advantage. However, this may not be the case. The price of insurance contracts cannot perfectly reflect the true accident risks of each individual who takes out insurance due to the transaction costs. Given variation in risks, some customers, namely those with high accident risks, capture value in excess of what they pay for (i.e., 'adverse selection;' Akerlof, 1984). At the limit, all of the rents from the new strategy will be eroded through the value capture/adverse selection of customers.

This example implies that protection of resource value goes beyond keeping resources non-imitable. Resources are not fully protected from value erosion unless they are protected from *all* kinds of capture. In the example, the proper way to protect value would be to segment the customer base. The example further indicates that EPR has implications for value creation, appropriation, and sustained competitive advantage, implications which add to the RBV. In order to explore these implications, we first examine value creation and appropriation in a setting where transaction costs are zero, which is the setting underlying the *Coase theorem* (Coase, 1988). The zero transaction cost setting serves as a useful benchmark, because it represents a state in which maximum value is created. We then explicitly consider transaction costs, and examine their implications for value creation and appropriation relative to the benchmark situation.

RELATING TRANSACTION COSTS TO VALUE CREATION AND APPROPRIATION

The Coase theorem

In short, the Coase theorem states that all value that *can* be created from the exchange and use

of an economy's available goods *will*, in fact, be created when transaction costs are absent. The underlying assumptions are that in such a surplus-maximizing equilibrium strategizers have full information,[8] there are no costs of defining and protecting resource property rights, and there are no bargaining costs.

As the costs of exchanging property rights are zero, all property rights to all attributes can be exchanged and are optimally bundled into resources.[9] In this situation, there will still be constraints on the use rights over resources, but these constraints will be defined in a value-maximizing manner. In other words, externalities cause no avoidable loss of value. Given the optimal constraints and costless exchange, resources will be put to their best possible uses. In this benchmark situation, *the maximum value that resources can create will be realized.*

Another way of stating that the cost of exchanging property rights is zero is that the prices for all those resource uses that are realized in the value-maximizing equilibrium emerge immediately from costless bargaining processes. For example, consider a parking space that is located adjacent to a supermarket. Since information and bargaining costs are zero, the supermarket owner will bargain with all users of the parking space so that all property rights to the various attributes of the parking space will be priced. Relevant attributes may be the time, date, and proximity to the supermarket entrance. Different prices for different bundles of property rights for these attributes will likely emerge. Since prices are perfect signals of scarcities, all attributes will be perfectly rationed, so that no queues emerge and reallocating the use rights for the parking space cannot increase created value. However, while the zero transaction cost condition implies that total resource value will be at its maximum, the issue of value appropriation is not directly addressed. For this, further theoretical apparatus, namely bargaining theory (Lippman and Rumelt, 2003a), is required.

As bargaining is costless, the value created by the use of resources is always independent of the value that each individual resource owner appropriates. One may think of parties to transactions

[8] This is a strong version of the Coase theorem (as in Coase, 1988; and Barzel, 1997).

[9] However, the very notion of a 'resource' becomes somewhat redundant in this extreme, as many exchanges will involve property rights over attributes rather than resources per se.

(i.e., resource owners) as first agreeing to maximize the value that can be created from their resources, and then splitting this value through bargaining to define each party's share of the created value (Milgrom and Roberts, 1992). Since all promises are enforceable, resource owners will always receive at least their opportunity costs and resource investments will always be covered (Hart, 1995). In other words, *value creation is independent of value appropriation when transaction costs are zero.*

The zero transaction cost setting does not imply long-run, perfect competition, and is therefore compatible with resource owners earning rents. As Coase (1988) notes, rents may be earned when the supply of input resources is not perfectly elastic, independent of whether transaction costs exist or not. As property rights are perfectly protected, these rents are sustainable. However, since bargaining (and forming coalitions) is costless, the owner of a scarce resource is unlikely to appropriate all rents.

While the rudiments of the resource-based view of sustainable competitive advantage (Barney, 1991; Peteraf, 1993) are thus far consistent with the zero transaction cost assumption, this assumption only leaves limited room for understanding the links between resources and sustained competitive advantage. In order to explore these links in detail, the assumption that transaction costs are zero must be abandoned.

The introduction of transaction costs brings both bad and good news to strategizers. The bad news is that in a positive transaction cost world realizing the full potential of all resources is impossible with respect to value creation. Moreover, resource value can be eroded in numerous ways by the creative attempts of other strategizers to capture value. The good news is that the presence of transaction costs generates sources of value creation and appropriation (i.e., strategic opportunities) that would not exist if the transaction costs were zero.

Value dissipation and value erosion: Bad news for strategizers

In a positive transaction cost world, some *value dissipation* is strictly unavoidable. Dissipation results because protecting property rights is costly and because a lack of protection induces strategizers to expend resources on costly capture. If a strategizer increases the protection of her property rights in order to reduce others' capture,

she may reduce one kind of value dissipation while increasing another one. Similarly, reducing protection in order to save on protection costs increases others' capture efforts. Therefore, for a given strategizer there is an optimal amount of dissipation, namely the amount that maximizes appropriated value.[10] Given such an optimum, changes in the costs of protection and capture change the amount of dissipation. For example, a strategizer's cost of protection may decrease because he adopts or creates new sales practices (as in the DeBeers example), contractual forms, or sorting or monitoring technologies. Capture and protection efforts will be different in the new equilibrium.

Direct and indirect dissipation

Two kinds of dissipation exist. Protection and capture *directly* reduce realized value compared to the zero transaction cost situation because the efforts themselves are costly and therefore consume value. Protection efforts, such as attribute measurement and exclusion of non-owners, are examples of direct dissipation. An example of capture that directly dissipates value is customers who sort between unsorted goods of varying qualities in order to select only those that have a higher value than the posted price.

Protection may also lead to *indirect dissipation* to the extent that the value-creating exchange of property rights is hindered, as when knowledge is kept in-house in order to protect against imitation (cf. Reed and DeFilippi, 1990). The knowledge does not then become an object of know-how exchange within a network of reciprocating firms (Von Hippel, 1988). Losses in the form of unrealized gains from knowledge exchange constitute one form of indirect dissipation, while capture may be another. For example, if many consumers sort the product, rather than just one, value is comparatively wasted. Moreover, customers may engage in costly competition over unprotected property rights (Barzel, 1997). If capture is sufficiently intensive, indirect dissipation emerges in the form of reduced transaction volume in the market. Other sources of indirect dissipation arise from morally hazardous behavior that induces suboptimal levels of production, and from holdup and imitative efforts that diminish investments.

---

[10] Value creation therefore requires that resource owners consider not only their own costs of protection, but also the costs to other strategizers of engaging in capture (Skaperdas, 1994).

Value erosion

The RBV notion of value erosion (Dierickx and Cool, 1989)—value dissipation as seen from the perspective of a resource owner—is easily aligned with the EPR notion of dissipation. Specifically, value erosion refers to the reduction in a resource's value that is induced by a reduction in others' capture costs or by an increase in the resource owner's own protection costs. Value erosion thus measures the change in a resource owner's appropriated value due to changes in the equilibrium between capture efforts and protection costs. For example, producers of digital products experience value erosion due to the declining cost of copies for private users. Value erosion is caused by both direct dissipation (i.e., users' capture costs and producers' protection costs) and indirect dissipation (i.e., investments in intellectual assets decline).

Unowned resources and value erosion

Supporters of the RBV sometimes argue that unique locations are rent sources (see Lippman and Rumelt, 2003b). For example, a unique, non-imitable riverside location for a production site may have the potential of creating sustained competitive advantage due to the low transportation costs it provides to the firm. However, the interdependence between the resource (the site) and the public good (the river) creates a problem of sustaining rents that has not been considered in the RBV literature. While the location may stay inimitable, *ex post* competition may develop for use of the river as other firms located further inland develop less expensive means to bring goods to the river (i.e., the equilibrium is disturbed by a technological innovation). These other firms will also use the river for transportation. If congestion occurs, the actual cost to the firm of transportation is high although the monetary price it pays is low. In the extreme, the firm's locational rents may be completely eroded by queuing costs.

This example illustrates a situation in which a firm can fully protect its own property rights to resource attributes, with the exception of its income rights related to the location of the land. Rents are initially earned because of complementary relations between resources. However, only one resource is under the control of the firm, which makes it harder for the firm to limit indirect dissipation. Even if all resources were owned by

the firm, efficiently rationing the use of resources may be costly. For this reason, some property rights over attributes may be left uncontrolled with respect to their use internally in the firm. In those instances, resources are not necessarily sources of sustained rents, since increases in the demand of some attributes may result in value erosion of other resources. In sum, the EPR clarifies value erosion in the RBV (Dierickx and Cool, 1989: 1508).

Sources of value creation: Good news for strategizers

The above reasoning points to two main methods of value creation that emerge with the introduction of transaction costs. The first is to reduce protection costs so that *direct* value dissipation diminishes. The second is to reduce *indirect* dissipation. The following example illustrates how the reduction of direct and indirect dissipation translates into value creation.

Consider a uniquely located (hence, inimitable) parking area that is adjacent to and owned by a supermarket.[11] In this case, customers value the combined good, namely the combination of what the supermarket offers and the parking spaces. This will be reflected in both the demand the supermarket faces and the prices it can charge. The supermarket will earn a profit from being located next to the parking space. The source of this profit is the positive externality in consumption. Thus, use rights to the parking space are unprotected in the sense that non-owners can use this attribute without directly compensating the owner. However, the owner will still make the parking space available to non-owners when she can appropriate its value through its complementarity to the supermarket's offerings.

Assume now that the supermarket's pricing decisions can be represented in terms of the monopoly diagram familiar from economics textbooks (see Figure 1).

D_1 is the demand curve that the supermarket would face in the absence of the parking space. Created value is represented by the area *IJHC*.

---

[11] If instead the supermarket did not own the parking space, it would be more costly for it to take measures to control dissipation of the value created by the parking space: patrons of other shops would compete with the supermarket's customers for the parking space, and such competition would gradually erode the rents earned by the supermarket on its location. This is the same situation as in the above example of the riverside location.

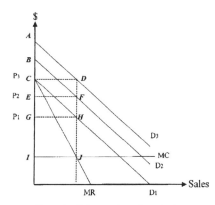

Figure 1.   Value-creating price rationing

However, if the supermarket constructs a parking space and does not restrict its use, D_2 is the combined demand curve for the goods offered by the supermarket *and* the free services of the parking space. The price is lower in the absence of the parking space (P_1), because consumers value having access to a parking space. Total created value increases by **BFHC** to **IJFB**. The supermarket can appropriate **EFHG** (= **BFHC**) by charging the higher price (P_2) for its goods. However, when a limited number of parking spaces are offered for free, customers queue for those spaces. This results in direct dissipation of value in the form of waiting time and indirect dissipation in the form of a smaller transaction volume than would have obtained if queuing costs were zero. (In Figure 1 it is assumed that not all value is dissipated in this way).

Value dissipation can be reduced if the supermarket extends the number of parking spaces, or if it protects its property rights and charges patrons for parking. The demand curve will shift outwards because customers have to expend fewer resources on queuing. Total created value increases by **ADFB** to **IJDA**. If the supermarket charges the equilibrium price that fully rations parking space (i.e., $P_3 - P_1$), and prices supermarket goods at P_1, it can appropriate the extra value (**CDFE**) generated by pricing the parking space.[12] The cost of

pricing the parking space has to be subtracted from **CFDE**, so as long as this cost is less than **CFDE**, to the supermarket gains value by pricing the parking services.

We have thus far assumed that the value of each parking space to customers is independent of location and time. However, in reality customers value parking spaces next to the entrance higher than other spaces, and they value parking at peak shopping hours more than at other hours. A single price will therefore not perfectly ration the use of parking spaces. If the supermarket can devise means of reducing the cost of pricing and enforcing property rights to these attributes, it will appropriate an even greater portion of the resource's value. In the case of a parking space, this may require investments in resources such as ticket and control systems. The ability to reduce indirect dissipation and capture a greater share of the value of attributes provides incentives to invest in such transaction cost-reducing technology.[13]

Pricing the parking lot is not the only means by which the supermarket can limit indirect dissipation. Alternatively, the supermarket can limit the time cars are allowed to park or it can limit access. However, the only way to *fully* limit indirect dissipation is to price each parking space according to its attractiveness to costumers. This may suggest that resource attributes should always be priced to fully realize their value-creating potential. This intuition is incorrect, as pricing is costly in the presence of transaction costs (Coase, 1988).[14]

Resource attributes are not priced when it is prohibitively costly to exclude non-owners from

---

[12] Here we have assumed that extending the parking lot is more costly than pricing parking services. Although customers are never worse off in the example, the monopolist supermarket captures all created value from the parking space and from

pricing parking spaces. In other words, customers have no bargaining power. Also, we have assumed that customers have similar queuing costs and valuations of parking spaces. Relaxing these assumptions does not compromise the overall conclusion.
[13] Will the supermarket earn rent on the parking lot? The answer to this question depends on: (1) its ability to keep the transaction cost-reducing resources inimitable; (2) the costs of acquiring these resources; and (3) its bargaining with landowners and construction companies as well as other strategizers who are interested in acquiring the land for resale to the supermarket. It may be common knowledge that parking spaces adjacent to supermarkets create value for the supermarket, although the supermarket is unable to price each parking space. Rents may then be captured by suppliers, or by strategizers who acquire the land for resale to the supermarket. The amount of rent captured by third parties depends on the specificities of the bargaining situation.
[14] Cf. Lippman and Rumelt's (2003a: 1085) observation that '... intuition suggests that a resource bundle will be more valuable if it can be accurately priced.' Transaction costs determine whether resources 'can be accurately priced.'

capturing property rights to the attributes, when attributes are costly to define and measure in verifiable ways, and when resource attributes are not in demand. More generally, some attributes and entire resources are more costly to price accurately than others, making it more costly to constrain dissipation for these resources. However, by restricting access to such resources, firms can limit dissipation and maximize value. This type of restriction arises when resources are kept in-house, a key theme in the RBV (Dierickx and Cool, 1989; Reed and DeFilippi, 1990).[15]

TRANSACTION COSTS AND SUSTAINED COMPETITIVE ADVANTAGE

The EPR is not a strategic perspective per se and does not directly address the issues of why some firms are persistently more successful than others. Thus, the issues of why firms are heterogeneous and pursue different strategies are not directly addressed by EPR. In contrast, firm heterogeneity is central to the RBV and much research has been directed towards establishing the circumstances under which firms earn sustainable rents from superior resources. Unlike the RBV, the EPR does not distinguish between the resources that give rise to sustained rent and those that do not. Nevertheless, the EPR can contribute directly to strategic analysis.

EPR's contribution to the analysis of sustained competitive advantage starts with the central point of the preceding discussion. The value that strategizers will realize and appropriate from resources depends on transaction costs. Thus, the rent differentials that resources create are partly a function of the differential costs of protecting resource attributes from capture. If a resource owner is able to create and appropriate more value from her bundle of resources compared to the competition, she has the potential of enjoying a sustained competitive advantage. In other words, sustained competitive advantage depends on transaction costs.

Determining the conditions under which firms enjoy a sustained competitive advantage is one of the main issues in the RBV. Barriers to competition are particularly important here (e.g., in the notions of *ex ante* and *ex post* limits to competition; Peteraf, 1993), and much effort has been put into the identification of factors (such as the nature of the resource or the resource accumulation process) that create such barriers. Competition is also important in the EPR (Alchian, 1977), but the main focus is on competition for less than perfectly protected property rights (Barzel, 1997; Hirshleifer, 2001). As has been argued, such competition is important in determining the value that a resource can create and the value that the owner of the resource can appropriate. Analysis of how transaction costs influence competition over less than perfectly protected property rights, therefore, provides important contributions to the RBV with respect to understanding the conditions for sustained competitive advantage.

Peteraf (1993) has elegantly summarized much of the RBV into 'four cornerstones of competitive advantage' that represent necessary conditions for sustained competitive advantage. In the following, these cornerstones serve as a means of more precisely identifying the contribution of EPR to furthering the RBV analysis of sustained competitive advantage.

Heterogeneity

The RBV analysis of heterogeneity stresses inherent efficiencies of resources (Peteraf, 1993) and differences in resource complementarities (Dierickx and Cool, 1989; Denrell, Fang, and Winter, 2003) as sources of firm heterogeneity. The EPR contributes a further dimension to resource and firm heterogeneity by stressing that resources are composed of property rights to attributes. Property rights are typically bundled in resources due to the cost of exchanging individual property rights and the cost of protecting these rights. Resources are therefore outcomes of processes of economizing transaction costs, and they vary in their efficiencies and potential for being combined in a complementary manner because they encompass different attributes.

By implication, resource heterogeneity fluctuates with innovations in sales practices, contracting practices, and other transaction cost-reducing technologies as well as with changes in legislation and norms. Firms thus have heterogeneous resources

---

[15] Resources may also not be priced because they are extremely firm specific (Lippman and Rumelt, 1982). Such resources are best used in-house. The fact that there are no prices on such resources does not imply a potential for value creation. However, we doubt that such resources are common.

not just because of different initial resource endowments and subsequent learning effects, but also because they are subject to different regulations (i.e., constraints on use rights), and face different costs of protecting and utilizing resource attributes in production or exchange. When resources change with changes in transaction costs and legislation, so do the values they can create and that the firm can appropriate.

Barriers to *ex ante* competition

The RBV stresses *informational* barriers to *ex ante* competition as a necessary condition for rents (Barney, 1986; Makadok and Barney, 2001). The EPR adds a different mechanism by which discrepancies between value and price may be established on strategic factor markets.

In the EPR, resource heterogeneity is caused by variations in the types and levels of valued attributes that resources embody. Such variation requires costly measurement (Barzel, 1997). Costly measurement implies that not all attributes are priced and that some strategizers may be able to capture value from non-priced attributes (Barzel, 1982). Strategizers on strategic factor markets that have low costs of capture because of superior efficiencies in searching and/or low opportunity costs for searches will be able to purchase resources — bundles of property rights over attributes, *including* the highly valued one — at prices below their value to the seller. This indicates that rent capture is connected to transaction costs (in this case, measurement costs), and that variation in the attributes of resources is a dimension that is important for understanding rent capture.

Barriers to *ex post* competition

The general lesson from both the RBV and the EPR is that barriers to *ex post* competition are a necessary condition for the sustainability of competitive advantage. However, *ex post* competition may be conceptualized more broadly in the EPR than in the RBV. In the RBV, *ex post* competition is mainly a matter of competitive imitation and resource substitution (Barney, 1991).

The EPR adds to this by pointing to *ex post* capture in many other forms, such as moral hazard, adverse selection and holdup, and to other elements of competition over less than perfectly protected attributes (see further Barzel, 1997). All

of these capture activities can be subsumed under *ex post* competition for unprotected property rights over resource attributes. The value that the focal firm can appropriate from its resources is determined by the capture activities of other firms, the firm's bargaining power *vis-à-vis* suppliers, buyers and employees, and the capture of employees. If capture activities are fully foreseen before the resource is acquired, their impact on value creation and appropriation will be taken into account in the reservation price of buyers (or sellers). However, if there are (transaction) costs for estimating capture or unforeseen changes in transaction costs, value erosion will occur. Thus, when forming expectations about future resource values (Makadok and Barney, 2001), managers should also assess the capture potential that is associated with these resources.

The EPR can expand the avenue of research pursued in the RBV with respect to identifying resource characteristics that may limit *ex post* competition and contribute to sustained competitive advantage. In the RBV, causal ambiguity is often seen as a characteristic that supports sustainability (Lippman and Rumelt, 1982). However, from an EPR perspective, causal ambiguity may also make it costly to write contracts and enforce performance norms. Causal ambiguity may therefore reduce value creation and appropriation. This creates a trade-off between protecting against imitation and protecting against other forms of capture.

Immobility

While the RBV suggests that resource immobility is preferable from the firm's point of view, transaction costs imply that immobility leads to underinvestment. Granting resources outside options, such as giving patent rights to research scientists, may increase their bargaining power (make them more 'mobile') *and* improve their investment incentives (Hart, 1995). This points to a trade-off in certain situations between immobility and value creation, and therefore refines the analysis of immobility as a condition of sustained competitive advantage.

CONCLUSION

Contribution to theory

Coase's (1992: 716) insight that '... a large part of what we think of as economic activity is designed to accomplish what high transaction costs would otherwise prevent' has important implications for the RBV of strategic management. Incorporating transaction costs more fully into the RBV introduces new sources of value dissipation and erosion. As suggested by Coase, strategizers will actively seek to reduce the value dissipation and erosion caused by transaction costs. In essence, strategic opportunities arise from reducing transaction costs.

The purpose of this work has been to clarify how transaction costs create opportunities for value creation and appropriation. The argument used the EPR lens to develop a more refined understanding of the notion of a resource and of the determinants of resource value. Resources can usefully be conceptualized as bundles of property rights to resource attributes, where the relevant property rights are subject to potential capture and therefore need protection. Capture and protection are costly activities that directly and indirectly diminish created value relative to the maximum value attainable if transaction costs are zero. Thus, transaction costs, along with conditions of scarcity, demand, imitability, and sustainability, influence resource value. Strategizers have incentives to create value by reducing dissipation, taking into account that such reduction is also costly and provided they can appropriate a sufficient part of the created value. The reduction of dissipation takes various forms, including the pricing and protecting of resource attributes. These insights refine the RBV analysis of sustained competitive advantage by adding new dimensions to notions of resource heterogeneity, *ex post* and *ex ante* competition, and immobility (Peteraf, 1993).

Taken together, all this indicates that the EPR can significantly contribute to the RBV analysis of strategic opportunities. According to Lippman and Rumelt (2003a: 1080), the RBV predicts that firms will focus their energies on developing 'complex "homegrown" resources ... Yet a glance at corporate reality reveals that much more effort is devoted to combinations, deals, mergers, acquisition, joint venture and the like.' They therefore suggest that more attention be devoted to such resource assembly, particularly under conditions of super-modularity. We concur, but argue that created value is not only constrained by knowledge of resource complementarities, but also by the transaction costs that attend the exchange aspects of 'combinations, deals, mergers, acquisition, joint

venture and the like.' Even more generally, the EPR indicates that resource value is significantly influenced by transaction costs, and that strategic opportunities arise when the transaction costs of defining, protecting, capturing, and exchanging property rights change.

Future work

The present paper is among the first applications of EPR to the RBV (see also Foss and Foss, 2000; Kim and Mahoney, 2002; Foss, 2003). Much work remains to be done. Among the many new avenues for development of the RBV that are implied by the EPR are the following.

Further theoretical development

This work has primarily examined how notions of transaction costs and property rights refine the understanding of resources and value creation and appropriation. Further theoretical development may proceed along at least three paths. The first begins with the observations that resource value is threatened by all sorts of capture efforts, and that competitive activities may be understood in terms of the capture and protection of property rights (Barzel, 1994). EPR may help to integrate the RBV with strategic theory that is more concerned with the external environment (Porter, 1980). A second path of development is to address those resources that create value because they economize transaction costs, such as specific ways of sorting goods (e.g., in retail and in such markets as fruit and vegetables), sorting customers (e.g., credit classes in banking), contracting, and the use of private orderings (Barzel, 1997; Williamson, 1996). While such resources have been neglected in the RBV (but see Mahoney, 1992; Chi, 1994), they are important sources of value creation. A third path is to connect with the significant amount of literature on technological spillovers (externalities) (Shy, 2001).[16] This literature highlights the central trade-off between limiting spillovers to other firms (i.e., protect property rights to knowledge resources) vs. sharing with these firms (and under what circumstances), and the links this trade-off has with R&D investment incentives. While EPR can frame the central ideas of the spillover literature, the latter adds

---

[16] We are grateful to an anonymous reviewer for this suggestion.

an emphasis on competitive dynamics that is not included in this paper's approach.

Formal modeling

The development of mathematical RBV models has recently begun (e.g., Makadok, 2003). The EPR draws attention to many variables, margins, and trade-offs (Foss and Foss, 2001). Formal modeling is necessary to fully clarify the potentials and limits of this approach with respect to furthering the RBV. One attractive line of research is to apply and develop formal game theory models on contests over insecure (i.e., costly to protect) property rights, and how such contests dissipate value (e.g., Skaperdas, 1994; Hirshleifer, 2001). In these treatments, strategizers are explicitly modeled as having (in our terminology) capture and protection functions, and differential endowments of resources to spend on these activities. Predictions as to which player will win in contests over insecure property rights, how much value will be dissipated, and how alternative kinds of social organization may reduce such dissipation can therefore be made. The relevance of this formal, game-theoretical approach to the non-formal approach developed in the present paper is that the formal apparatus can give precise meanings to such key EPR concepts such as capture, protection, and dissipation. The formal approach can also model the interaction between strategizers that have differential resource endowments, and between different capture and protection efficiencies (i.e., differential capabilities in these activities).

Empirical research

One avenue of empirical research in the RBV has been to pursue the implications for performance of different resource types. For example, Miller and Shamsie (1996) discuss the sources and sustainability of competitive advantage in the Hollywood film studios in terms of 'property' and 'knowledge-based' resources. Empirical RBV work can accommodate the unique insights that EPR brings to the RBV by incorporating in such exercises the 'transaction cost resources' mentioned above—forms of contracting, sorting systems, credit rationing systems, and other practices that firms adopt to protect resource value. While there is reason to suspect that such resources are very important in a number of industries, extremely little is empirically known about their contribution to sustained competitive advantage. Work on this issue may utilize operationalizations and measures that have been developed in the empirical literature on transaction cost economics (David and Han, 2004).

ACKNOWLEDGMENTS

We are grateful to Yoram Barzel, Jean Jules Boddewyn, Eirik Furubotn, Lasse Lien, Sara McGaughey, Joe Mahoney, Claude Ménard, Will Mitchell, Jackson Nickerson, Dan Spulber, seminar audiences at Copenhagen Business School, the Norwegian School of Economics and Business Administration, Southern Denmark University, and Université Paris (Sorbonne), as well as two anonymous reviewers for comments on numerous earlier versions of this paper.

REFERENCES

Akerlof G. 1984. The market for lemons (originally published 1970). Reprinted in *An Economic Theorist's Book of Tales*. Cambridge University Press: Cambridge, U.K.

Alchian AA. 1977. Some economics of property rights (originally published 1965). Reprinted in *Economic Forces at Work*. Liberty Press: Indianapolis, IN; 127–150.

Argyres NS, Liebeskind JP. 1998. Privatizing the intellectual commons: universities and the commercialization of biotechnology. *Journal of Economic Behavior and Organization* **35**: 427–454.

Barney JB. 1986. Strategic factor markets. *Management Science* **32**: 1231–1241.

Barney JB. 1991. Firm resources and sustained competitive advantage. *Journal of Management* **17**: 99–120.

Barzel Y. 1982. Measurement costs and the organization of markets. *Journal of Law and Economics* **25**: 27–48.

Barzel Y. 1994. The capture of wealth by monopolists and the protection of property rights. *International Review of Law and Economics* **14**: 393–409.

Barzel Y. 1997. *Economic Analysis of Property Rights* (2nd edn). Cambridge University Press: Cambridge, U.K.

Chi T. 1994. Trading in strategic resources: necessary conditions, transaction cost problems, and choice of exchange structure. *Strategic Management Journal* **15**(4): 271–290.

Coase RH. 1988. The problem of social cost (originally published 1960). Reprinted in *The Firm, the Market and the Law*. University of Chicago Press: Chicago, IL; 104–116.

Coase RH. 1992. The institutional structure of production. *American Economic Review* **82**: 713–719.

David RJ, Han S. 2004. A systematic assessment of the empirical support for transaction cost economics. *Strategic Management Journal* **25**(1): 39–58.

Demsetz H. 1988. Toward a theory of property rights (originally published 1967). Reprinted in *Ownership, Control, and the Firm*. Basil Blackwell: Oxford.

Denrell J, Fang C, Winter SG. 2003. The economics of strategic opportunity. *Strategic Management Journal* **24**(10): 977–990.

Dierickx I, Cool K. 1989. Asset stock accumulation and the sustainability of competitive advantage. *Management Science* **35**: 1504–1511.

Eggertson T. 1990. *Economic Behavior and Institutions.* Cambridge University Press: Cambridge, U.K.

Elzinga K, Mills D. 2001. Independent service organizations and economic efficiency. *Economic Inquiry* **39**: 549–560.

Foss NJ. 2003. The strategic management and transaction cost nexus: past debates, central questions, and future research possibilities. *Strategic Organization* **1**: 139–169.

Foss K, Foss NJ. 2000. Competence and governance perspectives: how much do they differ? And how does it matter? In *Competence, Governance, and Entrepreneurship*, Foss NJ, Mahnke V (eds). Oxford University Press: Oxford; 55–79.

Foss K, Foss NJ. 2001. Assets, attributes and ownership. *International Journal of the Economics of Business* **8**: 19–37.

Grant R. 1991. The resource-based theory of competitive advantage: implications for strategy formulation. *California Management Review* **33**: 114–136.

Hart O. 1995. *Firms, Contracts and Financial Structure.* Oxford University Press: Oxford.

Hirshleifer J. 2001. *The Dark Side of the Force: Economic Foundations of Conflict Theory*. Cambridge University Press: Cambridge, U.K.

Kenney RW, Klein B. 1983. The economics of block booking. *Journal of Law and Economics* **26**: 497–540.

Kim J, Mahoney JT. 2002. Resource-based and property rights perspectives on value creation: the case of oil field unitization. *Managerial and Decision Economics* **23**: 225–245.

Lippman SA, Rumelt RP. 1982. Uncertain imitability: an analysis of interfirm differences under competition. *Bell Journal of Economics* **13**: 418–438.

Lippman SA, Rumelt RP. 2003a. A bargaining perspective on resource advantage. *Strategic Management Journal* **24**(11): 1069–1086.

Lippman SA, Rumelt RP. 2003b. The payments perspective: micro-foundations of resource analysis. *Strategic Management Journal*, Special Issue **24**: 903–927.

Mahoney JT. 1992. The choice of organizational form: vertical financial ownership versus other methods of vertical integration. *Strategic Management Journal* **13**(8): 559–584.

Makadok R. 2003. Doing the right thing and knowing the right thing to do: why the whole is greater than the sum of the parts. *Strategic Management Journal*, Special Issue **24**: 1043–1055.

Makadok R, Barney JB. 2001. Strategic factor market intelligence: an application of information economics to strategy formulation and competitor intelligence. *Management Science* **47**: 1621–1638.

Milgrom P, Roberts J. 1992. *Economics, Organization, and Management.* Prentice-Hall: Englewood Cliffs, NJ.

Miller D, Shamsie J. 1996. The resource-based view of the firm in two environments: the Hollywood film studios from 1936 to 1965. *Academy of Management Journal* **39**: 519–543.

Oxley JE. 1999. Institutional environment and the mechanism of governance: the impact of intellectual property protection on the structure of inter-firm alliances. *Journal of Economic Behavior and Organization* **38**: 283–309.

Penrose ET. 1959. *The Theory of the Growth of the Firm*. Oxford University Press: Oxford.

Peteraf MA. 1993. The cornerstones of competitive advantage: a resource-based view. *Strategic Management Journal* **14**(3): 179–191.

Porter ME. 1980. *Competitive Strategy*. Free Press: New York.

Reed R, DeFilippi R. 1990. Causal ambiguity, barriers to imitation and sustainable competitive advantage. *Academy of Management Review* **15**: 88–102.

Shy O. 2001. *The Economics of Network Industries*. Cambridge University Press: Cambridge, U.K.

Skaperdas S. 1994. Contest success functions. *Journal of Economic Theory* **7**: 283–290.

Teece DJ. 1988. Profiting from technological innovation: implications for integration, collaboration, licensing and public policy (originally published 1986). Reprinted in *Readings in the Management of Innovation*, Tushman ML, Moore WL (eds). Ballinger: Cambridge, MA; 621–648.

Tirole J. 1988. *The Theory of Industrial Organization.* MIT Press: Cambridge, MA.

Von Hippel E. 1988. *The Sources of Innovation.* Cambridge University Press: Cambridge, U.K.

Wernerfelt B. 1984. A resource-based theory of the firm. *Strategic Management Journal* **5**(2): 171–180.

Williamson OE. 1996. *The Mechanisms of Governance.* Oxford University Press: Oxford.

Peripheral Vision

Original and Derived Judgment: An Entrepreneurial Theory of Economic Organization

Kirsten Foss, Nicolai J. Foss and Peter G. Klein

Kirsten Foss
Copenhagen
Business School,
Denmark

Nicolai J. Foss
Norwegian School
of Economics and
Business
Administration;
Copenhagen
Business School,
Denmark

Peter G. Klein
University of
Missouri, USA

Abstract

Recent work links entrepreneurship to the economic theory of the firm, using the concept of entrepreneurship as judgment introduced by Frank Knight. When judgment is complementary to other assets, it makes sense for entrepreneurs to hire labour and to own assets. The entrepreneur's role, then, is to arrange or organize the human and capital assets under his or her control. We extend this Knightian concept of the firm by developing a theory of delegation under Knightian uncetainty. What we call *original judgment* belongs exclusively to owners, but owners may delegate a wide range of decision rights to subordinates, who exercise *derived judgment*. We call these employees 'proxy-entrepreneurs', and ask how the firm's organizational structure — its formal and informal systems of rewards and punishments, rules for settling disputes and renegotiating agreements, means of evaluating performance and so on — can be designed to encourage forms of proxy entrepreneurship that increase firm value while discouraging actions that destroy value. Building on key ideas from the entrepreneurship literature, Austrian economics and the economic theory of the firm, we develop a framework for analysing the trade-off between productive and destructive proxy entrepreneurship. We link this analysis to the employment relation and ownership structure, providing new insights into these and related issues in the economic theory of the firm.

Keywords: judgment, entrepreneur, delegation, employment relation, ownership

Introduction

Modern firms are increasingly encouraging entrepreneurship at all levels of the oganization (e.g. Day and Wendler 1998; Yonekura and Lynskey 2002). To foster entrepreneurial attitudes and behaviour, managers must give significant discretion to employees. Delegated rights can, however, be used in both beneficial and harmful ways, presenting managers with a trade-off between encouraging beneficial entrepreneurship and facilitating harmful entrepreneurship inside the firm. Building on key ideas from the economics of entrepreneurship (Knight 1921; Casson 1982), Austrian economics (e.g. Von Hayek 1945; Von Mises 1949; Kirzner 1973) and the

Organization
Studies
28(12): 1893–1912
ISSN 0170–8406
Copyright © 2007
SAGE Publications
(Los Angeles,
London, New Delhi
and Singapore)

theory of the firm (Coase 1937; Holmström 1979; Hart 1995; Williamson 1996), we develop a framework for analysing this trade-off. We link this analysis to issues of the employment relation and asset ownership, arguing that our entrepreneurial perspective provides a fresh look at these classical issues in organizational theory.

We begin with recent work linking entrepreneurship to the economic theory of the firm using the Knightian concept of entrepreneurship as judgment (Casson 1982; Foss 1993; Langlois and Cosgel 1993; Foss and Klein 2005). The foundation of this approach is the proposition that entrepreneurial judgment is costly to trade, an idea originally suggested by Knight (1921). When judgment is complementary to other assets, it makes sense for entrepreneurs to hire labour and own assets. The entrepreneur's role, then, is to arrange or organize the human and capital assets under his or her control. This role becomes particularly important in a dynamic economy where agents face unforeseen changes, so that sequential decision-making, such as revising business plans that embody entrepreneurial judgment, is necessary (Coase 1937; Von Hayek 1945; Williamson 1996). Asset ownership plays a critical role in facilitating the entrepreneur's revision of such plans. Thus, the exercise of entrpreneurship is closely tied to resource ownership and the employment relation, providing a rationale for the existence of the firm.

The claim that entrepreneurial judgment is manifested in ownership is straightforward for small firms with one or few owners. It is harder to see the entrepreneurial element in ownership within large, complex organizations with fragmented ownership and decentralized decision-making.[1] We argue that a type of Knightian entrepreneurship — what we term *original judgment* — is inseparable from resource ownership, and is exercised by owners even if they delegate most day-to-day decisions to subordinates. In firms with decentralized organizational structures, employees have considerable latitude, but, as non-owners, their discretion is limited or constrained. In our framework, employees holding decision authority can be described as 'proxy entrepreneurs',' exercising delegated or *derived judgment* on behalf of their employers. Such employees are expected not to carry out routine instructions in a mechanical, passive way, but to apply their own judgment to new circumstances or situations that may be unknown to the employer. This type of arrangement is typically seen in the management literature as a form of empowerment, simultaneously encouraging employees to utilize the knowledge best known to them and giving them strong incentives to do so (e.g. Hill and Amabile 1993; Osterloh and Frey 2000; Gagné and Deci 2005). Such discretion is ultimately limited, because owners retain the rights to hire and fire employees and to acquire or dispose of complementary capital goods.[2] The precise manner in which employees' discretion is limited is given by the firm's organizational structure — its formal and informal systems of rewards and punishments, rules for settling disputes and renegotiating agreements, means of evaluating performance and so on. Under some organizational structures, the employment relation is highly constrained, giving employees few opportunities to engage in proxy entrepreneurship. In other firms the employment relation may be much more open. Granting such latitude to employees brings benefits and costs. As agents become less constrained, they are likely to engage in both 'productive' proxy entrepreneurship — activities that increase joint surplus — and 'destructive' proxy entrepreneurship, meaning activities that reduce joint surplus. One important function of contracts and organizational design is to balance productive and destructive proxy entrepreneurship by selecting and enforcing the proper contractual constraints. The optimal organizational structure, in the Knightian perspective, is one that encourages employees to use derived judgment in ways that increase firm value while discouraging unproductive rent-seeking, influence activities and other forms of proxy entrepreneurship that destroy value. The allocation of ownership rights and the characteristics of the employment relation thus matter for the efficient exercise of judgment. While not at variance with established approaches to the economic theory of the firm (e.g. Holmström 1979; Hart 1995; Williamson 1996), our approach goes beyond this literature.

The paper proceeds as follows. We begin by outlining the judgment approach to entrepreneurship, linking it to resource ownership, and distinguishing between original and derived forms of judgment. Next, we model, by means of a simple graphical example, the trade-offs between destructive and productive derived judgment. We argue that ownership of assets is a means for an entrepreneur holding original judgment to implement his or her preferred extent of derived judgment in the firm. The overall contribution of this paper is to show how the notion of entrepreneurship as judgment enriches the theory of economic organization. The Knightian approach to entrepreneurship, we argue, complements traditional approaches to the modern economic theory of the firm (i.e. moral hazard, the hold-up problem) (Holmström 1979; Hart 1995; Williamson 1996; Kim and Mahoney 2005).

Judgment and Delegation

Entrepreneurship as Judgment

Foss and Klein (2005) show how the theory of entrepreneurship and the theory of the firm can be linked using the concept of entrepreneurship as judgment. This view traces its origins to the first systematic treatment of entrepreneurship in economics, Richard Cantillon's *Essai sur la nature de commerce en géneral* (1755). It conceives entrepreneurship as judgmental decision-making under conditions of uncertainty. Judgment refers primarily to business decision-making when the range of possible future outcomes, let alone the likelihood of individual outcomes, is generally unknown (what Knight terms 'uncertainty', rather than mere probabilistic risk). More generally, judgment is required 'when no obviously correct model or decision rule is available or when relevant data is unreliable or incomplete' (Casson 1993).

As such, judgment is distinct from notions prevalent in the entrepreneurship literature, such as boldness, daring or imagination (Begley and Boyd 1987; Chandler and Jansen 1992; Aldrich and Wiedenmayer 1993; Hood and Young 1993; Lumpkin and Dess 1996), innovation (Schumpeter 1911), alertness (Kirzner 1973), leadership (Witt 1998a, 1998b) and other concepts of entrepreneurship that appear in the economics and management literatures. Judgment must be exercised in mundane circumstances, as Knight (1921) emphasized, for ongoing operations as well as new ventures. Alertness is the ability to react to *existing* opportunities, while judgment refers to the creation of *new* opportunities.[3] Those who specialize in judgmental decision-making may be dynamic, charismatic leaders, but they need not possess these traits. In short, decision-making under uncertainty is entrepreneurial, whether it involves imagination, creativity, leadership and related factors or not.

Knight (1921) introduces judgment to link profit and the firm to uncertainty. Judgment primarily refers to the process of businesspeople forming estimates of future events in situations in which the relevant probability distributions are themselves unknown.[4] Entrepreneurship represents a particular form of judgment, one that cannot be assessed in terms of its marginal product and which cannot, accordingly, be paid a wage (Knight 1921: 311). Various reasons for this asserted non-contractibility are given in the literature. The 'decisive factors', Knight argues, 'are so largely on the inside of the person making the decision that the "instances" are not amenable to objective description and external control' (Knight 1921: 251). Kirzner (1979: 181) argues that 'entrepreneurship reveals to the market what the market did not realize was available, or indeed, needed at all'. Casson (1982: 14) takes a more Schumpeterian position, arguing that '[t]he entrepreneur believes he is right, while everyone else is wrong. Thus the essence of entrepreneurship is being different — being different because one has a different perception of the situation' (see also Casson 1997; Demsetz 1988). The implication of these arguments is that there is no market for the judgment that entrepreneurs rely on, and therefore exercising judgment requires the person with judgment to start a firm. Of course, entrepreneurs can hire consultants, forecasters, technical experts and so on. However, in doing so they are exercising their own entrepreneurial judgment about whom to hire.

Original and Derived Judgment

Original judgment refers to the entrepreneurial formation and execution of a business idea. The idea may be anything from a loose, overall concept of how to combine inputs into outputs to a carefully specified, detailed business plan. A business plan involves the identification and coordination of inputs and activities designed to make the business profitable. If the plan is highly detailed, the entrepreneur may delegate parts of its implementation to agents. However, in this case the entrepreneur will limit the employees' entrepreneurial behaviour, as the essential actions to be taken are already laid out in the plan. If the entrepreneur recognizes a need for ongoing adjustment of the business plan, and wishes to take advantage of specific knowledge he or she does not possess, he or she will delegate the right to exercise derived judgment to employees.[5]

The hierarchy of delegation may be deep and nested. Owners may choose to exercise original judgment directly, in the day-to-day management of assets, or to delegate some or all proximate decision rights to subordinates. Owners may be represented by a board of directors that decides which decision rights to delegate to managers, who exercise derived judgment over resource uses (and try to communicate such judgments to the board). Managers may then further delegate their own derived judgment rights to lower-level employees. As Knight (1921) argued, corporate governance is a nested hierarchy of judgment. In an important sense, however, original judgment remains with the owner, because as a minimum, even the most 'passive' owners must choose someone to manage the asset. As Rothbard (1962: 538) puts it:

'Hired managers may successfully direct production or choose production processes. But the ultimate responsibility and control of production rests inevitably with the owner, with the businessman whose property the product is until it is sold. It is the owners who make the decision concerning how much capital to invest and in what particular processes. And particularly, it is the owners who must choose the managers. The ultimate decisions concerning the use of their property and the choice of the men to manage it must therefore be made by the owners and by no one else.'[6]

The claim that owners make the 'ultimate' decisions about resource use does not imply that owners supply the complete *content* of the firm's entrepreneurial plans. Instead, the owners, or the board of directors on behalf of the owners, may rely on plans and proposals developed by hired managers or outside consultants. In this situation, the board's judgment consists of deciding whether to commit resources to implement the business plan presented by the manager or consultant. In Fama and Jensen's (1983) terminology, owners exercise *decision control* while delegating *decision management* to non-owners.

In large, complex organizations, judgment is delegated across many levels. As the success of the business plan likely depends on the actions of top managers, the board delegates considerable discretion to them. These managers, in turn, delegate discretion to their own subordinates, and so on throughout the organization. Thus, all levels below the owners exercise judgment that is derived from the original judgment of the owners. For ease of exposition, in the following we focus on a simple model of a single entrepreneur–owner holding original judgment, and an employee who can exercise derived judgment. This employee exercises derived judgment in the sense that the entrepreneur delegates discretion to him but constrains his entrepreneurial activities, where the relevant constraints are derived from the original business plan and relate to, for example, the type of activities and the means of coordination described in that plan.

Derived Entrepreneurship: Productive and Destructive

The Productive/Destructive Distinction

In most of the entrepreneurship literature, both in economics and in management, there is a general, though usually implicit claim that all entrepreneurial activity is socially beneficial (e.g. Von Mises 1949; Kirzner 1973; Yonekura and Lynskey 2002; Shane 2003). However, as Baumol (1990) pointed out, entrepreneurship may be socially harmful if it takes the form of rent-seeking, or attempts to influence governments or management to redistribute income in a way that consumes resources and brings about a social loss. It is therefore necessary to introduce a distinction between productive and destructive entrepreneurship. This distinction applies in principle to both original and derived entrepreneurship. However, in the following we only consider the distinction in the context of derived entrepreneurship.

1898   Organization Studies 28(12)

For employees to exercise derived judgment they must have some discretion. When employees use their discretion to expend effort creating or discovering new attributes and taking control of these in such a way that value creation is reduced, we shall speak of 'destructive entrepreneurship'. Thus, discovering new forms of moral hazard (Holmström 1979), creating hold-ups (Williamson 1996) and inventing new ways of engaging in rent-seeking activities (Baumol 1990) are examples of destructive entrepreneurship. 'Productive entrepreneurship' refers to the creation or discovery of new attributes that lead to an increase in value creation. For example, a franchisee may discover new local tastes that, in turn, may form the basis for new products for the entire chain; an employee may figure out better uses of production assets and communicate this to the total quality management (TQM) team of which he is a member; etc. In the following, we use this distinction to sketch an entrepreneurial approach to internal organization.

As described above, we assume that employees, while not exercising the original judgment, exercise derived judgment through decision rights that are delegated to them. As proxy entrepreneurs, they make decisions about the use of resources owned by others.[7] These decisions may be value-creating (productive) or value-destroying (destructive). Although original judgment cannot be assigned a marginal product, owners can form expectations about the costs and benefits of employees' derived judgments.

Managing Derived Judgment

Many firms operate on the presumption that beneficial effects can be produced by giving employees more rights to work with company assets, monitoring them less and trusting them more. We shall call this a matter of 'reducing constraints on employees' in various dimensions. For example, firms such as 3M allocate time to research employees that they are basically free to use however they wish. This practice, it is hoped, will result in serendipitous discoveries. Many consulting firms have adopted similar practices. Industrial firms have long known that employees with many decision rights — researchers, for example — must be monitored and constrained in different, and typically much looser, ways than those employees charged only with routine tasks. More broadly, the increasing emphasis on 'empowerment' during recent decades reflects a recognition that employees derive a benefit from controlling aspects of their job situation (Osterloh and Frey 2000; Gagné and Deci 2005). The total quality movement emphasizes that delegating various rights to employees motivates them to find new ways to increase the mean and reduce the variance of quality (Jensen and Wruck 1994). To the extent that such activities increase created value, they represent productive entrepreneurship.[8]

Stimulating the productive creation and discovery of new asset attributes by reducing constraints on employees results in principal-agent relationships that are more open-ended, because agents get opportunities to exercise their own, often far-reaching, judgments. However, reducing the constraints that agents face introduces potentially destructive proxy entrepreneurship. Managing the trade-off between productive and destructive proxy entrepreneurship thus becomes a critical management task.

How can firms reduce the chance that derived judgment will be exercised in ways that are detrimental to the firm? In other words, how can destructive proxy entrepreneurship be minimized? Firms may delimit employees' use of assets, such as telephone and internet, by specifying their use rights over the relevant assets, instructing them to act in a proper manner towards customers, to exercise care when operating the firm's equipment, and the like. However, firms are unlikely to succeed entirely in their attempt to curb such activities. Monitoring employees may be costly; moreover, employees may creatively circumvent constraints, for example by inventing ways to hide their behaviour. Although firms may know that such destructive entrepreneurship takes place, they may prefer not to try to constrain it further. This is because the various constraints that firms impose on employees (or, more generally, that contracting partners impose on each other) to curb destructive entrepreneurship may have the unwanted side effect that productive entrepreneurship is stifled (see Kirzner 1985). More generally, imposing (too many) constraints on employees may reduce their propensity to create or discover new attributes of productive assets within the limits set by the business plan.

In this context, the employment relation and asset ownership are important because they give owner–entrepreneurs the rights and the ability to define formal and informal contractual constraints, that is, to choose their own preferred trade-offs. Ownership by conferring authority allows the employer-entrepreneur to establish his or her preferred organizational structure — and therefore a certain combination of productive and destructive entrepreneurship — at lowest cost. This function of ownership is particularly important in a dynamic world (Schumpeter 1911; Kirzner 1973; Littlechild 1986: D'Aveni 1994), where the trade-offs between productive and destructive entrepreneurship inside the firm are likely to change as the entrepreneur-owner revises his judgment.

An Example

Consider a relation between two actors, Jack and Jill. Cooperation between Jack and Jill generates gains from trade because their services are complementary. Each can exercise either original or derived judgment. Assume that the relation is an employment relation and that it involves the use of an asset. The relation is only productive if the asset is used (cf. our earlier remarks on judgment and asset ownership). This asset has multiple attributes (Barzel 1997), that is, multiple functions, uses and characteristics. Given Knightian ignorance and uncertainty, Jack and Jill do not know all relevant present and future attributes of the asset. Instead, attributes must be discovered, over time, as the asset is deployed in production. The relation can be organized so that Jack is employer and Jill employee, or vice versa. The asset may be owned by Jack or by Jill. In this mini-economy (cf. Holmström 1999), what allocation of ownership and assignment of roles of employer and employee maximizes value?

The employer exercises original judgment by conceiving and implementing a business plan. The employee exercises derived judgment in executing all or elements of that plan. The employer puts the plan in place by instructing and monitoring the employee in accordance with the plan; for example, by monitoring whether the employee maintains the value of the business plan by keeping the required quality levels of the product or service, physical assets, suppliers, etc. The employer not only forms original judgment, but also revises the business plan in the course of the relation as he discovers new uses of the assets in the project. As the employee is also equipped with entrepreneurial abilities; he or she may discover hitherto undiscovered attributes of the asset in the relation. Some of these discoveries will add to the value of the business plan, either by adding elements to the plan or increasing the effectiveness of the implementation of the plan. For example, in a restaurant chain, the discovery, by a local manager, of a new dish may add value to the overall chain.

The employment relation is constrained in several dimensions. There are limits to what the employee can do, as well as when, how, with whom, etc. In other words, the decision (property) rights held by employee are circumscribed by the employer (cf. Jones 1983). The number, scope and character of such constraints are choice variables (imposing them on the employee obviously requires bargaining power; we deal with this later). The employer may issue more or less detailed instructions. At one end of the spectrum, the employer instructs the employee about everything; no scope is left for derived judgment. At the other end, the employee has very considerable discretion; he has virtually full scope for exercising his or her derived judgment. Here we use the terminology that the relation can be made more or less 'incomplete.'[9] Less complete relations are those that give the employee more discretion. To abstract from enforcement issues (which are well treated in the modern economic theory of the firm), we assume that all the constraints that the employer specifies can be costlessly enforced, once implemented. What may require bargaining power, however, is the implementation of the employer's preferred constraints.

Value Creation as a Function of Entrepreneurship

A suggested above, there are costs as well as benefits associated with the relaxation of employment constraints, and, hence, an optimum level of incompleteness that is larger than zero. Figure 1 maps Jack and Jill's expectations (we assume these coincide) with respect to the effect on firm value of the employee's productive and destructive proxy entrepreneurship as functions of the incompleteness of the relation when combined with the employer's original judgment, as embodied in the business concept. The trade-off may be regulated by means of the constraints that are placed on the employee, for example, by determining the budgets to which employees have access (Jensen and Meckling 1992), the activities they can engage in (Holmström 1989), the people with whom they can work (Holmström and Milgrom 1990), the type of equipment to which they have access and how they are allowed to operate that equipment (Barzel 1997).[10] Such specifications of decision rights are simultaneously specifications of incompleteness. To simplify, one may think of 'the degree of incompleteness' in terms of the time that the employee is allowed to use corporate resources (including their own work time) to conduct 'research', that is, activities that are not directly prescribed by the employer—owner, as in the above example of 3M allowing their research personnel very considerable discretion.

Figure 1.
Monetary Surplus
as a Function of
Entrepreneurship

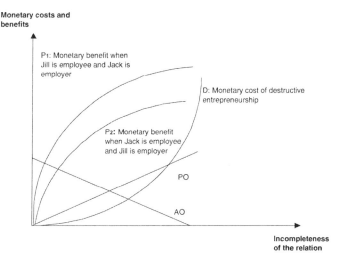

The P-curve then shows the benefits that may result from such *productive* proxy entrepreneurship as a function of the free time the agent is given. The P-curve thus maps those new discoveries of the employee that, when implemented, complements the employer's original judgment. The claim is that, as the employee is given more freedom, there is a greater probability that he or she will discover more beneficial attributes of the productive asset he or she operates. For example, the probability increases that the employee may discover new ways of making the asset more effective or new markets to which the asset's services may be deployed. The relation between total benefits and more free time is a strictly concave one. The decreasing marginal returns from new discoveries may be caused by the increasing difficulties of implementing the new discoveries, given that the employer and the employee are constrained in terms of the time that is available for productive activities. Alternatively, the employee's attention is more focused on making valuable discoveries when he or she has less free time than when he or she has more.

Because of differential entrepreneurial capabilities, and the complementarities between Jack and Jill's judgments, it matters for the joint monetary surplus from the relation who assumes the role of employer, the principal, and who is the agent (and as we argue later, who owns the asset). As shown in Figure 1, joint monetary surplus is higher when Jill is employee and Jack is employer.

However, there are also costs to giving the employee more free time for discovery, namely destructive entrepreneurial activities. The D-curve shows the costs from *destructive* proxy entrepreneurship as a function of the free time the employee is given.[11] The claim is that, as the employee is given more freedom, there is a greater probability that he or she will discover new ways of destroying value. For example, the probability increases that the employee may discover new ways of misusing equipment, engaging in wasteful new projects, etc. Thus, with increased discretion over the multi-attribute asset, the employee will discover more new ways of controlling attributes, which increases the employee's own benefit, but reduces expected joint surplus.

The Parties' Preferred Constraints

Although the different degrees of incompleteness represent differences in created value for the different teams (i.e. {Jack as employer, Jill as employee}, {Jill as employer, Jack as employee}), we cannot identify the preferred points of the parties until we have taken full account of their costs and benefits, that is, their opportunity costs and the way in which they share the joint monetary surplus from the relation.

With respect to the *employee*, we assume that she realizes relationship-specific private benefits (i.e. a non-transferable utility) of engaging in entrepreneurial activities and that this provides her sufficient motivation.[12] Because of these benefits, the employee suffers opportunity costs of being constrained.

The AO curve in Figure 1, assumed to be linear, represents the employee's opportunity costs of being constrained. These costs are inversely related to the degree of incompleteness. The employer suffers opportunity costs (the PO curve) of letting the employee exercise judgment by spending work time and other corporate resources on activities that may lead to discovery, because such resources could have been spent on routine activities. We assume that these costs are a linear function of the time given to the employee. Both parties share the monetary joint surplus in some proportion. We can assume, as is conventional, that they share 50:50. The employee's total benefits are thus the sum of her share of the joint surplus plus her private benefits, while the employer's net benefits are simply his share of the surplus minus his opportunity costs. Given the way these curves have been drawn, the team that maximizes net created value (monetary) is the one where Jack is employer and Jill is employee.

Given the specification of costs (including opportunity costs) and benefits in Figure 1, Figure 2 shows the preferred constraints of the parties. Figure 2 depicts a curve, Esurp., which represents the employer's share of the created value (minus his opportunity costs)[13] and a curve, esurp., which represents the employee's share of the surplus plus her private benefits.[14] Given this, the employer's preferred degree of contractual incompleteness is given by I^*_E and the employee's is given by I^*_e. Thus, the parties disagree about how many constraints should be imposed upon the employee! The parties may strike any contract between I^*_E and I^*_e (this will always be beneficial compared to a situation of no contract). However, given the assumption that a part of the employee's total benefits and the employer's costs are private, bargaining is likely to be costly and dissipate value.

In fact, as the example is constructed, no sharing rule can generate agreement on the preferred degree of contractual incompleteness, and any sharing rule will therefore cause some inefficiency. Moreover, according to Figure 2, it is more lucrative to be an employee than to be a principal, which may imply that the party who holds comparative advantages in forming original judgment (i.e. Jack, in Figure 1) may prefer to be an employee with the party who is comparatively

Figure 2.
The Parties' Preferred
Degree of Incompleteness

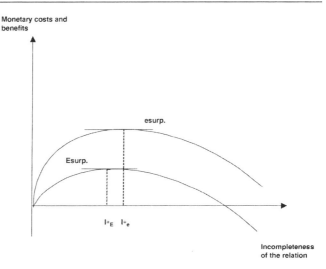

disadvantaged in forming original judgment as a employer (i.e. Jill, in Figure 1). This is clearly inefficient: As the example has been constructed, the team in which Jack is employer and Jill is employee creates more value than the other team.

In a zero transaction cost world, this inefficiency may be handled through the appropriate choices of sharing rules, bribes, and contractual constraints (Coase 1960). However, bargaining costs may swamp the benefits from such arrangements (Wernerfelt 1997). Given bargaining costs, it matters who sets sharing rules and contractual constraints. If, for example, the employee can set the constraints but cannot bribe the principal, not even 100 % residual claimancy will make it attractive to become employer, since, in this case, the agent will prefer total absence of constraints, which in turn means that joint monetary surplus will be zero (and the employer still has to suffer the opportunity costs of the employee's entrepreneurial activities). The question, then, is how these inefficiencies are minimized, that is, choosing the efficient team (i.e, team {Jack is employer, Jill is employee} or {Jill is employer, Jack is employee}), sharing rules and contractual constraints. We argue that ownership to the asset in the relation plays a key role with respect to all three issues.

Asset Ownership

Ownership Facilitates Entrepreneurship

Ownership plays a key role in easing entrepreneurship and exchange (i.e. minimizing costs of dissipation). Asset ownership confers a *bundle* of rights, including rights to hitherto unknown attributes of the relevant asset. Ownership reduces information, communication and contracting costs relative to a situation in which it was necessary to contract over all these rights. Thus, ownership eases the implementation of entrepreneurial judgment in a productive venture by allowing entrepreneurs to acquire, in one transaction, a bundle of rights to attributes (i.e. a distinct asset). This means that the parties do not have to engage in costly bargaining over many rights to single attributes (Barzel 1997). The dissipation of value is at a minimum. Moreover, ownership also facilitates the use of entrepreneurial judgment in a productive venture by conferring a legally recognized right to define contractual constraints (Coase 1937; Williamson 1996).

Recall now the possible inefficiency caused by the individual with comparative advantages in forming original judgment (here, Jack) wishing to assume the role of employee and being directed by the comparatively disadvantaged individual (here, Jill) because this would give him higher returns. This inefficiency may be avoided if somehow Jack can be made just as well off as employer in the efficient team as employee in the inefficient team. Simply adjusting the sharing rule with respect to the monetary surplus to compensate Jack will not do: If Jack receives, for example, 100% of the surplus, this will not compensate him, if Jill keeps the right to set the constraints. In fact, the greater the employer's share in the surplus, the greater will be the employee's incentive to choose constraints that maximize his or her own private benefits at the cost of the joint monetary surplus.

The power to set constraints is conferred by asset ownership. Thus, an employer who owns the asset can set constraints in such a way that he or she can influence the size of the surplus that will be shared among the parties, and in this way make sure that he or she will be actually be compensated for assuming the role of principal in the efficient team. In other words, ownership has the function, in our example, of minimizing the dissipation of value — it means that Jack and Jill do not have to engage in costly bargaining — and of selecting the efficient team, that is, the one that best utilizes the parties' comparative advantages in forming original and derived judgment. To put it in a compact manner, ownership is a means of implementing the principal's preferred degree of incompleteness in a low-cost way.

Although we have presented our arguments in the context of a static setting, the above functions of ownership are particularly important in a dynamic context, because in such a context an ongoing process of entrepreneurial creation and discovery will require that constraints in a relation are redefined. Thus, in terms of Figure 1, the slopes of the D- and the P-curves are likely to change over time as a result of entrepreneurial activities on the part of both the agent and the principal. The power conferred by ownership allows the principal to adjust the level of contractual constraints to ensure that he or she has incentives to maintain the role of principal in the efficient team, realizing comparative advantages of entrepreneurship. Indeed, as noted below, the notion that contractual constraints define the scope of entrepreneurship, rather than simply allowing agents to choose the values of particular variables with known distributions, is an inherently dynamic, forward-looking concept of organizational design.

Other Applications

Our theory of ownership as a means of implementing a preferred set of constraints in a productive relation, and therefore a certain combination of productive and destructive entrepreneurship, has application beyond the determination of who should be the owner. It can also cast light over the more general issue of why a certain agent owns a certain asset, independent of his relationships with other agents. The theory of ownership presented in Hart (1995) revolves around the hold-up problem: One should own those assets that are complementary to one's (non-contractible) human capital investments, since this increases (ex post) bargaining power and therefore the rents that may be expected from investments. This seems to be a less-than-general explanation: people own many things, the ownership of which cannot be explained by hold-up considerations (e.g. standard kitchen utensils in a household).

Another common idea is that those who discover new knowledge have an incentive to use it themselves because of the transaction costs of knowledge transfer. Given this, there is a general tendency for ownership of complementary assets to move to the knowledge source (rather than the other way round), because knowledge is harder to trade than most other resources (Foss 1993; Casson 1997). The problem with this explanation is that it is does not allow to distinguish analytically between ownership and rental agreements. Our theory can do this, however.

For example, suppose that a car rental company put very few constraints in the contracts they offer renters, so that the latter could use the company's cars for the purpose of running a taxi business or a truck operation. Thus, the company does not much constrain productive *and* destructive proxy entrepreneurship. In reality, however, a car rental company will normally prefer to circumscribe, in a relatively detailed way, the possible productive and destructive entrepreneurship that the renter can engage in. For example, usually, rental cars cannot be used for commercial purposes, among other things because the company fears that the car will not be driven in a proper way, and that this will diminish the demand of other renters for the car's services. Thus, in order to maintain demand and control externalities, the company constrains the use of the car in many ways. However, a renter who wishes to use a rental car for entrepreneurial, commercial purposes is not likely to find the constraints imposed by the car rental company to be optimal. Hence, that person may prefer to own the car in order to be able to impose his or her own preferred way of using the car: that is, he or she owns the car in order to carry out his or her own entrepreneurial plans.[15]

Conclusion

Contribution to Theory

In the entrepreneurial judgment approach, the theory of the firm becomes a theory of how the entrepreneur arranges his or her capital assets, including which combinations of assets they will seek to acquire and which assets they may later divest in an attempt to carry out the commercial experiment that embodies their judgment (Knight 1921; Casson 1982; Foss 1993; Langlois and Cosgel 1993; Foss and Klein 2005). The present paper extends this approach by explaining how entrepreneur–owners delegate decision rights to employees and how the employees' exercise of derived judgment is best circumscribed.

In established economic theories of organizational design, delegation is usually analysed with a principal–agent model. Such models have been exhaustively treated in the economics literature. A basic implication of this apparatus is that more complete contracts are preferable to less complete contracts. However, if agents are allowed to exercise derived judgment, as in our approach, this conclusion changes. There is a positive level of incompleteness, not because complete contracts are costly to draft (as in Crocker and Reynolds 1993), but because complete contracts curb entrepreneurial activities, both productive and destructive. More generally, in the kind of open-ended world envisaged by Knight (1921) as well as Austrian economists (Von Mises 1949; Shackle 1972; O'Driscoll and Rizzo 1985; Koppl and Minniti 2003), limiting employee discretion involves more than simply making formal, written contracts more complete. Discretion is constrained by organizational structure, which includes not only formal contracts, but also the complementary elements of informal norms ('corporate culture' and other implicit contracts), official and unofficial means for resolving disputes (Williamson 1996), and so on. Ownership conveys the right to define key elements of this organizational structure.[16]

Moreover, in contrast to the new property rights approach (Hart 1995), ownership has broad implications for firm performance. In our approach, the arrangement of property titles affects not only ex ante relationship-specific investments (as in the new property rights approach). but also how the firm will perform through time (original judgment rights should be allocated to the party best able to exercise them); likewise, internal organization affects not only current performance (as in agency theory, mechanism design, etc.), but also dynamics — how derived judgment will be exercised through time. The judgment approach to organizational design is thus inherently dynamic.

Implications for Future Research

As already indicated, the approach of this paper is in some important ways different from the mainstream in the economic theory of the firm. Thus, we have sidestepped the issue of motivating the agent by means of explicit incentives, by assuming that the agent realized a private benefit from having the freedom to engage in entrepreneurial activities that provide sufficient motivation for them to engage in these activities. This is not because we consider explicit incentives unimportant, but rather because we think the assumption that the agents can be (partly) motivated by being given more influence over their job situation is a realistic one (and a neglected one, too). Incorporating explicit incentives into the analysis should provide additional insight into optimal organizational design, however.

Our approach also suggests that existing studies of contractual completeness, by focusing narrowly on the presence or absence of certain clauses in formal, written contracts, may not adequately capture the actual discretion possessed by parties in economic relationships. Agents may have substantial rights to exercise derived judgment even when they are subject to strong, formal contractual restrictions. This is because, under Knightian uncertainty, the contracting space is always open-ended, so that new margins may be created or discovered over which agents may optimize their gains.[17] To give our approach empirical content, however, it is necessary to specify some observable proxies for derived judgment. It is unclear how such proxies could be identified in a large sample of firms, suggesting that case studies and quantitative analysis based on surveys of employee perceptions are necessary.

Conceiving of owners as entrepreneurs has further implications for the economic theory of the firm. Our analysis has focused on the judgment rights delegated to employees and the importance of stimulating productive proxy entrepreneurship. This does not imply, however, that we regard the entrepreneur–owner's original judgment rights as purely formal and symbolic. On the contrary, we view owners — even corporate shareholders — as critical decision makers, not simply passive providers of capital.[18] As such, their behaviour belongs at the forefront of research on the economics of organization. For example, if owners are entrepreneurs, then the firm should be viewed not as a production process, a stock of knowledge, or a governance structure, but as an *investment*. The firm-as-investment literature (Gabor and Pearce 1952, 1958; Vickers 1970, 1987; Moroney 1972; Klein 1999) challenges several aspects of conventional micro-economics, such as the claim that managers should expand output to the point where marginal revenue equals marginal cost, rather than the point where the return on the last dollar of money capital is just equal to the opportunity cost of that last dollar of money capital.[19] The firm-as-investment concept relates closely to an emerging literature on merger as a form of firm-level investment (Bittlingmayer 1996; Andrade and Stafford 2004).

Finally, we note some implications of our perspective for ongoing work in the tradition of Austrian economics. Much of the contemporary Austrian literature focuses on the organic, 'spontaneous' nature of market exchange, the distribution of tacit knowledge (Von Hayek 1945), and the failure of top-down, central planning (Von Mises 1920). However, in our view, the emphasis on 'market' over 'hierarchy' (to use Williamsonian terms) has resulted in a lack of attention to organizations, the ubiquitous, central features of all modern economies (Simon 1991).[20] In Foss's (2001) terminology, even in 'Hayekian settings' there is a role for 'Misesian ownership' and 'Coasian authority'. We hope the analysis presented in the present paper encourages further research in the Knightian and Austrian traditions on the functions of ownership, authority and delegation within firms and other organizations.

Notes

1   While much of the modern entrepreneurship literature focuses on start-ups and sole proprietorships, it is striking that none of the major contributions to the economic theory of entrepreneurship — those of Schumpeter, Knight, Mises, Kirzner and others — dealt specifically with small or new firms.

2   To state the issue differently: decentralized decision rights and incentive compensation approximate the high-powered incentives of private property and the price mechanism, but not perfectly (Foss 2003). De facto discretion is not a perfect substitute for de jure discretion. We thus

stand with Coase (1937), Williamson (1985, 1996) and Hart (1995) and against Alchian and Demsetz (1977) and Jensen and Meckling (1976), in seeing firm and market as alternative mechanisms for resource allocation, rather than simply different sets of contractual relations.

3   In the treatment of Austrian economist Israel Kirzner, entrepreneurship is characterized as 'a *responding* agency. I view the entrepreneur not as a source of innovative ideas ex nihilo, but as being *alert* to the opportunities that exist *already* and are waiting to be noticed' (Kirzner 1973: 74).

4   There is a long debate on whether Knightian uncertainty is meaningful, or whether 'uncertainty' is simply highly subjective, and therefore not insurable, risk (e.g. Demsetz 1988). We are agnostic on this issue, which does not seem to matter for our argument. Relatedly, it may be open to discussion whether Knightian uncertainty includes ignorance in the sense of unforeseen contingencies (Shackle 1972; Littlechild 1986; Williamson 1996). Unforeseen contingencies are important in our framework.

5   Note that the notion of 'derived judgment' does not imply a subordinate position in economic or legal significance; the notions of original and derived judgment are hierarchical (and temporal).

6   Kirzner (1973: 68) argues, similarly, that entrepreneurial alertness cannot be fully delegated: 'It is true that "alertness" ... may be hired; but one who hires an employee alert to possibilities of discovering knowledge has himself displayed alertness of a still higher order .... The entrepreneurial decision to hire is thus the ultimate hiring decision, responsible in the last resort for all factors that are directly or indirectly hired for his project.' Kirzner goes on to quote Knight (1921: 291): 'What we call "control" consists mainly of selecting someone else to do the "controlling"' Unlike Knightian judgment, however, Kirznerian alertness can be exercised without asset ownership. For more on the contrast between Knight and Kirzner, see Foss and Klein (2005).

7   Of course, to the extent that the proxy entrepreneur's decisions affect the value of his or her own personal reputation, human capital and so on, that person is acting as an entrepreneur–owner, exercising original judgment with regard to these intangible, personal assets.

8   Our notion of 'more constrained' and 'less constrained' employment relations includes, but is broader than, the notion of contractual completeness in the transaction cost literature (e.g. Crocker and Masten 1991; Crocker and Reyonlds 1993; Saussier 2000). Crocker and Reynolds (1993) define completeness as the probability that a contingency not covered by prior contractual agreement arises. Under Knightian uncertainty, all contracts are incomplete, meaning that it is impossible to specify all contingencies ex ante. The firm's organizational structure, governing the employment relation more broadly, can constrain employee opportunism even when formal contracts are highly incomplete in the Crocker and Reynolds sense.

9   As described above, we have in mind a broader notion of 'completeness' than what is found in modern contract theory.

10 For example, regulating with whom an employee is allowed to interact clearly influences destructive as well as productive entrepreneurship: on the one hand, it may lead to destructive collusion among agents (as in Holmström and Milgrom 1990); on the other hand it may lead to the generation of new ideas as the TQM literature emphasizes (Jensen and Wruck 1994).

11 Of course, one may envisage not only different P-curves, but also different D-curves.

12 Aghion and Tirole (1997) make a similar, clearly heroic, assumption. As justification, one may point to the fact that the ability to more or less freely dispose of a certain percentage of one's working hours has become increasingly part of many employment packages, particularly in 'dynamic' industries (IT, biotech, consulting, etc.).

13 More precisely, the employer receives Esurp. = ½ (P − D).

14 More precisely, the employee receives esurp. = ½ (P − D) + (k − AO), where k represents the value of AO when incompleteness is zero.

15 Of course, in this situation, car rental companies may increase earnings by offering differentiated products, where rental fees and contractual constraints differ for different segments of the market, or new firms may arise for special-purpose segments of the market. However, even those firms that offer cars with fewer or other contractual constraints may be too constraining for some, particularly those who (expect that they) are likely to discover so far unimagined activities (i.e. entrepreneurs). They will still want to become owners.

16 We do not claim that the informal aspects of organizational structure are *completely* controlled, or 'designed,' by owners. We certainly recognize that, for example, corporate culture can grow and evolve organically, that there is an element of 'spontaneous order' within the firm. But we maintain that formal constraints, established and revised by owners, are the ultimate drivers of organizational form.

17 See Foss and Foss (2000) for a discussion of how this heuristic contrasts with the conventional modelling approach in economic contract theory. Of course, in actual modelling, contracting spaces are somehow closed, because of the immense mathematical complexities of working

with open spaces. Foss and Foss invoke the notion of an open contracting space as a feature of the interpretation and application of the model.

18 These claims of course apply a fortiori to large block-holders, institutional investors, venture capitalists or angel investors in venture-backed firms, and other 'active' investors or investment groups.

19 If the firm is earning positive net returns at its current level of output, instead of increasing output until marginal net returns fall to zero, the firm could simply take those returns and employ them elsewhere, either to set up a new firm in the same industry or to diversify into a new industry (Gabor and Pearce 1952: 253). The efficient scale of production is determined by outside investment opportunities, not simply the marginal returns from producing a single output.

20 An obvious exception is Von Mises (1944).

References

Aghion, Philippe, and Jean Tirole
1997 'Formal and real authority in organization'. *Journal of Political Economy* 105: 1–29.

Alchian, Armen A., and Harold Demsetz
1977 'Production, information costs, and economic organization' in *Economic forces at work*. Armen A. Alchian (ed.). Indianapolis: Liberty Press.

Aldrich, Howard E., and Gabriele Wiedenmayer
1993 'From traits to rates: An ecological perspective on organizational foundings' in *Advances in entrepreneurship, firm emergence, and growth*. Jerome Katz and Robert Brockhaus (eds), 145–195. Greenwich, CN: JAI Press.

Andrade, Gregor, and Erik Stafford
2004 'Investigating the economic role of mergers'. *Journal of Corporate Finance* 10: 1–36.

Barzel, Yoram
1997 *Economic analysis of property rights*, 2nd edn. Cambridge: Cambridge University Press.

Baumol, William J.
1990 'Entrepreneurship: Productive, unproductive and destructive'. *Journal of Political Economy* 98: 893–919.

Begley, Thomas, and David Boyd
1987 'Psychological characteristics associated with performance in entrepreneurial firms and smaller businesses'. *Journal of Business Venturing* 2: 79–93

Bittlingmayer, George
1996 'Merger as a form of investment'. *Kyklos* 49: 127–153.

Cantillon, Richard
1755 *Essai sur la nature de commerce en général*. 1931 edn, Henry Higgs (ed.) London: Macmillan.

Casson, Mark C.
1982 *The entrepreneur: An economic theory*. Oxford: Martin Robertson.

Casson, Mark C.
1993 'Entrepreneurship' in *The Fortune encyclopedia of economics*. David H. Henderson (ed.). New York: Warner Books.

Casson, Mark
1997 *Information and organization*. Oxford: Oxford University Press.

Chandler, G. N., and E. Jansen
1992 'The founder's self-assessed competence and venture performance'. *Journal of Business Venturing* 7: 223–236.

Coase, Ronald H.
1937 'The nature of the firm' in *The theory of the firm: Critical perspectives in business and management*, Vol. II. (1999) Nicolai J. Foss (ed.). London: Routledge.

Coase, Ronald H.
1960 'The problem of social cost' in, Coase (1988) *The firm, the market and the state*. Chicago: University of Chicago Press.

Crocker, Keith J., and Scott E. Masten
1991 'Pretia ex machina? Prices and process in long-term contracts'. *Journal of Law and Economics* 24: 69–99.

Crocker, Keith J., and Kenneth J. Reynolds
1993 'The efficiency of incomplete contracts: An empirical analysis of engine airforce procurement'. *Rand Journal of Economics* 24: 126–146.

D'Aveni, R. A.
1994 *Hypercompetition: Managing the dynamics of strategic maneuvering*. New York: Free Press.

Day, Jonathan, and Jim Wendler
1998   'The new economics of organization'.
        The McKinsey Quarterly 1: 4–18.

Demsetz, Harold
1988   'Profit as a functional return:
        Reconsidering Knight's views'.
        *Ownership, control and the firm. The
        organization of economic activity,*
        Vol. 1. Oxford and New York:
        Blackwell.

Fama, Eugene F., and Michael C. Jensen
1983   'Separation of ownership and
        control'. *Journal of Law and
        Economics* 26: 301–326.

Foss, Kirsten, and Nicolai J. Foss
2000   'Theoretical isolation in contract
        theory: Suppressing margins and
        entrepreneurship'. *Journal of
        Economic Methodology* 7: 313–339.

Foss, Nicolai J.
1993   'Theories of the firm: Contractual
        and competence perspectives'.
        Journal of Evolutionary Economics
        3: 127–144.

Foss, Nicolai J.
2001   'Misesian ownership and Coasian
        authority in Hayekian settings: The
        case of the knowledge economy'.
        *Quarterly Journal of Austrian
        Economics* 4: 3–24.

Foss, Nicolai J.
2003   'Selective intervention and internal
        hybrids: Interpreting and learning
        from the rise and decline of the
        Oticon Spaghetti Organization'.
        Organization Science 14: 331–349.

Foss, Nicolai J., and Peter G. Klein
2005   'Entrepreneurship and the economic
        theory of the firm: Any gains from
        trade?' in *Handbook of
        entrepreneurship: Disciplinary
        perspectives* . Rajshree Agarwal,
        Sharon A. Alvarez, and Olav
        Sorenson (eds). Norwell, MA:
        Kluwer.

Gabor, André, and Ivor F. Pearce
1952   ' 'A new approach to the theory of the
        firm'. *Oxford Economic Papers* 4:
        252–265.

Gabor, André, and Ivor F. Pearce
1958   'The place of money capital in the
        theory of production'. *Quarterly
        Journal of Economics* 72: 537–557.

Gagné, Maryléne, and Edward L. Deci
2005   'Self-determination theory and

        work motivation'. *Journal
        of Organizational Behavior*
        26: 331–362.

Hart, Oliver
1995   *Firms, contracts and financial
        structure.* Oxford: Clarendon Press.

Hill, K.G., and T. M. Amabile
1993   'A social-psychological perspective
        on creativity: Intrinsic motivation and
        creativity in the classroom and
        workplace' in *Understanding and
        recognizing creativity.* S. G. Isaksen,
        M. C. Murdoch, R. L. Firestien, and
        D. J. Treffinger (eds). Norwoord, NJ:
        Ablex.

Holmström, Bengt
1979   'Moral hazard and observability'.
        Bell Journal of Economics 10: 74–91.

Holmström, Bengt
1989   'Agency costs and innovation',
        *Journal of Economic Behavior and
        Organiztion* 12: 305–327.

Holmström, Bengt
1999   'The firm as a subeconomy'. *Journal
        of Law, Economics and Organization*
        15: 74–102.

Holmström, Bengt, and Paul Milgrom
1990   'Regulating trade among
        agents'. *Journal of Institutional
        and Theoretical Economics*
        146: 85–105.

Hood, J. N., and J. E. Young
1993   'Entrepreneurship's area's of
        development: A survey of top
        executives in successful firms'.
        Journal of Business Venturing 8:
        115–135.

Jensen, Michael C., and William Meckling
1976   'Theory of the firm: Managerial
        behavior, agency costs, and capital
        structure'. *Journal of Financial
        Economics* 3: 305–360.

Jensen, Michael C., and William Meckling
1992   'Specific and general knowledge
        and organizational structure' in
        Contract economics. Lars Werin
        and Hans Wijkander (eds).
        Oxford: Basil Blackwell.

Jensen, Michael C., and Karen Wruck
1994   'Science, specific knowledge
        and total quality management'.
        *Journal of Accounting and
        Economics* 18: 247–287.

Jones, G. R.
1983 'Transaction costs, property rights, and organizational culture: An exchange perspective'. *Administrative Science Quarterly* 28: 454–467.

Kim, J., and J. T. Mahoney
2005 'Property rights theory, transaction costs theory and agency theory: An oganizational economics approach to strategic management'. *Managerial and Decision Economics* 26: 223–242.

Kirzner, Israel M.
1973 *Entrepreneurship and competition.* Chicago: University of Chicago Press.

Kirzner, Israel M.
1979 *Perception, opportunity and profit: Studies in the theory of entrepreneurship.* Reprinted 1983. Chicago and London: University of Chicago Press.

Kirzner, Israel M.
1985 'The perils of regulation'. *Discovery and the capitalist process.* Chicago: University of Chicago Press.

Klein, Peter G.
1999 'Entrepreneurship and corporate governance'. *Quarterly Journal of Austrian Economics* 2: 19–42.

Knight, Frank H.
1921 *Risk, uncertainty, and profit.* New York: August M. Kelley.

Koppl, Roger, and Maria Minniti
2003 'Market processes and entrepreneurial studies' in *Handbook of entrepreneurial Research.* Zoltan Acs and David B. Audretsch (eds). Boston: Kluwer.

Langlois, Richard N., and Metin Cosgel
1993 'Frank Knight on risk, uncertainty, and the rirm: A new interpretation'. *Economic Inquiry* 31: 456–465.

Littlechild, Stephen
1986 Three types of market process' in. *Economics as a process: Essays in the new institutional economics.* Richard N. Langlois, (ed). Cambridge: Cambridge University Press.

Lumpkin, G. T., and G. G. Dess
1996 'Clarifying the entrepreneurial orientation construct and linking it to performance'. *Academy of Management Review* 21: 135–172.

Moroney, J. R.
1972 'The current state of money and production theory'. *American Economic Review*: 335–343.

O'Driscoll, Gerald P., and Mario Rizzo
1985 *The economics of time and ignorance.* Oxford: Basil Blackwell.

Osterloh, Margit, and Bruno Frey
2000 'Motivation, knowledge transfer and organizational form'. *Organization Science* 11: 538–550.

Rothbard, Murray N.
1962 *Man, economy, and state: A treatise on economic principles.* Princeton, NJ: Van Nostrand.

Saussier, Stéphane
2000 Transaction costs and contractual incompleteness: The case of Electricité de France'. *Journal of Economic Behavior and Organization* 42: 189–206.

Schumpeter, Joseph A.
[1911] 1934. *The theory of economic development: An inquiry into profits, capital, credit, interest, and the business cycle.* Trans by Redvers Opie. Cambridge, MA: Harvard University Press.

Shackle, George L. S.
1972 *Epistemics and economics.* Cambridge: Cambridge University Press.

Shane, Scott
2003 *A general theory of entrepreneurship.* Cheltenham: Edward Elgar.

Simon, H. A.
1991 'Organizations and markets'. *Journal of Economic Perspectives* 5: 25–44

Vickers, Douglas
1970 'The cost of capital and the structure of the firm'. *Journal of Finance* 25: 1061–1080.

Vickers, Douglas
1987 *Money capital in the theory of the firm: A preliminary analysis.* Cambridge: Cambridge University Press.

Von Hayek, Friedrich A.
1945 'The use of knowledge in society', in Von Hayek (1948) *Individualism and economic order.* Chicago: University of Chicago Press.

1912   Organization Studies 28(12)

Von Mises, Ludwig
1920   'Economic calculation in the socialist
        commonwealth' in (1935) *Collectivist
        Economic Planning*. F. A. Hayek,
        (ed.). London: Routledge and Sons.

Von Mises, Ludwig
1944   *Bureaucracy*. New Haven: Yale
        University Press.

Von Mises, Ludwig
1949   *Human action*. New Haven: Yale
        University Press.

Wernerfelt, Birger
1997   'On the nature and scope of the firm:
        An adjustment cost theory'. *Journal
        of Business* 70: 489–514.

Williamson, Oliver E.
1985   *The economic institutions of
        capitalism*. New York: Free Press.

Williamson, Oliver E.
1996   *The mechanisms of governance*.
        Oxford: Oxford University Press.

Witt, Ulrich
1998a   'Imagination and leadership: The
        neglected dimension of an
        evolutionary theory of the firm'.
        *Journal of Economic Behavior
        and Organization* 35: 161–177.

Witt, Ulrich
1998b   'Do entrepreneurs need firms?'
        Review of Austrian Economics 11:
        99–109.

Yonekura, S., and M. J. Lynskey (eds)
2002   *Entrepreneurship and organization*.
        Oxford: Oxford University Press.

Kirsten Foss   Kirsten Foss is Associate Professor at the Centre for Strategic Management and
                         Globalization, Copenhagen Business School. Her main research interests are organiza-
                         tional design, modularity and the economics of organization. Her work has been pub-
                         lished in such journals as *Strategic Management Journal, Research Policy, Industrial
                         and Corporate Change*, and others.
                         Address: SMG-CBS, Copenhagen Business School, Porcelainshaven 24 2000
                         Frederiksberg, Denmark.
                         Email: kf.smg@cbs.dk

Nicolai J. Foss   Nicolai J Foss is a Professor at the Department of Strategy and Management, Norwegian
                         School of Economics and Business Administration, and a Professor of Economic
                         Organization and Strategy and Director of the Centre for Strategic Management and
                         Globalization, Copenhagen Business School. He has published numerous papers on
                         strategic management, the theory of the firm and the methodology of the social sciences.
                         Address: SMG-CBS, Copenhagen Business School, Porcelainshaven 24 2000
                         Frederiksberg, Denmark.
                         Email: njf.smg@cbs.dk

Peter G. Klein   Peter G. Klein is Assistant Professor of Applied Social Sciences at the University of
                         Missouri and Associate Director of the Contracting and Organizations Research
                         Institute. His research focuses on the economics of organizations with applications to
                         entrepreneurship, innovation, financial economics and corporate governance. His work
                         has appeared in the *RAND Journal of Economics*, the *Journal of Law, Economics, and
                         Organization, Economic Inquiry*, the *International Journal of the Economics of Business*
                         and other outlets. He taught previously at the University of Georgia and the Copenhagen
                         Business School and was a Senior Economist on the Council of Economic Advisers.
                         Address: Contracting and Organizations Research Institute, 135 Mumford Hall,
                         University of Missouri, Columbia, MO 65211, USA.
                         Email: pklein@missouri.edu

[16]

Public Choice (2008) 134: 307–328
DOI 10.1007/s11127-007-9229-y

Economic freedom and entrepreneurial activity:
Some cross-country evidence

Christian Bjørnskov · Nicolai J. Foss

Received: 22 November 2006 / Accepted: 15 August 2007 / Published online: 29 September 2007
© Springer Science+Business Media, BV 2007

Abstract While much attention has been devoted to analyzing how the institutional framework and entrepreneurship impact growth, how economic policy and institutional design
affect entrepreneurship appears to be much less analyzed. We try to explain cross-country
differences in the level of entrepreneurship by differences in economic policy and institutional design. Specifically, we use the Economic Freedom Index from the Fraser Institute
to ask which elements of economic policy making and the institutional framework are con-
ducive to the supply of entrepreneurship, measured by data on entrepreneurship from the
Global Entrepreneurship Monitor. We find that the size of government is negatively correlated and sound money is positively correlated with entrepreneurial activity. Other measures
of economic freedom are not significantly correlated with entrepreneurship.

Keywords Economic freedom · Entrepreneurship · Cross-country variation

JEL Classification M13 · O31 · O50

1 Introduction

Societies do not grow and prosper without entrepreneurs. Entrepreneurs are here defined
as those individuals who exercise their ability and willingness to perceive new economic
opportunities and to introduce their specific ways of seizing these opportunities into the

C. Bjørnskov (✉)
Department of Economics, Aarhus School of Business, University of Aarhus, Prismet, Silkeborgvej 2,
8000 Aarhus C, Denmark
e-mail: ChBj@asb.dk

N.J. Foss
Center for Strategic Management and Globalization, Copenhagen Business School, Porcelainshaven 24,
2000 Frederiksberg, Denmark
e-mail: njf.smg@cbs.dk

N.J. Foss
Department of Strategy and Management, Norwegian School of Economics and Business
Administration, Breiviksveien 40, 5045 Bergen, Norway

 Springer

308   Public Choice (2008) 134: 307–328

market in the face of uncertainty (Knight 1921; Wennekers and Thurik 1999: 46-7). They may do so by starting up firms or by instituting changes within established firms. As Baumol (1990) argues, entrepreneurial creativity need not necessarily be socially beneficial;[1] still, new products, processes, ways of organizing, etc., all essential aspects of the growth process, are outcomes of entrepreneurship (Schumpeter 1911; Rosenberg 1992; Wennekers and Thurik 1999). Not surprisingly, the history of all rich societies is ripe with entrepreneurs: Julius Caesar's friend Balbus went to Rome from a far-away province (Spain) and worked his way up through the ranks to become one of the richest people in the Empire, and on his way built both theatres and public baths; Thomas Edison's inventions both made him one of the most famous people of his age and brought electric light and many other modern appliances to ordinary people; and in more recent years, Bill Gates founded one of the world's largest personal fortunes by bringing the computer age into people's homes. Common to these three individuals and countless others less known is entrepreneurial ability and will. Indeed, while culture may vary, it is arguable that the particular characteristics of entrepreneurs are anthropological constants (Mises 1949; Kirzner 1997; Russell and Rath 2002).

Yet, we observe rather large differences in the supply and allocation of entrepreneurial activity across countries and time, particularly if entrepreneurship is proxied by such measures as self-employment, new firm formation, and the like (Blau 1987; Blanchflower 2000). Some countries are ripe with entrepreneurs who found firms in many different industries (e.g., United States), while in other countries new firm formation is more of an exception (e.g., Sweden). In this paper, we try to explain such cross-country differences by differences in economic policy and institutions. We take "economic policy" to mean government actions intended to improve overall (intertemporal) resource allocation. While institutions may be outcomes of such actions, institutions typically have a longer term existence, and in general may be understood as the designed or undersigned "rules of the game" as defined by property rights regimes, norms and mores, etc. (cf. North 1990).[2] Specifically, we use the well-known economic freedom indices (Gwartney and Lawson 2005) to ask which elements of economic policy making and the institutional framework affect the supply of entrepreneurship in societies. Our data on entrepreneurship are derived from the Global Entrepreneurship Monitor (http://www.gemconsortium.org), a research consortium that collects cross-national data on numerous aspects of entrepreneurship. The combination of these two datasets is unique in the literature.

Part of the background of this paper is that the interest in institutions (North 1990; Dixit 1996), growth (Romer 1990; Temple 1999) and entrepreneurship (Segerstrom et al. 1990; Baumol 1993) has strongly increased in economics in the last two to three decades.[3] In particular, the intersections between these three areas have been fertile ground for research. Thus, much of recent growth theory has been concerned with exploring cross-country links between institutions, economic policies and growth (e.g., Olson 1982; Barro 1991; Sachs

---

[1] Entrepreneurship may well be unproductive and even destructive. For example, entrepreneurship may be exercised in criminal or rent-seeking activities. As such, entrepreneurship can also be one of Bhagwati's (1982) Directly Unproductive Profit-Seeking Activities.

[2] It should be stressed the distinction between "pure" economic policy and institutional design is not always easy to make. In the following, we think of economic policy as a set of factors that can be changed within a shorter time-span, and institutions as a set of factors that are stable in the medium run and only change over longer periods of time. What separates the two concepts is thus their degree of persistence over time.

[3] Although, roughly speaking, interest in institutions and growth is still much larger than interest in entrepreneurship; cf. Bianchi and Henrekson (2005).

🍂 Springer

Public Choice (2008) 134: 307–328

and Warner 1997; Temple 1999; Glaeser et al. 2004), and there has also been some interest in linking entrepreneurship and growth (Aghion and Howitt 1992; Baumol 1993; Wennekers and Thurik 1999; Audretsch and Thurik 2001), although it seems fair to say theory in this area is ahead of empirical work.

Less interest has been devoted to the issue of how institutions and economic policy impact the supply and allocation of entrepreneurship (e.g., within-firm entrepreneurship or upstart firms, or between Baumol's three categories of entrepreneurship).[4] This lacuna may be caused by the well-known difficulties of modelling the entrepreneurial function and measuring the incidence and effects of entrepreneurship (cf. Bianchi and Henrekson 2005). This is a gap in the literature, because the link from the institutional framework and economic policies to economic growth may well be mediated by entrepreneurial activity (i.e., the supply and allocation of entrepreneurship). In Kirzner's (1980) terms, the entrepreneur is the "prime mover of progress," and neglecting the entrepreneur may mean neglecting an important mechanism in the growth process (Wennekers and Thurik 1999).

The design of the paper is the following. First, we outline some existing theories of entrepreneurial activity. Most economic theories of entrepreneurship are extremely abstract and do not enter into specific discussions of the institutional and economic policy determinants of entrepreneurship. Accordingly, we provide such a discussion. Secondly, we report a set of cross-country regressions that explain various measures of entrepreneurship in terms of variables drawn from the economic freedom indices. Finally, we discuss the findings and conclude with a set of policy recommendations for countries wanting to increase their entrepreneurial dynamism.

Two limitations of our analysis may be stated at the outset. First, the country sample, encompassing 29 developed, developing, and transition countries, is admittedly small. This smallness is not due to a choice on our part *per se*, but stems from the Global Entrepreneurship Monitor data only including 29 countries with full data. Second, while it is theoretically, and perhaps also empirically, important to distinguish between the supply and the allocation of entrepreneurship (cf. Baumol 1990), we essentially sidestep this distinction by taking start-up firms as the relevant measure of entrepreneurship. Start-ups *may* well capture the supply as well as the allocation of entrepreneurship, but to the extent that, for example, much entrepreneurship takes place inside firms, it is also conceivable that it only captures an aspect of the allocation of entrepreneurship. Unfortunately, the data do not allow us to introduce the distinction in the empirical analysis.

2 Theories of entrepreneurship and its determinants

2.1 The phenomenon of entrepreneurship

Because entrepreneurs in many ways personify market forces, one might expect entrepreneurs to be *the* central figures in economics, that is, to be recognized as "the single most important player in a modern economy" (Lazear 2002: 1). As numerous writers—from Hayek (1946) over Baumol (1968) to Bianchi and Henrekson (2005)—have lamented, the real-world importance of entrepreneurs is not reflected in economic theorizing. Yet, what is usually seen as the founding contribution to the economics of entrepreneurship, namely Cantillon (1755), actually precedes the *Wealth of Nations* by more than two decades, and

---

[4]However, see Audretsch et al. (2002) for some cross-country comparisons and Kreft and Sobel (2005) for cross-state comparisons in a US context.

many different conceptions of entrepreneurship have been developed in the economics literature, although usually at the fringes of economics, such as in non-mainstream traditions. In the following, we briefly survey the main conceptions.

Entrepreneurship as innovation   The most cited conception of entrepreneurship in economics is Schumpeter's idea of the entrepreneur as innovator (e.g., Segerstrom et al. 1990; Aghion and Howitt 1992; Baumol 1993). Schumpeter's entrepreneur introduces "new combinations" (Schumpeter 1911)—new products, production methods, markets, sources of supply, or industrial combinations—shaking the economy out of its previous equilibrium through a process Schumpeter termed "creative destruction" (Schumpeter 1942). Realizing that the entrepreneur has no place in the general equilibrium system of Walras, Schumpeter gave the entrepreneur a role as the source of economic change.[5] Schumpeter distinguished the entrepreneur from the capitalist; thus, the Schumpeterian entrepreneur need not own capital, or even work within the confines of a business firm at all. In Schumpeter's conception, "people act as entrepreneurs only when they actually carry out new combinations, and lose the character of entrepreneurs as soon as they have built up their business, after which they settle down to running it as other people run their businesses" (Ekelund and Hébert 1990: 569).[6]

Entrepreneurship as alertness and discovery   A rather different notion of entrepreneurship is the notion of "alertness" to profit opportunities. While already present in Cantillon's (1755) notion of entrepreneurship, this concept has been elaborated most fully by Kirzner (e.g., 1997). Kirzner follows Hayek (1968) in describing competition as a discovery process. The starting point of the analysis is thus disequilibrium, not equilibrium as in Schumpeter (1911). The source of entrepreneurial profit is alertness—the discovery of something (new products, cost-saving technology) unknown to other market participants. The simplest case is that of the arbitrageur, who discovers a discrepancy in present prices that can be exploited for financial gain. In a more typical case, the entrepreneur is alert to a new product or a superior production process and therefore steps in to fill this market gap before others. Profit comes not from following a well-specified maximization problem, but from having some knowledge or insight that no one else has—that is, from something beyond the given optimization framework. Kirzner's view of superior foresight thus differs from search theory in which the value of new knowledge is known in advance and available to anyone willing to pay the relevant search costs. In Ricketts's (1987: 58) words, the difference consists in that the searcher of search theory "... decides how much time it is worth spending rummaging through dusty attics and untidy drawers looking for a sketch which (the family recalls) Aunt Enid thought might be by Lautrec. Kirzner's entrepreneur enters a house and glances lazily at the pictures which have been hanging in the same place for years. 'Isn't that a Lautrec on the wall?'"

Entrepreneurship as judgment   A third conception is that entrepreneurship consists of judgmental decision-making under conditions of uncertainty. In the treatment of Knight (1921), the best known advocate of this view, judgment refers primarily to business decision-making when the range of possible future outcomes, let alone the likelihood of individual

---

[5]This includes, but is not limited to, the formation of new business ventures.

[6]Thus, even if by innovating the entrepreneur succeeds in establishing a monopoly that gives rise to indefinite returns, "... the flow of gains to the entrepreneur in *her entrepreneurial role* must be very temporary" (Baumol 1993: 7).

outcomes, is generally unknown, i.e., he faces uncertainty rather than probabilistic risk. While alertness tends to be passive, judgment is active. Entrepreneurs "are those who seek to profit by actively promoting adjustment to change. They are not content to passively adjust their [...] activities to readily foreseeable changes or changes that have already occurred in their circumstances; rather, they regard change itself as an opportunity to meliorate their own conditions and aggressively attempt to anticipate and exploit it" (Salerno 1993: 123). Because judgment in this view is something that is entirely idiosyncratic to the entrepreneur, the transaction costs of trading judgment are prohibitive (Foss and Klein 2005). Knight therefore argues that entrepreneurship and new firm formation are two sides of the same coin because the exploitation of entrepreneurial opportunity requires the start up of a new venture.

Defining entrepreneurship.   The above conceptions of entrepreneurship all arguably capture relevant aspects of the phenomenon. Drawing on the above contributions to the economics of entrepreneurship, and echoing Wennekers and Thurik (1999: 46-7), we therefore define "entrepreneurship as the manifest ability and willingness of individuals" to perceive new economic opportunities and to introduce their ways of seizing these opportunities into the market in the face of uncertainty. These opportunities may consist in new products, new processes, new modes of organization, and new product-market combinations, but they may also consist in spotting new opportunities for inter- and intra-market arbitrage. Individuals may exercise this ability and willingness on their own, as manager/owners of firms, as 'intrapreneurs' within firms, and as part of teams inside firms—although this is an aspect that we cannot capture in the empirical analysis that follows.

2.2 Determinants of entrepreneurship

The above summaries of classical contributions to the economics of entrepreneurship suggest several immediate determinants of entrepreneurship. Thus, Schumpeter and Knight both focus on determinants that are inherent to potential entrepreneurs, such as the degree to which a person is "venturesome" (Knight 1921) or has the "ambition" and "intelligence" to exercise "leadership" (Schumpeter 1911). In contrast, there is rather little specificity in the classical contributions on the institutional and economic policy prerequisites for (successful) entrepreneurship, although both Knight and Schumpeter stress the availability of credit. Schumpeter also links the exercise of entrepreneurship to the supply of other opportunities for social distinction.

However, one seeks in vain in the classical statements for more precise discussions of the institutional and economic policy antecedents to entrepreneurial activity, perhaps because the notion—now entirely commonplace—that institutions imply systems of incentives (e.g., North 1990) was not widespread at the time when Schumpeter and Knight wrote. Moreover, state apparatuses did not have anything like the size they do in contemporary welfare states, so it is perhaps understandable that the classical contributions missed out on this and in general emphasized individual-level determinants.

A partial exception is constituted by the (admittedly much more recent) work of Kirzner (1985). Kirzner (1985: 11) argues that the opportunity of profit switches on entrepreneurial alertness. Price discrepancies, representing profit opportunities, are "flashing red lights" that alert entrepreneurs to pockets of ignorance in the market. By closing these pockets, that is, exploiting gains from trade, entrepreneurs equilibrate the market. However, the signaling system of the market can be hampered in various ways. Thus, Kirzner argues that government intervention, such as minimum prices, price ceilings, and outright nationalization,

312   Public Choice (2008) 134: 307–328

destroys the informational signaling process of the market. Government intervention which aims to improve market outcomes is based on the presumption that government bureaucrats know in advance what the market will reveal. In addition to this fundamental knowledge problem comes the motivational problem that government bureaucrats, unlike entrepreneurs, do not have sufficient incentives to discover the correct prices.

2.3 Institutional determinants of entrepreneurship

How institutions affect the supply, quality and allocation (e.g., across Baumol's (1990) categories of productive, unproductive and destructive entrepreneurship) of entrepreneurial efforts, as well as how they affect whether entrepreneurship is associated with commercial success, has been a relatively under-researched area in mainstream economics.[7] The set of possible determinants of entrepreneurship is very large indeed, including the size of the government, the degree of administrative complexity/bureaucracy, the tax environment, the intellectual property rights regime, the enforcement of property rights in general, the level of trust, competition law, political freedom, labour laws, social security regime, bankruptcy law, corruption, crime, the ethnic composition of the population, availability of finance capital, etc. Some of these have been examined in previous work. For example, Brunetti et al. (1997) in a survey of private sector obstacles show that the most frequently mentioned obstacles to entrepreneurs are taxes, labour and safety regulations, and access to finance.[8] In a series of papers, Grilo and Thurik (e.g., 2004) build what they term an "eclectic framework" of determinants of entrepreneurship, highlighting demography, various kinds of government intervention, unemployment levels, the risk-reward profiles of self-employment versus other types of employment, etc. While elements of their framework relate to economic freedom, and it may be possible to build indices of economic freedom from this framework, they do not directly build theory concerning how such freedom impacts entrepreneurship, a generally neglected focus in the academic literature.

2.4 Economic freedom and entrepreneurship

In order to relate economic freedom to entrepreneurship, operational definitions of economic freedom are needed. Economists have typically treated economic freedom as a composite construct that includes such components that all ultimately boil down to the security and extent of property rights, but include, for example, the freedom to save, to change jobs, to devise contracts, to keep income, etc. In the following we discuss these components and relate them to the supply of entrepreneurship.

   Many scholars, and certainly those with a leaning towards classical liberalism (e.g., Friedman 1962), have used the *size of government* in a broad sense—that is, the extent to which the government intervenes in the economy through government consumption, redistribution through transfer schemes, public investments, and marginal taxation—as a good measure of economic freedom (e.g., Gwartney et al. 1999; Carlsson and Lundström 2002). There are many reasons why the size of government may be expected on *a priori* grounds to influence entrepreneurship.

---

[7] However, much applied research in small business economics, economic geography, innovation studies, etc. has dealt with how institutions and economic policy influence small-firm formation and the rate of innovation.

[8] It is arguable how much finance really matters. For example, Kreft and Sobel (2005) apply Granger causality testing to US panel data, and argue that venture capital follows entrepreneurial activity rather than the other way around. For the contrary view, see Kortum and Lerner (2000).

Public Choice (2008) 134: 307–328 313

Most directly, if economic activities in certain industries or sectors have essentially been nationalized, the scope for entrepreneurship is reduced, as nationalization often (but not necessarily) implies a public monopoly. In most parts of the Western industrialized world this is clearly the case of child care, health care, and care of the elderly. More indirect governmental control, such as requirements that certain trades be certified, may also reduce entrepreneurial activity for example, because certification amounts to barriers to entry (Demsetz 1982).

To the extent that a large government is associated with high levels of publicly financed provision of various services (e.g., care of the elderly, education, etc.) and with generous social security systems, the incentives to engage in entrepreneurial acts in order to make a living (what may be called "necessity entrepreneurship") are reduced because a relatively high reservation wage is practically guaranteed.[9] However, such schemes also reduce incentives for individual wealth formation which may be expected to negatively influence the level of entrepreneurial activity (Henrekson 2005: 11). One reason has to do with entrepreneurial judgment being idiosyncratic and often hard to clearly communicate to potential investors (Knight 1921). The entrepreneur may have to finance his venture himself, at least in the start-up phase. If individual wealth formation is reduced because of generous public transfer schemes, etc., this makes such financing difficult. Moreover, if entrepreneurs are only able to commit small amounts of personal capital to their entrepreneurial venture, their signal to potential outside investors concerning their commitment to the venture is correspondingly weaker.[10]

A large government also needs to be financed, ultimately by taxation. As Henrekson (2005: 9) rightly points out, "[i]n order to analyze how the tax system impacts on entrepreneurial behaviour, it is not sufficient to focus on the taxation of owners of firms. To a large extent, the return on entrepreneurial effort is taxed as wage income." One reason is that parts of the income that accrue from closely held companies may be paid out as wage income (depending on the specific tax regime), and that entrepreneurial activity may be carried out by employees. Rewards for entrepreneurial behaviour in firms (e.g., stock options, bonuses for suggesting improvements, etc.) are taxed as wage income. Henrekson (2005: 14) also points out that a high level of taxation moves many household-related services out of the reach for entrepreneurial exploitation: "... higher rates of personal taxation discourage the market provision of goods and services that substitute closely for home-produced services" (p. 15).

A related, yet distinct, item in an overall measure of economic freedom relates to the enforcement of property rights, that is, the extent to which property rights are secure over time (North 1990; Barzel 2005). Huge literatures in economic history, on intellectual property rights, and on innovation stress the importance for entrepreneurial activity at the micro level and economic development at the macro level of property rights being well-defined and enforced (e.g., Rosenberg and Birdzell 1986; North et al. 2000; Falvey et al. 2004; Glaeser et al. 2004). Well-defined and enforced property rights reduce the transaction costs of carrying out the commercial experimentation that we associate with entrepreneurship (Rosenberg 1992), because well-defined property rights usually imply that contracting costs are relatively low, and it is thus less costly to search for, negotiate with and conclude bargains with owners

---

[9]It may be argued, however, that welfare systems, by providing a safety system, may make people more prone to take entrepreneurial actions, because they know that if they fail, they need not starve. Thus, what may be called "opportunity entrepreneurship" could conceivable be positively influenced through this mechanism (see Sinn, 1995, 1997). Thanks to Niclas Berggren for pointing this out.

[10]De Soto (2003) points out that if property rights to assets, such as homes, that may function as collateral are poorly defined, this may reduce the ability of would-be entrepreneurs to obtain loans.

 Springer

314   Public Choice (2008) 134: 307–328

of those inputs that enter into entrepreneurial ventures. Well-defined and enforced income rights imply that the risk of undertaking entrepreneurial activities is reduced, which may also stimulate the supply of entrepreneurship. If so, it should be expected that institutional features, such as the quality of regulations and the judicial system, affect overall level of entrepreneurial activity.

A third important item in an economic freedom measure arguably is sound money (Friedman 1962), in particular the rate and variability of inflation. While anticipations of future relative prices are important in general for economic decision makers, it is arguable that they matter particularly much for entrepreneurs because entrepreneurs are essentially speculators who receive a residual income (Knight 1921; Kirzner 1997). Inflation, and particularly erratic inflation, "jams" the signalling effects of relative prices (Friedman 1977). While this may be less of a problem for risk-loving entrepreneurs, many entrepreneurs may well be risk-averse, particularly those who engage in necessity entrepreneurship or activity within well-developed sectors. In addition, the concept and measurement of sound money is associated with the level of financial development and financial depth, and as such a proxy for the access to capital, which classical theories stress as a crucial condition of entrepreneurship.

The fourth area of economic freedom is the degree of openness to international trade and investment. Larger trade flows through a country may arguably imply more access to international price signals, thus allowing potential entrepreneurs to take advantage of not only national but also international opportunities. In addition, freedom to invest could, as is often found in empirical studies, increase the rate of technology adoption (cf. Wacziarg 2001), providing further impetus for entrepreneurial discovery although also further competition from foreign entrepreneurs. In addition, the absence of capital restrictions also implies that entrepreneurs gain easier access to international capital markets, thereby potentially increasing the supply of venture capital.

Finally, following Kirzner (1985) public regulation is an important item in an economic freedom measure that is relevant to explaining the prevalence of entrepreneurial activity. Arguably, regulations can both help and hinder entrepreneurs who need clear rules and predictable enforcement of those rules. On the other hand, excessive regulations impose burdens on all firms, not the least start-ups, that may imply prohibitive start-up costs. In addition, Baumol (1990) made the point that individuals operating in heavily regulated economic environment may have larger gains from engaging in rent-seeking activities within the public sector—what he termed "destructive entrepreneurship"—than in real economic activities.

3 Empirical evidence

3.1 Data sources, variables, and models

The data used in this study are drawn from three different sources and are summarized in Table 1. First, the dependent variables in the following are from the Global Entrepreneurship Monitor Consortium (GEM) 2001 dataset, a rich large-scale questionnaire survey conducted in 29 countries in representative samples of individuals between 18 and 64 years; in total, approximately 77,000 respondents are included. The data contain answers to a large array of questions on both entrepreneurial activity, the reasons for the activities, how they were

Public Choice (2008) 134: 307–328

Table 1 Descriptive statistics

Variable	Mean	Minimum	Maximum	Std. deviation	Observations
TEA	8.0874	2.900	20.209	3.911	29
TEAOPP	5.519	1.250	13.307	2.807	29
TEANEC	2.095	0.209	6.753	1.836	29
Log GDP	9.731	7.816	10.414	0.584	29
Postcommunist	0.103	0	1	0.309	29
Number of MSME	51.126	20.0	99.6	21.251	27
Education	105.708	48.70	160.76	24.039	
Income inequality	35.458	25.60	62.30	9.197	29
Investment price level	1.050	0.792	2.022	0.299	29
Employment, ag.	3.679	0	18.6	3.603	29
Employment, man.	30.100	20.4	46.0	6.196	29
Market capitalization	96.528	17.611	271.116	68.972	28
Exchange rate volatility	0.291	0	1.177	0.255	29
Government size	5.449	2.540	8.080	1.548	29
Consumption, % of GDP	23.031	4.200	36.800	8.849	29
Transfers, % of GDP	15.961	4.900	29.800	6.908	28
Investment	11.844	4.000	31.000	6.515	18
Lack of taxation	4.586	1.00	10.00	2.151	29
Legal quality	7.348	3.300	9.500	1.763	29
Sound money	8.879	3.800	9.800	1.394	29
International trade	7.821	6.400	9.500	0.774	29
Regulatory quality	6.241	4.800	7.600	0.847	29

financed as well as a battery of background questions. We use three variables constructed from the data. The variables, aggregated at the country level, are:[11]

- *TEA* denotes the level of total entrepreneurial activity, measured by the proportion of respondents in each country who answer that they engaged in the upstart of an economic activity—starting a firm—within the sampling period. As such, the variable measures *all* firm upstarts regardless of the type of firm and the reason for the activity.

    Since the GEM database also includes questions on the reason why respondents may have started a firm of their own, we can distinguish between two broad types of entrepreneurial activity, "opportunity entrepreneurship" and "necessity entrepreneurship". These variables logically sum to the overall TEA index.

- *TEAOPP* is the proportion of the same sample who state that they have engaged in an activity for the reason that they perceive that it represents an economic opportunity to them ("opportunity entrepreneurship"); and

---

[11] For readers who may want to use the GEM database themselves, we use the variables denoted "tea01", "tea01opp" and "tea01nec" to form our aggregate data.

316   Public Choice (2008) 134: 307–328

Table 2   Countries included in this study

Country	TEA	TEAOPP	TEANEC	Country	TEA	TEAOPP	TEANEC
Argentina	9.6	5.3	4.1	Mexico	20.2	13.3	6.8
Australia	12.1	9.9	1.9	Netherlands	4.8	4.0	0.3
Belgium	3.4	2.6	0.6	New Zealand	15.2	12.4	2.5
Brazil	12.9	7.8	5.3	Norway	7.0	5.9	0.2
Canada	9.1	6.2	2.6	Poland	7.1	3.4	3.5
Denmark	5.6	4.6	0.3	Portugal	6.6	5.1	1.4
Finland	5.1	3.9	0.5	Russia	6.0	4.3	1.0
France	4.3	2.1	0.9	Singapore	5.9	4.6	1.1
Germany	5.8	4.1	1.4	South Africa	8.2	5.5	2.3
Hungary	10.9	7.6	3.2	South Korea	13.4	7.2	5.2
India	11.7	5.0	6.6	Spain	6.0	4.0	1.4
Ireland	9.7	7.2	1.8	Sweden	4.9	4.0	0.6
Israel	3.8	1.4	0.5	United Kingdom	5.2	3.5	0.9
Italy	8.2	6.3	1.7	USA	9.1	7.8	1.2
Japan	2.9	1.3	1.2				

- *TEANEC* is the proportion of the same sample who state that they engaged in an activity for the reason that they perceived it as "necessary", probably in order to uphold a decent standard of living or, in developing countries, to be able to support their family ("necessity entrepreneurship").

It should be stressed again that we thus only measure the actual economic entrepreneurial activity *through firm upstarts.* Hence, it must be emphasized that we neither capture whatever entrepreneurial activity occurs within existing firms, nor do we in any way measure the potential activity that there may have been in a country, had barriers to such activity not been in place. It is nevertheless clear that there is a substantial amount of cross-country variation, even in a small sample consisting of only 29 countries. The TEA data are distributed between a minimum of 2.9% of the sample population (Japan) and a maximum of 20.2% (Mexico); the opportunity index is distributed between 1.3% (Japan) and 13.3% (Mexico), while the necessity index is distributed between 0.2% (Denmark) and 6.8% (Mexico). The country-level data on entrepreneurship are summarized in Table 2.

While we prefer to keep the specification as parsimonious as possible, we add a few control variables. In the following, we control for the potentially important effects of overall economic development, which could influence both the ease with which new firms are set up as well as the economic incentives for individuals to do so, by including the logarithm to GDP *per capita*, measured in purchasing power parity-adjusted 1995 US dollars and taken from the Penn World Tables, Mark 6.1 (Heston et al. 2002). We also control for regional variations by including dummies for Sub-Saharan Africa, North Africa and the Middle East, Latin America, and the post-communist countries in Eastern Europe and Central Asia. Regarding the regional differences, Latin America and the postcommunist countries in particular might have different entrepreneurial traditions and underlying institutions due to the detrimental effects of decades of import-substituting industrialization policies and communism, respectively. As such, we hold the baseline specification as simple as possible, given the small number of observations while controlling for the most obvious potential factors.

To test the robustness of our results further, we employ a set of additional variables. These variables, that may all be argued to influence or proxy for influences on entrepreneurial activity, include the rate of market capitalization as percent of GDP, enrolment rates in secondary education, and the share of micro, small and medium companies in the economy, all from World Bank (2006); income inequality as measured by Gini coefficients from UNU (2006); the relative price of investments (as ratio of the overall price level) and the ten-year average coefficient of variation of the real exchange rate from Heston et al. (2002); and the shares of the workforce employed in agriculture and manufacturing as a proxy for industry structure, derived from CIA (2006).[12]

Our policy variables are from the freedom data, assembled by the Canadian Fraser Institute and published annually in Gwartney and Lawson (2005). The economic freedom indices have been used in a large number of studies documenting, among other things, their substantial effects on economic growth rates (e.g., Berggren 2003). In the use of this type of data in this context, we follow Kreft and Sobel (2005). We use all five sub-indices of economic freedom. These are:

- *Government size*—which measures the extent to which the government intervenes in the economy through consumption, redistribution through transfer schemes, public investments, and marginal taxation. For this particular index, we alternatively split it into its four sub-components.
- *Legal quality*—which measures the protection and respect for the rights of people to their own lives and rightfully acquired property. The legal quality index is composed of indicators of judicial independence, impartiality of the courts, protection of intellectual property rights, military interference in law and politics, and integrity of the legal system.
- *Sound money*—which consists of the rate and variability of inflation and monetary controls, which is a measure of the consistency of monetary policy. As such, this index also captures broader notions of financial sector development and financial depth.
- *International trade*—which measures the extent of trade and barriers to trade and capital flows, both through actual trade and investment flows and through indicators of tariff and non-tariff barriers to trade and capital.
- *Regulatory quality*—which is composed of three sub-indices measuring the freedom from government regulations and controls in the labour market, financial markets, and the price controls in the markets for goods and services. These three areas are again composed of: (1) the impact of minimum wages, hiring and firing practices, the share of the labour force with wages set in centralized bargaining, the generosity of unemployment benefits, and the use of conscript military personnel; (2) the percentage of deposits held in privately owned banks, bank competition, percentage of credit extended to the private sector, and the extent of interest rate controls; and (3) price controls, administrative procedures that are obstacles to business, time spent with the bureaucracy, the ease of starting new businesses, and the necessity of irregular payments.

As such, we employ a rather simple baseline for a number of reasons. First, as this in essence is an exploratory study we aim at capturing parsimonious effects of economic freedom. Second, as part of our small sample consists of developing or transition countries, a

---

[12]The inclusion of exchange rate volatility and market capitalization is evidently important, as sound money may simply proxy for the effects of import and export price volatility, and may be a poor proxy for financial depth. However, in the present sample it is only significantly associated with the alternative measure of real exchange rate volatility from World Bank (2006), which only is available for 23 observations here. Evidently, sound money picks up a somewhat different aspect of economic policy.

 Springer

318   Public Choice (2008) 134: 307–328

subset of the ideal data to be included is either unavailable or highly questionable. All results
in the following therefore need to be interpreted with this qualification in mind.

3.2 Some cross-country tests

We include these variables in a set of OLS regressions explaining either the full TEA scores
or the TEAOPP or TEANEC variables; Table 3 shows the results of the regressions including
all five areas of economic freedom. It also reports the results of using the robust regression
technique, which iteratively downweighs potential outlier observations based on the size of
their residuals (Huber 1964). This alternative procedure solves the well-known problem of
OLS regressions having a breakdown point of zero—i.e., a single outlier observation can
in principle induce an infinite bias—and thus tests whether results obtained by OLS can
be generalized to the full 29-country sample or are driven by single countries, which is an
especially important potential problem given our small sample size. When reading this and
the following tables, it should be kept in mind that due to severe limitations of the GEM
dataset, the sample is rather small; i.e., the size and significance of the results should be
interpreted accordingly.

The table shows that even with such a small sample, the specification does a fairly
good job at explaining the variation. The explanatory power (R squared) varies between
40 and 83%, and all F-tests for joint inclusion of the specification are significant, although

Table 3 Macro determinants of entrepreneurial activity

	TEA OLS	TEA RR	TEAOPP OLS	TEAOPP RR	TEANEC OLS	TEANEC RR
Log GDP	−3.909***	−3.989*	−1.725	−1.706	−2.413***	−2.547***
	(1.325)	(2.144)	(1.038)	(1.495)	(0.338)	(0.505)
Postcommunist	0.863	0.469	0.886	0.842	0.378	0.308
	(1.318)	(2.807)	(1.136)	(1.958)	(0.456)	(0.804)
Government size	2.124***	2.321***	1.740***	1.712***	0.558**	0.600***
	(0.692)	(0.721)	(0.404)	(0.503)	(0.243)	(0.210)
Legal quality	0.434	0.797	0.491	0.741	0.062	0.111
	(0.644)	(0.883)	(0.494)	(0.616)	(0.197)	(0.259)
Sound money	2.077***	2.582	1.304***	1.729	0.899***	0.937***
	(0.714)	(1.728)	(0.493)	(1.205)	(0.213)	(0.247)
International	−1.255	−1.840	−0.787	−1.131	−0.545**	−0.529*
trade	(0.793)	(1.144)	(0.566)	(0.798)	(0.250)	(0.312)
Regulatory	−0.785	−1.442	−0.449	−0.872	−0.420	−0.596
quality	(1.670)	(1.757)	(1.047)	(1.225)	(0.565)	(0.508)
Observations	29	29	29	29	29	29
Adjusted R^2	0.526	–	0.409	–	0.832	–
F statistic	4.11	2.52	2.94	2.22	14.86	11.24
RMSE	2.740	–	2.196	–	0.766	–

Note: all regressions include dummies for Asia, Sub-Saharan African, Latin America and the Caribbean, and
the Middle East and North Africa region; *** (**) [*] denotes significance at $p < 0.01$ ($p < 0.05$) [$p < 0.10$].
The variance inflation factor is 3.76 in all OLS regressions

Public Choice (2008) 134: 307–328   319

TEAOPP fails the 1% level. The inclusion of all five indices of economic freedom neither proves to be a problem as indicated by the low variance inflation factor (see footnote of Table 3). We are therefore able to include the five indices separately instead of the summary index, which allows us to gain a more precise impression of the importance of distinct dimensions of economic freedom.[13]

It is immediately apparent from the table that economic development (GDP per capita) is strongly and negatively associated with entrepreneurial activity. Hence, even though such activity forms an important determinant of the growth of average income, it tends to decrease with the level of incomes. However, this relation is not significant for opportunity activity (TEAOPP) while being strongly so for necessity activity (TEANEC). As such, development seems to reduce the amount of entrepreneurial activity which is caused by the *need* to engage in such activity, which is the main reason for the latter type while not necessarily reducing the perceived opportunities. The table also shows that, as of 2001, the post-communist countries do not deviate systematically from other comparable countries. Even though one might fear so, we do not find any sign of path dependency of a system that strongly discouraged private activity.

Turning to the policy variables, we first of all find that the size of government is strongly positively related to both total activity as well as the shares arising from opportunity or necessity. Remembering that a *larger* score on this index means *less* government intervention, this is quite clear evidence of a depressing effect of government activity, which we explore further in Table 5. The estimate suggests a substantial effect, as a positive one standard deviation change results in a rise in entrepreneurial opportunity activity of roughly 85% of a standard deviation. Second, we fail to find any effects of legal quality, the freedom to trade internationally, or the extent of the regulatory framework.[14] We do, however, also find evidence of a strong effect of having access to sound money on both the level of total activity as well as on opportunity and necessity entrepreneurship. Here, a positive one standard deviation change of sound money is associated with an increase of 53% of a standard deviation of TEAOPP and a 49% increase of TEANEC. The effect is evidently somewhat stronger at the margin for entrepreneurial activity based on the presumption of opportunity, yet it is not robust to being estimated by robust regressions. Further tests show that the insignificance of sound money using either TEA or TEAOPP is due to the influence of the three richest countries in the sample that also score highest on this index. As such, there seem to be decreasing returns to sound money as indicated in Table 4 further down where we instead use the logarithm to sound money. This has the specific effect of allowing for larger effects of having very poor monetary consistency, the reason being that once a country passes a certain threshold of economic development, it is likely to have set up independent monetary authorities to ensure that citizens have access to stable and predictable money. As such, there is very little variation at the top of the sound money index, which prevents identification of an average linear effect in the presence of decreasing returns. The further results in Table 4, that allow of a logarithmic association between economic freedom and entrepreneurial activity rather clearly support this notion, as the logarithm to sound money is strongly significant throughout.

---

[13] Even though all regressions include the regional dummies, the latter are generally not individually significant, but only jointly. In other words, these dummies tend to pick up variation that is difficult to interpret. We therefore opt for not presenting them in the tables.

[14] It should be noted that if we instead use actual trade volumes, which can also be obtained from the Penn World Tables, we obtain the same non-result as with the trade index from the Fraser Institute.

 Springer

Table 4 Macro determinants of entrepreneurial activity: Logged independent variables

	TEA OLS	TEA RR	TEAOPP OLS	TEAOPP RR	TEANEC OLS	TEANEC RR
Log GDP	−3.293**	−5.019**	−1.283	−2.715	−2.179***	−2.499***
	(1.402)	(2.224)	(1.046)	(1.676)	(0.364)	(0.447)
Postcommunist	0.285	−0.869	0.423	−0.483	0.226	0.049
	(1.507)	(3.065)	(1.236)	(2.309)	(0.437)	(0.728)
Log government	8.763***	7.933**	7.344***	6.731**	2.283**	1.494*
size	(3.139)	(3.332)	(1.972)	(2.511)	(1.066)	(0.814)
Log legal quality	0.282	−0.996	1.413	0.334	−0.456	−0.893
	(4.789)	(6.253)	(3.774)	(4.712)	(1.284)	(1.523)
Log sound	10.509***	29.309**	6.084**	21.588**	5.123***	4.022***
money	(4.029)	(14.408)	(2.862)	(10.856)	(1.132)	(1.326)
Log international	−5.763	−11.849	−3.222	−7.590	−3.066	−2.029
trade	(6.479)	(9.699)	(4.717)	(7.308)	(1.964)	(2.198)
Log regulatory	−0.332	3.679	0.707	3.669	−1.397	1.330
quality	(10.403)	(10.865)	(6.979)	(8.186)	(3.242)	(2.586)
Observations	29	29	29	29	29	29
Adjusted R^2	0.476	–	0.365	–	0.821	–
F statistic	3.55	2.86	2.61	2.39	13.80	12.41
RMSE	2.880	–	2.277	–	0.791	–

Note: all regressions include dummies for Asia, Sub-Saharan African, Latin America and the Caribbean, and the Middle East and North Africa region; *** (**) [*] denotes significance at $p < 0.01$ ($p < 0.05$) [$p < 0.10$]. The variance inflation factor is 3.41 in all OLS regressions

In sum, Tables 3 and 4 show substantial evidence for the effects of one type of economic freedom on the level of entrepreneurial activity and some support for another type.[15] However, the government size index covers a fairly disparate set of sub-indices (cf. Sturm et al. 2002). We therefore split this index into its component parts in Table 5, in which we keep the logarithm to GDP per capita, the post-communist dummy and the sound money index in the specification while excluding the three insignificant freedom indices. It should also be noted that for three of the four sub-indices, we use the underlying real data. Hence, "government consumption" is measured as the share of government consumption in total consumption; transfers and subsidies as a percentage of total GDP; and public investment as a share of total investments. The exception is the (lack of marginal) taxation index, which we keep as an index since it includes both the size of marginal taxes as well as the share of the labour force that face the highest marginal tax rate. Again, the regressions do a fairly decent job of explaining the cross-country variation although the R squared is much larger

---

[15] It should be noted that our results are robust to including a number of variables that may arguably proxy for similar underlying economic and institutional features mentioned in the literature. These variables include (but are not restricted to) measures of trade volume, discrepancies of domestic price levels from international levels, both absolute price levels and relative prices of capital goods, and alternative institutional measures such as the Freedom House democracy index and the World Bank index on the rigidity of employment rules. We do not report these additional results here but they are available on request from the authors.

Table 5 Effects of specific factors of government size

	TEA 1	TEA 2	TEA 3	TEA 4	TEANEC 5	TEANEC 6	TEANEC 7	TEANEC 8	TEAOPP 9	TEAOPP 10	TEAOPP 11	TEAOPP 12
Log GDP	-2.087**	-2.990*	-6.282**	-3.808**	-2.159***	-2.332***	-2.598***	-2.588***	0.008	-0.746	-4.021*	-1.345
	(0.841)	(1.742)	(2.799)	(1.436)	(0.279)	(0.596)	(0.488)	(0.394)	(0.782)	(1.324)	(2.335)	(1.176)
Postcommunist	-2.477*	0.934	12.323	0.811	-0.417	0.566	2.334	0.476	-1.895	0.619	9.514	0.591
	(1.357)	(1.813)	(0.327)	(1.707)	(0.775)	(0.654)	(1.602)	(0.491)	(1.207)	(1.687)	(6.458)	(1.705)
Sound money	1.649***	1.738***	3.994**	1.579***	0.706***	0.659***	1.113***	0.652***	1.015***	1.132***	2.862*	1.007*
	(0.351)	(0.545)	(1.969)	(0.593)	(0.146)	(0.129)	(0.378)	(0.122)	(0.306)	(0.513)	(1.534)	(0.537)
Government:												
Consumption, % of GDP	-0.376***				-0.104***				-0.282***			
	(0.070)				(0.021)				(0.062)			
Transfers, % of GDP		-0.338**				-0.060				-0.277**		
		(0.143)				(0.038)				(0.131)		
Investment			-0.149				-0.106				-0.019	
			(0.297)				(0.069)				(0.227)	
Lack of taxation				0.658*				0.139				0.549**
				(0.341)				(0.093)				(0.272)
Observations	29	28	18	29	29	28	18	29	29	28	29	29
Adjusted R Square	0.583	0.442	0.134	0.283	0.874	0.792	0.786	0.785	0.353	0.211	0.109	0.286
F statistic	6.59	4.06	1.38	2.58	28.84	15.70	9.89	13.53	3.18	2.03	–	
RMSE	2.571	2.931	4.158	3.370	0.662	0.863	1.001	0.919	2.298	2.475	3.315	2.788

Note: all regressions include dummies for Asia, Sub-Saharan African, Latin America and the Caribbean, and the Middle East and North Africa region

322   Public Choice (2008) 134: 307–328

when TEANEC is the dependent variable, which is due to the strong and significant impact of economic development.[16]

This point is clear as the logarithm of GDP per capita is consistently significant with a very large coefficient in the first four columns while it only becomes statistically significant in one of the four right-hand side columns. Again, the post-communist dummy is never significant, indicating that the Eastern European countries have rapidly come to resemble the rest of the Free World on this count. Likewise, sound money is significant in both statistical and economic terms throughout the table with either TEANEC or TEAOPP as the dependent variable.

Turning to the government size variables and starting in the four left-hand columns of Table 5, in which the necessity component of total entrepreneurial activity is the dependent variable, only one of the four underlying variables is statistically significant.[17] This variable, government consumption, may proxy for unemployment benefits and other welfare programs that lower the chances of having to set up a business out of necessity.

The results are different when we turn to the determinants of opportunity entrepreneurship. First of all, the share of total consumption pertaining to the government sector has a strong negative influence on TEAOPP. The coefficient, which is almost three times larger than with TEANEC, indicates that a one standard deviation increase in government consumption in this sample would induce a loss of opportunity entrepreneurship of about 90% of a standard deviation. Second, the share of transfers and subsidies in total GDP also exerts a negative influence on TEAOPP. Here, the estimate suggests that a one standard deviation increase in transfers would induce a loss of about 70% of a standard deviation.

Finally, the lack of taxation index also has a positive influence, that is, raising the marginal income tax rate or expanding the share of the labour force paying this rate affects the level of opportunity entrepreneurship negatively. The estimate here suggests that a one standard deviation deterioration of the index would induce a loss of about 40% of a standard deviation. Overall, we thus find that both the access to sound money and three different components of government size are strongly associated with national levels of opportunity entrepreneurship, while sound money and one of the government indices are associated with necessity entrepreneurship.

Naturally, all findings here must be interpreted with some care as they are based on a fairly small sample of countries. However, as a final exercise Table 6 reports the estimates of overall government size and sound money when adding one of the additional control variables; the estimates also include the full baseline specification although we only report the central estimates. As such, Table 6 provides a simple robustness test of the general findings. The table shows that even in such a small sample, the effects of two types of economic freedom remain significant at conventional levels, and none of the coefficients vary significantly from the estimates in Table 3. At first sight, the findings therefore seem to be robust

---

[16]The indices on all five areas are composed of sub-indices, but we opt for including only the index that is significant. Moreover, the government size index has been criticized for being composed of particularly disparate elements, which warrants further specific testing (cf. de Haan and Sturm 2000; Sturm et al. 2002). We have also performed tests with, for example, the three constituent sub-indices—labour, credit and business regulations—forming the overall regulation variable. These results are not reported here as they show no association. Hence, the extent of regulations and controls in the labour market seem unassociated with entrepreneurship in this sample even though other studies have argued for a strong correlation (e.g. Kreft and Sobel 2005). In addition, all results in Table 5 also survive being estimated with the robust regression technique although we do not report them due to space constraints.

[17]It is worth mentioning that the regressions with public investment contain many missing observations. If we attempt to substitute the missing observations with data from other sources, we get a negative association between necessity entrepreneurship and public investment, but no relation with opportunity activity.

Table 6 Additional robustness tests

	TEA Government size	TEA Sound money	TEAOPP Government size	TEAOPP Sound money	TEANEC Government size	TEANEC Sound money
Inclusion of:						
Number of MSME	2.156***	2.095**	1.780***	1.286**	0.611**	1.077***
	(0.719)	(0.825)	(0.420)	(0.651)	(0.272)	(0.217)
Education	2.085**	1.998**	1.719***	1.319**	0.543**	0.848***
	(0.734)	(0.727)	(0.447)	(0.574)	(0.249)	(0.212)
Income inequality	1.921**	1.976**	1.408**	1.137**	0.662**	0.951***
	(0.802)	(0.774)	(0.515)	(0.537)	(0.256)	(0.211)
Investment price level	1.739**	2.010***	1.584***	1.277**	0.387	0.869***
	(0.636)	(0.647)	(0.436)	(0.473)	(0.249)	(0.184)
Sectoral employment	1.710**	1.768***	1.501***	1.099**	0.492*	0.853***
	(0.684)	(0.566)	(0.438)	(0.415)	(0.277)	(0.216)
Market capitalization, % of GDP	2.053**	1.817**	1.650***	1.080**	0.509**	0.851***
	(0.755)	(0.784)	(0.437)	(0.552)	(0.245)	(0.226)
Exchange rate volatility	2.117***	2.148**	1.729***	1.421**	0.561**	0.876***
	(0.712)	(0.802)	(0.420)	(0.525)	(0.249)	(0.239)

Note: all regressions include the full baseline specification; *** (**) [*] denotes significance at $p < 0.01$ ($p < 0.05$) [$p < 0.10$]

324   Public Choice (2008) 134: 307–328

and stable.[18] In addition, the results are fairly robust to adding two extra control variables (not shown), even though the variance inflation factor tends to be disturbingly large.[19] In the following, we discuss the potential reasons for these effects and their economic significance.

4 Concluding discussion

The literature on entrepreneurship mainly focuses on individual-level characteristics of entrepreneurs and tends to ignore the political and institutional environment. The contribution of this work is to discuss the importance of economic policy and institutions as captured by the concept of economic freedom. We report a set of cross-country tests of the relation between entrepreneurship and economic freedom, and interpret our findings within the context of the existing theoretical literature. We thus contribute to the small literature on macroeconomic determinants of entrepreneurship as well as the much larger literature on economic freedom and economic growth.[20]

Fundamentally, we show that the size of government, the quality of the monetary policy and overall financial environment are strong determinants of entrepreneurship across the small sample of 29 countries for which there are comparable data. The basic access to sound money appears to be critical to both opportunity and necessity entrepreneurship (although this index shows decreasing returns to scale). On the other hand, only governments' share in total consumption affects *necessity* entrepreneurship, while government consumption, transfers, subsidies and the extent of taxation are negatively associated with *opportunity* entrepreneurship.

To exemplify the findings, we first summarize those pertaining to government size in Fig. 1, which reports the average level of entrepreneurial activity in the half of the sample with a small government sector and a large government sector, respectively. The figure provides an illustration of the economic significance of government interventions, and thereby also provides a "feel" for the size of the differences as the height of the columns are percent of the sample average.

According to the results, if, for example, Denmark was to raise its current score on the government size index (3.75) to the average of the remaining four areas—legal quality, sound money, freedom to trade, and regulatory freedom—(8.5), it would raise its TEAOPP by about eight points. While this is quite clearly an overestimate insofar as it represents more than two standard deviations of the TEAOPP variable—the GEM survey shows that only about 4.5% of the Danish population engage in entrepreneurship—it nevertheless indicates the substantial effect of having a very large-scale government sector. On the other

---

[18] It should be noted that we have performed a set of additional robustness tests although Table 6 only reports those for which the variables cover almost the entire sample. In particular, sound money also remains significant even if we include the volatility of the real exchange rate or actual inflation data in levels or variance from World Bank (2006). Hence, even if sound money may be the theoretically most worrisome of the five indices, as a referee correctly pointed out to us, the results are robust to including a set of other measures of financial development and related concepts.

[19] We chose not to report these results fully due to space constraints. As noted in the text, the findings are reasonably robust throughout and remain significant in the cases where the variance inflation factor remains below a level of approximately 20. We do, however, note that a full robustness test must await future research with more cross-country information.

[20] The study that is closest to the present work is Kreft and Sobel (2005) who show that across the US states, the level of entrepreneurial activity is significantly associated with economic freedom.

Public Choice (2008) 134: 307–328

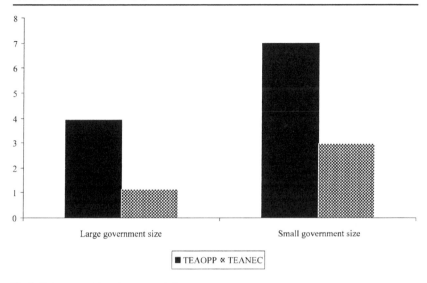

Fig. 1 Entrepreneurship and government size

hand, it would move Denmark to a position of about that of New Zealand, another rich country that in most other respects has noticeably similar formal institutions and cultural traits. Differences in individuals' access to sound money are also important but with about half the effect as that of the overall government index and most probable with decreasing returns.

That government consumption has a negative effect on the level of necessity entrepreneurship is hardly surprising as this variable includes, among other expenditures, both unemployment benefit expenditures and various public goods that, if not provided by the government, might entail a financial burden for the poor. However, the effect on opportunity entrepreneurship is approximately three times larger than that on necessity entrepreneurship. This finding would seem to contradict claims made recently by Scandinavian politicians that the 'welfare state' increases economic dynamism by protecting people from adverse effects of failing.[21] Instead, the empirical findings rather clearly indicate that central traits of the welfare state—strong redistribution by either public goods, reflected in government consumption, regressive transfers or high marginal taxation—are all strongly negatively associated with opportunity entrepreneurship.

As suggested already, this work contributes to the extensive literature on economic freedom. This literature has first and foremost demonstrated that aspects of economic freedom and other institutional measures are strongly associated with economic performance and economic growth (Grubel 1998; Carlsson and Lundström 2002; Berggren 2003; de Haan et al. 2006). Whether this association comes about through the effects of economic freedom on factor accumulation or productivity growth is still uncertain. However, using a set of alternative institutional indices related to economic freedom, Méon and Weill (2006)

---

[21] Interested readers can, for example, compare the present results to Henrekson's (2005) analysis of how the welfare state (in casu: the Swedish welfare state) stifles incentives for entrepreneurship. In addition, welfare states may also create moral hazard by providing entrepreneurs with incentives to undertake more risky ventures than otherwise.

326   Public Choice (2008) 134: 307–328

find evidence suggesting that such factors are strongly related to total factor productivity. Our study suggests that at least part of the association may come about through the effects of economic freedom on the degree of entrepreneurship and thus the degree of dynamism in the economy. Here, both direct and indirect channels may be important. The policy focus is usually on high-tech entrepreneurial activity à la Microsoft. Some start-up firms may indeed end up as major international players, and increased entrepreneurial activity resulting from increased economic freedom will probably increase the likelihood that such firms arise.

Yet, it should also be stressed that entrepreneurial activity need not be of a sophisticated technological nature to add to economic performance. As stressed by Hayek (1968), competition has important dynamic effects. Part of the effect of economic freedom on growth could therefore arise from more mundane reasons, for example if new firms increase the competition in product markets or in the production of factor inputs and intermediate goods. Given that economic freedom, through its effects on entrepreneurial activity, increases the competition and efficiency in intermediate goods markets, it could also result in improved efficiency in the production of final goods and thereby in improved economic performance.

However, a note of caution is called for when interpreting these results. First, note that our results do not inform us about the *survival* of firms resulting from entrepreneurial activities, only the likelihood of such activity occurring. Second, the results also do not inform us about the degree to which entrepreneurship is productive or not (cf. Baumol 1993). Third, our results cannot capture the within-firm entrepreneurship that also takes place. It is therefore entirely possible that a casual examination of the cross-country differences in total entrepreneurial activity might overstate the benefits of entrepreneurship potentially available to single countries if (1) there are country-level decreasing marginal returns to total activity; (2) a higher level of activity also reflects a larger proportion of such activities failing; or (3) there are large variations in the social returns to such activities. We are also likely to understate the degree of entrepreneurship for the third reason above, although the downward bias induced by this problem is unlikely to be systematic. Fourth, a final limitation of our analysis is that it cannot tell us whether government size mainly affects the context in which potential entrepreneurs work and their incentives to unfold their entrepreneurial abilities, or whether systems with large governments instead mainly limit entrepreneurship by transforming norms and privately held beliefs about society.[22]

However, in spite of the obvious limitations on analysis derived from cross-country empirical work consisting of simple entrepreneurial activity in only 29 countries, the findings in this paper fit well within a broader and much more extensive literature on economic freedom. Hence, the cross-country differences should neither be under- nor overestimated, but simply treated with the usual caution. Keeping the limitations of this analysis in mind, we conclude that these findings outline what may be costs of a lack of economic freedom that have seldom been discussed in the literature.

Acknowledgements   We are grateful to Niclas Berggren, Keld Laursen, Magnus Henrekson, Bill Shughart and two anonymous referees for helpful comments on earlier versions and to the Center for Political Studies, Denmark, for financing part of the work on this paper.

---

[22]While this to some might seem a slightly farfetched possibility, it is worth stressing that Lindbeck et al. (1999) argue theoretically for the risk that welfare states can undermine citizens' economic norms. Mokyr (2006) makes a similar argument that cultural beliefs played an important role in the Industrial Revolution, which was above anything else an entrepreneurial event.

Public Choice (2008) 134: 307–328   327

References

Aghion, P., & Howitt, P. (1992). A model of growth through creative destruction. *Econometrica*, *60*, 323–351.
Audretsch, D. B., & Thurik, R. (2001). Linking entrepreneurship to growth. OECD Science, Technology and Industry Working Papers, OECD Publishing.
Audretsch, D. B., Thurik, R., Verheul, I., & Wennekers, S. (2002). *Entrepreneurship: Determinants and policy in a European–US comparison*. Boston: Springer.
Barro, R. J. (1991). Economic growth in a cross-section of countries. *Quarterly Journal of Economics*, *106*, 407–443.
Barzel, Y. (2005). *A theory of the state*. Cambridge: Cambridge University Press.
Baumol, W. (1968). Entrepreneurship in economic theory. *American Economic Review*, *58*, 64–71.
Baumol, W. (1990). Entrepreneurship: productive, unproductive, and destructive. *Journal of Political Economy*, *98*, 893–921.
Baumol, W. (1993). *Entrepreneurship, management, and the structure of payoffs*. Cambridge: MIT.
Berggren, N. (2003). The benefits of economic freedom: a survey. *Independent Review*, *8*, 193–211.
Bhagwati, J. (1982). Directly-unproductive profit-seeking (DUP) activities. *Journal of Political Economy*, *90*, 988–1002.
Bianchi, M., & Henrekson, M. (2005). Is neoclassical economics still entrepreneurless? *Kyklos*, *58*, 353–377.
Blanchflower, D. G. (2000). Self-employment in OECD countries. *Labour Economics*, *7*, 471–505.
Blau, D. (1987). A time-series analysis of self-employment in the United States. *Journal of Political Economy*, *95*, 445–467.
Brunetti, A., Kisunko, G., & Weder, G. (1997). Institutional obstacles to doing business: region-by-region results from a worldwide survey of the private sector. Background paper for World Development Report 1997, Policy Research Working Paper 1759, Washington D.C.: World Bank.
Cantillon, R. (1755). In H. Higgs (Ed.), *Essai sur la nature de commerce en général*. London: Macmillan, 1931.
Carlsson, F., & Lundström, S. (2002). Economic freedom and growth: decomposing the effects. *Public Choice*, *112*, 335–344.
De Haan, J., Lundström, S., & Sturm, J.-E. (2006). Market-oriented institutions and policies and economic growth: a critical survey. *Journal of Economic Surveys*, *20*, 157–191.
Demsetz, H. (1982). Barriers to entry. *American Economic Review*, *72*, 47–57.
De Soto, H. (2003). *The mystery of capital: Why capitalism triumphs in the West and Fails everywhere else*. New York: Basic Books.
Dixit, A. (1996). *The making of economic policy: A transaction cost perspective*. Cambridge: MIT.
Ekelund, R. B., & Hébert, R. F. (1990). *A history of economic thought and method* (3rd ed.). New York: McGraw-Hill.
Falvey, R., Foster, D., & Greenaway, R. (2004). Intellectual property rights and economic growth. GEP Research Paper, Nottingham University, Nottingham.
Foss, N. J., & Klein, P. G. (2005). Entrepreneurship and the economic theory of the firm: Any gains from trade? In R. Agarwal, S. A. Alvarez & O. Sorenson (Eds.), *Handbook of entrepreneurship: Disciplinary perspectives*. Boston: Kluwer.
Friedman, M. (1962). *Capitalism and freedom*. Chicago: University of Chicago Press.
Friedman, M. (1977). Nobel lecture: inflation and unemployment. *Journal of Political Economy*, *85*, 451–472.
Glaeser, E., La Porta, R., Lopez de Silanes, F., & Shleifer, A. (2004). Do institutions cause growth? *Journal of Economic Growth*, *9*, 271–303.
Grilo, I., & Thurik, R. (2004). Determinants of entrepreneurship in Europe. Discussion Paper no. 3004, Max Planck Institute for Research Into Economic Systems, Group Entrepreneurship, Growth and Public Policy.
Grubel, H. G. (1998). Economic freedom and human welfare: some empirical findings. *Cato Journal*, *18*, 287–304.
Gwartney, J., & Lawson, R. (2005). *Economic freedom of the world 2005*. Downloadable from http://www.freetheworld.com/download.html.
Gwartney, J., Lawson, R., & Holcombe, R. (1999). Economic freedom and the environment for economic growth. *Journal of Institutional and Theoretical Economics*, *155*, 643–663.
De Haan, J., & Sturm, J.-E. (2000). On the relationship between economic freedom and economic growth. *European Journal of Political Economy*, *16*, 215–241.
Hayek, F. A. (1946). The meaning of competition. In *Individualism and economic order*. Chicago: University of Chicago Press.
Hayek, F. A. (1968). Competition as a discovery procedure. In *New studies in economics, politics, philosophy, and the history of ideas*. London: Routledge.

Henrekson, M. (2005). Entrepreneurship: a weak link in the welfare state? *Industrial and Corporate Change*, *14*, 437–467.

Heston, A., Summers, R., & Aten, B. (2002). Penn world tables, mark 6.1. Center for International Comparisons (CICUP), University of Pennsylvania.

Huber, P. J. (1964). Robust estimation of a location parameter. *Annals of Mathematical Statistics*, *35*, 73–101.

Kirzner, I. (1980). The prime mover of progress. In I. Kirzner & A. Seldon (Eds.), *The entrepreneur in capitalism and socialism*. London: Institute of Economic Affairs.

Kirzner, I. (1985). *Discovery and the capitalist process*. Chicago: University of Chicago Press.

Kirzner, I. (1997). Entrepreneurial discovery and the competitive market process: An Austrian approach. *Journal of Economic Literature*, *35*, 60–85.

Knight, F. (1921). *Risk, uncertainity, and profit*. Reprint 1965. New York: Houghton Mifflin.

Kortum, S., & Lerner, J. (2000). Assessing the contribution of venture capital to innovation. *Rand Journal of Economics*, *31*, 674–691.

Kreft, S. F., & Sobel, R. S. (2005). Public policy, entrepreneurship, and economic freedom. *Cato Journal*, *25*, 595–616.

Lazear, E. M. (2002). Entrepreneurship. NBER working paper 9109.

Lindbeck, A., Nyberg, S., & Weibull, J. (1999). Social norms and economic incentives in the welfare state. *Quarterly Journal of Economics*, *114*, 1–35.

Méon, P.-G., & Weill, L. (2006). Does better governance foster efficiency? An aggregate frontier analysis. *Economics of Governance*, *6*, 75–90.

von Mises, L. (1949). *Human action*. London: William Hodge.

Mokyr, J. (2006). Long-term economic growth and the history of technology. In P. Aghion & S. Durlauf (Eds.), *Handbook of economic growth*. Oxford: Oxford University Press.

North, D. C. (1990). *Institutions, institutional change, and economic performance*. Cambridge: Cambridge University Press.

North, D. C., Summerhill, W. R., & Weingast, B. (2000). Order, disorder and economic change: Latin America vs. North America. In B. B. de Mesquita & H. Root (Eds.), *Governing for prosperity*. New Haven: Yale University Press.

Olson, M. (1982). *The rise and decline of nations: Economic growth, stagflation, and social rigidities*. New Haven: Yale University Press.

Ricketts, M. (1987). *The new industrial economics: An introduction to modern theories of the firm*. New York: St. Martin's Press.

Romer, P. (1990). Endogenous technological change. *Journal of Political Economy*, *98*, 71–102.

Rosenberg, N. (1992). Economic experiments. *Industrial and Corporate Change*, *1*, 181–203.

Rosenberg, N., & Birdzell, L. (1986). *How the West grew rich*. New York: Basic Books.

Russell, A., & Rath, J. (2002). *Unravelling the rag trade: Immigrant entrepreneurship in seven world cities*. Oxford: Berg Publishers.

Sachs, J. D., & Warner, A. M. (1997). Fundamental sources of long-run growth. *American Economic Review*, *87*, 184–188.

Salerno, J. T. (1993). Mises and Hayek dehomogenized. *Review of Austrian Economics*, *6*, 113–146.

Schumpeter, J. A. (1911/1934). *The theory of economic development*. Cambridge: Harvard University Press.

Schumpeter, J. A. (1942). *Capitalism, socialism, and democracy*. London: Harper Perennial.

Segerstrom, P. S., Anant, T. C. A., & Dinopoulos, E. (1990). A Schumpeterian model of the product life cycle. *American Economic Review*, *80*, 1077–1091.

Sinn, H.-W. (1995). A theory of the welfare state. *Scandinavian Journal of Economics*, *97*, 495–526.

Sinn, H.-W. (1997). The selection principle and market failure in systems competition. *Journal of Public Economics*, *66*, 247–274.

Sturm, J.-E., Leertouwer, E., & de Haan, J. (2002). Which economic freedoms contribute to growth? A comment. *Kyklos 55*, 403–416.

Temple, J. (1999). The new growth evidence. *Journal of Economic Literature*, *37*, 112–156.

UNU. (2006). *World income inequality database, v2.0*. Helsinki: United Nations University-World Institute for Development Economics Research.

Wacziarg, R. (2001). Measuring the dynamic gains from trade. *World Bank Economic Review*, *15*, 393–429.

Wennekers, S., & Thurik, R. (1999). Linking entrepreneurship and economic growth. *Small Business Economics*, *13*, 27–55.

World Bank. (2006). *World development indicators*. Online database. Washington, DC: the World Bank.

Index